THE COMPLETE ENCYCLOPEDIA OF SUBMARINES 1578–2006

THE COMPLETE ENCYCLOPEDIA OF SUBMARINES

1578–2006

JOHN BATCHELOR & CHRIS CHANT

REBO PUBLISHERS

Published by Rebo International b.v., Lisse, Netherlands
in association with Publishing Solutions (www) Ltd. England.

Text: Christopher Chant
Illustrations: John Batchelor
Production, layout and typesetting: The Minster Press, 5 Mill Lane, Wimborne, Dorset, BH21 1JQ, England
Pre-press services: AMOS studio s.r.o., Prague, Czech Republic
Cover design: The Minster Press
Copy editor: Erin Ferretti Slattery

ISBN 978 90 366 2454 1

Contents

Introduction 7

Individual Submarine Sections 26–285

Index 287

Introduction

A type of naval vessel which has a long history but came into practical existence late in the nineteenth century, the submarine was a potentially decisive weapon in World War I (1914-18) and decisive weapon in World War II (1939-45), a major factor in the Cold War (1947-91) for both offensive and defensive purposes, and is still one of the most important warships operated by the world's more important navies. The submarine is a particular type of vessel designed to operate below the surface of the sea. The promise of invisibility provided by a vessel able to submerge, navigate below the surface of the sea, attack an unwitting target, and then escape to surface once more, has been a major spur to inventors. These last have been impractical visionaries, but there are few records of the achievements of any such men before the sixteenth century.

There are records of a sort for some seventeen designs dating to the period between 1578 and 1763, and among the pioneers of this period were William Bourne, Cornelius van Drebbel, David Bushnell, and Robert Fulton. The importance of the last two of these is especially significant in paving the way to the development of the practical submarine. With the introduction of metal as the successor to wood as the primary material for ship construction, further impetus was given to the design of such vessels, and in the latter half of the nineteenth century both U.S. and French engineers produced a number of models, none of them sufficiently successful to attract serious attention from their countries' naval authorities. Late in the nineteenth century, invention of the internal combustion engine combined with that of the electric motor, effective storage battery, and the Whitehead locomotive torpedo to make effective progress in the creation of a warship of this type.

The hull of a submarine must be circular in cross-section to allow it to withstand the pressure of the water to which it is subjected when submerged, this pressure increasing with

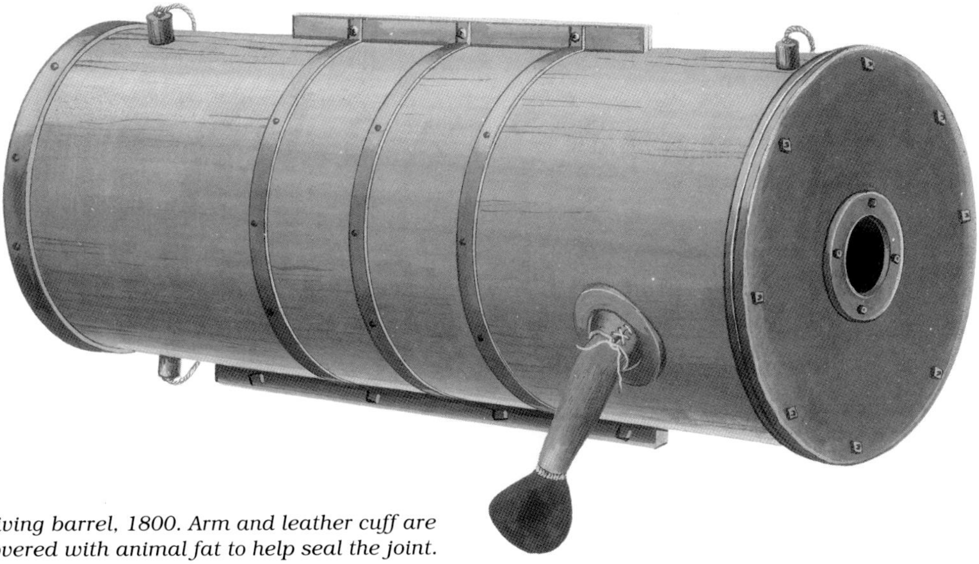

Diving barrel, 1800. Arm and leather cuff are covered with animal fat to help seal the joint.

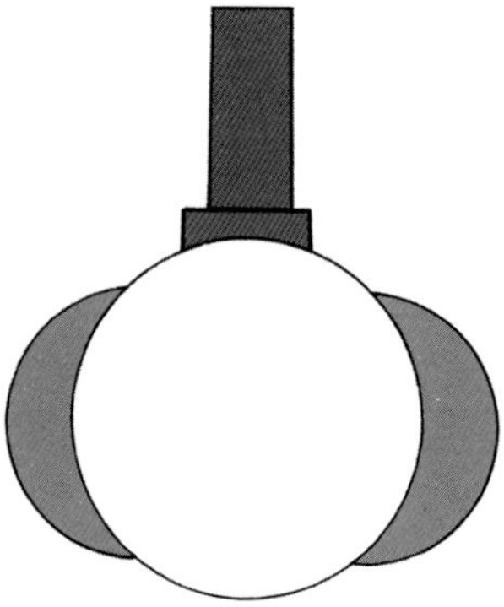

Single hull with saddle tanks.

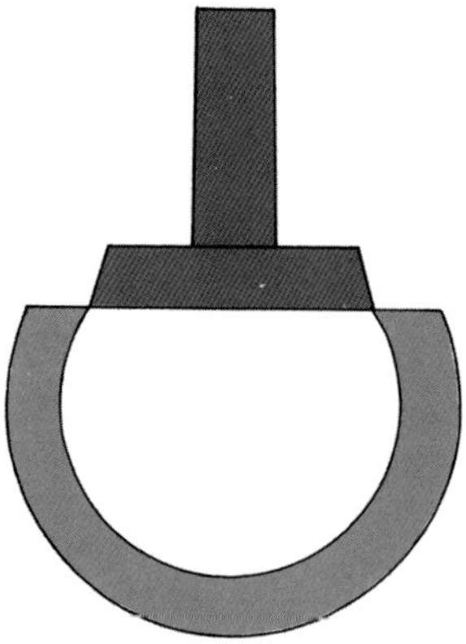

Modern double hull with deck casing.

Modern double hull with deck casing.

depth. The submarine must be fitted with ballast tanks to which water can be admitted to overcome its positive buoyancy when it submerges, or "dives," and from which it can be expelled by compressed air when the boat rises to the surface once more. Located inside or outside the hull, or between the pressure hull and the outer hull off a double-hulled submarine, ballast tanks are of two types, namely the main and auxiliary ballast tanks. The main ballast tanks, fitted internally in the submarine's pressure hull, or externally in the form of blisters outside the main hull, are designed to admit seawater when required, and so overcome the positive buoyancy of the vessel and thus allow it to submerge. When the ballast tanks are emptied, by expelling or "blowing" the seawater with the greater pressure of compressed air, positive buoyancy is restored and the submarine rises to the surface. The only task of the main ballast tanks is therefore to destroy or restore the submarine's positive buoyancy for the purpose of diving or surfacing. Such tanks are normally filled with air or water, according to whether the submarine is surfaced or submerged, but it was not uncommon for the captains of submarines in World Wars I and II to order the main ballast tanks to be partially filled to lower the boat slightly in the water and thereby reduce its visual silhouette and, at the same time, reduce the time required for a crash dive if surprised on the surface. In this condition, the submarine was said to be "trimmed down."

Auxiliary ballast tanks are situated inside the submarine's pressure hull, and their role is to allow the submarine, when submerged, to be trimmed so that it is in a state of equilibrium, possessing neither positive nor negative buoyancy in the ambient conditions. The weight of water in each of the tanks is adjustable either by admitting more seawater, or by pumping some back out into the sea, or by pumping water between tanks. As they are located along the length of the hull, the auxiliary tanks also allow a correct balance to be achieved, so keeping the submarine stable in the horizontal plane.

To control its depth when under way submerged, the submarine needs horizontal rudders or planes, which perform essentially the same task as the trim tanks by hydrodynamic means, and a vertical rudder or rudders to control its course. When dived, the submarine must have a propulsion system capable of operating without an air supply. Until the advent of a nuclear propulsion plant in the 1950s, this could be provided only by electric motors drawing current from batteries of considerable bulk and weight, yet which provided only a modest endurance. It should be noted, though, that experiments were made with alternative propulsion arrangements such as the decomposition of hydrogen peroxide. Along its longitudinal axis, the hull of the first practical submarines was generally cigar-shaped, but as a result of experimental work in the 1950s it is now known that the best results are derived from a hull of teardrop shape.

Another feature of all but a few of the earliest practical submarines, has been the tower-like structure found on the submarine's upper surface and known in U.S. and British terminology as the "sail" and "fin," respectively. Whatever its name, this usually accommodates the conning tower whose upper surface was the platform or, on larger boats, the bridge from which the boat could be

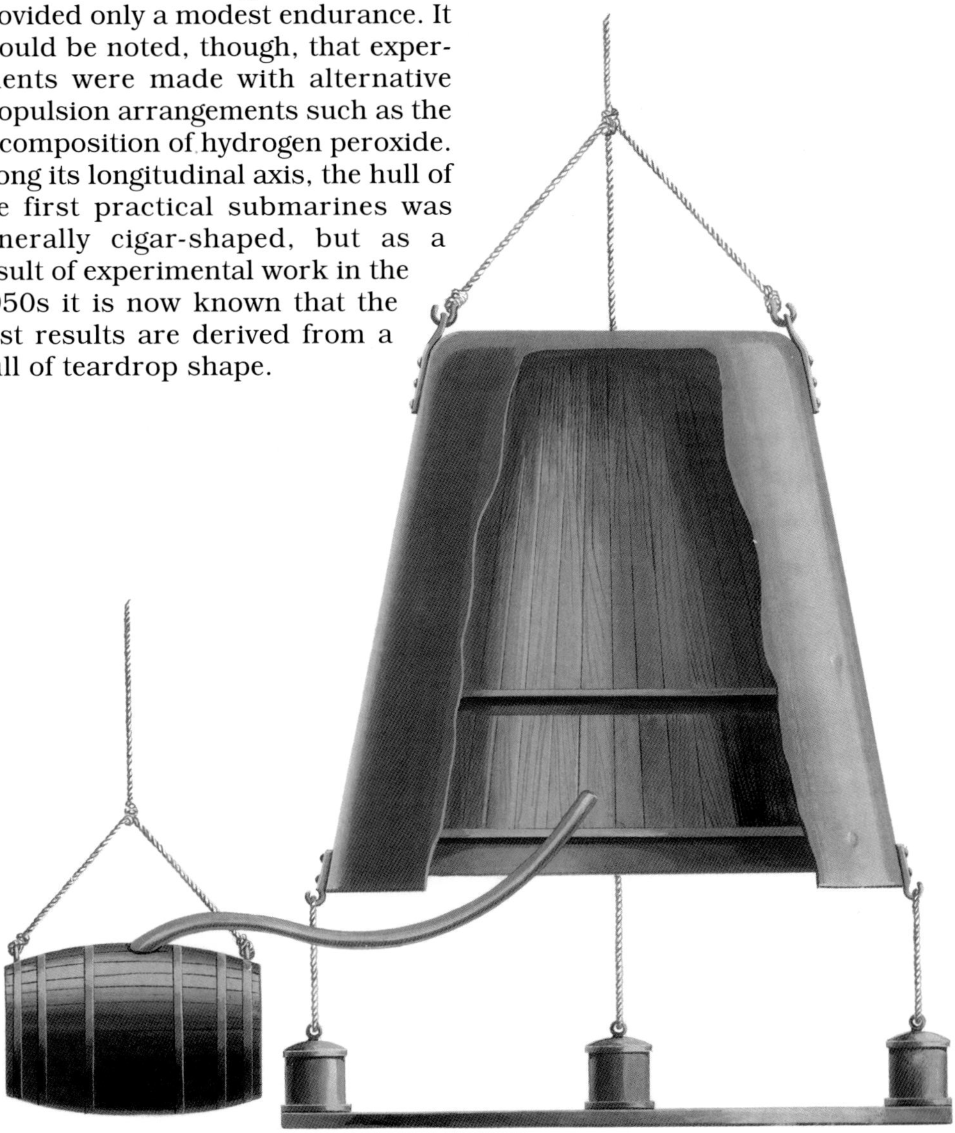

Diving bell, one of many attempts to allow a man to work beneath the sea.

conned or controlled with the aid of fields of vision better than could be provided by lifting of the head out of a hatch. The conning tower soon gained communication devices providing a link with the crew inside the submarine, and, as the submarine developed, provided the ideal location for the periscope or periscopes, radio antennae, radar masts, snorting mast, and the command and communications data center. In World War II the conning tower's primary function, as a small watertight compartment inside the sail, was the accommodation of the surveillance and attack periscopes required for the commanding officer to direct the boat and launch torpedo attacks. As such, it should not be confused with the submarine's control room located directly below it in the main pressure hull, or the bridge, an open or semi-enclosed platform at the top of the sail.

The periscope has traditionally been the way in which a member of the crew of a submarine, submerged at a shallow or periscope depth, to search visually above the surface of the water for possible targets and also for surface and air threats. When not in use, the periscope is retracted as much as 40 ft. (12.2 m) into the hull. The periscope therefore offers very useful capabilities, but the commander of a submarine must also consider carefully before using the periscope as it creates a small but nonetheless observable wake when the submarine is moving, and may also be detectable by radar. A simple naval periscope of fixed type and based on angled mirrors was built by a Frenchman, Marie Davey, in 1854. Thomas H. Doughty of the U.S. Navy invented a prismatic version. The 1902 invention of the collapsible or retractable periscope for submarine service is usually credited to Simon Lake, who called this the "omniscope" or "skalomniscope," but there are suggestions that an Italian, one Triulzi, demonstrated such a device as the "cleptoscope," one year earlier. Another early use of a primitive fixed periscope were the periscopes installed on the experimental French submarines *Gymnote* and *Gustave Zédé* by Captain Arthur Krebs in the late 1980s and early 1990s.

A modern submarine periscope incorporates lenses for magnification, and generally employs prisms and total internal reflection instead of mirrors, as prisms require no coatings and are thus more rugged than mirrors. The periscope may have other optical facilities including range-finding and targeting. The mechanical systems to raise and lower submarine periscopes are normally based on hydraulic power, and the periscope has to be strong to withstand the drag through water without suffering damage or deformation. Another way in which the periscope chassis can be put to good use is the carriage of radio or radar antennae.

Most submarines had two periscopes: one for navigation and observation, and the other for the commander's use in targeting. The diesel-electric submarines, which had narrow hulls, had their periscopes mounted in the conning tower, one behind the other, to provide adequate "drop" into the rest of the hull when they were retracted. In the much wider hulls of recent nuclear-powered submarines of the U.S. Navy, the two periscopes are disposed side-by-side. The observation scope was designed to scan the surface of the sea and also the sky, and generally possessed a wide field of view and either no magnification or low-power magnification. The targeting or attack periscope, on the other hand, had a narrower field of view and higher magnification. In World-War-II era submarines and in earlier submarines, it was the only means available for the gathering of accurate targeting information for the generation of a useful torpedo plot, for sonar of the day was not suitable for this purpose and almost all torpedoes were unguided.

The most modern submarines are no longer reliant on optical periscopes. The U.S. Navy's "Virginia" class of nuclear-powered attack submarines, for example, have photonics masts, which lift an electronic imaging sensor above the water. The signals for this sensor are relayed electronically to workstations in the submarine's control center. While the cables carrying the signal have to penetrate the submarine's pressure hull, this is smaller and more easily rendered watertight than any aperture for an optical periscope's tube. It is also less expensive and safer. Another positive factor of the elimination of the telescoping tube rising through the conning tower is that it widens the scope of the designer in deciding the location of internal equipment.

The first submarine that included all these features was designed by an Irish-born American, John P. Holland, whose design was accepted by the U.S. Navy. The first five submarines built in the UK were also based on the same design, which included surface propulsion by a petrol engine. Germany, on the other hand, preferred to wait until the diesel engine had been raised to the level of initial maturity. The diesel engine is considerably more frugal in fuel-consumption terms, meaning a greater range on a given quantity of fuel, but its most important attribute is that it runs on a heavier oil product of much lower volatility, reducing to a minimum the possibility of the build-up of a flammable fuel/air vapor in the submarine. Thus the diesel engine was standard for Germany's *Unterseeboote* ("undersea boats") or

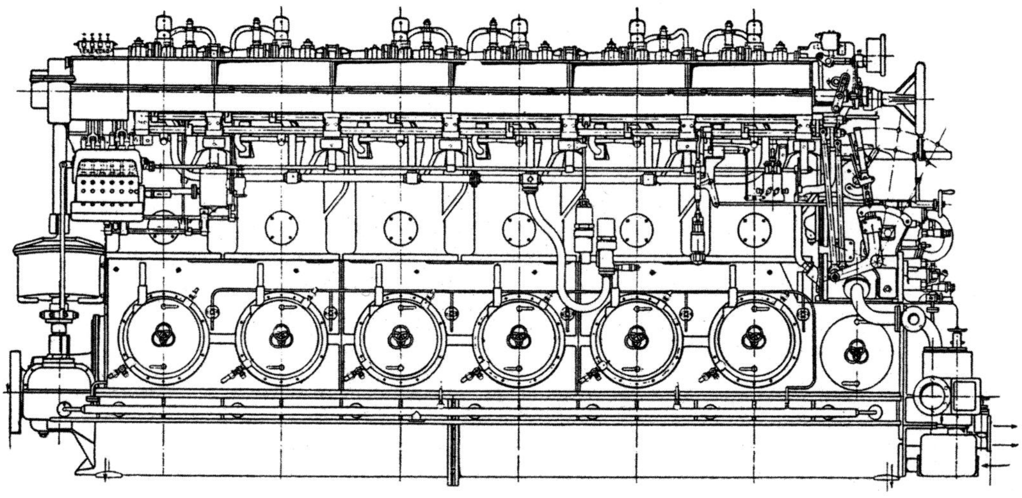

530 hp U-boat diesel engine.

"U-boats" right from the start. Other navies quickly followed suit.

At the start of World War I, there were about 400 submarines in service with some 16 navies, but about half of the total was comprised of British and French boats. The Royal Navy entered World War I with 74 submarines in service and other 31 under construction, while the Imperial German navy had just 33 boats in service with another 28 under construction. But while most of the British boats were of the coastal type, small and carrying only a limited armament, most of the German U-boats were sea-going boats of greater size and endurance, carrying a somewhat heavier armament. In the course of the war, each side constructed large numbers of submarines, not just of the attack type but for other roles such as mine-laying, which proved to be a task for which the submarine was eminently well suited. German construction in World War I was considerably greater than anything attempted by the UK and France, Germany's primary opponents, and the Imperial German navy was therefore able to operate a force which ranged in size and capability between the UB type of coastal U-boats with displacements between 125 to 250 tons, to the very large ocean-going cruiser types with displacements between 1,700 and 3,200 tons, with the range capability to cross the Atlantic. The largest British submarines built in World War I were the off K-class boats, which were designed to work as scouts ahead of the fleet: this was a role which demanded a high surface speed, and the 1,780-ton K-class boats were thus built with a steam propulsion arrangement for a speed of 21 knots, but the need to retract funnels and ensure watertight integrity was a lengthy process which meant very extended diving times and building up of a head of stream after any such boats had surfaced.

After World War I, the UK and France each built a large cruiser submarine. There were also experiments with submarine monitors mounting a single 12-inch (305 mm) gun, and with submarines capable of carrying a dismantled airplane which could be assembled and launched, when the boat was on the surface, to reconnoiter for targets beyond the submarine's visual horizon, and then spot for its gun armament in the following surface engagement. These experiments proved that while aircraft could be operated from submarines, it was a laborious process with little practical advantage, so the work remained at the experimental stage except in the Far East, where the Imperial Japanese navy adopted the idea with considerable enthusiasm. Many Japanese submarines of World War II were very large boats carrying one or more seaplanes, and later in the war the

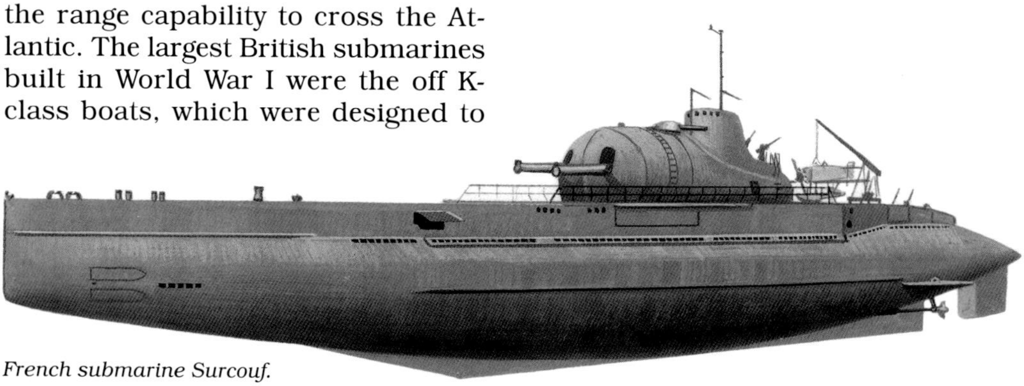

French submarine Surcouf.

Insignia from the conning towers of three German U-boats. Top; U 99; middle: U 92 and bottom: U 213.

concept was expanded to allow submarines to carry bombers intended for attacks on major targets such as the Panama Canal and U.S. fleet anchorages in the atolls of the Pacific Ocean.

The armament of submarines in World War I, the inter-war period, and through World War II included both guns and torpedoes, as the submarine of the time was designed for both surface and submerged actions. During this period, the submarine was in fact a submersible warship that could submerge for a short time, rather than a true submarine that could spend the majority of its operational time under the water. This resulted from the fact that the batteries of the time held sufficient charge to run the boat's essential systems and electric motors for only a limited period. Thus submerged speeds and ranges were low, and submarines spent long periods on the surface first to make long-range transits feasible, and, second, to recharge the batteries for underwater capability in combat. There were improvements in submarines in the period between the two world wars, but these were mostly in relation to increased range, improved habitability, and enhancement of the engines and equipment.

The submarine was more important in World War II than in World War I. The German navy once again sought to sever the British maritime lines of communications with the U.S., and fought the campaign with a greater intensity than it had managed in World War I. After a slow start, occasioned by the fact that it had only a small U-boat force, the German U-boat arm operated first in the North Sea and eastern part of the Atlantic, but then spread its net farther, especially after the U.S.'s December 1941 entry into the war, so that the U-boat "wolf packs" roamed the North and South Atlantic, the Baltic, Caribbean and Mediterranean Seas, and even the Indian and Arctic Oceans. The Battle of the Atlantic, as the primary campaign came to be called, became one of the most crucial parts of the entire war, for if Germany had managed to isolate the UK, the UK would have faced physical and industrial starvation and been forced to capitulate. This was not a one-sided war, however, and British submarines waged a hard-fought and largely successful offensive in the Mediterranean where, in company with surface warships and aircraft, they crippled the lines of supply between Italy and North Africa, where the German and Italian forces could survive only with men, equipment, fuel, and food delivered from Italy.

In a campaign fought over a larger area but otherwise analogous to the German effort in the Atlantic, the U.S. submarine arm swept the Pacific clear of Japanese merchant shipping. This isolated the Japanese home islands from the oil and other raw materials they needed to sustain the war effort, and effectively isolated the Japanese forces in the Pacific and South-East Asia. The U.S. submarine effort was based on the knowledge of Japan's industrial limitations, and the destruction of the Japanese merchant navy was a war-winning effort. Moreover, with its long range and heavy armament, the U.S. Navy's submarines also offered a potent capability against Japanese warships, many of which succumbed to torpedo attack. Available in ever larger numbers as a result of concentration on a few excellent designs, the U.S. Navy's fleet submarines also scouted for the surface forces and warplanes of the U.S. Navy, radioing essential information and only then picking off any ships they could, proving invaluable for the rescue of airmen forced down onto the water.

The Italian and Japanese submarine arms had many boats and fought with great courage, but failed to accomplish as much as they might have done as a result largely of faulty tactics. But the threat the Italian and Japanese submarines offered nonetheless exercised considerable

influence on Allied strategy. The miniature or midget-type submarines manned by a crew of up to four which were used to attack ships in harbor proved themselves capable of penetrating even the most heavily defended ports. A similar capability, pioneered by the Italians but then taken up by the British, was the human torpedo, based on a torpedo whose warhead the human crew could detach and affix to the hull of a target vessel before escaping.

The greatest developments in the concept of the submarine both appeared toward the end of the war, and were brought to fruition by the Germans, albeit too late to play any major part in operations. By 1943, the U-boats were facing such a difficult time running on the surface in the face of rampant Allied air superiority that they took a Dutch idea of the time just before the war and perfected it as the *Schnorchel* ("snorkel"), a breathing tube which could be extended from the sail so that its head was above the surface of the water. This made it possible for the U-boat to operate its diesel engines while the boat was submerged, providing a higher speed and allowing the batteries to be recharged while the boat remained at periscope depth. As well as providing this capability, the *Schnorchel*'s head was also a considerably smaller radar target than the U-boat or even its sail, reducing the Allies' chances of detecting a boat thus equipped. The other greater development was the Type XXI-class U-boat with greater battery capacity and a considerably more refined hull, which allowed a virtual doubling of underwater speed as well as greater range on electrical power. Germany also worked on the development of a gas turbine using a mixture of diesel fuel and hydrogen peroxide, which would enable a U-boat so fitted to reach a very high underwater speed, although for a limited period only. World War II ended before the work could be completed, though two developmental submarines of this type were constructed in the UK after the war.

The Allies examined Germany's late-war developments very closely in the period after the war's end and learned much, especially with regard to boosting submerged speeds by careful shaping and streamlining of exterior lines, but the single most important advance came from the U.S. Atomic Energy Commission's 1948 award of a contract to the Westinghouse Electrical Company to develop a nuclear propulsion plant suitable for submarine service, and on June 14, 1952, the keel of the first nuclear-powered submarine, the *Nautilus*, was laid. The completion and successful trials of this vessel two years later meant that the true submarine had become a reality at last, for the power derived from the nuclear reactor was more than sufficient for high underwater speed and all the submarine's electrical systems, including seawater desalinization and

HMS Superb.

air purification. The heat of the nuclear reactor is used to generate steam by means of a heat exchanger, keeping irradiated water separate from the water turned to steam to drive the turbine, thus removing the possibility of radiation damage to the submarine's crew. Since the reactor requires an exterior source of air, the only factor limiting the time the submarine can remain submerged is the revitalization of the air needed by the crew. This is provided by the installation of an air-purification plant, and the submarine can therefore remain submerged until a crew change or food supplies are required.

The great power which can be provided by a nuclear propulsion arrangement also allows the submarine to travel under the surfaced at or near its maximum speed without interruption. This facility was exploited first by designing the first such submarines along the lines pioneered by the Germans in their Type XXI-class U-boats, and then by adopting a hull of the optimum elongated teardrop shape, opening the way to submerged speeds much greater than had been achieved before, and comparable with the speed of all but the fastest warships on the surface. Moreover, while surface warships can seldom sustain their maximum speeds for long, especially in the face of deteriorating sea and weather conditions, the nuclear-powered submarine is immune to these factors. The nuclear-powered submarine thus marked the dawn of a new age in naval warfare.

The capabilities of nuclear power also opened the way to the construction of considerably larger submarines. Thus, while the first nuclear-powered submarines were of the hunter/killer type, designed to search out and destroy an enemy's submarines and surface warships with increasingly advanced torpedoes, the facility for greater size was exploited to allow the creation of the nuclear-powered ballistic missile submarine. The first missile submarines had been of the conventional diesel-electric type, carrying winged cruise missiles or, later, short-range ballistic missiles in small numbers for surface launch.

The combination of improved missile technologies and greater submarine size made possible the development of the submarine into a true component of deterrent warfare. The result, emerging in the late 1950s and early 1960s, was the nuclear-powered ballistic-missile submarine carrying up to 16 intermediate-range missiles such as the Polaris and, later, the Poseidon types, which could be launched from the submerged submarine. Further evolution along the same basic path resulted in weapons such as the Trident I, and current Trident II with greater range, and independently targeted warheads whose greater accuracy allowed the nuclear yield to be reduced. In addition to the U.S., China, the UK, France, and the USSR constructed nuclear-powered submarines of large size for the strategic missile role and of smaller size for the tactical attack roles, the latter often with their advanced torpedoes supplemented by an assortment of tube-launched misiles for the anti-ship, anti-submarine and land attack tasks.

For navies not wanting to adopt nuclear propulsion because of its cost, political, or ecological consequences, a possible answer to the creation of a real submarine, independent of the surface for a significant time, is air-independent propulsion. This is a phrase embracing several technologies that can allow a submarine to operate without the need to surface or use a snorkel, and generally describes the means whereby the diesel-electric propulsion of conventional submarines can be augmented or replaced. AIP is most commonly used as an auxiliary power source, generating electricity to power the electric motors, or recharge the submarine's batteries, or power life-support equipment and thereby reduce the demand on the batteries. Such systems are comparatively small, and can therefore be retrofitted into existing submarine hulls by the insertion of an additional hull section. The system does not normally possess the power or endurance to replace the standard diesel-electric propulsion, but its presence allows the submarine to remain submerged for considerably longer than it could on its standard propulsion arrangement.

The origins of AIP can be found in German research during World War II, when the Walter Company experimented with the use of concentrated hydrogen peroxide as the source of oxygen for submerged submarines. The Walter system was based on steam turbines, employing steam heated by burning diesel fuel in the hydrogen/oxygen atmosphere created by the decomposition of concentrated hydrogen peroxide by a catalyst. Several experimental U-boats were produced. One of these was the U-1407, which was scuttled by its crew at the end of the war, but salvaged by the British and commissioned as the *Meteorite*. The British built two improved boats in the late 1950s as the *Explorer* and *Excalibur*. The Soviets also undertook experiments with the same technology.

Hydrogen peroxide was a dead end for manned submarines, as it was highly dangerous, highly reactive in contact with a number of metals, very volatile, and quickly consumed. Hydrogen peroxide was nonetheless retained as a torpedo propellant by both the UK and USSR, although it was abandoned by the British following the explosion of a hydrogen peroxide torpedo in the submarine *Sidon* in June 1959. The Russian submarine *Kursk* was also lost in August 2000, with all hands, after the explosion of a hydrogen-peroxide torpedo.

Closed-cycle diesel engine technology uses an engine that can be operated conventionally on the surface, but can be provided with oxidant, usually stored as liquid oxygen, to continue running when submerged. Since the metal of an engine will burn in pure oxygen, the oxygen is usually diluted with recycled exhaust gases, but, as there are no exhaust gases as the engine is started, argon gas is used at this stage. The USSR invested heavily in this technology, and built 30 examples of the 650-ton "Quebec" boat with such an arrangement in 1953/56. The "Quebec"-class boat had three diesel engines, which were two conventional units and one closed-cycle unit to use liquid oxygen. The "Quebec"-class boats had a poor safety record; one was lost after an explosion and fire, and the last of them were scrapped in the early 1970s. The West German Type 205 boat *U-1* was fitted with an experimental closed-cycle diesel engine delivering 3,000 hp (2237 kW).

The closed-cycle steam turbine concept is epitomized by the French MESMA (Module d'Energie Sous-Marine Autonome) system, and such a unit has been retrofitted in an Agosta 90B-class submarine of the Pakistani navy. This is a modified version of the French nuclear propulsion system with heat generated by ethanol and compressed oxygen. The Swedish shipbuilder Kockums has built three Gotland class submarines for the Swedish navy with a Stirling-cycle auxiliary engine. This burns liquid oxygen and diesel fuel to drive 75-kW generators whose current can be used either for propulsion or battery charging. The AIP endurance of these 1,490-ton boats is about 14 days at 5 knots. In Germany, the Siemens company had created a 30/50-kW fuel cell unit, and nine of these are used in the U-31, lead boat of the Type 212A class of 1,830-ton submarines. The other three boats of this class, and the AIP-equipped export Type 209 and Type 214 boats each have two 120-kW modules from the same manufacturer.

In the first 50 years or so of its existence as a practical warship, the submarine matured from a very limited coastal and harbor defense weapon into a long-ranged ocean-going weapon with the capability to inflict serious, if not fatal, damage on an enemy's maritime trade and surface fleet. The limitations which prevented the conventional diesel-electric submarine from becoming wholly dominant disappeared with the advent of nuclear propulsion and the introduction of weapons such as long-range torpedoes guided by their own homing system or guided by commands sent down a wire from the parent submarine, and ballistic missiles of truly devastating destruction.

The means of locating and defeating submarines have improved steadily over the years, but are by no means yet perfect. Sonar systems have improved for service on warships and aircraft, the latter being longer-range fixed-wing machines which can drop one-shot sonobuoys and shorter-range helicopters often carried by dedicated anti-submarine warplanes and fitted with dunking or dipping sonar whose senor is lowered into the water to listen for underwater noise and then lifted at the end of the search. The standard anti-submarine weapon has developed from the "dumb" depth charge and ahead-throwing projectors of World War II to the "smart" torpedo. This can be delivered by submarines, surface warships, and aircraft, and sometimes as the payload of a medium-range unguided rocket fired from as warship, incorporating in its guidance package an advanced computer to allow the torpedo to locate, home in on, and destroy a target submarine by the detonation of a shaped-charge warhead on the target's most vulnerable point.

Even so, the submarine remains a major threat, and evidence of this can be found in the large sums of money and numbers of warships and aircraft devoted to the anti-submarine task by countries with major navies and large merchant marines. Moreover, while the threat to major navies and merchant marines in the world's oceans comes primarily from nuclear-powered attack submarines, the threat in shallower and coastal waters comes primarily from diesel-electric submarines, which are smaller and quieter than nuclear-powered submarines yet carry the same advanced anti-ship torpedoes. Additionally, these latest conventionally powered submarines are altogether more affordable to build and operate than a nuclear-powered submarine, and are therefore in service with a greater number of the world's navies, especially in regions of low political or economic stability or where the country in question can control a valuable maritime chokepoint such as a strait.

For the immediate future, therefore, the submarine will in all probability remain a major element of any well-balanced naval force for its abilities as an offensive platform and, in its nuclear-powered form, for the creation of a real deterrent capability when carrying nuclear-armed missiles and for the waging of offensive and defensive undersea warfare in its hunter/killer form. This latter can thus be offensive operations against enemy naval and merchant ships, and defensive operations to help protect major naval assets such as carrier battle groups against the efforts of an enemy's submarines with nuclear or conventional propulsion. It should be noted, however, that the submarine is still limited, in its modern form just as in its predecessors, although to a less restricted extent, by the nature of the environment in which it operates: the submarine can see or hear no farther than the range limits of its own sonar systems, and radio communications with a submerged submarine are limited: messages can be received, but it is dangerous to send messages as this almost invariably demands that an antenna be raised above the surface, increasing the chances of the submarine's detection.

Given submarines' ability to remain submerged for very extended periods, and the tactical advantages of doing so, navigation would have been a major problem, unless the boat was prepared to surface, or at least to come close to the surface, to take celestial sightings or receive radio-based navigation data, but for the development of the ship's inertial navigation system. This was developed after World War II specifically for service in nuclear-powered submarines, and is comparatively simple in concept although it requires a very high degree of

engineering and electronic precision, both of which make any such system costly. If a submarine's position is accurately plotted at the start of its voyage, and all subsequent accelerations in component vectors can be measured, they can be translated by calculation into speeds and distances which, when added to the initial position, give the current position. By this means, the navigator of a nuclear-powered submarine fitted with a SINS is provided with a continuous presentation of his submarine's position, even though there may have been no external sight taken for weeks, if not months. Inertial navigation is, in effect, a sophisticated form of dead reckoning, with accelerometers used in place of other mechanical or human sensors. The system can measure every acceleration due to speed and course changes, but is also designed to eliminate all accelerations resulting from gravity, pitching, rolling, etc. The system provides very accurate navigational data.

The first major trial and demonstration of the system's remarkable accuracy was undertaken in 1958, when the U.S. nuclear-powered submarines *Nautilus* and *Skate* navigated under the North Polar ice cap. Since then, nuclear submarines have made complete circumnavigations while remaining submerged, again relying on their SINSs. Such is the system's accuracy that an error of no more than 110 to 220 yards (100 to 200 m) is typical after a circumnavigation of the world, though it should be conceded that, in a voyage of such a length, occasional visual sights are taken to verify the accuracy of the system, as there is inevitably a certain amount of drift in any inertial navigation system no matter how well made.

The weapon most associated with the submarine is the torpedo. Derived from the name of a fish able to give a powerful electric shock, the term "torpedo" was initially used for an explosive charge moored in the sea, which later became known as a sea mine. The name followed the weapon when an explosive charge was attached to the end of a spar projecting from the bow of small craft to create the spar torpedo, or was towed by a boat, the tow rope being carried out at an angle by an otter board to create the Harvey torpedo. The spar torpedo was effectively used during the American Civil War (1861-65) by the Confederate submersible *H. L. Hunley* to sink the Federal ship *Housatonic* in 1864, and was still in service some 20 years later when it was use in the French defeat of a Chinese fleet in the Battle of the Min River.

In 1865, however, the first steps were taken toward the development of what is now known as the torpedo, namely a self-propelled missile. An Austro-Hungarian officer, one Luppis, devised a clockwork-powered boat-shaped craft, guided by lines attached to its rudder, for the defense of harbors. This was too crude for service, and Luppis approached Robert Whitehead, the English manager of a marine engine factory at Fiume (now Rijeka, Croatia), to create what became known as the Luppis-Whitehead locomotive torpedo. This first appeared in 1867 as a spindle-shaped underwater missile driven by a compressed-air engine at 6 knots over a distance of just a few hundred yards with a warhead based on 18 lb. (8.2 kg) of dynamite. The running

depth was controlled by a hydrostatic valve and, in 1868, the basic design was upgraded with a balance chamber in which a pendulum connected to horizontal rudders automatically corrected any fore-and-aft tilt.

The Austro-Hungarian government refused to buy the exclusive manufacturing rights, and in 1869 Whitehead accepted an invitation to bring to England the two torpedoes (14 and 16 inches, or 356 and 406 mm in diameter) developed by that time. These were exhaustively evaluated under Admiralty supervision at Sheerness, and the British government then bought the manufacturing rights. The Royal Laboratory at Woolwich was allocated the task of developing this basic weapon, and initially concentrated its efforts on the 16-inch (406 mm) model. This was propelled by a pair of contra-rotating propellers for ranges of 1,000 yards (915 m) at 7 knots or 300 yards (275 m) at 12.5 knots. Such a weapon became the first locomotive torpedo used in combat, when the British ship *Shah* fought an inconclusive action against the Peruvian monitor *Huascar* in 1877. By this time, Whitehead torpedoes were being supplied to most navies, and in 1878 they claimed their first victim when, during the Russo-Turkish War, a Turkish cutter was sunk by two Russian torpedo boats, each of which obtained a hit. The first warship to be so sunk was the Chilean rebel battleship *Blanco Encalada* during 1891.

The locomotive torpedo's greatest failing was its poor directional stability, but this problem was largely overcome in 1878-89 by the introduction a gyro-controlled steering apparatus invented by L. Obry of

Trieste, Italy. Another weapon of comparable concept pioneered in 1881 was the Brennan torpedo for harbor defense. This was, in effect, the world's first guided missile. Designed in 1877 by an Australian inventor, Louis Brennan, the weapon was operated by a pair of contra-rotating propellers turned by the rapid extraction (by shore-based winches) of wires wound around drums inside the torpedo. Differential speed on the wires connected to the shore station allowed the torpedo to be guided to its target, up to 2,000 yards (1830 m) distant.

By 1909, the standard Whitehead torpedo was an 18-inch (456 mm) weapon with a range of 2,000 yards (1830 m) at 35 knots or 4,000 yards (3660 m) at 29 knots. The next core improvement to the torpedo was a boost in performance derived from the enrichment of the compressed air driving the engine. In British Whitehead torpedoes, this took the form of a mix of steam and gas from the evaporation of water into superheated steam in a so-called generator by a jet of burning shale oil. In the U.S. Navy, the Bliss-Leavitt torpedo was driven by a turbine powered by steam generated by forcing a spray of water through an alcohol torch.

By 1914, and the outbreak of World War I, the typical torpedo was of 18-inch or 21-inch (457 or 533 mm) diameter, with a length in the order of 17.5 and 22 ft. (5.3 and 6.7 m), respectively, with ranges of 3,750 yards (3420 m) at 44 knots or 10,000 yards (9145 m) at 28 knots. With the exception of improved performance and enhancements such as pre-set course changes and the introduction of a magnetic firing pistol as an alternative to the standard impact firing pistol, the torpedo remained essentially unaltered in conceptual terms until the outbreak of World War II. The one major exception was the introduction of a notably high-performance Japanese torpedo. This was of 24-inch (610 mm) diameter, powered by liquid oxygen, and was developed by the Japanese, who made extensive and notably successful use of the weapon.

During World War II, the Germans developed a submarine-launched torpedo with electric propulsion: this left no trace of bubbles in the water, and was therefore difficult to detect except with sonar. The weapon was produced in several forms, including one that homed in automatically on the sound of a turning propeller. This G7e may be regarded as the first modern torpedo. Most modern torpedoes now carry their own electronically-based autonomic guidance systems to operate from the moment of launch or in the event of a break or other problem with the wires along.

Thus, several types of homing torpedo have been developed, particularly as anti-submarine weapons. These generally have advanced propulsion systems for high speed and/or long range, can dive as deep as the modern deep-diving submarine, can be launched from ships or submarines, and possess passive or active acoustic homing systems and/or wire guidance working in concert with the launch vessel's advanced electronic sensors. Great advances in the science and art of miniaturization have made feasible the creation of small, lightweight torpedoes for launch from ships, fixed-wing aircraft and helicopters, or for carriage as the payload of anti-submarine rockets, which release the torpedo payload over the target's supposed location. Earlier models are electrically propelled, but the most modern torpedoes have engines based on advanced solid or liquid propellants or oil.

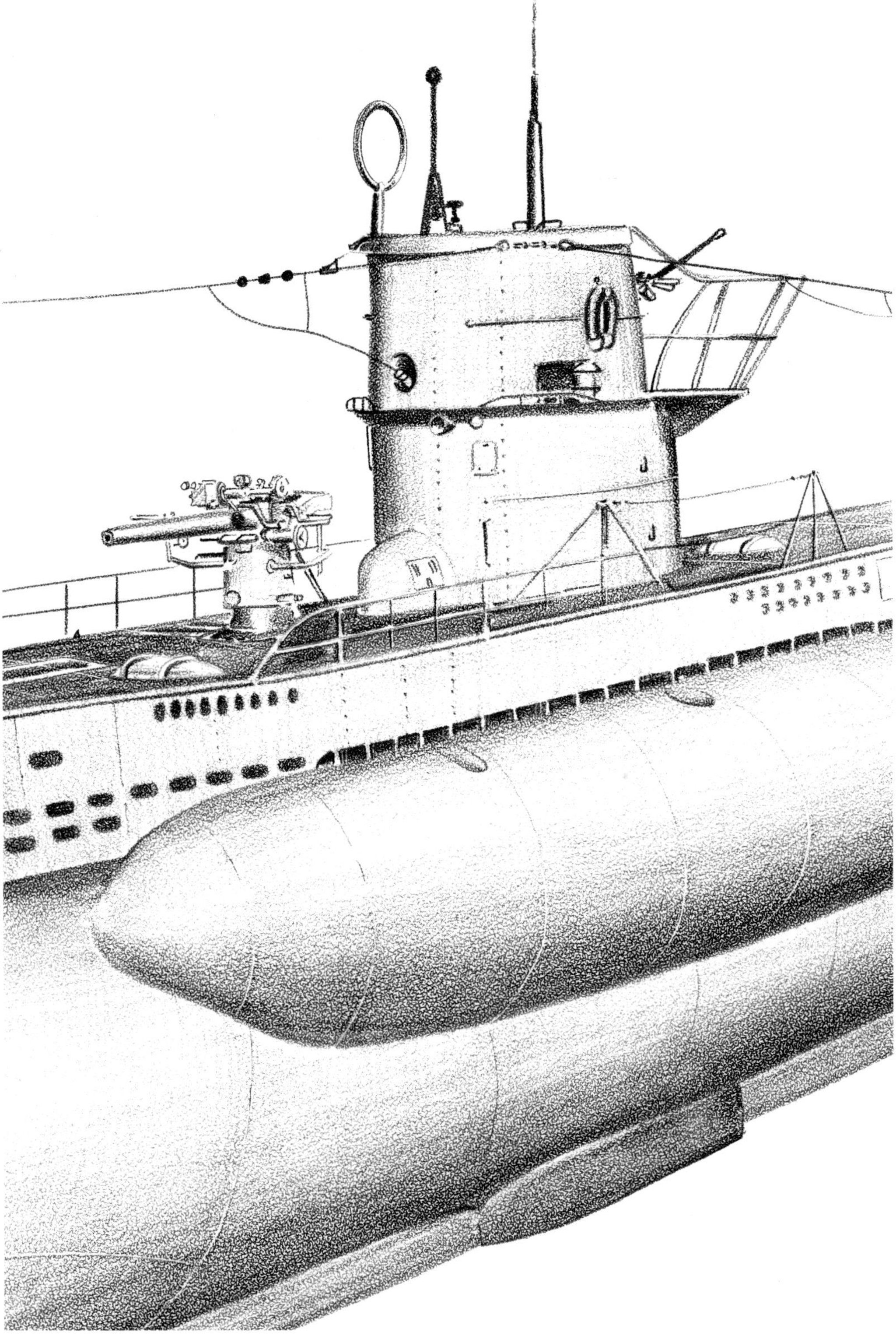

Bourne concept submarine (1578)

The notion of a vessel able to travel under the surface of the water dates from antiquity. The very first report of someone attempting to put the idea into practice seems to have been an attempt by Alexander the Great who, according to his teacher, the philosopher Aristotle, had developed a primitive submersible for reconnaissance by 332 BC.

In the modern era, however, the first person to propose a submarine that could have been workable was an Englishman, William Bourne, who was better known as a mathematician and who designed a prototype submersible. Bourne's notion was based on a boat-like hull of conventional construction but with its bilges fitted with leather ballast tanks for water admitted through hull openings below the waterline to cause the boat to sink. Buoyancy could then be restored by the movement of a couple of screw presses to squeeze the leather ballast tanks and expel the water. Air for the crew was drawn through a hollow mast whose head extended above the water when the boat was submerged. Bourne's concept did not include any way to propel his submersible boat.

By the seventeenth century, Cossacks of Ukraine were using a *chaika*

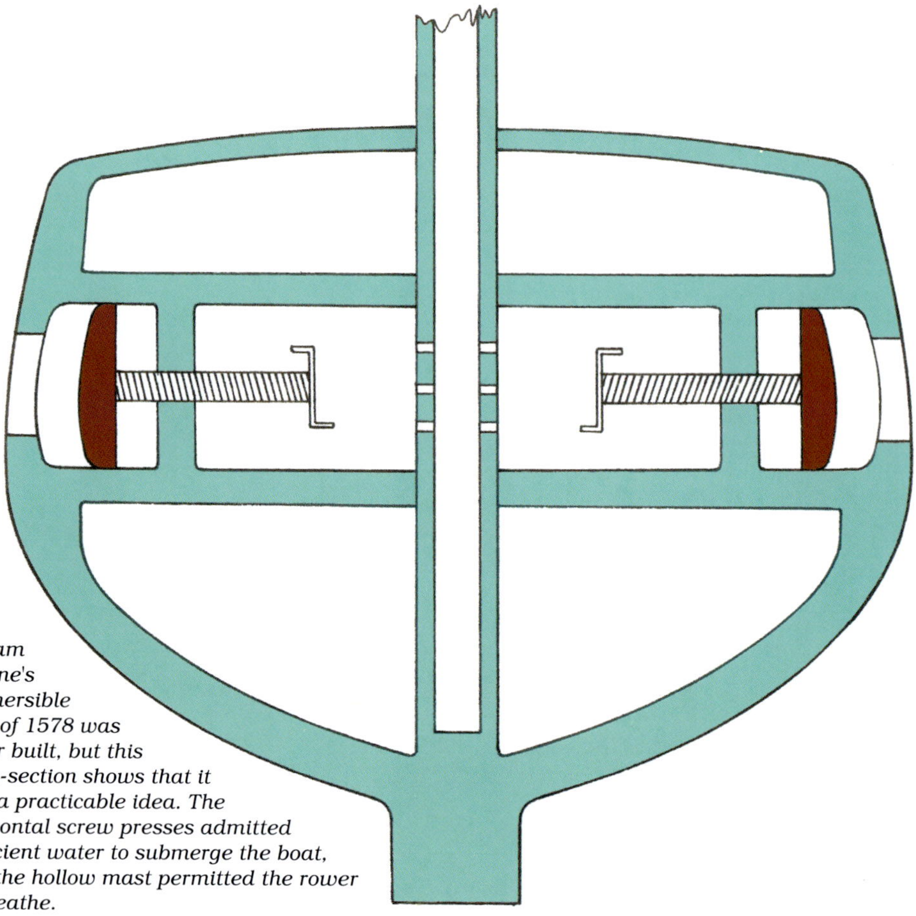

William Bourne's submersible boat of 1578 was never built, but this cross-section shows that it was a practicable idea. The horizontal screw presses admitted sufficient water to submerge the boat, and the hollow mast permitted the rower to breathe.

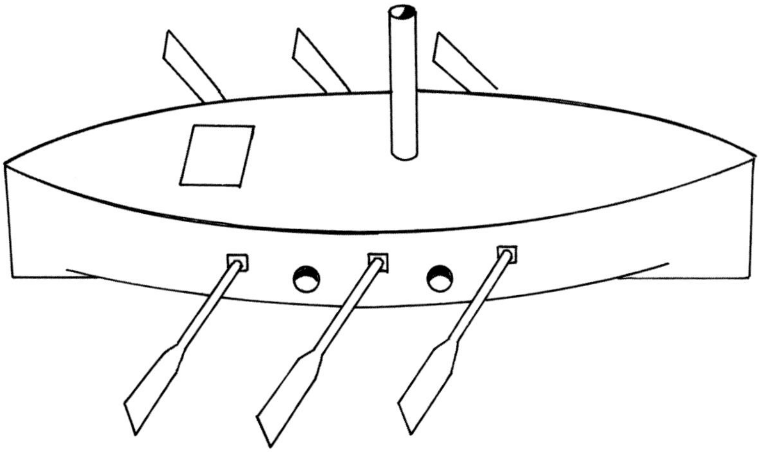

Sketch showing the propulsion system of the first true submersible, built by Jacobszoon Drebbel.

("gull") riverboat, which could be submerged, for reconnaissance and the delivery of "special forces." This appears to have been akin to the submersible boat ascribed by Aristotle to Alexander the Great. The *chaika* could readily capsize and submerge so that the crew was able to breathe the air trapped in the overturned hull and move the boat by walking on the river bottom. Weights were used to aid the submerging process, and there were pipes for additional breathing.

The first true submersible to be built, however, was the 1620 device of a multi-talented inventor, Cornelius Jacobszoon Drebbel, a Dutchman in the service of King James I. Drebbel built his boat while working for the British navy. Using Bourne's design of 1578 as his basis, Drebbel built a steerable submarine with a leather-covered wooden frame. The precise nature of Drebbel's boat is a matter of some dispute: some claim that it was not even a true submersible, as it lacked any means to alter its displacement by the admission and later expulsion of water: thus the boat relied on the efforts of the oarsmen to drive it partially under the surface so that it was merely running awash.

Between 1620 and 1624, Drebbel successfully built and tested two more submarines, each one bigger than the previous example. The third and final model was propelled by six oars and could carry up to 16 passengers. This model was demonstrated to the king and several thousand Londoners. The submarine remained under the surface of the water for three hours, and could travel from Westminster to Greenwich and back, cruising at a depth of from 12 to 15 feet (4 to 5 m). Drebbel even took the king for a test dive below the surface of the River Thames in the submarine boat, making James I the first monarch to travel underwater. Drebbel's third submarine was tested many times in the Thames, but did not attract enough Admiralty interest for the furtherance of the trials and possibly the construction of an operational boat, and was therefore never used in combat.

In 2002 the English boatbuilder Mark Edwards constructed a wooden submarine based on the original seventeenth century version of Drebbel. This was successfully tested underwater with two oarsmen at Dorney Lake near Windsor. Legal considerations prevented further trials in the River Thames.

De Son submarine (1653)

The first submarines had been seen by designers and, on occasion, builders, as being suitable for the exploration of the sea bed and the clandestine delivery of raiders, but the accolade of first conceiving the submarine as a weapon of war must go to a Frenchman, one M. de Son, who in 1653 had built in Rotterdam a submarine which, it was claimed, could cross the English Channel to attack the English fleet and "doeth undertake in one day to destroy a hondered ships." De Son certainly had a gift for self-promotion, for he also claimed that his boat would have the speed of a bird and "no fire, nor Storme, no Bullets can hinder her, unless it please God."

De Son's boat was also the world's first mechanically driven submarine. The boat was some 72 feet (21.9 m) long, and built largely of wood on the basis of a side-by-side pair of hulls. Each of these was based on a long central beam, metal-shod at its ends, surrounded by a spindle-shaped hull in which a short central section of cylindrical section verged into conical fore-and-aft sections. The air inside the hulls was sufficient to keep one man alive for three hours, it has been calculated, and a hatch in the upper surface of one of the cylindrical sections provided access to a small

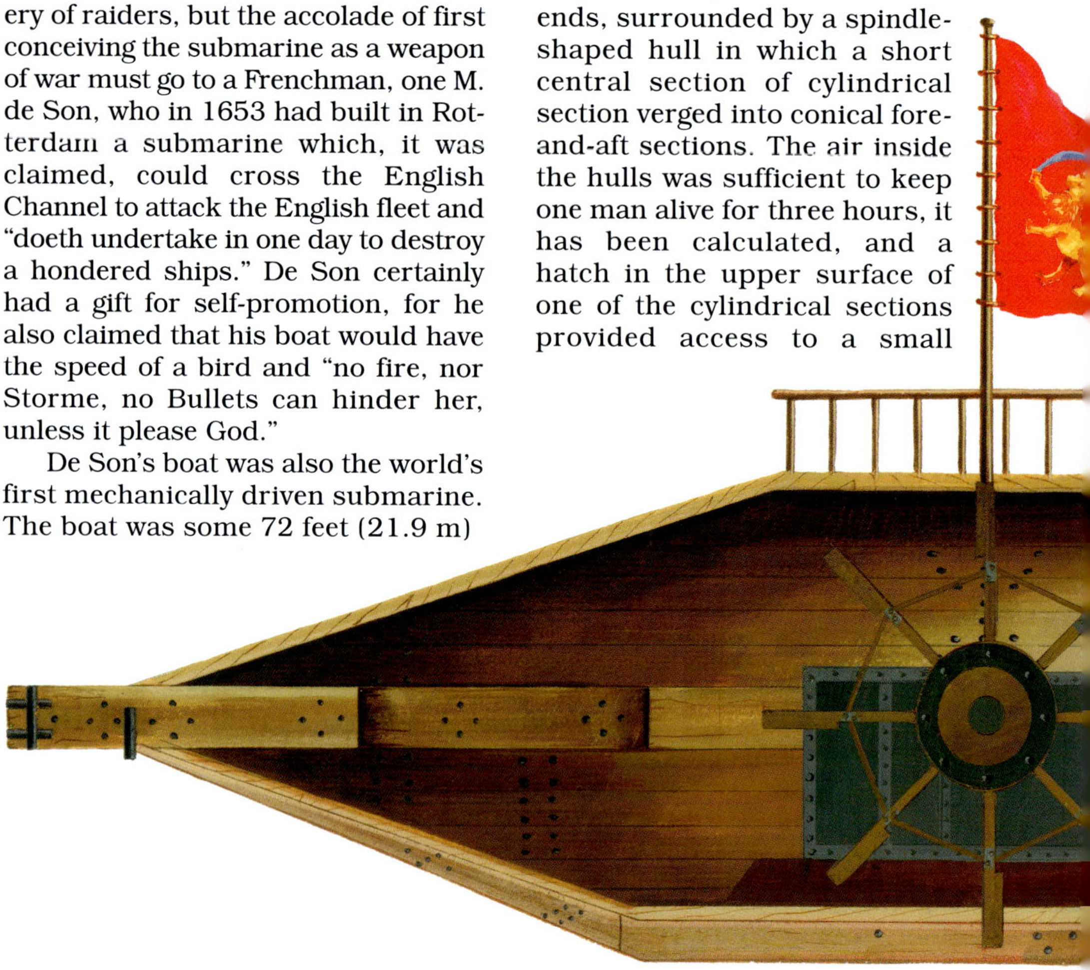

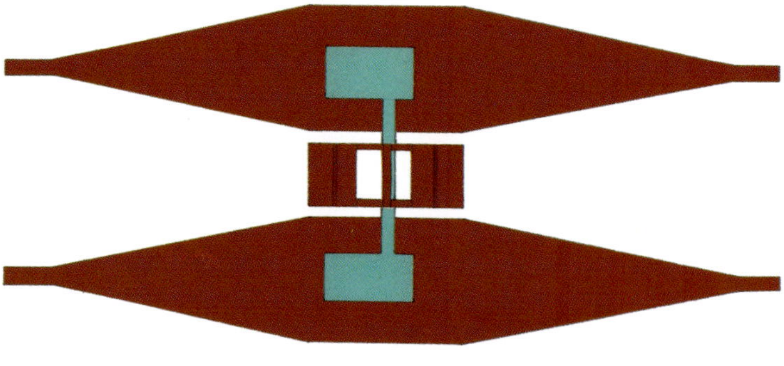

For the paddle to work, the top half would have had to be out of the water, so the vessel could never have been a true submersible.

"bridge," which was little more than a railed platform.

The two hulls were connected by a beam around which revolved a paddle wheel. This was driven by clockwork mechanisms in the hulls. However, initial trials revealed that the clockwork mechanism was too weak even to move de Son's catamaran boat, let alone provide it with the speed of a bird! The documents of the period

provide no evidence of a means of altering the boat's buoyancy by the admission and expulsion of water, so de Son's boat should be regarded not as a prototype powered submarine, but rather as the first attempt to create a powered submersible that, had it succeeded, would have run awash.

The tactical method envisaged by de Son for his boat was ramming attack, with the boat approaching its target undetected to drive the two metal-sheathed central beams against the side of the target ship and so punching holes through which the water would enter and sink her.

Although craft such as de Son's now seem almost quaint in their concept and execution, there was sound thinking behind the design. The real submarine would have to await the invention of the internal combustion engine in the 1880s before becoming a truly practical proposition.

There is no evidence that Italian Giovanni Borelli built a submarine, but an illustration of 1680 reveals elements of his thinking, including an understanding of the basic principle of displacement (volume versus weight). But Borelli illustrated a totally impractical ballast system in which weight was increased by allowing a bank of goat-skin bags to fill with water, then decreased by squeezing the water out of them once more to allow the boat to rise.

In 1696 Denis Papin, a professor of mathematics, built two submarines, using an air pump to control internal pressure relative to external water pressure, thus controlling buoyancy through the in-and-out flow of water into the hull. His selected propulsive method was sails on the surface and oars under the water. Papin's boats featured "certain holes" through which the operator might "touch enemy vessels and ruin them in sundry ways." Papin tested his first boat, but his patron lost interest and the second boat was never finished.

Turtle (1776)

The *Turtle* is of key importance in naval history as the world's first submarine to be operated in combat. It was designed in Connecticut in 1775 by the U.S. patriot David Bushnell as a means of approaching, without detection, and for the purpose of attaching explosive charges, ships anchored or moored in a harbor.

So named for its shape, the *Turtle* resembled a large clam as much as a turtle. Built of wood, the craft was 7 ft., 6 in. (2.3 m) long, 6 ft. (1.8 m) high and about 3 ft. (0.9 m) wide, and was based on a pair of wooden shells covered with tar. The craft was submerged by allowing water into the hull, and then brought back to the

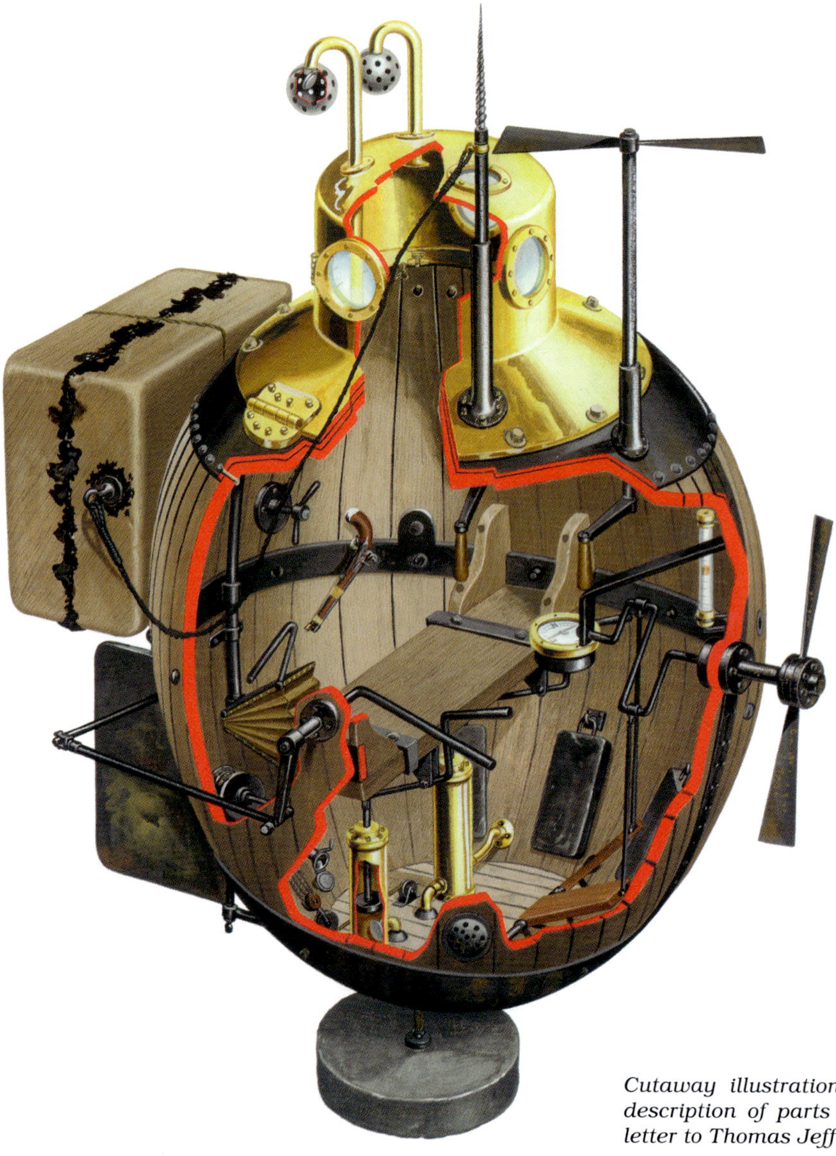

Cutaway illustration developed from description of parts in the designer's letter to Thomas Jefferson.

Extract from David Bushnell's letter to Thomas Jefferson, 1787.

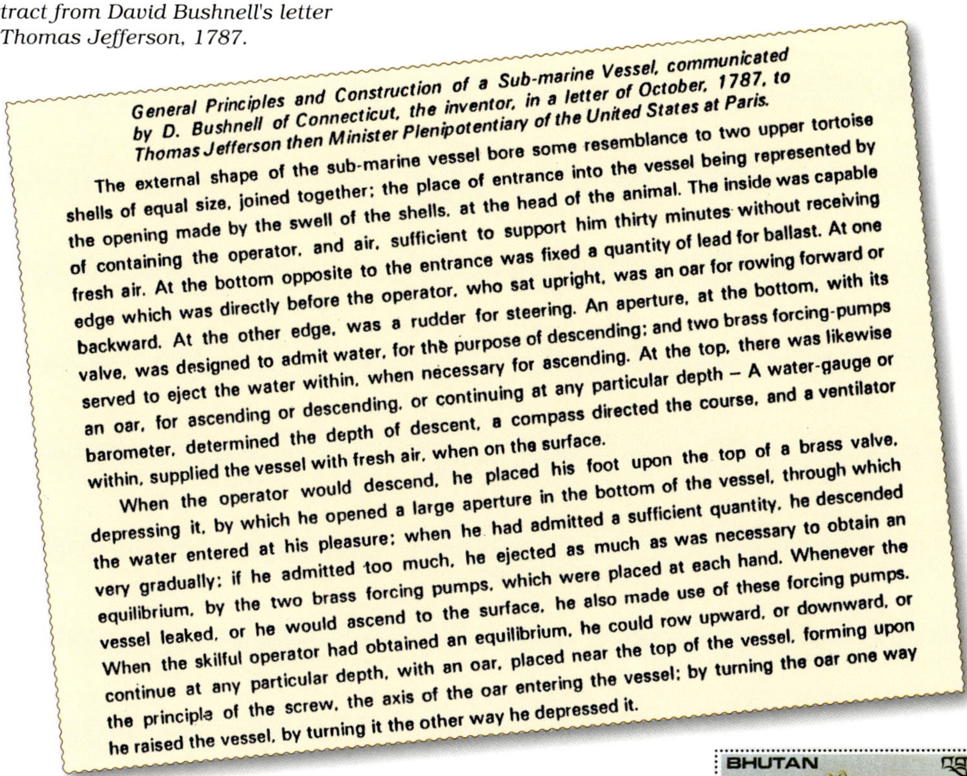

General Principles and Construction of a Sub-marine Vessel, communicated by D. Bushnell of Connecticut, the inventor, in a letter of October, 1787, to Thomas Jefferson then Minister Plenipotentiary of the United States at Paris.

The external shape of the sub-marine vessel bore some resemblance to two upper tortoise shells of equal size, joined together; the place of entrance into the vessel being represented by the opening made by the swell of the shells, at the head of the animal. The inside was capable of containing the operator, and air, sufficient to support him thirty minutes without receiving fresh air. At the bottom opposite to the entrance was fixed a quantity of lead for ballast. At one edge which was directly before the operator, who sat upright, was an oar for rowing forward or backward. At the other edge, was a rudder for steering. An aperture, at the bottom, with its valve, was designed to admit water, for the purpose of descending; and two brass forcing-pumps served to eject the water within, when necessary for ascending. At the top, there was likewise an oar, for ascending or descending, or continuing at any particular depth – A water-gauge or barometer, determined the depth of descent, a compass directed the course, and a ventilator within, supplied the vessel with fresh air, when on the surface.

When the operator would descend, he placed his foot upon the top of a brass valve, depressing it, by which he opened a large aperture in the bottom of the vessel, through which the water entered at his pleasure; when he had admitted a sufficient quantity, he descended very gradually; if he admitted too much, he ejected as much as was necessary to obtain an equilibrium, by the two brass forcing pumps, which were placed at each hand. Whenever the vessel leaked, or he would ascend to the surface, he also made use of these forcing pumps. When the skilful operator had obtained an equilibrium, he could row upward, or downward, or continue at any particular depth, with an oar, placed near the top of the vessel, forming upon the principle of the screw, the axis of the oar entering the vessel; by turning the oar one way he raised the vessel, by turning it the other way he depressed it.

surface by expelling the water, sloshing in the bilge, via the agency of a foot-operated pump. The *Turtle* also carried some 700 lb. (318 kg) of lead ballast to reduce its buoyancy, and of this ballast 200 lb. (91 kg) could be jettisoned in an emergency. The craft was propelled vertically and horizontally by hand-cranked propellers: this was in fact the first recorded use of the screw propeller for the propulsion of a water vessel. A steering capability was provided by a rear-mounted rudder whose tiller was braced between the operator's body and right arm, and the craft was manned and operated by just one person, The operator sat with his head in a raised and windowed "conning tower" whose upper surface constituted the hatch through which the operator entered and left the craft. The conning tower also carried a pair of snorkel-type air pipes fitted with check valves, and the air in the *Turtle* was sufficient for 30 minutes under the water. The *Turtle*'s equipment included compass and a depth gauge.

The *Turtle* was created and constructed specifically as a naval weapon, and in service was designed so that the operator, again using a hand device, could drill into the target ship's hull and plant a special casing, filled with 150 lb. (68 kg) of gunpowder. The operator then detached the mine to rest beside the target vessel; a timer ensured the detonation of the charge one hour after the *Turtle* and its "torpedo" had separated.

The Turtle, here in profile, was a very radical change to all previous ideas for ships or boats.

Testing was undertaken by the inventor's brother, Ezra, in the Connecticut River. Bushnell was defeated by the problem of providing a measure of lighting inside the craft and, after learning that the burning of a candle would much speed the use of the oxygen in the limited air supply inside the craft, sought help from Benjamin Franklin. The latter suggested the notion of using foxfire, a bioluminescent wood, to provide illumination for the compass and depth gauge. The light given by the material was said to be sufficient, though likely dimmer than expected, because the craft was cooled by the water around it and bioluminescent organisms are temperature-dependent.

General George Washington provided the funds to transport the *Turtle* to New York, from which the American forces wished to expel the British, in the War of Independence. On September 7, 1776, the *Turtle*, operated by a volunteer, Sergeant Ezra Lee (as David Bushnell was too old and Ezra Bushnell was ill), attacked the 64-gun HMS *Eagle*, flagship of Vice Admiral Richard

John Batchelor looks into the full-size model of the Turtle on show at the Submarine Museum at Gosport, England. This model was built from the cutaway illustration John researched at the Smithsonian Institute in Washington, D.C.

Howe. The ship was moored off what is today Liberty Island, but Lee could not bore through the copper-sheeted hull. When he attempted another spot in the hull, he lost sight of the target, rose to the surface, decided to abandon the effort, and made for the shore. The *Turtle* was spotted by a British gunboat near Governors Island, so Lee released the "torpedo," which detonated one hour later and caused great alarm among the ships of the British fleet.

The Americans made two more attempts to use the *Turtle*, but both were unsuccessful. The craft's final fate remains unknown, although it is likely that it was burned to prevent it falling into the hands of the British when they took New York City.

Turtle

Type:	attack submarine
Tonnage:	1 ton surfaced
Dimensions:	length 7 ft., 6 in. (2.3 m); height 6 ft. (1.8 m); beam 3 ft. (0.9 m)
Propulsion:	manually-powered propeller for 2-3 knots
Armament:	one detachable "torpedo" carrying 150 lb. (68 kg) of gunpowder
Complement:	1

Nautilus (1801)

Of major historical importance as the world's first practical submarine, the *Nautilus* was commissioned by First Consul Napoleon Bonaparte, and designed by the very gifted American inventor Robert Fulton, who was living and working in the French First Republic.

Though best remembered in the U.S. as a pioneer of the steam-powered surface vessel, such as the *North River Steamboat* (otherwise *Clermont*) of 1807, Fulton first came to prominence as a result of his submarine experiments. On December 13, 1797, Fulton wrote to the Executive Directory ruling France with his proposal for a system of submarine warfare, which included a rate schedule for the destruction of British ships ("4000 Livers [livres] per Gun for each British ship over 40 Guns...and 200 Livers per Gun for All vessels of war under 40 tons"). The concept offered, in theory at least and at only modest initial cost, a capability that the French navy could not readily provide at this time, and a single experimental vessel was ordered.

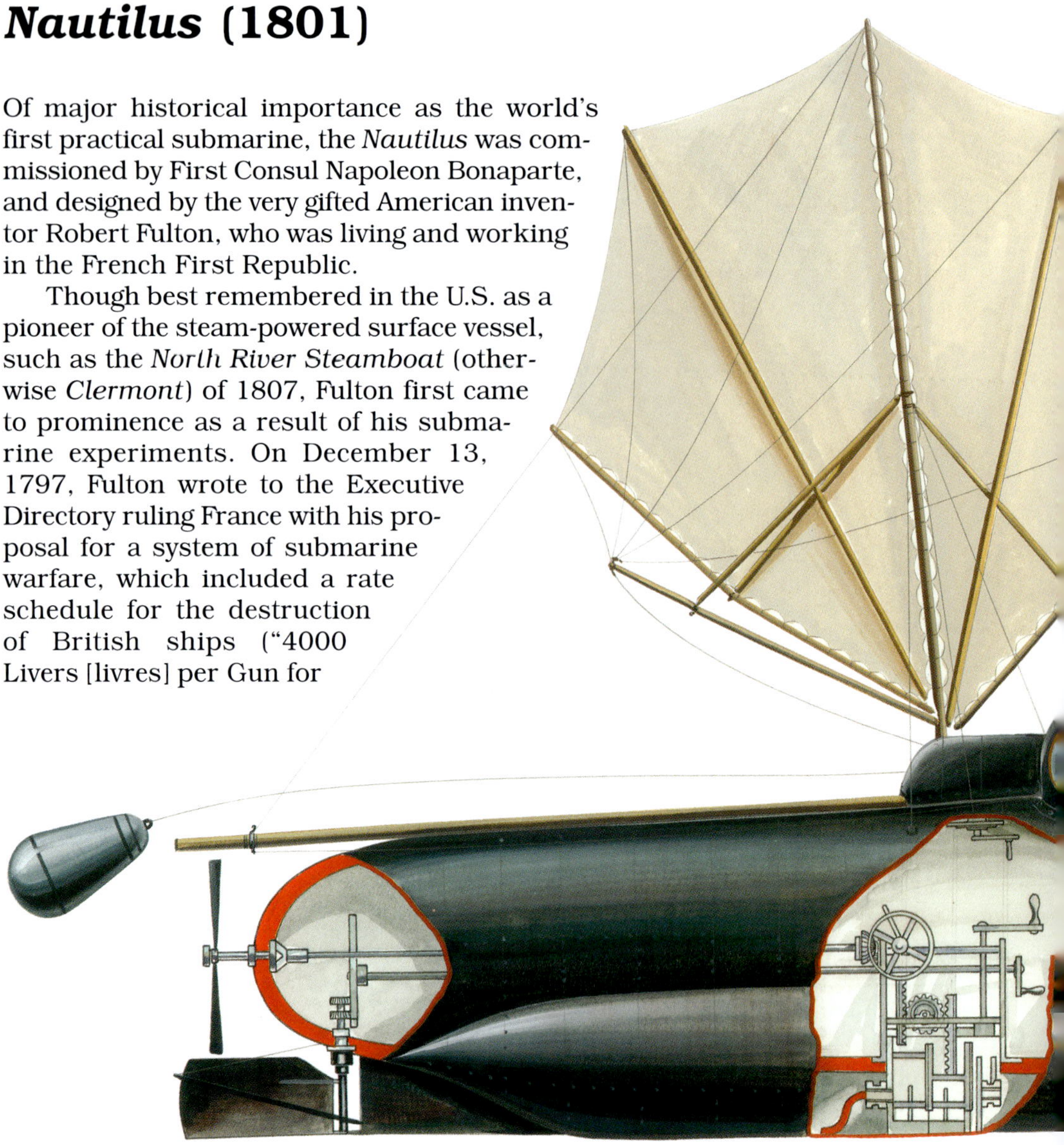

Built by J. C. Périer in Paris and completed in 1801, the *Nautilus* in many respects pioneered the submarine concept that would became standard much later in the same century. The vessel was based on a cylindrical hull that tapered sharply to a pointed bow and tapered slightly in diameter toward the hemispherical stern. The hull was fabricated of copper sheeting over iron ribs, and was 21 ft., 4 in. (6.5 m) long with a domed conning tower which also served as the hatch, was fitted with a periscope, and carried thin tubes which could be employed to freshen the air inside the vessel when it was moving just below the surface of the water. The vessel had a rudder under the stern for directional control and a forward-mounted diving plane for horizontal control, and thus introduced the basic combination of surfaces used right up to the present day. As initially conceived, the *Nautilus* contained air sufficient for four men and two burning candles over a period of three hours. In 1802 Fulton experimented with the use of a canister of compressed air to provide a submerged endurance of six hours, and the need for candles was removed by the insertion of a pane of glass, three-quarters of an inch (11.9 cm) thick, in the conning tower: this provided enough light, it was claimed, to read a watch at a depth of 25 feet (7.6 m). Diving and surfacing were regulated by the flow of water into and out of ballast tanks, and the process of expelling the water was powered by compressed air. When submerged, the *Nautilus* was driven at 2 knots by a hand-cranked four-blade propeller, and was driven on the surface by a sail supported by a mast designed to fold abaft the conning tower before the vessel submerged.

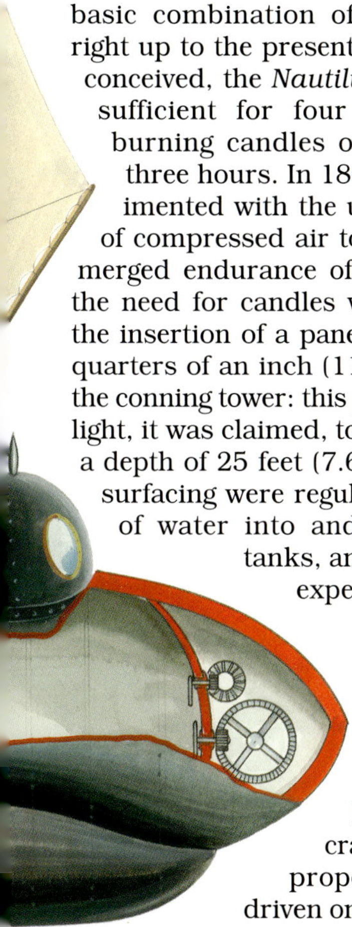

The *Nautilus* was tested in France in 1800-1801, when Fulton and three mechanics descended to a depth of 26 ft., 3 in. (8 m) using the ballast tanks. The original design included an auger extending above the conning tower, which was to have been used to drill a hole in the bottom of the target ship and so permit the attachment of an explosive charge that would be detonated only after the submarine had departed.

On September 12, 1801, Fulton and his crew of three departed from Le Havre in the *Nautilus*, reaching Cap de la Hogue five days later after a voyage of 70 miles (113 km). Fulton tried to approach two British brigs, but these sailed before he could reach and attack either of them. During the following year, the *Nautilus* sank a trial target using a gunpowder charge, which Fulton called a "torpedo" after the electric ray. Napoleon asked to see the vessel, but Fulton replied that it had been "dismantled as a result of rot," and his French funding ended in 1804.

Fulton took the *Nautilus* to England, where he gained the interest of Prime Minister William Pitt. In 1805 Fulton sank a 300-ton brig, but the Royal Navy was not interested and Fulton turned to surface vessels. It is worth noting that Fulton believed the submarine to be so decisive a weapon that he called it "A Curious Machine for Mending Politics" and so ending war.

Nautilus

Type:	attack submarine
Tonnage:	19 tons surfaced
Dimensions:	length 21 ft., 3 in. (6.5 m); beam 6 ft., 4 in. (1.9m); draft 3 ft., 7 in. (1.2 m)
Propulsion:	sail and hand-cranked propeller for 2 knots
Armament:	one "torpedo"
Complement:	3 or 4

Brandtaucher (1851)

During the War of 1812, an American named Silas Halsey lost his life in an unsuccessful submarine attack of 1814 on a British warship in the harbor of New London, and in 1834 a Russian naval designer, Karl Shilder, built and tested a submarine of all-metal construction in the harbor of St Petersburg. This boat was armed with six Congreve rockets.

However, the next major advance in the concept and practice of submarine warfare arrived in 1850, when Wilhelm Bauer, a non-commissioned officer in the army of Bavaria, designed and built a submarine called the *Brandtaucher* (fire diver), sometimes also called the *Plongeur Marin* (sea diver). At this time, the powerful Danish fleet was blockading the German coast, and with the financial backing of several important citizens of the port city of Kiel (which was suffering as a result of the blockade), Bauer's boat was laid down in the private shipyard of August Howaldt.

The *Brandtaucher* included some features that had first appeared in the *Nautilus*, but this German submarine was built entirely of sheet iron, and in basic terms resembled a large oblong tank. Water was admitted into a double bottom to ballast the boat down, but when awash a heavy weight was moved backwards and forwards to produce a series of dips.

No matter how complex and ingenious, the submarine would not work until fitted with internal combustion and/or electric motors.

Despite its severe limitations, the *Brandtaucher* offered sufficient threat or persuaded the Danes that it might be able to do so, to cause the Danes to standard considerably farther out to sea. However, in February 1851, Bauer again took the lead, in an altogether different manner presaging a too-frequent occurrence of later submarine history, when his submarine's hull plating buckled under the pressure of the water, and the *Brandtaucher* settled on the bottom of the Kiel harbor. It took all of Bauer's considerable strength of personality to badger the two terrified seamen with him to accept that only one thing would save them. This was to let more water to the boat until the pressure was equalized. Only then could the two hatches be opened and all three men escape to the surface. In 1887 the *Brandtaucher* was rediscovered during dredging operations, and the vessel was subsequently exhibited at the Naval School in Kiel before settling in the Military History Museum of Dresden, Germany, where it still rests.

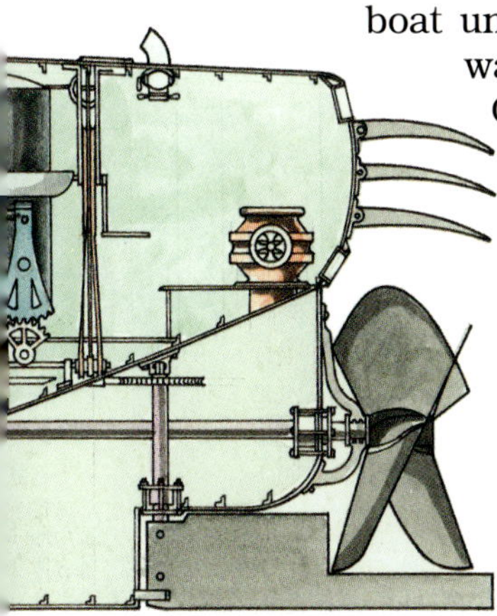

Apparently, Bauer was deserted by his backers at this stage, and he therefore approached the Austrian authorities. Any chance of securing Austrian backing was then lost in the mire of Austrian politics, and Bauer decided to try his luck in England. His work caught the attention of Prince Albert, but again he had little success. Bauer's next stop was Russia, where he was permitted to build the *Diable Marin* ("sea devil"). Almost nothing is known of this boat other than the fact that in 1856 Bauer took his submarine below the surface of the Kronshtadt harbor with several musicians during the coronation of Tsar Aleksandr II, and, during the royal salute, the band struck up "God Preserve the Tsar." The *Diable Marin* was later sunk, and thereafter Bauer drifted into obscurity.

Brandtaucher

Type:	attack submarine
Tonnage:	not available
Dimensions:	length 26 ft., 6 in. (8.07 m); beam 6 ft., 8 in. (2.02 m); draft 8 ft.. 8 in. (2.63 m)
Propulsion:	propeller powered by three men on treadwheels for 3 knots
Armament:	not known (if any)
Complement:	3 or 4

Alstitt boat (1863)

During the American Civil War (1861-65), considerable strides were made in the development of the submarine as a viable if not yet fully practical weapon of war. The Union side was the first to field a submarine. The *Alligator*, designed by the French engineer Brutus de Villeroi and built by the Neafie and Levy yard of Philadelphia, Pennsylvania, was the first U.S. Navy submarine and the first boat with an effective compressed air system for the supply of breathing air, and the first with an air filtration system. The *Alligator* was also the first submarine equipped with a diver lock, which made it possible for a diver to exit the submarine and return after planting mines against the underside of an enemy ship's hull for later detonation by electrical means. The *Alligator* was initially propelled by 16 oars for a speed of 3 to 4 knots, but after six months the boat was taken in hand for conversion to screw propeller propulsion by means of a hand-operated crank for a speed of 7 knots. Larger than the Confederate submarines of the Civil War, the basically cylindrical *Alligator* had a crew of 21 men and was 47 feet (14.3 m) long with a maximum diameter of about 4 ft., 8 in. (1.4 m). The armament was two spar torpedoes. This submarine was lost in a storm off Cape Hatteras on April 2, 1863, fortunately without loss of life, as it was being towed unmanned to its first operational deployment at Charleston, South Carolina.

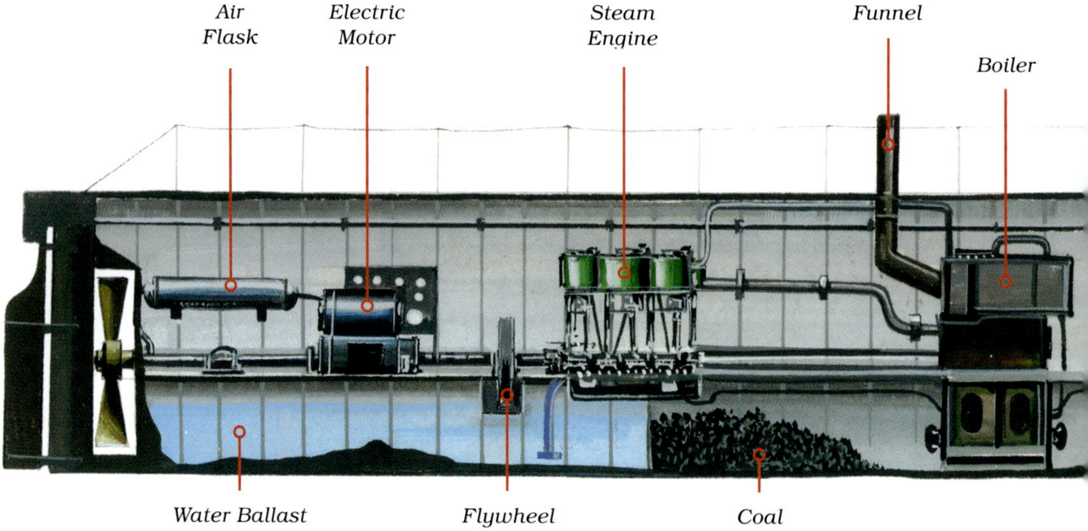

Despite the fact that the American *Plunger* of 1897 and French *Narval* of two years later are generally credited with being the world's first two submarines with a mixed propulsion arrangement, this accolade should in fact go to the boat designed in 1863 by an American engineer, one Alstitt, and built at Mobile, Alabama, for the Confederacy. One of the reasons for the boat's almost immediate failure was the location of the diving planes at the bow rather than abaft the propeller, and this positioning made the boat almost completely unmanageable.

The Alstitt boat's mixed-propulsion arrangement, driving one large four-blade propeller located just ahead of the rudder, had steam and electric elements. The former was used for surface running, and was based on a boiler located below and just abaft the conning tower with its funnel emerging through the deck above and abaft the boiler. Coal for the boiler's furnace was carried in two compartments below the boiler installation. The boiler's steam was ducted to an engine farther toward the boat's stern, and this engine turned a propeller shaft fitted with a substantial flywheel. Electrical power was used for underwater running, and was based on elements in the bow and stern. Filling most of the boat forward of the conning tower was a large assembly of electrical batteries, and these supplied current to an electric motor which drove the propeller shaft at a point abaft the flywheel.

The locomotive or free-running torpedo had not been invented by this time, so the Alstitt boat was fitted with large, watertight but buoyant cases of gunpowder arranged along each side of the vessel. These cases were held by chains connected to positions inside the boat, and when freed floated up to the surface under the moored ship being attacked, and were then detonated electrically. For attacks on moving targets, the intention was to scatter contact-fused mines in its path—any of which did not detonate were then collected at leisure! A third option was the spar torpedo, comprising an explosive charge at the end of a long pole, or spar, extending ahead of the boat. Designed during the American Civil War by E. C. Singer, the weapon was used by running the end of the spar into the ship being attacked. The spar's tip was often equipped with a barb to fix itself into the wood of the target hull. The Singer spar torpedo was detonated by means of a trigger mechanism adapted from a rifle lock, its spring-loaded trigger being detonated via the agency of a long cord attached to the attacking vessel. The attacking vessel rammed its target, embedding the barbed torpedo in its hull, then backed off, and as the trigger cord became fully extended it pulled the trigger to detonate the torpedo with the attacking vessel, it was hoped, at a safe distance.

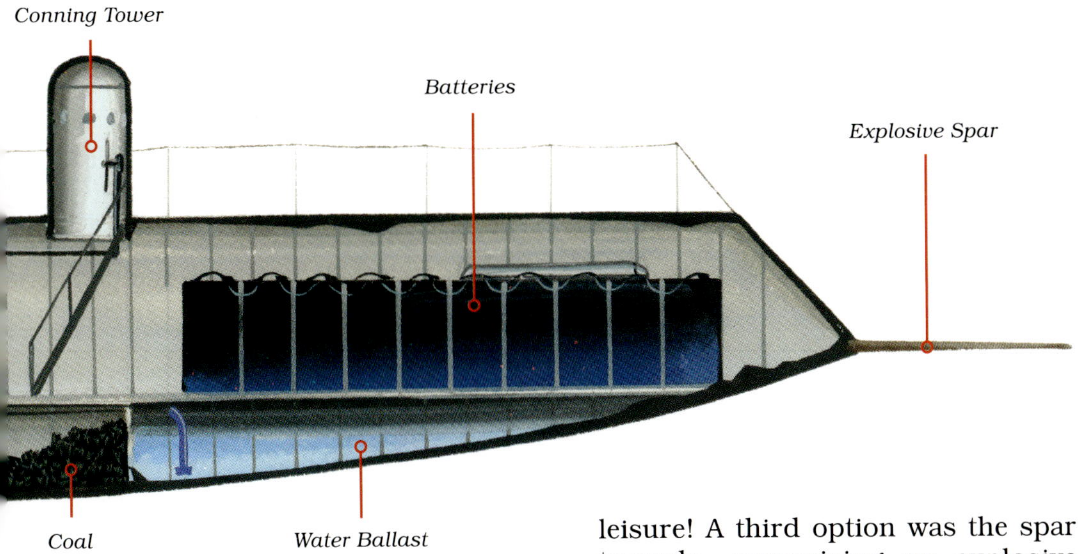

David (1863)

The *David* was built as a private venture by T. Stoney at Charleston, South Carolina in 1863, and was put under command of the Confederate States Navy. The cigar-shaped *David* was armed with a single spar torpedo carrying a 60 or 70 lb. (27 or 32 kg) gunpowder charge at the tip of the spar projecting dead ahead from her bow. Designed to operate very low in the water, the *David* resembled a submarine in her overall shape, but was nonetheless a surface vessel designed to operate no lower than awash in the water. Operating on dark nights, and with her boiler burning anthracite coal, which gives off little if any smoke, the *David* was in practical terms as difficult to see as a genuine submarine of the period.

On the night of October 5, 1863, the *David*, under the command of Lieutenant William T. Glassell, steamed unobtrusively down the harbor of Charleston to attack the USS *New Ironsides*, an ironclad warship with casemated guns. The torpedo boat approached undetected until it was within 50 yards (46 m) of the warship, which was part of the Union squadron blockading Charleston. When hailed by a lookout on the *New Ironsides*, Glassell fired his shotgun at the Union vessel and drove his own vessel straight forward to strike the *New Ironsides*. The *David*'s spar torpedo detonated under the *New Ironside*'s starboard quarter, projecting water into the air, which then fell on the Confederate vessel and extinguished her boiler fires. Dead in the water, the *David* floated under the quarter of the *New Ironsides* as the latter's men peppered the water around the torpedo boat with fire.

Believing that the *David* was about to sink, Glassell and two others jumped overboard. The pilot, Walker Cannon, could not swim and elected to remain on board. A short time later, Assistant Engineer J. H. Tomb swam back to the *David* and reboarded her. Tomb got the *David*'s engine working once more and, and with Cannon at the wheel, the torpedo boat steamed up the channel to safety. Glassell and James Sullivan, the *David*'s fireman, were captured. The *New Ironsides* was seriously damaged by the spar torpedo's detonation, but did not sink. The next period of the *David*'s existence, over a time of some four months, remains obscure. It or other torpedo boats attempted

further attacks on the ships of the Union blockade squadron: reports from different ships suggest three such undertakings, all of them unsuccessful, during the remainder of October 1863.

On March 6, 1864, the *David* was used for an attack in the USS *Memphis* in the North Edisto River. The torpedo boat struck the Union ship on the port quarter but the torpedo did not explode. The *Memphis* slipped her anchor chain to get under way as rapidly as possible, and at the same time her crew fired ineffectually at the *David* with their small arms. The Confederate torpedo boat then returned to the attack and once again hit the *Memphis*, this time a glancing blow on the starboard quarter, but yet again the torpedo did not detonate. The *Memphis* had by now started to fire on her attacker with heavy guns, so the *David*, which had lost part of her funnel when it rammed the larger ship, retreated up the river out of gun range. The *Memphis*, which had suffered no damage, resumed her role in the blockade.

The *David*'s final confirmed action occurred on April 18, 1864, when the torpedo boat made an attempt to sink the screw frigate USS *Wabash*. But the look-outs on the Union blockade vessel were alert and spotted the movement of the *David* early enough to allow the Union frigate to slip her anchor chain, avoid the attack, and open fire on the torpedo boat. Neither of the vessels suffered any damage.

The *David*'s fate is uncertain. Several torpedo boats of this type were seized when the Union forces captured Charleston during February 1865, and the *David* may well have been among them.

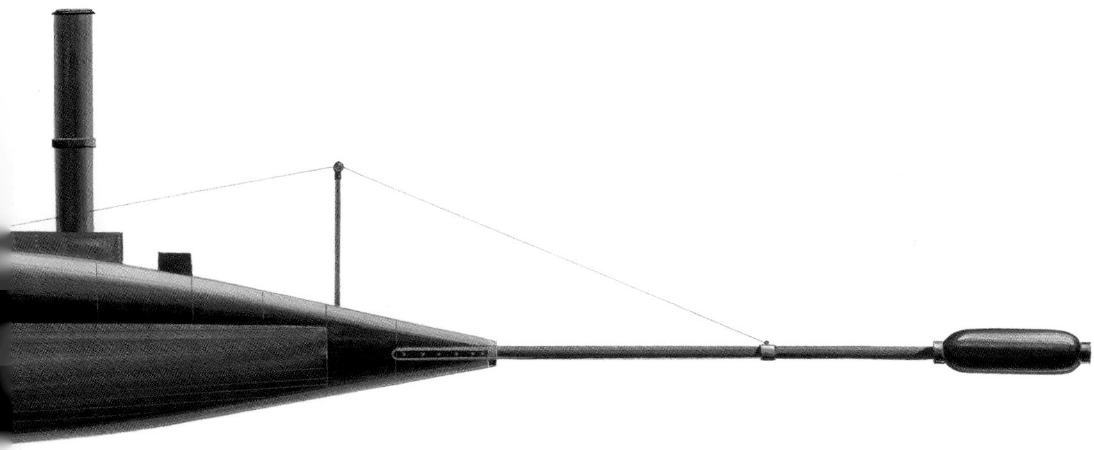

David

Type:	attack torpedo boat
Tonnage:	not known
Dimensions:	50 ft., 0 in. (15.2 m); beam 6 ft., 0 in. (1.8 m); draft 5 ft., 0 in (1.5 m)
Propulsion:	one steam-engine powered one propeller
Armament:	one spar torpedo
Complement:	4

H. L. Hunley (1863)

A vessel of the Confederate States Navy, the *H. L. Hunley* was the first submarine in the world to sink a warship in action. The *H. L. Hunley* was the third vessel, following the *Pioneer* and *American Diver*, designed, funded, and constructed by a group of inventors and investors drawn by the lure of a Confederate promise in the U.S. Civil War (1861-65) of prize money equal to 20% of the value of any Union warship sunk. Among the private-enterprise group was an officer of the Confederate army, Captain Horace Lawson Hunley. In essence a modified cylindrical steam boiler of riveted iron construction, the *H. L. Hunley* was steered by one member of the crew, had its dive controlled by a pair of hand-operated planes on the sides of the forward hull, and powered by eight others hand-cranking the shaft for the shrouded single propeller located just forward of the rudder. There were two small raised and windowed cupolas each topped by a hatch. The armament was typically simple, in accord with the standards of the day, and comprised one spar torpedo.

Initially known as the *Fish Boat*, and built at Mobile, Alabama, by Thomas B. Park and Thomas W. Lyons, the boat undertook successful trials in Mobile Harbor during August 1863 and was then moved by train to Charleston, South Carolina. The boat's first skipper was James R. McClintock, one of the venture's partners, but under his leadership the boat failed in its attacks on the ships of the Union blockade squadron off Charleston and commissioned into the Confederate States Navy with a volunteer crew under the command of Lieutenant John A. Payne. Five of this naval crew were killed when the boat sank accidentally, and another nine, Hunley among them, were lost when the boat sank again on October 15.

The *H. L. Hunley* nonetheless managed to attract another crew. On the night of February 17, 1864, the *H. L. Hunley* moved into Charleston

Harbor and attacked the screw sloop USS *Housatonic*, which sank with the loss of five men. Neither the *H. L. Hunley* nor its crew returned from this mission, and the remains of the boat that had made the world's first successful submarine attack were thought lost forever.

Although the *H. L. Hunley* can be regarded as only a qualified technical success, having killed less than one of the enemy for every four of her own crew, her destruction of the *Housatonic* nonetheless marked the emergence of the submarine as the

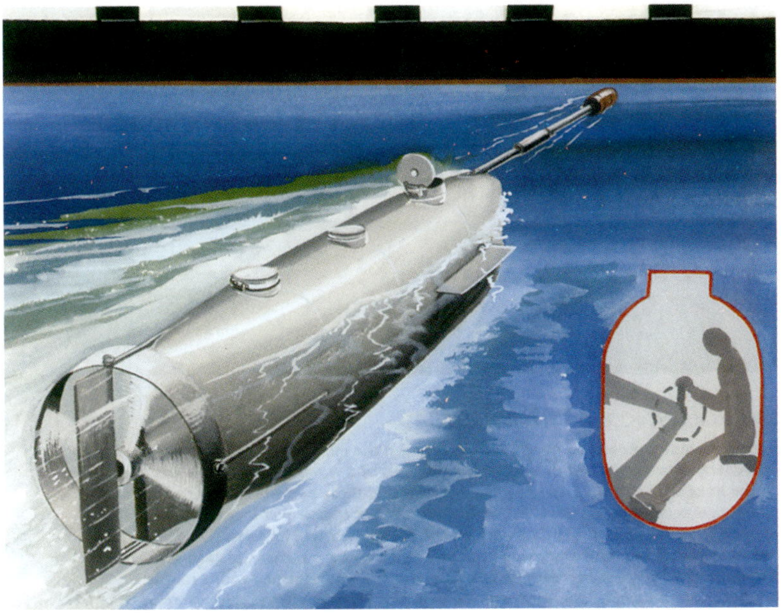

Left:
The claustrophobic conditions inside the Hunley can only be imagined.

Below left:
Most of the Hunley hull was taken up with the means of propulsion: men.

agent of a new form of warfare which would start to fulfill its promise, or rather its threat, just over half a century later in World War I (1914-18).

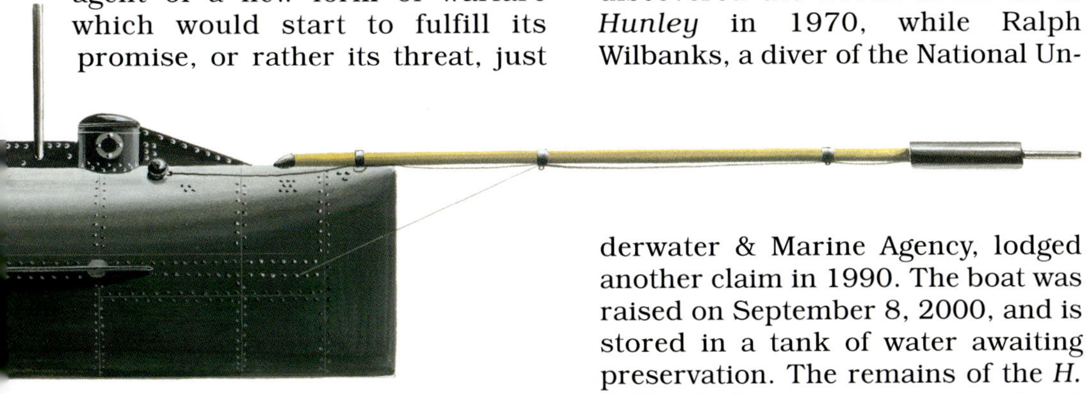

E. Lee Spence, an underwater archaeologist, claimed that he had discovered the wreck of the *H. L. Hunley* in 1970, while Ralph Wilbanks, a diver of the National Underwater & Marine Agency, lodged another claim in 1990. The boat was raised on September 8, 2000, and is stored in a tank of water awaiting preservation. The remains of the *H. L. Hunley*'s crew were removed and accorded a full military funeral before a crowd of up to 50,000 people, including 10,000 Civil War re-enactors.

H. L. Hunley

Type:	attack submarine
Tonnage:	7.5 tons surfaced
Dimensions:	39 ft., 6 in. (12.0 m); beam 30 ft., 10 in. (1.2 m); draft 5 ft., 0 in. (1.5 m)
Propulsion:	hand-cranked propeller for 4 knots surfaced
Armament:	one spar torpedo
Complement:	9

Intelligent Whale (1863)

The origins of the *Intelligent Whale* can be discerned in the fears of the Union side in the American Civil War (1861-65) that the Confederate side was beginning to develop a technical superiority in the matter of underwater warfare, and could well threaten the ships of the squadrons with which the Union side was closely blockading the Confederacy's major ports.

The *Intelligent Whale* was an experimental submarine with hand-cranked propulsion, and was designed by Scovel S. Meriam in 1863 for construction by Augustus Price and Cornelius S. Bushnell, whose interests were bought out in 1864 with the creation of the American Submarine Company. There followed many years of litigation over the ownership of the *Intelligent Whale*, whose acquisition had first been mooted by the U.S. Navy in 1864. When the title was finally fixed by the courts, the submarine was sold on October 29, 1869, to the U.S. Navy, with most of the price to be paid after the boat had completed successful trials. In September 1872 the first trial was held and was deemed by the U.S. Navy to have been only partially successful; the Department of the Navy refused to consider any further payments and the whole project was abandoned.

Built entirely of iron plates, and of cylindrical sections tapering curvaceously from a point of maximum diameter amidships to a finer point at the bow and a cut-off point at the stern, where the shrouded propeller

was located, the *Intelligent Whale* submerged by allowing water to enter the boat's special flooding compartments, and was returned to the surface by expelling the water through the use of pumps and compressed air. Longitudinal control of the boat below the surface of the water was entrusted to a pair of diving planes hinged to the rear of two fixed horizontal surfaces. It was estimated that the *Intelligent Whale* carried sufficient air to allow the boat to remain under the surface of the water for about ten hours. While accommodation was provided for a maximum of 13 men, a crew of only six men was required to operate the vessel safely.

The only known trial of the *Intelligent Whale*, which carried no inbuilt armament and not had been conceived as a vehicle for the delivery of clandestine or "sneak" attacks, was made by a certain General Sweeney and two others. They submerged the boat in 16 feet (4.9 m) of water and Sweeney, wearing a diver's suit, left the boat via a hole in her bottom, placed a charge under a target scow (barge), and then returned to the *Intelligent Whale* to re-enter the vessel via the hole in the bottom. The charge was then exploded by the operation of a friction primer by hauling on a lanyard, the detonation of the charge sinking the target scow.

The *Intelligent Whale* was then placed on display at the Brooklyn Navy Yard before being transferred in 1966 to Washington Navy Yard for long-term display in its Navy Memorial Museum. At present, the submarine is displayed in the New Jersey National Guard Militia Museum, Sea Girt, New Jersey.

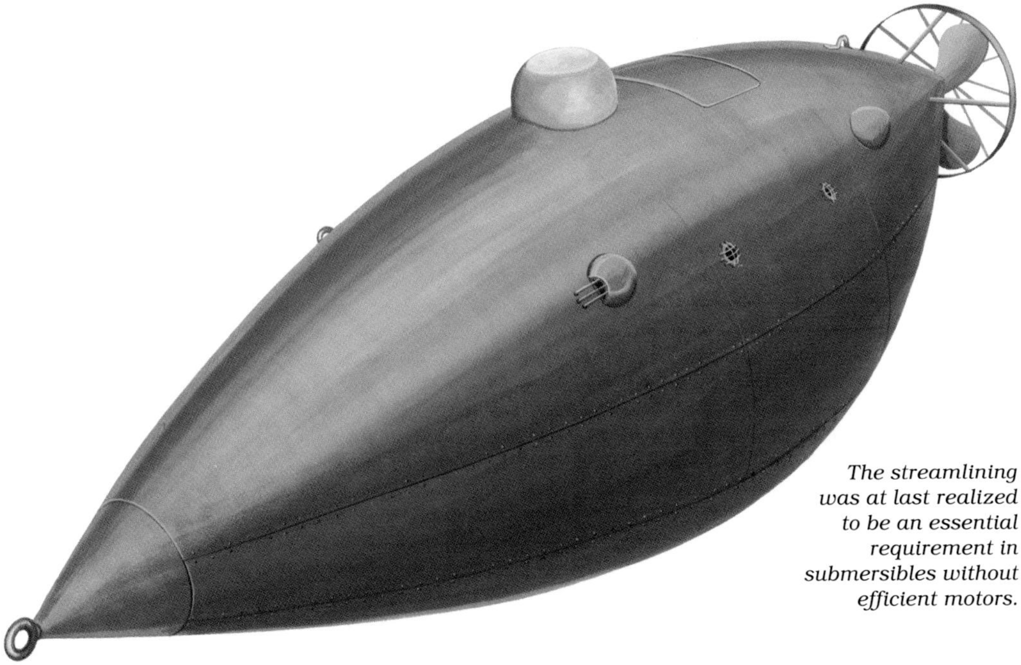

The streamlining was at last realized to be an essential requirement in submersibles without efficient motors.

Intelligent Whale

Type:	experimental submarine
Tonnage:	2 tons surfaced
Dimensions:	length 28 ft., 8 in. (8.75 m); beam 7 ft., 0 in. (2.1 m); draft 9 ft., 0 in. (2.75 m)
Propulsion:	hand-cranked propeller for 4 knots surfaced
Armament:	none
Complement:	6/13

Whitehead Torpedo (1868)

What made the submarine an effective weapon of war, once its mechanical problems had been overcome and an effective means of propulsion created, was the availability of the locomotive (self-propelled) torpedo as successor to the spar torpedo and other such weapons that required the submarine to close within spitting distance of its target.

The locomotive torpedo was the creation of Robert Whitehead, an Englishman who was born in 1823 and died in 1905. Whitehead trained as an engineer and draftsman, attended the Mechanics Institute in Manchester, initially worked in a shipyard in Toulon, France, and then became a consultant engineer in Milan, Italy, before removing to Trieste, on the Austro-Hungarian coast of the Adriatic Sea. Here, the locomotive torpedo of which the first prototypes had been tested in 1860. Luppis had recently retired from the Austro-Hungarian navy, and now sought to bring to fruition his long-time notion of a "coast savior" weapon, which was a low-profile surface craft driven by compressed air and controlled by ropes from the shore.

Whitehead's efforts led to the Minenschiff ("mine ship"), a pioneering locomotive torpedo presented to the Austro-Hungarian navy on December 21, 1866. A gunboat was adapted to launch the weapon by means of a barrel, also designed by Whitehead.

The key elements of the locomotive torpedo as finally perfected were propulsion by a small reciprocating engine running on compressed air;

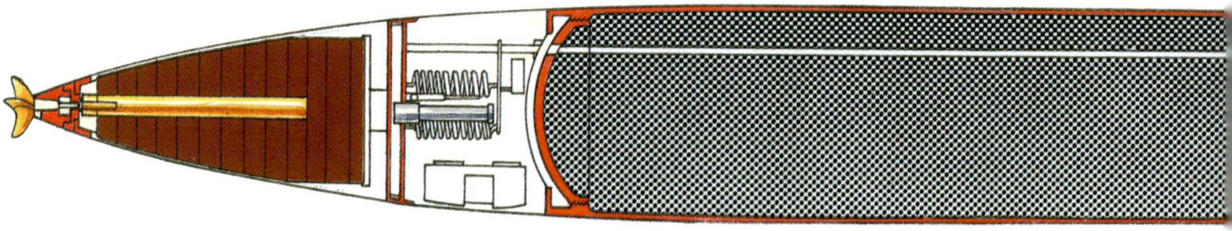

Whitehead's work came to the attention of the Fonderia Metalli foundry in Fiume (now Rijeka, Croatia), and in 1856 Whitehead became the manager of this company, whose name he changed to the "Stabilimento Tecnico di Fiume." The STF began to design and build ship's steam boilers and engines, which were the most modern products of that era.

In the early 1860s, Whitehead met a local engineer, Giovanni Biagio Luppis, and agreed to collaborate on the perfection of Luppis's invention, from 1868, a self-regulating device which kept the torpedo at a pre-set and constant depth through the use of a hydrostatic valve and pendulum balance, connected to a horizontal rudder, which controlled the depth at which the torpedo ran; and from 1898, when he bought it from its Austro-Hungarian inventor, Ludwig Obry, a gyroscopic mechanism which stabilized the torpedo directionally.

Whitehead bought the assets in 1875 and turned the STF into a private company called the Torpedo-Fabrik

Fine engineering skills can be appreciated from this photograph of the aft end of a Whitehead torpedo.

von Robert Whitehead, later floated as Whitehead & Co. Società per Azioni.

Most of the world's major navies had started to take note of the development of the locomotive device by the late 1880s. A trio of naval actions during the late nineteenth century changed the perception of the torpedo.

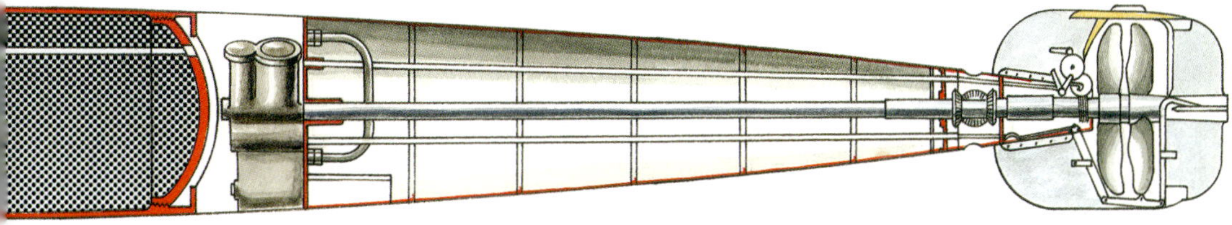

In 1891, in the midst of the Chilean Civil War, the Chilean naval vessel *Almirante Lynch* torpedoed and sank in port the rebel Chilean armoured vessel *Blanco Encalada* with a 14-inch (356 mm) Whitehead torpedo at the close range of 100 yards (90 m). In 1894, in the midst of the Brazilian Civil War, the rebel vessel *Aquidaban* was torpedoed and sunk at night while moored in a roadstead by the torpedo gunboat *Gustavo Sampaio* with a 14-inch (356 mm) Schwartzkopf torpedo. In 1895, during the Sino-Japanese War, the Chinese battleship *Ting Yuen* was crippled in port by multiple torpedo hits over the course of two nights by several Japanese torpedo boats.

Whitehead torpedo (1868)

Type:	locomotive torpedo
Weight:	650 lb. (295 kg)
Dimensions:	length 14 ft., 1 in. (4.29 m); diameter 16 in. (406 mm)
Propulsion:	V-2 compressed air engine for 7 knots over 600 yards (550 m)
Warhead:	67 lb. (30 kg) of explosive

Resurgam (1879)

Two British submarines carried the name *Resurgam* ("I will arise"), both of them designed by the Reverend Mr. George Garrett of Moss-side in Manchester, England, in his search for a weapon capable of penetrating the type of chain netting which had become standard since the development of the locomotive torpedo, fired by the newly emerged torpedo boat, as an effective weapon against moored vessels. Suspended in the water from wire-braced booms extending laterally from the sides of major warships' hulls, the chain netting was designed to prevent the torpedo from reaching the hull of its intended target.

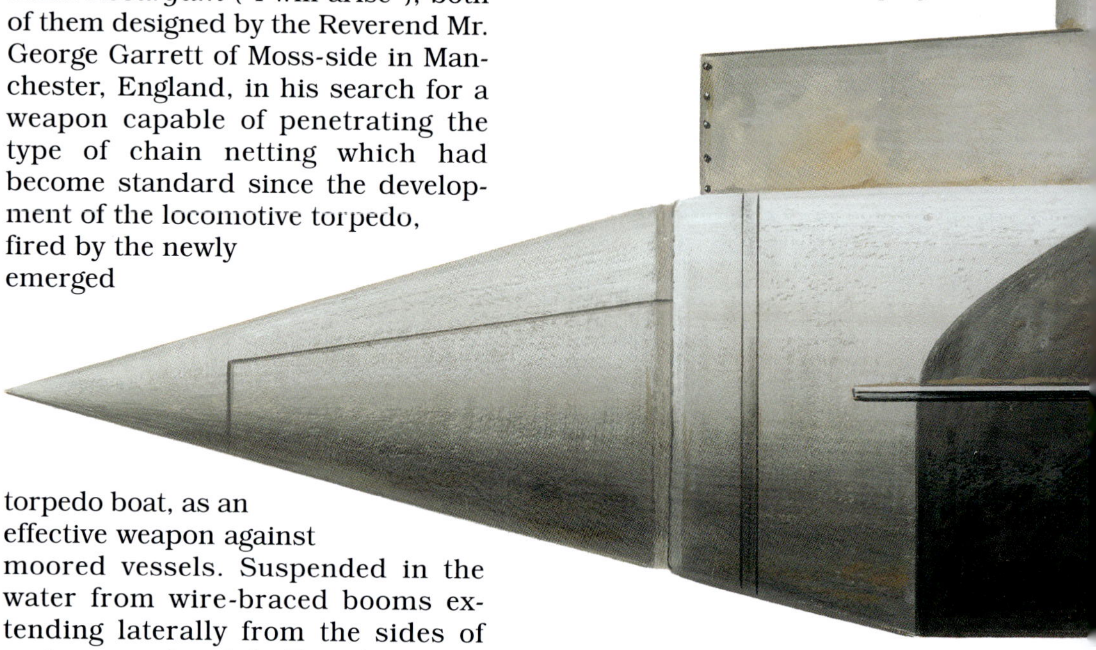

The standard shape of the future submarine can be seen in the Reqsurgam.

The first *Resurgam*, built in 1878, was a small vessel only some 14 feet (4.25 m) long, and propelled by a single propeller operated by a hand-crank. Nicknamed the "curate's egg" for its shape and design by a man of the cloth, the *Resurgam* was intended for operation by a single man, but its small size and inadequate manning would have rendered in useless for any operational purpose.

The second vessel was the *Resurgam II* of 1879. This was of a more practical concept and built of iron to a design stressed to provide a diving depth of about 150 feet (45.5 m). The *Resurgam II* was based on a central hull section of essentially cylindrical section with conical bow and stern sections tapering to a point and to a small-diameter flat stern through which emerged the shaft for the propeller just abaft the upper and lower section of the rudder. The superstructure was itself surmounted by a small cylindrical turret with a hatch at its top. There was no

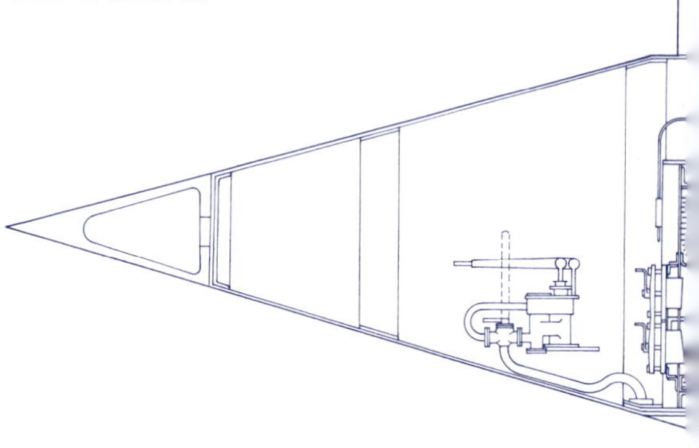

"Packing it all in" has always been a problem with submarines. There was little room for the crew to work in.

periscope, and, as it had no lighting, the submarine's interior was illuminated by candles.

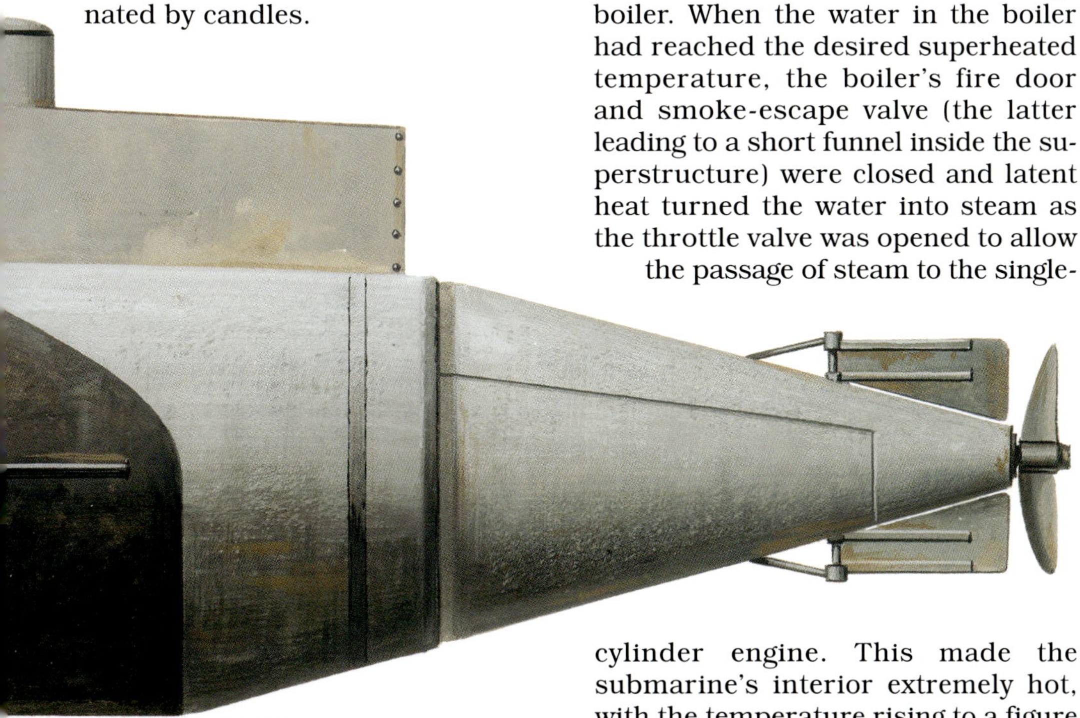

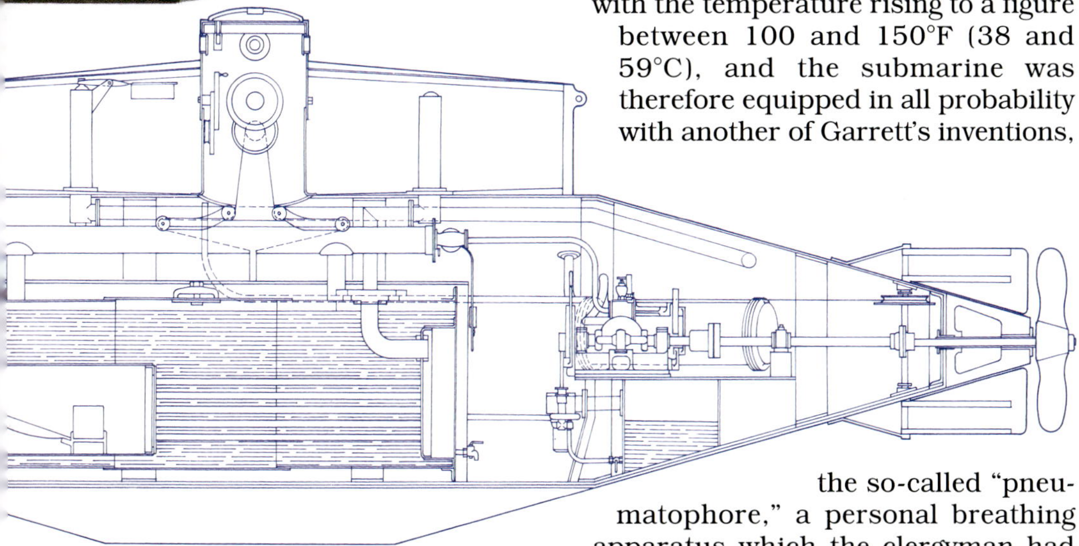

No record has survived of how the *Resurgam II* dived and surfaced, how it was ballasted, or how it was kept stable.

The *Resurgam II*'s propulsion arrangement was based on a steam boiler working on the Lamm flameless principle. In this, a coal-fired furnace heated the water in a large boiler. When the water in the boiler had reached the desired superheated temperature, the boiler's fire door and smoke-escape valve (the latter leading to a short funnel inside the superstructure) were closed and latent heat turned the water into steam as the throttle valve was opened to allow the passage of steam to the single-cylinder engine. This made the submarine's interior extremely hot, with the temperature rising to a figure between 100 and 150°F (38 and 59°C), and the submarine was therefore equipped in all probability with another of Garrett's inventions, the so-called "pneumatophore," a personal breathing apparatus which the clergyman had designed for use of trapped miners.

Resulting from a private order placed by the 27-year old Garrett, the *Resurgam II* was built, for a price of £15,000 and over a period of eight months, by Cochrane & Company, and launched from the constructor's yard in Birkenhead, opposite Liverpool on the estuary of the Mersey river, on November 26, 1879. After some initial, and apparently encouraging trials in the Mersey estuary, the *Resurgam II* departed for a base Garrett had established at Rhyl, on the north coast of Wales. It is not known how much of the voyage was made underwater, but at one stage the intrepid Garrett and the other member of the crew became lost in Liverpool Bay and had to inquire of a passing ship where they were. The ship's captain provided the information, and added that they were the biggest fools he had ever met. The *Resurgam II* reached Rhyl and undertook further trials.

Garrett then hired a steam yacht to tow the submarine around Wales and the southwest of England, to Portsmouth, on the south coast of England. This was the Royal Navy's largest base, and Garrett hoped to impress the Royal Navy with the capabilities of his boat. The yacht, with the *Resurgam II* in tow, left Rhyl on February 24. The weather was already deteriorating, and, during the following day, the yacht's engine failed. Garrett and his mechanic transferred to the yacht to assist in the repairs to the engine. The tow rope then broke in the steadily mounting seas, and Garrett could only watch as the *Resurgam II* foundered and sank, fortunately without loss of life.

Garrett went on to design submarines for the Turkish navy, and finally emigrated to the U.S., where he reached the rank of corporal in the U.S. Army's Corps of Engineers. Garrett died in New York in 1902, the final stages of his life having been spent in obscurity and failing health, the latter probably as a result of the carbon monoxide his body had absorbed during the working of the Lamm steam-engine system.

The wreck of the *Resurgam II* was discovered in 1995 by an experienced wreck diver, Keith Hurley, as he was trying to clear snagged fishing nets in

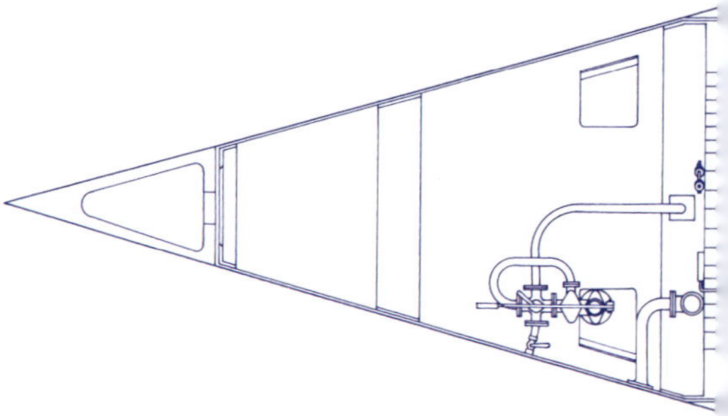

60 feet (18 m) of water, and the wreck was designated under the Protection of Wrecks Act on July 4, 1996. The hull is intact although partially damaged, but remains at risk from trawling and illegal diving. After the location of the wreck, the conning tower steering wheel was broken and portable items have apparently been taken. In 1997, a project undertaken by the Archaeological Diving Unit and more than 100 volunteer divers coordinated by the Nautical Archaeology Society surveyed the structure of the hull and the colonizing marine life, and also used remote sensing equipment to search for debris in the surrounding area. The wreck is cur-

rently protected against further erosion. As of 2007, plans to raise this important technical and industrial artifact have not yet materialized, and in October 2007 further work was started to help preserve the wreck in situ pending any definitive recovery effort.

A replica of the *Resurgam II* was put on display at Woodside, Birkenhead, United Kingdom, in 1997

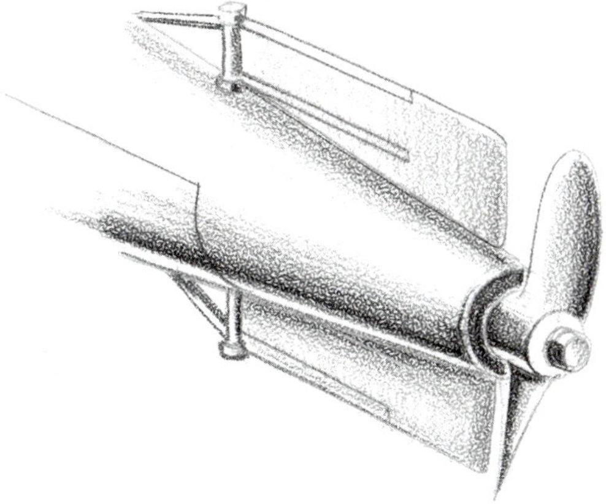

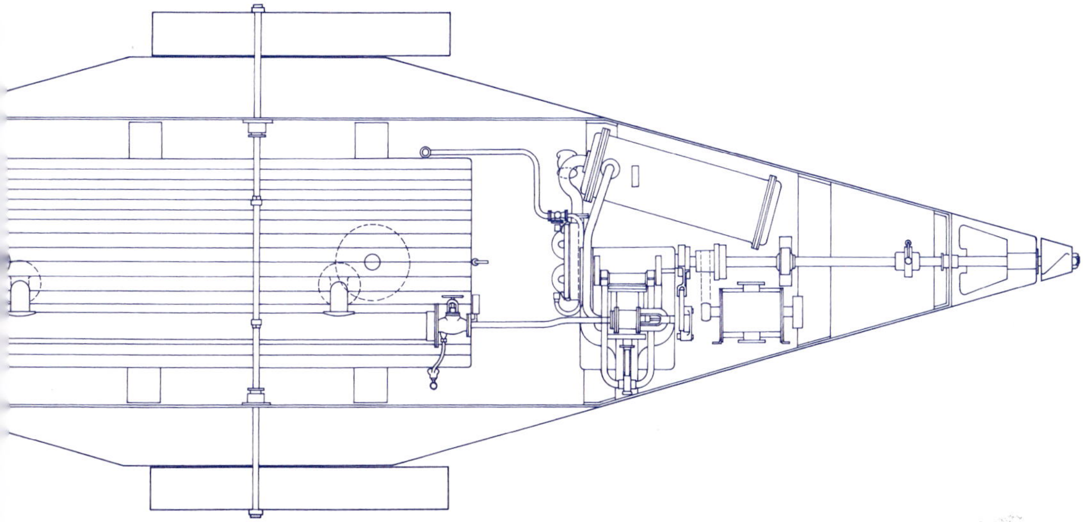

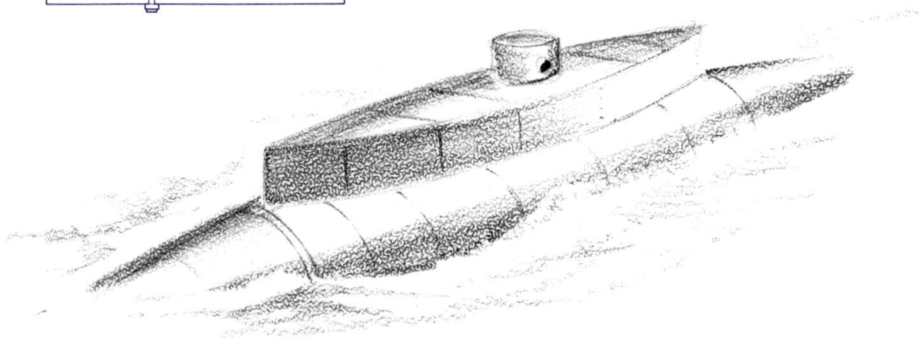

Resurgam II

Type:	submarine
Tonnage:	30 tons surfaced
Dimensions:	length 45 ft., 0 in. (13.7 m); beam 7 ft., 0 in. (2.1 m); draft not available
Propulsion:	one Lamm steam propulsion system for 3 knots surfaced
Armament:	none
Complement:	2

Fenian Ram (1881)

The *Fenian Ram* was created by John Philip Holland, an Irish-born American, for use by the Clan na Gael (Irish Republican Brotherhood, or Fenians) against the British. The construction launch of the *Fenian Ram* by Delamater-Robinson at the Delamater Iron Company in New York was funded by the IRB's Skirmishing Fund after trials of a prototype, 14 ft., 6 in. (4.4 m) long, in May 1878. This boat resulted from Holland's meeting with John J. Breslin, who had recently recovered six Irish convicts from Australia. The prototype remained under water for one hour in the Passaic River, New Jersey, and, after proving the essential soundness of Holland's notions, was scuttled. The prototype was later raised at exhibited as the *Holland No. 1*.

The design of the *Fenian Ram*, as the new boat was dubbed by the New York *Sun*, was derived, at least in part, from the Whitehead torpedo; like the weapon, the submarine was of basically cylindrical section, although tapered fore and aft from a parallel-section amidships portion surmounted by a shallow conning tower fitted with a hatch, with its control fins (two horizontal diving planes ands one vertical rudder) located just forward of the stern-mounted single propeller. Built of iron, the boat was not designed to submerge by taking on ballast water, but was intended to maintain a slight positive buoyancy which would be overcome in forward motion by the angling of the diving planes to drive the boat under the surface.

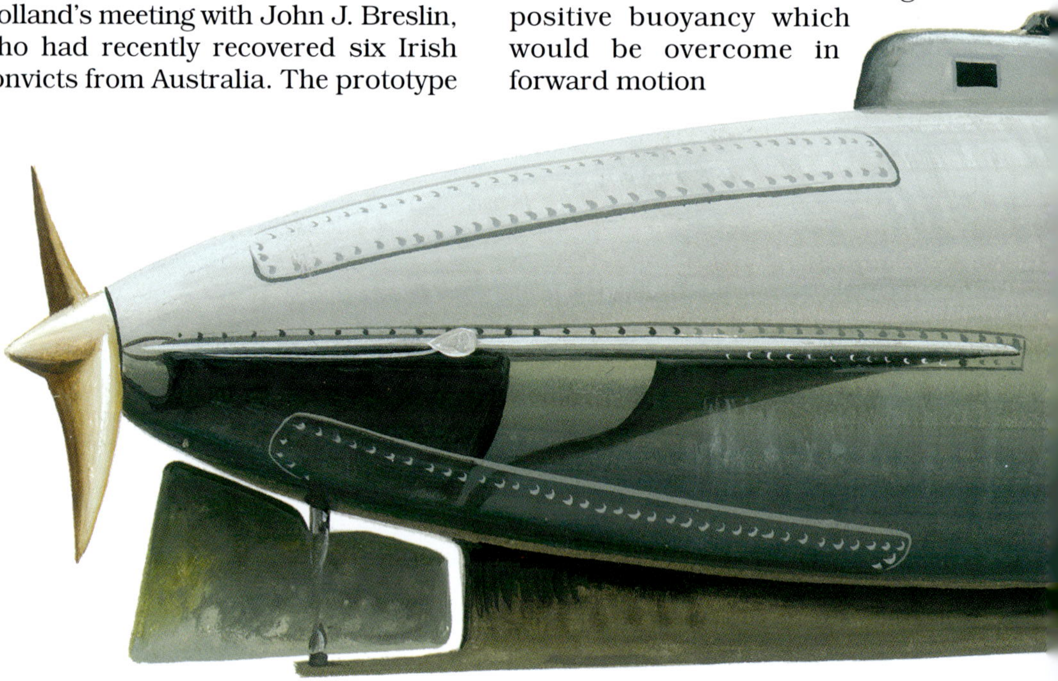

The *Fenian Ram* was fitted with a 9-inch (229 mm) pneumatic gun. About 11 feet (3.35 m) long, this was mounted along the boat's centerline and fired out of her bow. The gun was conceptually similar to the modern torpedo tube. With the bow cap closed, an explosive-filled projectile 6 feet (1.83 m) long was loaded into the tube from the boat's interior of the submarine via an inner door, which was then closed before the outer door was opened by a remote mechanism to allow the tube to flood. Finally, air at a pressure of 400 lb/in^2 (2.8 MPa) shot the projectile out of the tube. Reloading involved the closure of the outer door once more, the blowing of the water from it into a ballast tank by more compressed air, and the opening of the inner door.

After completion in May 1881, the boat was taken in hand for trials: several dives were made in the area of New York Harbor, down to a depth of 60 feet (18.3 m) and for periods of up to 2 hours 30 minutes, and the test-firing of inert projectiles was also undertaken.

As a result of funding disputes within the IRB, and also of disagreement over payments from the IRB to Holland, the Fenians stole the *Fenian Ram*—and also the *Holland III* prototype—before the matter of the boat's ownership could be decided by the courts, in November 1883. They took the submarine to New Haven, Connecticut, but, once there, discovered that they had no way to train the three-man crew to operate the submarine. Holland refused to help and, unable either to use or to sell the boat, the Fenians had the *Fenian Ram* hauled into a shed on the Mill River. Her 17 hp (12.7 kW) gasoline engine was scavenged to operate a forge in a brass foundry.

In 1916 the *Fenian Ram* was exhibited in Madison Square Garden to raise funds for victims of the Easter Rising in Dublin. After this, the boat was moved to the New York State Marine School. In 1927, Edward Browne purchased her and moved her to Paterson, New Jersey, where it can still be seen.

Fenian Ram

Type:	attack submarine
Tonnage:	19 tons surfaced
Dimensions:	length 31 ft., 0 in. (9.45 m); beam 6 ft., 0 in. (1.8 m); draft 7 ft., 3 in. (2.2 m)
Propulsion:	one 17 hp (12.7 kW) gasoline engine for 99 knots surfaced
Armament:	one 9-inch (229 mm) pneumatic gun
Complement:	3

Goubet II (1886)

In the last quarter of the nineteenth century, France and the UK regarded each other as primary potential adversaries in any European or colonial war which might break out. France was uncomfortably aware that, despite its greater land area and larger population, it was inferior to the UK in naval strength as a result of historical factors, and also in the size and capabilities of its industrial sector. In an attempt to offset the Royal Navy's overwhelming superiority in oceanic

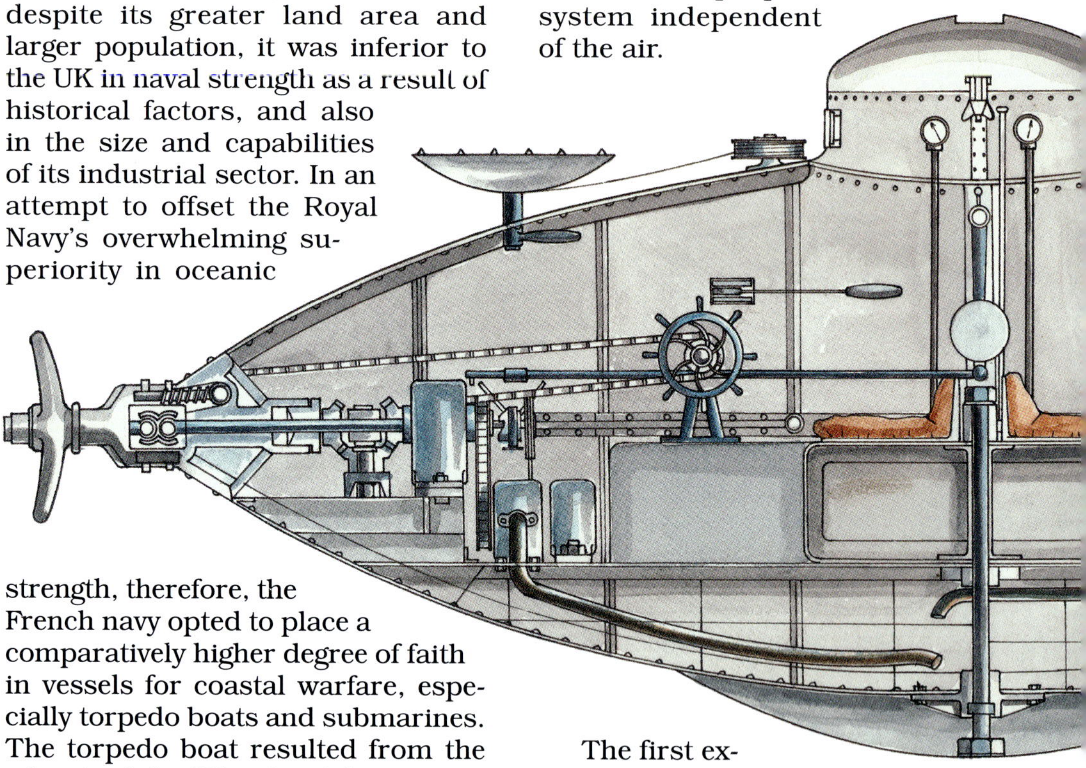

strength, therefore, the French navy opted to place a comparatively higher degree of faith in vessels for coastal warfare, especially torpedo boats and submarines. The torpedo boat resulted from the advent of the Whitehead locomotive torpedo. The submarine was beginning to emerge as a viable weapon if it could be adapted for the underwater launch of the torpedo, and provided with an effective means of underwater propulsion that did not demand a large supply of air.

The possibilities of steam from latent heat and of compressed air for underwater propulsion were already being evaluated, but clearly had distinct limitations. Greater potential in the longer term had been presaged in 1859 by Gaston Planté's invention, in France, of the lead-acid rechargeable battery. This was improved in 1880 by the loading of the surfaces with red lead, and this finally offered the designers of submarines the real opportunity to create boats with an underwater propulsion system independent of the air.

The first expression of this new capability came in 1887 with the *Goubet I*, a small two-man boat designed by a civil engineer, Claude Goubet. This was 16 ft., 5 in. (1.7 m) long with a beam of 5 ft., 10 in. (1.7 m) and draft of 3 ft., 3 in. (1 m), and had surfaced and submerged displacements of 1.6 and 1.8 tons, respectively. The hull was of cylindrical section tapering to a pointed bow and stern from the amidships section, where there was a glazed cupola/hatch above and a ballast keel below. The batteries were grouped in the bow, and an electric motor toward the stern drove a small propeller for a speed of 5 knots surfaced.

Though workable, the *Goubet I* was too small to be of any practical use and distinctly tricky to handle, as Goubet had provided no means of keeping longitudinal stability. Even so, the *Goubet I* is of great historical significance as the world's first electrically powered submarine.

Dominated by the officers of the "Jeune Ecole" ("young school"), which emphasized the advantages of indirect attack by cheap vessels, the French navy was sufficiently impressed that Goubet now moved forward to the design of a larger boat, the *Goubet II*. This was built at Cherbourg in 1886-89 with a bronze hull. The boat was similar in concept to its predecessor, and was again manned by a pair of men sitting back-to-back in the center of the hull. The boat was propelled by an electric engine initially designed for motor car use, and drew its current from a battery of Laurent-Cely accumulator batteries in the lower part of the hull. The boat was submerged by allowing water to flood freely into the ballast tanks until the boat was awash, and then by admitting more water until the boat's reserve buoyancy had been overcome. The batteries held sufficient charge to propel the boat for a full-speed distance of 23.5 miles (38 km).

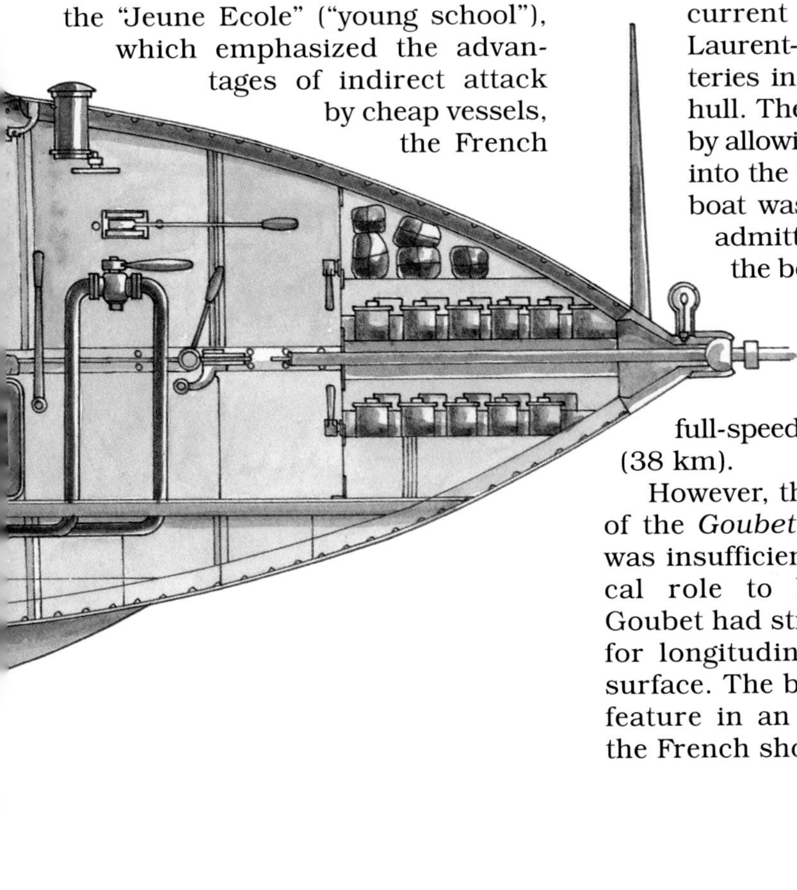

However, the increase in the size of the *Goubet II* over the *Goubet I* was insufficient to allow any practical role to be considered, and Goubet had still not made provision for longitudinal control under the surface. The boat ended its life as a feature in an amusement park on the French shores of Lake Geneva.

Goubet II

Type:	experimental submarine
Tonnage:	5 tons surfaced and 5.5 tons submerged
Dimensions:	length 26 ft., 3 in. (8 m); beam 6 ft. (1.8 m); draft 6 ft. (1.8 m)
Propulsion:	one 4 hp (3 kW) Siemens electric motor for 6 knots surfaced
Armament:	none
Complement:	2

Peral (1886)

One of the major problems with the creation of an effective submarine was underwater propulsion, and even as the electrical battery was being created and brought to the initial level of development in which it was suitable for demanding tasks such as powering submerged submarines via electric motors, some designers were searching along other of the technical paths which the industrial revolution and the Victorian age had opened. The Reverend Mr George Garrett of the UK saw the future of latent heat of a shutdown steam boiler, and in this he was supported by a rich Swedish inventor, Thorsten Nordenfelt, one of those to whom Garrett wanted to display his *Resurgam II* when the boat was being towed from North Wales to Portsmouth but foundered during the voyage.

The other primary course of endeavor was the electrical battery as pioneered in submarine use by a French engineer, Claude Goubet. Goubet's mantle was next assumed by a Spanish naval officer, Lieutenant Isaac Peral y Caballero, who had been born in Cartagena in June 1851. Peral was not the first Spanish proponent of the submarine: this accolade fell to Narsisco Monturiol and Cosma Garcia who, some 20 years earlier, had produced *El Ictineo*, which was in effect a copy of Bauer's submarine with the type of armament first used by Bushnell nearly a century before. The gun armament of the wooden-hulled *El Ictineo* was supplemented by a steam-powered auger in the bow with which to bore holes in the hull of a target ship. Looking like a great swordfish, *El Ictineo* made 60 successful dives before the project died, probably from a lack of any official interest.

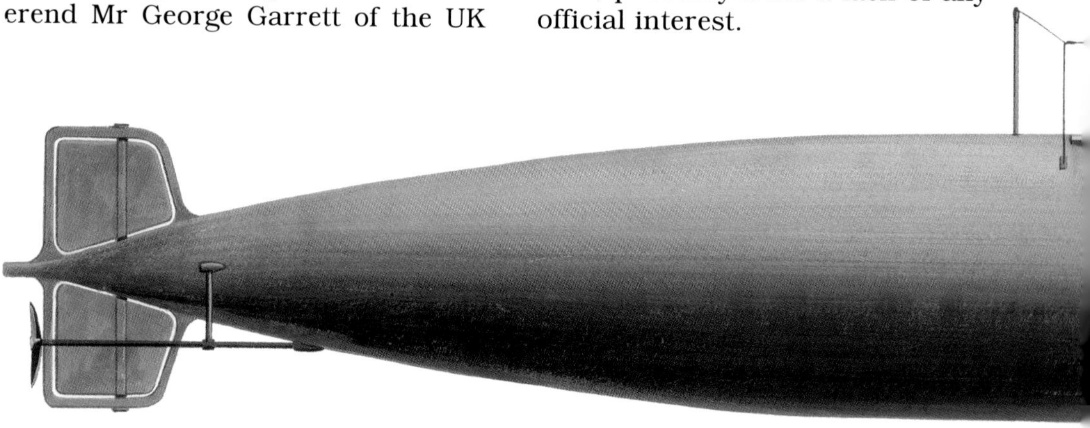

The first submarine with a combustion engine was *El Ictineo II*, designed by Monturiol. Originally launched in 1864 at a Barcelona yard, the boat was converted to peroxide propulsion and steam in 1867. Some 46 feet (14 m) long, this two-man boat could dive to a depth of 100 feet (30 m) and remain under the water for two hours. On the surface the boat ran on a steam engine, but underwater such an engine would quickly have used all of the submarine's oxygen. Monturiol therefore invented an anaerobic engine: the most notable feature of this engine was the fact that even as it powered the propeller through the decomposition of hydrogen peroxide, it released oxygen which was used in the hull for the crew and also fed an auxiliary steam engine.

Peral was a scientist and inventor as well as a naval officer, and based his submarine, generally known as the *Peral*, on sound principles and with electric underwater propulsion. This propulsion arrangement was based on a battery of 420 accumulators which provided current to a pair of main motors, each developing 30 hp (22.4 kW) and driving a three-blade propeller outboard of the stern-mounted rudders and two small diving planes, as well as three smaller electric motors, each delivering 5 hp (3.7 kW) for pumping out the ballast tanks. The least satisfactory feature of the *Peral* was the retention of vertical propellers, of the type pioneered by Nordenfelt, inset at bow and stern for longitudinal control under the water.

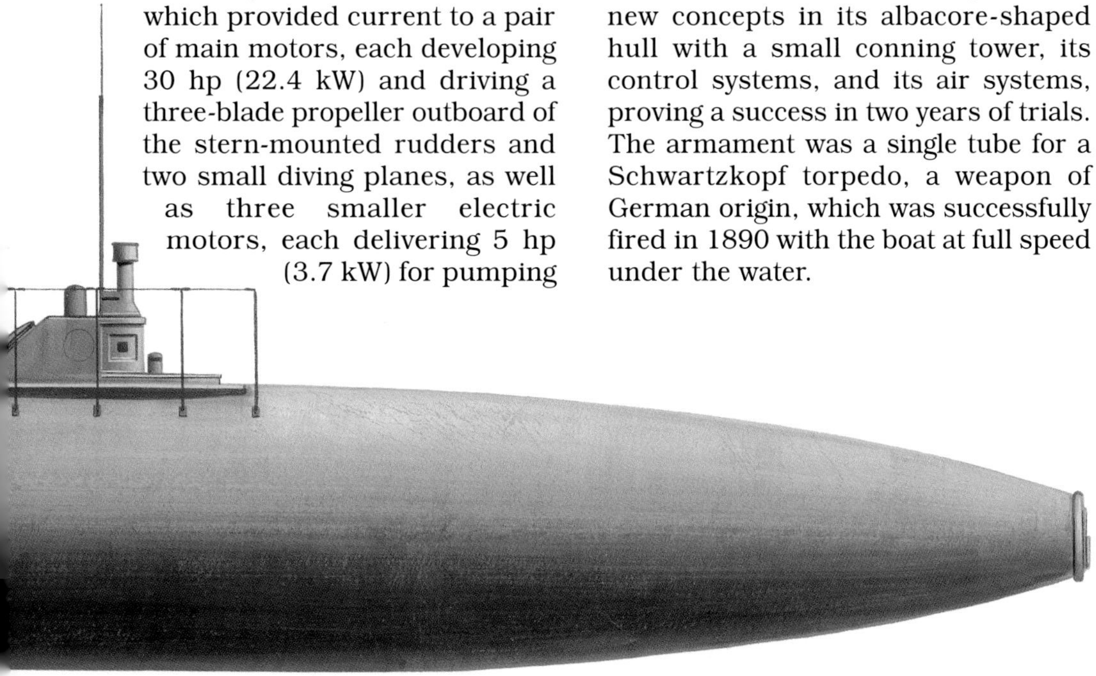

The *Peral* was laid down in 1884 at the Carraca yard in Cadiz and, launched only four years later in September 1888, was intended from the outset for naval service in the attack role. The boat was arguably the first "modern" submarine, as it was capable of firing its primary weapon underwater, at full speed, and under complete control of the crew. The *Peral* pioneered new concepts in its albacore-shaped hull with a small conning tower, its control systems, and its air systems, proving a success in two years of trials. The armament was a single tube for a Schwartzkopf torpedo, a weapon of German origin, which was successfully fired in 1890 with the boat at full speed under the water.

Like *El Ictineo II*, the *Peral* failed not because of an intrinsic deficiency but as a result of the lethargy of the Spanish government and disinterest of the Spanish navy. The *Peral* was removed from naval service in 1909 and is now displayed in Cartagena, Spain.

Peral

Type:	attack submarine
Tonnage:	87 tons surfaced
Dimensions:	length 70 ft. (21.3 m); beam 8 ft., 6 in. (2.6 m); draft not available
Propulsion:	two 30 hp (22.4 kW) electric motors for 120 knots surfaced
Armament:	one tube for three torpedoes
Complement:	about 6

Abdul Medjid (1887)

While the Reverend Mr George Garrett of the UK and Thorsten Nordenfelt of Sweden were collaborating on securing a major world position in the design and production of submarines, as presaged by the completion of the *Nordenfelt I* in 1885, there began to spread a series of rumors that Imperial Russia was acquiring a fleet of 50 small submarines. The rumors did not suggest the task for which these small boats were being procured, but the plan was changed after the poor success of some early trials, and the boats were instead adapted as pontoons and buoys.

the supervision of Garret, commissioned as a commander in the Turkish navy specifically for this task. Ultimately, only the *Abdul Medjid*, locally called the "Whale Ship," was assembled and launched.

The Turkish boat was half as long again as the *Nordenfelt I*, and the Lamm compound steam engine, with a steam accumulator for underwater propulsion, was a good deal more potent: speeds of 10 knots surfaced and 5 knots submerged were projected. The armament consisted of two internal torpedo tubes mounted vertically, and two 1-inch (25 mm) guns. The diving depth was 50 feet (15 m).

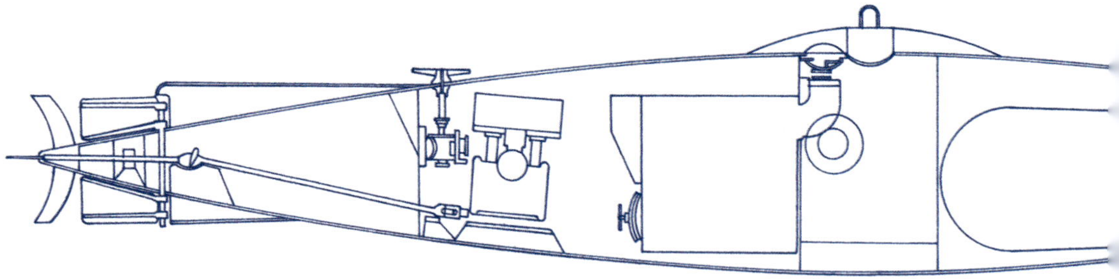

As a nation often at loggerheads with Russia but not actually at war with it, Turkey had been thoroughly alarmed by the supposed threat and, following the unprofitable visit to John P. Holland in the U.S., the Turkish naval authorities decided to order two Nordenfelt submarines to be built in the UK by the Des Vignes Company at Chertsey on the River Thames. The two boats were built as the *Nordenfelt II* and *Nordenfelt III*, to be named *Abdul Medjid* and *Abdul Hamid*, respectively, in Turkish service. The two boats were shipped in sections to Constantinople (now Istanbul) for reassembly under

The boats certainly appeared to the Turkish authorities to represent a powerful supplement to their armed forces, for the boats were theoretically superior to anything operated by its "natural enemies," Russia and Greece: the latter had acquired the *Nordenfelt I*. The *Abdul Medjid* was, like all boats of the period, full of problems, as suggested by the Nordenfelt company's representative, Captain P. W. D'Alton, at one time the chief engineer of the Central London Railway and the expert on the "Lamm Fireless Locomotive" propulsion arrangement. D'Alton commented that the major problem was the boat's total lack of longitudinal stability: as soon as the boat pitched forward or aft, the water in her boiler and ballast tanks surged and increased the inclination. The boat therefore proceeded in a series of scarcely controlled pitching movements, and on the one occasion, a torpedo was fired the lightened bow rose and the boat descended almost stern first toward the bottom before being brought onto an even keel.

This was a problem with all of the Nordenfelt

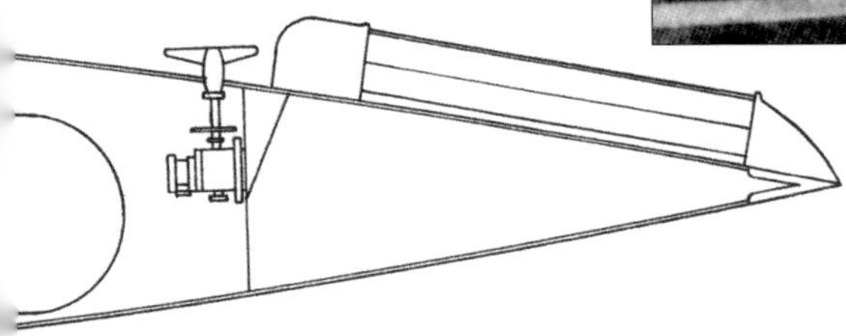

Above:
This section of a Nordenfelt boat shows the tightly packed engine room area. Note the suited man alongside the engine.

Left:
A longitudinal section, again, shows how little space there was for the crew.

boats, but the company refused to admit the fact, let alone rectify it. The Turkish navy found it impossible to find a volunteer crew. The remains of the two boats were discovered, derelict, by a German naval mission that reached Constantinople (now Istanbul) in 1914.

Abdul Medjid

Type:	attack submarine
Tonnage:	100 tons surfaced and 160 tons submerged
Dimensions:	length 100 ft. (30.5 m); beam 12 ft., 2 in. (3.7 m); draft not available
Propulsion:	one 250 ihp (186.4 kW) Lamm steam compound engine and steam accumulator for 8 knots surfaced and 4-5 knots submerged
Armament:	two torpedo tubes and two 1-inch (25 mm) guns
Complement:	7

Nordenfelt submarines

Born in Sweden during 1842, Thorsten Nordenfelt was an inventor and industrialist. The son of a colonel in the Swedish army, Nordenfelt (sometimes spelled "Nordenfeldt") worked for a Swedish company in London from 1862 to 1866, and formally immigrated to the UK in 1867, when he married Emma Stansfeld Grundy. In this same year, Nordenfelt and his brother-in-law started a small business to import Swedish steel for the manufacture of rails for the British railway industry, and later established the Nordenfelt Guns and Ammunition Co. Ltd. to develop a type of multi-barrel machine gun designed by Helge Palmcrantz and universally called the "Nordenfelt gun." His company also designed a range of quick-firing naval guns of small caliber (37 to 57 mm) for use against torpedo boats, which were then seen as a primary threat to capital ships. The guns were manufactured in Erith in the English county of Kent; in Stockholm, Sweden; and also in Spain. Under pressure from the Rothschild banking and Vickers industrial empires, Nordenfelt merged his company with that of Sir Hiram Maxim in 1888.

Meetings between Nordenfelt and the Reverend Mr George Garrett, designer of the pioneering *Resurgam* submarine, led to the design and manufacture of a small series of steam-powered submarine boats. The first of these was the 56-ton *Nordenfelt I* of 1885, a vessel 64 feet (19.5 m) long and very similar to the ill-fated *Resurgam* of 1879. This boat had a range of 145 miles (240 km) and was armed with a single torpedo. The *Nordenfelt I* was built by Bolinders in Stockholm and, like the *Resurgam*, operated on the surface by conventional steam power, and under the surface on the latent heat of the tank of superheated steam remaining after the boiler had been shut down. At a time of major Balkan tensions, and concerned lest Ottoman Turkey attempt to reconquer it, Greece bought the boat but found it of no practical use, as Nordenfelt had yet to come to grips with the problem of effective longitudinal control.

The Ottoman Sultan Abdülhamid, also concerned about the level of Greco-Turkish tension, instructed his naval ministry to buy two submarines from Nordenfelt. These were each to be capable of firing three torpedoes, were to be built in the UK, and then, by the terms of the contract, were to be dismantled, put into cradles, and shipped to Constantinople. The final assembly of the submarines was to be done in the Taskizak shipyard on the Golden Horn. The construction of the boats in England proceeded according to schedule, but there were problems during the transport of the parts to Istanbul and during the final assembly in the Taskizak shipyard. The Reverent Garrett had to travel to Istanbul on several occasions to supervise the work.

The first boat was launched on September 6, 1886, and started its trials on February 5, 1887. As the results of the trials were not satisfactory, this *Abdülhamid* was returned to shipyard hands. The second boat was the *Abdülmecid*, launched on August 4, 1887.

After a series of trials held in the Golden Horn and Bosporus, the two submarines proceeded on January 13, 1888 under their own power to the Bay of Izmit. Here, all efforts to dive them fully or to steam them submerged failed. But the submarines were able to fire torpedoes successfully. The Ottoman navy thus became the first in the world to fire a torpedo from a submarine and hit the target. After these trials, both submarines returned to the naval yard at the Golden Horn and were left to rust.

Nordenfelt's efforts in the creation of an effective submarine culminated with the *Nordenfelt IV*, which had twin steam engines delivering 1,200 hp (895 kW) and two torpedo tubes. The boat had a displacement of 245 tons submerged, was 125 feet (38.1 m) long, and had a surfaced range of 1,000 miles (1610 km). The boat was not spindle-shaped like its predecessors, but was squared off vertically at the bow and stern, where it was tapered horizontally on each end. There was a propeller embedded vertically in each end in an unsuccessful effort to deal with the underwater stability problems that had beset the earlier boats. The *Nordenfelt IV* was launched in 1887 and sold to the Russian navy. However, the boat ran aground off Jutland during its delivery voyage. The crew escaped without harm and the boat was recovered, but the Russians had doubts about their purchase and refused to accept the boat, which was scrapped.

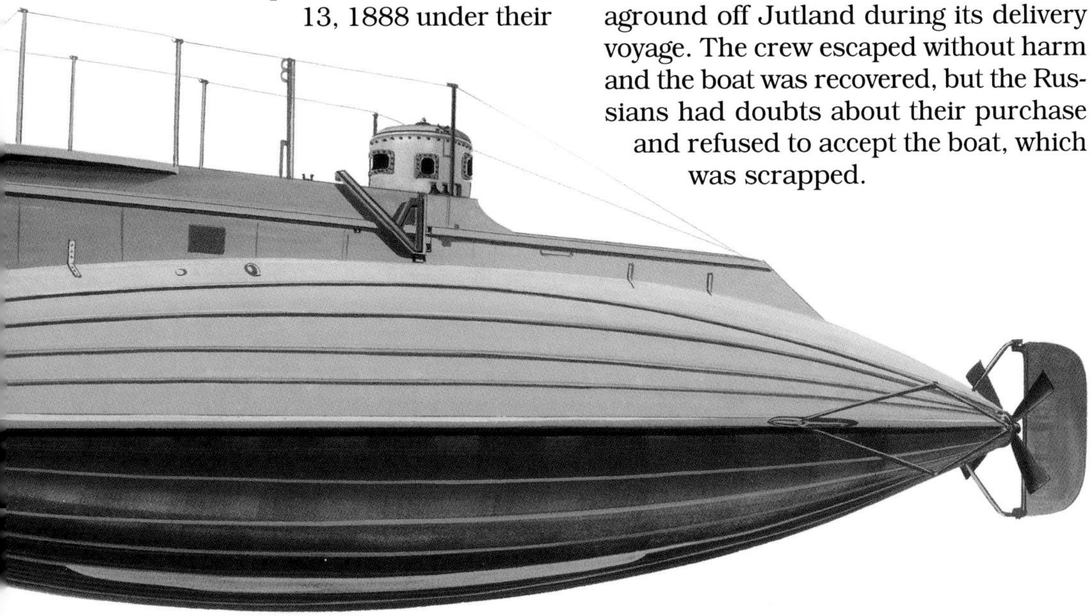

One of the two Nordenfelt submarines to be built in Germany.

A number of other countries, including Germany, toyed with the Nordenfelt submarine concept, but none of these concepts reached the hardware stage.

After personal bankruptcy, Nordenfelt was forced out of the Nordenfelt-Maxim company in 1890 and left England for France, where his new company, the Société Nordenfelt, designed the eccentric screw breech used on the first piece of modern field artillery, the French "75" of 3-inch (75 mm) caliber. In 1903 Nordenfelt returned to Sweden to retire, and died in 1920.

Gymnote (1888)

Limited but useful thinking about the submarine continued in France through much of the nineteenth century, and in the second half of the century began to bear fruit. France had a number of very talented designers involved with the Jeune Ecole ("young school") of far-sighted naval officers who believed in the creation of a balanced French navy with, among better prepared in the number of its submarines than either the UK or the U.S. How effective the French submarines would have been is more problematical, but at the superficial level the French submarine arm seemed to be a formidable force.

The French navy was a firm believer in the torpedo, carried by small vessels, as the means of

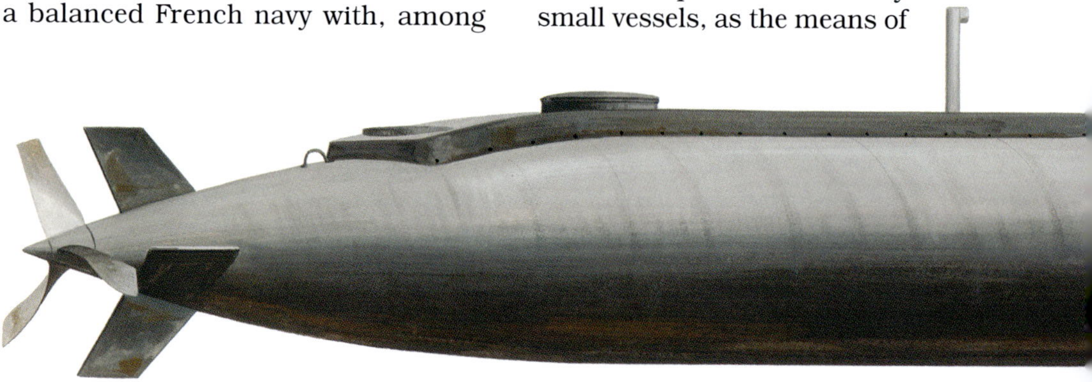

other things, a strong capability for the destruction of an enemy's maritime trade. Such a *guerre de course* was conceived with the British merchant marine as its primary target. Admiral Aube wrote in 1879 that the armored ship was obsolete and that a new navy was thus needed to fight a running battle and wage war against commerce. Aube was highly respected by his contemporaries and, as minister of the navy in the French government, was responsible for the establishment of a submarine service. This was not an easy course for the French, who had more than their fair share of oddities, a tendency exacerbated for the French penchant of the time for over-complexity.

Nothing that the French did was technically equal to the work of John Philip Holland but, if underwater war happened, France was for long far

offsetting the British navy's overwhelming numerical and technical superiority in warships with powerful gun armament. There was no way of armoring small vessels to withstand the fire of heavy warships, so such vessels had to be very fast, agile, and, where possible, operate awash. There was no real need to submerge completely, although the facility to do so would provide an opportunity to gain surprise. Semi-submersibles, operating mainly on the surface and possessing good range, seemed the best type of vessel for offensive attacks or breaking a blockade. But in coastal warfare the submarine had advantage, despite its shorter range, as it would be all but invisible.

Factors such as these led France to build three quite distinct types of such craft: semi-submersibles, submersibles, and submarines. There was much controversy about which type was best. Submersibles were not good sea boats, largely because they had a reserve buoyancy of only some 7%, and were therefore suited to only the calmest of waters. French thinking led to the development of steam and steam-electric propulsion for semi-submersibles and submersibles and to all-electric propulsion for submarines, the latter being defined as a type that was not dependent, at least for a short time, on any connection with the air.

The well-known French engineer Henri Dupuy de Lôme conceived the first significant French submersible in the 1880s as the *Gymnote* (a type of electrical fish). Like the American pioneer Robert Fulton, de Lôme was an extremely talented inventor, although his work on airship design and his important work on the Panama Canal have been forgotten. De Lôme died before the submarine project could be brought into being, but his friend and associate Gustave Zédé continued the task and, with sundry modifications, completed the *Gymnote*, which was launched on September 24, 1888, as a submarine with all-electric propulsion using no fewer than 564 accumulators for the current to power a 55 hp (41 kW) electric motor which turned the propeller at the inefficiently high rate of 2,000 revolutions per minute.

The submarine was built with a steel single hull, a detachable lead keel, and three hydroplanes on each side. It made more than 2,000 dives. The boat was reconstructed in 1898 with a raised conning tower, casing, and drop collars for two 14-inch (356 mm) torpedoes. The boat sank at Toulon, France, in 1907, and was raised, but was then scrapped in the following year.

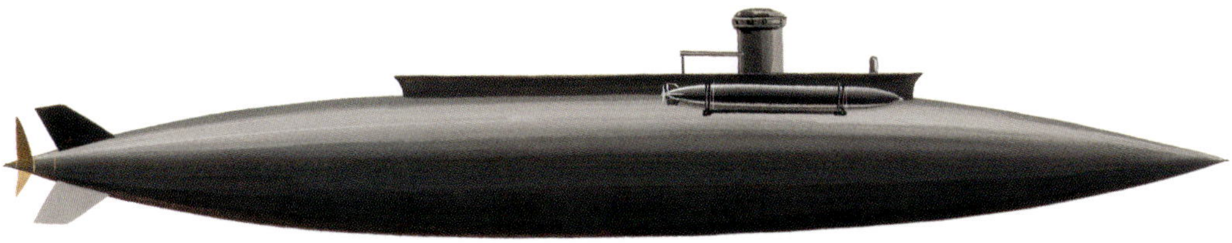

***Gymnote* (1898 standard)**

Type:	experimental submarine
Tonnage:	30 tons surfaced and 31 tons submerged
Dimensions:	length 58 ft., 5 in. (17.8 m); beam 6 ft. (1.8 m); draft 5 ft., 6 in. (1.6 m)
Propulsion:	one electric motor delivering 55 hp (41 kW) for 7.3 knots surfaced and 4.2 knots submerged
Armament:	(trials only) two drop collars for two 14-inch (356 mm) torpedoes
Complement:	5

Gustave Zédé (1893)

With the concept of the all-electric submarine pushed forward by the *Gymnote*, albeit only for coastal and harbor defense purposes as a result of its short range, the French naval ministry ordered a larger boat with which the development of such craft could be expanded, especially a more fully optimized torpedo armament. The task of designing the new boat was entrusted to one M. Ramazzotti and, following the untimely death Gustave Zédé, an associate of Dupuy de Lôme, the new boat was named for him.

The *Gustave Zédé* was launched on June 1, 1893. The boat had a circular-section hull that tapered fore and aft but, unlike most submarines of the era, was not symmetrical fore and aft. The boat was based on 76 frames connected by longitudinal braces covered by plates of Roma (a bronze alloy) to avoid corrosion. The superstructure extended from the bow to within 50 feet (15.2 m) of the stern, and there were two entrance hatches as well as a conning tower. To surface, the boat expelled water from the tanks using air compressed by electrically powered Thirion pumps.

Propulsion was provided by two electric motors connected to the same shaft. The motors were manufactured by Sautter Harlé and each rated at 360 hp (268 kW). Each motor weighed 13.5 tons and ran at 250 revolutions per minute. Electric power was originally provided by a 130-ton battery of Laurent-Cély accumulators, and consisted of 720 elements producing 1800 ampères at 300 volts. This battery began to be plagued by short circuits after only a few days of operation, and had to be replaced. The new battery exploded as the process of charging it started, however, and there followed a fire. As a result, the number of cells was reduced by half, and the design speed was thus trimmed from 15 knots. Another problem was the release of acid vapor, which made the crew sick.

On her first trip, the *Gustave Zédé* became unstable as soon as it submerged and yawed so

much that it was impossible to hold a straight course for more than a few minutes. Following the initial trials, the battery was replaced by a larger-capacity unit, the canvas conning tower was replaced by a metal tower, the Thirion pumps were modified, and a new system of diving rudders was installed. This last had two planes forward, two amidships, and two aft. These modifications took four years, but the result was significantly improved stability and greater speed.

The conning tower was a little over 3 ft., 3 in. (1 m) high, and fitted with a periscope with a diameter of about 14 in. (355 mm), offering a field of vision from -7° to +20°. The image was very distorted and indistinct, rendering it virtually useless for any practical purpose, but this was nonetheless a pioneering feature. The armament consisted of three 18-inch (450 mm) Whitehead torpedoes launched by means of one tube in the bow.

The *Gustave Zédé* made more than 2,500 dives, once traveled submerged from Toulon to Marseille, France (a distance of 41 miles, or 66 km), and was decommissioned in 1909.

Gustave Zédé

Type:	developmental submarine
Tonnage:	265 tons surfaced and 274 tons submerged
Dimensions:	length 159 ft., (48.5 m); beam 10 ft., 6 in. (3.2 m); draft 10 ft., 6 in. (3.2 m)
Propulsion:	two electric motors delivering 720 hp (537 kW) for 9.2 knots surfaced and 6.5 knots submerged
Armament:	one 18-inch (450 mm) tube (bow) for three torpedoes
Complement:	19

Argonaut (1897)

Since reading Jules Verne's 1870 novel *20,000 Leagues Under the Sea*, the American engineer Simon Lake had been fascinated by the concept of underwater travel and exploration. So when the U.S. Navy announced a submarine design competition for 1893, following similar competitions in 1887 and 1888-89, Lake decided to enter.

The design reflected Lake's interest in the submarine for commercial and salvage purposes. It was intended to submerge on an even keel using a combination of judicious ballasting and horizontal control planes, and to move mainly on the bottom, using powered wheels for propulsion. The engine was to have been a compound steam engine, whose boiler would be shut down before the vessel submerged, when compressed air replaced steam to drive both the propeller and wheels. Lake's plans included a lock-in/lock-out chamber for a diver, a crude "viewing tube" for vision above water, and automatic mechanisms to control depth and attitude.

The eight contenders included Lake and also John Holland, and the latter won, as he had the two previous competitions. Though unhappy, Lake was still determined to create a commercially viable underwater craft, and within 12 months he had completed a simple wooden demonstrator, the *Argonaut Junior*. This was little more than a large, triangular wooden box that could be ballasted to sink to the bottom, where it could be made to crawl forward on a set of man-powered wheels. Stored compressed air was used both to blow the ballast tanks for returning to the surface and to pressurize the interior to keep water out when a trap door was opened in the floor to give access to the bottom.

Lake demonstrated the *Argonaut Junior* successfully in a river near Atlantic Highlands, New Jersey, in December 1894, and so won enough investment capital to establish the Lake Submarine Company and embark on the design and construction of true submarine. This *Argonaut I* was built in the same graving dock at Baltimore, Maryland, at the same time as Holland's unsuccessful *Plunger*. The *Argonaut I* kept most of the distinctive features of Lake's 1893 design, including powered wheels for bottom crawling and a diver's lock. The boat was driven by a petrol engine, and a float-supported hose allowed air to be drawn in which the boat was submerged. Even so, the boat carried enough compressed air for deeper dive and a submerged endurance of up to 24 hours.

Designed for salvage and exploration, the *Argonaut I* usually traveled on the surface to where its capability was needed, at which point it descended vertically, by ballasting down or using haul-down anchors in the keel, before moving along the bottom on its wheels.

Completed in 1897, the *Argonaut I* undertook initial trials and was then used to salvage the cargoes of vessels sunk in Chesapeake Bay. Lake took the boat into open water in 1898, moving generally on the surface but submerging to investigate wrecks. This voyage revealed the need for improved seaworthiness, so Lake had the boat rebuilt during the following year in Brooklyn, New York, largely by lengthening the boat to 56 feet (17.1 m) and adding a superstructure, to create the *New Argonaut* or *Argonaut II*. From his new base at Bridgeport, Connecticut, Lake started to recover sunken cargo on a commercial basis, and in the next few years he recovered the contents of more than 30 ships that had gone down in Long Island Sound. For this, Lake added special improvements to the boat, as well as a "submarine wrecking car" used to bring salvaged commodities, such as coal, to the surface.

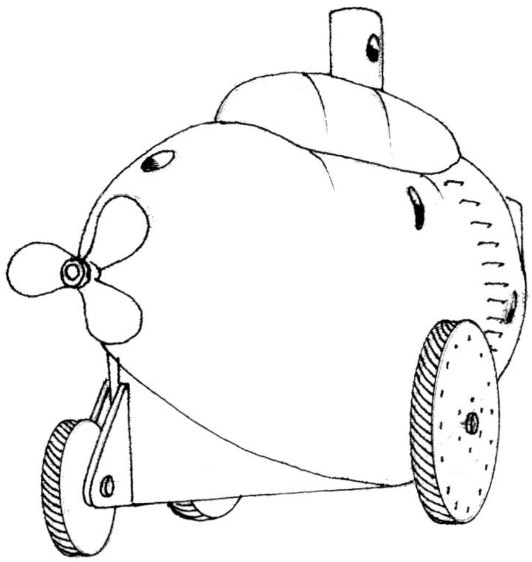

Argonaut I

Type:	salvage submarine
Tonnage:	59 tons submerged
Dimensions:	length 36 ft. (11 m); beam 9 ft. (2.7 m); draft not relevant
Propulsion:	one petrol engine delivering 30 hp (22.4 kW) for 5 knots surfaced and 5 knots submerged
Armament:	none

Narval (1899)

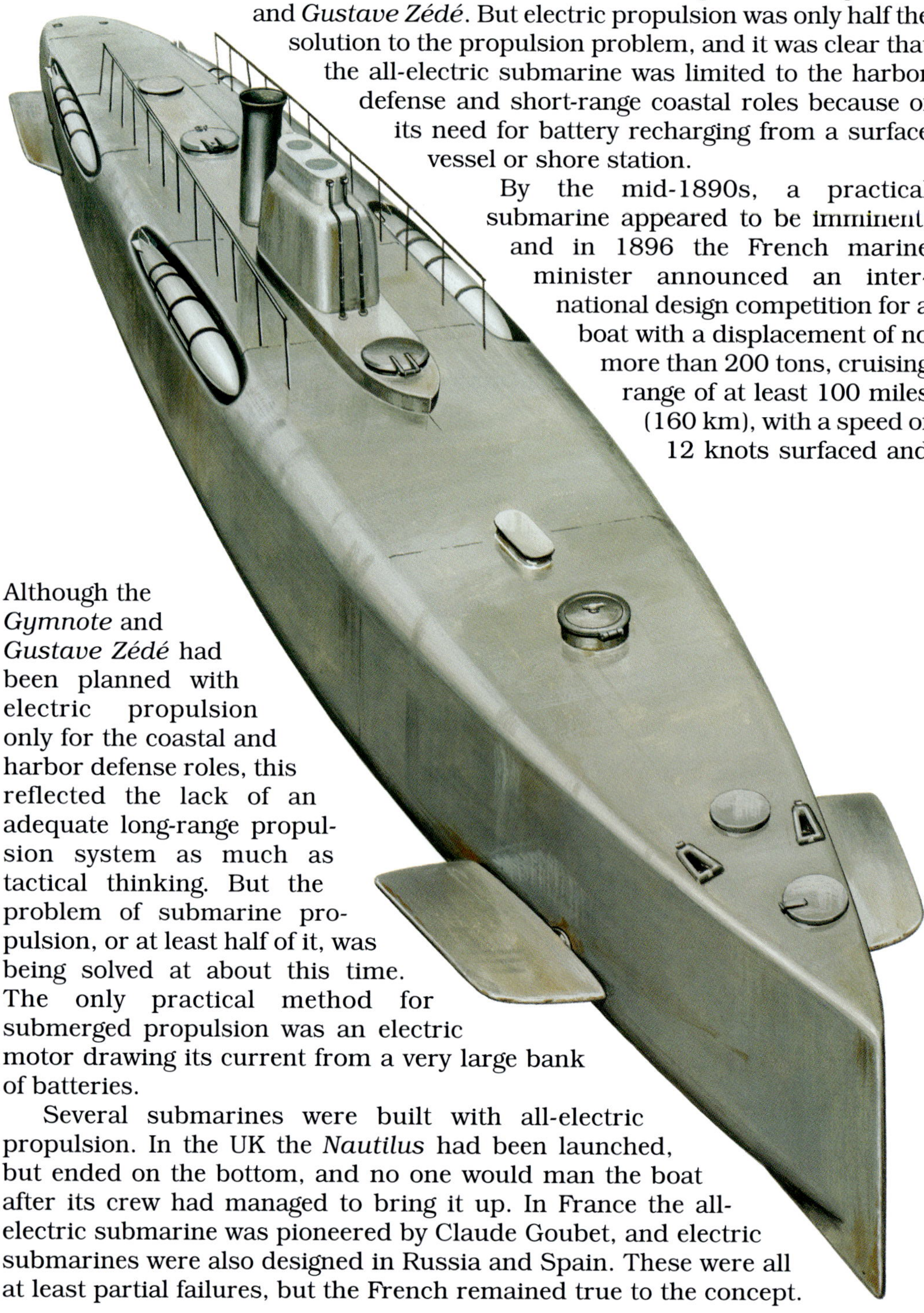

Evidence of the French affiliation to the concept are the *Gymnote* and *Gustave Zédé*. But electric propulsion was only half the solution to the propulsion problem, and it was clear that the all-electric submarine was limited to the harbor defense and short-range coastal roles because of its need for battery recharging from a surface vessel or shore station.

By the mid-1890s, a practical submarine appeared to be imminent, and in 1896 the French marine minister announced an international design competition for a boat with a displacement of no more than 200 tons, cruising range of at least 100 miles (160 km), with a speed of 12 knots surfaced and

Although the *Gymnote* and *Gustave Zédé* had been planned with electric propulsion only for the coastal and harbor defense roles, this reflected the lack of an adequate long-range propulsion system as much as tactical thinking. But the problem of submarine propulsion, or at least half of it, was being solved at about this time. The only practical method for submerged propulsion was an electric motor drawing its current from a very large bank of batteries.

Several submarines were built with all-electric propulsion. In the UK the *Nautilus* had been launched, but ended on the bottom, and no one would man the boat after its crew had managed to bring it up. In France the all-electric submarine was pioneered by Claude Goubet, and electric submarines were also designed in Russia and Spain. These were all at least partial failures, but the French remained true to the concept.

8 knots submerged. At least 29 designs were submitted, and the winner was the *Narval,* from a French designer, Maxime Laubeuf.

The boat was launched in 1899, and was notably advanced in its overall appearance as well as its propulsion. There were pairs of diving planes fore and aft, a flat casing, three hatches, a small conning tower flanked by two sets of rails which extended well aft and, the one feature odd to modern eyes, a funnel with a flared top abaft the conning tower. The *Narval* was based on two propulsion systems. For surface running, there was a steam engine with oil-burning boilers, which provided a range of 500 miles (800 km) at 7.5 knots or 250 miles (400 km) at 11 knots. For submerged running, there was an electric motor powered from a large battery for 71 miles (115 km) at 5 knots or 25 miles (40 km) at 8 knots. The single most important feature of the *Narval*'s propulsion was the coupling of the steam engine to the electric motors so that the batteries could be recharged while the submarine was on the surface: running in reverse, the electric motors became dynamos. This clever and efficient system steadily became the norm for all submarine design before nuclear propulsion.

The *Narval* did not wholly solve the propulsion problem, however, as a steam engine was, in general, too hot to be located inside the small and cramped engine room of a craft as small as a submarine, and the tasks of closing down the burners before the boat could submerge, and then of lighting them and getting up a head of steam after the vessel had surfaced, were a time-consuming tactical nightmare.

The *Narval* was also one of the first submarines of the double-hull type, with an inner hull that withstood the pressure of the water when the boat was submerged, and also accommodated the crew, and an outer hull that contained ballast and fuel tanks and provided the desired hydrodynamic outer shape. Such a double-hull design was extremely strong, and did much to improve the reliability of submarines.

The armament was based on four torpedoes carried externally in a pair of drop collars on each beam abreast the conning tower and farther aft. The bow was also strengthened for ramming, a feature much in vogue at this time.

Despite its defects, the *Narval* was closer to the right answer than any submarine before it. It should be noted, however, that at the much the same time, two U.S. inventors, John Holland and Simon Lake, were developing submarines which were at least as advanced and perhaps even more so.

Narval

Type:	attack submarine
Tonnage:	136 tons surfaced
Dimensions:	length 111 ft., 6.5 in. (34 m); beam not available; draft not available
Propulsion:	one steam engine delivering 220 hp (164 kW) for 11 knots surfaced and one electric motor delivering 80 hp (59.6 kW) for 8.1 knots submerged
Armament:	four drop collars for four torpedoes
Complement:	not available

Holland VI (1897)

John Philip Holland was born on February 29, 1840, in Ireland, later immigrated to the U.S., and died there on August 12, 1914. Holland is universally credited with being the creator of the first truly practical submarine, and Holland boats were the first such craft commissioned into U.S. and British naval service. One of four brothers born in Liscannor, County Clare, John and his brother Michael were active members of the Irish Republican Brotherhood, otherwise known as the Fenians, the forerunner of the Irish Republican Army. Holland and the Fenians developed a plan to build a submarine small enough to be carried on a merchant ship to an area near an unsuspecting British warship, where submarine would be released from the bottom of the merchantman to attack the warship.

Holland immigrated to the U.S. in 1873, and two years later offered his first plan for a submarine to the U.S. Navy, which rejected his concept as unworkable. The Fenians still funded development at a level that made it possible for Holland to quit his teaching position. The *Fenian Ram* was launched in 1881, but soon after this Holland and the Fenians parted company on bad terms, largely as a result of financial matters within the Fenian organization and also between the Fenians and Holland.

John Holland emerging from Holland No. VI in April 1898. 25 years of hard work, disappointment, and frustration had elapsed before this famous photograph was taken.
Photo: Naval Historical Centre.

Holland continued to develop his designs, and also worked on several experimental boats. The first of these to enjoy any measure of real success was the *Holland No. 1*, launched in 1878 by the Albany Iron Works. This boat was of angular riveted metal construction with a small hatch-topped conning tower, and a

From the beginning, Holland hull designs showed the way of future submarines.

pair of hydroplanes on the side of the hull forward of the conning tower. As initially planned, the *Holland No. 1* was to be hand-powered by a crank driving a two-blade propeller, but the development of a moderately effective petrol engine, in this case a 4 hp (3 kW) Brayton unit, allowed Holland to complete the boat to a more effective standard. The *Holland No. 1* had a displacement of 2.2 tons surfaced, length of 14 ft., 6 in. (4.4 m) and beam of 3 ft. (0.9 m), but all other details are missing. The *Holland No. 1* completed its trials and then, after the engine had been removed, was scuttled in the Upper Passaic River in about 14 feet (4.2 m) of water. The hull was later discovered and raised, and it is now a museum exhibit.

The importance of the *Holland No. 1*, which was too small for any practical purpose, was the fact that Holland had realized the importance of the internal combustion engine for surfaced running. Other submarine pioneers of the time were still thinking in terms of steam propulsion for surfaced running. The petrol engine was not the perfect solution, but was better than the steam engine.

On May 17, 1897, the *Holland VI* was launched as Holland's and indeed the world's first truly successful submarine. This was the first boat with sufficient power to run submerged for any useful distance, and also the first boat in which the propulsion arrangements were entrusted to the combination of a battery-powered electric motor for submerged running and a petrol engine for surfaced running.

The *Holland VI* was built by the Crescent Shipyard of Elizabeth, New Jersey. Crescent undertook the task to a contract from Holland's company, known at the time as the Holland Torpedo Boat

Holland VI *continued*

Company. The new boat was constructed under the personal supervision of Holland, who designed the vessel and its details in collaboration with Crescent's chief constructor, Arthur L. Busch. After meeting Holland in 1896, Busch "translated" Holland's concepts and sketches into the blueprints that allowed the cutting of metal and the construction of the submarine.

The *Holland VI* incorporated all of the major features which submarines of the early twentieth century would possess, albeit in more advanced forms as the art and science of submarine design and construction developed. The *Holland VI* had both an internal combustion engine for surfaced running and an electric one for submerged operation. The boat also had armament in the form of an 18-inch (457 mm) torpedo tube for which two reload weapons were carried, and a deck gun, in this case a pneumatically operated 8-inch (203 mm) "Dynamite Gun." There was a low conning tower, with a hatch in its upper surface, from which the boat and its weapons could be controlled. Finally, the *Holland VI* had all ballast and trim tanks required for the boat to make precise changes in its depth and attitude, once submerged below the surface of the water. Propulsion was provided by a single four-bladed propeller which was flanked by two vertical rudders and two horizontal hydroplanes.

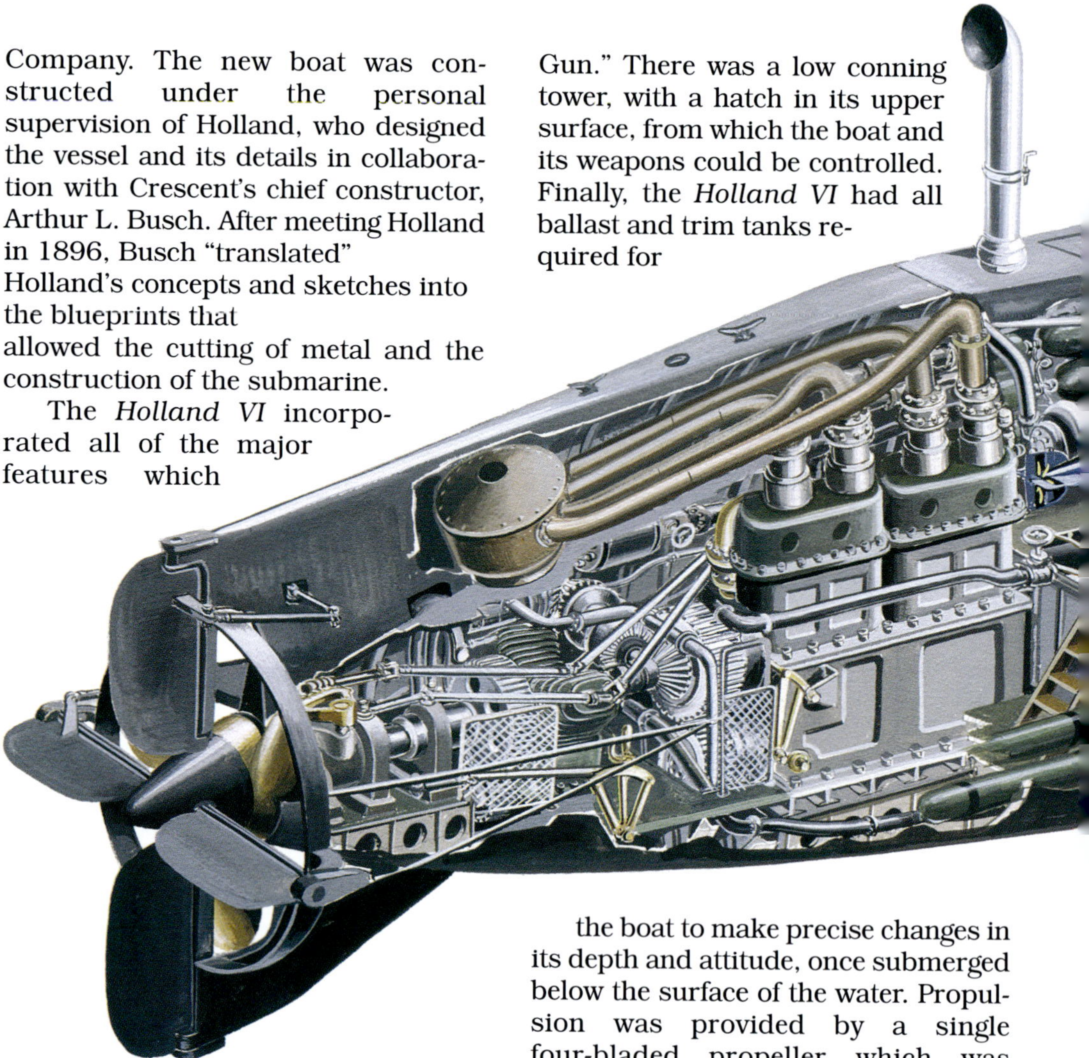

The *Holland VI* underwent a lengthy period of trials and development. After surface trials and a 30-minute static dive, the *Holland VI* recorded its first under-way dive on March 17, 1898, off Staten Island, New York. Ten days later, the boat began its official trials; one of the witnesses was Secretary of the Navy Theodore Roosevelt, who was strongly in favor of the U.S. Navy's purchase of the vessel. It fact it was not until April 11, 1900, that the *Holland VI* was

This cutaway illustration clearly shows the well-thought-out interior of this Holland IV boat.

U.S. Navy, and later acquired the aircraft manufacturer Convair (originally Consolidated and Vultee).

The *Holland* was thus the first commissioned submarine of the U.S. Navy and, as such, the first of the unbroken line of submarines in the U.S. Navy. However, the *Holland* was in fact the third submarine to be owned by the U.S. Navy: the first had been the *Submarine Propeller* (also known as the *Alligator*) and the second, the *Intelligent Whale*. Neither of these had been commissioned boats, however.

bought by the U.S. government, and the boat was commissioned into the U.S. Navy on October 12 of the same year as the *Holland* (SS-1).

Together with seven later submarines of the same basic design, the *Holland* was based at New Suffolk, New York, on the North Fork of Long Island, between 1899 and 1905. The success of this and the other early Holland submarines assured Holland that he had been right to establish the Electric Boat Company. This had been incorporated in New Jersey with the financial assistance of Isaac Leopold Rice, on February 7, 1899, and is now the Electric Boat Division of the General Dynamic Corporation, which grew out of the submarine company's enormous technical and financial success as the primary builder of submarines for the

On October 16, 1900, the *Holland* left Newport under tow of the tug *Leyden* bound for Annapolis, Maryland, where it was used in the training of midshipmen (cadets) of the U.S. Naval Academy as well as the officers and enlisted men who had been selected for the training vital in readying them for service as the crews of this and later submarines ordered for the U.S. Navy's new submarine arm.

The *Holland* proved valuable for experimental purposes in collecting

Holland VI continued

The dynamite guns are seen facing fore and aft, angled upwards. The normal torpedo faces forward, below the Zalinsky dynamite gun.

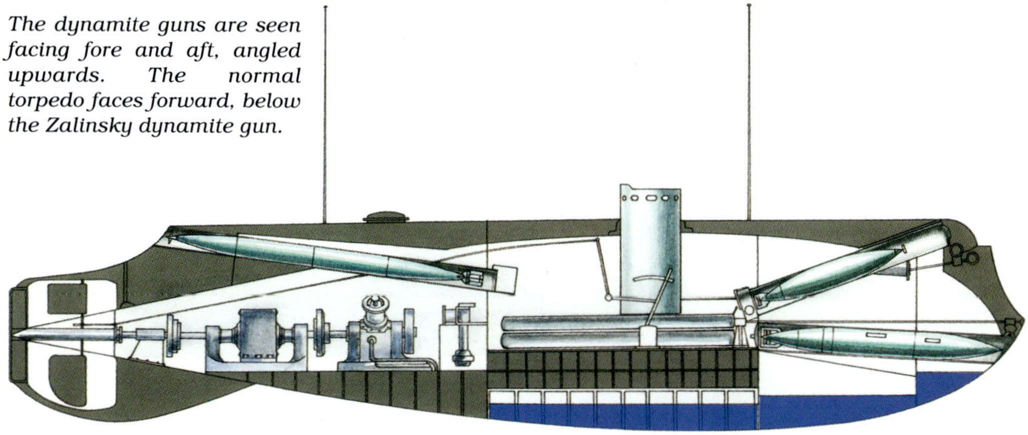

data that allowed improvement in submarines being designed or even under construction. The boat's surfaced run of 166 miles (267 km) Annapolis to Norfolk, Virginia, between January 8-10, 1901, provided other useful data on her performance while underway over an extended period.

Except for the period between June 15 and October 1, 1901, when the boat was used in the training of cadets at the Naval Torpedo Station, Newport, Rhode Island, the *Holland* remained at Annapolis until July 17, 1905, in its primary role of training. From Annapolis, the *Holland* was transferred to the great naval base at Norfolk, Virginia, where it remained until the submarine was stricken on November 21, 1910. The discarded boat was sold as scrap to Henry A. Hitner & Sons, of Philadelphia, Pennsylvania, on June 18, 1913, for just $100, the buyer being required to post a $5,000 bond as assurance that the submarine would be broken up and not used as a ship.

The construction of another five Holland-type boats, with the submerged displacement increased to 123 tons and the length to 64 feet (19.5 m), was also undertaken by the Crescent Shipyard, these boats being the A-

class submarines *Plunger*, *Adder*, *Moccasin*, *Porpoise*, and *Shark* intended primarily for the harbor defense role, and another two were built by the Union Iron Works as the *Grampus* and *Pike*. The boats were all launched between 1901 and 1903 and with the exception of the first, which was stricken in 1913, survived to 1921-22, when they too were stricken and used at targets. The last six boats had constituted the 1st Submarine Division of the Asiatic Torpedo Fleet after being shipped in pairs to the Philippines in 1908, 1909, and 1915.

Although the Royal Navy had publicly disowned the concept of the submarine, the growth of the French submarine arm at a time of strong British and French rivalry at the start of the twentieth century led to a revision. After Electric Boat had offered to build Holland-type submarines for the Royal Navy, the Admiralty secured a license for five boats to be constructed by Vickers at Barrow-in-Furness, United Kingdom. These were launched between October 1910 and June 1902 as *No. 1* to *No. 6* after completion to a design with a displacement of 122 tons submerged, length of 63 ft., 10 in. (19.5 m), surfaced and submerged speeds of 7.5 and 5 knots, respectively, armament of one 18-inch (457 mm) bow tube for three torpedoes and complement of eight. The boats were used almost exclusively for experimental and development work, and remained in service for 10 years.

The Holland type of boat was also the Imperial Japanese navy's first submarine, of which five were ordered from the Fore River Company under Electric

Boat license. These were the *No. 1* to *No. 5*, shipped as sets of components to Japan late in 1904 and then assembled after some delay and with great difficulty. The boats had a displacement of 124 tons submerged, length of 67 feet (20.4 m), surfaced and submerged speeds of 8 and 7 knots, respectively; armament of one 18-inch (457 mm) tube for two torpedoes, and complement of 13.

Holland

Type:	experimental and training submarine
Tonnage:	64 tons surfaced and 74 tons submerged
Dimensions:	length 53 ft., 10 in. (16.4 m); beam 10 ft., 2 in. (3.1 m); draft 8 ft., 6 in. (2.6 m)
Propulsion:	one Otto petrol engine delivering 45 hp (33.5 kW) for 8 knots surfaced and one electric motor delivering 50 hp (37.3 kW) for 5 knots submerged
Armament:	one 8-inch (203 mm) "Dynamite Gun" and one 18-inch (457 mm) tube (bow) for three torpedoes
Complement:	7

Naïade class (1904)

By the time of the *Gustave Zédé*, the French navy understood the submarine's suitability for a navy which could not match its main rival in the numbers and capabilities of its major warships, but could hope to check it in a coastal war through the massed use of small craft (both surface and underwater) firing torpedoes.

An early clue toward this tendency could be found in the *Morse*, which had been built by the Arsenal de Cherbourg. Laid down in July 1899 and stricken in November 1909, this was a single-hull boat of Roma bronze designed, like the *Gustave Zédé*, by M. Romazotti, to combine the best features of the *Gymnote* and *Gustave Zédé*. The boat carried a detachable lead keel, and its life was short, as the basic design was quickly overtaken by that of the *Narval*. The data for the *Morse*, which had a range of only 104 miles (167 km) at 4.3 knots surfaced, included a displacement of 143 tons surfaced and 149 tons submerged, length of 119 ft., 9 in. (36.5 m), beam of 9 ft. (2.7 m), draft of 9 ft., 3 in. (2.8 m), propulsion by one electric motor delivering 284 hp (211.75 kW) for 7.25 knots surface and 5.5 knots submerged, armament of one 18-inch (450 mm) bow tube for three torpedoes, and complement of 13.

Resulting from France's fascination with torpedo craft of all types, the *Narval* had a submerged displacement of 202 tons, length of 111 ft., 7 in. (34 m) and armament of four drop collars for four 18-inch (450 mm) torpedoes. The *Narval* was designed by Maxime Laubeuf and built by the Arsenal de Cherbourg for launch in October 1899. Laubeuf's concept was a torpedo boat which could submerge to make its attack and departure, and its major innovation was a triple-expansion steam engine powered by steam from an oil-fired boiler for surface running and battery charging. The steam plant provided a speed of 9.9 knots, and the electric motor offered a submerged speed of 5.3 knots. The *Narval* was the first double-hulled French submersible boat: the strongly constructed inner cigar-shaped hull contained all major equipment and the thin outer hull had the lines of a torpedo boat. The ballast tanks were situated between the two hulls, and the result made the

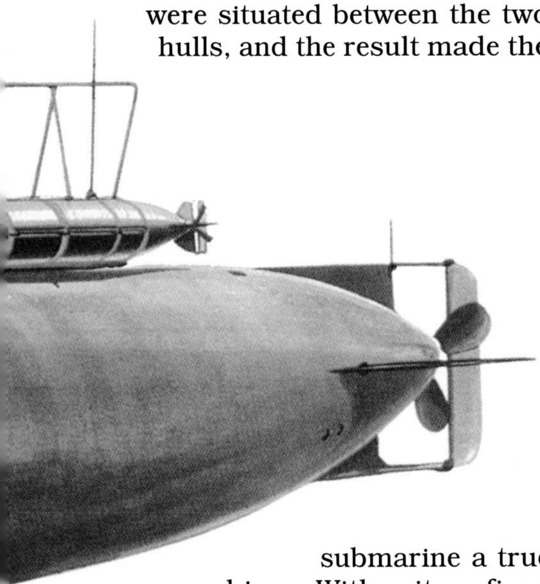

submarine a true warship. With its fixed conning tower in the center of the hull's flat upper surface, and a periscope, the *Narval* pioneered the look of the definitive submarine, despite its funnel. It required as long as 21 (later reduced to 12) minutes to cool the boiler and blow off steam before diving. The boat was stricken in 1909.

There followed the Sirène, Farfadet, and Morse classes of four, four, and two submarines, respectively, the first and last built by the Arsenal de Cherbourg and the second by the Arsenal de Rochefort. The first class, essentially of a modified Narval type, comprised the *Espadon*, *Silure*, *Sirène*, and *Triton* with mixed steam and electric propulsion for 9.75 knots surfaced and 5.8 knots submerged, a submerged displacement of 213 tons, length of 99 ft., 3 in. (32.5 m), armament of four drop collars for four 18-inch (450 mm) torpedoes; all the boats were stricken in 1919. The second was of the single-hulled type designed by M. Maugas, and comprised the *Farfadet*, *Gnôme*, *Korrigan*, and *Lutin* with all-electric propulsion for 6.1 knots surfaced and 4.3 knots submerged; submerged displacement of 202 tons, length of 135 ft., 6 in. (41.3 m), and armament of four drop collars for four 18-inch (450 mm) torpedoes; all the boats were stricken between 1906 and 1913. And the third was also of the single-hulled type designed by Romazotti, and comprised the *Algerien* and *Français* also with all-electric propulsion for 10.1 knots surfaced and 8.3 knots submerged, submerged displacement of 160.1 tons, length of 120 ft., 5 in. (36.7 m), and armament of one bow tube and two drop collars for three 18-inch (450 mm) torpedoes; both of the boats were stricken in 1914.

These three classes paved the way for the 20 boats of the Naïade class, which were single-hulled submarines of Romazotti design with a gasoline engine for surface running and battery charging. The boats were built by the Arsenal de Cherbourg (three boats), Rochefort (six boats) and Toulon (eleven boats) for launch between 1903 and 1905, but had only short ranges and were all stricken, between 1912 and May 1914. The boats were the *Alose*, *Anguille*, *Bonite*, *Castor*, *Dorade*, *Esturgeon*, *Grondin*, *Loutre*, *Ludion*, *Lynx*, *Méduse*, *Naïade*, *Otarie*, *Oursin*, *Perle*, *Phoque*, *Protée*, *Souffleur*, *Thon*, and *Truite*.

Protector (1902)

In 1985 Simon Lake established the Lake Submarine Company in New Jersey, and hoped to compete with John P. Holland in gaining an order from the U.S. Navy for a new genera-

Comparatively small wheels would have been less an asset than a hindrance, running on an unseen seabed.

tion of submarines offering, for the first time, genuine operational capability. Ultimately, the order went to Holland, for he was able to demonstrate his *Holland VI,* whereas Lake had only the obsolete *Argonaut* to demonstrate, as his latest boat was not ready. This last was the *Protector*, which was launched on November 1, 1902, at Bridgeport, Connecticut, where Lake had his headquarters. The *Protector* was a logical development of the Argonaut with greater size, improved capabilities, torpedo armament in bow and stern, and considerable comfort for the crew. The boat was the first of Lake's level-keel type of submarines, and also the first boat in the world with hydroplanes forward of the conning tower complemented, in this boat, by stern-mounted hydroplanes. Other features of the boat were an omniscope (primitive form of periscope) emerging from the upper surface of the conning tower, an arrangement of retractable wheels so that the boat could run along the bottom, and external keels which could be jettisoned in an emergency.

The *Protector* was designed for coastal defense, and there was considerable controversy between the

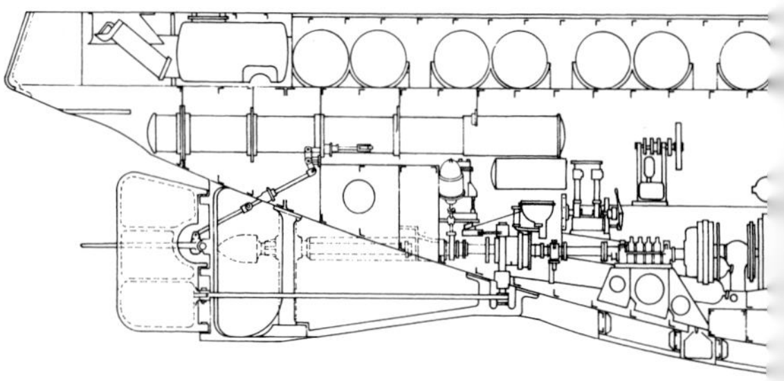

adherents of the Lake and Holland types of submarine. Many officials were strongly in favor of the Lake-type submarine, which was designed to operate on an even keel, but there were just as many who preferred the Holland type of boat designed to dive and rise by angling the hull down or up. The deciding factor was that the U.S. Navy already had experience with the Holland type of boat.

At this time there was growing hostility between Japan and Russia about the latter's possessions and rights in the Far East, culminating in the Russo-Japanese War (1904-05), won decisively by Japan. As the tensions between the two Imperial nations rose, both Japanese and Russian navies expressed a keen interest in the *Protector*. Lake sold the boat to the Russians, dismantled it, and shipped the components to St Petersburg during the course of the Russo-Japanese War. It was assembled and trialed as the *Osetr*. From St Petersburg, the boat was then moved some 6,000 miles (9655 km) across Russia on the Trans-Siberian Railway to Vladivostok, on the Pacific coast. Special cars had been built for the purpose, bridges were strengthened, and extraordinary provision was made to pass the boat through some tunnels. The *Osetr* was so successful that the Russian navy ordered five more boats of this type. These were the *Bychok*, *Kefal*, *Paltus*, *Plotva*, and *Sig*, manufactured by Newport News Shipbuilding in 1905 and shipped to Russia. The boats were stricken between 1913 and 1915 after having constituted the Russian navy's first submarine force of practical naval submarines.

The significant achievement of the *Protector* submarine is that it established on a worldwide basis the precedent for submarines of the even-keel type. Unfortunately, the U.S. did not properly acknowledge this fact until 1912, after the navies of several other countries had achieved considerable success with submarine of the Lake type.

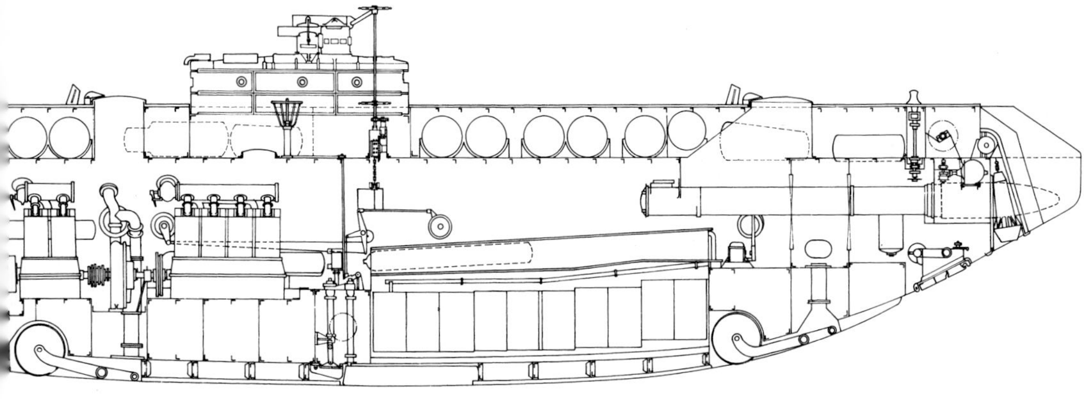

Protector (as Osetr)

Type: submarine

Tonnage:	136 tons surfaced and 174 tons submerged
Dimensions:	length 67 ft., 6 in. (20.6 m); beam 14 ft., 2 in. (4.3 m); draft not available
Propulsion:	two petrol engines delivering 240 hp (179 kW) for 10 knots and two electric motors delivering 110 hp (82 kW) for 6 knots submerged
Armament:	three 18-inch (457 mm) tubes (two bow and one stern) for three torpedoes
Complement:	7

Forel (1902)

During the advent of the submarine as a practical weapon of war, the navies of the world's major powers seemed to be fascinated by the concept of the midget submarine. This was perhaps the result, in part at least, of the perception by many of the more senior naval officers that the submarine was an underhand weapon, which led more junior officers to see the submarine as a vehicle for their more dashing ambitions. At a more practical level, however, the midget submarine was cheap to build and operate; the midget submarine had only very limited manning requirements. Moreover, such boats could offer a small radius of action, which effectively removed the need for the crew to be provided with anything more than the most vestigial living features on board, for they would live ashore or on a mother vessel, and occupy their boat only on the type of short-endurance operation which was all that boats of this type could hope to undertake.

On the tactical level, the midget submarine could be used for both offensive and defensive missions. Its small size, and therefore its very low visibility, even when running awash, meant that the type was admirably suited for attacks on an enemy's coastal installations, most especially his harbors. Such boats would be transported by their mother vessel, either on board or under tow, and be committed to their tasks from as close to the target areas as possible, their crews fully rested and their batteries charged to capacity. The boats would then penetrate the harbor as and when they found the opportunity past defenses such as nets, and torpedo or mine the ships posing the greatest threats to their own navy's major warships. Only after this would the boats seek to escape and regain their mother vessel.

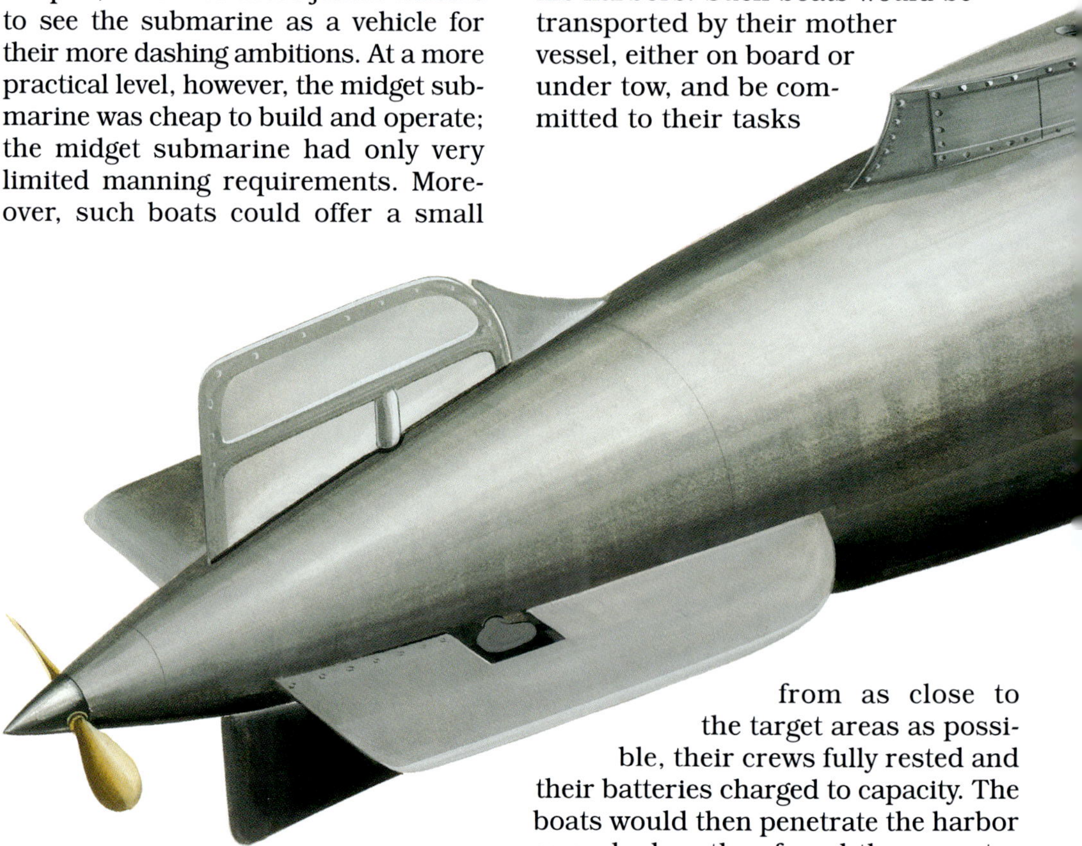

For defensive operations, the midget submarine could be deployed at major bases with their crews ready to board if and when an enemy force approached. The boats would then slip out of harbor to tackle the enemy's major warships and then return, if possible, to their base for rearmament and for their batteries to be recharged against the possibility of another sortie.

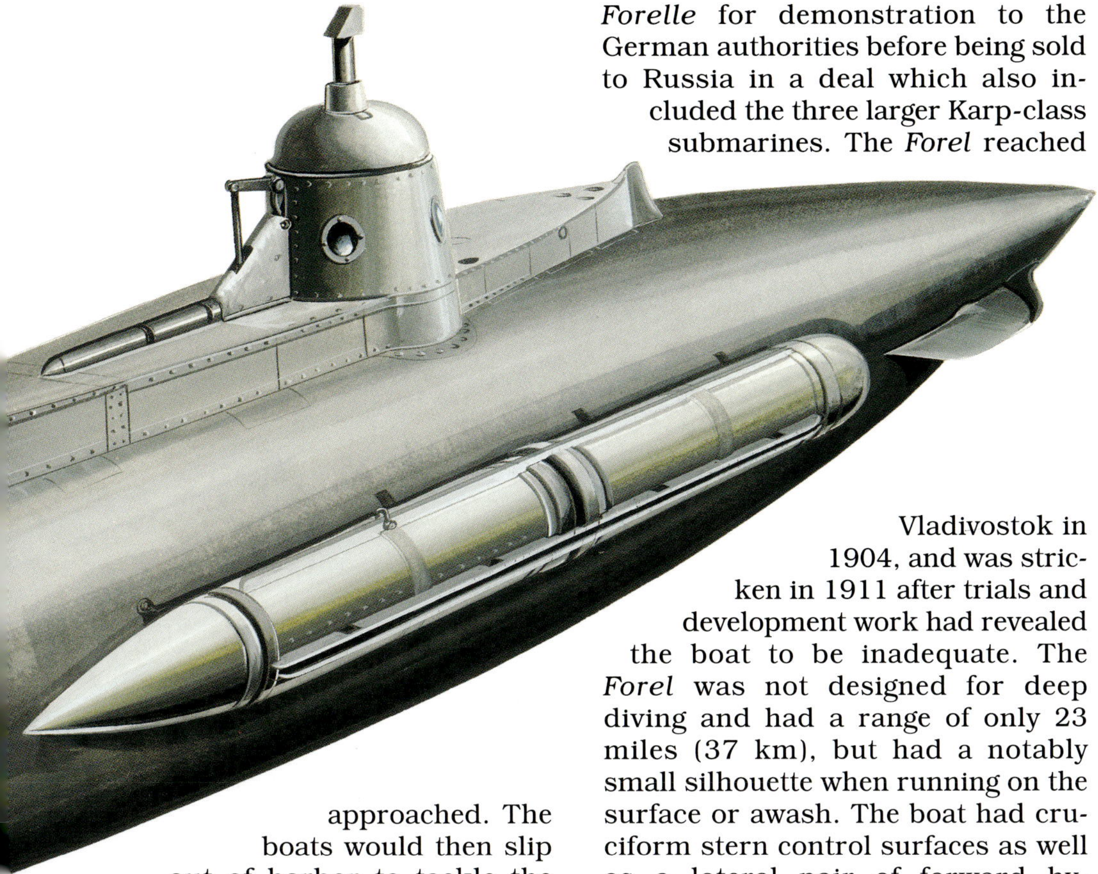

The Imperial Russian navy's first experiment in this direction was the *Forel*, which was launched in 1902 in Germany by the Germaniawerft as the *Forelle* for demonstration to the German authorities before being sold to Russia in a deal which also included the three larger Karp-class submarines. The *Forel* reached Vladivostok in 1904, and was stricken in 1911 after trials and development work had revealed the boat to be inadequate. The *Forel* was not designed for deep diving and had a range of only 23 miles (37 km), but had a notably small silhouette when running on the surface or awash. The boat had cruciform stern control surfaces as well as a lateral pair of forward hydroplanes, and its coming tower carried a primitive periscope. The hull was too small for the installation of any internal torpedo armament, especially as the hull was spindle shaped with a finely tapered bow, so the armament was limited to torpedoes carried by one external drop collar on each beam.

Forel

Type:	midget submarine
Tonnage:	16 tons surfaced and 17 tons submerged
Dimensions:	length 43 ft. (13.1 m); beam 7 ft. (2.1 m); draft 7 ft. (2.1 m)
Propulsion:	one electric motor delivering 70 hp (44.7 kW) for 4 knots
Armament:	two drop collars for two torpedoes
Complement:	not available

Hajen (1904)

The *Hajen* ("shark") was the first submarine designed and built in Sweden. The boat was launched from the Örlogsvarvet ("navy yard") at Stockholm on July 16, 1904. The boat resulted from a 1900 decision to despatch the naval engineer Carl Richson to the U.S. to learn all he could about the design and construction of submarines, and on arrival in the U.S. Richson felt that the thinking of John P. Holland was superior to that of Simon Lake. Richson therefore learned as much as possible about the work of *Holland*, who was currently on the verge of creating the first practical submarine for eventual purchase by the U.S. Navy, and returned to Sweden to design his country's first submarine.

In 1902 the Swedish parliament voted to allocate funds for a pioneering Swedish submarine, and in November 1902 the king of Sweden formally approved the allocation. Richson completed work on the design and construction was started, in conditions of the greatest possible secrecy, in the old "galley yard" within the Stockholm naval shipyard. The resulting boat was, in its final iteration after a rebuild in 1916, of somewhat unusual and highly distinctive appearance. It was almost as if the forward section of a torpedo boat, with a torpedo tube incorporated in the lower part of its bow, had been dropped into a large opening cut into the upper

surface of an elongated melon. The flat deck of this boat was surrounded by wire railing, and in its center was a low and short superstructure with an outward-curving upper edge. This carried a circular-section windowed conning tower surmounted by a hatch, and abaft it was the primitive periscope. The stern of the submarine reflected its Holland-derived origins in comprising horizontal and vertical pairs of surfaces to control the boat's diving and direction keeping. These surfaces surrounded the propeller.

The Avance paraffin engine, for which 2.2 tons of fuel were carried, never provided the reliability which had been expected, and when the *Hajen* was rebuilt in 1916 by at Bergsunds

Mekaniska Verkstad, in Stockholm, it was replaced by a four-cylinder diesel engine delivering 135 hp (101 kW). Other changes included a platform deck (see above) and a longer bow increasing the length from 70 ft., 10 in. (21.6 m) to 76 ft., 5 in. (23.3 m). The *Hajen* had only a short first-line operational career, for with the arrival in service of the *Hvalen* in 1909, the boat was reclassified as a second-class submarine, and was then used primarily for training.

The *Hajen* was stricken in 1922. The boat was stripped of machinery and all the fittings inside the hull and then used until 1932 as a moored depot vessel. The submarine is now a prized exhibit at the Swedish Naval Museum in Karlskrona.

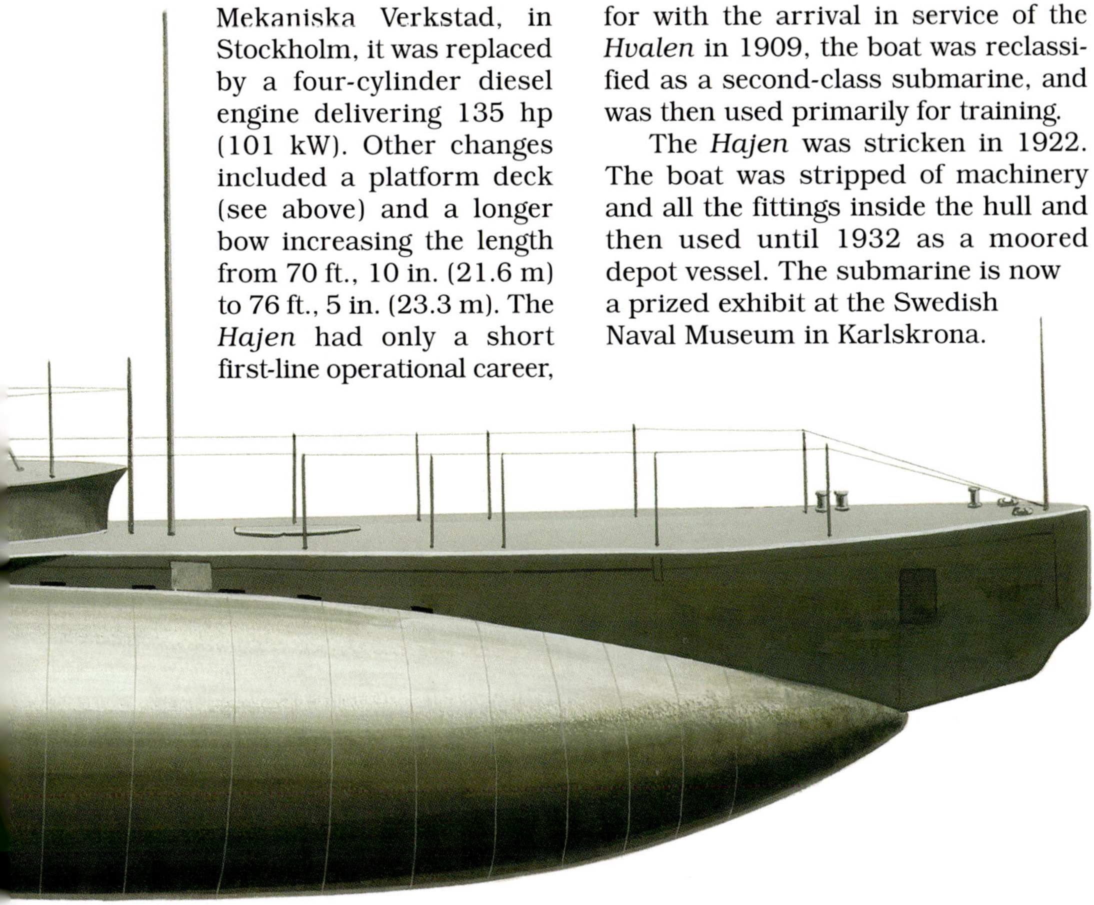

Sporting a very advanced shape, the Hajen was nevertheless based on the designs of John P. Holland.

Hajen

Type:	submarine
Tonnage:	111 tons surfaced and 127 tons submerged
Dimensions:	length 70 ft., 10 in. (21.6 m); beam 11 ft., 10 in. (3.6 m); draft 9 ft., 10 in. (3 m)
Propulsion:	one Avance paraffin engine delivering 200 hp (149 kW) for 9.5 knots surfaced, and one Luth & Rosen electric motor delivering 70 hp (52.2 kW) for 7 knots submerged
Armament:	one 18-inch (457 mm) tube for three torpedoes
Complement:	8-11

U-1 (1906)

The history of the European development of the submarine, in its first form as a practical submersible, lies in 1850 when the Bavarian inventor and engineer Wilhelm Bauer built his *Brandtaucher* at Kiel. This craft sank during the first diving trial, and Bauer could make no progress in the following years despite unceasing efforts to convince the authorities that his type of submersible would really work.

Between 1840 and 1902, only two other submersible boats were built in Germany, both at the Howaldtswerke, one in 1891 and another in 1897. The next move toward the construction of a submarine in a German shipyard came in 1902, when a Spanish engineer, Raymondo Lorenzo d'Equevilley-Montjustin, who had formerly been an assistant of the French submarine designer Maxime Laubeuf, was taken onto the payroll of the Germaniawerft at Kiel, a yard recently bought by the great steel and armaments magnate Friedrich Krupp. The new employee's first design was the tiny spindle-shaped midget submarine *Forelle*, which was sold after numerous demonstrations to the German naval authorities to the navy of imperial Russia together with the three Karp-class boats.

Until 1904, the opinion of Admiral Alfred von Tirpitz, secretary of state of the Reichsmarineamt (Imperial Naval Office) was essentially negative, but after the Forelle had proved itself technically successful, von Tirpitz instructed the Torpedoinspektsion ("torpedo inspection"), which was the Reichsmarineamt department with overall responsibility for all underwater weapons development, to embark on the design of an effective submarine. As the German navy had virtually no practical experience in such matters, it simultaneously ordered a submarine from Germaniawerft so that the two types could be subjected to a comparative evaluation.

The boat ordered from Germaniawerft was the double-hulled *U-1*, but major design revisions compared to the Karp-class boats built for Russia (a slightly enlarged pressure hull and an improved external hull, which prevented oil leakage from the external tanks) meant that the new submarine was launched only on August 4, 1908, and commissioned only in December of the same year. The boat designed by the navy was the *U-2*, which was laid down at the imperial navy yard at Kiel and not launched until June 18, 1908.

Sections through the U show the use of space, which would be copied by most other countries.

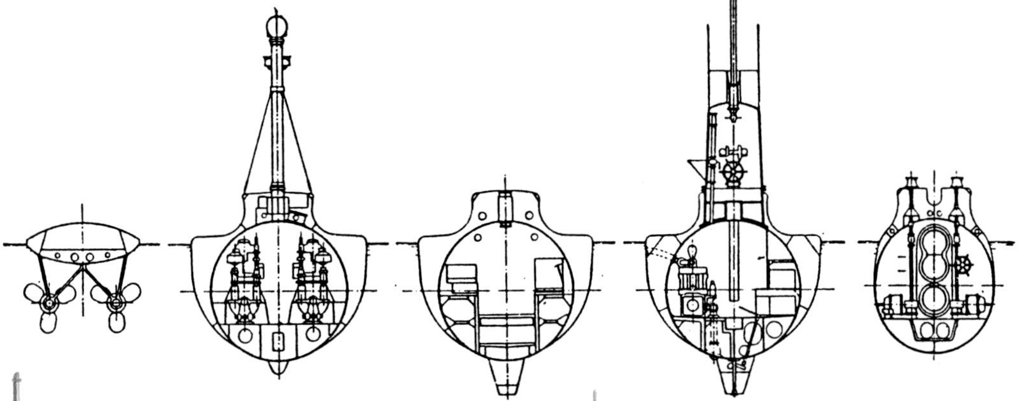

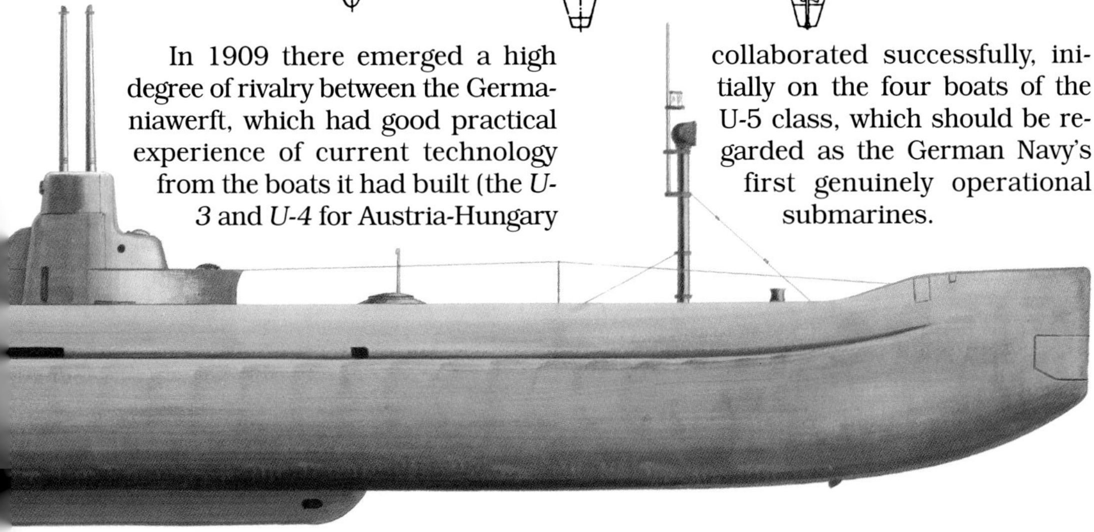

In 1909 there emerged a high degree of rivalry between the Germaniawerft, which had good practical experience of current technology from the boats it had built (the *U-3* and *U-4* for Austria-Hungary and the *Kobben* for Norway) and the Torpedoinspektsion, which had superior design capability. The rivalry was defused by d'Equevilley's departure from the Germaniawerft, after which the two groups collaborated successfully, initially on the four boats of the U-5 class, which should be regarded as the German Navy's first genuinely operational submarines.

The *U-1* was used only for trials and training, and stricken in 1919 after a collision, but later rebuilt as a permanent exhibit in the Deutsches Museum in Munich, Germany.

U-1

Type:	submarine
Tonnage:	238 tons surfaced and 283 tons submerged
Dimensions:	length 138 ft., 9 in. (42.4 m); beam 12 ft., 6 in. (3.8 m); draft 10 ft., 6 in. (3.2 m)
Propulsion:	two Körting kerosene engines delivering 400 hp (298 kW) for 10.8 knots surfaced, and two electric motors delivering 400 hp (298 kW) for 8.7 knots submerged
Armament:	one 18-inch (450 mm) tube for three torpedoes
Complement:	12

Minoga (1908)

On January 4, 1901, the Russian ministry of marine allocated the task of designing an operational submarine for service with the imperial Russian navy to a pair of engineering officers, Lieutenants M. N. Beklemishev and I. S. Goryunov, with the technical support of Naval Architect Senior Assistant I.G. Bubnov. Bubnov was employed by the ministry-owned Baltic Works shipyard at St Petersburg, where the resulting submarine was to be built. This three-man design team presented its concept to the ministry on May 3, 1901. The design received formal approval in the following July, and the Baltic Works shipyard was contracted to build *Torpedo Boat No. 113*, which was later renamed as the *Delfin*. Bubnov was then appointed to lead the Construction Commission for Submarines. Bubnov then designed the follow-on Kasatka class of six boats, again of the single-hulled type and built by the Baltic Works, but the exigencies of the Russo-Japanese War (1904-05) also persuaded the Russian navy to order seven Holland-type boats from the Nevskiy Yard of St Petersburg, six Lake-type boats assembled from kits by the arsenal at Libau, three Karp-class boats from Germaniawerft, and four improved Lake-type boats of the Kaiman class from the Crichton Yard of St Petersburg.

The next submarine of Russian design was therefore the *Minoga*, a Bubnov design ordered in February 1906 from the Baltic Works. This was a single-hulled submarine with saddle tanks, and planned for a maximum diving depth of 96 feet (29 m). The design was prepared using data provided by the operations of Russian boats in the waters of the Pacific Ocean off Vladivostok. One of the main changes was the introduction, for the first time in a Russian submarine, was surfaced propulsion by diesel engines, but these were unreliable and additional complexity was added by the incorporation of a blade-pitch control mechanism so that the single propeller could usefully absorb the power of the different engines.

The *Minoga* was launched in October 1908 and soon found to be too cramped for genuinely effective service use. The 11 tons of diesel oil provided a surfaced range of only 690 miles 1110 km) at 10 knots, while the battery power was sufficient for 57.5 miles

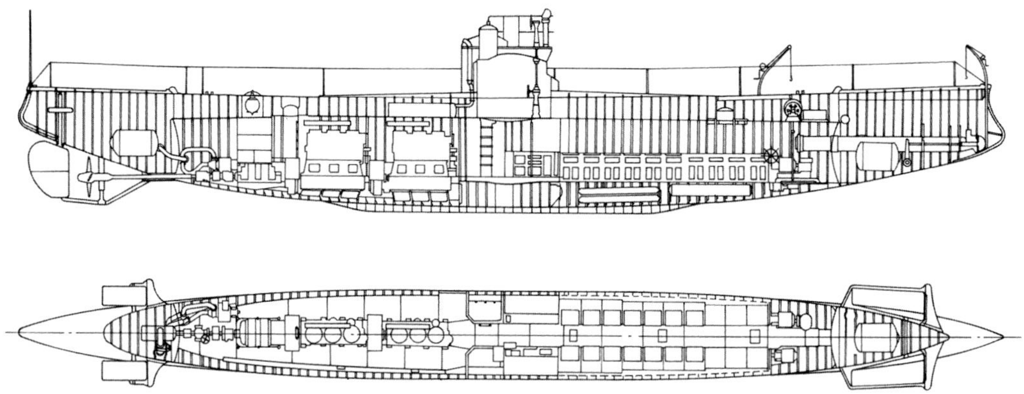

Using the best of Holland and Lake designs, Russia's second home-built submarine was quite advanced.

(92.5 km) at 5.3 knots submerged. The boat was on the strength of the 1st Submarine Flotilla after being commissioned, before passing to the 4th Submarine Flotilla in 1913. The boat was transferred to the Caspian Sea in 1918, and deleted for scrapping in 1922.

By 1918 the Russian navy had received 73 Russian-designed boats of the Kasatka, Minoga, Akula, Morzh, and Bars classes, and four more were being built to the new Major General Bubnov or B-class design. Thirty-two of these boats were built to the designs of Bubnov, who had become Major General of the Naval Architect Corps and Honoured Professor at the Nikolayev Marine Academy.

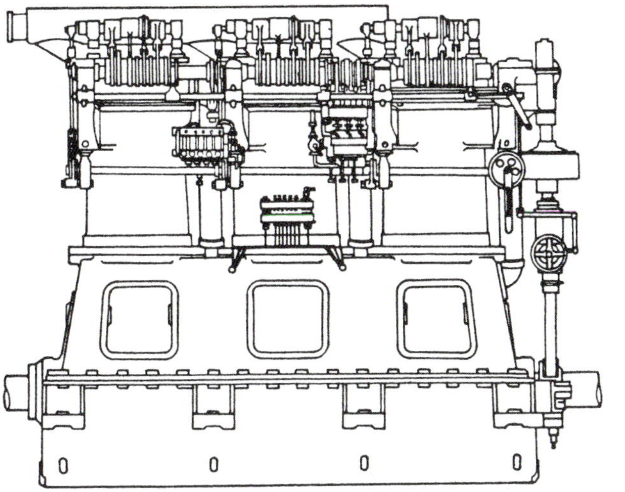

Minoga

Type:	submarine
Tonnage:	123 tons surfaced and 155 tons submerged
Dimensions:	length 107 ft., 0 in. (32.6 m); beam 9 ft., 0 in. (2.8 m); draft 9 ft., 0 in. (2.8 m)
Propulsion:	two diesel engines delivering 240 hp (179 kW) for 11 knots surfaced, and one electric motor delivering 70 hp (52.2 kW) for 5 knots submerged
Armament:	one 1 ½-inch (37 mm) gun, and two 18-inch (457 mm) tubes (bow) for two torpedoes
Complement:	22

D class (1908)

Following the five Holland-type submarines that pioneered the use of underwater craft in British service in the first decade of the twentieth century, the Royal Navy progressed slowly by means of three classes of small submarines optimized for coastal and harbor protection. These were the 13 Vickers-built A-class submarines with a submerged displacement of 207 tons, the 11 generally similar but improved Vickers-built B-class submarines with a submerged displacement of 316 tons, and the 38 generally similar C-class submarines built by Vickers (32 boats) and Chatham Dockyard (six boats) with a submerged displacement of 320 tons. The first four of these 62 boats carried one 18-inch (457 mm) bow tube for three torpedoes, while all of the others were fitted with two 18-inch (457 mm) bow tubes for four torpedoes.

The following D-class boats were the Royal Navy's first submarines capable of operating significantly beyond coastal waters in the overseas patrol task which was of great importance in the defense of the UK's imperial and trade interests. These submarines were also the first British boats with diesel rather than gasoline engines, and also the first British boats fitted with radio transmitters, using an antenna which was attached to a mast erected on their conning towers when the boats were on the surface. Earlier submarines had possessed only receiving apparatus.

The D-class patrol submarine was developed out of the C-class coastal submarine with greater displacement and length, diesel engines to avoid the safety problems associated with gasoline engines but with the added benefit of greater fuel economy, and optimization for overseas service with much improved habitability for a larger crew and a designed range of 2,880 miles (4635 km) at 10 knots surfaced.

The D-class design also included two propellers rather than the single propeller of earlier classes, this change allowing the absorption of greater power, increasing reliability and, most importantly, significantly enhancing maneuverability. The boats were single-hulled, and fitted with saddle tanks, in a change that enlarged the useful volume inside the pressure hull. Starting with the *D-6*, the D-class boats were also the first British submarines fitted with a deck gun forward of the conning tower. The design also included a bridge structure larger than that of earlier classes, and this feature gave the boats the recognizable aspect of the modern submarine.

The D-class design was considered so innovative that the first of the class, the *D-1*, was, in effect, a prototype built in conditions of great secrecy in a securely guarded building shed at the Vickers yard at Barrow-in-Furness. The boat was launched with equal secrecy on May 16, 1908, and was then fitted out in secrecy at a screened berth. Once moved to the fitting-out berth, it was once again screened from view. The details of the *D-1* differed from those of the main-sequence boats, starting with the *D-3*, in a displacement of 483 tons surfaced and 595 tons submerged, length of 163 ft., 0 in. (49.7 m) and beam of 20 ft., 6 in. (6.25 m). The following *D-2*, launched on May 25, 1910, had a displacement of 489 tons surfaced and 603 tons submerged, a length of 162 ft., 1 in. (49.4 m) and beam of 20 ft., 6 in. (6.25 m).

The D-class boats were based at Harwich, Immingham, Blyth and Dover, and their primary tasking was the location and destruction of German warships, a role in which the boats worked until a time later in World War I, when they were relegated to the training role at Portsmouth. During World War I, the boats patrolled the North Sea and the Heligoland Bight, and protected cross-Channel troopships. During the war, the *D-2*, *D-3*, *D-5*, and *D-6* were lost; the *D-1* was expended as a target in October 1918; and the *D-4*, *D-7*, and *D-8* were paid off in July 1919. There were to have been another two boats in the class, but the *D-9* and *D-10* were built by Chatham Dockyard as the *E-1* and *E-2*, the first two units of the following E class.

D-3 class

Type:	patrol submarine
Tonnage:	495 tons surfaced and 620 tons submerged
Dimensions:	length 164 ft., 7 in. (50.2 m); beam 20 ft., 5 in. (6.3 m); draft 11 ft., 5 in. (3.5 m)
Propulsion:	two diesel engines delivering 1,200 hp (895 kW) for 14 knots surfaced, and two electric motors delivering 550 hp (410 kW) for 9 knots submerged
Armament:	one 12 pdr gun, and three 18-inch (457 mm) tubes (two bow and one stern) for six torpedoes
Complement:	25

E class (1912)

The British E-class submarine, of which large numbers were built in three groups, began as an improved version of the D-class boat, of which eight were built (two by Chatham Dockyard and the other six by Vickers) for launch between May 1908 and January 1911. All 10 of the boats in the first group (the *E-1* to *E-8* for the Royal Navy and the *AE-1* and *AE-2* for the Royal Australian Navy) and some of the 12 boats in the second group (*E-9* to *E-20*) built by the same two yards had been completed before the start of World War I. The 34 boats of the third group (*E-21* to *E-56* excluding *E-28*) were completed by a number of yards (Vickers at Barrow-in-Furness, Chatham Dockyard, William Beardmore at Dalmuir, Yarrow at Scotstoun, Scotts at Greenock, Fairfield at Govan, Swan Hunter at Wallsend-on-Tyne, Cammell Laird at Birkenhead, William Denny at Dumbarton, John Brown at Clydebank, John Thornycroft at Woolston, and Armstrong Whitworth at Newcastle upon Tyne) during the course of World War I.

The construction of the boats in three groups reflected the development in the technology of submarine construction and operation. The boats of the E class operated mainly in the North and Baltic Seas against the Germans, but a sizeable number also saw service in the Aegean Sea and Dardanelles against the Turks. Some of the boats also served with the Russians in Russian coastal waters before these four boats were blown up and scuttled at Helsingfors in 1918 to avoid their seizure as the Bolsheviks gained control of Russia for the White forces. The E-class submarines served right through World War I as numerically the most important element of the Royal Navy's submarine arm, but were replaced later in the war by the L-class boats as these became available. Three of the British "Group 1" boats and both Australian boats were lost, nine of the "Group 2" boats were lost, and 10 of the "Group 3" boats were lost. The surviving boats were had all been

withdrawn from service by 1922 and sold for scrapping.

The British boats of the first or E-1 group differed from the boats of the third group in details such as their displacement of 665 tons surfaced and 796 tons submerged, length of 178 ft., 0 in. (54.25 m), propulsion by two Vickers diesel engines delivering 1,750 hp (1305 kW) for 15 knots surfaced and two electric motors delivering 600 hp (447.5 kW) for 9.5 knots submerged, range of 3,455 miles (5560 km) at 10 knots surfaced, and armament of four 18-inch (457 mm) tubes (one bow, two beam and one stern) for eight torpedoes. The two Australian boats differed from the group one boats mainly in their displacement of 664 tons surfaced and 780 tons submerged, and length of 176 ft., 0 in. (53.6 m). The boats of the second or E-9 class represented a stage in the development toward the Group 3 (otherwise, the E-21 class) boats, and their data included a displacement of 662 tons surfaced and 807 tons submerged, length of 181 ft., 0 in. (55.2 m), propulsion by two Vickers diesel engines delivering 1,600 hp (1193 kW) for 15.25 knots surfaced and two electric motors delivering 840 hp (626 kW) for 10.25 knots, and armament of one 12 pdr gun and five 18-inch (457 mm) tubes (two bow, two beam, and one stern) for 10 torpedoes. Some of the Group 3 boats were used as minelayers, their torpedo armament being reduced to three 18-inch (457 mm) tubes (two bow and one stern) for six torpedoes, the omission of the beam tubes allowing the incorporation of tubes for up to 20 mines.

Some E-class boats were fitted out to deliver mines to enemy territory. Fast on the surface and submerged, they were useful boats.

E (Group 3) class

Type:	patrol submarine
Tonnage:	662 tons surfaced and 807 tons submerged
Dimensions:	length 181 ft., 0 in. (55.2 m); beam 15 ft., 1 in. (4.6 m); draft 12 ft., 6 in. (3.8 m)
Propulsion:	two Vickers diesel engines delivering 1,600 hp (1193 kW) for 15 knots surfaced, and two electric motors delivering 840 hp (626 kW) for 10 knots submerged
Armament:	one 12 pdr gun, and five 18-inch (457 mm) tubes (two bow, two beam and one stern) for 10 torpedoes
Complement:	30

Skipjack class (1911)

Since the purchase of John P. Holland's privately built *Holland VI* boat for entry into U.S. Navy service as the *Holland*, the service's first commissioned submarine, the U.S. Navy had progressed only slowly in the furtherance of this arm. The seven A-class boats (*Plunger, Adder, Grampus, Moccasin, Pike, Porpoise,* and *Shark*) were built to an improved Holland standard. The three B-class boats (*Viper, Cuttlefish and Tarantula*) were of Electric Boat design but built by Fore River with a slight increase in displacement from 123 to 173 tons submerged, size and performance over the A-class boats but a doubling of the torpedo tubes from two to four, although with only four rather than five torpedoes. The five C-class submarines (*Octopus, Stingray, Tarpon, Bonita,* and *Snapper*) built by Fore River were somewhat enlarged quasi-brothers of the B-class submarines with a submerged displacement of 275 tons, length of 105 ft., 4 in. (32.1 m), speed of 10.5 knots surfaced and 5 knots submerged, and armament of two 18-inch (457 mm) tubes for four torpedoes. The U.S. Navy's preference at this stage for the Holland type of diving submarine, rather than the Lake type of level-keel boat, was further reflected in the three D-class boats (*Narwhal, Grayling,* and *Salmon*) built by Fore River to a standard which included a submerged displacement of 337 tons, length of 134 ft., 10 in. (41.1 m), speed of 12 knots surfaced and 9.5 knots submerged, and armament of four 18-inch (457 mm) tubes for only four torpedoes.

A major change became evident in the following E class, whose two units were the *Skipjack* and *Sturgeon,* both built by Fore River for launch in May and June 1911, respectively. In common with other U.S. Navy submarines, the boats were renamed on November 17, 1911, becoming *E-1* and *E-2,* respectively. For the first time in the short history of the U.S. Navy submarine arm, the boats of this class were lighter and smaller than those of the preceding class, which the Submarine Flotilla considered a retrograde step. But the boats were also the first American submarines with diesel rather than gasoline engines for surfaced running and battery charging, though these were unreliable and changed in 1915; the first U.S. boats with bow hydroplanes; and the first U.S. boats with radio equipment. Their designed diving depth was 2,090 feet (91 m), and their

range was 2,420 miles (3895 km) at 11 knots surfaced and 115 miles (185 km) at 5 knots submerged. The submarines were used as coastal and harbor defense boats before World War I, when they were reallocated to the training role, and also used for the testing of tactics and new equipment.

The *E-1* (*SS-24*, from July 1920) was commissioned on February 14, 1912, and six days later left Boston for Norfolk, Virginia, via Newport and New York. Off Virginia, the boat underwent trials throughout April, and entered operational service off southern New England before reaching New York Navy Yard on September 28 for alterations, repairs and the installation of the Sperry gyro-compass, for which it was a pioneer underwater test ship. It also experimented with submerged radio transmission.

The *E-1* continued important experimental development and training with the Atlantic Fleet for the next five years until December 4, 1917, when it left Newport for the Azores for patrols from January 12, 1918, between Ponta Delgada and Horta, protecting the islands from German attack and use as a haven by U-boats. The boat returned to New London on September 17 and, after a refit, was used in the training of new submariners and the testing of experimental listening gear. Placed in reserve on March 20, 1920, the *E-1* reached Norfolk on April 22 to be placed in ordinary on July 18, 1921. On September 17, the boat sailed for Philadelphia, where it was decommissioned on October 20, 1921, and sold on April 19, 1922, in accordance with the terms of the Washington Naval Treaty.

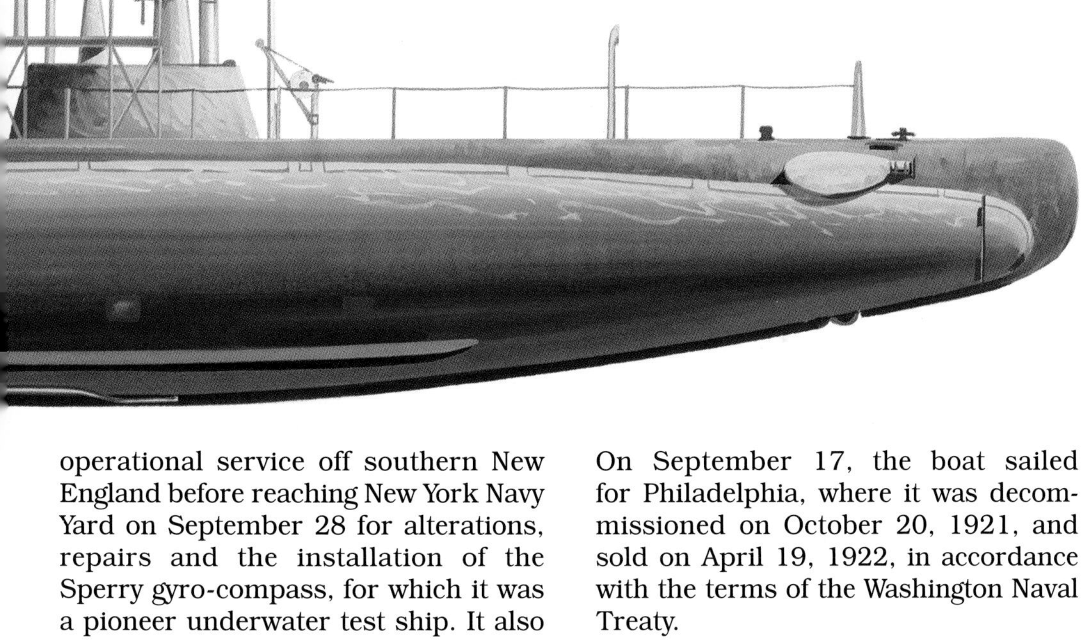

Skipjack class

Type:	coastal and harbor defense submarine
Tonnage:	287 tons surfaced and 342 tons submerged
Dimensions:	length 135 ft., 2 in. (41.2 m); beam 14 ft., 5 in. (4.4 m); draft 11 ft., 10 in. (3.6 m)
Propulsion:	two diesel engines delivering 700 hp (522 kW) for 13.5 knots surfaced, and two electric motors delivering 600 hp (447.5 kW) for 11.5 knots submerged
Armament:	four 18-inch (457 mm) tubes for four torpedoes

Ferre class (1912)

The Peruvian navy had been effectively destroyed during Peru's defeat in the War of the Pacific (1879-84) against Peru and Bolivia. By 1906, the Peruvian navy was only just starting to emerge from very low state to which it had fallen in the aftermath of this war, and the process of rebuilding effectively began with the receipt in 1906-07 of the two 3,100-ton scout cruisers of the Almirante Grau, ordered from the Armstrong Yard of Elswick-on-Tyne in the UK. The two

vessels, armed with two 6-inch (152 mm) and eight 3-inch (76 mm) guns, and possessing a speed of 24 knots, were the service's first modern warships in many years.

However, the single most influential factor in the development of the Peruvian navy during this era was a French naval mission, which began its operations in Peru in 1908 but soon grew to six officers. As an almost inevitable consequence of this French influence, not to mention lobbying for French yards, Peru bought from France one second-hand Chasseur-class destroyer, the 520-ton *Rodriguez,* and two new submarines, as well as almost purchasing a cruiser. As it was, the argument about the procurement of this *Comandante Aguirre*, which had been the French navy's *Dupuy de Lôme*, combined with the outbreak of World War I to lead to the end of the mission's endeavors in 1914. During the early years of the war, the scout cruisers *Almirante Grau* and *Coronel Bolognese* operated in the task of escorting merchant ships in Peruvian territorial waters (one Peruvian merchant vessel, the *Lorton*, was torpedoed in World War I, during February 1917). On September 29, 1917, Peru imposed armed guards on board eight German ships interned in Callao, and on June 14, 1918, broke diplomatic relations with Germany and seized the interned ships. During World War I, Peru was unable to increase the strength of its navy, which was therefore still in a poor state when a U.S. naval mission started work in the country during 1920. The first warships procured under the stimulus of the U.S. mission were R-class submarines ordered late in the 1920s to replace the Ferre-class boat, which had been stricken in 1919.

The two Ferre submarines ordered under the influence of the French naval mission were the Laubeuf-type *Ferre* and *Palacios*, built by Schneider-Creusot and launched in 1912 and 1913, respectively. The two submarines were transported to Peru by the *Kangaroo*, which was specially designed and constructed for the long-distance delivery of submarines. The service life of these two French-built boats was shortened by the constant scarcity of batteries and essential spare parts. There is some dispute as to the armament of the boats; some sources claim that it was four bow tubes for six Smulders torpedoes, and others that it had one internal bow tube for two torpedoes and four external drop collars for four torpedoes. The boats had a range of 2,300 miles (3700 km) at 10 knots surfaced.

There had been one other submarine in Peru before this time, a boat built in 1879 by its designer, the inventor Federico Blume. Little is known about the boat, which was possibly without armament. The boat could undertake no operations during the War of the Pacific, and was destroyed to prevent it from falling into Chilean hands.

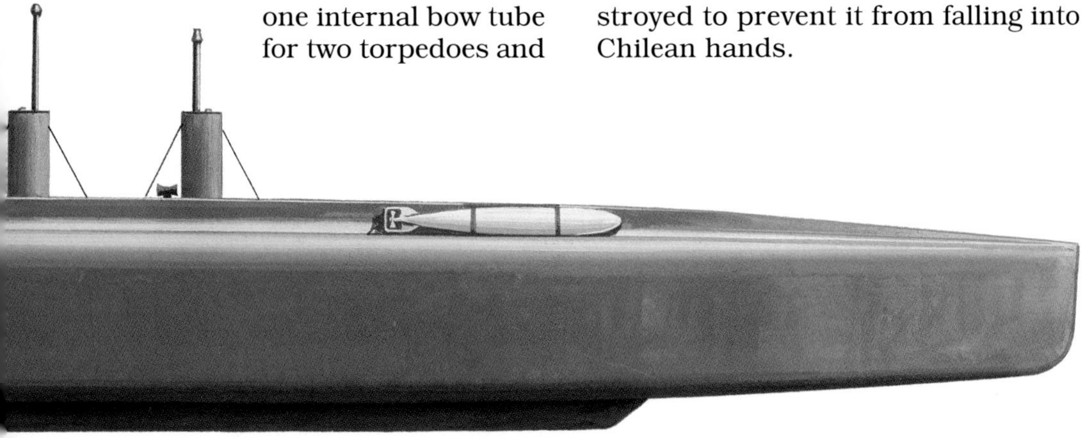

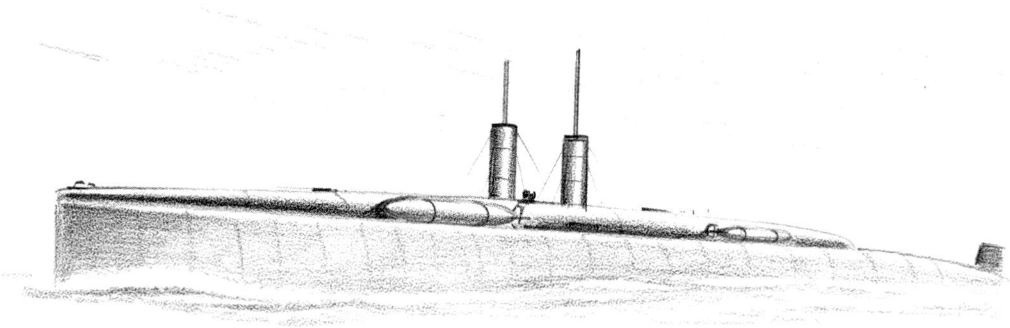

Ferre class

Type:	submarine
Tonnage:	300 tons surfaced and 400 tons submerged
Dimensions:	no data available
Propulsion:	two Schneider-Carels diesel engines delivering 400 hp (298 kW) for 13 knots surfaced, and two electric motors delivering 200 hp (149 kW) for 8 knots submerged
Armament:	four 18-inch (457 mm) tubes (all bow) for four torpedoes

Laubeuf submarines

After his celebrated steam-powered submarine *Narval*, which was a semi-submersible launched in 1899 and technically successful despite its slow diving time, Maxime Laubeuf designed for the French navy the Sirène class of four steam-powered submersible boats, launched in 1902; the twin-hulled Aigrette class of two diesel-electric submersible boats, launched in 1904; and the Circe class of two diesel-electric submersible boats, launched in 1907.

Laubeuf returned to steam power with the Pluviôse class of 18 boats constructed under the 1905 French program, laid down in 1906, and completed between October 1908 and January 1911. Twin-hulled, these boats were named after scientists and the months of the French revolutionary calendar (as were the boats of the succeeding Brumaire class). Their steam-powered reciprocating engines prevented quick submergence, but the vessels were good sea boats. Despite the main limitation of a protracted diving time, the boats of the class were remained in steady service throughout World War I. By 1914, only the *Floréal*, *Germinal*, *Monge*, and *Ventôse* retained the bow tube originally installed to supplement the two drop collars and four cradles for six torpedoes. The *Pluviôse* was rammed and sunk with all hands near Calais by the cross-Channel steamer *Pas-de-Calais* on May 26, 1910, but was raised and restored to service. The *Floréal* was sunk in a collision with the British armed boarding steamer *Hazel* off Mudros on August 2, 1918. The *Fresnel* was torpedoed off Durazzo by Austro-Hungarian destroyers and exploded on December 5, 1915. The *Monge* was sunk in the south Adriatic by the Austro-Hungarian cruiser *Helgoland* on December 29, 1915. The *Vendémiaire* collided with the French battleship *St Louis* and was lost on June 8, 1912. The *Prairial* collided off Le Havre with the British steamship *Tropic* and was lost on April 29, 1912. The surviving boats were stricken in 1919.

In 1909 the Greek navy ordered two Laubeuf submarines as its Delfin-class boats *Delfin* and *Xifias*. These were built by Schneider at Châlons, and delivered in 1912. The boats had one internal bow tube (with a reload torpedo) and four external tubes.

The *Delfin* was based at the island of Tenedos in the Aegean Sea, and during the 1st Balkan War (1912-13) made the first modern submarine torpedo attack on December 9, 1912. The boat's commander sighted the Turkish 3,250-ton cruiser *Medjidieh* emerging from the Dardanelles with five escorts and, after an hour maneuvering into position, fired a torpedo at a range of 545 yards (500 m), but the weapon did not run properly and sank.

Both the submarines served under the French flag in 1917-18, were stricken in 1920, and were sold for scrap in 1921.

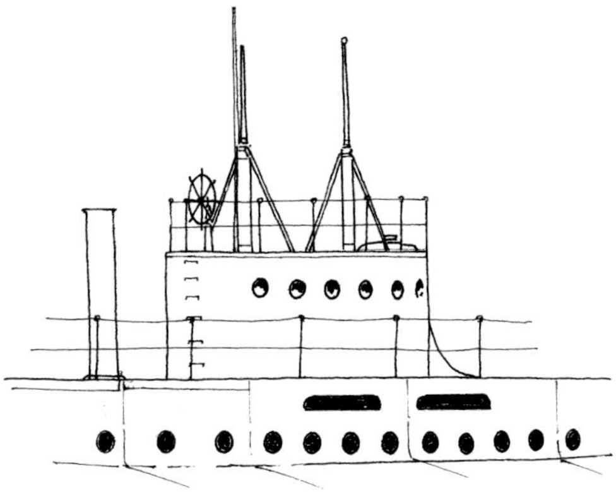

Note the very exposed steering position used by the Quartermaster when on the surface. Right behind him was the funnel.

Delfin class

Type:	submarine
Tonnage:	310 tons surfaced and 460 tons submerged
Dimensions:	length 164 ft. (50 m); beam 15 ft., 5 in. (4.7 m); draft 9 ft. (2.7 m)
Propulsion:	two Schneider diesel engines delivering 720 hp (537 kW) for 13 knots surfaced, and two electric motors delivering 460 hp (343 kW) for 8.5 knots submerged
Armament:	five 17.7-inch (450 mm) tubes (four bow and one stern) for five torpedoes
Complement:	24

F class (1916)

As part of its 1904 ship-building program, the Brazilian navy had ordered three small F-class coastal submarines from Fiat-San Giorgio of Italy. All launched in 1913, these were Laurenti-Fiat type submarines, and were supported by the *Ceara*, a tender which was also ordered from the same yard and launched in 1915. These F-class submarines were the first underwater boats procured by the Brazilian navy. In the latter part of the nineteenth century, Brazil had made a part payment on the submarine *Goubet II*, designed by the French inventor Claude Goubet, a pioneer of submarine design and an important figure in the development of both the French and Russian submarine arms. The *Goubet II* remained in France, however, and was finally auctioned. Numerous contemporary English-language naval magazines reported that Brazil had purchased the original submarine, the *Goubet I* as well as five examples of the improved *Goubet II*, but these reports were erroneous.

The Brazilian submarines had a displacement of 250 tons surfaced and 305 tons submerged, length of 150 ft., 11 in. (46 m), propulsion by two diesel engines delivering 700 hp (522 kW) for 13.5 knots surfaced and two electric motors delivering 500 hp (373 kW) for 8 knots submerged, armament of two 18-inch (457 mm) bow tubes, and complement of 20. All of these *F-1*, *F-3*, and *F-5* boats were all stricken in November 1933.

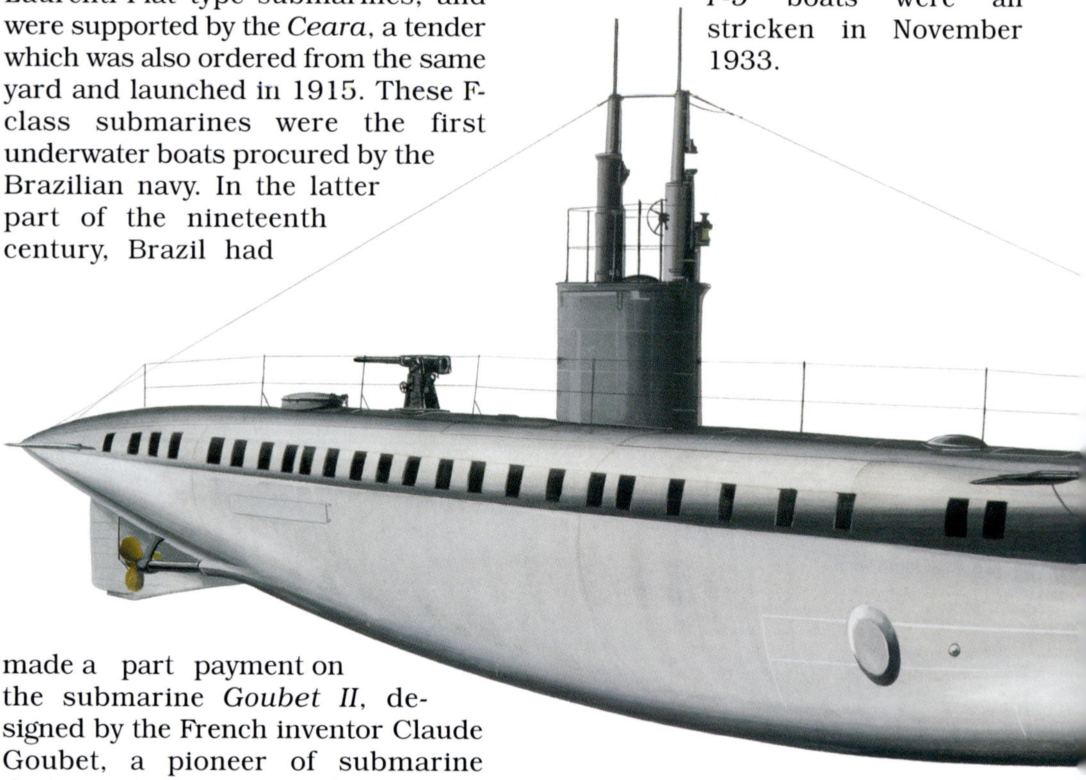

Designed at the Fiat-San Giorgio yard under the overall supervision of Engineer Major Cesare Laurenti, the Italian F-class submarine had a slightly greater displacement and marginally different dimensions to the Brazilian boats; it was an improved version of the Medusa class of coastal submarine, of which the Italian navy had received eight examples in 1912-13. By comparison with the Medusa class, the F class provided faster diving, an additional periscope, a gyro-compass, Fessenden acoustic submarine signaling gear, and armament boosted by the addition of one 3-inch (76 mm) anti-aircraft gun. The boats also had high levels of agility in both their surfaced and submerged trims,

The original orders of 1915 envisioned a total of 24 boats for the Italian navy as the *F-1* to *F-24*, but the *F-19*, *F-20*, and *F-21* were sold to the Portuguese navy, in whose service they became the *Foca*, *Golfinho*, and *Hidra*. The *F-22*, *F-23*, and *F-24* were sold to the Spanish navy, in whose service they became the *A-1* (*Monturiol*), *A-2* (*Garcia*), and *A-3* (no name).

The Italian navy then contracted for another three boats to keep its total at 21. The new boats were the *F-19* (ii), *F-20* (ii) and *F-21* (ii). The boats were built by Fiat-San Giorgio at La Spezia (thirteen boats), Odero at Sestri (three boats), and Orlando at Livorno (five boats).

The boats were completed between September 1916 and August 1918. The *F-8* sank on February 14, 1917, off La Spezia during a trial but was refloated and put back into service in September. The *F-14* was sunk in error on August 6, 1928, by the destroyer *Giuseppe Missori*, which rammed the boat while it was surfacing during an exercise off Pola. The boat was raised on August 7, 1928, and scrapped. The *F-3* was stricken in 1919, but the other boats survived until stricken between the late 1920s and mid-1930s.

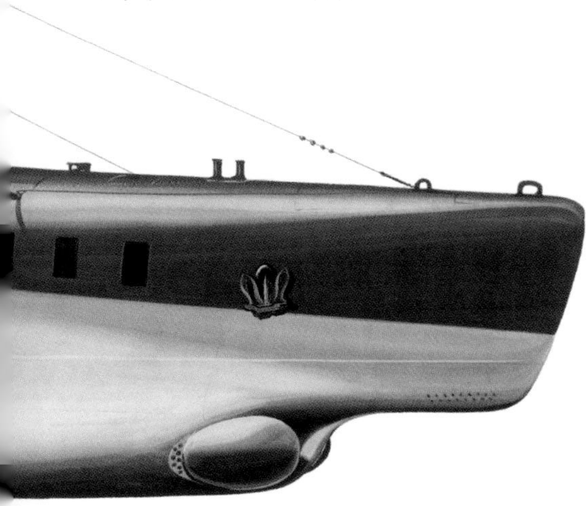

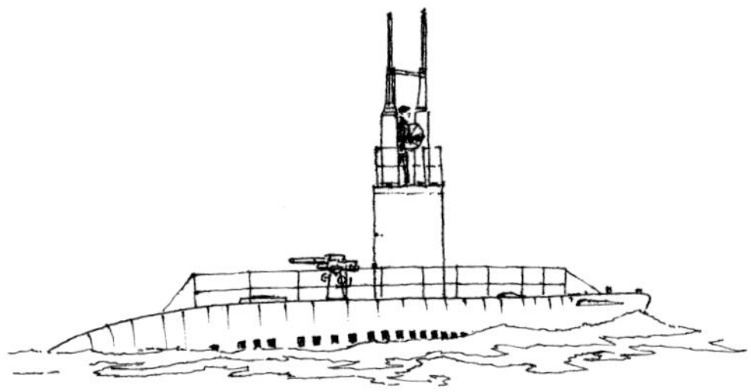

F class

Type:	coastal submarine
Tonnage:	262 tons surfaced and 319 tons submerged
Dimensions:	length 149 ft., 7 in. (45.6 m); beam 13 ft., 9 in. (4.2 m); draft 10 ft., 2 in. (3.1 m)
Propulsion:	two Fiat diesel engines delivering 670 hp (500 kW) for 12.5 knots surfaced, and two Savigliano electric motors delivering 500 hp (373 kW) for 8.2 knots submerged
Armament:	one 3-inch (76 mm) gun, and two 18-inch (450 mm) tubes (both bow) for four torpedoes
Complement:	26

UB I class (1915)

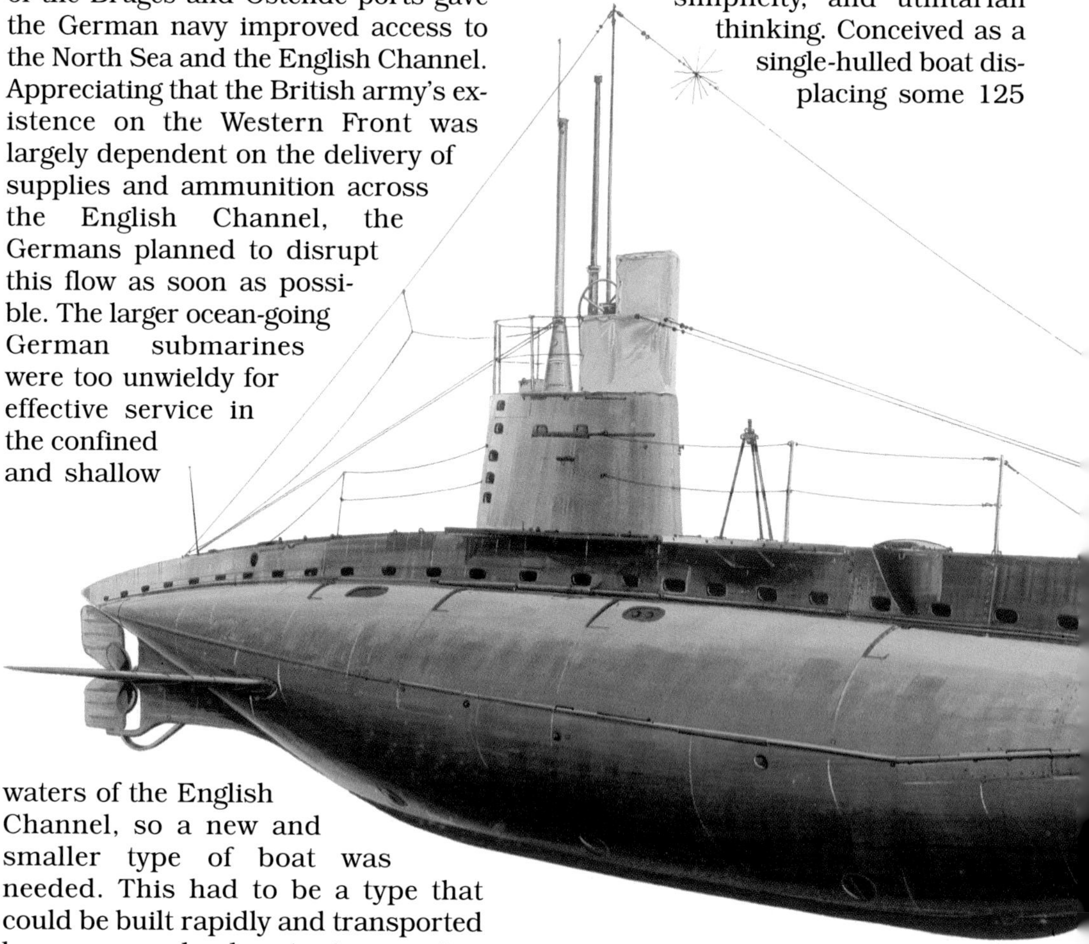

The development of the UB I class of coastal submarines resulted from the German army's offensive into Belgium at the start of World War I. The capture of the Bruges and Ostende ports gave the German navy improved access to the North Sea and the English Channel. Appreciating that the British army's existence on the Western Front was largely dependent on the delivery of supplies and ammunition across the English Channel, the Germans planned to disrupt this flow as soon as possible. The larger ocean-going German submarines were too unwieldy for effective service in the confined and shallow waters of the English Channel, so a new and smaller type of boat was needed. This had to be a type that could be built rapidly and transported by secure overland routes to operating bases in Flanders. In October 1914 a small stock of Daimler marine diesel engines was allocated for naval service and, in combination with two 18-inch (450 mm) torpedo tubes, formed the basis of the design of the UB I class.

The U-Boot Inspektsion, under the Reichsmarineamt (Imperial Naval Office) drafted the specification for this Project 34 type, which could be built in as little as four months. Created under the direction of Dr Hans Techel of the Germaniawerft yard, the UB I class boat was a capable blend of minimal resources, compact dimensions, simplicity, and utilitarian thinking. Conceived as a single-hulled boat displacing some 125 tons, the UB I design was driven by two factors: maximum permissible width for rail transport, which was fixed at 10 ft., 4 in. (3.15 m), and construction which was straightforward and simple construction, the latter translating into a design without compound curves and complex assemblies.

Only one propeller was used, and as the supply of Daimler engines was limited, this was used in only the first group of boats (*UB-1* to *UB-8*) built by Germaniawerft, a similarly rated Körting diesel engine being used for the boats of the A. G. Weser-built second group (*UB-9* to *UB-17*). The riveted pressure hull was created from cylindrical and truncated conical boiler plate sections and, while simple to fabricate, gave the boats a distinctively angular shape below the water, where it had a horizontal bow cap of elliptical shape to accommodate side-by-side torpedo tubes. A narrow, free-flooding deck casing blended into the bow cap and extended along the full length of the hull, and a relatively large conning tower was positioned amidships. To facilitate torpedo loading, the hull had no bulkheads forward of a position abaft the conning tower, where there was a torpedo loading hatch.

Oil fuel comprised 3.5 and 3 tons in the boats of the first and second groups, respectively, giving a range of 1,895 and 1,740 miles (3050 and 2800 km) at 7.5 and 5 knots. The submerged range was 52 miles (85 km) at 4 knots. The boats could submerge in a mere 33 seconds, and the design diving depth was 165 feet (50 m).

Contracts for 15 boats were signed in October 1914, but in November, Weser's order was increased from seven to nine boats after it had been decided to transfer the *UB-1* and *UB-15* to the Austro-Hungarian navy for Mediterranean operations as the *U-10* and *U-11*. This service also ordered three more boats, the *U-15* to *U-17*.

Construction times were incredibly short: the lead boat was built in just 75 days, and the entire class had been completed by April 21, 1915. The *UB-10*, *UB-12*, *UB-16*, and *UB-17* were converted into minelayers in 1918: their hulls were lengthened to 105 feet (32 m), and the torpedo tubes were replaced by four 39-inch (100 cm) tubes for eight mines. Seven of the German boats and one of the Austro-Hungarian boats were lost in the war.

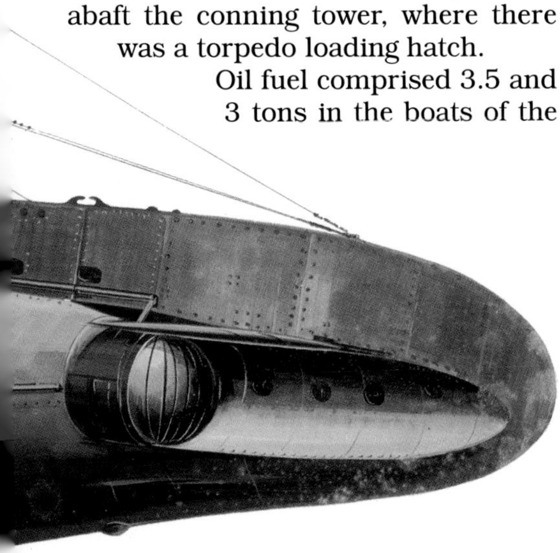

UB I class (Group 1)

Type:	coastal submarine
Tonnage:	127 tons surfaced and 342 tons submerged
Dimensions:	length 92 ft., 2 in. (28.1 m); beam 10 ft., 6 in. (3.2 m); draft 9 ft., 10 in. (3 m)
Propulsion:	one Daimler diesel engine delivering 60 hp (44.7 kW) for 6.5 knots surfaced and one Siemens Schuckert Werke electric motor delivering 120 hp (89.5 kW) for 5.5 knots submerged
Armament:	two 18-inch (450 mm) tubes (both bow) for two torpedoes
Complement:	14

B class (1904)

Used by the Royal Navy, the B class contained 11 small submarines optimized for the coastal and harbor defense roles. All of the boats were built by Vickers and launched between October 1904 and March 1906. Most of the boats served in World War I.

The submarines of the B class were essentially similar in design terms to the 13 boats of the preceding Vickers-built A class, which was the first British-designed class after the Holland-type boats with which the Royal Navy had started exploring underwater craft. Like their predecessors, the B-class boats had petrol engines for surface propulsion and battery-powered electric motors for underwater propulsion. Whereas the A-class boats each had one 16-cylinder Wolseley engine delivering 350 hp (261 kW), the larger B-class boats each had one 16-cylinder Vickers engine delivering 600 hp (447.5 kW). The greater danger represented by surface propulsion by the gasoline engine, which burns lighter and more volatile fuel than the diesel engine, and could lead to a build-up of an explosive fuel/air vapor inside the submarine, was wholly ignored at this time.

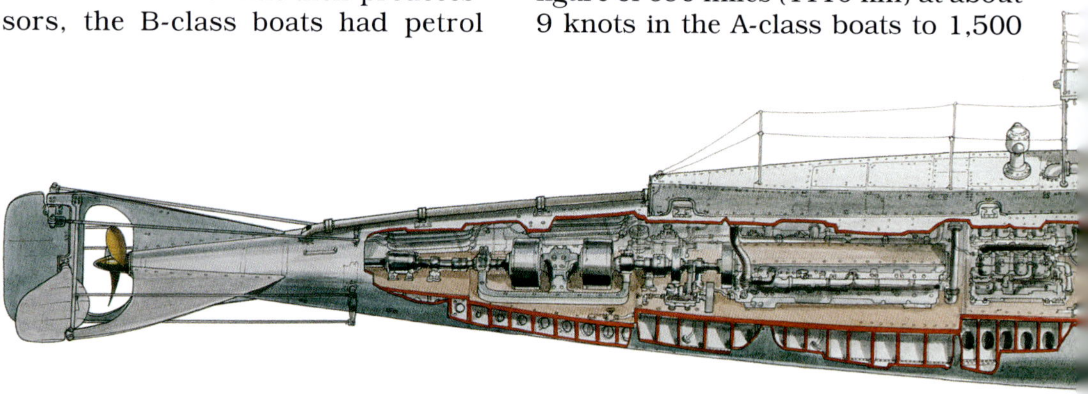

The greater installed power reflected the fact that the design was created specifically to overcome the speed, endurance, and sea-keeping limitations that had adversely affected the boats of the A class, and the B-class boats were therefore substantially longer and heavier. Improvements were made to surfaced speed, which was increased by 2 knots over the 10 knots of the A-class boats, but the submerged speed declined by 1 knot from the 7 knots typical of the A-class boats despite the use of a more powerful electric motor. The surfaced range was also improved from the figure of 690 miles (1110 km) at about 9 knots in the A-class boats to 1,500 miles (2415 km) at a similar speed in the B-class boats.

Sea-keeping was improved by the addition of a deck casing, and underwater maneuverability was significantly enhanced by the addition of a pair of hydroplanes at the forward end of the conning tower.

The *B-2* sank off Dover on October 4, 1912, after colliding with the SS *Amerika*, so by the start of World War I in August 1914 the class contained 10 boats. By this time, the submarines of the B class could be regarded only as obsolete, and some of them were quickly relegated to training duties.

The *B-6* to *B-11* were sent to the Mediterranean at the outbreak of World War I. On December 13, 1914, under the commanded of Lieutenant Norman Douglas Holbrook, the *B-11* entered the Dardanelles and torpedoed the Turkish battleship *Mesudiye*. By the end of 1915, the boats were essentially unserviceable for lack of spares, and all operational use of the submarines had ended by the first part of 1916. In 1917 England arranged with Italy to rebuild six of the boats at Venice as surface patrol vessels by removing the electric motor and association batteries, building up the fore casing to create forecastle, creating a small bridge structure, and adding a 12 pdr deck gun. The *B-10* was sunk by an Austro-Hungarian air attack on August 9, 1916, while being converted, and the five revised boats were used in the Adriatic Sea and later at Malta, where they were sold for scrapping in 1919.

B class

Type:	coastal submarine
Tonnage:	287 tons surfaced and 316 tons submerged
Dimensions:	length 142 ft., 2.5 in. (43.5 m); beam 13 ft., 7 in. (4.1 m); draft 11 ft., 7 in. (3.4 m)
Propulsion:	one Vickers patrol engine delivering 600 hp (447.5 kW) for 12 knots surfaced, and one electric motor delivering 290 hp (216 kW) for 6 knots submerged
Armament:	two 18-inch (457 mm) tubes (both bow) for four torpedoes
Complement:	15

UB II & UB III classes (1915 & 1917)

While it did achieve its primary objective of very rapidly creating a tactically useful force of small submarines for the coastal role with its UB I class, the imperial German navy appreciated from an early stage of World War I's naval effort that these early boats were too small for genuinely effective use. They had been designed on the basis of existing diesel engines (initially produced for use in motor launches) and could therefore carry only two torpedo tubes without reload weapons.

The result was a larger and more effective UB II class of coastal submarines, which were of the single-hulled types with saddle tanks, a designed diving depth of 165 feet (50 m) and a diving time which varied from 45 seconds in the boats of the first group, built by Blohm & Voss, to 30 seconds in the boats of the second group, built by A. G. Weser. The first group comprised a pair of subgroups, the first launched between August 21 and October 9, 1915, and the second between November 16, 1915, and May 6, 1916. The *UB-18* to *UB-23* comprised the first subgroup and the *UB-30* to *UB-41*, the second. The second group also included two subgroups launched between October 18 and December 31, 1915, and March 4 and June 17, 1916. These second-group boats were the *UB-24* to *UB-28* and the *UB-42* to *UB-47*.

There were a number of differences between the subgroups. For instance, the *UB-24* to *UB-29* and *UB-30* to *UB-47* had one 3 ½-inch (88 mm) L/30 deck gun in place of the earlier boats' 2-inch (50 mm) L/40 deck gun, and the larger-caliber weapon also replaced the smaller gun on the *UB-18* and *UB-21* to *UB-23* in 1916-17. The *UB-21*, *UB-22*, *UB-27*, *UB-34*, *UB-35*, and *UB-41* also had a pair of 20-inch (500 m) rearward-firing torpedo tubes located externally when their bow tubes were revised for the laying of mines. The *UB-43* and *UB-47* were sold to Austria-Hungary in 1917 and recommissioned as the *U-43* and *U-47*: the boats survived the war and were allocated to Italy as reparations before being scrapped.

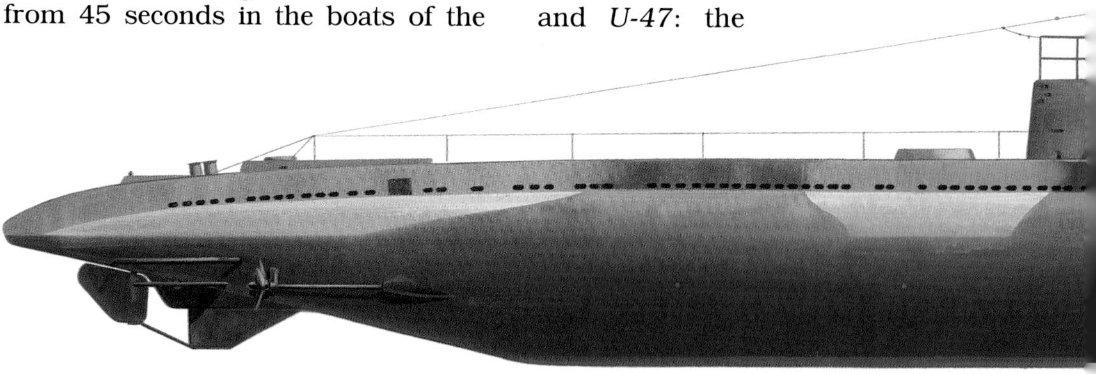

Of the nineteen German boats lost in the war to a whole host of causes including mining, capture, air attack, ramming, and attack by ships ranging upward from drifters and Q-ships, the *UB-26* was raised, became the French *Lieutenant Morillot*, and was scrapped in 1931. The *UB-23* was interned in Spain, but also became a French reparation and was scrapped. The *UB-24*, *UB-25*, *UB-28*, and *UB-42* became

British war reparations and were scrapped; the *UB-21* sank during transfer to the UK; and the *UB-40* was scuttled during the German retreat from Flanders.

The 85 UB III class boats also comprised several subgroups varying from each other in displacement, dimensions and machinery, the last including surfaced propulsion by AEG, Benz, Körting, or MAN diesel engines. These boats' submerged range was about 63 miles (102 km) at 4 knots, but their surfaced range at 6 knots varied from about 10,400 miles (16735 km) in the *UB-48*, *UB-54*, *UB-66*, *UB-133*, and *UB-170* subgroups to about 9,785 miles (15750 km) in the *UB-60*, *UB-72* and *UB-75* subgroups, 9,420 miles (15160 km) in the *UB-80* subgroup, and 8,290 miles (13340 km) in the *UB-88*, *UB-103*, *UB-118*, *UB-142* and later subgroups.

The basic data for the UB III class submarine included a displacement of 516 to 533 tons surfaced and 651 increasing to 656 tons submerged; length of 181 ft., 5 in. (55.2 m) increasing to 183 ft., 3 in. (55.9 m); beam of 19 ft. (5.8 m); draft of 12 ft., 2 in. (3.7 m); propulsion by two diesel engines delivering 1,100 hp (820 kW) for 13.5 knots surfaced and two electric motors delivering 788 hp (588 kW) for 7.5 knots submerged; primary armament of five 20-inch (500 m) tubes (four bow and one stern) for 10 torpedoes; and complement of 34.

Built by Blohm & Voss at Hamburg, A. G. Wester at Bremen, Vulcan at

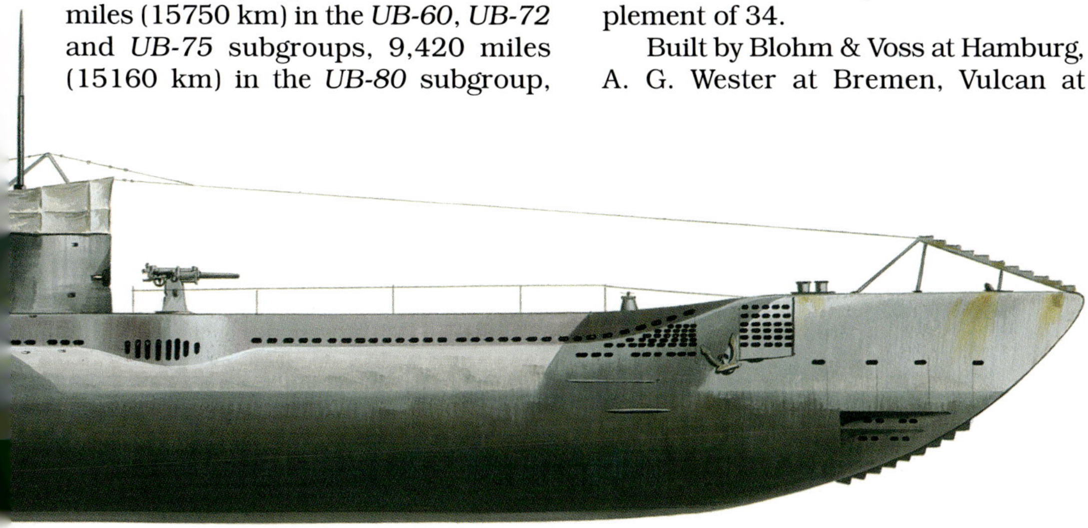

UB II class (Group 2)

Type:	coastal submarine
Tonnage:	279 tons surfaced and 305 tons submerged
Dimensions:	length 121 ft. (36.9 m); beam 14 ft., 5 in. (4.4 m); draft 12 ft., 2 in. (3.7 m)
Propulsion:	two Daimler, Körting, or Benz diesel engines delivering between 270 and 284 hp (201 and 212 kW) for 9 knots surfaced, and two Siemens Schuckert Werke electric motors delivering 280 hp (209 kW) for 5.8 knots submerged
Armament:	one 2-inch (50 mm) gun and two 20-inch (500 m) tubes (both bow) for four or later six torpedoes
Complement:	22

Hamburg and Germaniawerft at Kiel, the UB III class submarine was more akin to the very successful UC II class of mine-laying submarines than to the preceding UB II class of torpedo-armed attack submarine. The UC II class boats had gained an excellent reputation by sinking more than 1,800 Allied and neutral vessels, and in this design the Germans saw an opportunity to create still greater capability by incorporating some of the features of the UC II class boat into the UB III class design.

The UB III class of submarines entered service early in 1917 as World War I was starting to turn against Germany, a process accelerated by the U.S.'s entry into the war on the Allied side in April

1917, and the Allied introduction of the convoy system for its merchant vessels. Even so, the UB III class of submarines proved very effective, being credited with the destruction of 567 vessels before the end of hostilities in November 1918. The Germans lost 37 of the boats. Most of the survivors were broken up in the UK, but a number were lost en route to the breakers. The *UB-73*, *UB-84*, *UB-87*, *UB-142,* and *UB-154* were broken up in France, and three others saw service in the French Navy, The *UB-114*, *UB-121*, *UB-126,* and *UB-130* were expended in explosive trials in France. The *UB-59* was scuttled during the German retreat from Flanders; likewise, the *UB-48* and *UB-129* were scuttled at Pola after the Austro-Hungarian armistice. The *UB-80*, *UB-95*, and *UB-102* were broken up in Italy, and the *UB-125* and *UB-143* in Japan after brief service in the Japanese navy.

UB II class (second group)

Type:	coastal submarine
Tonnage:	279 tons surfaced and 305 tons submerged
Dimensions:	length 121 ft 0 in (36.9 m); beam 14 ft 5 in (4.4 m); draught 12 ft 2 in (3.7 m)
Propulsion:	two Daimler, Körting or Benz diesel engines delivering between 270 and 284 hp (201 and 212 kW) for 9 kt surfaced, and two Siemens Schuckert Werke electric motors delivering 280 hp (209 kW) for 5.8 kt submerged
Armament:	one 1.98 in (50 mm) gun and two 19.7 in (500 m) tubes (both bow) for four or later six torpedoes
Complement:	22

U-9 class (1910)

Designed by the imperial German navy's own team, the Torpedo-Inspektsion department, the *U-2* was laid down at Kiel Navy Yard but not completed until 1908, too late for realistic trials with the *U-1*, designed and built by the Germaniawerft yard at Kiel. In 1909 there emerged a measure of rivalry between the two teams based on Germaniawerft's proved construction capability and the navy's superior theoretical design capability, and the tension was relieved only after 1914, the *U-6* to a torpedo from the British submarine *E-6* in September 1915, the *U-7* to a torpedo fired wrongly by the *U-22* in January 1915, and the *U-8* by the British destroyers *Gurkha* and *Maori* in March 1915.

In 1910-11 the German navy felt itself ready at last to undertake its initial series of trials to evaluate U-boat tactics and operational procedures, but these trials were adversely

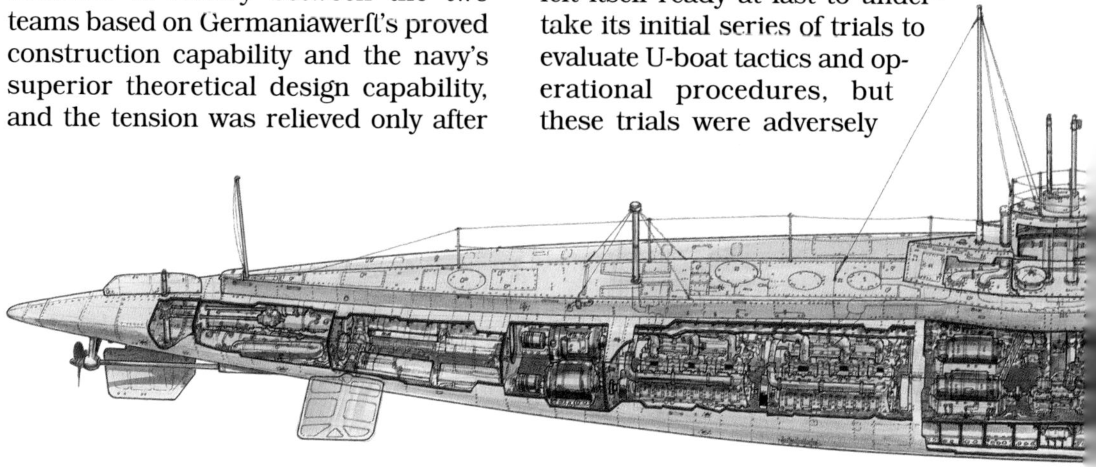

the departure of Germaniawerft's chief designer, the expatriate Spaniard Raymondo Lorenzo d'Equevilley-Montjustin. After this, the two teams worked more harmoniously. The first fruit of the new relationship was the U-5 class, comprising the *U-5, U-6, U-7*, and *U-8*, built by Germaniawerft. The class before this had been the U-3 class, comprised of the *U-3* and *U-4* built by the Danzig Navy Yard. The *U-2* had pioneered the standard armament for the U-boats of the period, namely two bow and two stern tubes for six 18-inch (450 mm) torpedoes. The U-5 submarines pushed forward the technological art, as far as German submarine design and construction were concerned, but were also the first U-boats with any real measure of operational utility. All four boats saw service in the first part of World War I: the *U-5* being lost to a mine in December affected by the loss of the *U-3* in a diving accident in November 1911: the boat was later raised, and sank finally while under tow to the UK in 1918.

One of the most important lessons learned in these first trials was the danger inherent in the use of surface propulsion engines running on lighter oil products, such as the kerosene burned by the Körting engines of these early U-boats. The answer was the diesel engine burning considerably a heavier and less volatile oil fraction, but the development of such engines to adequate power and a useful level of reliability at only a modest weight was difficult, and it was not until the advent of the four U-19 class of submarines in 1913 that diesel propulsion became standard in German boats.

After the trials of 1910-11, the Torpedo-Inspeknotsion offered an initial

U9 is seen here with full surface running rig of tall exhaust, masts, and aerials. It changed the perception of submarine warfare by sinking 3 British cruisers.

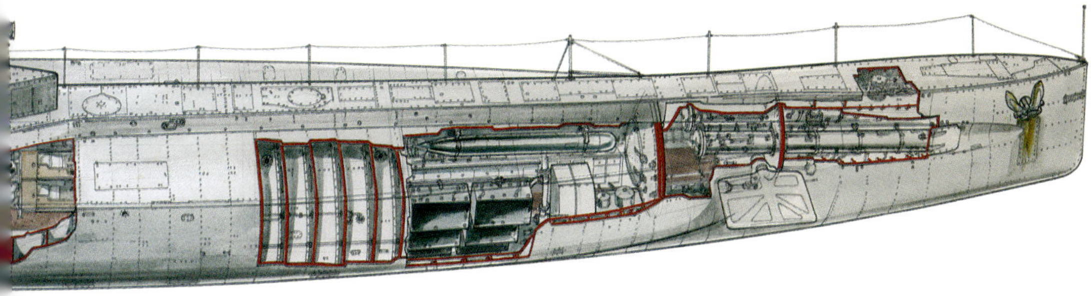

scheme, acceptable to the senior commanders of the High Seas Fleet, for the creation of an effective U-boat service. The four major elements of this scheme were the use of 36 U-boats (24 operational and 12 in reserve) for the creation of a perimeter patrol securing the Heligoland Bight, 12 U-boats for the defense of Kiel Bay in the Baltic Sea, 12 U-boats for offensive operations in the North Sea, and 10 U-boats as a general reserve. At this time, the High Seas Fleet was focused primarily on the great success expected of its major surface warships in any future naval war, and therefore saw the fledgling U-boat arm as a defensive "weapon." Even so, the German navy requested that the U-boat arm be built to a strength of 70 boats by 1919.

Another development in 1912 was the decision to explore diesel-engine technology from Italy by means of the purchase of a diesel-propelled submarine from Fiat-Laurenti at La Spezia. The boat was scheduled for completion in 1915, but not delivered as Italy had entered World War I on the Allied side by that time.

By 1912 it had become clear that the Torpedo-Inspeknotsion lacked the size and remit to cope with every aspect of what was now a steadily growing new arm of the naval service. The solution was found in the creation of the Inspektsion des U-Bootwesens ("Submarine Inspection") department as a stand-alone administrative body.

Meanwhile the design and construction of more U-boats with kerosene engines for surfaced propulsion was continuing as the German navy continued its evolutionary development of the submarine via classes of just a few boats. The first of these after the U-5 class was the U-9 class, containing the *U-9, U-10, U-11* and *U-12*. All four boats were built by the Danzig Naval Yard in 1910-11.

The Inspektsion des U-Bootwesens created the designation system adopted to differentiate the submarines built in German yards. "U" was used to indicate sea- and ocean-going patrol/attack submarines for the German navy; "UA" and "UD" for submarines built for the Norwegian and Austro-Hungarian navies, respectively; "UB" for coastal attack/defense submarines for the German navy; "UC" for coastal minelayers for the German navy with first-generation wet stowage of the mines; "UE" for improved mine-layers for the German navy with dry stowage for 34 mines as well as two external torpedo tubes; and "UF" for a variant for the German navy with all-torpedo armament as a small coastal type which could be built cheaply and quickly by mass production methods. The UF type was later rejected in favor of the Ms ocean-going boats.

The lead boat of the U-9 class first demonstrated the capabilities of the submarine in modern warfare. The U-9 had been ordered on July 15, 1908, and her keel was laid down by the Kaiserliche Werft in Danzig for launch on February 22, 1910, and commissioning on April 18, 1910. On July 16, 1914, only two weeks before the outbreak of World War I, the U-9's crew reloaded the boat's torpedo tubes while submerged, the first time this had been achieved in any submarine.

Kapitänleutnant Otto Weddigen, the captain of U-9.

U-9 class

Type:	patrol submarine
Tonnage:	493 tons surfaced and 611 tons submerged
Dimensions:	length 188 ft., 4 in. (57.4 m); beam 19 ft., 8 in. (6 m); draft 10 ft., 2 in. (3.1 m)
Propulsion:	four Körting kerosene engines delivering 1,050 hp (783 kW) for 14.2 knots surfaced, and two Siemens Schuckert Werke electric motors delivering 1,160 hp (865 kW) for 8.1 knots submerged
Armament:	four 18-inch (450 mm) tubes (two bow and two stern) for six torpedoes
Complement:	29

On August 1, 1914, Kapitänleutnant Otto Weddigen took command. On September 22, while patrolling the "Broad Fourteens," an area in the southern part of the North Sea, the boat found a squadron of three obsolescent British Cressy-class armored cruisers, assigned to the task of denying German surface vessels access into the eastern end of the English Channel. The U-9 fired all six of her torpedoes, reloading while submerged, and in less than an hour sank the *Aboukir*, *Hogue* and *Cressy*, resulting in the loss of 1,459 British sailors.

It was one of most notable submarine actions ever undertaken, albeit against obsolete warships. On October 15, the U-9 sank another British armored cruiser, the *Hawke*. On January 12 of the following year, Weddigen was succeeded in command by Johannes Spiess, who commanded the boat until April 19, 1916. During this period, the U-9 sank 13 ships, totaling 8,635 tons, in the form of 10 small fishing vessels and the British steamers *Don*, *Queen Wilhelmina* and *Serbino*.

After this, the U-9 was relegated to training service, survived the war, and was scrapped in 1919. Of the other three boats, the U-10 was lost in the Baltic during May 1916, probably to a mine; the U-11 was mined in the Straits of Dover in December 1914, and the U-12 was rammed and sunk by the destroyer Ariel off Fife Ness in March 1915.

Akula (1907)

After its first six Lake-type level-diving submarines, ordered from the U.S. and assembled at the Arsenal of Libau for launch in 1905, the imperial Russian navy decided in 1906 to order another class of Lake-type submarines for manufacture and constriction wholly in Russia. This was the Kaiman class of four boats, namely the *Kaiman*, *Alligator*, *Drakon*, and *Krokodil*. Characterized by a displacement of 409 tons surfaced and 482 tons submerged, length of 132 ft. (40.2 m), propulsion by two patrol engines delivering 1,200 hp (895 kW) for 10.5 knots surfaced and two electric motors delivering 400 hp (298 kW) for 7 knots submerged, and armament of four 18-inch (457 mm) tubes (two bow and two stern) for torpedoes, the boats were built by the Crichton Yard of numerous design and construction faults, as well as a displacement some 12 tons greater than had been planned.

When it learned that the yard then intended to sell the boats to another navy, the Russian naval ministry decided to take control of the boats without paying the yard the final installment of the price. The money thus saved was used for a conversion program in 1911. This included the removal of one three-cylinder section from each petrol engine, which provided a surfaced power of 800 hp (496.5 kW) for 8.4 knots on surface, and the installation of new ballast pumps in the volume this saved, so reducing the diving time from 10 to three minutes. Two drop-collars for 18-inch (457 mm) torpedoes were also added.

in St Petersburg and launched in 1907-08.

This Lake-type design was developed from that of the *Protector*, with the displacement increased to allow the incorporation of more powerful armament and a greater fuel capacity designed to increase the boats' range so that they operate off the Japanese coast from bases on Russia's Pacific coast. Completed in December 1910, the boats were not accepted because

The boats were finally commissioned at the end of 1911 and from 1913 constituted the Baltic Fleet's 2nd Submarine Flotilla, which was redesignated as the 3rd Submarine Flotilla in 1915. The boats saw significant service in the first part of World War I, but were stricken on November 1916 to release experienced crews for the service on the boats of the AG class. The *Krokodil* became a battery-charging hull, and all four of the boats were at Reval on February 25, 1918, so that they would not be captured by the Germans.

Ordered in December 1906 as a Bubnov version of the Kaiman-class submarines, the *Akula* in many respects represented an enlarged version of the *Minoga* with a more reliable propulsion arrangement driving three rather than one propellers.

The boat was built by the Baltic Works of St Petersburg and launched on September 4, 1907, but suffered severe teething problems. Propulsion was the most severe of these: the original 225 hp (168 kW) electric engine was replaced by a 300 hp (224 kW) unit, and all three propellers were changed.

The *Akula* was of the single-hull type with saddle tanks and a designed diving depth of 150 feet (45 m). The most successful of the pre-war Russian submarines, the *Akula* was mined off Windau, in the Baltic Sea, on November 28, 1915.

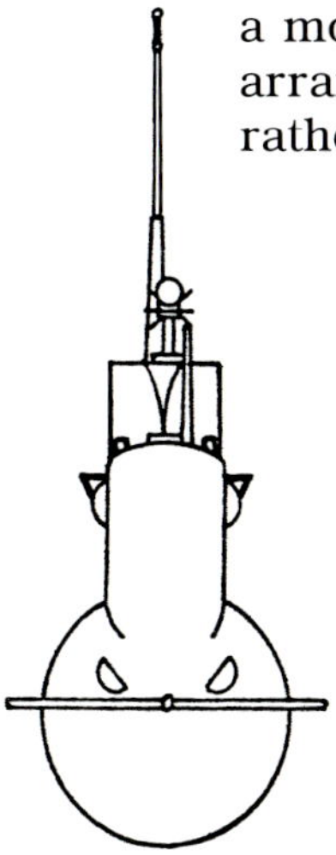

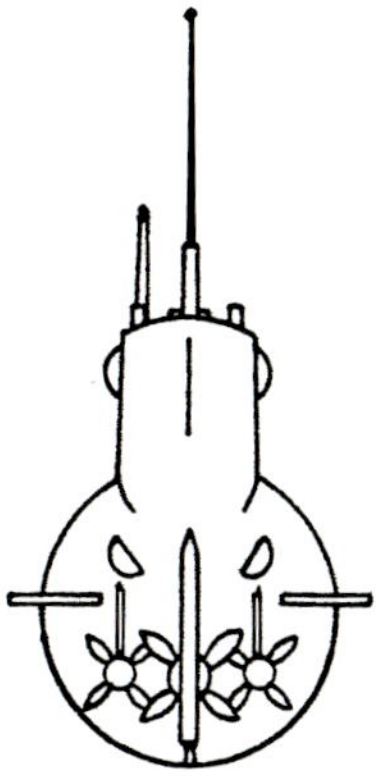

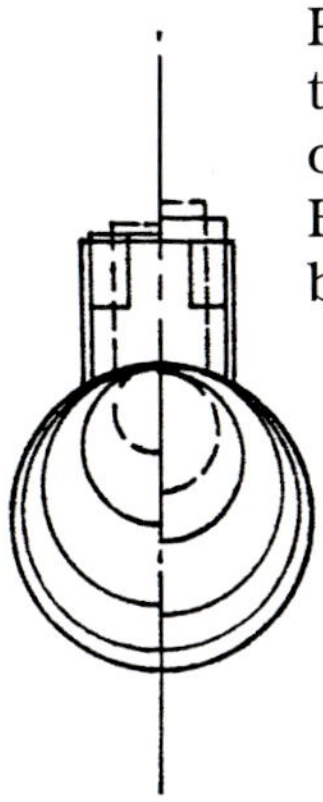

Akula

Type:	submarine
Tonnage:	370 tons surfaced and 475 tons submerged
Dimensions:	length 184 ft. (56 m); beam 12 ft. (3.6 m); draft 11 ft. (3.4 m)
Propulsion:	three diesel engines delivering 900 hp (671 kW) for 10.6 knots surfaced and one electric motor delivering 300 hp (224 kW) for 6.6 knots submerged
Armament:	one 1 7/8-inch (47 mm) gun, four 18-inch (457 mm) tubes (two bow and two stern) and four drop collars for eight torpedoes, and four mines
Complement:	34

Krab (1912)

The imperial Russian navy had considerable experience and skill in the design, manufacturing, and use of moored sea mines by the start of the twentieth century, and rightly saw this weapon as being an essential component of its capability to defend its own coastal waters with only a comparatively small number of major surface warships: carefully sited minefields could cause severe damage to an enemy's attacking fleet, and also channel surviving units into areas where the Russian surface warships and submarines operated to best advantage.

For this essentially defensive purpose, and also the offensive purpose of mining the waters off an enemy's major ports, the Russian navy was an early adherent of the concept of using the submarine as a mine layer. The *Krab*, designed by M. N. Naletov, was thus planned and designed as the world's first submarine mine layer. The boat was ordered in 1908 from the Nikolayev Navy Yard, but was launched only on September 1, 1912, and then completed only in July 1915, by which time the imperial Germany navy's first UC I class of submarine minelayers had entered service.

The *Krab* was of the single-hulled type with a designed diving depth of 150 feet (45 m) and a range of 1,960 miles (3155 km) at

The mine-laying tubes and doors are clearly shown.

hulls, and two propeller shafts flanking the fin-and-rudder unit.

The core of the boat's design and construction was its mine-laying capability, vested in a pair of parallel tubes located in the after part of the boat between the pressure hull and the casing. Up to a total of 60 mines were carried horizontally in the two tubes, and moved steadily toward the stern by electrically powered chain conveyors. Here at the stern, well to the rear of the rudder and propellers, the mines were dropped after the doors covering the rear of the tubes had been opened.

On its first cruise in World War I, when the boat was based in the black Sea, the *Krab* sailed under commercial colors and laid a field off the northern end of the Bosporus, the strait separating the small part of Turkey in Europe, which included Constantinople (now Istanbul), from the major part in Asia Minor. In World War I Turkey was allied with Germany in the Central

7 knots surfaced or 95 miles (155 km) at 4 knots submerged. The boat was configured in the normal fashion of a Lake-type vessel with level-diving submarine pairs of hydroplanes, each protected against the possibility of snagging on a net or mine riser wire by a metal tube frame, fore and aft, a long conning tower set comparatively far forward and carrying two periscopes, a single fin and rudder under the rear of the

Krab continued

Powers, and Russia with France and the UK in the Allied powers. This initial minefield caused damage to the Turkish gunboat *Isa Reis*. The *Krab* participated in a second mining oper-

ation off the northern end of the Bosporus in 1916, and later in the same year laid a minefield off Varna on the coast of Bulgaria, on the western side of the black Sea, which cost the Bulgarian navy its torpedo boat *Shumni*, which was sunk, and at the same time damaged a sister vessel, the *Strogi*.

With the military and political collapse of Russia in 1917-18, Ukraine declared its independence, and the former Russian ports on the northern coast of the Black Sea came under Ukrainian rule. Thus the *Krab* served

Automatically inflating balloons stabilized the mines for their drop to the ocean bed. Weighted sensors "felt" the approach to landing, to set in motion the eviction of the cradle.

under Ukrainian colors in April 1918, but was then seized as the Germans overran much of Ukraine. The Germans surrendered the *Krab* to the UK as British forces moved into the region to support the anti-Bolshevik White Russian forces in November 1918. The boat was finally scuttled off Sevastopol in Crimea on April 26, 1919, so that it would not be captured by the advancing Bolshevik forces of the Red Army. The wreck was eventually raised in 1935 and scrapped.

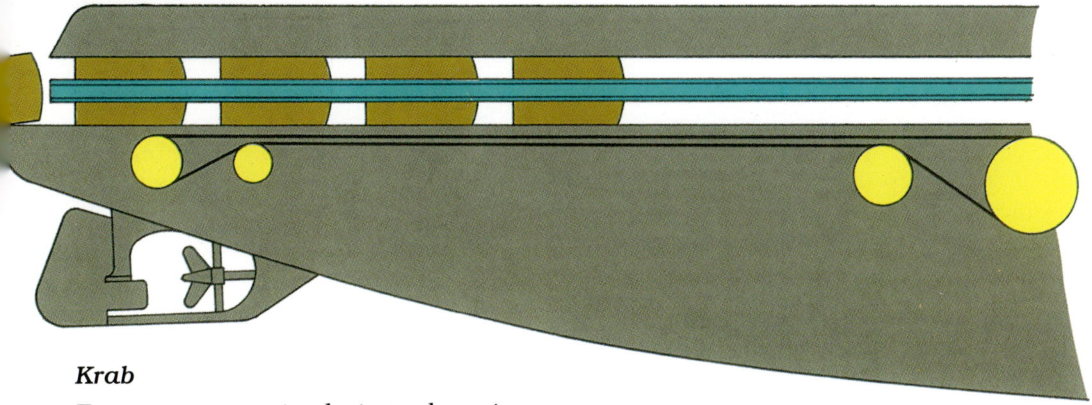

Krab

Type:	mine-laying submarine
Tonnage:	560 tons surfaced and 740 tons submerged
Dimensions:	length 173 ft., 3 in. (52.8 m); beam 14 ft., 0 in. (4.3 m); draft 12 ft., 9 in. (3.9 m)
Propulsion:	four patrol engines delivering 1,200 hp (895 kW) for 11.8 knots surfaced, and two electric motors delivering 400 hp (298 kW) for 7.1 knots submerged
Armament:	one 3-inch (75 mm) gun, two 18-inch (457 mm) tubes (both bow), two drop collars for six torpedoes, and two stern chutes for 60 mines
Complement:	50

C class (1906)

The C class of submarines were the last gasoline-engine boats built for the Royal Navy, and, as such, marked the end of the British development of the Holland-type submarine for British service. The class totaled 38 boats built as the *C-1* to *C-38* between 1905 and 1910, and these served right through World War I. The lead yard was that of Vickers at Barrow-in-Furness, but five of the boats (*C-17*, *C-18*, *C-19*, *C-20*, *C-33* and *C-34*) were built by Chatham Dockyard to ensure that the royal yards were kept abreast of the latest technical developments .

War I the others operated mostly in the coastal-defense role from bases at Leith, Harwich, Hartlepool, Grimsby and Dover, England. Some of the boats were also adapted to operate within the Q-ship concept and decoy U-boats into tactical traps. The technique was for a trawler to tow the boat by means of a cable that also carried a telephone wire. When a U-boat surfaced to shell the trawler, the surface vessel informed the boat, which then slipped its tow and attempt to torpedo the U-boat.

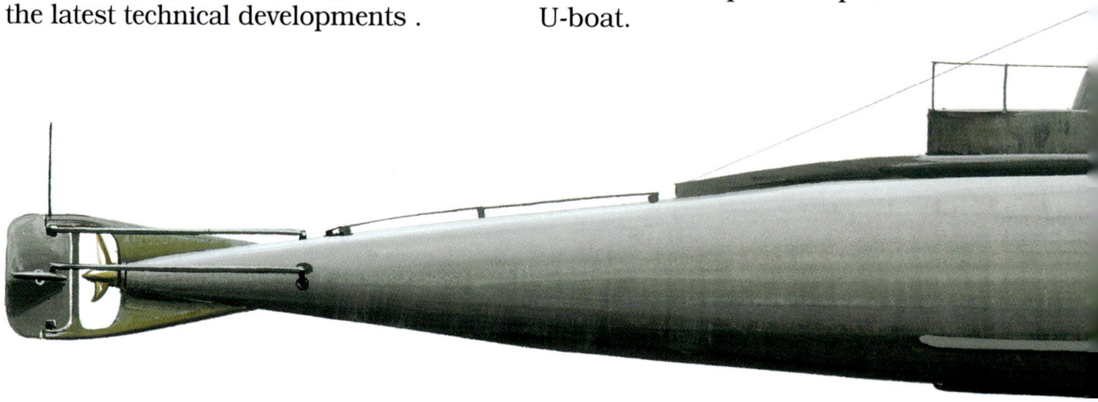

With just a 10% reserve of buoyancy over its surface displacement, the C-class boat was a poor surface vessel, and also limited to the coastal and harbor defense roles by its short range of only 1,150 miles (1850 km) at 8.75 knots surfaced. This was primarily the responsibility of Admiral Sir John "Jackie" Fisher, the First Sea Lord, who was a firm proponent of a powerful surface navy and believed that submarines could be relegated to secondary tasks such as serving as mobile alternatives to minefields in the local defense role. But the boat was based on a long spindle-shaped hull, which contributed to good underwater performance, in comparison with that of other boats of the time.

Three of the boats had been sent to Hong Kong in 1911, and during World

The first boat commissioned, the now-elderly and completely obsolete *C-3*, was packed with explosives and blown up in an attempt to destroy a viaduct during the classic raid on the German naval base at Zeebrugge in occupied Belgium on April 23, 1918. Four of the C-class boats operated in the Baltic Sea, from a base at Reval (now Tallinn, Estonia), as part of the blockade which the imposed in this region to prevent Germany's imports of high-grade iron ore from Sweden. The boats were dispatched in September 1915 by means of an extremely lengthy and tortuous route around the North Cape of Norway to Arkhangyel'sk, where they were loaded on barges for movement via the White Sea Canal to Kronshtadt, at the head

Despite its good shape, the C-class boat suffered from poor surface running performance and was therefore kept to coastal defense roles.

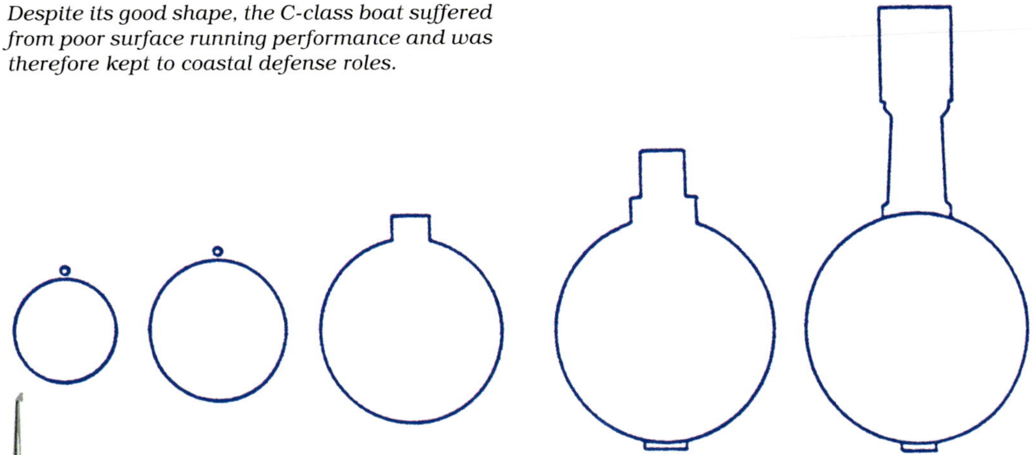

of the Gulf of Finland near St Petersburg, where they were relaunched. Three of the boats were destroyed outside Helsingfors (now Helsinki, Finland) in 1918 to prevent their capture by German troops who had landed nearby.

Some 10 of the class were lost during the war, including the *C-16*, which was mistakenly rammed by the destroyer *Melampus*. The surviving boats were stricken at the end of World War I with the sole exception of the *C-4*, which was retained for trials until into 1922.

C class

Type:	coastal submarine
Tonnage:	287 to 290 tons surfaced and 316 to 320 tons submerged
Dimensions:	length 142 ft., 2.5 in. (43.3 m); beam 13 ft., 7 in. (4.1 m); draft 11 ft., 2 in. (3.4 m) to 11 ft., 6 in. (3.5 m)
Propulsion:	one Vickers petrol engine delivering 600 hp (447.5 kW) for 13 knots surfaced, and one electric motor delivering 300 hp (224 kW) for 7.5 knots submerged
Armament:	two 18-inch (457 mm) tubes (both bow) for four torpedoes
Complement:	16

U-31 class (1914)

Preceded by the four U-boats of the U-27 class, which were themselves developed from the four boats of the U-23 class and four boats of the U-19 class, which had basically the same dimensions, identical armament, and a conceptually similar propulsion arrangement of steadily increasing power for improved performance class by class, the U-31 class appeared in 1914. The 11 boats were built by the Germaniawerft yard of Kiel as the *U-31* to *U-41* for launch between January and October 1914.

The U-31 class submarine was a double-hulled type designed under the leadership of Hans Techel, who was also responsible for the six U-51, three U-63 and six U-81-class boats. The U-31-class submarine had the same dimensions as the U-23-class boat except for a slight increase in draft, the same power plant except for slightly upgraded diesel engines, greater fuel capacity, and basically the same armament fit. The increase in oil bunkerage resulted in a surfaced range of 8,980 miles (14450 km) at 8 knots, and the submerged range was 95 miles (150 km) at 5 knots. The boats could dive in 1 minute, 40 seconds. While the torpedo armament remained unaltered, there were certain revisions to the gun armament in the light of operational experience in World War I. Thus the *U-31* had no deck gun at all at the time it was sunk in January 1915, the *U-32*, *U-36* and *U-37* for a time had two 3 1/2 inch (88 mm) guns fore and aft of the conning tower, in 1917 the *U-32* had one 4-inch (105 mm) gun, and this weapon became standard for the boats which survived into 1916-17.

The *U-32* was sunk by the British sloop *Wallflower* on May 8, 1915; the *U-33* survived to be scrapped in 1919-20; the *U-34* was sunk by the Q-ship *Privet* on November 9, 1918; the

Surrendered U-boats tied up either at Harwich or Weymouth (UK) after capitulation.

U-35 survived to be broken up in 1919-20; the *U-36* was sunk by the Q-ship *Prince Charles* on July 24, 1915; the *U-37* was mined on April 1, 1215; the *U-38* survived to be scrapped in 1921; the *U-39* survived to be scrapped in 1923; the *U-40* was torpedoed by the British submarine *C-34* on June 23, 1915; and the *U-41* was sunk by the Q-ship *Wyandra* on September 24, 1915.

The most celebrated, and indeed the most successful submarine of all times in terms of the tonnage sunk, was the *U-35*, which operated in the Mediterranean Sea during World War I and was involved in the sinking of 224 ships totaling 539.741 gross registered tons. The *U-35*'s keel was laid on December 20, 1912, at Friedrich Krupp's Germaniawerft yard in Kiel. The boat was to have been delivered on March 1, 1914, but was delayed as a result of development problems with its diesel engines. The *U-35* officially entered service on November 3, 1914, under the command of Kapitänleutnant Waldemar Kophamel as a boat of the 2nd U-Boat Flotilla based at Heligoland. The *U-35* completed its first two patrols, without success, in the North Sea. In its following three patrols, the boat sank 17 merchant ships totaling 25,716 tons. Later, it was paired with *U-34* after an action trained at Pola in Austria-Hungary, von Arnauld de la Perière was given command of the *U-35* on November 18, 1915, and in the course of 15 patrols sank 189 merchant vessels totaling 446,708 tons. Under his command, the *U-35* also sank the British gunboat *Primula* on February 29, 1916 and the French gunboat *Rigel* on October 2, 1916.

The *U-35*'s fourteenth patrol, between July 26 and August 20, under de la Perière was the single most successful submarine patrol of all time. During that period, the boat sank 54 merchant ships totaling 90,350 tons.

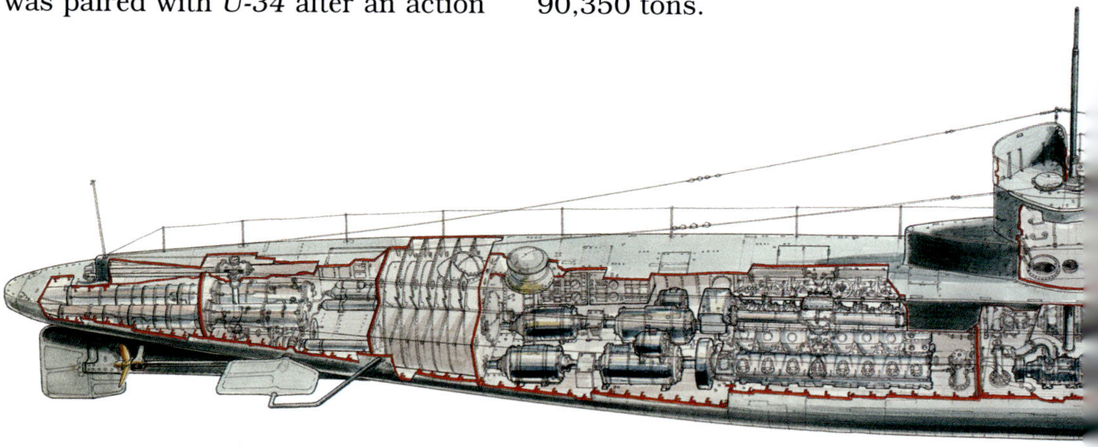

off Cattaro in Montenegro, and sank three merchant ships totaling 4,067. The *U-35* then made two more solo patrols and destroyed 15 more merchant ships totaling 59,409 tons.

The boat's longest-serving commander was *Kapitänleutnant* Lothar von Arnauld de la Perière, who became much acclaimed for allowing the crews of merchant vessels to launch and embark in lifeboats and then giving them directions to the nearest port before sinking their ships. After being

Kapitänleutnant Ernst von Voigt assumed command of the *U-35* on March 17, 1918, and undertook two operations (an operation patrol and a redeployment) between September 7 and October 9, 1918, but both were curtailed by engine damage. On October 14, 1918, Kapitänleutnant Heino von Heimburg assumed command and the *U-35* was transferred to Kiel. At the end of World War I, the *U-35* was transferred to England and docked in Blyth in 1919-20 before being scrapped.

The control room of a German U-boat. On the left is one of the hydroplane wheels; the wheel mid-picture operates the rudder.

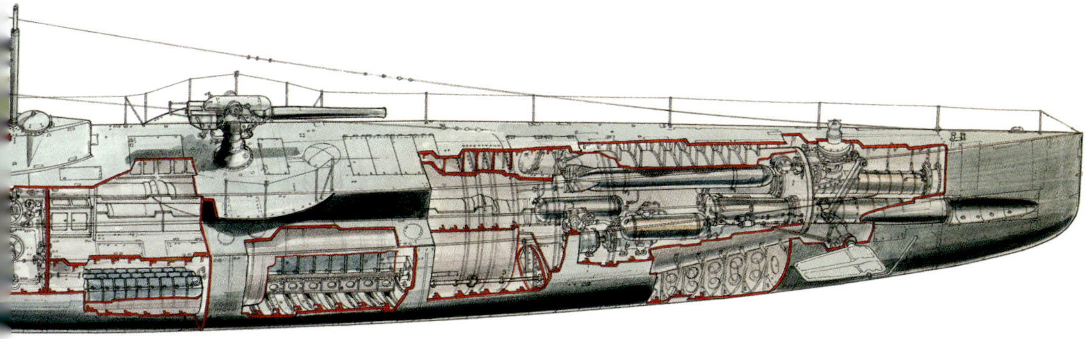

U-31 class

Type:	patrol submarine
Tonnage:	685 tons surfaced and 878 tons submerged
Dimensions:	length 212 ft., 3 in. (64.7 m); beam 20 ft., 8 in. (6.3 m); draft 11 ft., 10 in. (3.6 m)
Propulsion:	two Man diesel engines delivering 1,850 hp (1379 kW) for 16.4 knots surfaced, and two electric motors delivering 1,200 hp (895 kW) for 9.7 knots submerged
Armament:	one $3^1/_2$-inch (88 mm) gun and four 18-inch (500 mm) tubes (two bow and two stern) for six torpedoes
Complement:	35

E class

The 56 British and two Australian E-class submarines saw extensive and widespread service. The origins of the class can be found in the 1910-11 building program, in which the Admiralty ordered six improved D-class boats, but without any major change, as the D boats were highly successful. The two important changes were the addition of a pair of watertight bulkheads, and the enlargement of the hull to allow the incorporation of two beam-firing torpedo tubes, which the Royal Navy believed made possible short-range firing of greater accuracy. The E-class boat was thus designed with single bow and stern tubes, and a pair of beam-firing tubes amidships. The diesel engines were the standard Vickers four-stroke type in all but the *E-3*, which had two-stroke Carel diesel engines. These Belgian units proved inadequate, and were soon replaced by Vickers engines.

At the outbreak of World War I in August 1914, it was ordered that two boats of the 1911-12 program, the *E-7* and *E-8*, should be built to the initial E-1 class standard rather than the improved standard of the follow-on boats of what now became the E-9 class. The basic design proved highly successful, and construction continued into 1917. The E class boats lost nearly half of their number, but also gained excellent

results in the campaigns of the Sea of Marmara and the Baltic Sea. Although the standard deck gun was a 12 pdr gun, the *E-7* was fitted with 6 pdr weapon in 1915, and the *E-2* with a 4-inch (102 mm) weapon for use in the Sea of Marmara.

The *E-1* was despatched to the Baltic in October 1914 and was scuttled off Helsingfors (now Helsinki, Finland) in April 1918 to avoid capture. The *E-3* was torpedoed in the North Sea by the *U27*. The *E-4* was sunk in collision with the *E-41* on August 15, 1916, and, although raised, was not recommissioned. The *E-7* was trapped in anti-submarine nets in the Dardanelles and then destroyed by an explosive charge from the *UB-14*. The *E-8* operated in the Baltic and was scuttled off Helsingfors in August 1918. The *AE-1* was lost in September 1914, probably after hitting a reef off the Bismarck Islands archipelago. The *AE-2* was sent to the Mediterranean in March 1915 and had to be scuttled in the Sea of Marmora after sustaining severe damage from a Turkish torpedo boat in April 1915.

Five more E-class boats were proposed for the 1911-12 program, but with a range of significant enhancements indicated by operational experience with the D- and early E-class boats. Ultimately, the first two boats were completed to the initial E-class standard as noted above, and the Admiralty also ordained that only the most important improvements should be incorporated in what became the E-9 class to avoid delay of a mass-production type with the *E-12*, built by Chatham Dockyard, as the standard for all builders other than Vickers.

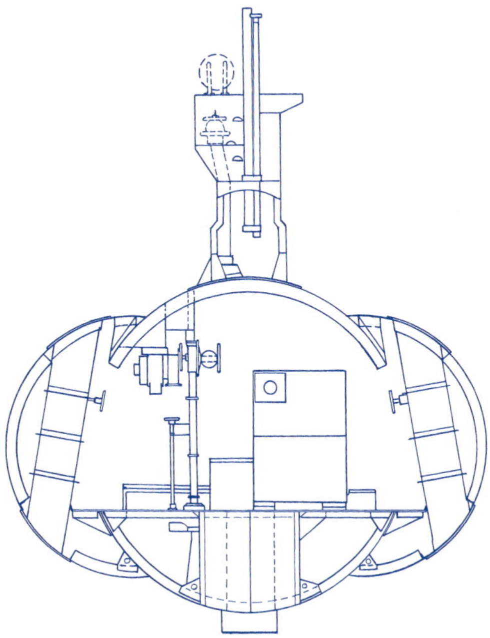

The E-9 class design was lengthened by 3 feet (0.9 m) to allow the addition of a second 18-inch (457 mm) bow tube. While the D-class boats had their two bow tubes in a superimposed pair providing a finer bow entry, the E-9 class of boats had a side-by-side pair as this allowed more protection for the bow caps and also eased torpedo loading, for which purpose the forward bulkhead was shifted 2 feet (0.6 m) aft. The position of the engines was pushed farther forward, the conning tower was enlarged to provide a steering position, and there was a third watertight bulkhead.

The *E-9* to *E-11* and *E-14* to *E-16* were ordered to this standard, but the Chatham Dockyard created a compromise between the original E-1 class and this modified type being built by Vickers. The most important change was the retention of the single bow tube, but as the *E-12* was the pattern for construction by yards other than Vickers, the paired bow tubes must have been readopted since all the later war-built boats had two bow tubes.

By the start of World War I, Vickers had already been contracted for the *E-17* and *E-18*, but the Admiralty needed rapid growth of the submarine arm, and on November 11, 1914, a conference was convened to allocate future construction of the *E-19* to *E-56*: these

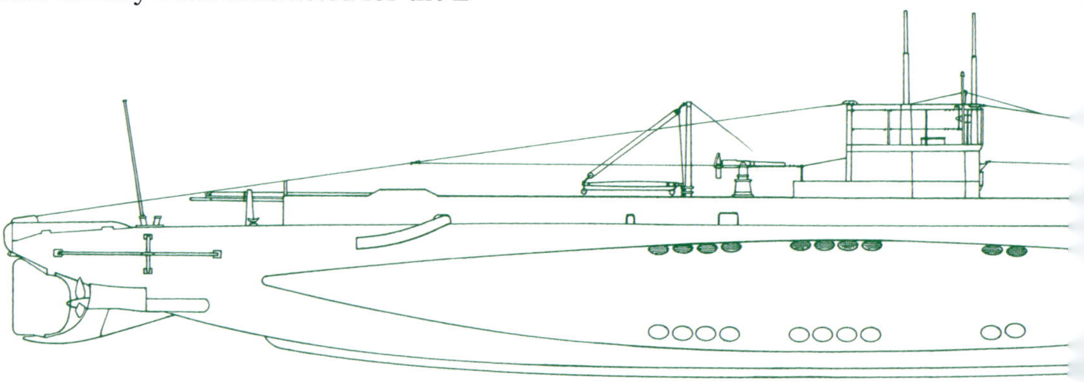

were ordered from Vickers (six boats), Beardmore (four boats), Scott (two boats), Yarrow (one boats), Armstrong (two boats), White (one boats), Thornycroft (three boats), John Brown (three boats), Fairfield (four boats), Palmer (two boats), Cammell Laird (four boats) and Denny (three boats). The total included two boats already ordered from Beardmore by Turkey, which now became the *E-25* and *E-26*. Yarrow's *E-27* and *E-28* were cancelled in April 1915 to allow the yard to concentrate on more important work, but the *E-27* was reinstated in August.

There were variations in the type of deck gun fitted, to make use of whatever weapon was available at the time. Operational experience in the Sea of Marmara had confirmed the utility of a deck gun, the shells of which were often more useful and cheaper than a torpedo, and among the weapons now added with the E-20's 6-inch (152 mm) howitzer fitted by the builder, the *E-11*'s 12 pdr gun, and the *E-12*'s 4-inch (102 mm) gun supplied by Malta Dockyard. Some of the North Sea boats received a 3-inch (76 mm) or 12 pdr gun in 1916-17. Early in 1916, the *E-22* was fitted with a launch platform on its after superstructure to fly off two Sopwith Baby floatplanes for reconnaissance of the Heligoland Bight. In the Sea of Marmara, several boats carried spare torpedoes lashed to the casing. A change effected in all the boats during World War I was the removal of the upper rudder.

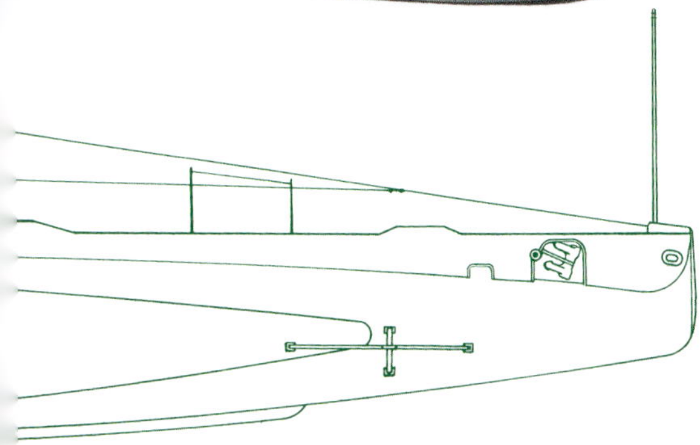

The *E-9* went to the Baltic in October 1914 and was scuttled to avoid falling into German hands; the *E-19* was scuttled at the same time. The *E-13* was sent to the Baltic in August 1915 and, while trying to enter this sea ran aground on Saltholm and, after being disabled by German fire, was interned on August 18, 1915, by the Danes, and returned to the UK in November 1918. While trying to get through to the Sea of Marmara, the *E-15* ran aground off Kephez Point on April 15, 1915, and was disabled by shell fire. Numerous attempts were made to destroy her, including bombing, destroyer attack, long-range bombardment, and an attack by the *B-6*, but on the night of April 16, it was destroyed by 14-inch (356 mm) torpedoes launched by battleships' picket boats. The *E-18* was sunk off Bornholm by a German decoy ship. On exercises off Harwich on August 15, 1916, the *E-41* was rammed by the submerged *E-4*; both boats sank with heavy loss of life but were later salvaged.

Brumaire class (1911)

Ordered under the provisions of the French 1906 naval construction program, the Brumaire class of double-hulled submarines was designed by Maxime Laubeuf as a diesel-engined development of his own Pluviôse class of 18 boats, with two sets of reciprocating steam engines delivering 700 ihp (522 kW) for 12 knots surfaced. The Pluviôse-class submarines could not dive rapidly as a result of the time it required to shut down the steam plant and make the boats watertight. The surfaced range of the Pluviôse- class boats was 1,725 miles (2775 km) at 9 knots or 1,035 miles (1665 km) at 12 knots, and the submerged speed was 57.5 miles (92.5 km) at 5 knots.

The Pluviôse-class submarines were nonetheless good sea boats and therefore deemed worthy of further development and construction. The diesel engine selected for the Brumaire-class boats was a MAN-type four-stroke six-cylinder unit made in France by A. C. Loire, Sautter-Harlé, Normand, Indret, and Sabathé. These engines provided a surfaced range of 1,960 miles (3155 km) at 10 knots, while the battery-powered electric motors provided a submerged range of 97 miles (155 km) at 5 knots.

The boats were the *Arago*, *Bernouilli*, *Brumaire*, *Coulomb*, *Curie*, *Euler*, *Faraday*, *Foucault*, *Franklin*, *Frimaire*, *Joule*, *Le Verrier*, *Montgolfier*, *Newton*, *Nivôse*, and

Volta, which were launched between April 1911 and March 1913 by the Arsenals de Cherbourg (six boats), Rochefort (four boats) and Toulon (six boats). Some of the boats, such as the *Arago*, *Faraday* and *Le Verrier*, were upgraded in 1916 by the installation of a different deck gun, namely a 3-inch (75 mm) or 1 3/4-inch (47 mm) weapon.

The entire class was on the strength of the French navy's Mediterranean fleet, and spent the whole of World War I in this theatre. On April 4, 1916, the *Bernouilli* broke into the Austro-Hungarian base at Cattaro in occupied Montenegro and blew the stern off the destroyer *Csepel*. *Le Verrier* rammed the German *U-47* on July 28, 1918, by accident after each had launched torpedoes but failed to secure hits. The *Foucault* was sunk off Cattaro by Austro-Hungarian aircraft on September 15, 1915. The *Curie* was captured on December 20, 1914, at Pola, a more northerly Austro-Hungarian base, after getting into this port, and was recommissioned by the Austro-Hungarians as the *U-14* with a new battery and one 3 1/2-inch (88 mm) deck gun. The boat was recovered by the French after World War I. The *Joule* was mined in the Dardanelles on May 1, 1915.

The French planned in 1917 to adapt six of the boats to a mine-laying standard along the lines pioneered by the *Amarante* and *Astrée* of the later Amphitrite class, but the project was abandoned. The boats that survived World War I were all stricken in the first half of the 1920s.

Brumaire class

Type:	coastal submarine
Tonnage:	397 tons surfaced and 551 tons submerged
Dimensions:	length 170 ft., 11 in. (52.1 m); beam 17 ft., 9 in. (5.15 m); draft 10 ft., 2 in. (3.1 m)
Propulsion:	two diesel engines delivering 840 hp (653 kW) for 13 knots surfaced, and two electric motors delivering 660 hp (492 kW) for 8.8 knots submerged
Armament:	one 3 pdr gun, one 18-inch (450 mm) tube (bow) for two torpedoes, and four drop collars and two external cradles for six 18-inch (450 mm) torpedoes
Complement:	29

UC I, UC II, & UC III classes (1915)

In October 1914, only one month after the first UB I-class coastal submarines had been ordered, the imperial German navy ordered its first UB I-class coastal mine-layer to a single-hulled design with a diving depth of 165 feet (50 m), 12 mines carried in six near-vertical flooded tubes forward, and no torpedo armament although the *UC-11* was fitted with one 18-inch (450 mm) external tube aft in 1916.

The class was intended as much for the gathering of operational experience as combat mine-laying, and was therefore limited to just 15 boats, namely the *UC-1* to *UC-10* ordered from Vulcan of Hamburg and launched between April and July 1915, and the *UC-11* to *UC-15*, ordered from A. G. Weser of Bremen and launched in April and May 1915.

Analogues of the UB I-class coastal submarines, these had a displacement of 168 tons surfaced and 183 tons submerged, length of 111 ft., 6 in. (34 m), beam of 10 ft., 4 in. (3.2 m), propulsion by one Daimler or Benz diesel engines delivering 90 hp (67.1 kW) for 6.2 knots surfaced and one electric motor delivering 175 hp (130.5 kW) for 5.2 knots submerged, range of 900 miles (1450 km) at 5 knots surfaced or in the second group 1,050 miles (1690 km) at 5 knots surfaced and 57.5 miles (92.5 km) at 4 knots submerged, and range of 1400 miles.

Only one of the boats survived World War I. After it had been rammed and sunk by a British steamer in July 1915, the *UC-2* was raised by the British for display, and the *UC-12* was similarly raised by the Italians after being sunk by the detonation of one of its own mines, rebuilt and commissioned as the *X-1*, and scrapped in 1919. The *UC-13* was lost accidentally after grounding; the *UC-4* was scuttled during the German retreat from Flanders; the *UC-5* was stranded, captured, and put on display by the British; the *UC-8* was interned in the Netherlands after grounding, and was commissioned as the *M-1* between 1915 and 1932.

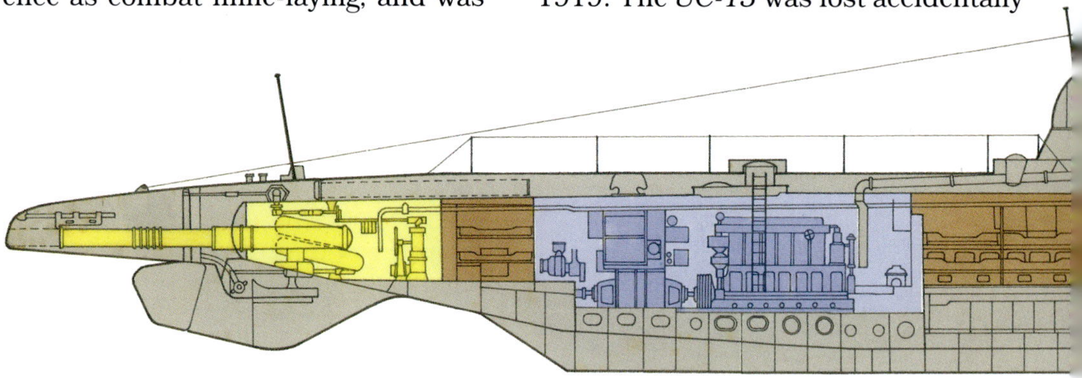

Operational experience with the UC I-class boats indicated the need for considerably greater size and other changes, leading to the design of the UB II class of coastal mine-laying submarines, of which 64 were ordered from Blohm & Voss of Hamburg, Vulcan of Hamburg, A. G. Wester and Germaniawerft for launch between February 1916 and March 1917.

The UC II class boat was of the double-hulled type with improved range and sea-keeping compared with the UC I class. The boats varied in a number of their details, especially in the shape of their bows, and propulsion machinery was increased in power to 600 hp (447.5 kW) for the diesel engine and 620 hp (462 kW) for the electric motor in the *UC-34*, *UC-46* and later groups. The submerged range was constant at about 61 miles (100 km) at 4 knots throughout the class, but the surfaced range varied from 8,380 miles (13,485 km) in the UC-46 group to 9,210 miles (14820 km) in the UC-61 group, to about 10,075 miles (16,215 km) in the *UC-49* and *UC-55* groups, to about 10,650 miles (17140 km) in the *UC-16*, *UC-25*, and *UC-40* groups, and to more than 11,515 miles (18530 km) in the *UC-34*, *UC-65*, and *UC-74* groups.

The other primary data for the UC II class was a displacement of 417 to 434 tons surfaced and 480 to 517 tons submerged, length of 162 ft., 0 in. (49.4 m) to 172 ft., 10 in. (52.7 m), beam of 17 ft., 2 in. (5.2 m), propulsion by two Daimler or Körting diesel engines delivering 500 hp (373 kW) for 11.4 knots surfaced and two electric motors delivering 460 hp (343 kW) for 7 knots submerged, armament of

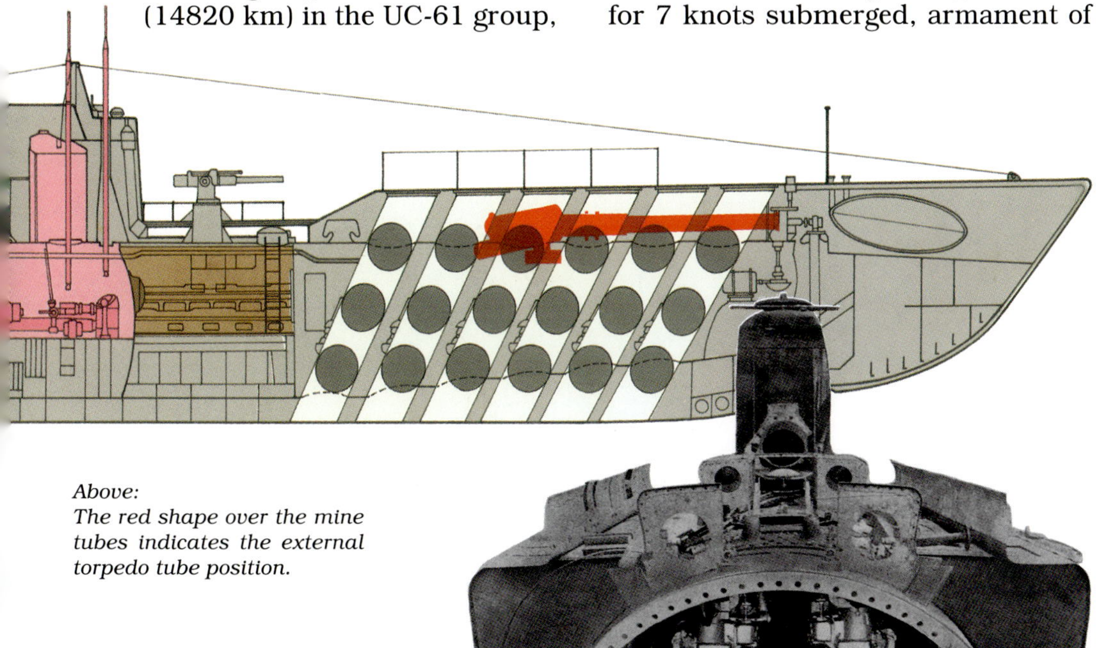

Above:
The red shape over the mine tubes indicates the external torpedo tube position.

Right:
This photograph of a boat before the stern section was fitted displays efficient use of the available space in the engine room.

UC I, UC II, & UC III classes *continued*

one 3 ½ inch (88 mm) gun in some boats, three 20-inch (500 mm) tubes (two external bow and one internal stern) for seven torpedoes and six 39-inch (100 cm) chutes for 18 mines, and complement of 26.

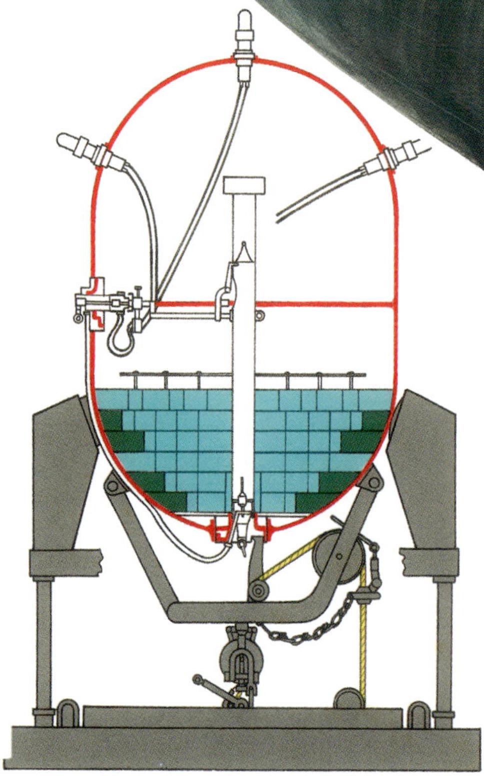

Germany lost 45 of these boats in the war. The *UC-32*, *UC-40*, and *UC-69* were lost in accidents, as was the *UC-45*, which was raised and surrendered to the UK. The Mediterranean-based *UC-25*, *UC-33*, *UC-53*, and *UC-57* were scuttled after the fall of Austria-Hungary, as was *UC-61*, which was scuttled by her crew after grounding. The *UC-48* was interned at Ferrol in Spain but then lost accidentally during the transfer to the UK. The

UC III class (UC-90 group)

Type:	coastal mine-laying submarine
Tonnage:	491 tons surfaced and 571 tons submerged
Dimensions:	length 214 ft., 10 in. (56.5 m); beam 18 ft., 0 in. (5.5 m); draft 12 ft., 6 in. (3.8 m)
Propulsion:	two MAN diesel engines delivering 600 hp (447.5 kW) for 11.5 knots surfaced, and two electric motors delivering 770 hp (574 kW) for 6.6 knots submerged
Armament:	one 4-inch (105 mm) gun (some boats only), three 20-inch (500 mm) tubes (two amidships external and one stern internal) for seven torpedoes, and six 39-inch (100 cm) tubes for 14 mines
Complement:	32

UC-76 was interned in Sweden, later transferred to the UK, and scrapped. France received the *UC-22*, *UC-23*, *UC-27*, *UC-28*, *UC-56*, *UC-58*, and *UC-74* as war reparations, and the other survivors were scrapped in the UK.

The UC III class should have consisted of the *UC-80* to *UC-192*, but only the 26 boats of the UC-90 group (*UC-90* to *UC-114*) were completed, in this instance by Blohm & Voss, which launched the boats between January and August 1918. The lower-numbered boats would have been shorter and later boats would have been longer, and would have had Benz or Körting diesel engines in some cases.

The UC III-class mine-laying submarine was significantly improved over its predecessors, and was of the double-hulled type, with a diving depth of 245 feet (75 m) and two 20-inch (500 mm) tubes mounted externally amidships to fire forward.

The *UC-91* was lost after an accident, and all of the other surviving boats were distributed as war reparations: the UK received the *UC-92*, *UC-95*, *UC-101* to *UC-103*, *UC-105*, *UC-106* and *UC-108* to *UC-114*, of which the *UC-110* was lost by accident during transfer; France received the *UC-100*, *UC-104* and *UC-107*, which were scrapped; Italy received the *UC-93*, *UC-94* and *UC-98*, which were soon scrapped; Japan received the *UC-90* and *UC-99*, and commissioned these as the *O-4* and *O-5*; and the U.S. received the *UC-97*, which was expended as a gunnery practice target after initial public display. The incomplete *UC-80* to *UC-89* and the *UC-115* to *UC-138* were broken up on their slips at Danzig, Bremen and Hamburg after the war, and the orders placed with Blohm & Voss for the *UC-139* to *UC-192* were cancelled in 1918-19.

M class (1917)

The M class of three submarines, namely the *M-1*, *M-2*, and *M-3*, was built by Vickers and Armstrong, who was also supposed to build the *M4*, launched in July 1919 to clear the slip after being cancelled in the previous year. These were doubled-hulled boats with diesel and electric propulsion, and their uniquc and most obvious feature was the 12-inch (305 mm) gun, for which 50 rounds were carried in a turret faired into the forward part of the conning tower.

The boats were ordered in 1916 in place of the last four boats, the *K-17* to *K-21*, of the first group of steam-powered K-class fleet submarines, which were cancelled. The type was designed for a diving depth of 200 feet (61 m), and its range was 2,300 miles (3700 km) at 15 knots or 5,180 miles (8335 km) at 10 knots surfaced, and 10.4 miles (16.75 knots at 9 knots or 92 miles (148 km) at 2 knots submerged.

The M-class submarines were intended as monitors (coastal bom-

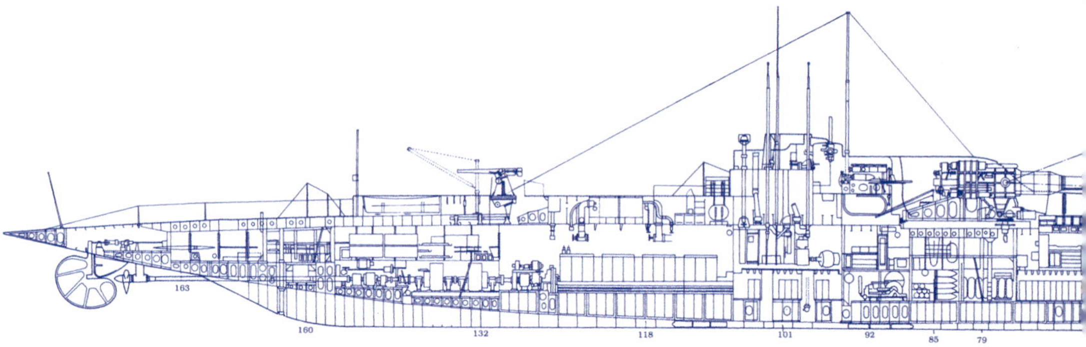

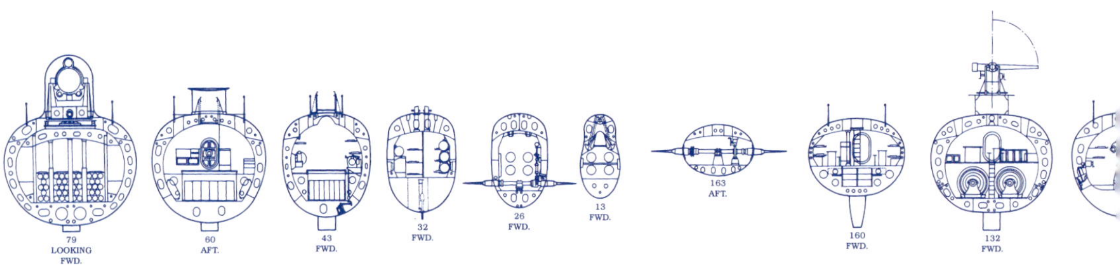

bardment vessels), but their role was already being revised before detailed design work had started. The definitive role was therefore the destruction of merchant vessels and smaller warships, which would be engaged at periscope depth or on the surface with shells rather than more expensive torpedoes. At the time the torpedo was seen as impractical against a moving warship at any range above 1,000 yards (915 m). Nevertheless, it is unlikely that a well-constructed ship would be sunk by a single 12-inch (305 mm) shell.

It was intended that the gun fire from periscope depth using a simple bead sight on the end of the gun aligned with the target, through the periscope, at a range of around 1,300 yards (1190 m), the exposure time of the gun above the surface being in the order of 75 seconds. The submarine had to surface to reload the gun, which would take about 3 minutes. The gun was an Mk IX L/40 weapon initially built for the Formidable class of pre-dreadnought battleships. The mounting allowed the elevation of the gun between -5° and +20°, and, in training, 15° port and starboard of the centerline, but in practice was not very successful.

The *M-1* and *M-2* also had four 18-inch (457 mm) torpedo tubes, and the *M-3* and *M-4* had 21-inch (533 mm) tubes and were 20 feet (6.1 m) longer to accommodate them.

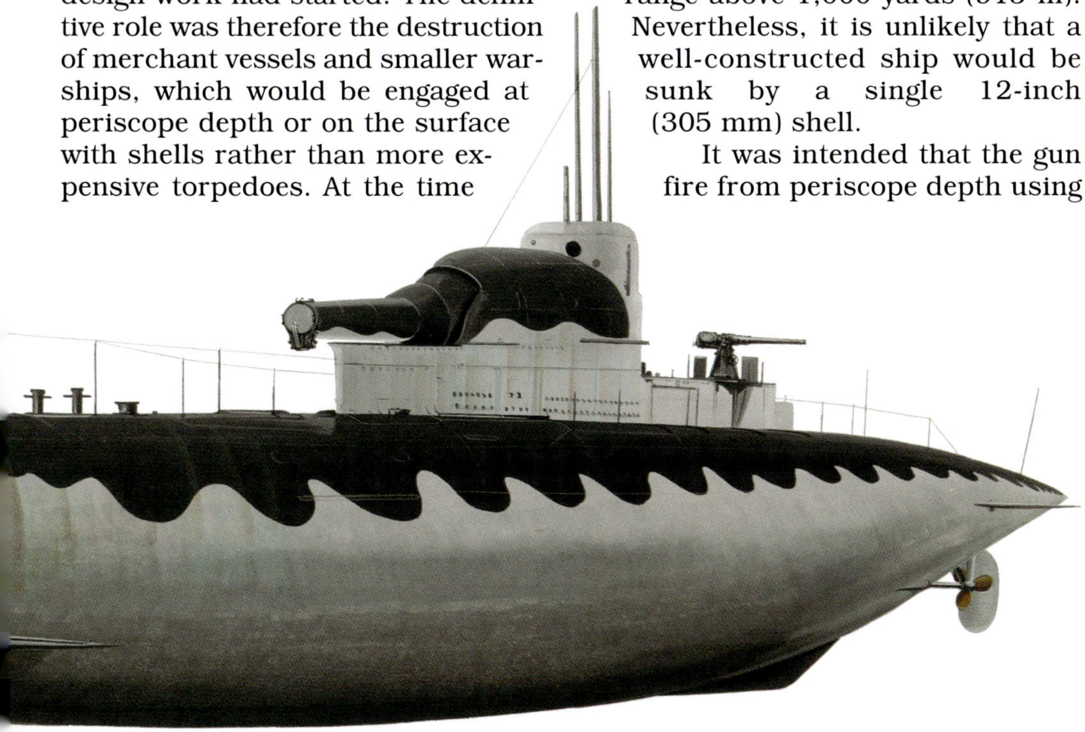

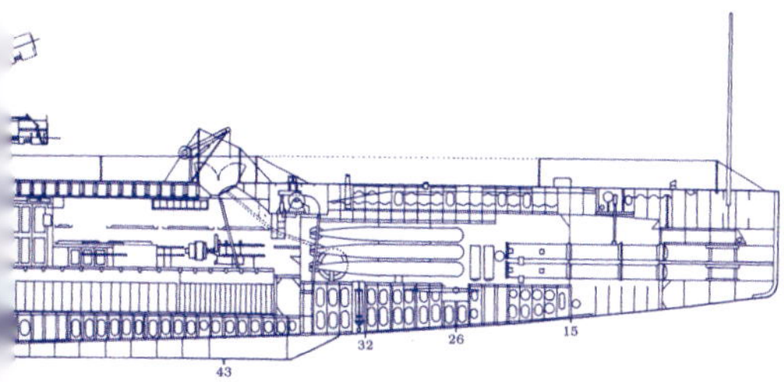

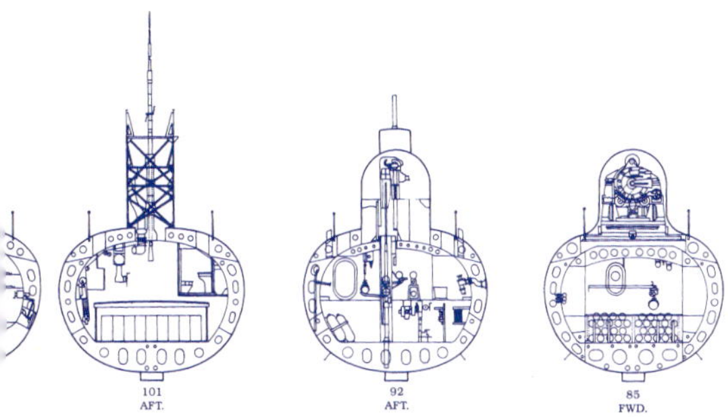

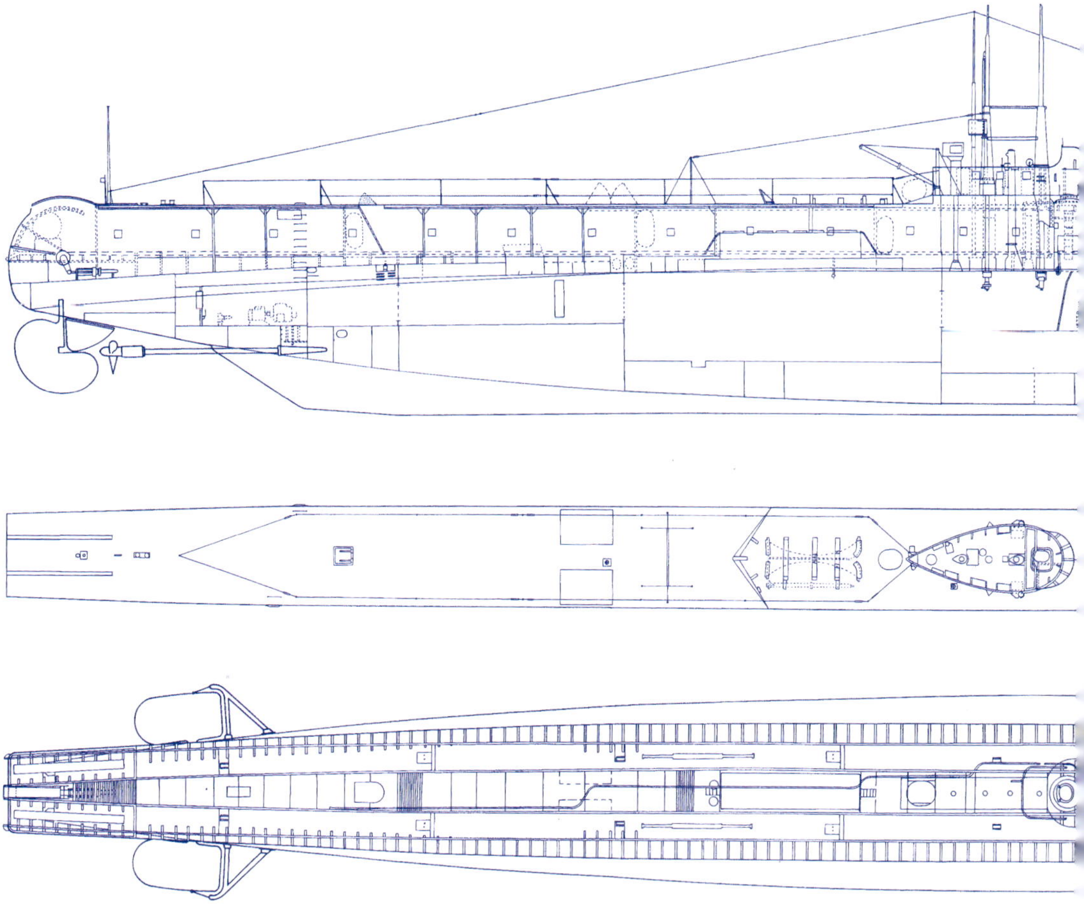

The *M-1* was the only member of the class to enter service before the end of World War I but see no action. The boat was lost with all hands on November 12, 1925, during an exercise in the English Channel near Start Point in Devon, after a collision with a Swedish collier, the *Vidar*. The wreck of the *M-1* was discovered by a diving team in 1999 at a depth of 240 feet (73 m).

The *M-2* was converted to a seaplane carrier in 1925, a hangar replacing the gun turret. The boat was lost off Chesil Beach on January 26, 1933, probably as a result of the premature opening of the hangar door. The submarine lies in much shallower water, 105 feet (32 m) deep, with the top of its conning tower only 66 feet (20 m) below the surface at low tide.

The *M-3* was converted into a mine layer in 1927 with stowage for 100 mines, primarily to test the mine-handling equipment intended for the Porpoise-class submarines. The mines were carried on a conveyor belt extending along the upper part of the boat's hull and covered by an enlarged casing. The mines were laid through a door at the stern. The *M-3* was scrapped in 1932 after the trials had been completed.

In 1924 all three completed members of the class were used to

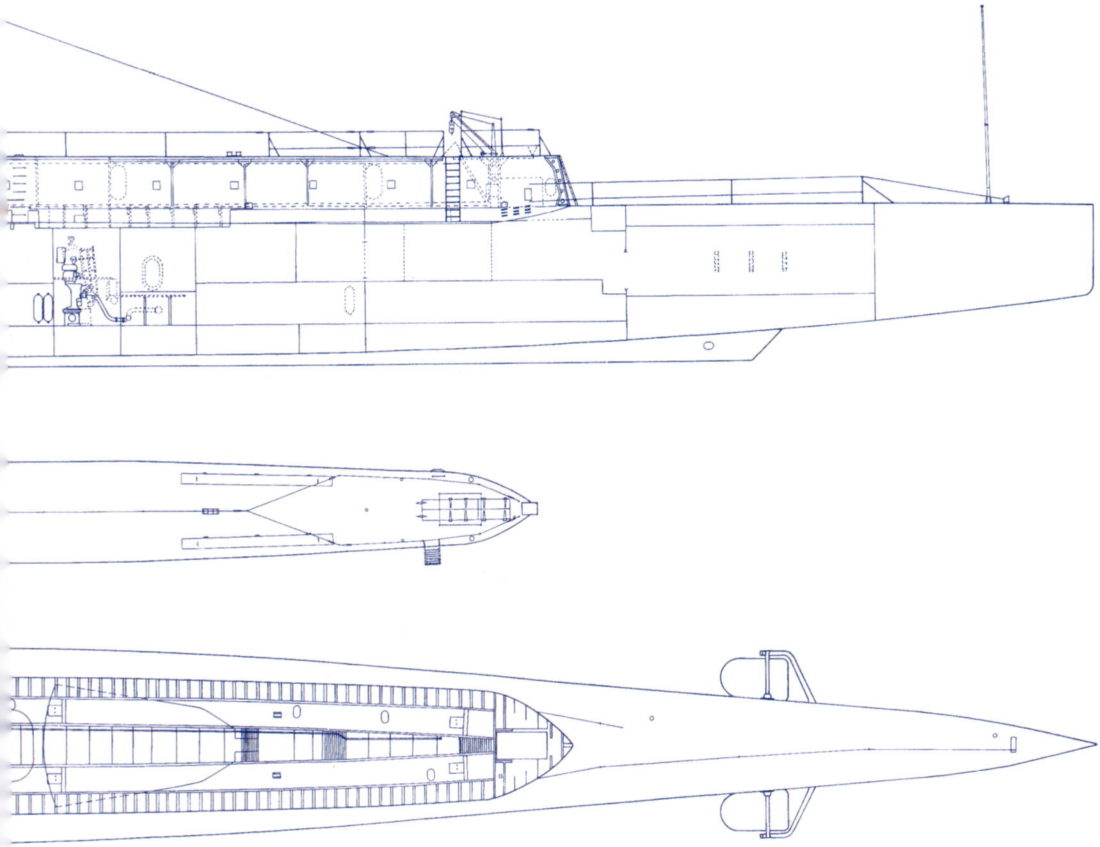

test hull camouflage in a program to investigate the ways in which submarines might be rendered less visible to aircraft: the *M-1* was painted grey-green, the *M-2* dark grey and the *M-3* dark blue.

M class (M-1, as built)

Type:	monitor submarine
Tonnage:	1,594 tons surfaced and 1,946 tons submerged
Dimensions:	length 295 ft., 9 in. (90.1 m); beam 24 ft., 8 in. (7.5 m); draft 15 ft., 11 in. (4.9 m)
Propulsion:	two Vickers diesel engines delivering 2,400 hp (1789 kW) for 15 knots surfaced, and four electric motors delivering 3,200 hp (2386 kW) for 9 knots submerged
Armament:	one 12-inch (305 mm) gun, one 3-inch (76 mm) AA gun, and four 18-inch (457 mm) tubes (all bow) for eight torpedoes
Complement:	65

J class (1915)

The British J-class submarine of WWI was created to counter U-boats thought wrongly to be capable of 22 knots. Yet the supposed threat of such boats was taken seriously enough for the J-class submarine to be planned on the basis of the standard diesel-electric propulsion in an arrangement unique within the Royal Navy, namely a three-shaft arrangement for a speed of 19.5 knots surfaced.

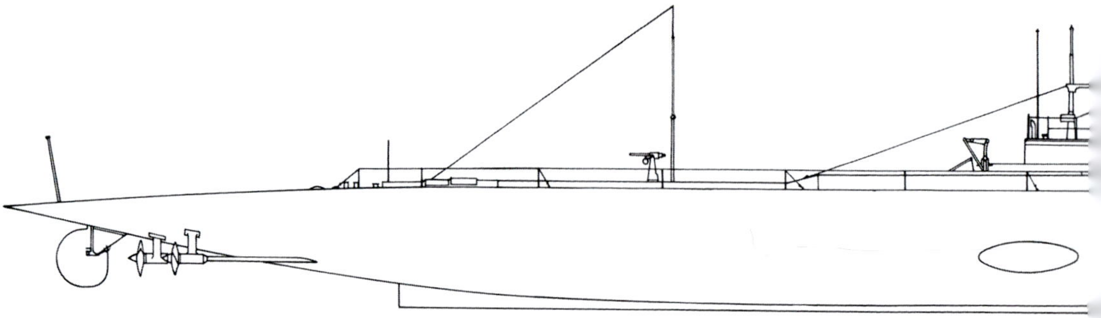

A class of eight boats was planned; seven boats were ultimately built by Portsmouth Dockyard (the first two boats), Pembroke Dockyard (the second two boats) and Devonport Dockyard (the last three boats). The design was of the partial double-hulled type, with the double hull occupying 56% of the length. Experience revealed that the large free-flooding casing brought the bow down in any sort of seaway, reducing the speed, so the casing was first sealed and then raised, which gave the boats a practical 17 knots. Their range was 5,750 miles (9255 km) at 12.5 knots surfaced.

The first boat was the *J-4*, which was commissioned on July 17, 1916, and assigned to the 11th Submarine Flotilla based at Blyth in Northumberland, where the boat was joined by its sisters. From Blyth, the boats were used operationally against German surface vessels and U-boats in the North Sea and off Gibraltar. One of the boats, the *J-6*, was sunk in error on October 15, 1918, by a British warship. The *J-7* was ordered by the Royal Australian Navy, which specified a number of changes including the movement farther aft of the control room from a point just forward of the beam torpedo tubes to the motor room

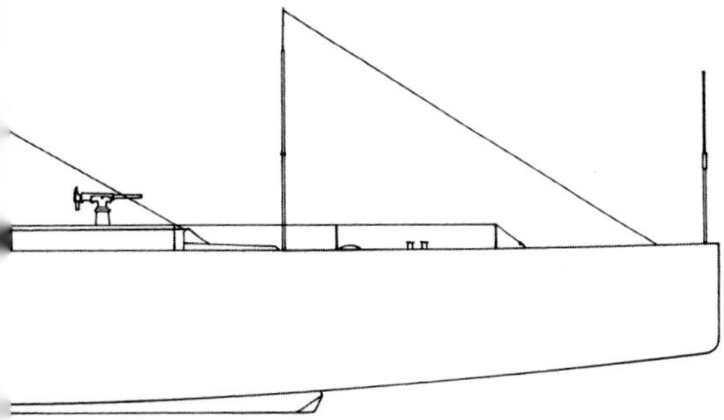

aft; the conning tower was also moved so that it was still above the control room.

After the end of World War I, the five surviving British boats were given to the Australian navy, and all six boats were transferred into the Australian reserve fleet at Westernport on July 12, 1922. The submarines were all scuttled in the mid-1920s onward, the *J-1*, *J-2*, *J-4*, and *J-5* in the Bass Strait, and the other two as breakwaters inside Port Phillip Bay.

J class

Type:	patrol submarine
Tonnage:	1,210 tons surfaced and 1,760 tons submerged
Dimensions:	length 274 ft., 9 in. (83.7 m); beam 23 ft., 1 in. (7 m); draft 16 ft., 0 in. (4.9 m)
Propulsion:	three Vickers diesel engines delivering 3,600 hp (2684 kW) for 19.5 knots surfaced, and three electric motors delivering 1,350 hp (1007 kW) for 9.5 knots submerged
Armament:	one 4-inch (102 mm) gun, and six 18-inch (457 mm) tubes (four bow and two beam) for 12 torpedoes
Complement:	44

F class (1911)

In the two boats of the E class, namely the *Skipjack* and *Sturgeon* built by Fore River to follow the three D-class submarines from the same yard, the growth in size of U.S. coastal submarines was reversed to a modest extent. Many saw this as a retrograde step but it was the forward step represented by the adoption of diesel engines for surfaced propulsion for the first time in any U.S. Navy submarine. Though the new type of engine was clearly the way forward, the units in the E class gave considerable difficulty and had to be replaced in 1915. Other more modern submarines possessing longer range and therefore an ocean-going capability, and were decommissioned during 1922 as part of U.S. compliance with the terms of the Washington naval treaty.

The F-class submarines which followed were again of the single-hulled Holland type, and the four boats were designed for the U.S. Navy by Electric Boat as early as 1909. Built in pairs by the Union Iron Works and Moran, the *Carp* (*F-1*), *Barracuda* (*F-2*), *Pickerel* (*F-3*), and *Skate* (*F-4*) were similar to the C-class and D-class submarines

enhanced features, appearing for the first time in an American submarine, were bow hydroplanes and radio equipment.

The class confirmed the tendency of all U.S. Navy submarine types before 1917 to desire underwater speed greater than that of comparable boats in other navies. The United States E-class submarines were used as coastal and harbor defense submarines prior to World War I. After the U.S. entered World War I, the boats were used for training, and for the evaluation of tactics and new equipment. The E-class boats were soon overtaken by built as well as designed by Electric Boat. Slightly longer than the D-class submarines, the F-class boats were based on circular sections along the hull's long axis and, like the E-class boats, had a pair of bow hydroplanes.

The hull was divided into three compartments which were, from bow to stern, the forward compartment with the torpedo room and its four 18-inch (457 mm) torpedo tubes; the control room with the ballast control valves, hydroplane controls, and the periscope; and the engine room with its two diesel engines. These diesel engines were connected to a common shaft which turned motors that could be used as generators for charging the batteries and also as conventional motors to drive the propellers. The boat's electrical charge battery was contained in an array of cells in rubber-lined and open-topped steel jars.

With the same type of propulsion arrangement as the E-class boats, the F class of submarines suffered the same type of problems, and had to be withdrawn for a time in 1915 to be re-engined. The designed diving depth was 200 feet (61 m), and the range was 2,650 miles (4265 km) at 11 knots surfaced, and 115 miles (185 km) at 5 knots submerged.

The *Skate* foundered off Pearl Harbor in the Hawaiian Islands on March 25, 1915, but was raised and scrapped. The *Carp* was lost in a collision with the *Pickerel* in foggy conditions during an exercise off the West Coast on December 17, 1917. The *Barracuda* and *Pickerel* survived to be stricken and sold for scrapping in August 1922.

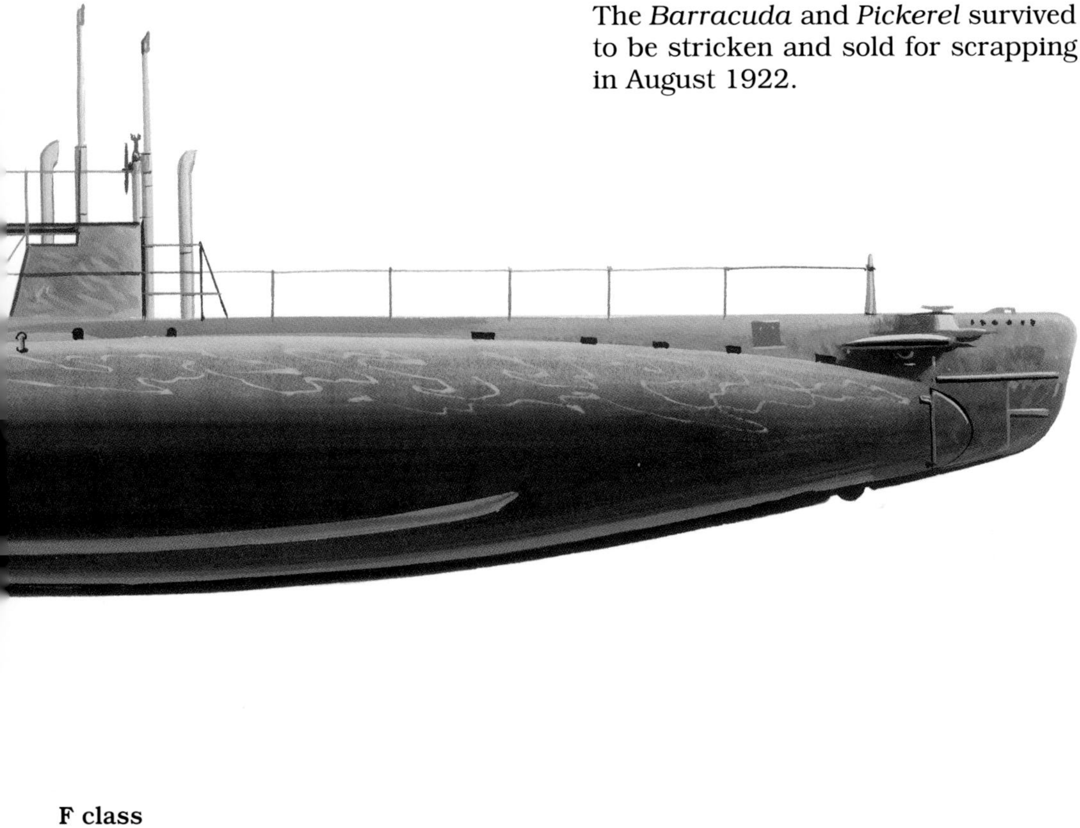

F class

Type:	coastal submarine
Tonnage:	330 tons surfaced and 400 tons submerged
Dimensions:	length 142 ft., 9 in. (43.5 m); beam 15 ft., 5 in. (4.7 m); draft 12 ft., 2 in. (3.7 m)
Propulsion:	two diesel engines delivering 800 hp (596.5 kW) for 13.5 knots surfaced, and two electric motors delivering 620 hp (462 kW) for 11.5 knots submerged
Armament:	four 18-inch (457 mm) tubes (all bow) for four torpedoes
Complement:	22

U151 class (1917)

The U-151 class comprised seven submarines built for the imperial German navy in World War I by Reiherstiegwerft of Hamburg (*U-152*, *U-153* and *U-154*), Flensburger Schiffbau of Flensburg (*U-151* and *U-155*), Atlas Werke of Bremen (*U-156*), and Stülcken Sohn of Hamburg (*U-157*).

The boats were conceived for the mercantile task, a fact reflecting the increasing tight and successful blockade with the British and, to a lesser extent the French, were imposing on Germany, which could to a large extent feed itself but was now suffering in industrial and military

terms from the lack of raw materials, such as rubber and specialized metals which had to be imported. Given the British command of the surface waters, the only option left to Germany was the blockade-running submarine, which could cruise on the surface but submerge to complete the first outward and last inward legs of its voyage, or if discovered at sea.

The first two such boats were the *Deutschland* and *Bremen*, built with private funding and operated by the Deutsche Ozean-Reederei subsidiary of the Norddeutscher Lloyd line. Launched on March 28, 1916, the boats had a wide beam to provide volume for cargo, of which 700 tons could be carried, much of it outside the pressure hull.

On its first voyage, which began on June 23, 1916, the *Deutschland* carried an export cargo of 163 tons of chemical dyes, medical drugs and mail. Traveling through the English Channel, the boat reached Baltimore, Maryland on July 8 and after discharging her cargo loaded 348 tons of rubber, 341 tons of nickel, and 93 tons of tin on board. The boat arrived back in Bremerhaven on August 25, 1916. The profit was four times the boat's cost. A second voyage to the U.S. was made between October and December 1916 and was also commercially successful, again trading chemicals, medicines, and gems for rubber, nickel, alloys, and tin. However, the *Deutschland* was lightly damaged during a collision with a tug in New London.

The *Bremen* was lost with all hands toward the start of its first transatlantic voyage in January 1917, possibly to a mine off the Orkney Islands. The third mercantile submarine, the *Oldenburg*, was never completed in its designed role.

A third voyage was planned for the *Deutschland* in January 1917, but was not attempted in the light of worsening German-U.S. relations, as indicated by the U.S. entry into the war on the Allied side in April 1917, largely as a result of Germany's policy of unrestricted U-boat warfare.

Photograph showing the control room - looking forward - with the steering wheel, depth gauge, electric high pressure air blower and wheels for operating the Kingston valves, etc. *Photo: John Batchelor Collection.*

U151 class *continued*

Mast and derricks were all removed before diving.

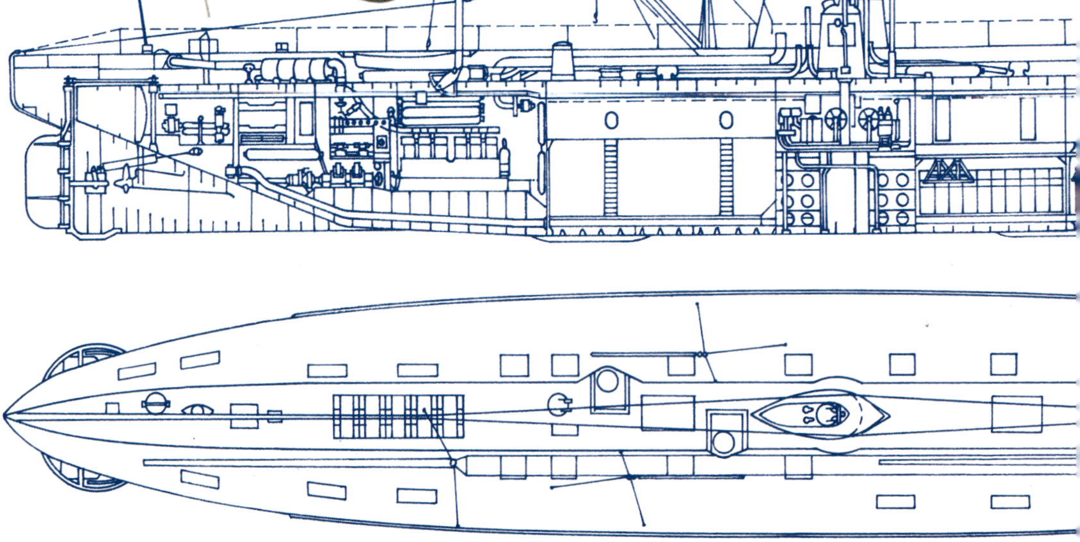

The *Deutschland* was then taken over by the German navy in February 1917 for conversion into the *U-155* cruiser submarine, and the incomplete *Oldenburg* was launched in April 1917 and completed as the *U-151*.

The other boats, also laid down in 1916, were also completed in 1917 to the cruiser submarine standard, their capacity of 328 tons of fuel for a range of about 28,790 miles (46330 km) at 5.5 knots surfaced reflecting their initial development for mercantile service. The other side of this coin was indifferent submerged performance, including a range of 75 miles (120 km) at 3 knots.

Commissioned into the German navy on February 17, 1917, with three twin tube mountings above the water and two 6-inch (150 mm) guns, the *U-155* completed three successful war

German Super Submarine The Deutschland at sea, showing wireless mast and gear. *Photo: John Batchelor Collection.*

patrols, sinking 43 ships. After the war, the boat was transferred to the UK in December 1918 and scrapped in 1921.

The *U-157* completed the longest patrol of World War I, totaling 129 days between November 27, 1917, and April 15, 1918. The *U-151* and *U-157* were delivered after the war to France as part of Germany's war reparations: the first was extended as a gunnery target in 1921, and the second was scrapped in the same year. Of the other boats, the *U-154* was torpedoed by the E-35 in May 1918, the *U-156* succumbed to a mine in September 1918, and the *U-152* and *U-153* were lost under tow to the breaker's yard in 1921.

U-151 class

Type:	cruiser submarine
Tonnage:	1,512 tons surfaced and 1,875 tons submerged
Dimensions:	length 213 ft., 3 in. (65 m); beam 29 ft., 2 in. (8.9 m); draft 17 ft., 4 in. (5.3 m)
Propulsion:	two Germania diesel engines delivering 800 hp (596.5 kW) for 12.4 knots surfaced, and two electric motors delivering 800 hp (596.5 kW) for 5.2 knots submerged
Armament:	two 4-inch (105 mm) or 3½-inch (88 mm) guns, and two 20-inch (500 mm) tubes (both bow) for 18 torpedoes
Complement:	56 plus provision for 20 supernumeraries as prize crew

L and S classes (1917)

The L class was the first attempt to create an ocean-going submarine class for the US Navy. The first boats were laid down early in 1914, but commissioned only two years later. The boats were built in two groups, the first consisting of the *L-1*, *L-2*, *L-3*, *L-4*, *L-9*, *L-10*, and *L-11* from Fore River; and

the second, of the *L-5*, *L-6*, and *L-7* from Lake as well as the *L-8* from the Portsmouth Navy Yard.

After service in the Atlantic Flotilla, most of the boats of the first group needed extensive refits for combat service in World War I when, in November 1917, all the boats were deployed to Bantry Bay in Ireland and the Azores Islands for patrols. After the war, the boats were used for trials of new torpedoes and hydrophone equipment before being decommissioned in 1922-23 and scrapped under the terms of the 1933 London Naval Treaty.

The data for the boats of the first group included a displacement of 542 tons submerged, length of 167 ft., 4 in., (51 m), beam of 17 ft., 6 in. (5.3 m), propulsion by two BS diesel engines delivering 1,200 hp (895 kW) for 14 knots surfaced and two electric motors delivering 800 hp (596.5 kW) for 10.5 knots submerged, armament of one 3-inch (76 mm) gun and four 18-inch (457 mm) tubes for seven torpedoes, and complement of 28. The boats of the second group had a slightly greater displacement and were slightly shorter but beamier.

The S-class boats were the first submarines built to a U.S. Navy concept.

The first boat was the *S-1* commissioned in 1918, and the class consisted of 51 boats, of which the last was commissioned in 1925. The boats were built in four groups, of slightly different design, as the first or "Electric Boat" group (*S-1* and *S-18* to *S-41*) from Bethlehem Steel (Fore River) and Union Iron Works; the second or "Navy Yard/Lake" type (*S-2* to *S-17*) from the Portsmouth Navy Yard and Lake Torpedo Boat; the third (*S-42* to *S-47*) from Bethlehem; and the fourth or "2nd Lake" type (*S-48* to *S-51*) from Bethlehem.

Three prototypes were built to the same specification as Electric Boat's *S-1*, which was launched on September 26, 1918, by Fore River, which was Electric Boat's subcontractor, but commissioned only on June 5, 1920, Lake's *S-2* and the Bureau of Construction & Repair's *S-3*. The Lake design was considered inferior, but second, improved groups of the Electric Boat and BuC&R boats were built.

The U.S. Navy commissioned the 48 operational S-class boats between 1920 and 1922. These marked a considerable improvement over the preceding O and R class in terms of range, speed, and more reload torpedoes for the same number of bow tubes, while a few later boats also had a stern tube. The boats saw service in World War II in both the Atlantic and the Pacific. Smaller and slower than many of the submarines produced for war service, lacking the range for Pacific patrols, and 20 years old, they were used in reconnaissance and supply roles. The boats were withdrawn in mid-1943 as fleet submarines became available, and used for anti-submarine training. The majority of surviving boats were scrapped in 1946. Some were transferred to other navies, such as the six to the Royal Navy.

S Group 1 class

Type:	patrol submarine
Tonnage:	854 tons surfaced and 1,062 tons submerged
Dimensions:	length 219 ft., 5 in. (66.9 m); beam 20 ft., 8 in. (6.3 m); draft 15 ft., 9 in. (4.8 m)
Propulsion:	two New London Ship and Engine Company diesel engines delivering 1,200 hp (895 kW) for 14 knots surfaced, and two Electro Dynamic, Ridgway or General Electric electric motors delivering 1,500 hp (1118 kW) for 11 knots submerged
Armament:	one 4-inch (102 mm) gun, and four 21-inch (533 mm) tubes (all bow) for 12 torpedoes
Complement:	38-42

R class (1918)

In March 1917 the department of the Director of Naval Construction in the Admiralty completed the design of a submarine with the capability to overtake any German U-boat, which would then be sunk by torpedo attack rather than gun fire. The Admiralty did not at the time approve of a concept so radical but when, later in the same year, the professional head of the Royal Navy's submarine arm suggested that the concept should be re-examined and further developed, high-level interest in the design was revised in a form with the torpedo armament based on six rather than four tubes.

Ordered in December 1917, the 12 R-class submarines were thus the first boats designed specifically to attack and sink other submarines, and as such can be regarded as the precursors of modern hunter/killer submarines. For this purpose, the R-class boats were designed to be faster underwater, at 14 knots, than on the surface, at 9 knots. In fact, the boats exceeded these design figures as a result of their streamlined hulls and conning towers, in combination with a notably powerful electric motor for submerged propulsion.

The R-class boat was designed on the basis of a streamlined spindle-shaped hull of circular section, reminiscent of the hulls of the Holland, A, B, and C classes of submarines, although to a considerably more refined degree. This terminated forward in a vertical bow, and at the after end in a well-tapered stern supporting the single propeller. Other notable features of the design were greatly increased battery capacity, six 18-inch (457 mm) bow tubes later replaced by 21-inch (533 mm) tubes, volume in the bow for the very sensitive hydrophone which provided a submarine-detection capability, a nicely streamlined conning tower, and no deck gun. To save time, the hull sections were identical to those of the Improved H class. The propulsion was in essence half of that used in the Improved H class, but the 220-cell battery of the much larger J-class boat was used for the power needed to create the very high submerged speed which was required. The boats had a designed diving depth of 250 feet (76 m), and their range was 2,300 miles (3700 km) at 8 knots surfaced.

The *R-1*, *R-2*, *R-3*, and *R-4* were ordered from Chatham Dockyard, the *R-5* and *R-6* from Devonport Dockyard (later changed to Pembroke Dockyard), the *R-7* and *R-8* from Vickers, the *R-9*

and *R-10* from Armstrong, and the *R-11* and *R-12* from Cammell Laird. World War I ended in November 1918, ending the threat of the U-boat, and in August 1919 *R-5* and *R-6* were cancelled, giving the Royal Navy a class of 10 boats, all launched between April and October 1918.

At 15 knots, the R-class submarines possessed a submerged speed not excelled for quarter of a century, and then only by experimental and developmental boats. Operating from Killybegs, in Donegal, Ireland, one of the class reportedly tracked a U-boat and fired on it in October 1918: the torpedo struck its target but failed to detonate.

All but *R-4* and *R-10* were stricken and sold for scrap in 1923. The two surviving boats were then used for training in anti-submarine warfare at Portland. Here their speed allowed the boats to outrun and outmaneuver the trawlers used to train crews. The *R-10* was sold in 1929, and the *R-4* in 1934, and it is arguable that the Royal Navy at the time and for some years to come did not fully appreciate the fact that the R-class boats led the way forward.

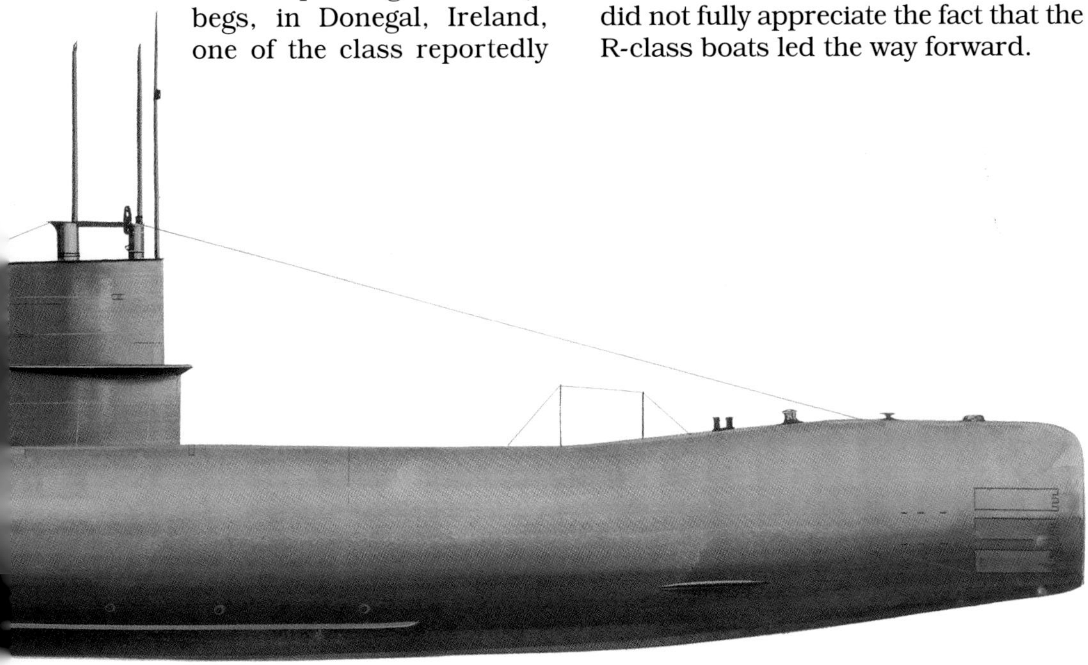

R class

Type:	attack submarine
Tonnage:	420 tons surfaced and 500 tons submerged
Dimensions:	length 163 ft., 9 in. (49.9 m); beam 15 ft., 3 in. (4.6 m); draft 11 ft., 6 in. (3.5 m)
Propulsion:	one diesel engine delivering 240 hp (179 kW) for 9.5 knots surfaced, and one electric motor delivering 1,200 hp (895 kW) for 15 knots submerged
Armament:	six 18-inch (457 mm) tubes (all bow) for 12 torpedoes
Complement:	22

German G/6 torpedo (1908)

The G/6 weapon was the standard torpedo of the German U-boat arm, and also large numbers of surface vessel classes, in World War I. The torpedo was of the standard dimensions for all torpedoes carried by larger U-boats of World War I: smaller U-boats were armed with a torpedo of 18-inch (450 mm) diameter. The G/6 heavyweight torpedo carried a TNT/Hexanite warhead weighing 362 lb. (164 kg) with an impact fuse, was a straight-running and unguided weapon stabilized by a gyroscope, and possessed a speed of 35 knots over a distance of 3,825 yards (3500 m), a lower speed producing an increased range of 6,560 yards (6000 m).

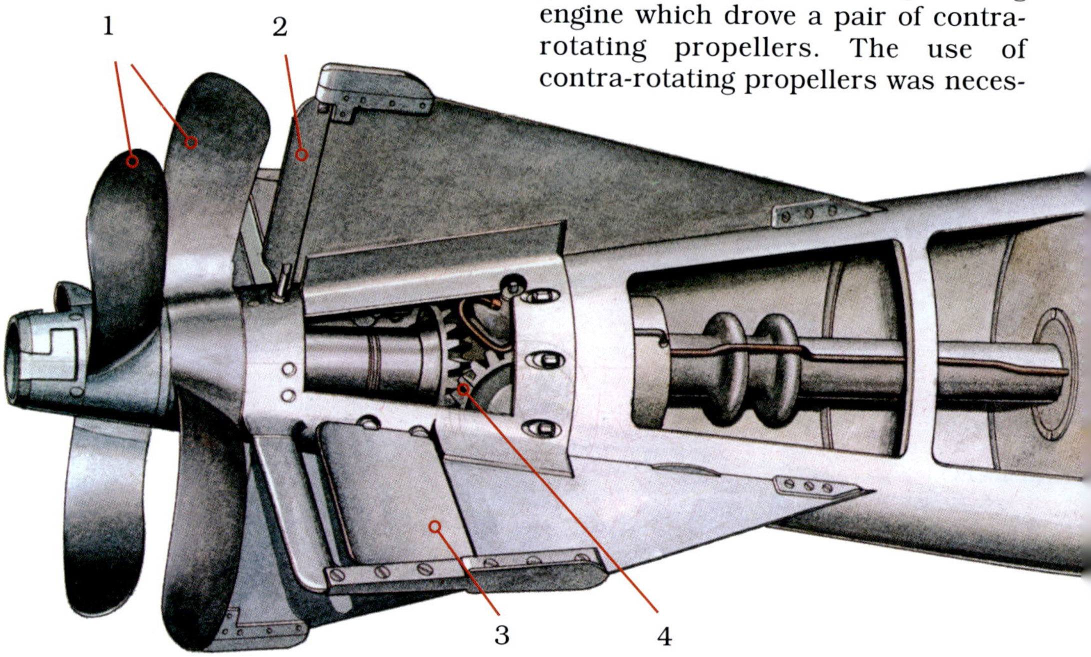

The G/6 was an early example of the wet heat propulsion system. The torpedo was fueled by a mixture of compressed gas, decalin or kerosene, and water. The compressed gas was forced into a combustion chamber along with the decalin or kerosene and the water, where the mixture was ignited. The superheated steam which resulted from this process then powered a four-cylinder reciprocating engine which drove a pair of contra-rotating propellers. The use of contra-rotating propellers was necessary to prevent the torque reaction that would otherwise have deflected the torpedo from its course.

Until 1908, torpedoes had been driven by compressed air alone, but the introduction of the wet heat propulsion system greatly enhanced speed and range. The problem was how to balance these attributes to best tactical effect: any increase in speed meant reduced range, and, conversely, any increase in range meant reduced speed.

Though this propulsion system gave the G/6 good speed and range, it was also very noisy and left a long wake of bubbles. The former was not of particular importance before the British development later in the war of

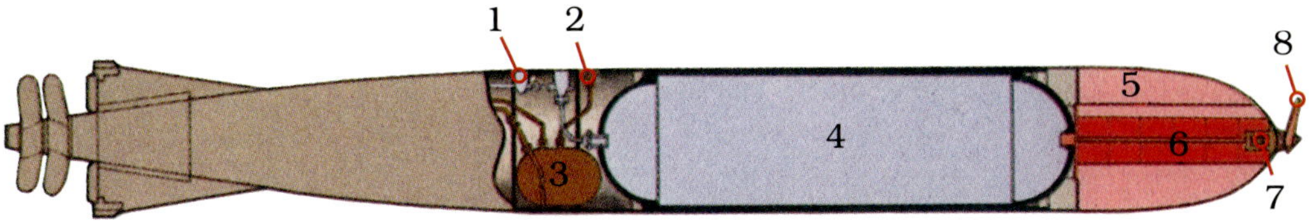

G/6 torpedo

1. Air-charging valve
2. Fuel-charging valve
3. Fuel tank
4. Air cylinder
5. Warhead
6. Exploder charge
7. Primer
8. Detonator horn

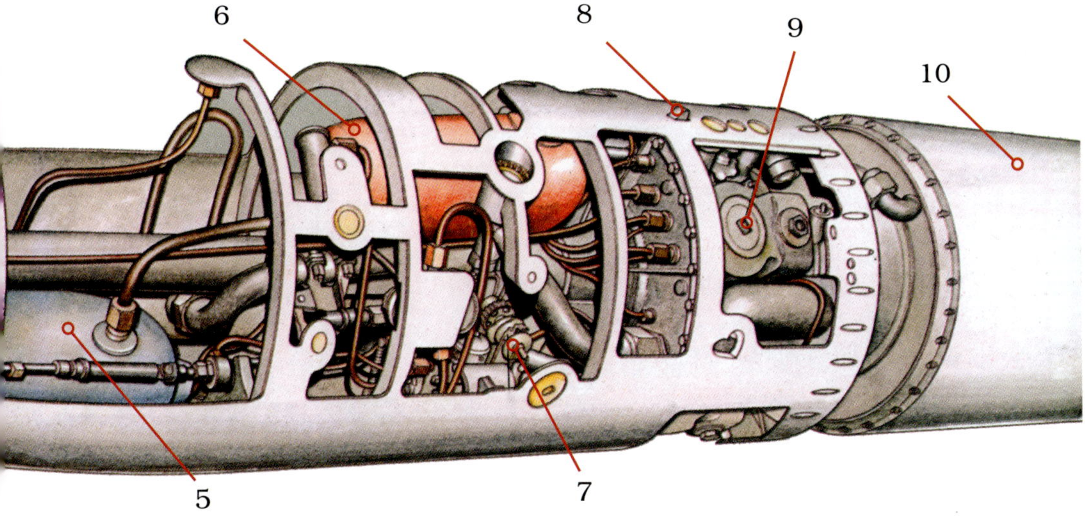

Motive parts of the G/6 torpedo

1. *Contra-rotating propellers* 2. *Rudder (one above and another below)* 3. *Hydroplane (left and right)* 4. *Propeller differential gearing* 5. *Fuel tank* 6. *Fuel tank* 7. *Hydrostatic depth-regulating mechanism* 8. *Starter latch, engaged as the torpedo was fired* 9. *One of the engine's four cylinder heads* 10. *Air cylinder*

ASDIC (Anti-Submarine Division-ic or, erroneously, Allied Submarine Detection Investigation Committee). Later known as "sonar," this underwater hydrophone detection system provided a passive means of detecting underwater sounds.

The latter provided a highly visible indication of a U-boat's intended victim and also of the position from which the boat fired the weapon. When convoys were introduced later in the war, escorting aircraft and airships often spotted such wakes.

G/6

Type:	anti-ship torpedo
Weights:	whole torpedo, 2,491 lb. (1130 kg); warhead, 362 lb. (164 kg)
Dimensions:	length 19 ft., 8¼ in. (6 m); diameter 19.7 in. (500 mm)
Propulsion:	wet heat combustion engine for 3,825 yards (3500 m) at 36 knots

Swordfish and K class submarine (1916)

In response to the recommendation of the British 1912 Submarine Committee that an "overseas submarine" have a displacement of 10,000 tons and a surface speed of 20 knots, Vickers produced a design which the company believed could be achieved by the standards of the day: a maximum surface speed of 17 knots and a displacement of at least 1,270 tons. Though unhappy with the company's response, the Admiralty nonetheless appreciated that Vickers possessed far greater, but limited, experience with diesel propulsion. The Fiat company was approached via Scott's yard about the engine, but was in accord with Vickers and only reluctantly prepared to guarantee the power of 1,850 hp (1582 kW) suggested by Vickers for the new 12-cylinder diesel engine. Fiat recommended a steam turbine installation, but this notion was rejected though adopted later for the Swordfish.

Vickers received a provisional order in October 1912 and laid the keel of the *Nautilus* in March 1913, one month before receiving the official order. As the company had predicted, the development of the powerful engine was very slow, and although the *Nautilus* was launched at the end of 1914 the boat was not completed until October 1917, four months after it had been numbered N-1. Although on the strength of the Portsmouth-based 6th Submarine Flotilla, the boat did not reach operational status but was instead used as depot ship, supplying battery-charging power to other submarines.

Though apparently a failure, the *Nautilus* was a considerable step forward in size and power, and the British experience with this boat provided useful data for later developments.

Despite its unhappiness with the performance suggested by Vickers for the *Nautilus*, the Admiralty still wanted to create a submarine with a surface speed of 20 knots. The proposal put forward by the Laurenti Company of Italy in 1912 was then dusted off, as it had promised 18 knots at a displacement of just 856 tons, and formed the conceptual basis for the Fiat 140bis design by Scott's yard with increased surface displacement, reduced endurance, and heavier armament. This led to the placement of an order in August

1913 for a new boat adhering closely to the Laurenti concept with a double hull for 75% of the length. A small folding funnel was incorporated which could be folded down by electrical power and then sealed to prevent an ingress of water. The gun armament was two 3-inch (76 mm) weapons, located fore and aft, on "disappearing mountings" that retracted under watertight covers. Shutting down the funnel required some 11 minutes, and the rise in heat inside the boat was noticeable.

Like the S-class boats, the *Swordfish* was divided into a greater number of watertight compartments than was typical of British boats of the period. Other features included safety buoys, a telephone buoy, a blowing arrangement with controls forward and aft as well as in the control room, and an emergency high-pressure air line to every compartment.

Numbered S-1 at the start of April 1916, the *Swordfish* was commissioned toward the end of the same month as a tender to the depot ship *Dolphin*. Although in theory operational with the 4th Submarine Flotilla following acceptance in July 1916, the new boat's trials continued for five months. The boat was laid up at Portsmouth in January 1917 as its future was assessed. The boat was taken in hand on

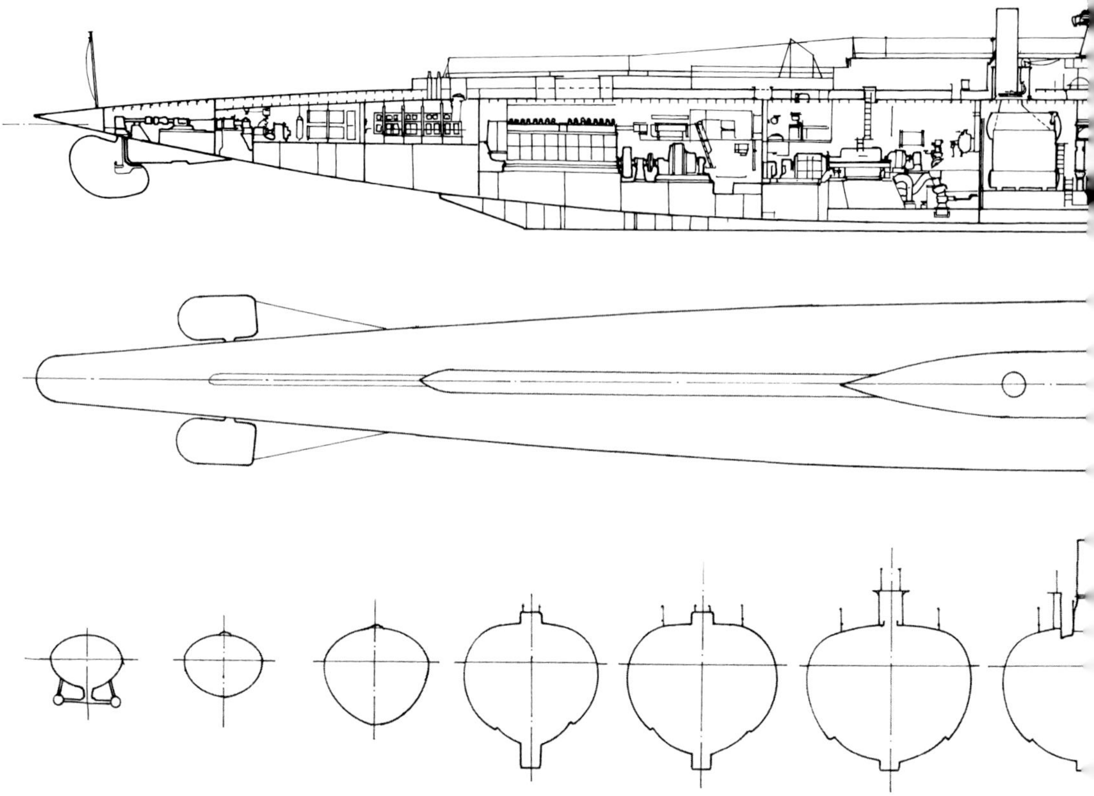

June 27, 1917, for conversion to a surface patrol boat and reverted to the name *Swordfish* in July. A new raised forecastle and wheelhouse were created, a new taller but fixed funnel was stepped, and the gun armament was revised to two 12 pdr guns supplemented by depth charges. The original steam machinery was retained, and the batteries were probably replaced by ballast. Commissioned on August 10, 1917, and accepted two months later, the *Swordfish* served as tender to the *Victory*, and did not become operational until January 1918.

The details of the *Swordfish* in its original form included displacements of 932 tons surfaced and 1,105 tons submerged, length of 231 ft., 3.5 in. (70.5 m), beam of 22 ft., 11 in. (7 m), surfaced propulsion by two Parsons geared steam turbines delivering 4,000 hp (2982 kW) for 18 knots, submerged propulsion by two electric motors delivering 1,400 kW (1044 kW) for 10 knots, armament of two 3-inch (76 mm) guns as well as two 21-inch (533 mm) bow and four 18-inch (457 mm) beam tubes for two and eight torpedoes, respectively, and crew of about 18.

Steam propulsion was again the dominating feature of the K-class submarine, whose concept had been drafted by the Director of Naval Construction as early as 1913 in an effort to

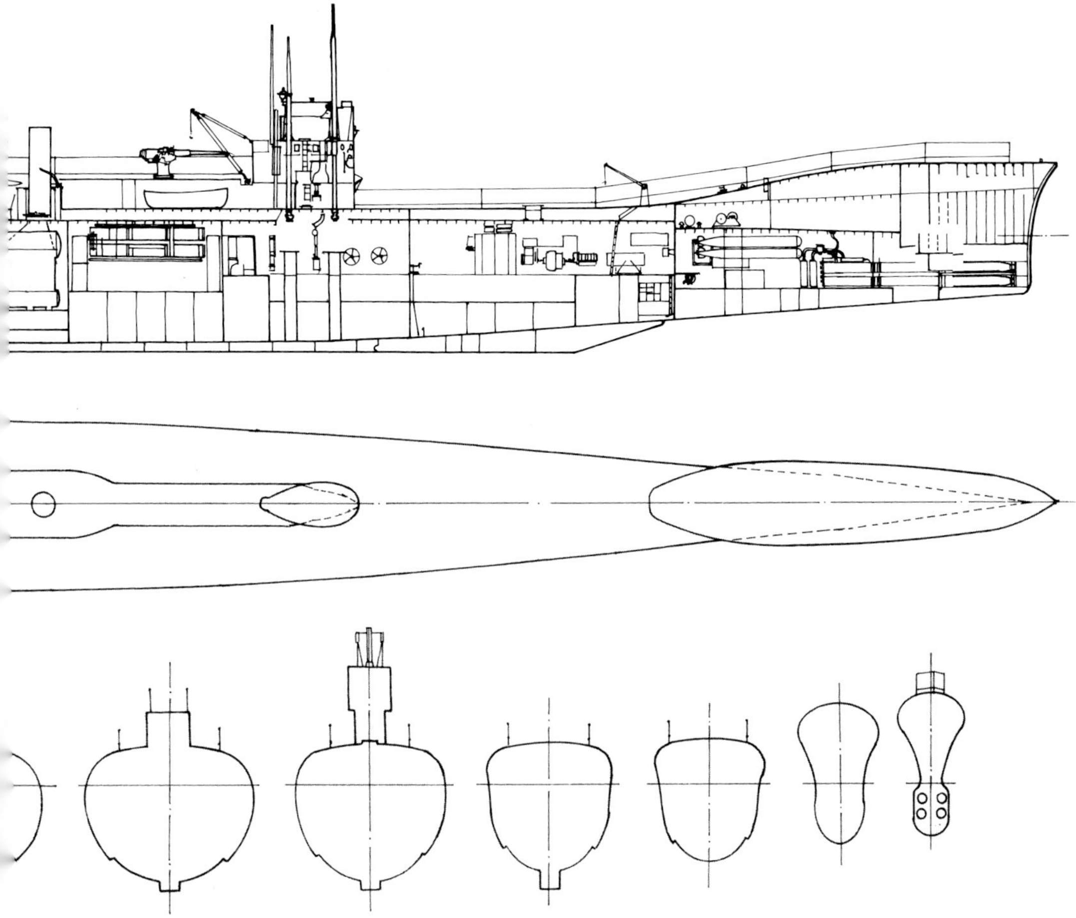

create large and fast boats possessing the speed and range to operate as scouts for the battle fleet. The boats were indeed large and fast, but became nicknamed the "Kalamity" class as a result of the many accidents which befell them: 18 K-class boats were built, and while the class suffered no combat losses, it lost six of its number in accidents. Only one K-class boat ever engaged an enemy vessel, hitting a U-boat amidships with a torpedo whose warhead did not detonate.

In 1913 the DNC drew up the outline of a design to operate with the fleet. This required a speed of at least 24 knots, and the only way this could be provided with the propulsion arrangements of the time was steam propulsion. The DNC recommended that in any fleet action, the steam-powered boats, after providing early warning of an enemy's presence, would then pass round the enemy's flank to tackle its ships as the enemy pulled back.

The boats were to be 338 feet (103 m) long, have a surfaced displacement of 1,700 tons, achieve 24 knots on 10,000 shp (7456 kW) and be armed with eight 21-inch (533 mm) tubes. The concept was then put on the back burner until the results of the trials of the *Nautilus* and *Swordfish* had been completed, and the slightly smaller J-class boats with three-shaft diesel-electric propulsion were ordered. However, by mid-1915, it had become clear that the J-class boats would not live up to expectations, especially as they would reach only 19 knots rather than the required 21. Admiral Sir John Jellicoe, commanding the Grand Fleet, asked for the matter of a high-speed scout submarine to be re-examined. The DNC's original design was then reconsidered in comparison with a new concept from Vickers for a 2,000-ton boat to reach 23 knots on 14,000 hp (10438 kW) and be armed with eight 18-inch (457 mm) tubes. This was deemed inadequate and, by an almost inevitable compromise, Vickers was contracted to rework the DNC's concept to create the K class.

An eventual total of 21 such boats was ordered from June 1915 at a unit price of £340,000. Ultimately, only 17 of the boats were built to the original pattern; the last four were cancelled in favor of the same number of great M-class boats. Six units of an Improved K-class design were ordered in October 1917, but the end of World War I in November 1918 meant that of these only the K 26 was completed.

The design of the K-class boats was based on a double hull, and although powered on the surface by two Brown-Curtis or Parsons geared turbines using steam from two oil-fired Yarrow boilers, they had four electric motors for submerged propulsion. Each of the boats was also fitted with an 800 hp (596 kW) diesel generator to charge the batteries and provide limited propulsive power if problems arose with the boilers.

This drove the displacements up to 1,980 tons surfaced and 2,566 tons submerged. The gun armament was two 4-inch (102 mm) surface weapons and one 3-inch (76 mm) anti-aircraft weapon, and the torpedo armament comprised ten 18-inch (457 mm) tubes as four in the bow, two on each beam and two in a revolving mount on the superstructure for night use. The last were later unshipped, as they were prone to damage in rough seas.

Each boat had a proper deckhouse built over and around the conning tower, providing the crew with better protection than the canvas screens which had been fitted in all previous Royal Navy submarines.

The boats' considerable size resulted in control and depth-keeping problems, especially as efficient remote controls were not yet available. This was made worse by the fact that the designed maximum diving depth was 200 feet, and in a boat of this length a sharp dive could well have lowered the bow below this depth while the stern was still on the surface. Moreover, the eight internal bulkheads were designed to stand a pressure equivalent to a mere 70 feet (20 m).

The first boat to be completed, in May 1916, was the *K 3*, whose trials revealed many problems. The most serious were the high temperatures in the boiler room, only partially mitigated by the installation of higher-capacity fans. Steaming at speed tended to push the bow into the water, worsening already indifferent sea-keeping, and to overcome this problem a bulbous swan bow was added. Nevertheless, there were still problems: the most embarrassing was that in a heavy sea, water could enter the boat through the twin funnels and put the boiler fires out.

The boats suffered numerous accidents, largely as a result of the design's poor maneuverability and the operation of the boats in conjunction with surface vessels.

The final, improved, boat was the *K 26*, which was completed at leisure for commissioning in 1923. It had six 21-inch (533 mm) bow torpedo tubes but retained the 18-inch (457 mm) beam tubes. Her higher casing almost cured the problems of seawater entering the boiler room and improved ballast tank arrangements cut the diving time to 3 minutes 12 seconds to get to 80 feet (24 m). It also had an increased maximum diving depth of 250 feet (75 m).

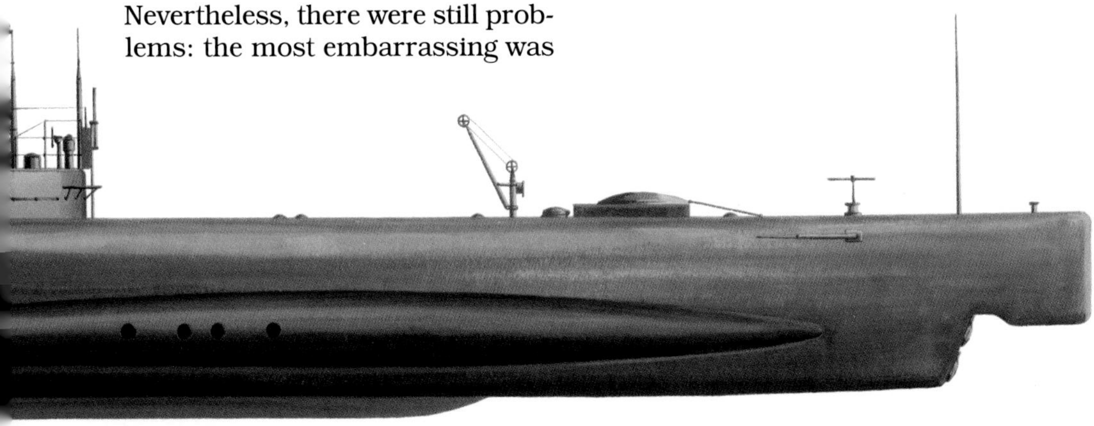

Most of the boats were scrapped in 1921-26 but the K 26 survived until 1931 only to be broken up because its displacement exceeded the limits for submarine displacement in the London Naval Treaty of 1930.

K class

Type:	fleet scouting and attack submarine
Tonnage:	1,980 tons surfaced and 2,566 tons submerged
Dimensions:	length 330 ft. (100.6 m); beam 26 ft., 6.75 in. (8.1 m); draft 17 ft. (5.2 m)
Propulsion:	two geared steam turbines delivering 10,500 hp (7829 kW) for 24 knots surfaced and four electric motors delivering 1,440 hp (1074 kW) for 9.5 knots submerged
Armament:	two 4-inch (102 mm) and one 3-inch (76 mm) guns, and 10 18-inch (457 mm) tubes for 18 torpedoes
Complement:	59

L class (1917)

By 1916 the Royal Navy was faced with the urgent requirement to replace its E class of submarines. Although it had experimented with double-hulled boats, the Admiralty now reverted to the well-established saddle-tank hull in a refined form. The first pair of new boats was ordered in February 1916 for completion in mid-1917 as the *E 57* and *E 58* of what originally had been intended merely as a lengthened version of the E class. Ultimately, these boats incorporated so many changes and improvements that they became the L 1 and L 2 of the new L class.

The *L 3* to *L 8*, completing the first group of L-class boats with a length of 231 ft., 1 in. (70.4 m), were ordered in May 1916 and completed between November 1917 and March 1918. The armament varied: the *L 1* had a 3-inch (76 mm) anti-aircraft gun on a disappearing mounting, and initially some had no gun at all, but eventually each boat had one 4-inch (102 mm) gun on a platform at the forward end of the conning tower, with its own access trunk. All the boats carried ten 18-inch (457 mm) torpedoes fired through four bow and two beam tubes.

The bow salvo was inadequate, so a second group was planned as *L 9* to *L 51*. Ultimately, only 19 boats were completed to a revised standard with four 21-inch (533 mm) bow tubes with eight torpedoes as well as the two 18-inch (457 mm) beam tubes. The *L 9* was ordered in August 1916, followed in December by the *L 10* to *L 35* (excluding L 13 as "unlucky"): the *L 28* to *L 32* were broken up after being laid down, and the *L 34* and *L 35* were cancelled before being laid down. Although *L 36* to *L 49* were planned, these were never ordered.

Five boats were completed as mine layers with vertical chutes, each carrying one mine, in the saddle tanks and the torpedo armament reduced to the bow tubes. *L 11*, *L 12*, *L 14* and *L 17* had 16 tubes but the *L 25* had only 14 tubes. The boats from the *L 12* on had the 4-inch (102 mm) gun raised to the bridge deck level, where it was served by an enclosed access trunk.

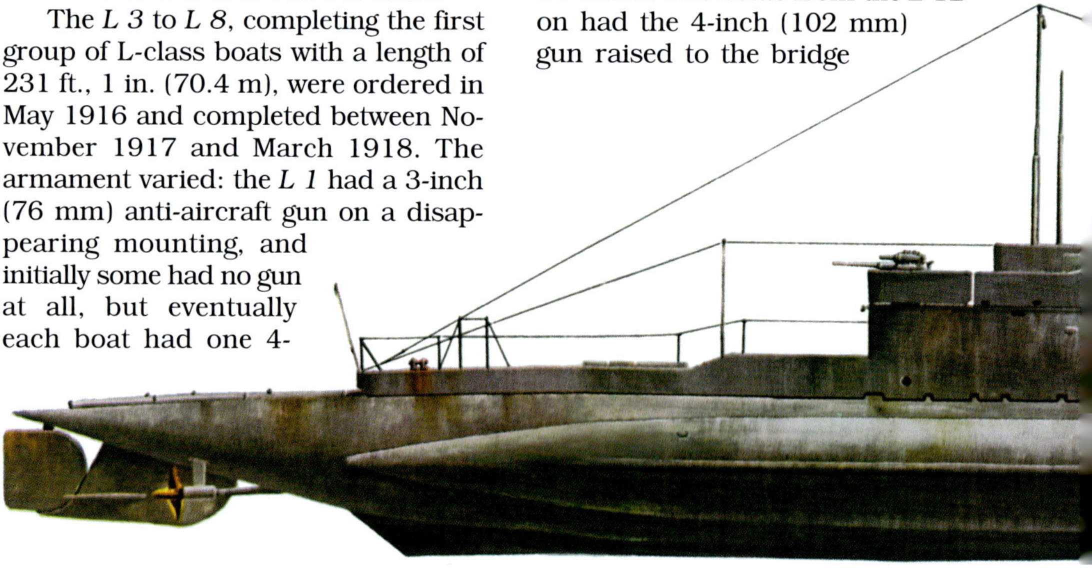

The boats of the second L-class group were significantly better than the E class, especially in accommodation and overall habitability. While the first group's boats were sold for breaking in the early 1930s, the boats of the second group were retained and three of them survived to 1945 as training submarines.

The main changes resulted from the change to 21-inch (533 mm) tubes. The pressure hull was lengthened by 7 ft.,

6 in. (2.3 m) and a watertight bulkhead was added abaft the bow tubes to separate the tube compartment from the forward torpedo room. From *L 18* on, the boats carried more fuel, and this enhancement was retrofitted to the *L 9* to *L 17* as well as the boats of the first group. No reload torpedoes were carried for the beam tubes.

A further expansion of the L-class design was authorized early in 1917 even before the boats of the first group had entered service, but when these proved successful it was decided merely to improve the armament of the boats of the third group, which was planned as *L 50* to *L 74*. The first two were ordered in January and February 1917, followed by *L 56* to *L 58* in April 1917 and *L 59* to *L 66* and *L 74* in April 1918. Most were still in an early stage of construction at the time of the Armistice, and *L 59* to *L 66* and *L 74* were cancelled in November 1918, followed by *L 50*, *L 51*, *L 57*, *L 58*, *L 67*, *L 68*, *L 70*, *L 72* and *L 73* in April 1919. The frames of *L 67* and *L 68* were used in 1927 for the Yugoslav *Hrabn* and *Nebojsa*.

The boats of the third group were distinguishable from their predecessors by having a second 4-inch (102 mm) gun platform at the after end of the conning tower. The bow salvo was increased to six 21-inch (533 mm) tubes for 12 torpedoes, and the beam tubes were omitted. The *L 55* was completed in 1918, sent to the Baltic early 1919, was sunk off Kronshtadt in 1919, and was later raised and repaired for Soviet naval service. The other boats were deleted in the late 1930s.

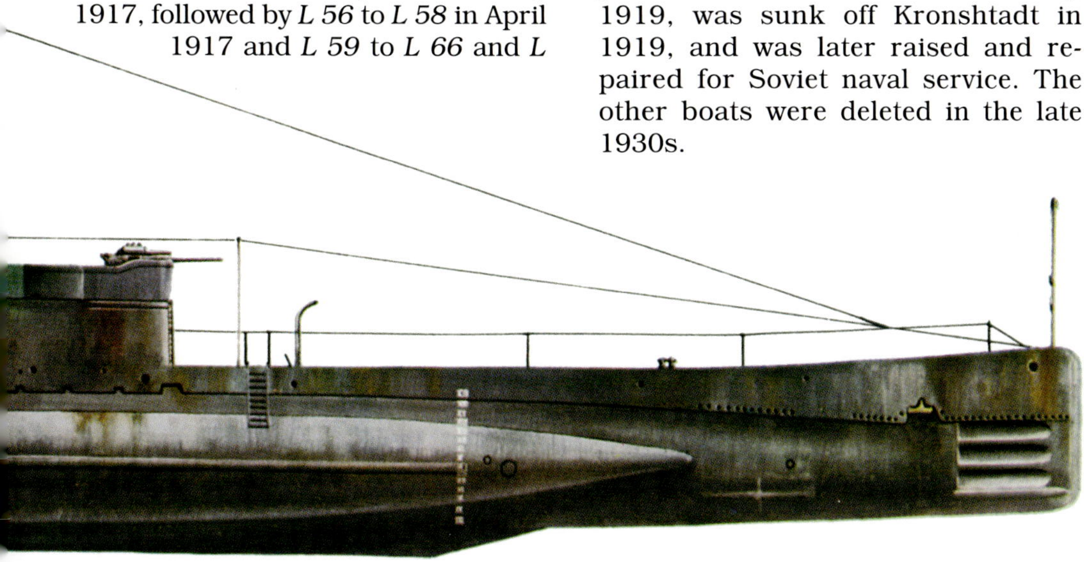

L class (third group)

Type:	attack submarine
Tonnage:	960 tons surfaced and 1,150 tons submerged
Dimensions:	length 235 ft. (71.6 m); beam 23 ft., 5.5 in. (7.15 m); draft 13 ft., 1.5 in. (4 m)
Propulsion:	diesel engines delivering 2,400 hp (1789 kW) for 17 knots surfaced and two electric motors delivering 1,600 hp (1193 kW) for 10.5 knots submerged
Armament:	two 4-inch (102 mm) guns and six 21-inch (533 mm) tubes for 12 torpedoes
Complement:	44

U-139 class (1917)

By the middle of 1915, the economic plight in which Germany found itself, largely as a result of the British naval blockade, meant that German war industries could not obtain adequate supplies of certain essential commodities and raw materials. The U.S. was still neutral at this time, and Germany decided that it would be useful to build a class of long-range, large submarines that could be used as blockade runners for the German trade with the U.S., with the ability to penetrate the British blockade by making the first and last parts of their voyages largely underwater.

A class of eight submarine freighters was therefore designed specifically for the task, and the first three were allocated the mercantile names *Deutschland*, *Bremen,* and *Oldenburg* rather than naval designations. The *Deutschland* was completed in time to make two voyages to and from the U.S. before the latter entered the war on the Allied side, but, even so, these were more propaganda than commercial successes. The *Bremen* was lost in the course of her first voyage. The *Oldenburg* was never commissioned as a submarine freighter, since by then the U.S. had entered the war. Beginning in February 1917, the two surviving boats were converted or completed as submarine cruisers, and the other five units of this type were built as such from keel up. The *U-154* and *U-156* were lost in action; the *U-152* and *U-153* became British war reparations, but were lost while on tow to the breakers in 1921. The *U-155* (ex-*Deutschland*) was ceded to the UK and was scrapped in 1922, and the *U-151* (ex-*Oldenburg*) and *U-157* became French war reparations. The first was sunk as a gunnery target in 1921 and the second scrapped in the same year.

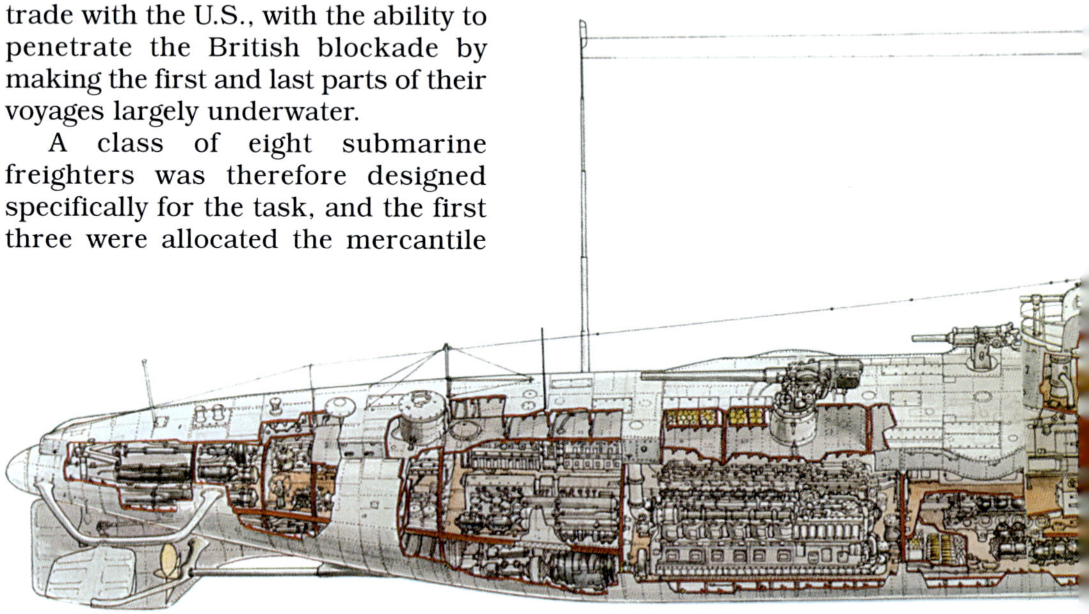

The long-range oceanic cruiser concept proved very attractive to the Germans, who laid down three more boats specifically for this role. These were the *U-139*, *U-140* and *U-141* of the U-139 or Projekt 46 class built by Germaniawerft, and the first two boats were to have been named as the *Kapitänleutnant Schwieger* and *Kapitänleutnant Weddigen*. The boats incorporated a measure of armor protection and had a diving depth of 245 feet (75 m). The boats carried between 440 and 450 tons of fuel for their diesel engines, which translated into a cruising range in the order of 20,450 miles (32910 km) for the second and third boats with the greater fuel capacity.

Launched between November 1917 and January 1918, all three of the boats survived the war and were handed over to the allies as war reparations: the *U-139* became the French *Halbronn*, which was discarded in 1935; the *U-140* was transferred to the U.S. and sunk as a gunnery target in 1921; and the *U-141* passed to the UK and was scrapped in 1923. Technically very successful, the boats caught the attention of several nations and were thus important in the development, in particular, of Japanese and U.S. long-range submarines.

U-139 class

Type:	oceanic cruiser submarine
Tonnage:	1,930 tons surfaced and 2,483 tons submerged
Dimensions:	length 301 ft., 10 in. (92 m); beam 29 ft., 10 in. (9.12 m); draft 17 ft., 4 in. (5.3 m)
Propulsion:	two diesel engines delivering 3,300 hp (2640 kW) for 15.3 knots surfaced and two electric motors delivering 1,690 hp (1260 kW) for 7.6 knots submerged
Armament:	two 6-inch (150 mm) guns and six 20-inch (550 mm) tubes (four bow and two stern) for 19 torpedoes
Complement:	66 plus accommodation for 20 men as prize crews

D, K and M classes (1917)

The three D-class submarines, all built by Fore River for launch in 1909-10, were the *Narwhal*, *Grayling* and *Salmon*, and in November 1911 were renamed as the *D 1*, *D 2* and *D 3*. These were Holland-type boats, the last U.S. submarines to be built with gasoline rather than diesel engines for surfaced running and battery charging, and had a designed diving depth of 200 feet (90 m). The boats started their lives along the Eastern Seaboard, but the *D-3* was reallocated to the Caribbean in 1912. The *D-2* sank alongside the dock at New London in September 1917 but was salvaged, and all three boats were sold for breaking in 1922.

Built by Fore River (four boats), Union Iron Works (three boats) and Moran (one boat) for launch between September 1913 and July 1914, the K-class boats were the *Haddock* (later *K 1*), *Cachalot* (later *K 2*), *Orca* (later *K 3*), *Walrus* (later *K 4*), *K 5*, *K 6*, *K 7* and *K 8*. As in the previous classes after the switch from gasoline-engined to diesel-engined propulsion, the NSLE engines proved very troublesome: three of the boats did not pass their engine trials, and even after considerable development work, three failed their final trials. The designed diving depth was 20 feet (90 m). Despite their engine problems, the boats of the K class achieved considerable success in cruising. The four boats based on the Western Coast cruised to Hawaii at a time late in 1915. The *K 1*, *K 2*, *K 4* and *K 6* were stationed in the Portuguese Azores for operations against German U-boats after the U.S.'s April 1917 entry into World War I, and all eight boats survived to be sold for breaking in 1931.

Constructed by Fore River and launched in September 1915, while the U.S. was still a neutral state in World War I, the *M 1* was the first double-hulled submarine built for the U.S. Navy, and a boat of this type was ordered as previous single-hulled boats had revealed themselves to lack adequate reserve buoyancy. Possessing basically the same military characteristics as the 11 boats of the preceding L class, the *M 1* was about one-fifth larger and had about 27% reserve buoyancy by comparison with abut 11.5% for Lake-type submarines and 15.5% for the Holland-type L-class boats.

Again possessing a designed diving depth of 200 feet (90 m), the *M 1* was found to have adequate seaworthiness, but was not popular with its crews, as its habitability was deemed poorer than that of the single-hulled boats and the interior was more crowded. The boat was also uncomfortable when submerging and surfacing, as it tended to take on a pronounced list. This metacentric height problem was resolved in the following three AA-class or T-class boats, which were the U.S. Navy's first fleet submarines. The *M 1* was discarded in 1922.

D class

Type:	attack submarine
Tonnage:	288 tons surfaced and 337 tons submerged
Dimensions:	length 134 ft., 10 in. (41.1 m); beam 13 ft., 9 in. (4.2 m); draft 11 ft., 10 in. (3.6 m)
Propulsion:	one petrol engine delivering 600 hp (447 kW) for 12 knots surfaced and two electric motors delivering 260 hp (194 kW) for 12 knots submerged
Armament:	four 18-inch (457 mm) tubes for four torpedoes
Complement:	15

K class

Type:	attack submarine
Tonnage:	392 tons surfaced and 521 tons submerged
Dimensions:	length 150 ft., 3 in. (45.8 m); beam 16 ft., 9 in. (5.1 m); draft 13 ft., 1 in. (4 m)
Propulsion:	two diesel engines delivering 950 hp (708 kW) for 14 knots surfaced and one electric motor delivering 680 hp (507 kW) for 10.5 knots submerged
Armament:	four 18-inch (457 mm) tubes for eight torpedoes
Complement:	28

M class

Type:	attack submarine
Tonnage:	488 tons surfaced and 676 tons submerged
Dimensions:	length 196 ft., 3 in. (59.8 m); beam 19 ft. (5.8 m); draft 11 ft., 2 in. (3.4 m)
Propulsion:	two diesel engines delivering 840 hp (626 kW) for 14 knots surfaced and two electric motors delivering 680 hp (507 kW) for 10.5 knots submerged
Armament:	one 3-inch (76 mm) gun and four 18-inch (457 mm) tubes for eight torpedoes
Complement:	28

Deck guns

Early naval operations in World War I provided striking evidence that the submarine already was and would rapidly develop further as a major weapon against warships and mercantile shipping. However, while it carried a powerful warhead with good effect against larger ships, the torpedo of the time had a number of limitations such as its comparatively short range for accurately delivered attacks, size and high cost. The size meant that only a few reload torpedoes could be carried, and the cost meant that it offered little return on investment when used on a small target such as a small coaster or fishing vessel.

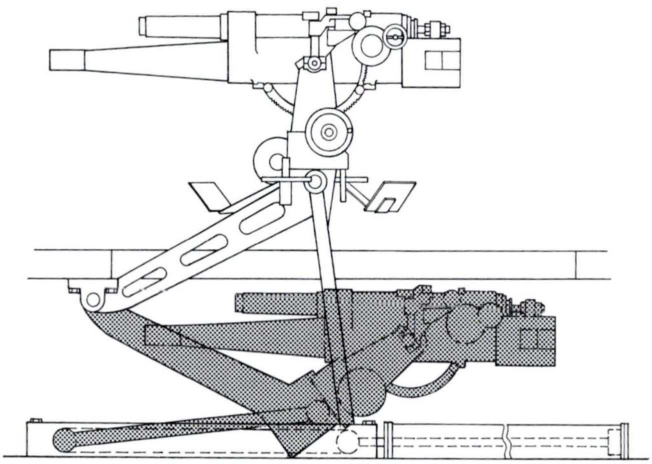

Retractable Submarine Gun. Several designs were produced but, during WWI, the gun was considered a more permanent part of the submarine's equipment. Years later saw the need to streamline hulls, thus producing a revival of the idea; all modern submarines have retractable deck fittings.

Inevitably, therefore, thought turned to a more cost-effective solution to the problem of destroying smaller targets. The solution was the deck gun, which was relatively simple to install, did not need any form of sophisticated fire-control system as targets of the type likely to be engaged

German 8.8 cm Submarine Gun
This gun on its disappearing mounting was a feature of the U19 Class. However, the housing mechanism was cumbersome and the gun crew had to get on deck as quickly as possible, with ammunition being passed up through the hatch.

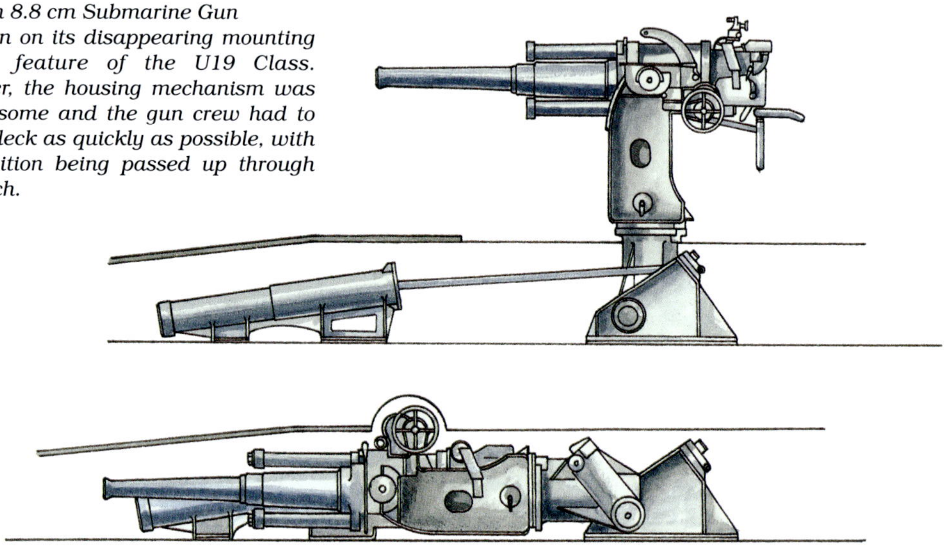

by a gun in a surfaced action were tackled at short range, and could be supplied with a useful number of rounds considerably smaller and cheaper than torpedoes yet just as effective against small targets.

There was an underwater drag penalty to be paid for a gun mounted above the hull, measures had to be taken to prevent water entering parts of the gun which might corrode, and more delicate items such as sights had to be removable for storage inside

The deck gun remained standard for boats designed and built in the period between the two world wars, and submarine operations from the start of World War II confirmed the continued utility of the deck gun for ship destruction and also, to a more limited degree and mostly in the Pacific theatre, shore bombardment purposes. The same change in World War II was the addition to the basic deck gun of provision for anti-aircraft weapons in ever larger calibers and

6-pounder Hotchkiss gun
This was fitted to many British submarines in 1915 as an emergency measure after the successful Sea of Marmora campaign. It had a range of 4500 yards. These types of guns were later handed over to the Army for use in the first tanks.

the boat when not needed. Some submarines also had their gun on a mounting that retracted into the casing, thus removing the drag burden at the price of greater weight and complexity.

In World War I, submarines carried deck guns of greatly different caliber, ranging at the lower end from the 3 pdr weapon with a 47 mm caliber to the 12-inch (305 mm) ex-battleship gun carried by the British M-class submarines. Typical calibers were in the range of 3 and 4 inches (76 and 102 mm), though some U-boats carried a 6-inch (150 mm) gun or howitzer.

numbers so that the submarine could fight it out, if necessary, with aircraft.

The German Type I, Type VII, Type IX, and Type X classes of U-boats were typical of the German approach, and carried one powerful deck gun forward of the conning tower. When served by a capable crew of between three and five, such a weapon could fire between 15 and 18 rounds per minute, and was often used to finish off vessels already damaged by a torpedo, or to sink smaller ships.

The weapon could be used, of course, only when the U-boat was on the surface, and because of the time it took to take the gun out of action and get the crew below, deck-gun action was generally not contemplated where there was the likelihood of attack from the air. It needed a chain of men, including three on deck, to move the ammunition from the main locker below the control room to the gun, and to return spent cases back blow. U-boats had a small watertight locker for ready-use ammunition on deck so that the crew could bring the gun into action as quickly as possible.

In 1937 it was planned to build the Type XI-class cruiser submarines. These would each have carried four 5-inch (127 mm) guns in two twin turrets, but none of the boats was built.

Thc Type VII-class boat carried the 3 1/2 inch (88 mm) C35 L/45 gun, a weapon not to be confused with the celebrated "88" anti/aircraft and anti-tank gun for land service.

The two weapons did not even fire the same ammunition; the naval weapon was generally supplied with 250 of its own 31-lb. (14 kg) rounds firing a 20-lb. (9 kg) shell. Beginning in June 1943, the boats operating in the Atlantic were generally stripped of their deck guns, and those working in the Mediterranean and North Sea kept the weapons for only a few months longer. In July 1944 some of the Type VIIC boats of the 8th U-Boat Flotilla

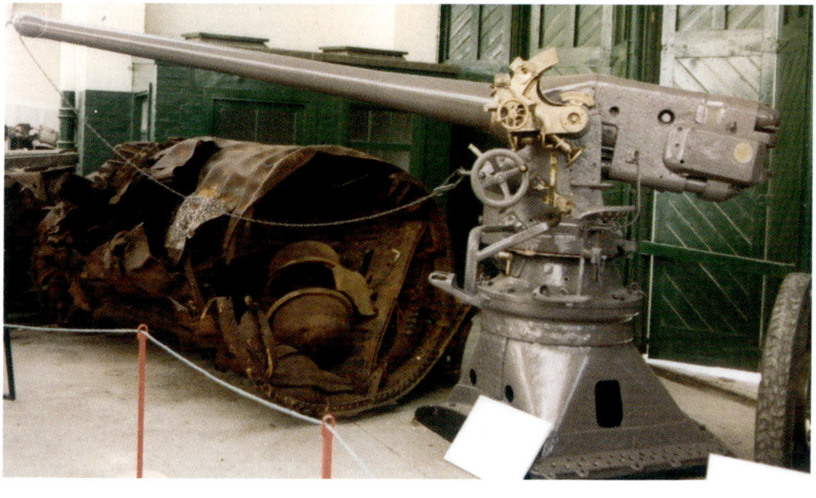

German U-boat gun, the L45 MkII. *Photo: John Batchelor.*

based at Königsberg, in the southeastern corner of the Baltic Sea, once again shipped their deck guns for patrols against the Soviets and for attacks on coastal targets.

The much wider deck of the larger Type I, Type IX, and Type X classes of U-boats could accommodate the more potent 4-inch (105 mm) C35 L/45 gun, for which some 110 rounds (250 in the Type IXD-class boats) were generally carried.

After the massive increase in the Allied powers' anti-submarine capability through the introduction of more and better optimized anti-submarine warships, starting in 1942 and reaching a decisive technical superiority in 1943, the deck guns were removed from almost all U-boats in 1943 and 1944. A few commanders were allowed to retain such weapons, most typically those operating U-boats in the Indian Ocean, where there were fewer opposing warships and aircraft and also fewer ways in which reload torpedoes could be provided. But from 1943 on, the deck gun was a thing of the past for most U-boats.

German 15 cm Submarine Gun.
This gun was mounted in the U-cruisers of the U151 and U139 Classes.

Submarine-launched aircraft

A major limitation of the attack submarine with the standard type of diesel/electric propulsion and limited, if any, electronic aids was the result of the boast' low elevation in the water. This made it hard for an enemy to spot the vessel even when in was running on the surface or awash, but at the same time it provided the submarine with only a very limited visual horizon.

From an early time, there were suggestions submarines could be fitted to embark a small airplane which could be carried in a watertight hangar or container for swift assembly and launch as the parent submarine's "eye in the sky," searching for targets, the approach of hostile warships, or spotting for the submarine in surfaced actions with the embarked gun.

After experimental use of a Friedrichshafen FF.29 floatplane carried to its operating area on the deck of a surfaced submarine, which then partially submerged so that the airplane floated off to take-off in conventional fashion, the Germans began to develop two more advanced aircraft, the Hansa-Brandenburg W.20 biplane and LFG V.19 monoplane. The first was designed in 1917 for use by cruiser U-boats but did not enter service, and the second was an experimental type too flimsy for practical use.

The Arado 231 Seaplane. This experimental machine had a limited range of only 310 miles (500 km) but could have been a useful spotter for a U-boat group in the vastness of the Atlantic Ocean. Disassembled and with the propeller removed, it would have fitted into a watertight tube of only 6 ft., 6 in. (2 m) wide.

Sopwith Baby.

Martin Kitten.

The British also trialed the aircraft-carrier submarine concept when the *E22* was fitted in 1916 to carry and launch two Sopwith Schneider or Baby floatplanes in 1916. The aircraft were carried on the deck, and the submarine could not submerge without losing them.

The *Surcouf* was a French submarine designed as a submarine cruiser to seek and engage in surface combat. The boat carried a Besson MB.411 observation floatplane in a hangar built into the after part of the conning tower.

In the late 1920s, the Italian navy developed the *Ettore Fieramosca* as a submarine with a waterproof hangar for a small reconnaissance floatplane. The two aircraft types created for possible service on this boat were the Macchi M.53 and Piaggio P.8, but the program was then cancelled, and the hangar was removed in December 1931 before the boat had been delivered.

Submarine-launched aircraft *continued*

After the loss of the British *M1*, armed with a 12-inch (305 mm) gun, the surviving M-class submarines were converted to other uses. By 1928 the *M2* had been fitted with a waterproof hangar and steam catapult and could launch and recover a small Parnall Peto airplane, the object being to scout ahead of the fleet. The *M2* was lost in 1932 and the Royal Navy abandoned this concept.

The idea of a submarine aircraft carrier was studied in the U.S. beginning in 1922. The U.S. Navy bought a pair of Caspar (Heinkel) U.1 floatplanes, which could be broken down into small and manageable assemblies, for assessment at the Naval Air Station at Anacostia. The service then ordered 12 examples of a submarine-based floatplane as six Cox-Klemin XS-1 and six Martin MS-1 machines. There were tested on the submarine *S-1* during October and November 1923. Later, Cox-Klemin developed its design with an XS-2 model, but the U.S. Navy had lost interest in the concept. In 1931 Loening offered its XSL-1 amphibian flying boat for submarine trials.

The German navy also embarked on the development of aircraft-equipped submarines, and ordered very large cruiser U-boats in early 1939. These boats were to be twice as large as any existing U-boat, contain a crew of 110, and were to have carried one Arado Ar 231 floatplane, but were cancelled at the start of World War II later in the year. The Type XI class was projected as a trio of boats each carrying one Ar 231 in a special deck hangar.

The Type IXD-2 class of boat was a long-range submarine operating in the Indian Ocean and Far East areas

The Norwegian Navy bought Farman floatplanes in 1916 for trials, and when they broke down or ran out of fuel the submarines were able to recover then by surfacing gently underneath.

The first Besson MB. 411, as fitted to the French submarine Surcouf. This plane was still aboard the Surcouf when the vessel escaped from Brest and reached Plymouth. The diminutive seaplane made several flights off the South Devon and Dorset coasts, causing some confusion among aircraft spotters!

Besson MB.411

Type:	two-seat submarine-launched reconnaissance/spotting floatplane
Powerplant:	one Salmson 9Nd radial engine rated at 175 hp (130 kW)
Dimensions:	wingspan 39 ft., 4 1/2 in. (12.0 m); length 27 ft., 3/4 in. (8.25 m); height 9 ft., 4 1/4 in. (2.85 m)
Performance:	maximum speed 118 mph (190 km/h); range 249 miles (400 km)
Armament:	none

from a base at Penang, in Japanese-occupied Malaya. To support the operations of these boats, the Focke-Achgelis Fa 330 Bachstelze towed kite autogyro was developed for limited service after mid-1942. It was also hoped to use the Flettner Fl 282A Kolibri helicopter, in a special version which could be dismantled, in the same role.

The Japanese applied the concept of the aircraft-carrying submarine most extensively, and 47 boats had the ability to carry aircraft. The most numerous single model was Type B1 class, whose 20 units could each carry and operate one reconnaissance float-plane, generally of the Yokosuka E6Y or E14Y type. The two large Type AM-class boats could each carry two aircraft, generally of the Aichi M6A bomber type. Finally, there were the three units of the truly huge I-400 class created for attacks on the Panama Canal and each carrying three M6A bombers.

X 1 class (1921)

Although the Royal Navy had considered the idea of a submarine commerce raider as early as 1915, it had initially decided that there was little need for such a submarine, as most of Germany's merchant navy was bottled up in harbor after the first few weeks of war by the tight blockade imposed by the Royal Navy's surface fleet. However, the technical success of the German freighter submarine *Deutschland*, and the impressive capability of the U-151 class of commerce-raiding submarines developed from the *Deutschland* and her sister ships led the Admiralty to reconsider its thinking in the period immediately following the end of World War I in November 1918.

The *X 1* was then planned and ordered as a submarine commerce raider for the Royal Navy, with the gun armament and fire-control arrangements which would allow the boat to tackle merchant vessels as well as any surface warship up to the size of a destroyer.

The *X 1* was laid down on November 2, 1921, at the Naval Dockyard Chatham, launched on June 16, 1923, and completed on September 23, 1925, before being commissioned in December 1925.

The *X 1* approached the double-hulled type of submarine more fully than any earlier British submarine. The plating of the pressure hull was one inch (25 mm) thick, the designed diving depth was 350 feet (107 m); the test depth, 200 feet (90 m). Fuel was clearly a major consideration in a boat intended for cruises over very long ranges, and amounted to 452 tons, of which just 40.5 tons was carried inside the pressure hull. Surface propulsion was, of course, the task of diesel engines. These comprised two Admiralty main engines each delivering 3,000 hp (2237 kW), and two MAN auxiliary diesels, each stripped from the surrendered German mine-laying submarine U-126 and delivering 1,200 hp (895 kW), to drive the generators used to charge the batteries. These generators could also drive the GEC electric motors directly, in which case the latter developed 1,000 hp (746 kW) each rather than the 1,200 hp (895 kW) resulting from the use of battery current. The total surface power theoretically available was thus 8,000 hp (5965 kW), but the auxiliary diesels never achieved their designed output, so their shaft revolutions, and hence those of the main diesels, were limited and some 1,000 hp (746 kW) were lost.

The Admiralty diesel engine was derived from the MAN diesel engine which had provided so successful in German U-boats during World War I, but the reliability and power of this engine were never as good as those of the German original, and the *X 1* therefore suffered from engine problems throughout its comparatively short life.

The *X 1* was larger than any earlier submarine, with an overall length of 363 ft., 6 in. (110.8 m), and in addition to its bow armament of six 21-inch (533 m) tubes for 12 Mk 4 torpedoes, the submarine carried two gun turrets, one forward of and the other abaft the conning tower, each carrying two 5-inch (132 mm) quick-firing guns. The availability of the guns' firing shells, which could be carried in considerably larger numbers than the torpedoes, considerably more costly as well as shorter-ranged, was intended to make commerce raiding very economical.

In theory, the *X 1* could achieve 19.5 knots on the surface, and at its 8 knots economical speed the submarine had a range of 21,535 miles (34655 km), which was greater than that of any naval cruiser. But even with its engines working perfectly, the *X 1* was slower and less agile than any destroyer. The submarine was therefore vulnerable to the fire of ships and bombing from the air. The *X 1* should have been able to sink or disable a destroyer at a range of 6,000 yards (5485 m) with her guns alone, but this was not feasible as the low height above the water of the range-finding equipment and its unsteadiness in the water rendered the boat inherently unsuitable as a gun platform.

The *X 1* was placed in reserve in 1933, taken off the active list in 1936, and scrapped in 1937.

X 1

Type:	commerce-raiding cruiser submarine
Tonnage:	3,050 tons surfaced and 3,600 tons submerged
Dimensions:	length 363 ft., 6 in. (110.8 m); beam 29 ft., 10 in. (9.1 m); draft 15 ft., 9 in. (4.8 m)
Propulsion:	two Admiralty and two MAN diesel engines delivering 7,000 hp (5219 kW) for 19.5 knots surfaced, and two GEC electric motors delivering 2,400 hp (1789 kW) for 8 knots submerged
Armament:	four 5-inch (132 mm) guns and six 21-inch (533 mm) tubes for 12 torpedoes
Complement:	110

O class (1917)

The U.S. Navy's O class of submarine was introduced shortly before the Armistice of November 1918, which brought World War I to an end. None of the new boats but *O-4* and *O-6* saw combat: on July 24, 1918, a British armed merchant vessel mistook the two for U-boats and fired on them, to no effect.

The 16 boats fell into two subclasses, the first comprising *O-1* to *O-10*, designed by the Electric Boat Company; and the second, the *O-11* to *O-16*, designed to a different standard by the Lake Torpedo Boat Company. The standard of the initial 10 boats (the first two built by the Portsmouth Navy Yard and the other eight by Fore River for launch between September 1918 and July 1918) included displacements of 348 tons surfaced and 629 tons submerged, length of 172 ft., 3 in. (52.5 m), beam of 18 ft., 1 in. (5.5 m), two NSLE diesel engines delivering 880 hp (656 kW) for 14 knots surfaced and two electric motors delivering 740 hp (552 kW) for 10.5 knots submerged, range of 6,335 miles (10195 km) at 11.5 knots surfaced, and diving depth of 200 feet (90 m).

The last six boats (the first three built by Lake and the last three by California Ship Building for launch between September 1917 and May 1918) were completed to a standard including greater length, reduced beam and BS rather than NSLE diesel engines. These boats were generally considered inferior to the first 10. Some of the boats served in the training role at various times from 1928 to the end of World War II in 1945, but the six Lake-designed boats were scrapped in 1930-31 in accordance with the provisions of the London Naval Treaty. The *O-5* and *O-9* were sunk in accidental collisions on October 28, 1923, and

June 20, 1941, respectively, the *O-1* was deleted in 1938, and the surviving units of the initial subclass were sold for breaking in 1945-46.

The *O-12* was sold out of the service in 1930 and leased for use as the *Nautilus* by the Wilkins-Ellsworth trans-Arctic submarine expedition, in which it was hoped to reach the of the North Pole by submarine to link up with the airship *Graf Zeppelin*. On June 4,

O-class boat on training duty. Note the 3-inch (76 mm) deck gun retracted into a tub built into the port side of the casing, forward of the conning tower
Photo: U.S. Navy.

1931, the *Nautilus* left New York with a 20-man crew led by Captain Sloan Danenhower to cross to England, but was nearly swamped in a storm when being towed by the battleship *Wyoming*. On August 5, the *Nautilus* headed along the English Channel and then along the Norwegian coast. A storm again damaged the boat, carrying away her bridge and giving her a permanent list, but after a stop in Tromsø on August 11, she successfully reached Spitsbergen, where Wilkins allowed just one day for repairs. The crew carried out the planned scientific experiments as the boat continued north, hindered by pack ice. The boat was poorly outfitted to deal with the cold, as it lacked both insulation and heaters. The fresh water system froze and the hull developed slow leaks. After ten days, the *Nautilus* reached 82° N, farther north than any other vessel had managed under its own power, and preparations began to dive and proceed under the ice. However, the boat refused to respond; the stern planes had been carried away at some unknown earlier time. Without them, the submarine could not control its depth while submerged, and the expedition had to be aborted, returning to Spitsbergen on September 20. The *Nautilus* was scuttled in deep Norwegian waters in November 1931.

O class (second group)

Type:	attack submarine
Tonnage:	491 tons surfaced and 566 tons submerged
Dimensions:	length 175 ft., 3 in. (53.4 m); beam 16 ft., 9 in. (6 m); draft 13 ft., 9 in. (4.2 m)
Propulsion:	two Busch-Sulzer diesel engines delivering 880 hp (656 kW) for 14 knots surfaced and two Diehl electric motors delivering 740 hp (552 kW) for 10.5 knots submerged
Armament:	one 3-inch (76 mm) gun and four 18-inch (457 mm) tubes for eight torpedoes
Complement:	29

Argonaut, *Narwal* and *Nautilus* (1927)

Built by Portsmouth Navy Yard and launched on November 10, 1927, the *V-4* was a very efficient submarine, unique among the submarines of the U.S. Navy in being the only American boat designed and constructed specifically as a mine-layer. The design of the boat evolved from a series of long-range cruiser studies launched in 1919 after the U.S. Navy had started to investigate the capabilities of U-boats surrendered by Germany at the end of World War I. Up until this time, the primary characteristics required of U.S. submarines had been high underwater speed and the ability to dive swiftly, and such boats

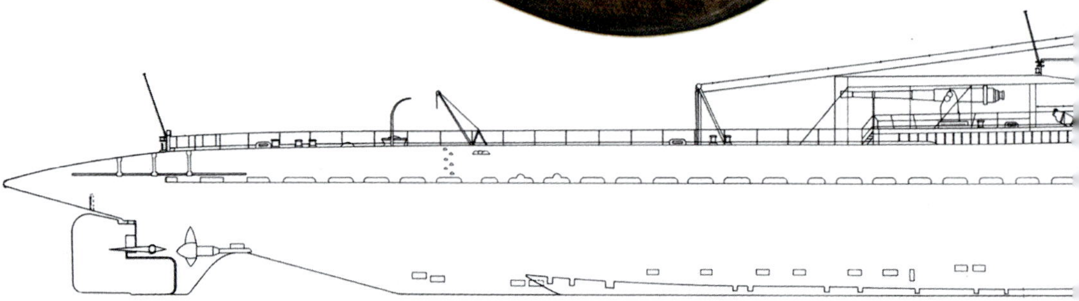

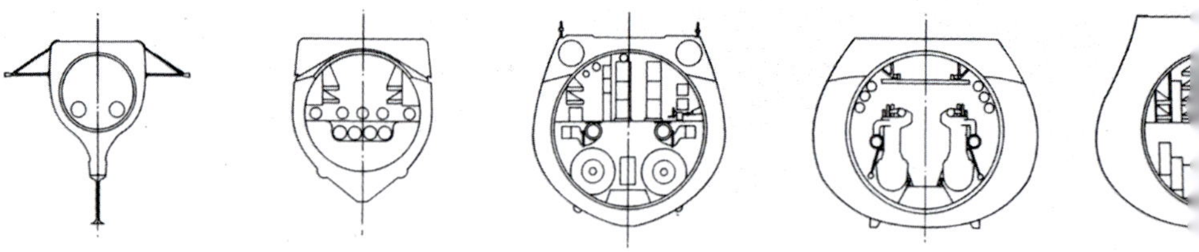

had not generally been seaworthy on the surface. The Germans, on the other hands, emphasized surface performance and seaworthiness, as they regarded the U-boat to be a submersible torpedo boat, using its underwater capabilities only for attack and escape.

In April 1923 the U.S. Navy called for a long-range mine-layer submarine able to dive to 300 feet (90 m) and possessing an endurance of 90 days with a radius of no less than 6,900 miles (11105 km) at 10 knots with standard fuel and 20,700 miles (33315 km) with maximum fuel. Speed was considered to be of secondary importance, but a sustained cruising speed of 15 knots was demanded for surfaced running. The requirement also demanded the carriage of a single observation/spotting airplane (never carried), four 21-inch (533 mm) tubes in the bow for 16 torpedoes, and two tubes aft for 60 mines.

Contemporary studies for cruiser submarines decided that greater size would be required, and demanded the potent surface armament in the form of two 6-inch (152 mm) L/53 guns in the *V-4*, but 7-inch and even 8-inch (178 and 208 mm) guns in the cruiser boats, as well as aircraft and mines. The design series started in 1919 and by October 1920 some concepts had indicated a displacement as great as 20,500 tons. This was clearly too great a technical leap, given that the largest submarine yet created had a displacement in the order of 2,000 tons, so the Bureau of Construction and Repair took a break in its thinking up to 1922, and then reverted to the original concept of 1919 for a less complex type of boat, many of whose design problems were already being addressed and overcome in the *V-1* to *V-3* of what would later be the Barracuda class, and many of whose detail features and devices had been trialed and proved on the *S-48* to *S-51*, the last units of the S class.

By this time, more data on the design of larger submarines had been gained from German sources, the plans of larger German U-boats could be examined, and the Bureau of Engineering

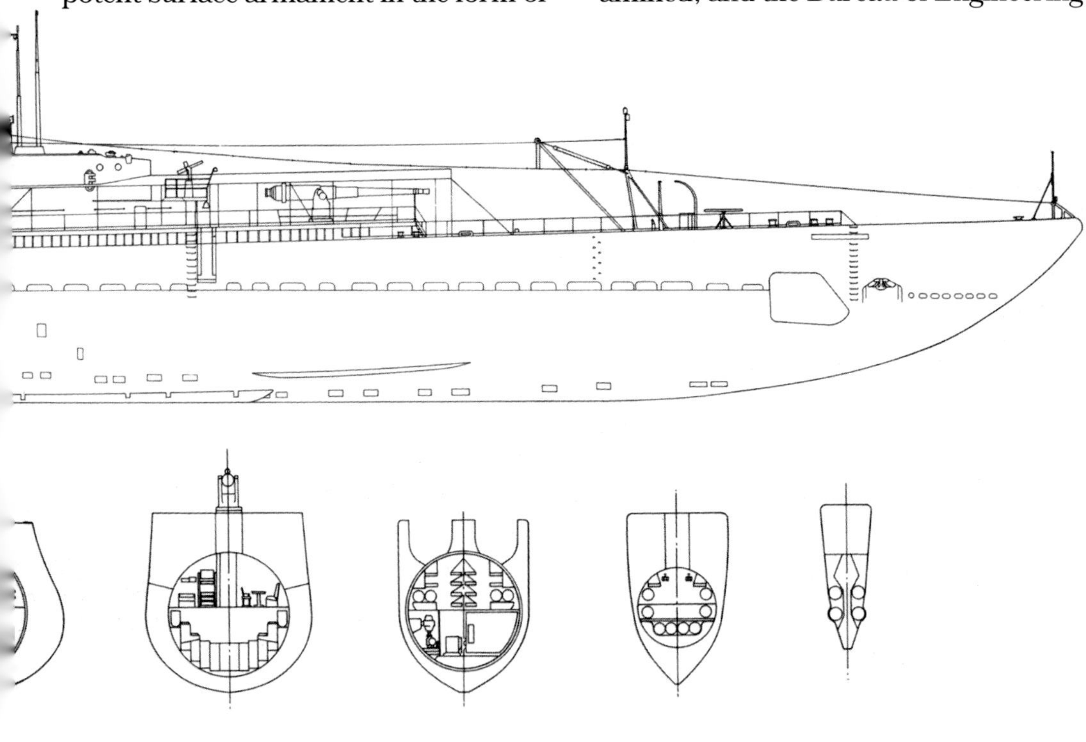

Argonaut, *Narwal* and *Nautilus* continued

A wartime picture of USS Narwhal showing her two 6-inch (150 mm) guns, used to bombard the Matsuwa airfield in 1943. Photo: U.S. Navy.

had decided in principle that the MAN type of diesel engines would become standard for U.S. submarines. The hull of the *V-4* was initially to have been modeled closely on that of the *V-1*, but after a request that the bulbous bow characteristic of U.S. submarines be compared with the typical U-boat bow, the latter was found to be far better.

When commissioned on April 2, 1928, the *V-4* was the largest submarine built in the U.S. with a displacement of 4,045 tons submerged and length of 381 feet (116.1 m), and served initially with Submarine Division 12 based at Newport, Rhode Island. In January and February 1929, the *V-4* underwent a series of trials, and dived to 318 feet (97 m), the greatest depth attained by any U.S. submarine up to this time. On February 6, 1929, the *V-4* was assigned to Division 20, Submarine Divisions, Battle Fleet, and arrived at San Diego, California, on March 23. The boat was renamed the *Argonaut* on February 19, 1931, and redesignated as SM-1 ("submarine minelayer number 1") on July 1 of that year. On June 30, 1932, it arrived at Pearl Harbor, was assigned to Submarine Division 7, and became the flagship of Submarine Squadron 4 in mid-1939. Although it had been planned to convert the boat with reliable General Motors diesels engines in place of her unreliable MAN engines in 1940-41, this was not done; the boat was converted as the APS-1 supply and transport submarine, and was lost on January 10, 1943.

Built by Portsmouth and Mare Island Navy Yards and launched in December 1927 and March 1930, respectively, the *V-5* and *V-6* (later *Narwhal* and *Nautilus*) were cruiser counterparts of the *V-4* with two 21-inch (533 mm) stern tubes rather than mine-laying tubes, and eight reload torpedoes were carried externally under the gun casing fore and aft. A surfaced speed of 17 knots was demanded and achieved, and there was no demand for the carriage of an airplane. The original MAN diesel engines were replaced by Fairbanks-Morse diesel engines in 1940-41 and their composite propulsion arrangement, of the type also used by the *Argonaut*, was replaced by a diesel-electric propulsion arrangement of the type used in more modern fleet boats. The range was 20,725 miles (33355 km) at 10 knots surfaced and 57.5 miles (92.5 km) at 5 knots submerged.

During World War II, the boats were used primarily for the delivery and extraction of raiding parties, and the major war alteration was the addition of four external tubes (two forward and two under the raised gun deck amidships) in place of reload torpedoes.

Both of the boats survived World War II and were sold for breaking in 1945.

Narwhal class

Type:	cruiser submarine
Tonnage:	2,987 tons surfaced and 4,050 tons submerged
Dimensions:	length 371 ft. (113.1 m); beam 33 ft., 3 in. (10.1 m); draft 16 ft., 1 in. (5.2 m)
Propulsion:	diesel-electric arrangement with two Fairbanks-Morse diesel engines delivering 5,400 hp (4026 kW) for 17 knots surfaced and two Westinghouse electric motors delivering 2,540 hp (1894 kW) for 8 knots submerged
Armament:	two 6-inch (152 mm) guns and six 21-inch (533 mm) tubes for 24 torpedoes
Complement:	89

Surcouf (1930)

The French navy was fascinated by the concept of a commerce-raiding and cruiser submarine armed with heavy guns to reduce demands on the number of torpedoes which could be carried and, to an extent, tackle warships up to light cruiser size. The resulting *Surcouf* was ordered in December 1927 from the Arsenal de Cherbourg, launched in October 1929, and commissioned in May 1934. At the beginning of World War II, the *Surcouf* was the largest submarine in the world.

The Washington Naval Treaty of 1922 had placed strict limits on naval construction by the major naval powers, but submarines had been omitted. The French navy thus decided to secure an advantage by the construction of three

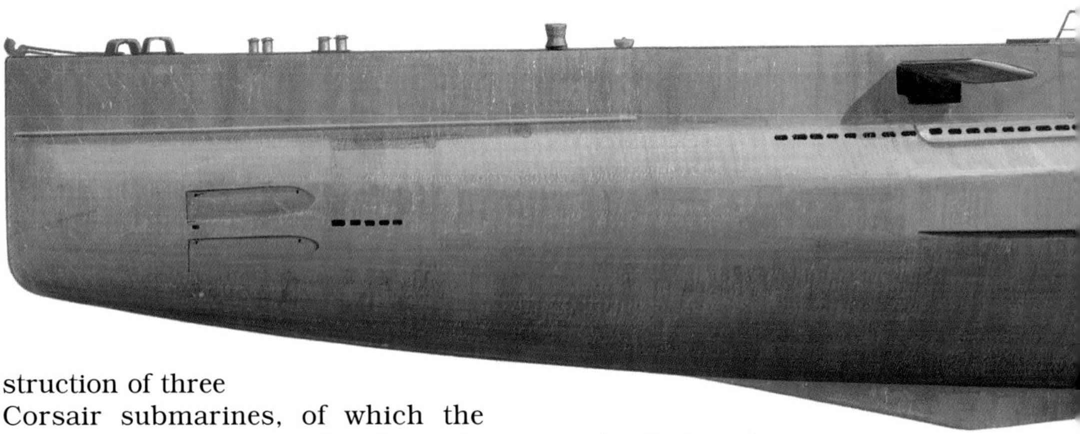

Corsair submarines, of which the *Surcouf* was the first and in fact only one. The *Surcouf* was designed to engage in surface combat, and carried a tiny Besson reconnaissance and spotting floatplane in a watertight hangar abaft the conning tower. The armament was centered on eight 22-inch (550 mm) tubes (four bow and four external in a trainable mounting on the rear casing) with 14 torpedoes, four 16-inch (400 mm) tubes (in another trainable mounting) with eight short-range but very fast torpedoes, and two 8-inch (203 mm) guns in a watertight turret forward of the conning tower. The guns were fed from a magazine holding 60 rounds and controlled by a director incorporating a rangefinder with a base length of 16 ft., 5 in. (5 m) and mounted high enough to provide a horizon of 12,030 yards (11000 m). It was also intended that the floatplane would direct the fire of the guns out to a range of 26,245 yards (24000 m). Two 1 ½ inch (37 mm) cannons and four half-inch (13.2 mm) machine guns were mounted on the top of the hangar for anti-aircraft use. The Surcouf also carried a 16 ft., 5 in. (5 m) boarding launch, later removed, and had a cargo compartment for 40 prisoners.

The fuel tanks carried 280 tons for a range of 11,515 miles (18530 km), and the boat could also carry all the supplies required for a patrol of 90-day endurance.

In 1940 the *Surcouf* was based in Cherbourg, but, at the time of the German invasion, was being refitted in Brest. The crew resisted a British attempt to seize the boat on July 3, and before surrendering lost one man to two British dead. By August 1940, the British had completed the *Surcouf*'s refit and handed the boat to the Free French navy under the command of the only officer of the original crew who had not demanded to be repatriated. There was a great deal of animosity between the crew of the *Surcouf* and the British, who claimed that *Surcouf* was attacking British ships: one officer and two sailors were later put on board for "liaison" purposes.

The *Surcouf* needed a crew of up to 130 men, equivalent to the crews of three more conventional boats, and this made the British reluctant to recommission the boat. In December 1941 the *Surcouf* was involved in the recapture of the Vichy French islands of St Pierre and Miquelon, just off Canada's east coast. In January 1942 the Free French decided to send the *Surcouf* to the Pacific theatre of war, where its range capabilities could be used to best effect. After taking on supplies at Bermuda, the boat headed south, but the movement triggered rumors that the boat was to be used to liberate Martinique. On February 18, 1942, the *Surcouf* was lost with all hands. An official joint U.S. and Free French report stated that the boat left Bermuda on February 12 and was accidentally rammed by the American freighter *Thompson Lykes* off the north coast of Panama near the Panama Canal.

Surcouf

Type:	cruiser submarine
Tonnage:	3,250 tons surfaced and 4,304 tons submerged
Dimensions:	length 360 ft., 10 in. (110 m); beam 29 ft., 6 in. (9 m); draft 23 ft., 10 in. (7.25 m)
Propulsion:	two Sulzer diesel engines 7,600 hp (5667 kW) for 18.5 knots surfaced and two electric motors delivering 3,400 hp (2535 kW) for 10 knots submerged
Armament:	eight 21 3/4 in. (550 mm) and four 15 3/4 in. (400 mm) torpedo tubes, two 8-inch (203 mm) gun, two 1 1/2-inch (37 mm) AA guns and four half-inch (13.2 mm) AA machine guns
Complement:	118

S class (1918/21)

The S-class submarines were the first boats built to a U.S. Navy design. The first was the *S-1*, commissioned in 1918; and the last, the S-51 of 1925. The S class was divided into five groups or subclasses of slightly different design. The first group were the Electric Boat-type *S-1* and *S-18* to *S-41* built by Fore River and Union Iron Works; the second was only the Lake-type *S-2* built by Lake; the third were the Navy Yard-type *S-3* to *S-17* built by Lake and the Portsmouth Navy Yard; the fourth group were the Navy Yard-type *S-42* to *S-47*, built by Fore River; and the fifth group were the second Lake-type *S-48* to *S-51*, built by Lake.

The *S-1*, *S-2*, and *S-3* were Electric Boat, Lake and Bureau of Construction and Repair (later Bureau of Ships) prototypes meeting a U.S. Navy specification. The Lake type was deemed the worst of the three, but improved groups of Electric Boat and Navy Yard boats were built, and the force was completed by the four improved Lake-type boats.

The U.S. Navy commissioned the 48 "production standard" boats between 1920 and 1922, and as a result the S-class boats constituted the main strength of the U.S. submarine arm throughout the 1920s and 1930s, and indeed fought in World War II, when (despite their obsolescence) ten of the boats sank fourteen

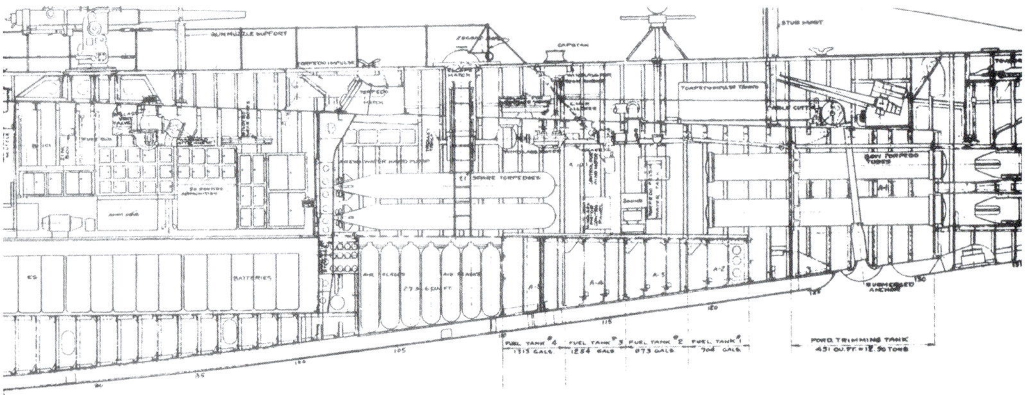

Japanese merchantmen and warships, and another six and one were passed to the Royal Navy and Polish navy in 1941-42 as training submarines.

The boats of the S class nonetheless marked a useful improvement over the boats of the O and R classes as they offered greater range (up to 3,950 miles/6355 km) at 6.5 knots surfaced), higher speed, and eight rather than four torpedo reloads for the same number of bow tubes.

In 1923 the *S-1* was used for experiments with an embarked seaplane, an idea taken further by the French and Japanese, and four similar boats were provided to Peru in 1926-28. Two had been sunk, one had foundered and two had been stricken during the 1920s and 1930s, but the surviving boats were used in World War II in both the Atlantic and the Pacific. Smaller and slower than most later submarines, and able to fire only an obsolete torpedo, they were used mainly for reconnaissance and supply roles, as well as for coastal defense. Seven of them were lost in the war and another two were expended in tests, but the *S-44* sank the Japanese heavy cruiser *Kako* in August 1942. The boats were withdrawn in mid-1943 as fleet submarines became available, and were relegated to training before being scrapped in 1946.

S class (Navy Yard type, second group)

Type:	attack submarine
Tonnage:	906 tons surfaced and 1,126 tons submerged
Dimensions:	length 225 ft., 5 in. (68.7 m); beam 20 ft., 8 in. (6.3 m); draft 16 ft., 1 in. (4.9 m)
Propulsion:	two Busch-Sulzer diesel engines delivering 1,200 hp (895 kW) for 14.5 knots surfaced and two Electro Dynamic electric motors delivering 1,200 hp (895 kW) for 11 knots submerged
Armament:	one 4-inch (102 mm) gun and four 21-inch (533 mm) tubes for 12 torpedoes
Complement:	38

Sjölejonet class (1936)

At the end of World War I, the Royal Swedish navy had some 15 submarines in service, all the submarines that had been built in Sweden up to that time. Sweden had been neutral in the war and had suffered no accidental losses. The oldest two boats, dating from 1914 and 1909, were deleted in 1922 and 1919, but the others remained in service until most of them were scrapped in the early part of the 1930s. During World War I, the Swedes had obtained a license to use the submarine plans of Weser A. G., plans they used in the development of their second Hajen class. Launched in 1917-18, these were three boats with an armament of four 18-inch (457 mm) bow tubes for eight torpedoes. Another three boats of a similar design were launched in 1921 as the Bävern class, with the same torpedo armament.

Impressed by the German navy's small U-boat coastal minelayers of the UC types, the Swedish navy ordered a comparable boat as the *Valen*, launched in 1925 and carrying 20 mines as well as four 18-inch

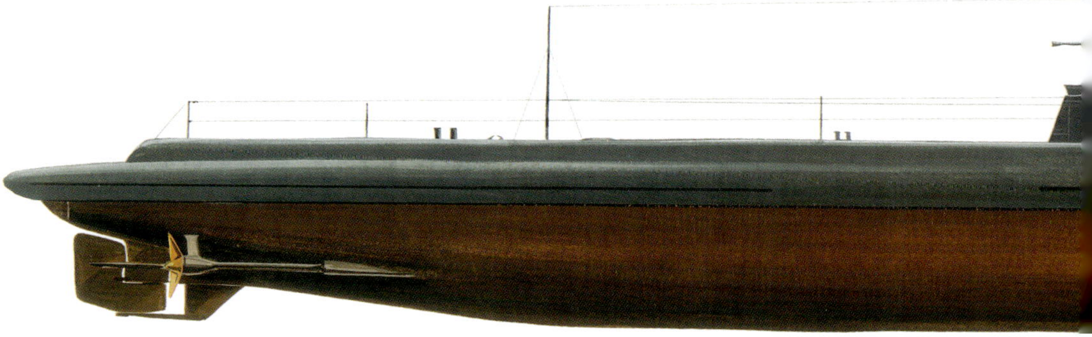

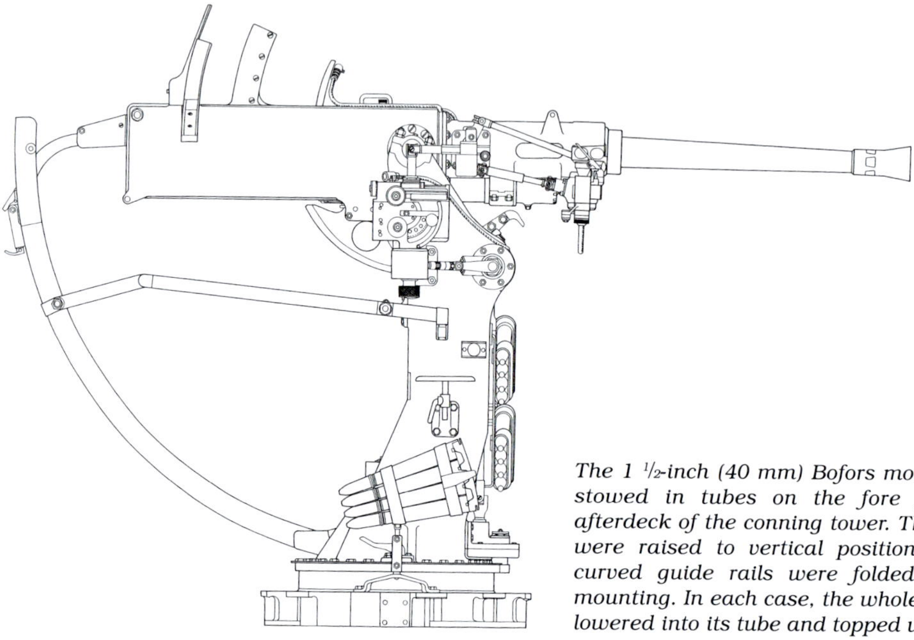

The 1 ½-inch (40 mm) Bofors mounts were stowed in tubes on the fore part and afterdeck of the conning tower. The barrels were raised to vertical position and the curved guide rails were folded into the mounting. In each case, the whole unit was lowered into its tube and topped with a lid.

(450 mm) torpedo tubes, a second group of three in 1934-35 as the Delfinen class, and a third group in 1942 as the Neptun class.

Sweden's second class of patrol submarines after World War I was the three-strong Draken class, launched in 1926-30. The largest submarines constructed in Sweden up to that time, with a displacement of 850 tons submerged, the boats were armed with four 21-inch (533 mm) bow tubes and one 4-inch (105 mm) gun. These were the only Swedish boats ever fitted with a large-caliber deck gun.

During the middle of the 1930s, the Swedish navy saw that another large war was probably inevitable. Responding to the need for ensuring neutrality though armed strength, it switched from ordering a class of three boats every five years to contracting for the nine-strong Sjölejonet. These were small boats intended for coastal operations in the Swedish archipelago. The boats were the *Sjölejonet*, *Sjöbjörnen*, *Sjöhunden*, *Svärdfisken*, *Tumlaren*, *Dykaren*, *Sjöhasten*, *Sjöormen*, and *Sjöborren*, all conventional except for the unusual arrangement of the tubes: three in the bow, one in the stern, and two in a traversing, remotely controlled mounting in the upper casing.

Commissioned between 1938 and 1942, the boats served for more than 20 years. The *Sjöborren* was in collision with another vessel and sank on September 4, 1942, but was raised, repaired and brought back into service. The boats were refitted in the 1950s and were deleted in 1959-1964.

Sjölejonet class

Type:	patrol submarine
Tonnage:	580 tons surfaced and 760 tons submerged
Dimensions:	length 210 ft., 8 in. (64.2 m); beam 21 ft. (6.4 m); draft 11 ft., 2 in. (3.4 m)
Propulsion:	two MAN diesel engines delivering 2,100 hp (1566 kW) for 16.2 knots surfaced and two electric motors delivering 1,000 hp (746 kW) for 10 knots submerged
Armament:	two 1 ½-inch (40 mm) Bofors AA guns and six 21-inch (533 mm) torpedo tubes
Complement:	38

B class (1915)

The first submarine of the Royal Danish navy was the *Dykkeren*, built by Fiat-San Giorgio of La Spezia in Italy and accepted by the Danish navy in October 1909. With a submerged displacement of 132 tons, length of 113 ft., 10 in. (34.7 m), armament of two 18-inch (457 mm) torpedo tubes and complement of nine, the boat was problematical from the start and suffered so many teething problems that it was taken in hand by the Copenhagen Naval Dockyard for the implementation of a number of largely successful fixes. The boat was lost in October 1916 after colliding with a Norwegian freighter, salvaged but then stricken in June 1917, and broken up in the following year.

Next in Danish service came six boats of the Havmanden or, later, the A class. The lead boat and two others were built at Fiume in Austria-Hungary (now Rijeka, Croatia) by Whitehead, and the other three were built in Denmark by the Copenhagen Naval Dockyard. The boats were launched between December 1911 and February 1914, and proved generally successful. The characteristics of the class included displacements of 164 tons surfaced and 204 tons submerged, length of 127 ft., 8 in. (38.9 m), propulsion by one Fiat or MAN diesel engine for 450 hp (335.5 kW) for 13 knots surfaced and two electric motors delivering 275 hp (205 kW) for 10 knots submerged, armament of two 18-inch (457 mm) bow tubes, and complement of 10 later increased to 14. The boats all survived to be stricken between 1928 and 1932, one of the boats first being used as a target.

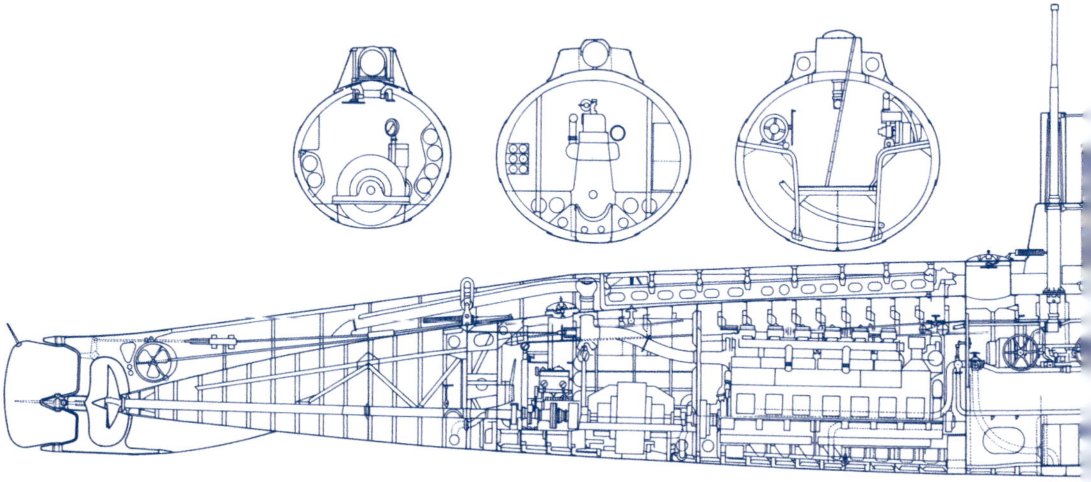

Soon after the advent of the first Havmanden boats, the Danish navy decided to move very slightly up the displacement ladder with its next class, the Ægir or B class, of which five examples were ordered from the Copenhagen Naval Dockyard. These boats were the *Ægir*, *Ran*, *Triton*, *Neptun*, and *Galathea*, which were launched between December 1914 and April 1916. A sixth boat was ordered after the loss of the *Dykkeren*, but although material was gathered for the boat it was in fact never laid down. The Ægir-class submarines had one stern tube as well as two bow tubes, and from 1917 carried a 57 mm deck gun for anti-aircraft purposes.

All of the boats survived into the 1930s, and while the *Ægir* and *Neptun* were stricken in April 1933, the other three units remained operational up to the time Denmark was overrun by the Germans in April 1940, and were then discarded, lying derelict until scrapped in 1946.

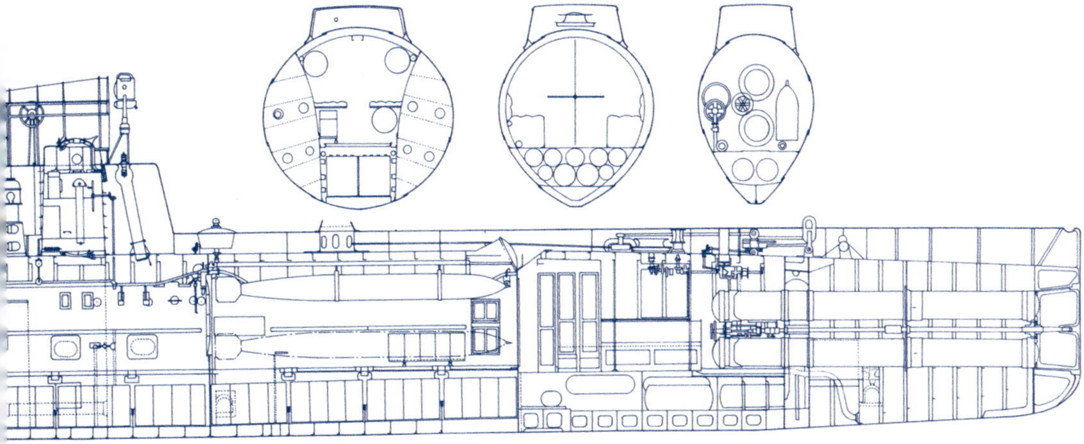

Ægir class

Type:	patrol submarine
Tonnage:	185 tons surfaced and 235 tons submerged
Dimensions:	length 133 ft., 2 in. (40.6 m); beam 12 ft., 2 in. (3.7 m); draft 7 ft., 11 in. (2.4 m)
Propulsion:	two Burmeister & Wain diesel engines delivering 450 hp (335.5 kW) for 13.5 knots surfaced and two electric motors delivering 340 hp (253.5 kW) for 9.8 knots submerged
Armament:	one 2 1/4-inch (57 mm) gun and three 18-inch (457 mm) tubes
Complement:	11 (later 14)

Orzeł class (1938)

Poland gained its independence from Russia only after World War I, and during the 1920s faced the very real possibility of Soviet aggression, a threat that survived into the 1930s and was then joined by the increasingly threatening stance of Germany as it rearmed under Nazi leadership. The Polish navy felt that the best way to secure Poland's Baltic Sea coast was by laying mines,

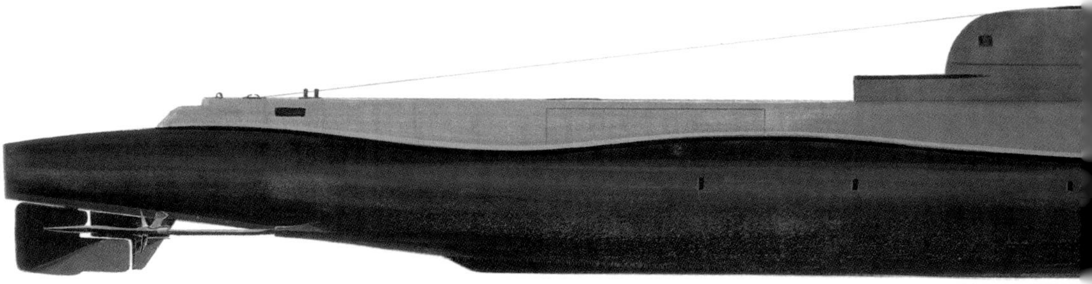

and to this end it ordered the three units of the Wilk-class coastal minelayer submarine from French yards in 1926. The boats proved technically successful although noisy, and with a submerged displacement of 1,250 tons carried 40 mines as well six 22-inch (550 mm) torpedoes for the six tubes (four fixed in the bow and two trainable on the pressure hull.

In the mid-1930s, the Polish navy decided to augment its submarine capability with a class of four patrol boats. The service's initial thinking was to order the boats from British yards, but all of the tenders received from such yards demanded a price which was too high. At the same time, the Admiralty claimed that the construction of a submarine possessing a surfaced speed in excess of 20 knots was technically impossible by the standards of the day.

The Polish navy therefore turned to the Netherlands, where it received a more encouraging response, and the design of the Orzeł class ocean-going submarine with mine-laying capability was modeled on that of the Royal Dutch navy's O-19 class.

Although it had originally been planned as a four-strong class, the Orzeł class was ordered to the extent of just two boats on January 29, 1935, the lead boat being funded by public subscription. The *Orzeł* ("eagle") was built by the de Schelde yard of Vlissingen and launched in January 1938, while the *Sep* ("vulture") was built by the Rotterdam Dockyard and launched in October of the same year. These large boats proved themselves to be excellent boats with good fighting qualities. The boats were of the double-hull type, the pressure hull was divided into five watertight compartments, the depth limit was 260 feet (80 m), and the ranges were 8,060 miles (12970 m) at 10 knots surfaced and 115 miles (185 km) at 5 knots submerged.

The *Orzeł* was commissioned in February 1939 and reached Gdynia two months later before the builder's trials had been concluded to avoid the possibility of German sabotage. The *Sep* was interned at Stavnas in Sweden in September 1939, 17 days after the German invasion of Poland. Two days earlier, the *Orzeł* had put in at Tallinn in Estonia as a result of mechanical problems and, in a manner contrary to international law but probably in response to German pressure, was interned on the same day. Despite the fact that the boat's charts, navigation equipment and part of the armament had been removed, the submarine escaped from Tallinn, avoiding an Estonian gunboat, three days later. The boat reached Rosyth, Scotland, on October 14, 1939. The boat was lost, probably to a mine in the North Sea on June 8, 1940. The *Sep* was returned to Poland in October 1945, and was discarded in 1970.

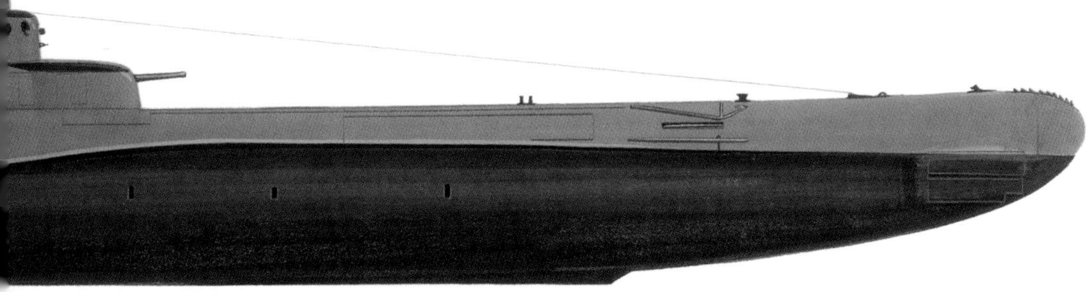

Orzeł class

Type:	patrol submarine
Tonnage:	1,100 tons surfaced and 1,650 tons submerged
Dimensions:	length 275 ft., 7 in. (84 m); beam 22 ft. (6.7 m); draft 13 ft., 8 in. (4.2 m)
Propulsion:	two Sulzer diesel engines delivering 4,740 hp (3535 kW) for 20 knots surfaced and two Brown-Boveri electric motors delivering 1,100 hp (820 kW) for 9 knots submerged
Armament:	one 4-inch (105 mm) gun, two 1 ½-inch (40 mm) guns and 20 22-inch (550 mm) tubes with 20 torpedoes
Complement:	60

Acciaio class (1941)

The Italian navy was very enthusiastic about the submarine, and from the late 1920s ordered large number of small submarines of the so-called Bernardis 600-ton type, which were cheap enough to be built in useful numbers. The first four types were the seven Argonauta-class boats of 1929, 12 Sirena-class boats of 1931, 10 Perla-class boats of 1935, and 17 Adua-class boats of 1936. The last iteration of the basic concept was found in the 13 Acciaio-class boats, namely the *Acciaio*, *Alabastro*, *Argento*, *Asteria*, *Avorio*, *Bronzo*, *Cobalto*, *Giada*, *Granito*, *Nichelio*, *Platino*, *Porfido*, and *Volframio*. The boats were laid down in 1940-41 by three yards and completed in 1941-42. The design was that of the Adua class, with a smaller conning tower to trim the visual silhouette, and more powerful diesel engines. The three Tosi-built boats had more powerful diesels than the other 10 submarines, although this meant the loss of the two stern tubes, for a designed speed of 14.7 knots on the surface, and had different electric motors. As completed the boats achieved 15 knots or more on the surface, but their sub-

merged speed was below that estimated.

Of the boats, the *Acciaio*, *Granito*, and *Porfido* were torpedoed by British submarines. The *Argento*, *Asteria*, and *Avorio* were scuttled to avoid capture after being damaged by surface ships. The *Alabastro* was sunk by aircraft, the *Cobalto* was rammed and sunk, and the *Bronzo* was captured and was placed in British service as the *P 714* before being transferred in 1944 to the Free French navy as the Narval. The *Volframio* was scuttled at La Spezia on September 8, 1943, salvaged by the Germans, and finally sunk in an Allied air raid. The *Nichelio* was transferred to the USSR as war reparations in 1949. The *Giada* remained with the Italian navy to become the battery-charger *PV2* in 1948-50 before being reinstated on the list as a training vessel after being rebuilt 1951-53. The boat was discarded in 1966.

Acciaio class

Type:	patrol submarine
Tonnage:	697 tons surfaced and 850 tons submerged
Dimensions:	length 197 ft., 6 in. (60.2 m); beam 21 ft., 2 in. (6.45 m); draft 15 ft., 8 in. (4.8 m)
Propulsion:	two Fiat diesel engines delivering 1,400 hp (1044 kW) for 14 knots surfaced and two CRDA electric motors delivering 800 hp (596 kW) for 7.7 knots submerged
Armament:	one 4-inch (100 mm) gun or two 20 mm cannon and six (four bow and two stern) or four 21-inch (533 mm) tubes
Complement:	45

Saphir class (1928)

After the authorization of the first ocean-going patrol submarines of the Redoutable class, which eventually numbered 31 boats in three generally successful groups, the French navy decided to introduce a new type of double-hulled mine-laying submarine of moderate displacement. This was the in the well-proved Normand-Fenaux system of external mine tubes, which was simple and safe, but in most other respects the Saphir-class boats were not in any way outstanding, although it should be recorded that the *Rubis* was the most successful mine-laying boat of World War I.

The maximum operational depth of the boats was 245 feet (75 m), with ranges of 10,605 miles (17065 km) at 7.5 knots surfaced and 90 miles (145 km) at 4 knots submerged. The torpedo armament comprised two 22-inch (550 mm) bow tubes for four torpedoes, and an external arrangement of one 22-inch (550 mm) and two 16-inch (400 mm) tubes aft.

The boats were launched only between December 1928 and July 1935 for completion from the early 1930s, and were thus still

Saphir class, whose first two units were the *Saphir* and *Turquoise* authorized in 1925. Another four boats were authorized singly as the *Nautilus*, *Rubis*, *Diamant*, and *Perle* in the years between 1926 and 1929, and all six of the boats were built by the Arsenal de Toulon in the south of France.

The design of the class was centered on the carriage of up to 32 mines comparatively new at the start of World War II in 1939. The first three were seized by Axis forces at Bizerta in North Africa on December 8, 1942; the first pair was taken over by the Italians as the *FR112* and *FR116*, but all three were scuttled or sunk as the allies closed on Bizerta during 1943. The *Diamant* was raised after being scuttled on November 27, 1942, but the hulk was bombed in 1944. The *Perle* was mistakenly bombed and sunk by British aircraft on July 8, 1944.

The *Rubis* was the most successful of the boats. During the Norwegian campaign, in May 1940, it laid mines off the Norwegian coast, which claimed four Norwegian vessels in May and June, and a further three merchantmen in July. At the time of the French surrender on June 25, 1940, the boat was in a British port and her crew swiftly joined the Free French forces.

While mine-laying off Norway in mid-1941, the *Rubis* met and torpedoed a Finnish merchantman. Later in the war, it laid mines in the Bay of Biscay, claiming three German auxiliary minesweepers, an armed trawler, and a French tug during 1942, and a fourth auxiliary minesweeper in 1943. Operating off the Norwegian coast near Stavanger in September 1944, its mines claimed two auxiliary submarine chasers and two merchantmen. In October and November, it continued in Norwegian waters, damaging two vessels but without any sinkings. On December 21, however, her mines claimed three auxiliary submarine chasers, a German merchantman, and a minesweeper.

Throughout the war, the boat made 22 operational patrols, laying nearly 700 mines and sinking some 21,000 tons of shipping. The submarine was taken out of service in April 1949, but was still in use as a sonar target at Toulon in 1957.

Saphir class

Type:	mine-laying submarine
Tonnage:	761 tons surfaced and 925 tons submerged
Dimensions:	length 216 ft., 2 in. (65.9 m); beam 23 ft., 7 in. (7.2 m); draft 14 ft., 1 in. (4.3 m)
Propulsion:	two Normand-Vickers diesel engines delivering 1,300 hp (969 kW) for 12 knots surfaced and two electric motors delivering 1,000 hp (746 kW) for 9 knots submerged
Armament:	one 3-inch (75 mm) gun, three 22-inch (550 mm) and two 15 ¾-inch (400 mm) torpedo tubes, and 32 mines
Complement:	42

Kalev class (1936)

Estonia had secured its independence from German and later from Soviet rule in 1920 with considerable aid from the British, who had captured two Soviet destroyers and presented them to the new country's fledgling navy. These were retired in 1933 and sold to Peru, and the Estonian navy then decided to base its contribution to the national defense capability largely on mine-laying submarines, as had been pioneered by Latvia, its southern counterpart on the eastern side of the Baltic Sea. Facing basically the same threat as Estonia and in similar geographical conditions, Latvia had ordered two boats from France, but, given the circumstances, it was natural for Estonia to turn to the UK for the design and construction of the two boats it desired.

The desire of both Estonia and Latvia to procure submarines with mine-laying capability was probably the result of the success with mines in Baltic operations during World War I and in the later Allied operations against the Soviets.

Estonia's order was placed with the British firm of Vickers-Armstrong, which based the design on that of the Parthian-class boats used by the Royal Navy, albeit on a reduced scale with a submerged displacement of 850 tons rather than the British boats' 2,040 tons. As in the Royal Navy's E-class and L-class minelayers of World War I, the mine chutes were located vertically in the saddle tanks, five on each side abreast the conning tower. Each tube carried two mines. The torpedo armament was based on four bow tubes, and there was no large-caliber deck gun, the Estonians preferring two different calibers of anti-aircraft gun.

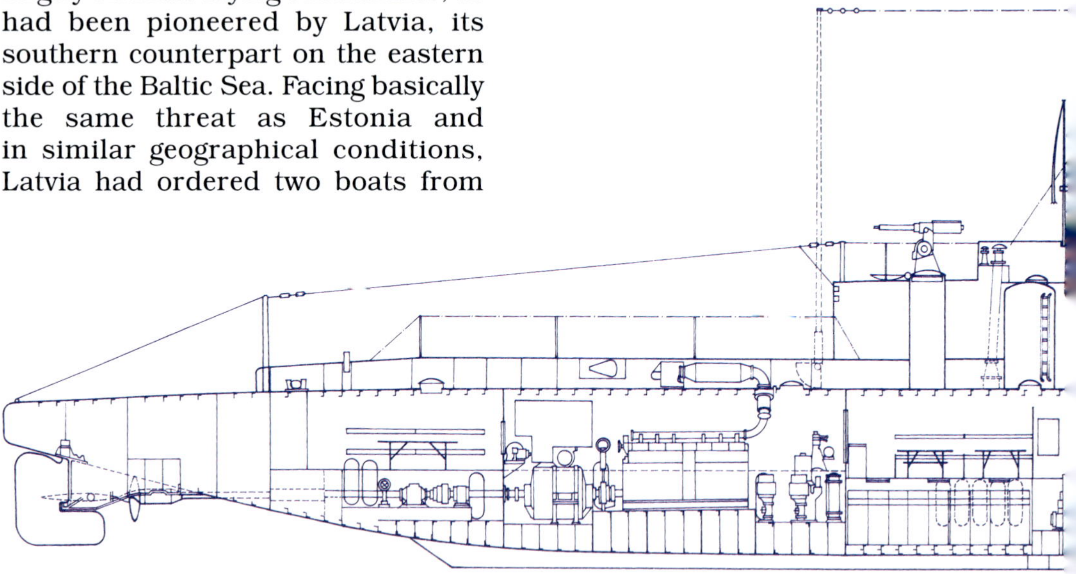

Built in Barrow-in-Furness for launch in 1937 and 1936, respectively, the two boats were the *Kalev* and *Lembit*. Both of the boats were commissioned in 1937, but enjoyed only a short period of service in Estonian colors before Estonia was compelled to accede to Soviet rule.

On August 6, 1940, the Estonian navy was absorbed into the Soviet navy, but the two boats retained their original names under the new colors.

Perhaps ironically, the *Kalev* was mined and sunk off Hangö, the southwesternmost tip of Finland, while operating as a transport submarine. The *Lembit* seems to have been used in her intended role as a mine-layer, and survived the war. In 1945 her name was changed to *U-1*, and in 1949 to *S-85*. The boat was then allocated to a Soviet naval shipyard and there used for a number of experimental purposes from 1956 into a time early in the 1970s. The boat was stricken in 1979 and moved to Tallinn, where it was preserved as a memorial.

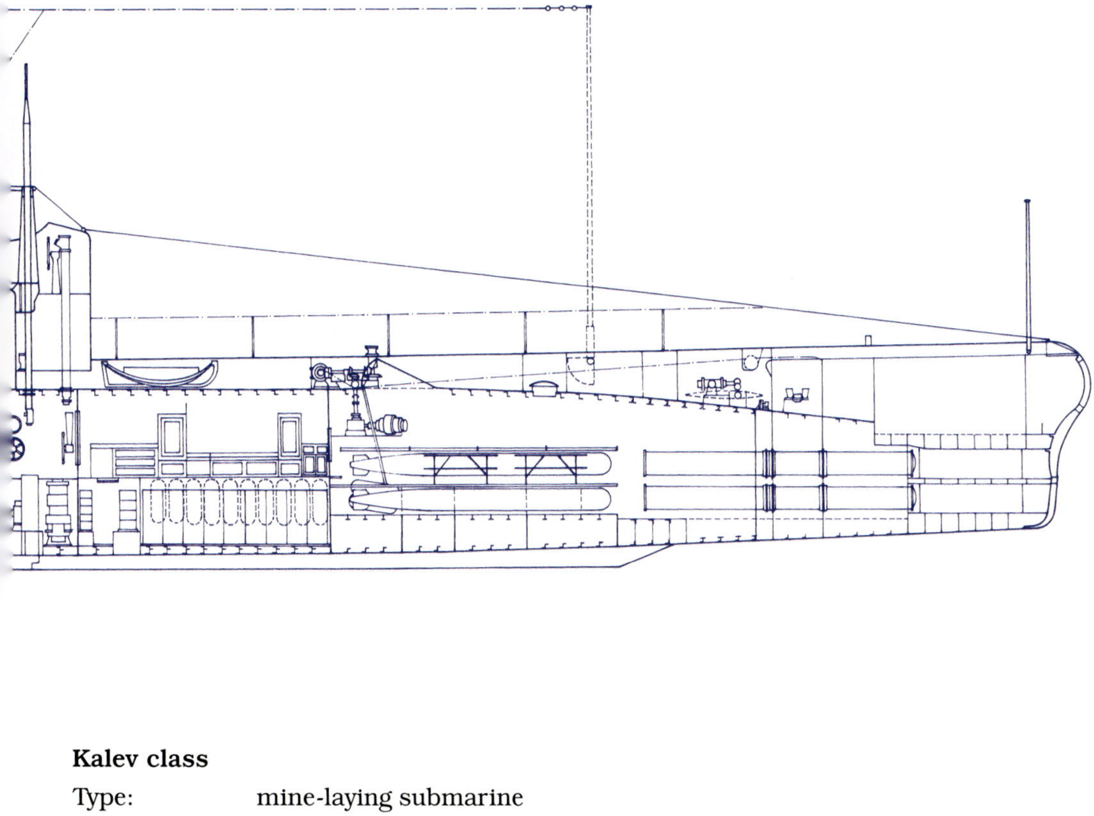

Kalev class

Type:	mine-laying submarine
Tonnage:	620 tons surfaced and 850 tons submerged
Dimensions:	length 190 ft., 3 in. (58 m); beam 23 ft., 11 in. (7.3 m); draft 10 ft., 10 in. (3.3 m)
Propulsion:	two Vickers diesel engines delivering 1,200 hp (895 kW) for 13.5 knots surfaced and two electric motors delivering 790 hp (589 kW) for 8.5 knots submerged
Armament:	one 1 ¾-inch (45 mm) and one 20 mm gun, four 21-inch (533 mm) tubes, and 20 mines
Complement:	38

ShCh class (1939)

The ShCh class of medium-sized patrol submarines comprised six series (or groups) of boats authorized from 1930: four Series III, 19 Series V, 12 Series V-bis, nine Series V-bis2, 33 Series X and 20 Series X-bis boats.

The first submarine design to be originated wholly in the USSR, the ShCh class had been created during the late 1920s and boats of this basic type remained in production from 1930 until the end of World War II. The design faults evident in the initial Series III boats were steadily eliminated in later series, which were therefore built in larger numbers. The boat was of the saddle-tank type, and the outer hull extended along some two-thirds of the boat's overall length. The maximum diving depth was 295 feet (90 m), and the pressure hull was subdivided into seven (six in the Series III) watertight compartments. The range for each type was Series III 6,900 miles (11105 km) at 8 knots surfaced and 140 miles (225 km) at 1.75 knots submerged, Series V 6,620 miles (10655 km) at 8.5 knots and 145 miles (235 km) at 2 knots, Series V-bis 10,710 miles (17235 km) at 8.5 knots and 145 miles (235 km) at 2 knots, Series V-bis2 8,235 miles (13255 km) at 8.5 knots and 125 miles (200 km) at 2 knots, Series X 7,485 miles (12045 km) at 8 knots and 125 miles (200 km) at 2.5 knots, and Series X-bis 4,205 miles (6765 km) at 8 knots and 140 miles (225 km) at unspecified speed.

The Series III boats were built by the Ordzhonikidze Yard, and three were lost to mines in World War II. Twelve, three and four Series V units were built by the Dalzavod, Marti, and Ordzhonikidze yards, respectively. All of the Dalzavod boats survived the war and were broken up in 1958; the first and second Marti boats were sunk in the war and the last was broken up in 1958; and first and last of the Ordzhonikidze boats were lost in the war and the other two discarded in the 1950s.

The Series V-bis boats were built by Dalzavod and Marti to the extent of nine and three boats, respectively, only the last of them being lost in the war, another being lost in the mid-1950s, and the rest being discarded during the 1950s. Of the Series v-bis2 boats, four, three, and two were built by Dalzavod, Marti, and the 61 Kommunar yards, respectively. Three of the boats were lost in World War II, and the others were discarded in the 1950s.

The Series X and Series X-bis submarines were generally similar to the earlier ShCh-class boats, but especial care was taken in their construction to reduce their levels of underwater noise, and the opportunity was taken in the Series X-bis final group to exploit the capabilities offered by the improved technology now available to reduce the building time required for each boat.

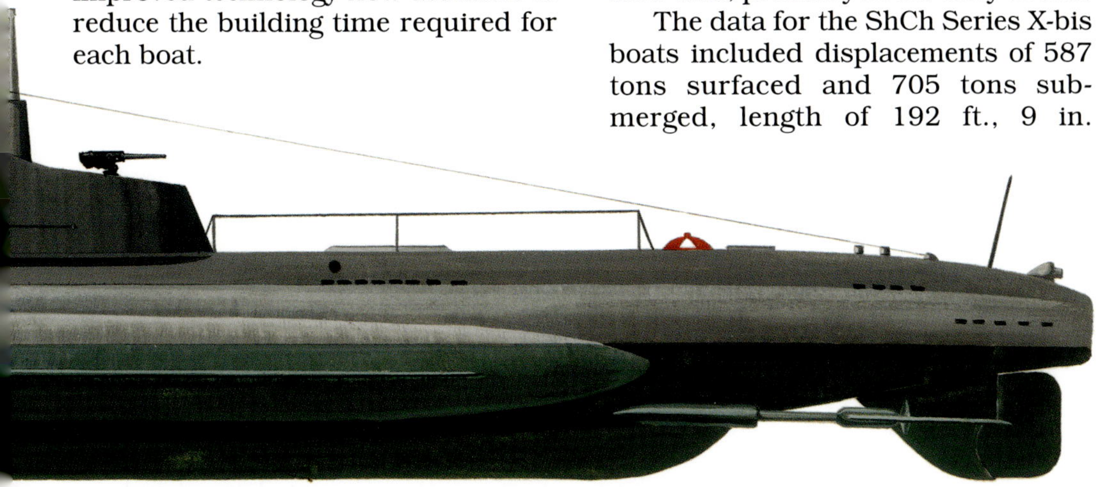

Of the Series X boats, five, sixteen, six, four, and two were built by Dalzavod, Marti at Leningrad and Nikolayev, Ordzhonikidze, 61 Kommunar, and Zhdanov yards, respectively. Some 13 of the boats were lost in World War II, two of them to mines, and the surviving boats were discarded during the 1950s. Finally, of the Series X-bis boats, four, one, and 15 were built by the Dalzavod, 61 Kommunar, and Marti yards (the last only at Leningrad). Four or possibly five of the boats were lost during the war, and of the surviving units two were broken up in the later 1940s, one was broken up in the 1950s, another discarded during the same decade, and the last of the submarines were discarded at a later date, probably in the early 1960s.

The data for the ShCh Series X-bis boats included displacements of 587 tons surfaced and 705 tons submerged, length of 192 ft., 9 in. (58.75 m), propulsion by two diesels and two electric motors delivering 1,600 and 800 hp (1193 and 596.5 kW) for speeds of 13.6 knots surfaced and 8 knots submerged, armament of two 1 ¾ inch (45 mm) guns and six 21-inch (533 mm) tubes (four bow and two stern) for 10 torpedoes, and complement of 39.

ShCh (Series V-bis) class

Type:	patrol submarine
Tonnage:	607 tons surfaced and 749 tons submerged
Dimensions:	length 192 ft., 9 in. (58.75 m); beam 20 ft., 4 in. (6.2 m); draft 14 ft., 1 in. (4.3 m)
Propulsion:	two diesel engines delivering 1,370 hp (1021.5 kW) for 12 knots surfaced and two electric motors delivering 800 hp (596.5 kW) for 7.5 knots submerged
Armament:	two 1 ¾-inch (45 mm) gun and six tubes for 10 torpedoes
Complement:	40

Redoutable class (1935)

Classified by the French navy as ocean-going submarines, the Redoutable class represented a major advance in capability over the smaller Requin class it succeeded. With a submerged displacement of 1,441 tons and length of 256 ft., 8 in. (78.25 m), these boats had been authorized in1922, and were the first ocean-going French boats designed after World War I.

The first two Redoutable class boats were authorized in 1924, with seven more in 1925 and five each in 1926 and 1927 to complete the first group's 19 boats (*Redoutable*, *Vengeur*, *Archimède*, *Fresnel*, *Henri Poincaré*, *Monge*, *Pascal*, *Pasteur*, *Poncelet*, *Achille*, *Ajax*, *Actéon*, *Achéron*, *Argo*, *Protée*, *Pégase*, *Persée*, *Phénix*, and *Promethée*). An improved second group (*L'Espoire*, *Le Glorieux*, *Le Centaure*, *Le Héros*, *Le Conquerant*, and *Le Tonnant*) was authorized in 1928/29, and the definitive third group (*Agosta*, *Sfax*, *Casabianca*, *Bévèziers*, *Ouessant*, and *Sidi Ferruch*) in 1930.

Of double-hull construction and possessing a diving depth of 245 feet (75 m), the Redoutable-class boats were excellent sea boats with the high surfaced speed required for long transits to and from their patrol areas. The poorest feature of the design was the diving time of 45 to 50 seconds. The class was deemed very successful, and the power of the diesel engines, and thus the surfaced speed, was increased from 6,000 hp (4474 kW) and 17 knots in the first group to 7,200 hp (5368 kW) and 19 knots in the second group and still more in the third group.

After 1941, the range could be increased by using some of the ballast tanks for fuel. As in earlier French boats, the torpedo armament included external and internal tubes. The former comprised two 22-inch (550 mm) and two 16-inch (400 mm) tubes in a single quadruple mounting aft (replaced in some boats during 1942 by three 22-inch/550 mm tubes) and a triple 22-inch (550 mm) mount abaft the conning tower; none of these tubes had reloads. The internal tubes were four 22-inch (550 mm) units in the bow with six torpedoes. The anti-aircraft armament of the surviving boats was increased after 1942.

The *Redoutable*, *Vengeur*, *Fresnel*, *Henri Poincaré*, *Pascal*, *Acheron*, and *L'Espoire* were scuttled at Toulon in November 1942, although some were raised but sunk later by Allied bombing. The *Pasteur*, *Achille*, *Agosta*, and *Ouessant* were scuttled at Brest. The *Monge*, *Poncelet*, *Ajax*, *Actéon*, *Persée*, *Le Heros*, *Le Conquerant*, *Le Tonnant*, *Bévèziers*, and *Sidi Ferruch* were lost during Allied attacks on French colonial possessions. The *Protée* was probably depth-charged by German patrol vessels; the *Pégase* was paid off at Saigon in September 1941 and later broken up there; and the *Sfax* was torpedoed by mistake by the *U-37* after the surrender of France.

French sailors working on torpedo tubes.

Redoutable class

Type:	patrol submarine
Tonnage:	1,570 tons surfaced and 2,084 tons submerged
Dimensions:	length 301 ft., 10 in. (92.3 m); beam 26 ft., 11 in. (8.2 m); draft 15 ft., 5 in. (4.7 m)
Propulsion:	two Sulzer or Schneider diesel engines delivering 8,000 hp (5965 kW) for 20 knots surfaced and two electric motors delivering 2,000 hp (1491 kW) for 10 knots submerged
Armament:	one 4-inch (100 mm) gun, nine 21 3/4 -inch (550 mm) tubes and two 15 3/4-inch (400 m) tubes
Complement:	61

B class (1940)

The Royal Norwegian navy moved into the submarine era in the first decade of the twentieth century with an order for one boat, similar to the Imperial German navy's *U-1*, placed with Germaniawerft. The *Kobben* (from 1913 *A 1*) was launched in May 1909 and entered service with a submerged displacement of 259 tons, length of 128 ft., 11 in. (39.3), speeds of 11.9 knots surfaced and 9.8 knots submerged, and armament of three 18-inch (457 mm) tubes located as one in the stern and two in the bow. The boat was sold in 1933. Norway's next three boats, out of an order for four, were also built by Germaniawerft in the period before World War I and, all launched in 1913, were the larger *A 2*, *A 3* and *A 4* with a submerged displacement of 355 tons, length of 152 ft., 7 in. (46.5 m), speeds of 14,5 knots surfaced and 9 knots submerged, and the same tube disposition as the *A 1* but with five rather than four torpedoes. The incomplete *A 5* was impressed for German service as the *UA* after the outbreak of World War I. The A 2 was broken up in 1940, and the other two Norwegian boats were scuttled on April 16, 1940, shortly after the German invasion of Norway in World War II.

Norway was neutral in World War I, and despite deciding before the outbreak of the war in 1914 to supple-

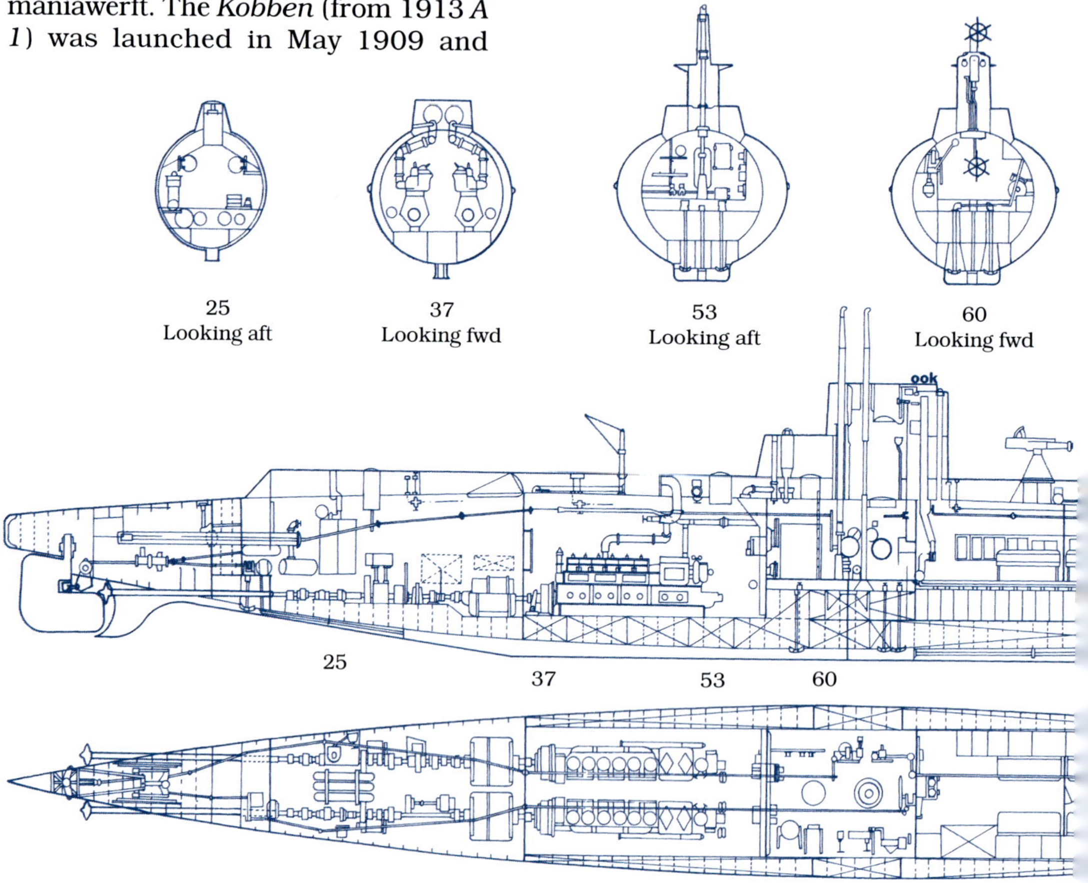

ment its planned five German-built small coastal submarines with a class of six slightly larger boats to a design by an American company, Electric Boat (Holland), it moved forward with construction only during and after the end of World War I. All of the boats were built under license to the Horten Naval Dockyard. The boats were laid down between 1915 and 1926, launched between 1922 and 1929, and completed between 1923 and 1930. The range of the boats was 3,340 miles (5375 km) at 9 knots surfaced and 175 miles (280 km) at 3 knots submerged, and their four torpedo tubes were all grouped in the bow.

All six of the boats were operational at the beginning of the war. The *B 1* was able to escape to the UK on June 8, 1940, joining the 7th Submarine Flotilla as a sonar training and target boat until discarded in April 1944 and breaking up in 1946. The *B 2* was captured by the Germans at Fiskå on April 11, 1940, but not used. The *B 3* was scuttled in Alsvåg, Vesterålen, on June 10, 1940, by its own crew to prevent its seizure by the Germans. The crew originally wanted to reach the UK but was prevented by a battery explosion. The *B 4* was captured by the Germans at Filtvet on April 10 but not used. The *B 5* was captured by the Germans at Fiskå on April 11, 1940, and the *B 6* was surrendered to the Germans on May 18, 1950, under threat that the town of Florø would otherwise be bombed. The *B 5* and *B 6* were taken into German service as the *UC-1* and *UC-2*, and were stricken in 1942 and 1944, respectively.

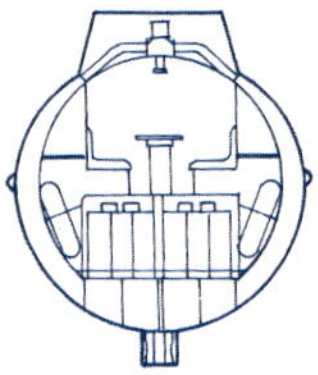

75
Looking aft

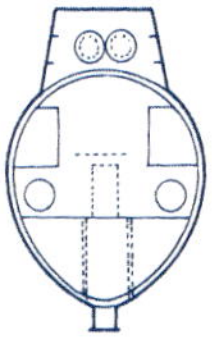

90
Looking fwd

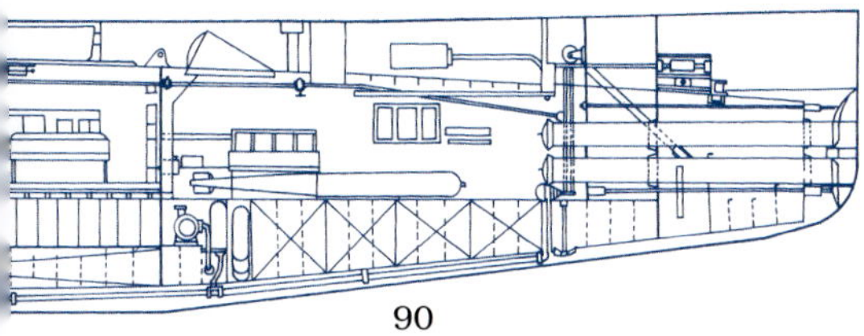

90

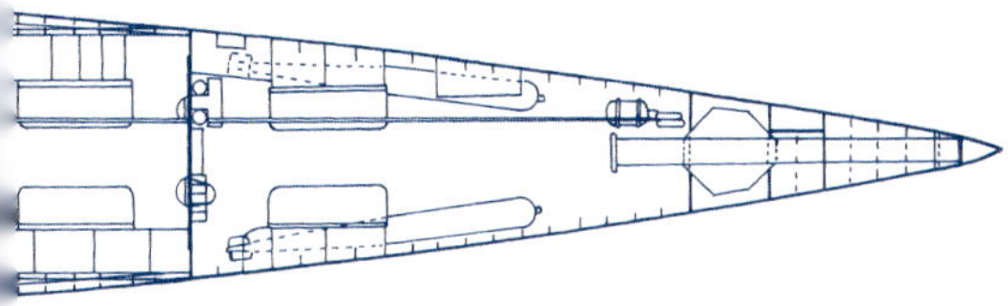

B class

Type:	patrol submarine
Tonnage:	365 tons surfaced and 545 tons submerged
Dimensions:	length 167 ft., 4 in. (51 m); beam 17 ft., 6 in. (5.33 m); draft 11 ft., 6 in. (3.5 m)
Propulsion:	two Sulzer diesel engines delivering 900 hp (671 kW) for 14 knots surfaced and two electric motors delivering 700 hp (522 kW) for 11 knots submerged
Armament:	one 3-inch (76 mm) gun and four 18-inch (457 mm) tubes
Complement:	23

K class (1938)

Otherwise known as Series XIV boats, the submarines of the K class were the largest underwater vessels ordered for the Soviet navy before the period following the end of World War II in 1945. The first nine of these large oceangoing submarines were authorized under the second five-year program (1933-38) and the last three under the third five-year program (1939-44). The first three and last three were built by the Marti Yard in Leningrad, and the middle six by the Ordzhonikidze Yard, also in Leningrad, and were intended for service with the Northern Fleet operating from bases along the USSR's Arctic coast.

Laid down 1936-38 and completed in 1939-45, the K-class submarines were the best as well as the largest of the USSR's boats of World War II. Created specifically for operations in the cold of the far north, the design was drafted from 1934, and to ensure that the limitations characteristic of the three boats of the preceding Pravda or Series IV class, which were poor sea boats and suffered from the effects of instability, poor diving time, and short range. A major experimental program was undertaken with the *Forel*, a Bars submarine that had been launched in 1916. It was originally intended that the K boats would each carry one example of the small SPL floatplane, which would be carried in dismantled form in a special watertight hangar and assembled only for scouting flights, but the idea was soon dropped.

The K-class design was based on the double-hull concept with the interior divided into seven watertight compartments. The diving depth was 230 feet (70 m), the diving time 50 seconds, and the ranges were 16,120 miles (25940 km) at

9 knots surfaced on the 250 tons of diesel fuel carried, and 185 miles (300 km) at 2.9 knots submerged using current from the four 60-cell batteries. A total of 24 torpedoes was carried for the ten 21-inch (533 mm tubes), which were installed as six fixed in the bow, two fixed in the stern, and two trainable on the pressure hull. There was also provision for the carriage and laying of up to 20 Type EM mines in the middle ballast tank. A surfaced speed of 22.5 knots had been demanded in the original requirement, but it was very unusual for the boats to achieve this in practice.

The *K 1* and *K 2* were transferred to the Northern Fleet in 1940. The boats traveled from the Baltic Sea near Leningrad to the White Sea via the Belomorsko-Baltiyskiy Kanal imeni

Stalina (Stalin White Sea-Baltic Sea Canal), which had been opened on August 2, 1933, after an appalling 20-month construction program in which it has been estimated that 100,000 gulag prisoners died, although some accounts put the figures both higher and lower. The canal runs partially along several rivers and a pair of larger bodies of water, namely Lake Onega and Lake Vygozero, and its length is 141 miles (227 km). The *K 3*, *K 21* and *K 23* followed via the same route during August 1941.

The Soviets had planned to deploy all of the K class to the Northern Fleet as they were completed, but after German and Finnish troops had managed to cut the canal link in September 1941 the other seven boats were instead allocated to the Baltic Fleet for the duration of hostilities in what the Soviets called the "Great Patriotic War."

The *K 1* was lost in the Kara Sea during October 1943, presumably as a result of striking a mine. The *K 2* failed to return from patrol off northern Norway in August and September 1942, and the *K 3* was sunk on March 21, 1943, by the *U-1102*, *U-1106* and *U-1111* off Batsfjord. The *K 21* was used in an unsuccessful attack on the German battleship *Tirpitz* during the PQ-17 operation on 5 July 1942, and survived to become a stationary training unit in 1959. The *K 22* was mined off Cape Harbaken on February 7, 1943, and the *K 23* was sunk by the *U-1101*, *U-1109* and *U-1110* off Olesafjord on May 12, 1942.

The *K 53* to *K 56* boats were accepted, though incomplete, by the Soviet navy during 1942, and had been completed and commissioned only by the end of 1945, The *K 51* to *K 56* were finally transferred to the Northern Fleet via the sea route through the Baltic, North and Norwegian Seas in August 1948, and these boats were discarded during the 1950s.

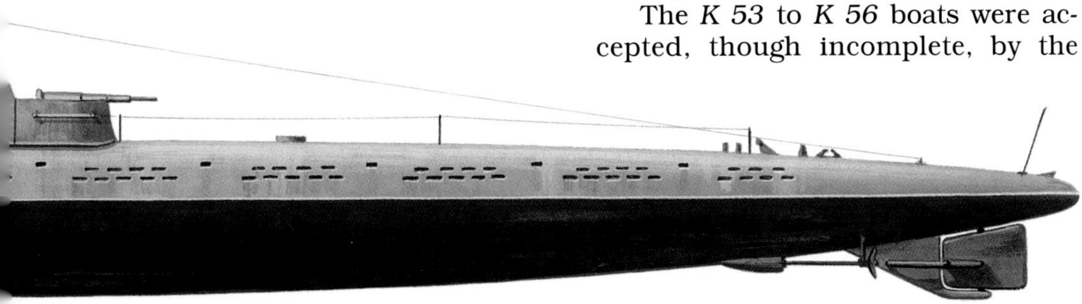

K class

Type:	patrol submarine
Tonnage:	2,104 tons surfaced and 2,600 tons submerged
Dimensions:	length 320 ft., 4 in. (97.65 m); beam 24 ft., 3 in. (7.4 m); draft 14 ft., 10 in. (4.5 m)
Propulsion:	diesel engines delivering 8,400 hp (6263 kW) for 21 knots surfaced and two electric motors delivering 2,400 hp (1789 kW) for 10 knots submerged
Armament:	two 4-inch (100 mm) and two 1 3/4-inch (45 mm) guns, 10 21-inch (533 mm) tubes, for 24 torpedoes, and 20 mines
Complement:	60

Odin class (1926)

Requiring a new class of boats to replace the submarine of the L class, of which 73 had been ordered in the later part of World War I but only 23 completed in 1917-19, the Admiralty started to plan a new type of patrol submarine in the first half of the 1920s with the range and endurance needed for operations in the Pacific Ocean. The design was of the saddle tank type, with fuel tanks of riveted construction on the outside of the pressure hull, and while the theoretical diving limit was 500 feet (150 m), no boat of this design was tested to a depth greater than 300 feet (90 m).

A prototype boat was laid down by Chatham Dockyard as the *Oberon* in 1924, launched in September 1926, and completed in 1927. The boat had a submerged displacement of 1,831 tons, length of 269 ft., 8 in. (82.2 m), speeds of 13.75 knots surfaced and 7.5 knots submerged on 2,950 hp (2200 kW) and 1,350 hp (1007 kW) respectively, and the armament was one 4-inch (102 mm) gun and 16 torpedoes launched from eight 21-inch (533 mm) tubes located as six in the bow and two in the stern. Trials revealed that considerable amounts of the 186 tons of diesel oil leaked from the riveted tanks, which were replaced by welded units, and the boat never attained its designed speeds of 15 knots surfaced and 9 knots submerged. The boat was laid up in 1944 and scrapped in the following year.

The Royal Australian Navy was sufficiently impressed with the performance

of the Oberon's design to order the *Otway* and *Oxley* from Vickers-Armstrong at Barrow-in-Furness to an improved design offering higher speeds. The boats were laid down in 1925, launched in 1926, and completed in 1927, but finding itself unable to operate the boats at a time of financial crisis in the "great depression," Australia transferred the two boats to the Royal Navy. The boats had displacements of 1,636 tons surfaced and 1,872 tons submerged, length of 275 ft. (83.8 m), speeds of 15 knots surfaced and 8.5 knots submerged on the 3,100 hp (2311 kW) provided by Vickers diesel engines and 1,350 hp (1007 kW) of the electric motors, and the same armament as the *Oberon*. The *Oxley* was accidentally torpedoed and sunk by the *Triton* on September 10, 1939, and the *Otway* was broken up in 1945.

This paved the way for the Odin class, which was in effect the *Oberon* with modifications for higher speed. The boats were the *Odin*, *Olympus*, *Orpheus*, *Osiris*, *Oswald*, and *Otus*, which were laid down in 1927, launched in 1928-29 and completed in 1929-30. Nearly all of the 174 tons of diesel fuel was in external tanks and, like the hull, these required stiffening. The torpedo tube arrangement was identical to that of the earlier boats, but the torpedo complement was 14 as to stern tube reloads were carried. Four of the boats were lost in World War II, the *Olympus* to a mine and the *Odin*, *Orpheus* and *Oswald* to Italian destroyers. The two surviving boats disappeared soon after the war's end.

Odin class

Type:	patrol submarine
Tonnage:	1,781 tons surfaced and 2,038 tons submerged
Dimensions:	length 283 ft., 6 in. (86.4m); beam 29 ft., 11 in. (9.1 m); draft 16 ft., 1 in. (4.9 m)
Propulsion:	Admiralty Standard Range diesel engines delivering 4,520 hp (3370 kW) for 17.5 knots surfaced and two electric motors delivering 1,390 hp (1036 kW) for 8 knots submerged
Armament:	one 4-inch (102 mm) gun and eight 21-inch (533 mm) tubes for 14 torpedoes
Complement:	53

Triton class (1936)

The British T (or Triton) class of patrol submarines was designed from 1934 as successor to the O, P and R classes. The design process was complicated by the terms of the London Naval Treaty of 1930, which restricted the total British submarine fleet to 52,700 tons, a maximum of 2,000 tons for any boat, and maximum armament of one 5-inch (130 mm) gun. The Repeat P design, as the new type was initially designated, was meant to yield a boat large and powerful enough to operate independently against Japanese vessels, and this demanded considerable size and great firepower, and the design ended with 10 forward-facing tubes and a maximum diving depth of 300 feet (90 m). The design was finalized in 1935, and in the middle of that year it was decided to drop the Repeat P designation and give the boats names starting with "T."

The lead boat, the *Triton*, was ordered in March 1936, launched in October 1937, and ran her trials in December 1938. Fifty-three T-class boats were built before and during World War II in three groups, with a number of small changes between the boats of any group.

The *Triton* and the other 14 pre-war boats were ordered in batches of one, four, seven and three in the programs of 1935 to 1938. The boats originally had a bulbous bow covering the two forward external torpedo tubes, the other two being amidships, but this reduced surface speed in rough weather.

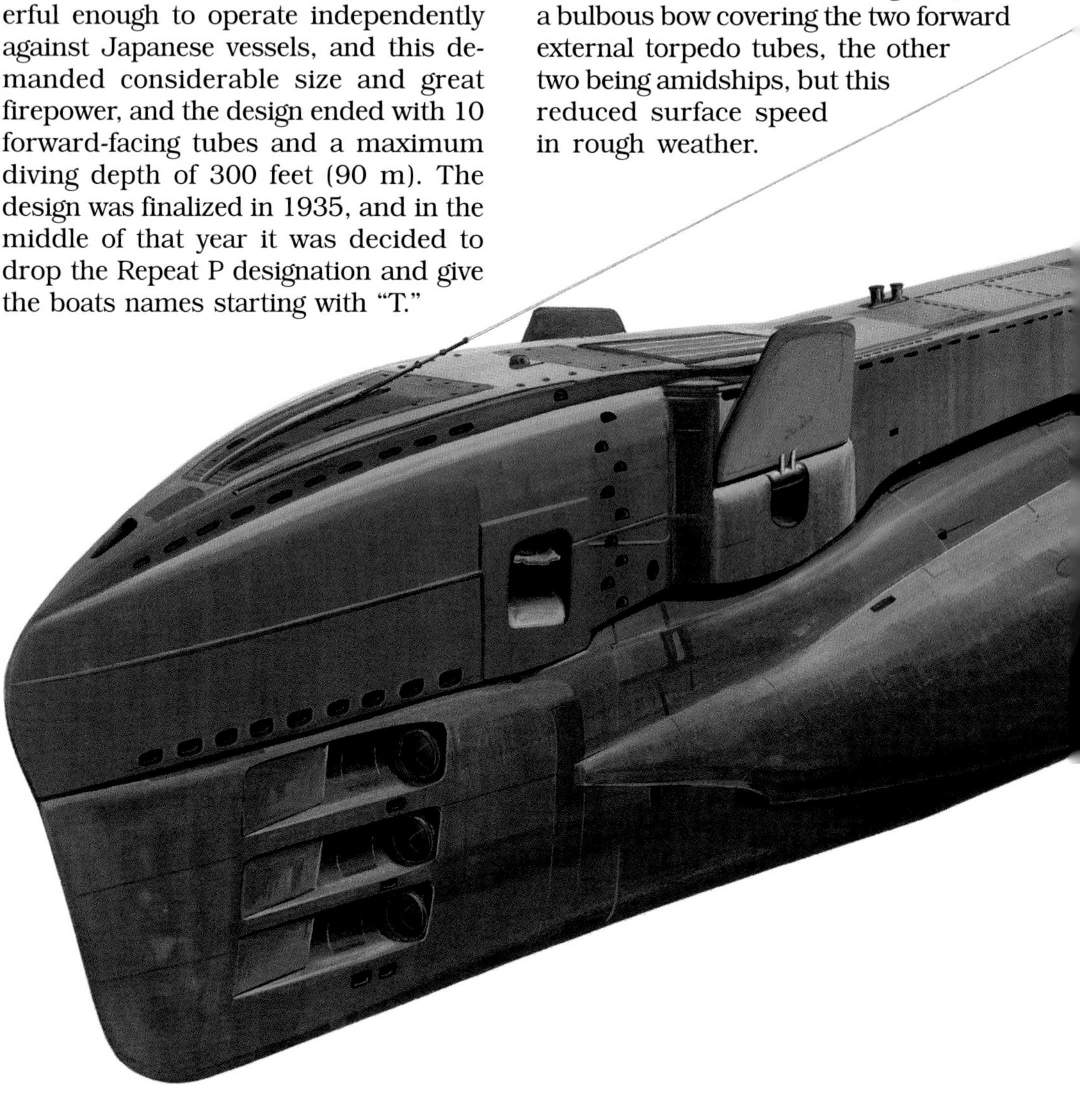

The tubes were removed from the *Triumph* during repairs after it had been damaged by a mine, and from the *Thetis* during the extensive repairs following her sinking and subsequent salvage for re-entry to service as the *Thunderbolt*. The other boats were the *Tribune*, *Trident*, *Taku*, *Tarpon*, *Thistle*, *Tigris*, *Triad*, *Truant*, *Tuna*, *Talisman*, *Tetrarch* (the only boat completed with mine-laying capability), and *Torbay*. Only six of these boats survived the war.

There followed the 16 boats of the War Emergency and 1940 Programs (seven and nine submarines, respectively). The first seven started with the *Thrasher*, launched in November 1940, and otherwise consisted of the *Tempest*, *Thorn*, *Traveller*, *Trooper*, *Trusty*, and *Turbulent*. The external bow torpedo tubes were shifted 7 feet (2.1 m) aft to improve sea keeping, the two external forward-angled tubes just forward of conning tower were reposi-

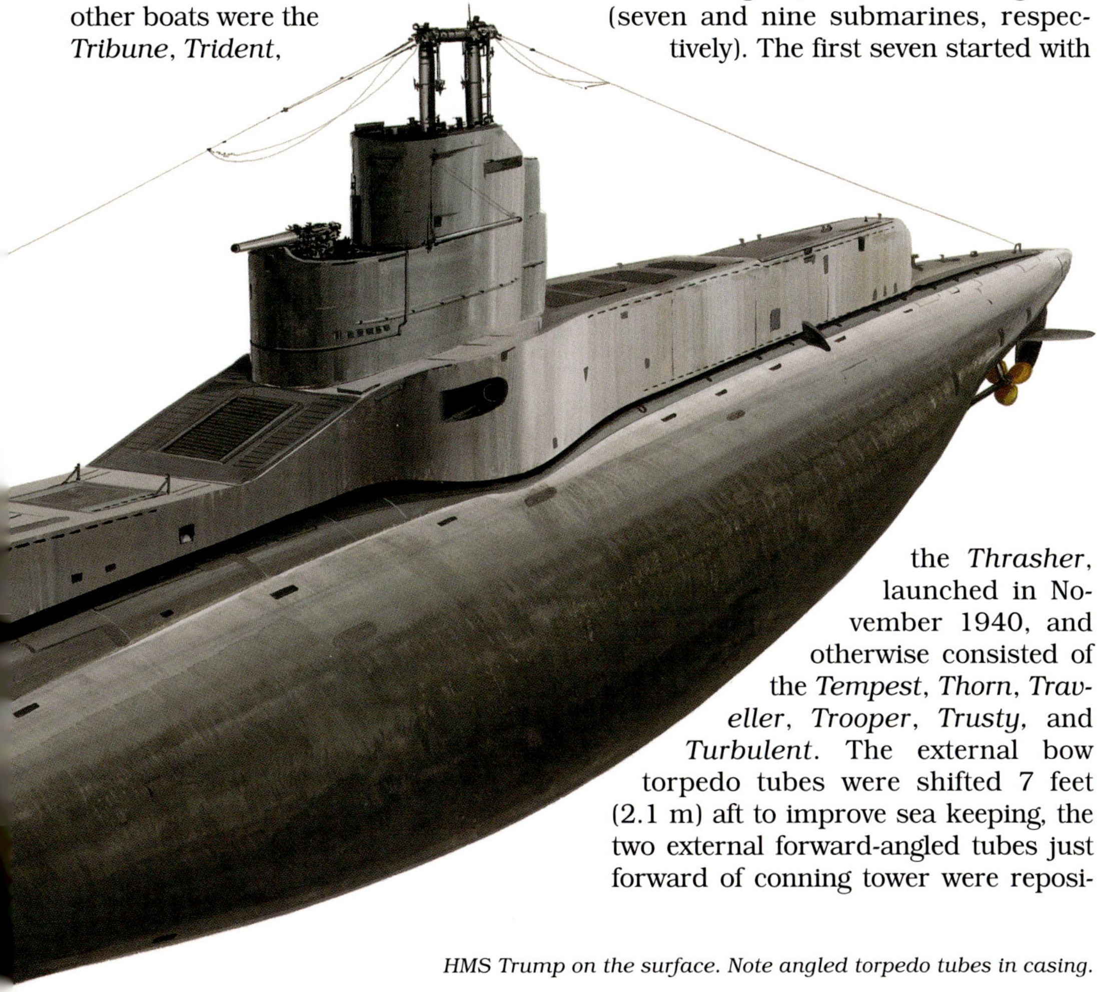

HMS Trump on the surface. Note angled torpedo tubes in casing.

tioned abaft it and angled to fire astern, and an external stern tube was also fitted. This gave a total of eight forward- and three rearward-facing tubes with 17 torpedoes. All of the boats operated in the Mediterranean, and only the *Thrasher* and *Trusty* survived. The *Turbulent* sank more than 90,000 tons of shipping, and was depth charged more than 250 times before succumbing in March 1943.

The boats of the 1940 program lacked many refinements, had only one anchor, and had much of the internal pipework of steel rather than copper. The first Group Three boat was *P311* (ex-*Tutankhamen*), launched in June 1942, and in the *Tactician*, *Tally Ho*, *Tantalus*, *Tantivy*, *Taurus*, *Templar*, *Trespasser*, and *Truculent* welding gradually replaced riveting, some boats being completely welded, which gave them a diving depth of 350 feet rather than 300 (107 m, rather than 90 m). The only boat lost in the war was the *P311*.

The third group consisted of the boats ordered under the 1941 and 1942 programs. The first of the 1941 boats, launched in June 1943, was the *Telemachus*, and the other boats were the *Talent* (transferred in 1943 to the Royal Dutch navy as the *Zwaardvisch*), *Taciturn*, *Talent* (ex-*Tasman*), *Tapir*, *Tarn*, *Teredo*, *Terrapin*, *Thorough*, *Thule*, *Tiptoe*, *Tireless*, *Token*, *Tradewind*, *Trenchant*, *Trump*, and *Tudor*. Most of these boats were completed too late for service in World War II.

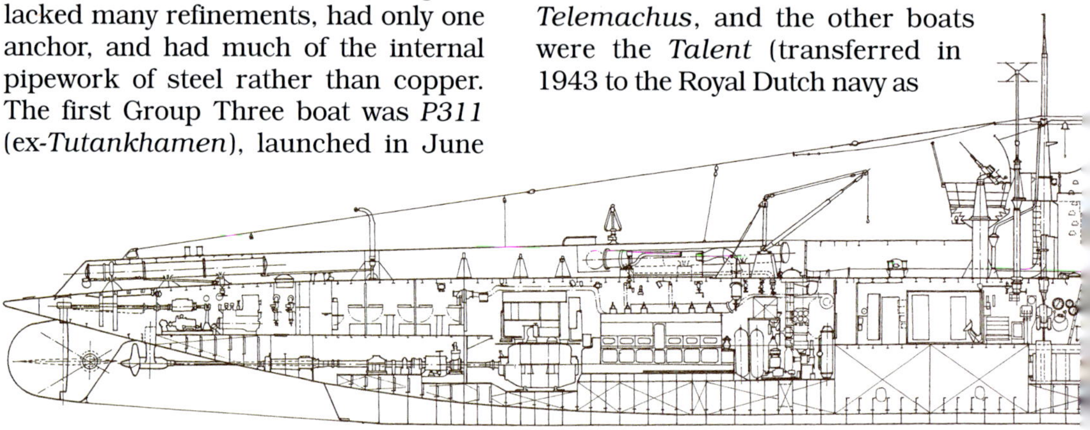

Some 14 submarines were ordered under the 1942 program, but only five of these were completed as the *Tabard*, *Thermopylae*, *Totem*, *Truncheon* and *Turpin*. In the mid-1980s, the last three were sold to Israel as the *Dakar*, *Dolphin* and *Leviathan*, the first of which was lost on passage to Israel.

The T-class submarines fought in all theatres of World War II and suffered 25% losses. They were particularly vulnerable in the Mediterranean, where their large size made them easily visible

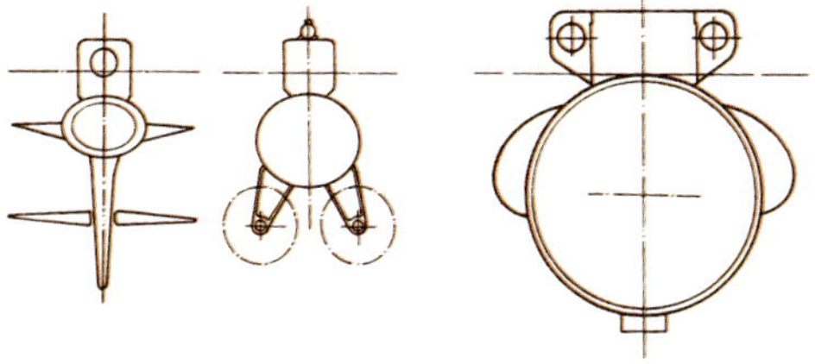
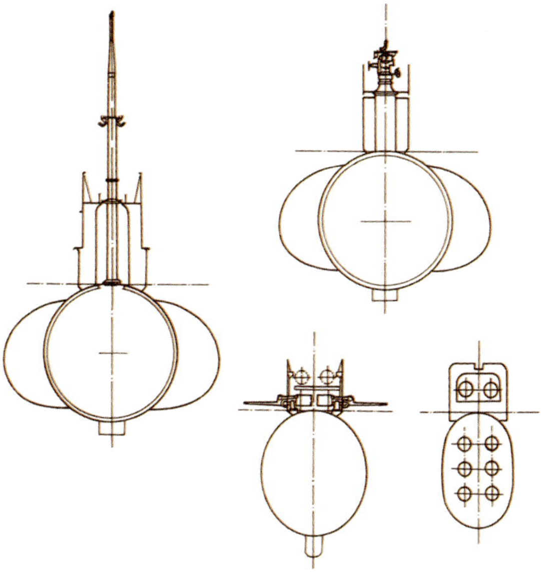

The British T Class went through many wartime modifications. This example (the Telemachus) shows how many changes had been made in the original design: a changed bow shape, external tubes facing aft, and a platform on the conning tower for a 3/4-inch (20-mm) AA gun. Completed in 1943, it was scrapped in 1961.

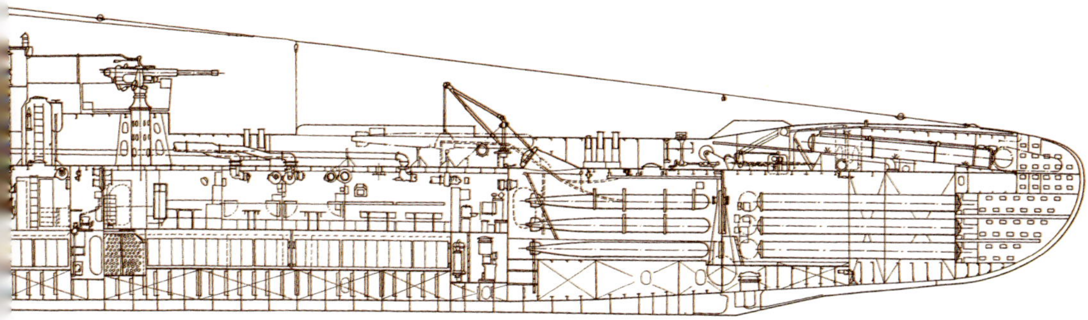

from the air in the clear waters, but they had much more success elsewhere. After the war, all surviving boats of the first two groups were scrapped and the others were revised with snorting masts as the first of many upgrade efforts. In addition to the boats sold to Israel, other exports were the made to the Netherlands. The first of these was the initial *Talent*, as already mentioned, and the other two were the *Tijgerhaai* (ex-*Tarn*), *Zeehond* (ex-*Tapir*) and *Dolfijn* (ex-*Taurus*). The last of the boats was the *Dolphin*, stricken by Israel in 1977.

T (1941 & 1942 Programs) class

Type:	patrol submarine
Tonnage:	1,319 tons surfaced and 1,571 tons submerged
Dimensions:	length 273 ft., 6 in. (83.4m); beam 26 ft., 7 in. (8.1 m); draft 14 ft., 10 in. (4.5 m)
Propulsion:	Admiralty Standard Range or Vickers diesel engines delivering 2,400 hp (1789.5 kW) for 15.25 knots surfaced and two electric motors delivering 1,450 hp (1081 kW) for 9 knots submerged
Armament:	one 4-inch (102 mm) gun and 11 21-inch (533 mm) tubes for 17 torpedoes
Complement:	61

U class (1940)

The British U class of submarine, most of which were built under the War Emergency 1940 and 1941 Programs, consisted of 71 small boats built just before and during World War II. The boats were initially intended as unarmed trainers to replace the aging H class, and thus to be operated as targets in anti-submarine training exercises.

The first three boats were the *Undine*, *Unity*, and *Ursula* ordered in 1936, but during construction the boats were modified with four internal and two external bow tubes. Apart from the *Undine* and *Unity*, all of the boats were also fitted with a 3-inch (76 mm) gun but there was no hatch for the gun crew, who had to use the main conning tower hatch. The first three U-class boats entered service in the latter half of 1938, and only the *Ursula* survived the war, spending 1944-49 in Soviet service, presaging later loans of U-class boats to the Soviets.

As war loomed, 12 more boats were ordered, although only the *Unique*, *Upholder*, *Upright*, and *Utmost* had the external tubes. These tubes were omitted from later vessels because they generated a large bow wave and made it tricky to hold periscope depth. The U-class boats were very useful in the confined waters of the North Sea and the Mediterranean, so another 34 vessels, forming the third group, were ordered in 1940-41. They were similar to the second group, but were lengthened slightly to improve the streamlining of the hull. Almost all of the 49 boats were built by Vickers, except for the *Umpire* and *Una*, which were built at Chatham Dockyard. Most of the boats operated with the 10th Submarine Flotilla based at Malta. Nineteen of the boats were lost during the war, thirteen of them in the Mediterranean and the other six in the North Sea and Atlantic Ocean. One boat, the *Untamed*, sank in May 1943 but was salvaged and recommissioned as the *Vitality*. From 1941, some of the boats were transferred to Soviet, Free French and other Allied navies. Later in the war the basic design was developed as the V class with a welded rather than riveted hull.

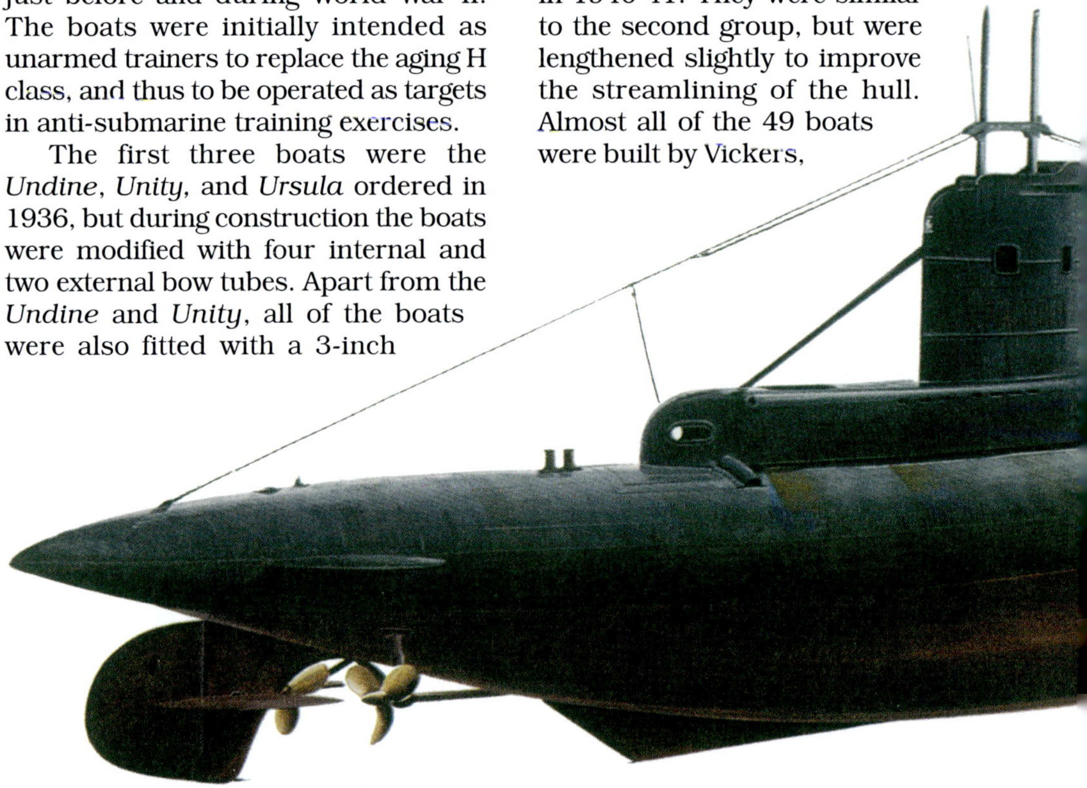

The 12 boats of the second U-class group were similar to the first three submarines but with modifications for better depth keeping. This group included several boats that later became highly celebrated. The *Urchin* was became the Polish *Sokół*, which sank a large amount of enemy shipping. The *Upholder* was commanded for its entire life by Lieutenant Commander Malcolm Wanklyn, who received a Victoria Cross for attacking a well-defended convoy on May 25, 1941, and sinking an Italian liner *Conte Rosso*. In an

operational career of 16 months spent in the Mediterranean before it was sunk in April 1942, the *Upholder* carried out 24 patrols and sank around 119,000 tons of Axis ships (three U-boats, one destroyer, 15 transport ships and possibly a cruiser and a destroyer). Losses among the boats of this group were high, and only three survived the war.

The third group constituted largest series of U-class boats: 34 boats were ordered in three batches. Given that submarine losses were expected to be high, it was decided in June 1940 to allocate P-series numbers rather than names, but at the end of 1942 the policy was revised, and names (four of them starting with V rather than P) were allocated to all but the eight that had already been sunk. Several were transferred to Allied navies, both before and after the war, and the last U-class boats were scrapped in the 1950s.

A final 22 boats, 2 and 20 with U and V names, were laid down in 1942-43 for completion in 1943-45 with finer bows and sterns lengthened by 7 ft., 8 in. (2.33 m) over those of the 1941 program's "short-hull" boats to reduce noise. The boats had welded frames and riveted hulls, and could dive to 300 feet (90 m). None was lost, four were transferred to Norway, and the British boats had gone by 1961.

U (1941 Long-Hull Program) class

Type:	patrol submarine
Tonnage:	662 tons surfaced and 740 tons submerged
Dimensions:	length 204 ft., 6 in. (62.3 m); beam 16 ft., 1 in. (4.9 m); draft 15 ft., 3 in. (4.65 m)
Propulsion:	Paxman diesel engines delivering 615 hp (458.5 kW) for 11.25 knots surfaced and four electric motors delivering 825 hp (615 kW) for 10 knots submerged
Armament:	one 3-inch (76 mm) gun and four 21-inch (533 mm) tubes for eight torpedoes
Complement:	33

S class (1931)

The Royal Navy's S-class submarines were designed and first built within the context of the modernization of the British submarine force in the early 1930s, and were intended to satisfy a requirement for smaller patrol boats to replace the H-class boats in service in the restricted waters of the North Sea and the Mediterranean Sea. Demand rose radically during World War II, and the S class became the most prolific submarine class ever built for the UK: over a 15-year period, 62 such boats were constructed, excluding 50 Improved S-class submarines launched in 1940-1945. The boats also operated in the Far East after being revised with additional tankage, and after the war the S-class boats continued in Royal Navy service into 1960s. The last to operate was the *Sea Devil*, launched in 1945 and scrapped in February 1966. S-class boats were also sold or loaned to the navies of France (four boats), Israel (two boats), the Netherlands (one boat) and Portugal (three boats), while four units of a modified version were ordered by the Turkish navy in 1939 as the Oruc Reis class.

The first group of S-class boats were the *Swordfish*, *Sturgeon*, *Seahorse* and *Starfish* of the Swordfish class, all built by Chatham Dockyard in 1930-1932. They were smaller and slower than later classes, and carried less armament, but could be crewed by fewer men. During the war, the boats operated in home waters,

A rating watches the hydroplane indicator in a British sub. The hydroplanes control the angle of ascent and descent of a submarine underwater.

especially in the English Channel, and off the Scandinavian coast. This resulted from the boats' limited fuel supply, and the boats of the second and third groups had their fuel capacities enlarged to allow them to operate farther afield. Only the *Sturgeon* survived at the war's end.

The data for these boats included displacements of 640 tons surfaced and 935 tons submerged, length of 202 ft., 6 in. (61.7 m), beam of 24 feet (7.3 m), propulsion by Admiralty diesel engines delivering 1,550 hp (1156 kW) for 13.75 knots surfaced and electric motors delivering 1,440 hp (1074 kW) for 10 knots submerged, armament of one 3-inch (76 mm) gun and six 21-inch (533 mm) bow tubes for 12 torpedoes, and complement of 36.

The second group totaled eight boats of the Shark class. These were larger than the boats of the Swordfish class, the extra length improving the streamlining and increasing the surfaced speed slightly despite the greater displacements and the retention of the original propulsion arrangement, and the complement was increased by one man. The construction of the boats was allocated to Chatham Dockyard (four boats) and the commercial yards of Scotts at Greenock (one boat) and Cammell Laird at Birkenhead (three boats). All of the boats were built between 1934 and 1937. The boats were the *Shark*, *Sealion*, *Salmon*, *Snapper*, *Seawolf*, *Spearfish*, *Sterlet*, and *Sunfish*. Like those of the first group, the boats of the second group operated mostly in home waters with farther limits of the Scandinavian coast and the Bay of Biscay. The *Sunfish* was assigned to the Soviet navy and operated in the Baltic Sea, but was sunk by friendly aircraft on July 27, 1944. Most of the boats were lost during the war; only the *Sealion* and *Seawolf* survived until the end of the war.

The third and by far the most numerous group of the S class totaled 50 boats. These were the largest and most powerfully armed of the S-class submarines, and each boat needed a complement of 48 men. The combination of greater length and more powerful diesel engines increased the surfaced speed by 1 knot, but the greater displacement and lower-powered electric motors reduced the submerged speed by 2 knots.

Most of the boats were built at the Scotts and Cammell Laird yards at Greenock and Birkenhead, respectively, but three were constructed by Chatham Dockyard and another three by the Vickers-Armstrong yard at Barrow-in-Furness. The construction program continued from 1941 to 1945. Completed with greater fuel tankage than the earlier boats of the class, the submarines of the 1939 War Emergency, 1940, 1941, 1942 and 1943 Programs were able to operate considerably farther afield, their patrol areas including the Mediterranean Sea and parts of the Pacific Ocean off the coast of the Asian mainland.

The 50 boats of these four building programs consisted of two distinct subgroups. The first were the 33 boats with a surfaced displacement of 842 tons and ordered under the 1939 War Emergency, 1940 and 1941 Programs (except the *Sea Devil* and *Scotsman*) plus the *Sturdy* and *Stygian* of the 1942 Program. These were characterized by an external stern tube in addition to the six bow tubes. The second subgroup were the 17 boats with a surfaced displacement of 814 tons and as such comprising the *Sea Devil* and *Scotsman* of the 1941 Program, plus those ordered under the 1942 and 1943 Programs (except the *Sturdy* and *Stygian*). None of these boats carried an external tube, but had a welded pressure hull of thicker steel providing an operational depth limit of 350 feet (107 m) rather than the 300 feet (91 m) limit in the first subgroup.

The data for the boats of the third group included displacements of between 814 and 842 tons surfaced and 990 tons submerged, length of 217 feet (66.1 m), beam of 23 ft., 9 in. (7.25 m), draft of 13 ft., 10 in. (4.2 m), propulsion by Admiralty diesel engines delivering 1,900 hp (1417 kW) for 14.75 knots surfaced and electric motors delivering 1,300 hp (969 kW) for 9 knots submerged, armament of a single 3-inch

(76 mm) and 20 mm guns and seven 21-inch (533 mm) tubes (six forward and one stern) for 13 torpedoes, and complement of 48.

Losses continued to be high. Nine of the boats (the *P222*, *Saracen*, *Sahib*, *Sickle*, *Simoom*, *Splendid*, *Stonehenge*, *Stratagem*, and *Syrtis*) were lost during the war, and the *Shakespeare* and *Strongbow* were damaged so severely that they were written off and scrapped. Many of the surviving boats remained in service after the war. Transferred to the French navy, the *Sportsman* was lost off Toulon in 1951, and the *Sidon* was sunk after a torpedo malfunction in 1955.

The boats of the 1939 War Emergency Program were the *Safari*, *Sahib*, *Saracen*, *Satyr*, and *Sceptre*. The boats of the 1940 Program, which had the external stern tube, one 20-mm AA cannon and air warning radar, were the *Seadog*, *Sibyl*, *Sea Rover*, *Seraph*, *Shakespeare*, *P222* (lost before a name could be allotted to her), *Sea Nymph*, *Sickle*, *Simoom*, *Sirdar*, *Spiteful*, *Splendid*, and *Sportsman*; the other seven (P81 to P87) ordered from Vickers-Armstrong were cancelled during 1943 before they had even been laid down. The boats of the 1941 Program were the *Stoic*, *Stonehenge*, *Storm*, *Stratagem*, *Strongbow*, *Spark*, *Scythian*, *Stubborn*, *Surf*, *Syrtis*, *Shalimar*, *Scotsman*, *Sea Devil*, *Spirit*, and *Statesman*. The boats of the 1942 Program were the *Sturdy*, *Stygian*, *Subtle*, *Supreme*, *Sea Scout*, *Selene*, *Seneschal*, *Sentinel*, *Sidon*, *Sleuth*, *Solent*, *Spearhead*, and *Springer*. Eight boats were ordered under the 1943 Program, but only four were completed as the *Saga*, *Scorcher*, *Spur*, and *Sanguine*; the other four (the *Sea Robin*, *Sprightly*, *Surface*, and *Surge*) were cancelled after the end of the war in 1945.

Shark class

Type:	patrol submarine
Tonnage:	758 tons surfaced and 960 tons submerged
Dimensions:	length 208 ft., 8 in. (63.6 m); beam 24 ft. (7.3 m); draft 11 ft., 10 in. (3.6 m)
Propulsion:	Admiralty Standard Range diesel engines delivering 1,550 hp (1156 kW) for 14 knots and electric motors delivering 1,440 hp (1074 kW) for 10 knots submerged
Armament:	one 3-inch (76 mm) gun and six 21-inch (533 mm) tubes for 12 torpedoes
Complement:	39

Type II classes (1935)

The Type II classes of U-boats were designed for coastal operations, and were modeled closely on the *CV-707*, designed by a Dutch-fronted German company set up after World War I to maintain and develop submarine technology and so evade the limitations imposed on Germany by the Treaty of Versailles in 1919. Derived from Germany's UB II class of coastal sub- of Kiel, was laid down on February 11, 1935. In this year Adolf Hitler reached agreement with the UK for a German navy up to 35% of the size of the Royal Navy in surface ships, but equal in submarine numbers. The *U-1* was launched 11 days after the June 18, 1935, signature of the agreement, and there followed five more boats up to the U-6.

marine, the *CV-707* was built in 1933 by the Crichton-Vulcan yard of Aabo in Finland and bought by the Finnish navy in 1936 as the *Vesikko*. This boat was used primarily for the training of new German submarine officers.

Beginning in the 1920s, Germany began to rebuild her armed forces in programs greatly accelerated by the rise to power of the Nazi party in 1933. The first of six Type IIA class boats, built by Deutsche Werke

The most readily apparent feature of the Type II class boats was their diminutive size, which led to the nickname *Einbaum* ("dug-out canoe"). However, the Type II class boats could operate in very shallow waters, dived very rapidly, and were difficult to spot on the surface, as their conning towers were low. These factors were offset by limited diving depth, short range, poor habitability, and only three bow tubes for five torpedoes. The boats were of the single-hulled type without watertight compartments.

Most Type II class boats saw operational service only in the early years of the war and were thereafter being relegated to training. But some were stripped down to just a hull, transported by barge and road vehicle to Linz, Austria, and reassembled in Romania for Black Sea service against the Soviets. In contrast with those of later U-boat classes, the losses in the U II class were few, a fact reflecting their use as training boats; even so, some boats were lost in accidents.

The Type IIA subclass, of which three were lost, had a submerged displacement of 298 tons, length of 134 ft., 2 in. (40.9 m), beam of 13 ft., 5 in. (4.12 m), the same surface propulsion as the other three subclasses for 13 knots surfaced but electric motors delivering only 180 hp (134 kW) for 6.9 knots submerged, and complement of 25. The 20 Type IIB class boats were the *U-7* to *U-24* plus *U-120* and *U-121* ordered by Yugoslavia, of which seven were lost, and these were built by Germaniawerft, Deutsche Werke and, in the case of the last two, Flenderwerft between 1935 and 1940. They differed from the Type IIA class boats in their submerged displacement of 324 tons, length of 140 feet (42.7 m) and longer range.

Deutsche Werke built eight Type IIC class boats, the *U-56* to *U-63*, of which two were lost, between 1937 and 1940. These boats had a submerged displacement of 336 tons, length of 144 feet (43.9 m), and electric motors delivering 205 hp (153 kW) for 7 knots submerged. Deutsche Werke also built 16 wider and longer-ranged Type IID class boats, the *U-137* to *U-152*, of which three were lost, in 1939-40.

Type IID class

Type:	coastal patrol submarine
Tonnage:	309 tons surfaced and 358 tons submerged
Dimensions:	length 144 ft., 4 in. (44 m); beam 16 ft. (4.9 m); draft 12 ft., 9 in. (3.9 m)
Propulsion:	two MWM diesel engines delivering 350 hp (337 kW) for 12.7 knots surfaced and two Siemens electric motors delivering 205 hp (153 kW) for 7.4 knots submerged
Armament:	one 20 mm gun and three 21-inch (533 mm) tubes for five torpedoes
Complement:	25

Type VII classes (1936)

The Type VII U-boat classes were the workhorses of the German submarine arm in World War II. The design was created on the basis of earlier types via a Dutch dummy company, IvS ("Ingenieurskantoor voor Scheepsbouw den Haag") established by Germany after World War I in order to maintain a design capability via boats built by yards in Finland and Spain. This paved the way to the Type VII and Type IA classes, the latter built by A. G. Weser but halted after two boats.

The Type IA led to the Type VII and Type IX, of which the former was built in larger numbers (more than 700) than any other submarine class in history. Given its numbers, the Type VII class was built in a number of subclasses.

The Type VIIA boat was designed in 1933-34. Deschimag of Bremen built six of the ten boats (*U-27* to *U-36*), the other four coming from Germaniawerft of Kiel. The Type VIIA boats were popular and much more powerful than the tiny Type II boats they replaced, with four internal bow and one external stern torpedo tubes, for which 11 torpedoes were normally carried. Each boat also shipped one 3 ½ inch (88 mm) deck gun. The boats were built in 1935-37, and all but two were sunk in World War II. The data for the Type VIIA class included a displacement of 616 tons surfaced and 733 tons submerged, length of 211 ft., 7 in. (64.5 m), beam of 19 feet (5.8 m), propulsion by two diesel

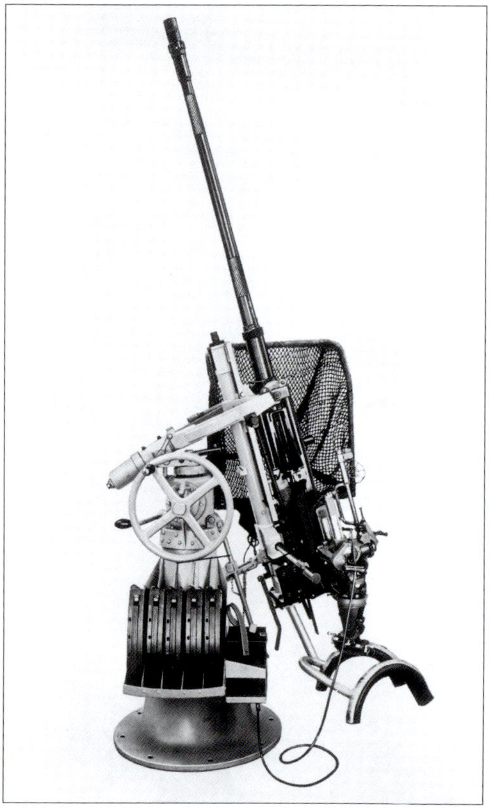

¾-inch (20 mm) AA cannon.

engines delivering 2,100 hp (1566 kW) or more for 16 knots surfaced and two electric motors delivering 750 hp (559 kW) for 8 knots submerged, and complement of 44.

The only major limitation of the Type VIIA was its fuel capacity, so 24 Type VIIB class boats were built in 1936-40 with an additional 33 tons of fuel in external saddle tanks for an additional 2,875 miles (2500 miles) to the range at 10 knots surfaced. The Type VIIB boats were also slightly faster than the Type VIIA submarines, and had two rudders rather than a single unit for enhanced maneuverability. The torpedo armament was also improved, the stern tube being moved from the original position outside the pressure hull to one within it: single reload torpedoes were carried below the deck plating of the after torpedo room, which also served as the electric motor room, and in two watertight compartments under the upper deck, giving a total of 14 torpedoes. On the surface, the Type VIIB boat was powered by two MAN or Germaniawerft diesel engines delivering 2,800 to 3,200 hp (2088 to 2386 kW) for 17.2 knots, and under the water by two AEG or BBC electric motors delivering 750 hp (559 kW) for 8.8 knots. The Type VIIB class included many of the most famous U-boats of World War II, including *U-48* (the most successful), Günther Prien's *U-47*, Otto Kretschmer's *U-99*, and Joachim Schepke's *U-100*.

The Type VIIC boat was built to the extent of 568 boats commissioned in 1940-45, the first of them the *U-69*. The Type VIIC class was very effective, and was also ubiquitous despite a range less than that of the larger Type IX boats. The Type VIIC was only slightly modified from the Type VIIB, having very similar engines and power but, being larger and heavier, was marginally slower. Many of these boats were fitted with the Schnorchel ("snorkel") in 1944-45. The Type VIIC boats had the same tube arrangement as their predecessors, with the exception of *U-72*, *U-78*, *U-80*, *U-554*, and *U-555* with only two bow tubes, and *U-203*, *U-331*, *U-351*, *U-401*, *U-431*, and *U-651* without a stern tube.

The U-Flak boats were the Type VIIC class *U-441*, *U-256*, *U-621* and *U-951* modified to be surface escorts for the attack U-boats operating from the French Atlantic bases. They had greatly increased anti-aircraft firepower in the form of one 1 ½ inch (37 mm) gun, two quadruple 20 mm cannon mountings and sometimes two single ¾-inch (20 mm) cannons. Only five torpedoes were carried to free volume for the

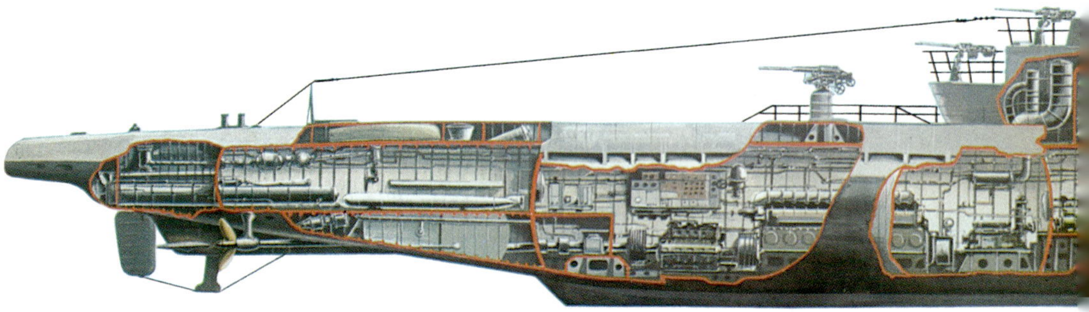

gunners and additional AA ammunition. The conversion of three other boats was started but not completed, and these eventually returned to service as standard Type VIIC boats. The modified boats became operational in June 1943 and gained initial success, winning the Germans some two more months of limited freedom to cross the Bay of Biscay on the surface until the British developed countermeasures. The U-Flak boats were then converted back to their original standard, which now included one ¾-inch (20 mm) quadruple mounting.

The Type VIIC/41 was a modified Type VIIC with the same armament and engines but a stronger pressure hull, giving it a deeper diving depth and lighter machinery to offset the greater mass of steel in the hull. This resulted in an overall slight decrease in displacements. Some 91 such boats were built, and from *U-1271* onward they lacked all mining capability.

The Type VIIC/42 was planned in 1942-43 as successor to the Type VIIC with a considerably stronger pressure hull to double the diving depth, two periscopes rather than one, and two more reload torpedoes. Orders were placed for 176 such boats, but the whole class was cancelled in September 1943 in favor of the new Type XXI.

The Type VIID, designed in 1939-40, was a version of the Type VIIC lengthened to 252 ft., 3 in. (68.7 m) to provide for three banks of five vertical mine tubes just abaft of the conning tower. The propulsion was essentially that of the Type VIIC. Six such boats were built, and only one survived to the end of the war.

The Type VIIF, designed in 1941, was created for the transport role to take reload torpedoes out to boats

Kap./Lt. Günther Prien's U47 enters Scapa Flow to sink HMS Royal Oak, October 13 or 14, 1939.

which had expended all their weapons but still had the fuel and other consumables for continued patrol. The Type VIIF boats were the largest and heaviest of all the Type VII boats built, with a displacement of 1,067 tons surfaced and 1,162 tons submerged, and a length of 254 ft., 7 in. (77.6 m). They had the same torpedo armament as the other Type VII boats but lacked any deck gun, and could carry up to 39 torpedoes. Only four Type VIIF boats were built. The *U-1062* and *U-1059* were sent to support U-boats in the Far East, while the *U-1060* and *U-1061* remained in the Atlantic. Only the last survived.

Type VIIC class

Type:	patrol submarine
Tonnage:	749 tons surfaced and 851 tons submerged
Dimensions:	length 220 ft., 2 in. (67.1 m); beam 20 ft., 4 in. (6.2 m); draft 15 ft., 9 in. (4.8 m)
Propulsion:	two diesel engines delivering 2,800 hp (2088 kW) for 17 knots surfaced and two electric motors delivering 750 hp (550 kW) for 7.6 knots submerged
Armament:	one 3 ½-inch (88 mm) gun, one 20 mm cannon, and five 21-inch (533 mm) tubes for 14 torpedoes or mines
Complement:	44

Type IX class (1938)

The Type IX class was designed in 1935-36 to provide the German navy's U-boat arm with a capability for extended ocean-going operations far from the support facilities offered by a home base. The range capability of these boats is attested by the fact that a modest number of them were used for extended patrols, over a comparatively short period of World War II known to the men of the U-boat service as the "second happy time," off the eastern seaboard of the U.S. and in the Caribbean Sea during the first months of 1942. However, the extended range of the Type IX class was achieved only at the cost of increased diving times and decreased agility. Thus, the smaller Type VII boats were built in greater numbers for service as the real workhorses of the U-boat arm.

The Type IX class U-boat was derived from the Type IA class boat, and was developed though several sub-classes. The standard features of the Type IX submarines included six torpedo tubes (four at the bow and two at the stern), and 16 reload torpedoes carried as six internally and 10 externally in five containers (two at the bow and three at the stern). The availability of 22 torpedoes in all allowed the captains of Type IX class submarines to follow a targeted convoy on the surface by day and then attack night after night as long as there were torpedoes available. The boats could also be used as mine-layers with 44 TMA or 66 TMB mines. For surface actions there was one 4-inch (105 mm) L./45 deck gun supplied with about 110 rounds, and an anti-aircraft capability was provided by a tertiary battery that differed in calibers and numbers during the course of the war. The conning tower was fitted

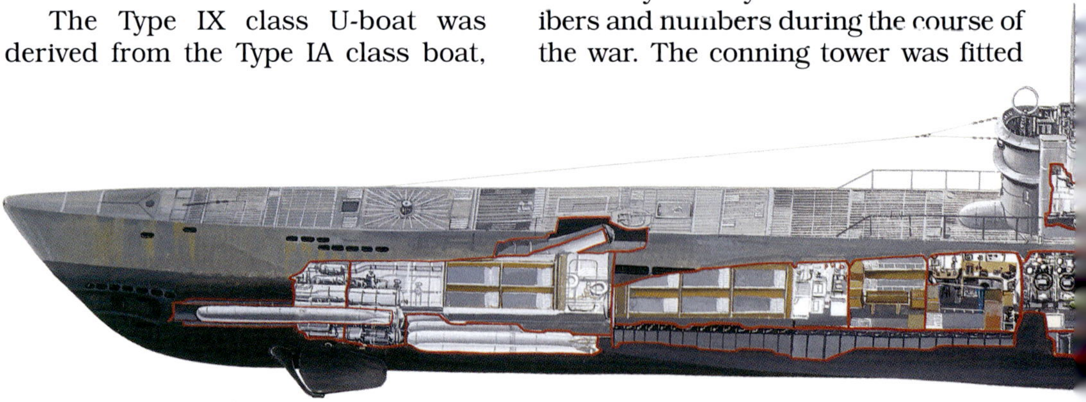

with two periscopes, and the Type IXA and Type IXB class boats had another periscope in the control room, but this was deemed unnecessarily complex and omitted from later boats.

Eight Type IXA class U-boats were built by A. G. Weser of Bremen as the *U-37* to *U-44*. All but the *U-37* and *U-38*

Captain Gallery on the bridge of the captured U-505, the first U.S. Navy capture of an enemy war vessel on the high seas since the War of 1812. Photo: U.S. Navy.

The conning tower of U-505 on display at the Museum of Science and Industry, Chicago, Illinois.
Photo: John Batchelor.

were lost in the war, and the crews of the two surviving scuttled their boats in May 1945. The data for this initial class differed from those of the Type IXD class in a displacement of 1,032 tons surfaced and 1,152 tons submerged, length of 251 ft., 4 in. (76.6 m), beam of 21 ft., 4 in. (6.5 m), draft of 15 ft., 5 in. (4.7 m), speed of 18.2 knots surfaced

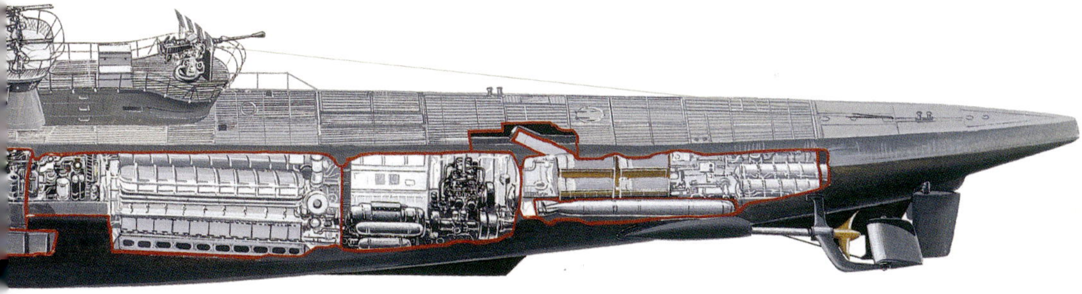

and 7.7 knots submerged, range of 12,070 miles (19425 km) at 10 knots surfaced and 89.5 miles (144 km) at 4 knots submerged, and complement of 48-56.

The Type IXB class was an improved Type IXA class with greater range and, with each boat sinking an average of 100,000 tons of shipping, this was the most successful variant. Celebrated boats included the *U-123* of *Kapitänleutnant* Reinhard Hardegen, which opened the campaign in US waters early in 1942, and the *U-107* of *Kapitänleutnant* Günther Hessler, which operated off West Africa and had the single most successful patrol of World War II with almost 100,000 tons of shipping sunk. Fourteen Type IXB class U-boats were built by A. G. Weser as the *U-64*, *U-65*, *U-103* to *U-111*, and *U-122* to *U-124* with data differing from those of the Type IXA class in details such as a displacement of 1,051 tons surfaced and 1,051 tons submerged, beam of 22 ft., 4 in. (6.8 m), speed of 7.3 knots submerged, and range of 13,795 miles (22200 km) at 10 knots surfaced and 73 miles (118 km) at 4 knots submerged. During 1944, the surviving boats, and those of other subclasses, were stripped of their 4-inch (105 mm) guns and received one

1 ½ inch (37 mm) and two 20 mm AA cannons. All but the *U-123* were lost in the war, which entered French service as the *Blaison*.

The Type IXC class was a further refinement with a submerged displacement of 1,213 tons and bunkerage for an additional 43 tons of fuel, increasing the range to 15,460 miles (24880 km) at 10 knots surfaced. As mine-layers, the boats could carry 44 TMA or 66 TMB mines, although 35 boats (the U-162 to U-170 and U-505 to U-550) were not fitted for mine operations. Fifty-four boats of this class were built by A. G. Weser, Seebeckwerft of Bremen, and Deutsche Werft of Hamburg. The boats were the *U-66* to *U-68*, *U-125* to *U-131*, *U-153* to *U-166*, *U-171* to *U-176*, *U-501* to *U-524*, and *U-533*. All but five were lost, and the *U-510* became the French *Bouan*.

The Type IXC/40 class was an improved Type IXC with a displacement of 1,237 tons submerged, speed of 19 knots surfaced, and range of 15,920 miles (25620 km) surfaced. Some 87 of this model were built by A. G. Weser, Seebeckwerft and Deutsche Werft as the *U-167* to *U-170*, *U-193* to *U-194*, *U-525* to *U-550*, *U-801* to *U-806*, *U-841* to *U-846*, *U-853* to *U-859*, *U-865* to *U-870*, *U-877* to *U-881*, *U-1221* to *U-1262* and *U-1501* to *U-1530*.

The Type IXD-2 class was longer and heavier than the Type IXC/40, and the Type IXD/42 was almost identical to the Type IXD-2 but for its diesel engines delivering 5,400 hp (4026 kW). In 1943 and 1944 the torpedo tubes were removed from some Type IXD-2 boats to allow them to carry 252 tons of freight to and from Japan, a task also undertaken by the *U-180* and *U-195* of the Type IXD-1 class with torpedo tubes and Germania rather than MAN diesel engines. A. G. Weser built 30 of the

Top: Forward torpedo room of U-505.

Bottom: Aft torpedo room of U-505. Note bunks squeezed into the restricted area.

Photos: John Batchelor.

Right:
One of the propellers of U-505. Note the twin rudders.
Photo: John Batchelor.

Left:
1 ½ inch (37 mm) anti-aircraft gun on "bandstand" at aft end of U-505 conning tower.
Photo: John Batchelor.

boats as the *U-177* to *U-182*, *U-195* to *U-200*, *U-847* to *U-852*, *U-859* to *U-864*, and *U-871* to *U-876*. Several Type IXD/42 boats were ordered from A. G. Weser of Bremen, but only the *U-883* was commissioned.

Type IXD class

Type:	patrol submarine
Tonnage:	1,610 tons surfaced and 1,799 tons submerged
Dimensions:	length 287 ft., 5 in. (87.6 m); beam 24 ft., 7 ¼ in. (7.5 m); draft 17 ft., 9 in. (5.4 m)
Propulsion:	two MAN M9V40/46 supercharged diesel engines delivering 4,400 hp (3281 kW) for 20.8 knots surfaced, and two Siemens-Schuckert Werke double-acting electric motors delivering 1,000 hp (746 kW) for 6.9 knots submerged
Armament:	one 4-inch (105 mm) gun and six 22-inch (550 mm) tubes (four bow and two stern) for 24 torpedoes
Complement:	55-63
Range:	surfaced 12,750 miles at 10 knots (23,600 km at 19 km/h), submerged 115 miles at 4 knots (213 km at 7 km/h)
Max depth:	750 ft. (230 m)

Brin class (1938)

The submarine arm was one of the best elements of the Italian armed forces in World War II, and its boats were generally operated with a high degree of professional skill, courage and enterprise. However, logistical support and the use of any coherent operational philosophy were both plagued by the fact that no fewer than 26 classes of submarine were built for the Regia Marina between the end of World War I and the armistice with the Allied powers during September 1943.

The five Brin-class boats built in the late 1930s were typical of the larger type of ocean-going Italian submarines. These were long-range submarines intended mostly for operations in the Red Sea and the Indian Ocean in the defense of Italy's East African empire. The class was built by Tosi at Taranto, and the design was based on that of the Archimede class, of which Tosi had built four units in 1931-35 with a submerged displacement of 1,259 tons. The Brin class had a partial double hull, but of a more streamlined shape than the hull of its predecessor, resulting in a higher speed on essentially the same power. In general, the boats proved to be highly satisfactory, and were the *Brin*, *Galvani*, *Guglielmotti*, *Archimede*, and *Torricelli*.

The armament was based on eight 21-inch (533 mm) torpedo tubes located as four each in the bow and stern. The boats each carried 12 reload torpedoes for a complement of 20 such weapons, a fact reflecting the boats' intended deployment in areas without much in the way of local bases. There was also a 4-inch (100 mm) L/43 gun mounted, somewhat unusually, at bridge deck level at the after end of the long conning tower. This feature was confined to the Brin class and the three somewhat larger units of the Foca class, another Italian design of the same period. It is not known what, if any, operational advantage was expected of this; early in World War II this mounting was removed from both the Brin and Foca classes and replaced by a 4 ¾-inch (120 mm) L/47 gun mounted on the foredeck.

The first three boats of the class were built openly, and launched in 1938. The final pair were the *Archimede* and *Torricelli*, which were built in secret to replace two boats of the same name covertly transferred to

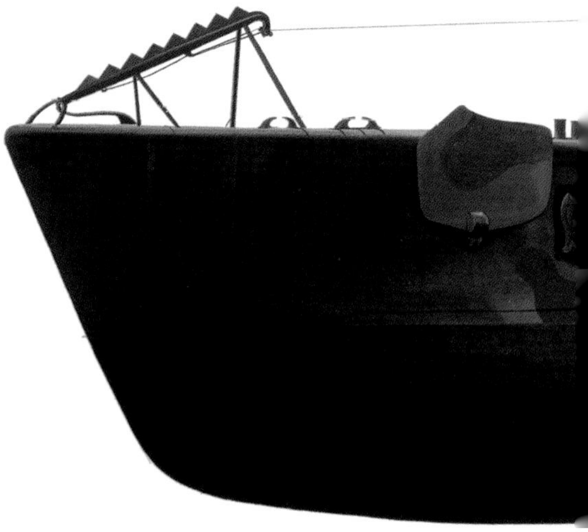

the navy of the Spanish Nationalist insurrectionist forces fighting the Republican government forces in the Spanish Civil War (1937-39).

In June 1940, when Italy entered World War II, all but the *Brin*, which had returned to Italy, were based in the Red Sea. Two of the boats succumbed after attack by British warships very early in the war: the *Torricelli* on June 23, 1940, and the Galvani just one day later but in a completely different action. The *Torricelli* was scuttled by her own crew after a heavy surface action in the Red Sea with three British destroyers, of which one was sunk, and a sloop. The *Galvani* fell victim to a British sloop off the Persian Gulf.

In May 1941 all the Italian boats operating to the east of Suez, including the *Archimede* and *Guglielmotti*, were ordered to Bordeaux on the west coast of German-occupied France, by way of the Cape of Good Hope, being replenished by the German armed merchant cruiser *Atlantis* en route. This voyage was in itself a considerable achievement as the boats had received no refits; at Bordeaux, they were joined by the *Brin* for Atlantic operations, in which they sank or damaged seven merchantmen totaling 53,200 tons.

The *Guglielmotti* was torpedoed by the British boat *Unbeaten* in the Mediterranean in March 1942, and the *Archimede* was sunk by the depth charges of a U.S. Navy PBY-5 flying boat off Brazil in April 1943. Only the *Brin* survived, and was surrendered to the Allies in 1943, sent to Ceylon (now Sri Lanka) as a training target until the war's end, and returned to Italy to be stricken in 1948.

Brin class

Type:	patrol submarine
Tonnage:	1,016 tons surfaced and 1,266 tons submerged
Dimensions:	length 237 ft., 8 in. (72.5 m); beam 21 ft., 1 in. (6.7 m); draft 14 ft., 11 in. (4.5 m)
Propulsion:	two Tosi diesel engines delivering 3,400 hp (2535 kW) for 17.3 knots surfaced and two Ansaldo electric motors delivering 1,300 hp (969 kW) for 8 knots submerged
Armament:	one 4 3/4-inch (120 mm) gun and eight 21-inch (533 mm) tubes for 20 torpedoes
Complement:	58

Type XIV class (1941)

The Type XIV U-boat was a development of the Type IXD-1 boat with a shorter and somewhat fuller hull, and was designed specifically for the resupply at sea of other U-boats, to extend the endurance of their patrols without the waste of time involved in return to base for supplies of oil and other consumables. The role of the boats inevitably led to their receipt of the nickname *milchkühe* ("milk cows"). To maximize their capabilities in the supply role, the boats lacked all offensive weaponry, and were therefore fitted only with Flak guns for self-defense. In addition to its own 203 tons of diesel fuel for a range of 10,700 miles (17225 km) at 12 knots, each of the boats could carry a cargo of 432 tons of diesel fuel and four torpedoes for transfer at sea and, in the case of some of the boats of this important class, bakery and flour storage so that fresh bread could be baked on passage and delivered to the crews being resupplied.

Midway through World War II, the availability of the Type XIV class boats made it possible for the smaller Type VIIC boats to operate off the east and southern coasts of the U.S. during the "second happy time" in the early months of 1942 before the U.S. had come fully to grips with the need for convoys and the dousing of navigation lights.

Given their importance in keeping patrol boats at sea in their operational areas, the Type XIV boats were inevitably a priority target for all Allied air and sea forces, and the availability

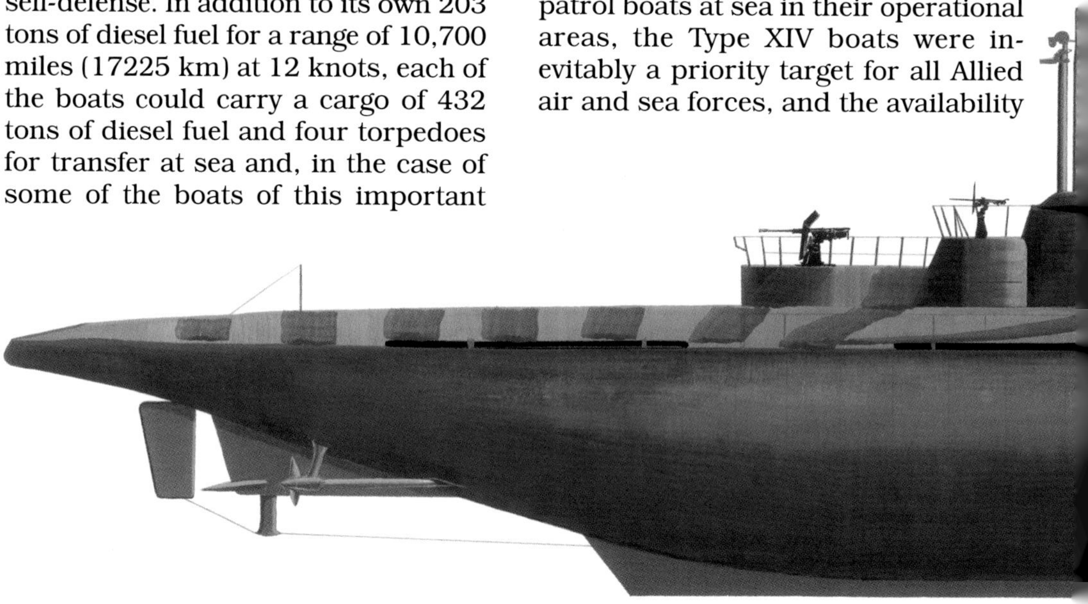

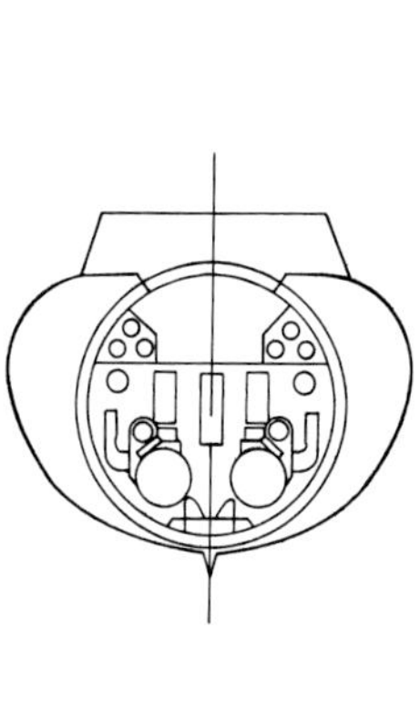

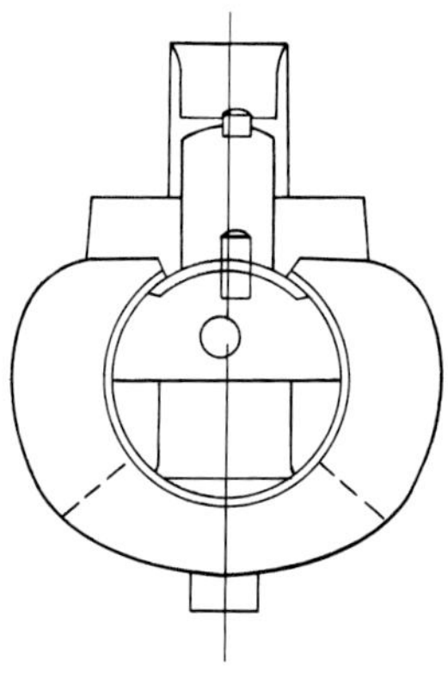

to the allies of improved radar and more extensive air coverage resulted in the destruction of all the Type XIV class boats in the course of 1943. Service in the boats of this class was very dangerous: out of an estimated 530 to 575 men who served in these boats, no fewer than 289 were killed. Of the 10 losses, nine were the result of attack by British on U.S. aircraft (five and four deaths, respectively) and the tenth to an attack by four destroyer escorts of the U.S. Navy.

Ten Type XIV boats ordered from Deutsche Werke of Kiel were launched in 1941-42 and later commissioned as the *U-459*, *U-460*, *U-461*, *U-462*, *U-463*, *U-464*, *U-487*, *U-488*, *U-489*, and *U-490*. Another 14 boats of this class were ordered but cancelled. Three of them, the *U-491*, *U-492* and *U-493*, were about 75% complete when work-stop order was given and were scrapped in July and August 1943. The other 11 had not been laid down before they were cancelled in May 1944.

On the same day *Grossadmiral* Karl Dönitz, commander-in-chief of the German navy, dropped all plans for the development of the Type XX U-boats, which were large transport boats that, with a submerged displacement of 2,962 tons, a length of 255 feet (77.7 m) and eight compartments for the carriage of wet or dry cargo, would have been able to deliver 800 tons of fuel but would not have been ready for service until the summer of 1945 at the earliest.

Type XIV class

Type:	replenishment submarine
Tonnage:	1,668 tons surfaced and 1,932 tons submerged
Dimensions:	length 220 ft., 2 in. (67.1 m); beam 30 ft., 8 in. (9.35 m); draft 21 ft., 4 in. (6.5 m)
Propulsion:	two Germaniawerft diesel engines delivering 3,200 hp (2386 kW) for 14.8 knots surfaced and two Siemens electric motors delivering 750 hp (559 kW) for 6.2 knots submerged
Armament:	two 1 ½-inch (37 mm) and two 20 mm AA guns
Complement:	53/60

Siluro a Lenta Corsa (1940)

Designs for a "human torpedo" or Siluro a Lenta Corsa ("low-speed torpedo") were first prepared in Italy during 1935 by two officers, one of them Teseo Tesei, at the base of La Spezia. This strange device, some 20 feet (6.1 m) long and 21 inches (533 mm) in diameter, had saddles and stirrups for two men, who worc free-diving gear. Thirty men were allocated to Tesei, and shortly before the end of 1935 the prototype was ready for trials. The SLC was driven by an electric motor turning a pair of contra-rotating propellers, and could operate for up to six hours at a speed of 3 knots. Tesei undertook some of the first trials, and declared his invention to be a *maiale* ("pig"), and the name stuck. Direction was controlled by movement of a lever to the left or right, while ascent and descent was controlled by movement of the control lever backward and forward. In front of the pilot was a small luminous dial which, down to a depth of 30 feet (9 m), allowed him to read his compass, amp meter, and pressure gauge. Behind the pilot, the other member of the team was tasked with maintaining the trim, using an electric pump to move water between the fore and aft tanks, and to help secure the front section of the *maiale*, which was a detachable warhead containing 551 lb. (250 kg) of HE, for attaching to the underside of the target ship. Special clamps were used to secure a wire between the bilge keels as a cradle for the warhead, which was fitted with a time fuse to allow the *maiale* to escape.

On June 10, 1940, the day when Italy entered World War II, the Italian merchant vessel *Fulgor* took refuge in Cadiz Bay, 80 miles (130 km) from the British base at Gibraltar. The Italians planned that the vessel would not go to sea again: it was to become a secret depot for their submarines in action in the Atlantic. Her regular crew was replaced by naval personnel, and large quantities of consumables were bought and loaded, while secret deliveries included torpedoes labeled as machinery. Crews for the *maiali* arrived on the merchant vessel, and in August 1941 the submarine *Scire*, with two *maiali*

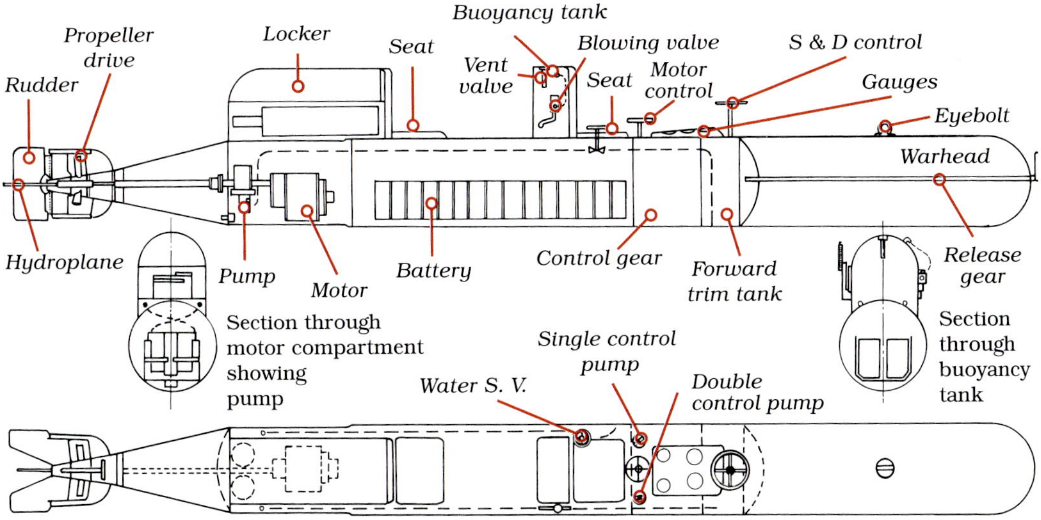

Above:
The diagrams show the relatively simple workings of the two-man Sea-Pig, with its huge detachable warhead.

Right:
The Italian "human torpedo" preserved in a park overlooking the sea in Catania, Sicily.
All photos: John Batchelor.

clamped to her, sneaked into Cadiz Bay and transferred the two *maiali* to the *Fulgor*, which received another three SLCs in September of the same year by the same means. Under the command of Lucio Visintini, the *maiali* were to force their way into the Gibraltar harbor and attack the British ships there, but the net defenses were lowered and the *maiali* followed a British destroyer into the harbor. Visintini attached his warhead to the hull of the naval tanker *Denbydale*. Hours later, the tanker's back was broken by an explosion. Soon after this, there were two other explosions, under the 10,900-ton cargo ship *Durham* and the 2,445-ton storage tanker *Fiona Shell*.

The *maiali* had proved their capability. But the Italians realized that it might no longer be necessary to continue using the *Fulgor*, as another Italian vessel, the *Olterra*, was available at Algeciras, in Spain just opposite Gibraltar. Visintini was smuggled onto the *Olterra* to supervise her conversion into a *maiale* base ship. A section some 25 feet (7.6 m) long was cut from the bulkhead separating the bow compartment from the small cargo hold and hinged as a hatch. The Italians next cut an opening, 4 feet (1.2 m) square, in the side of the bow some 6 feet (1.8 m) below the waterline, the plating being hinged to open inward as another hatch. Again delivered in the form of "machinery," the *maiali* were slung in water-filled bow to pass in and out through the hatch in the side.

Soon the first attack from the *Olterra* was launched, Visintini leading three *maiali*. Intelligence had advised that small explosive charges were detonated by the harbor gate, at intervals of about 10 minutes, to deter submarines, and the Italian party was gambling on breaking through between explosions. As they listened to the explosions, though, the Italians realized that the interval was only about three minutes. Visintini and his companion were killed by an explosion at the gate, and their *maiale* disappeared to the bottom. The rear-seater on the second *maiale* was dislodged by the force of the current somewhere in the bay and his colleague returned alone to the *Olterra*. The crew of the third *maiale* was hit while trying to cut through the underwater defensive net, and their human torpedo was damaged, so they pulled away and sank their weapon before swimming to shore.

It was May 1943 before the Italians were able to restock the *Olterra*, on which Ernesto Notari, a former destroyer captain, led the naval detachment. He decided against further attacks on the Gibraltar harbor, and opted to focus his team's efforts on ships in the open outer anchorage, which was protected only by patrol craft. On May 7 Notari led the next attack, which was a success: all three *maiali* returned safely and three ships were hit. These were the 7,000-ton Liberty ship *Pat Harrison* and 7,500-ton *Mahsud* (severely damaged), and the 4,875-ton *Camerata*, which was a total loss.

Locker behind 2nd crew member showing pneumatic ram and air bottle.

The third and final attack from the *Olterra* was launched on August 3, Notari again leading three *maiali*. Notari's target was the 7,000-ton Liberty ship *Harrison Grey Otis*, and below her Notari discovered a new defense in the form of a curtain of barbed wire hanging deep into the water from the vessel's sides. Notari went deep to get under the curtain, but soon the two men were in difficulty. While they were fixing the warhead, their *maiale* started to drift up, threatening to break the surface. Notari tried to rectify the matter by opening the diving valves, but too wide and too quickly, and the *maiale* plunged out of control. Notari hung on as the *maiale* dropped deeper, soon

Right:
The guard around the propeller.

Below right:
The forward control position, showing vital information on dials.

passing 115 feet (35 m), which was three times the maximum training depth. Then the *maiale* reversed direction and began a fast ascent toward the surface. Notari was almost ripped away, but still managed to cling on as the *maiale* broke surface with a great splash right beside the Liberty ship. To his amazement, no one on the ship spotted the event, so he set off back toward the *Olterra*, some 4 miles (6.4 km) away. Notari's rear-seater had been torn away during the dive and returned to the surface on the other side of the Liberty ship. Believing that Notari must be dead, Petty Officer Giannoli supported himself on the ship's rudder and then, believing that the warhead's detonation was due at any minute, shouted for help. Giannoli was pulled on board, and just as a patrol boat was being coming alongside to collect him, the warhead exploded, blowing a hole in the side of the ship. Two more explosions soon followed: the 10,000-ton Norwegian tanker *Thorshoudi* was broken in two and disaster had also overtaken the 6,000-ton British vessel *Stanridge*. All three ships sank.

Other *maiale* crews operated in the eastern Mediterranean. In December

1941 *maiali* penetrated the Alexandria harbor and targeted the British Mediterranean Fleet's only two battleships, the *Valiant* and *Queen Elizabeth*. Both had holes blown through their hulls. Although they were able to steam under their own power to dry dock for repair, the two battleships were out of commission for months, a fact the British were largely able to conceal. This was nonetheless a severe blow as it helped to tilt the balance of naval power.

O-19 class (1938)

Up until the two-boat O-19 class, the Dutch had differentiated between their O-type boats for service in home waters and K-class boats for service in the waters round the Dutch East Indies. The first of the South-East Asian boats had been the *K-I*, completed in 1913 with a displacement of 386 tons, whereas the O-2 class boats of the same period and intended for home service were considerably smaller at a displacement of only 150 tons. The boats for South-East Asian had, of course, to therefore entered service only in 1921-23. The K-II and K-V classes, amounting to one and three boats respectively, were akin to the *K-I* in being of the Hay-Denny type, but the K-III and K-VII classes switched to the Holland type.

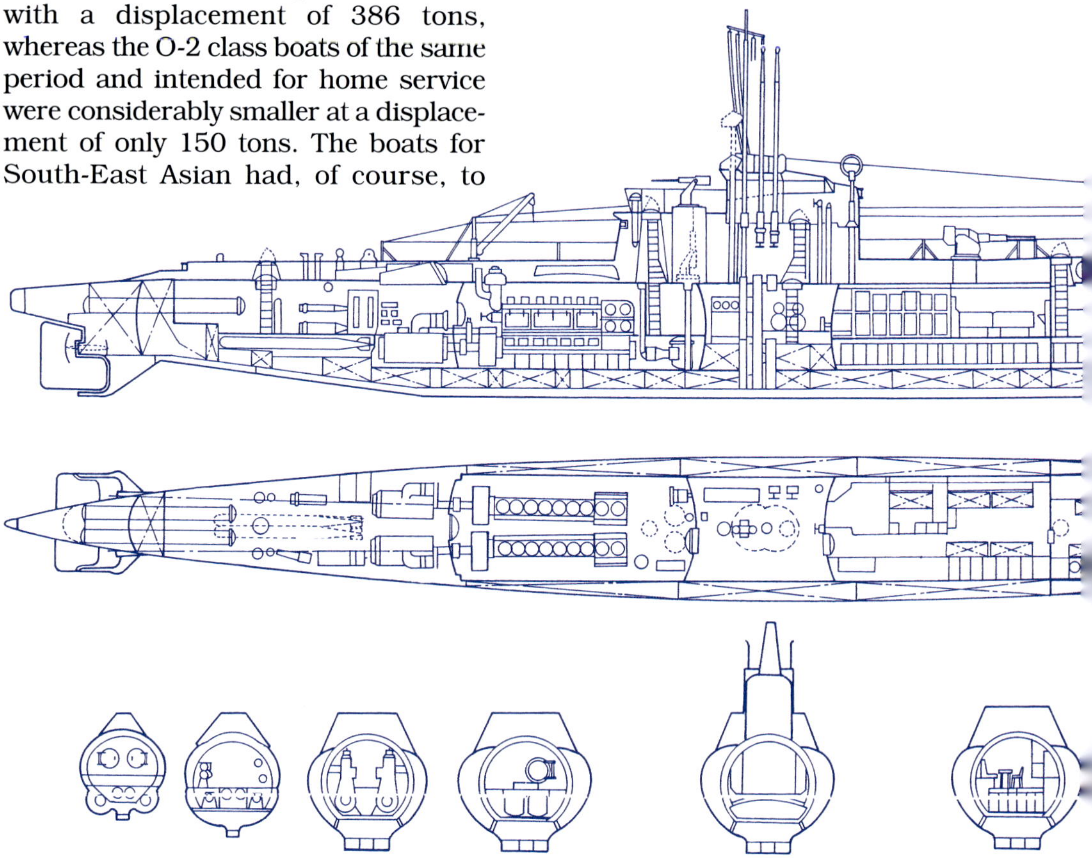

cope with much hotter temperatures and longer patrols, and therefore required greater volume inside the pressure hull.

No fewer than nine colonial submarines of four distinct classes had been laid down during World War I, even though the Netherlands remained neutral in this conflict, but all of these boats took a long time to complete, and

The first Dutch submarine of the period after World War I was the K-XI class of 815 tons submerged, and the three boats were completed in 1925. They were followed in the early 1930s by the K-XIV class, whose five units had a submerged displacement of 1,008 tons and were in effect enlarged versions of the O-12 class boats then building for use in home waters. The K-

XIV class boats were the largest submarines built by the Netherlands up to that time, and had a powerful armament of eight 21-inch (533 mm) torpedo tubes located as four in the bow, two in the stern and two on a trainable mounting in the upper casing.

The next submarines for Southeast Asian service were to have been the K-XIX class boats, but it was decided to drop the different prefixes previously used to distinguish between the two types of submarine and the new type thereupon became the O-19 class. The design was derived from that of two mine-laying boats, the *Orzel* and *Sep*, built for the Polish navy by Rotterdam Dry Dock two years earlier, but with engines offering some 60% more power than those of the O-16 class for a surfaced speed of slightly more than 19 knots. To allow the boats to cruise just under the surface on their diesel engines, and so avoid the worst of the tropical heat, a Dutch officer conceived the idea of an air-breathing tube, the prototype snorkel. First fitted in the O-19 class, this tube incorporated an air intake and an engine exhaust, with an automatic cut-off valve to prevent accidental flooding. The class had the same armament arrangement as the K-XIV class, and was also equipped to carry mines, using the French Normand-Fenaux system: 40 mines were carried in 20 vertical tubes, 10 on each side of the hull in the ballast tanks, each tube containing two mines.

The *O-19* and *O-20* were completed in time to escape the German invasion of May 1940 and reached the South-East Asia. On December 20, 1941, the *O-20* was severely damaged by depth charges from the Japanese destroyer *Uranami* and had to be scuttled. The *O-19* operated in Far Eastern waters throughout the war until it was wrecked in the South China Sea on July 8, 1945.

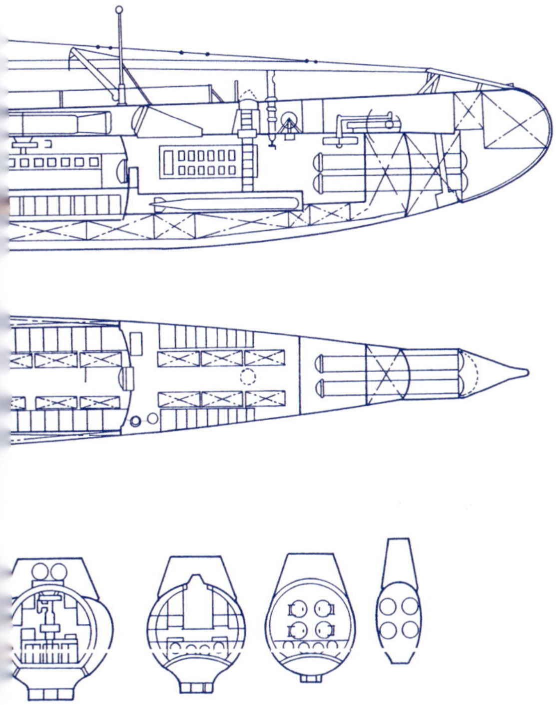

O-19 class

Type:	patrol submarine
Tonnage:	998 tons surfaced and 1,536 tons submerged
Dimensions:	length 265 ft., 9 in. (81 m); beam 24 ft., 7 in. (7.5 m); draft 13 ft., 1 in. (4 m)
Propulsion:	two Sulzer diesel engines delivering 5,200 hp (3879 kW) for 19.25 knots surfaced and two electric motors delivering 1,000 hp (746 kW) for 9 knots submerged
Armament:	one 3 1/2-inch (88 mm) and two 1 1/2-inch (40 mm) AA guns, and eight 21-inch (533 in) tubes for 14 torpedoes
Complement:	55

X class (1942)

The X-class submarines were a series of midget submarines built for the Royal Navy in World War II, used operationally in 1943-45. Known individually as "X-craft," the boats were designed to be towed to their operational areas by a larger submarine, most generally an S-class or T-class boat. The passage was normally made with the X-craft manned by a passage crew, and the operational crew exchanged places by means of a dinghy once the operational area had been reached. The X-craft carried only 2,434 lb. (1104 kg) of diesel fuel, sufficient for a range of 575 miles (925 km) on the surface, while its batteries provided a range of 95 miles (153 km) at 2 knots submerged. The maximum diving depth was 300 feet (90 m). With its attack completed, the X-craft was supposed to rendezvous with its "mother" boat and then be towed home.

The endurance was limited primarily by the endurance and determination of the crew, but was thought to be up to 14 days in the craft.

Each of the craft was powered on the surface by a Gardner four-cylinder diesel engine, adapted from a type used in London buses, and the standard crew was initially three men (commander, navigator, and engineer) but this was soon supplemented by a specialist diver, for whom an air lock or "wet and dry" compartment was provided.

The "weapons" carried by the X class of submarines consisted of two side-cargoes, which were explosive charges held on the sides of the hull and each containing two tons of Amatol HE. The X-craft was designed to position itself below the target vessel and drop these onto the sea bed before creeping off to safety, before time fuses initiated the detonation of the two charges.

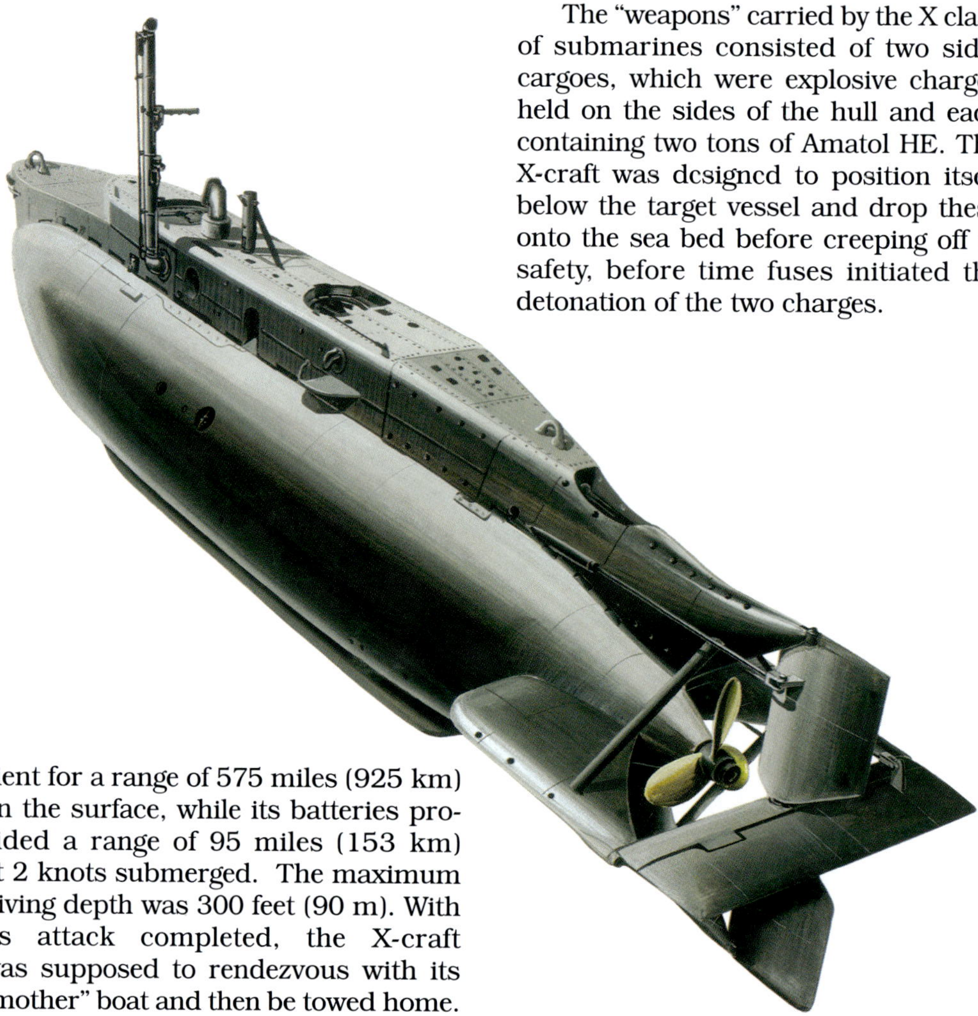

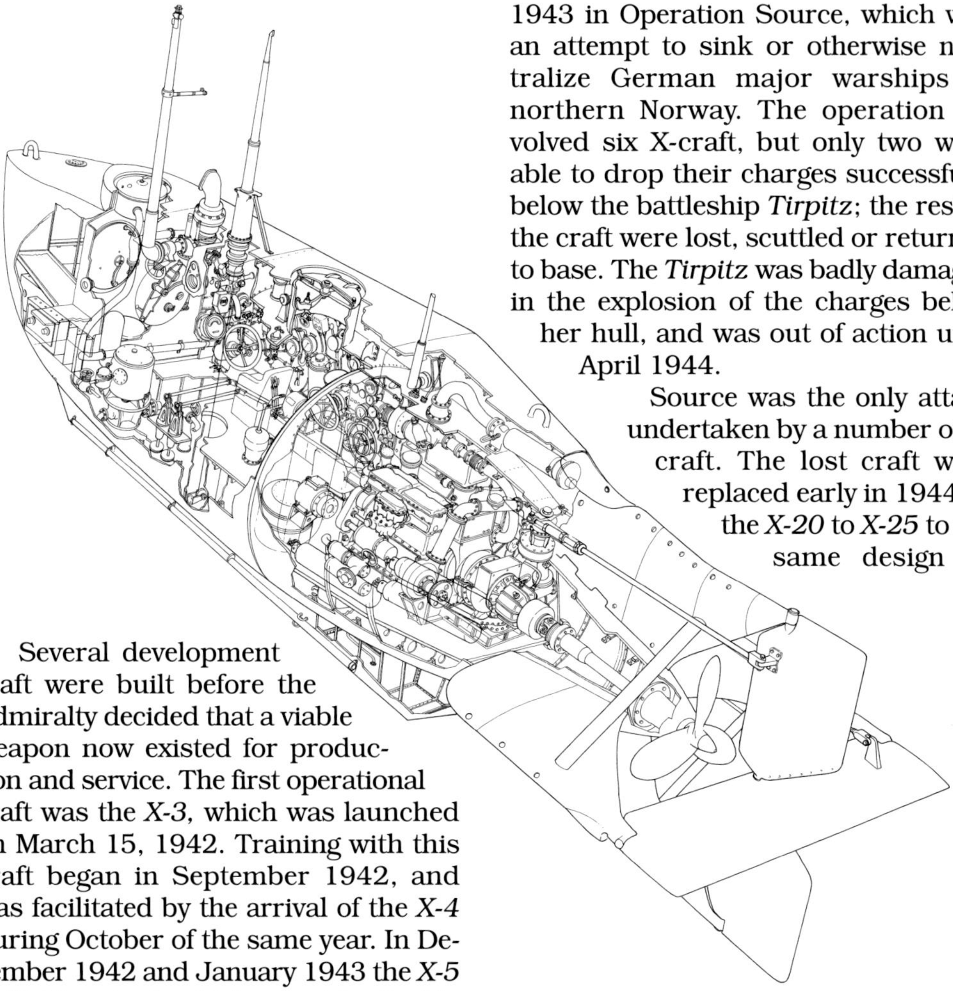

Several development craft were built before the Admiralty decided that a viable weapon now existed for production and service. The first operational craft was the *X-3,* which was launched on March 15, 1942. Training with this craft began in September 1942, and was facilitated by the arrival of the *X-4* during October of the same year. In December 1942 and January 1943 the *X-5* to *X-10* arrived, which were identical to the *X-3* and *X-4* externally but introduced a completely revised interior arrangement deemed necessary for use in combat operations.

The first operational use of the X-class boats took place in September 1943 in Operation Source, which was an attempt to sink or otherwise neutralize German major warships in northern Norway. The operation involved six X-craft, but only two were able to drop their charges successfully below the battleship *Tirpitz*; the rest of the craft were lost, scuttled or returned to base. The *Tirpitz* was badly damaged in the explosion of the charges below her hull, and was out of action until April 1944.

Source was the only attack undertaken by a number of X-craft. The lost craft were replaced early in 1944 by the *X-20* to *X-25* to the same design as

the *X-5* to *X-10* and the *XT-1* to *XT-6* were also introduced for use only as training craft with displacements of 26.7 tons surfaced and 29.8 tons submerged, slightly greater beam, and only 1,124 lb. (514 kg) of diesel fuel as only a shorter surfaced range was required.

On April 15, 1944, the *X-24* was used in an attack on the Laksevåg floating dock in the harbor of the German-occupied Norwegian city of Bergen. The *X-22* had been intended for the mission, but this boat had been rammed accidentally during training and lost with all hands. The *X-24*'s crew made its approach carefully and escaped successfully, but mistook the target and placed the charges not under the dock, which suffered only minor damage, but below the *Bärenfels*, a 7,500-ton merchant ship lying alongside the dock. The ship was sunk. On September 11 of the same year, *X-24* repeated the operation, this time in the hands of a different crew, and succeeded in sinking the dock.

X-craft were also involved in the preparations for Operation Overlord, Operation Postage Able involving surveys of the planned landing beaches by the *X-20*, which spent four days of January 1944 off the north coast of France. While the crew undertook periscope reconnaissance of the shoreline and echo soundings of the waters off the beaches by day, by night the boat approached the beaches and a pair of divers swam shore to collect beach samples. The divers landed on two nights to survey the beaches at Vierville-sur-Mer, Moulins St Laurent and Colleville-sur-Mer in the area of the U.S. landing forces on "Omaha" Beach. On the third night, the divers were scheduled to land in the estuary of the Orne river ("Sword" Beach) but the crew and the divers were exhausted after surviving on little more than benzedrine tablets, and the boat's commander called off this undertaking, steering the boat home to the south coast of England. During Overlord, the *X-20* and *X-23* operated as pilot craft in Operation Gambit, helping the Allied forces to land on the beaches assigned to them.

Six midget submarines were built as the *XE-1* to *XE-6* for use in the Far East. The boats were constructed as XE-class craft to an improved standard with a length of 53 ft., 1 in. (16.2 m) and submerged displacement of 33.6 tons. Each boat carried a four-man crew in the form, typically, of a lieutenant in command, a sub-lieutenant, an engine room artificer, and leading seaman or seaman; at least one of the men was a qualified diver. In addition to the two side charges, each boat carried at least six 200 lb. (91 kg) limpet mines for magnetic attachment to the target by the diver.

The six boats and their depot ship, *Bonaventure,* reached Labuan Island off in Borneo in July 1945, and four of the boats were used operationally. In August 1945 the *XE-1* and *XE-3* attacked Japanese heavy cruisers in Singapore harbor, severely damaging the *Takao* but missing the *Myoko*, and escaped successfully.

Another two operations were undertaken to cut the undersea telephone cables connecting Singapore, Saïgon, Hong Kong, and Tokyo, forcing the Japanese to use radio and make themselves open to message interception. The *XE-4* located and severed the cables from Saigon, and the *XE-5* achieved a similar success off Lamma Island, Hong Kong. The European boats were discarded in 1945, but some of the Far East boats survived until 1952-53.

X class

Type:	midget submarine
Tonnage:	27 tons surfaced and 30 tons submerged
Dimensions:	length 51 ft., 3 in. (15.6 m); beam 5 ft., 9 in. (1.75 m); draft 5 ft., 4 in. (1.6 m)
Propulsion:	one Gardner diesel engine delivering 42 hp (31.3 KW) for 6.5 knots surfaced and one Keith Blackman electric motor delivering 30 hp (22.3 kW) for 5.5 knots submerged
Armament:	two 4,400 lb. (1996 kg) detachable explosive charges
Complement:	4

"S" War Emergency & 1941 Programme classes (1941)

When World War II started in 1939, the Royal Navy had a pressing need for more submarines, and as the 12 boats of the pre-war Swordfish and Shark subclasses of the S class had proved excellent, more such submarines were ordered in four batches under the War Emergency, 1941, 1942 and 1943 Programs. Some 61 boats were ordered, but 11 were cancelled late in the war.

The hull was lengthened by comparison with those of the Swordfish and Shark classes, so the boats had greater displacement. Production encompassed the period when British yards were switching from riveted to welded construction, so while the boats of the War Emergency and 1941 Programs had a combination of welded and riveted construction, all but two of the boats of the 1942 and 1943 programs were all-welded, increasing the diving depth from 300 feet to 350 (91 m to 107). There was nothing radical in the design of the S-class boats, but from the start the type exhibited a harmonious blend of all that was right and thus emerged as reliable, safe, and agile, with sufficient armament and performance.

While the Swordfish and Shark classes had six 21-inch (533 mm) bow tubes for 12 torpedoes, in most of the boats ordered under the War Emergency and 1941 programs, another tube was added externally at the stern without a reload. Most of the boats could carry 12 mines instead of torpedoes. The standard deck gun was a 3-inch (76 mm) weapon, but the *Scotsman*, *Scythian*, and *Sea Devil* had a 4-inch (102 mm) weapon. In these boats, the stern tube had to be removed to offset the greater weight of the larger-caliber gun, and the stern tube was also omitted from the *Safari*, *P-222*, and *Strongbow*. Many of the boats were also given a 3/4-inch (20 mm) AA cannon on a platform at the after end of the conning tower.

The War Emergency and 1941 Program boats were the *Safari*, *Sahib*, *Saracen*, *Satyr*, *Sceptre*, *P-222*, *Seadog*, *Sea Nymph*, *Sea Rover*, *Seraph*, *Shakespeare*, *Sibyl*, *Sickle*, *Simoom*, *Sirdar*, *Spiteful*, *Splendid*, *Sportsman*, *Scotsman*, *Scythian*, *Sea Devil*, *Shalimar*, *Spark*, *Spirit*, *Statesman*, *Stoic*, *Stonehenge*, *Storm*, *Stratagem*, *Strongbow*, *Stubborn*, *Surf* and *Syrtis*. The standard fuel load was 45 tons carried in internal tanks, but in all except the *Safari*, *Scotsman*, and *Sea Devil* this was increased to 67 tons by converting part of two main tanks, and could be supplemented by a further 40 tons in *Scotsman* and *Sea Devil* or by 25 tons in most of the boats with 67 tons by using more of the main tanks for fuel.

Given the possibility that the Germans might be able to introduce large numbers of their high-speed Type XXI U-boats, between July and September 1944 the *Seraph* was converted at Devonport into a high-speed training target by cleaning-up the boat's hull and casing, removing the guns, and installing higher-capacity batteries, more powerful motors, and the coarser-pitch propellers of the T-class submarine: this resulted in a speed of 12.5 knots at periscope depth on 1,647 hp (1228 kW), and a surfaced speed of 16.75 knots. The boat was also given extra protection for use as a target for inert torpedoes. The *Sceptre*, *Satyr*, and *Statesman* were later converted similarly.

The *Sahib*, *Saracen*, and *P-222* were sunk by Italian torpedo boats or corvettes in April 1943, August 1943, and December 1942, respectively; the *Splendid* by a German and *Stratagem* by a Japanese destroyer in April 1943 and November 1944, respectively; and the *Sickle*, *Simoom* and *Syrtis* probably by mines in June 1944, November 1943 and March 1944, respectively; the *Stonehenge* was lost to unknown causes in the Malacca Straits in March 1944. The *Satyr*, *Spiteful*, *Sportsman*, and *Statesman* were transferred to France in 1951-52 to become the *Saphir*, *Sirène*, *Sibylle*, and *Sultane* in the anti-submarine training role. The *Sibylle* was lost in an accident, and the other three were later returned to the UK. The last British boats were scrapped in the early 1960s.

S (War Emergency and 1941 Programs) class

Type:	patrol submarine
Tonnage:	842 tons surfaced and 990 tons submerged
Dimensions:	length 217 ft. (66.1 m); beam 23 ft. 9 in. (7.25 m); draft 13 ft., 10 in. (4.2 m)
Propulsion:	two Admiralty Standard Range or Vickers diesel engines delivering 1,900 hp (1417 kW) for 14.75 knots surfaced and two electric motors delivering 1,300 hp (969 kW) for 9 knots submerged
Armament:	one 4-inch (102 mm) gun and seven 21-inch (533 mm) tubes for 13 torpedoes
Complement:	48

Vampire class (1943)

The Royal Navy's V-class submarine was more formally known as the U Long-Hull 1941-42 Program-class boat. Some 42 units of the class were ordered from Vickers-Armstrong for construction at either Barrow-in-Furness or Walker-on-Tyne, but only 22 were completed. Seven of the boats received names starting with "U," while four of the preceding U-class boats had received names starting with "V." The V-class submarines were very similar to the preceding U class except for their pressure hulls of three-quarter-inch steel rather than a half inch thick (19 mm rather than 12.7) for a deeper diving capability, and a lengthened stern and fining at the bows to reduce noise and improve underwater handling. The hulls had welded frames and riveted plates.

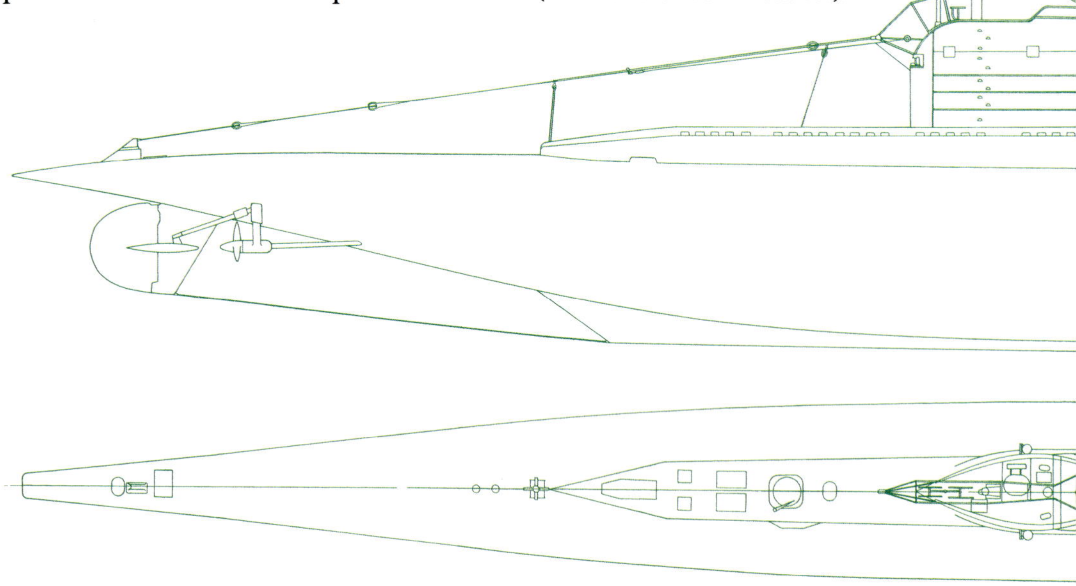

The first eight units were ordered on December 5, 1941, as the *Venturer* (later the Norwegian *Utstein*), *Viking* (later the Norwegian *Utvær*), *Veldt* (completed as the Greek *Pipinios*), *Vampire*, *Vox*, *Vigorous*, *Virtue*, and *Visigoth*. The next 18 boats were ordered on 21 May 1942, but six were cancelled early in 1944, so leaving the *Vivid*, *Voracious*, *Vulpine* (later the Danish *Storen*), *Varne*, *Upshot*, *Urtica*, *Vineyard* (completed as the French *Doris*), *Variance* (later the Norwegian *Utsira*), *Vengeful* (later the Greek *Delfin*), *Vortex* (completed as the French *Morse* before becoming the Danish *Saelen*), *Virulent* (later the Greek *Argonaftis*) and *Volatile* (later the Greek *Triaina*).

The cancelled boats would have been the *Veto*, *Virile*, *Visitant*, *Upas*, *Ulex* and *Utopia*. Another six boats were ordered on November 17, 1942, but four were cancelled in January 1944 to leave only the *Votary* (later the Norwegian *Uthaug*) and *Vagabond*. The cancelled boats would have been the *Vantage*, *Vehement*, *Venom* and *Verve*. Lastly, 10 boats were ordered but all cancelled in November 1943. The only two of these to receive names would have been the *Unbridled* and *Upward*.

Picture shows the Engine Room of a British WWII-era submarine.
Photo: Vickers.

The two Danish boats remained in service until 1958, the four Greek boats until 1957-58, and the last of the British boats into the late 1940s and early 1950s.

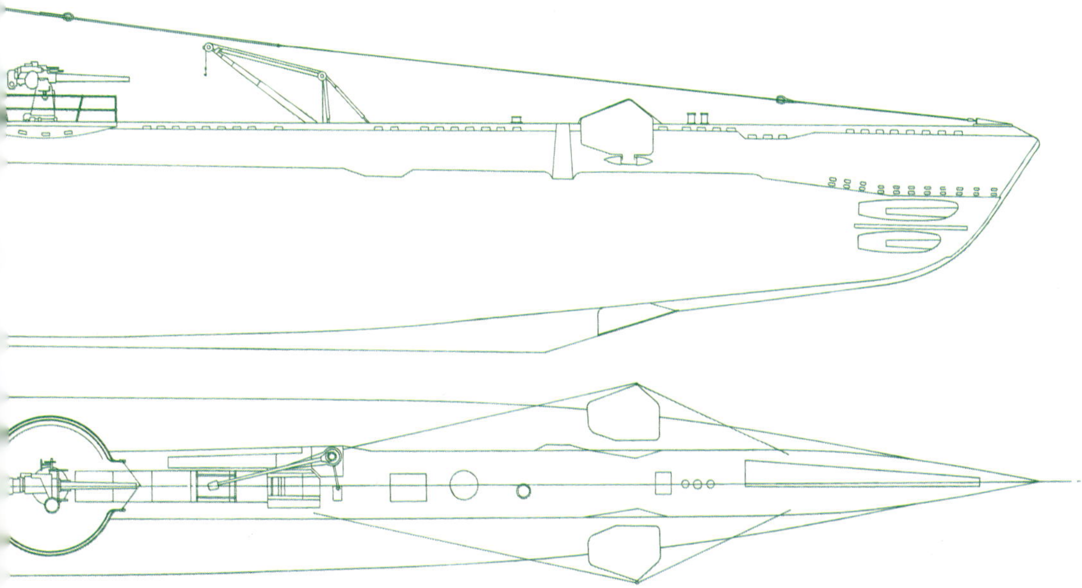

Vampire class

Type:	patrol submarine
Tonnage:	658 tons surfaced and 740 tons submerged
Dimensions:	length 204 ft., 6 in. (62.33 m); beam 16 ft., 1 in. (4.9 m); draft 15 ft., 3 in. (4.64 m)
Propulsion:	two Paxman diesel generators delivering 615 hp (459 kW) for 11.25 knots surfaced and two electric motors delivering 825 hp (615 kW) for 10 knots submerged
Armament:	one 3-inch (76 mm) gun and four 21-inch (533 mm) tubes for eight torpedoes
Complement:	33

Chariot human torpedo (1942)

The Italian navy pioneered the underwater human torpedo as a manned derivative of the torpedo operated by a two-man crew wearing diving suits and sitting astride the main body of the weapon. Electrically powered, the human torpedo carried a large warhead that could be attached to the target as the crew made their escape on the rear part of the vehicle. The torpedo was carried by another vessel, normally a submarine, and launched near the target.

The concept was first used with success by the Italian navy (Regia Marina) early in World War II and then copied by the British when they suffered the consequences of the Italian attacks. The official designation of the Italian craft was Siluro a Lenta Corsa ("slow-running torpedo"), but their riders nicknamed it the *maiale* (pig), as it was difficult to steer. The British copies were named Chariot, and British work on the development of the Chariot Mk I can be dated to April 1942. The Chariot Mk I had a theoretical diving depth of 150 feet (45 m) but practical limit of 60 feet (18 m) or less, and its endurance was six hours at maximum speed.

The first British Chariot attack was Operation Title, an abortive attack on the German battleship *Tirpitz* in Norwegian waters between October 26 and November 1, 1942. On October 26, the trawler *Arthur*, manned by three Norwegians, left British waters with seven British commando frogmen hidden on board and two Chariots secured below her hull. Two days later, the *Arthur* reached the Norwegian coast near Edøy and bluffed its way past the German patrols. On October 30 the two Chariots were freed from their fixings under the hull and the *Arthur* began to tow the torpedoes toward the target area. However, on October 31 a storm broke the fastening bolts of the Chariots, which were lost, and the operation had to be called off.

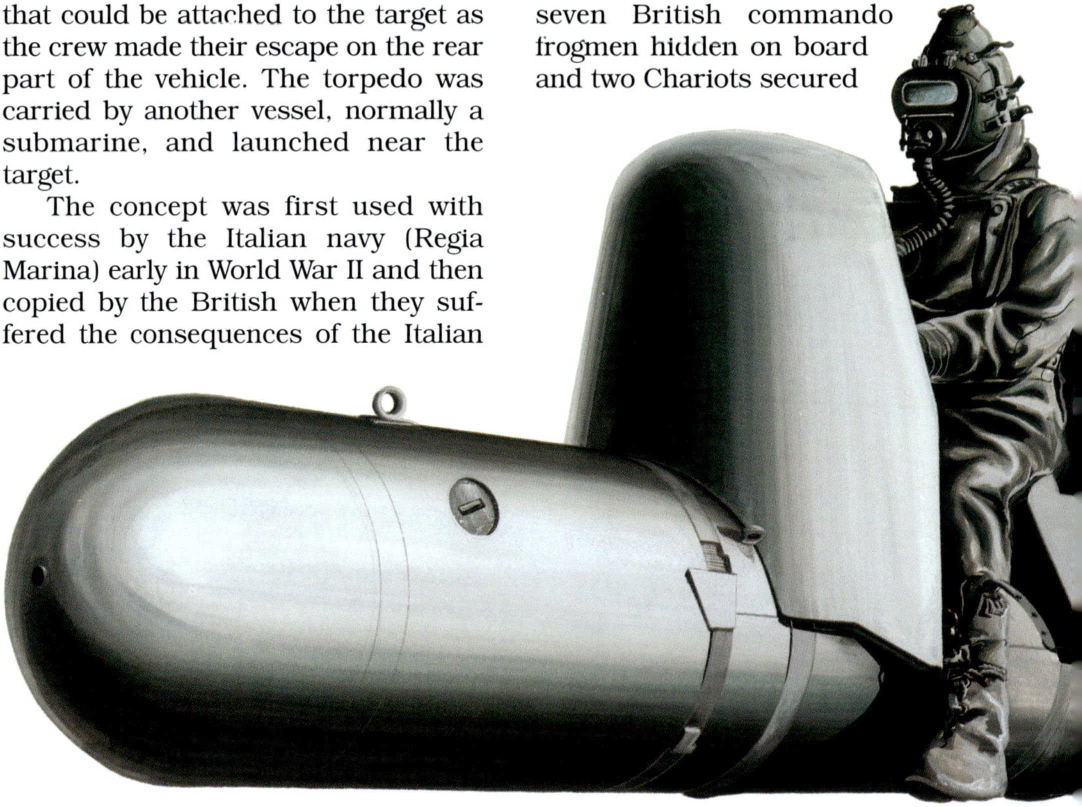

Operation Principal was the next British attack with Chariots, and was directed at targets in the Italian ports of Palermo on the island of Sicily and of La Maddalena on the island of Sardinia on January 2-3, 1943. In December 1942 the first Chariots reached Malta. The Chariots were despatched from Malta against Palermo and La Maddalena, just before the end of 1942. The *P311* and her three Chariots (and 10 "charioteers") were lost with all hands while en route to La Maddalena, but five other Chariots carried by the *Trooper* (three) and

Thunderbolt (two) penetrated into Palermo harbor, where the new light cruiser *Ulpio Traiano* was sunk and the large liner *Viminale* damaged on the night of January 2-3, 1943. All of the Chariots were lost by being scuttled, or as a result of equipment malfunction or human error. One "charioteer" died in the attack, and the *Unruffled* recovered two others. Five had to land and were taken prisoner; two later escaped.

The second half of the Principal undertaking left two 2.5-knot Chariot Mk Is and eight "charioteers" on Malta. On January 18-19, 1943, these two Chariots were carried by submarines in the Operation Childhood attack on the ships with which the Germans hoped to block the Tripoli harbor, a logistic base which was urgently needed by the British 8th Army as it advanced west across the northern coast of North Africa. The "charioteers" arrived too late and a blockship was sunk in the harbor mouth. None of the men or chariots returned to Malta.

On April 16 the British sent 14 new "charioteers" to Malta, following them with examples of the new 4.5-knot Chariot Mk II, on which the two "charioteers" sat back-to-back and which carried a 1,190 lb. (540 kg) warhead carrying 560 lb. (254 kg) of Torpex HE. In June the British submarine *Unseen* carried three Chariot Mk IIs from Malta to Sicily, where the "charioteers" surveyed 100 miles (160 km) of coast, examining beaches. Late in June, another six Chariots reached Malta for an operation planned against the Italian fleet anchorage at Taranto, but with the fall of Benito Mussolini and the installation of a government seeking an armistice with the Allies, the planned attack was cancelled and all the "charioteers" were sent to the main base at Loch Cairnbawm on the west coast of Scotland.

On September 24, four Chariot Mk IIs and 12 "charioteers" were dispatched from Loch Cairnbawm to Lunna Voe in the Shetland Islands to train in for operations among the Norwegian islands, and on October 14 a British light warship carrying two Chariots and four "charioteers" sailed from Lunna Voe to Tevik Bay in Norway, but German aircraft found the British vessel and attacked it, causing significant damage but not preventing its return to

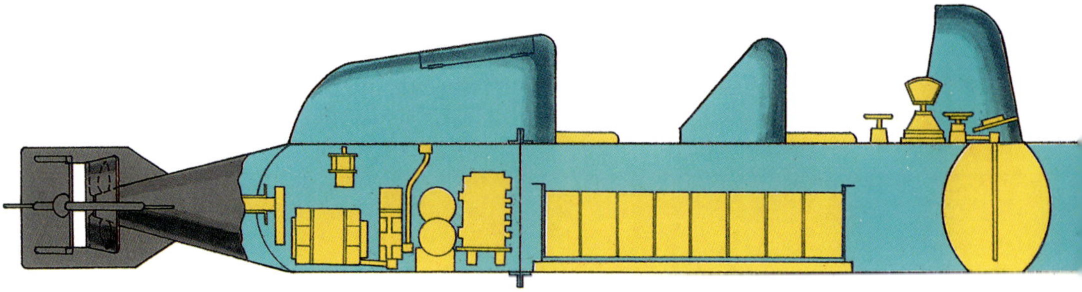

the UK. Later in the same year, another British vessel, with two Chariots and four "charioteers" left Lunna Voe for the Nordfjord in Norway, but no target for the Chariots was discovered and the vessel returned to the Shetland Islands. On November 11, another such effort was launched, with two Chariots and four "charioteers" delivered from Lunna Voe, in this instance to Tevik Bay, Norway, to attack any ship which entered the harbor of Askvoll. After two days, no German ship had arrived and there was a growing threat that the harbor would be closed by ice, so the British party set off back to the Shetland Islands, jettisoning the two Chariots en route because of adverse weather.

In May 1944 Chariots and "charioteers" were sent from the UK to Trincomalee in Sri Lanka, and at much the same time Chariots were used for a survey of the sea bed off the Normandy coast of German-occupied France in preparation for Overlord.

On June 2, after the amalgamation of the British and southern Italian manned torpedo forces in the Mediterranean, the Italian destroyer *Grecale* sailed from Bastia in Corsica to La Spezia carrying three motor torpedo boats and Italian frogmen including Luigi Durand De La Penne, and also two British Chariots, for an attack on the Italian heavy cruisers *Bolzano* and *Gorizia*, which had been seized by the Germans after the Italian armistice of September 9, 1943. The *Grecale* launched the boats, which then carried the Chariots and their "charioteers" to a release point 3 miles (4.8 km) off the harbor of La Spezia. One Chariot developed a leak in its buoyancy tank and was abandoned, but the other sank the *Bolzano*. This thwarted a German plan to sink the cruisers as blockships in

the harbor entrance. Only one of the "charioteers" escaped; the other three were captured.

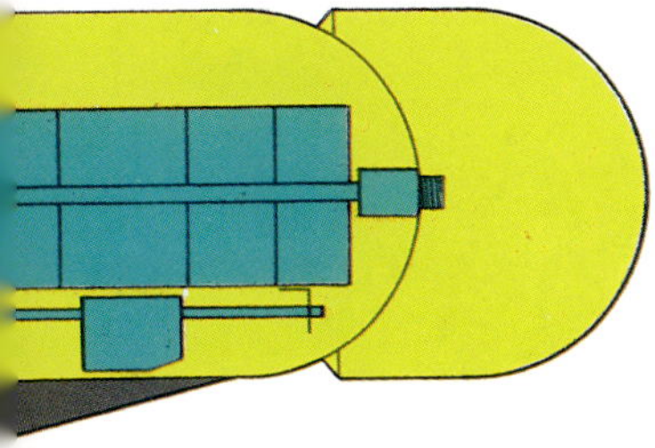

On October 27-28, the British submarine *Trenchant* carried two Chariots to an attack on the harbor of Phuket Island in Thailand. The submarine launched the Chariots 6 miles (9.7 km) from the harbor, where the only targets were a pair of commandeered Italian liners, the *Sumatra* and the *Volpi*, each of about 5,000 tons. Six hours later, the "charioteers" returned to their parent vessel with the Chariots (the only time this was achieved), but during the return voyage the submarine received a report of Japanese naval activity in the area and therefore jettisoned the Chariots so it could move more rapidly. The *Trenchant* delivered the four "charioteers" back to Trincomalee, Sri Lanka.

This is believed to have been the last combat operation undertaken by manned torpedoes, but after the end of World War II, the British used Chariots to aid in the clearance of mines and wrecks in harbors.

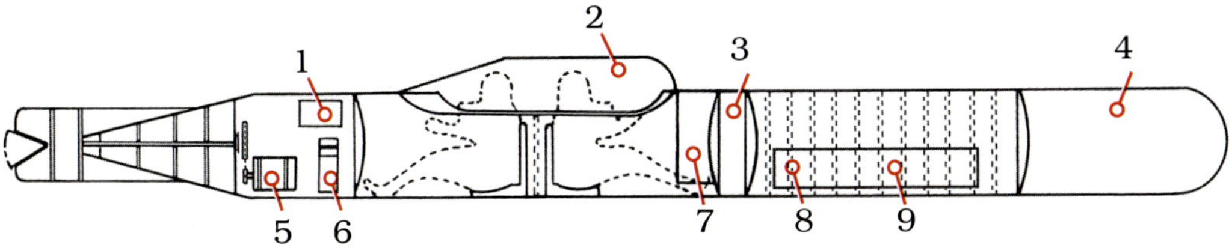

Chariot Mk. II

1	*Controller*	4	*Head*	8	*Stiffeners*
2	*Detachable Perspex Hood with sliding louvers*	5	*Motor*	9	*Battery*
3	*Bouyancy Tanks*	6	*Pump*		
		7	*Comp Tank*		

Chariot Mk I

Type:	human torpedo
Tonnage:	1.6 tons surfaced
Dimensions:	length 22 ft., 3 in. (6.8 m); beam 2 ft., 4 in. (0.7 m); draft 4 ft., 6 in. (1.4 m)
Propulsion:	one electric motor delivering 2 hp (1.5 kW) for 2.7 knots surfaced and 2.75 knots submerged
Armament:	one detachable 900-lb. (408 kg) warhead containing 600 lb. (272 kg) of HE
Complement:	2

German midget submarines (1943)

Impressed by the capabilities of British midget submarines and both British and Italian human torpedoes, the German navy proceeded along similar paths to create craft suitable for the defeat of large invasion fleets. The major conceptual difference between the German types and the British and Italian types was the Germans' decision to use the torpedo rather than side charges or a detachable warhead as the "weapon."

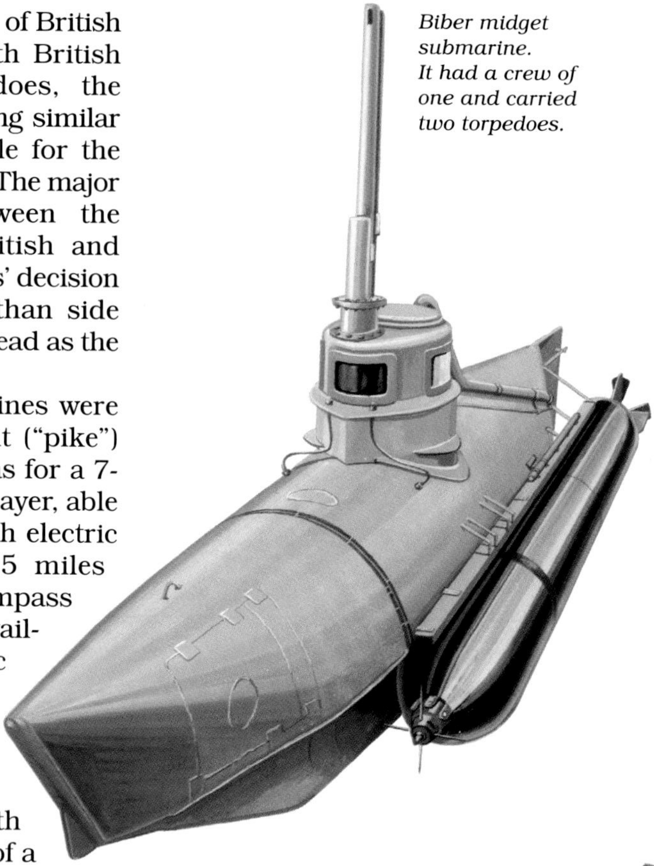

Biber midget submarine. It had a crew of one and carried two torpedoes.

The first midget submarines were of the Type XXVIIA or Hecht ("pike") class. The original design was for a 7-ton midget submarine mine-layer, able to stow one limpet mine, with electric drive and a range of 102.5 miles (165 km). As no suitable compass of small enough size was available, and standard gyroscopic equipment had therefore to be used, the size had to be increased, a fact with reduced the range. There then emerged difficulties with the provision and mounting of a suitable mine, so all notions of using the boats operationally were terminated and the craft were operated solely in the training role. The Type XXV1IA-class construction program was therefore trimmed radically, and only 53 (*U-2111* to *U-2113* and *U-2251* to *U-2300*) were delivered by Germaniawerft of Kiel from May 1944. Modifications in some of the boats included the replacement of the mine by an external torpedo slung underneath the hull, the use of the forward compartment, which originally housed the mine, for additional battery space to increase the range, or the adaptation of this compartment as a "wet and dry" compartment from which frogmen could leave or enter the craft.

Molch midget submarine, with crew of one and two torpedoes.

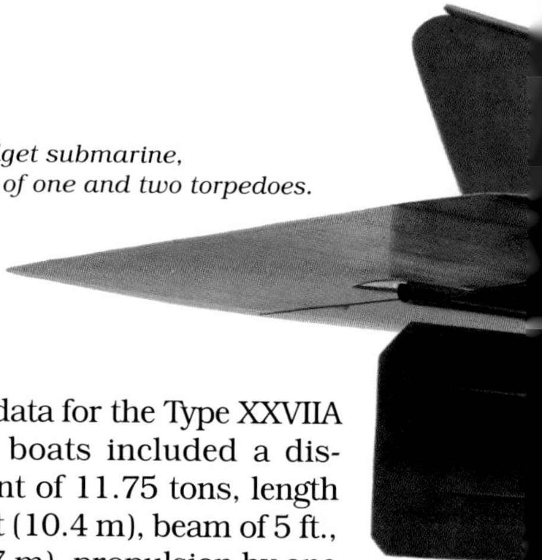

The data for the Type XXVIIA class of boats included a displacement of 11.75 tons, length of 34 feet (10.4 m), beam of 5 ft., 6 in. (1.7 m), propulsion by one electric motor delivering 13 hp (9.7 kW) for 5.75 knots surfaced and 6 knots submerged, range of 90 miles (145 km) at 3 knots surfaced and 44

Marder midget submarine, with crew of one and one torpedo.

miles (70 km) at 6 knots submerged increased to 79 miles (125 km) with additional battery capacity, armament of one mine or 21-inch (533 mm) torpedo, and complement of two.

The Type XXVIIB or Seehund ("seal") class was a logical development from the Type XXVIIA class, and was a successful type. Designed in 1944, and operated by a two-man crew, the boats were used with limited success in the final months of the war, sinking nine merchant vessels and damaging another three, but losing 35 of their own number, mostly to adverse weather.

After several attempts to perfect a midget submarine, the Seehund class was designed early in 1944, and in September of the same year the first three prototypes were produced in Kiel. Although 1,000 units of the Seehund class were planned, only 285 Seehund craft had been completed by the end of the war, and of these just 138 (*U-5001* to *U-5118* and *U-5251* to *U-5269*) had been commissioned by April 1945. Its small size, speed and agility made the Seehund virtually undetectable and difficult to destroy as a result of its ability to be tossed about without breaking up

German midget submarines *continued*

during depth charge attacks. The boats operated mainly around the German coast and in the English Channel, and could attack on the surface in turbulent weather, but had to be almost stationary for submerged attacks. In the final months of the war, the Seehund boats were used as supply boats, replenishing much needed supplies to beleaguered German garrisons along the coast. The range of the Seehund was 185 miles (300 km) at 7 knots surfaced and 71.5 miles (115 km) at 3 knots submerged, but about 50 of the craft were fitted with external tankage increasing the surfaced range to 575 miles (925 km) at 7 knots.

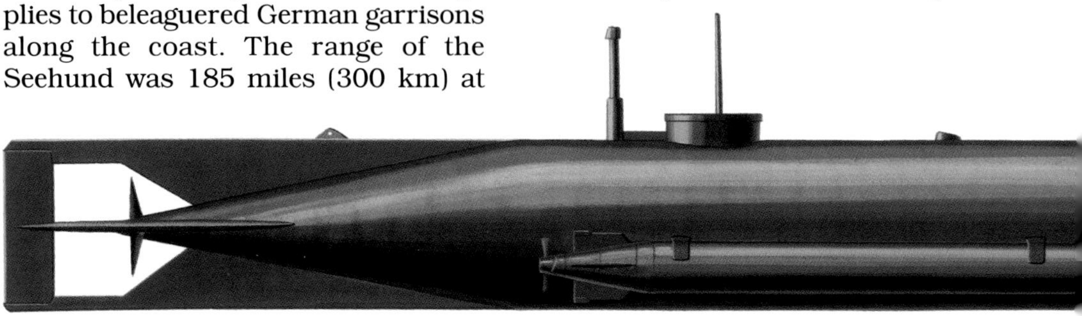

Above: Hecht type XXVIIA.

Below: Type XXIII midget submarine.

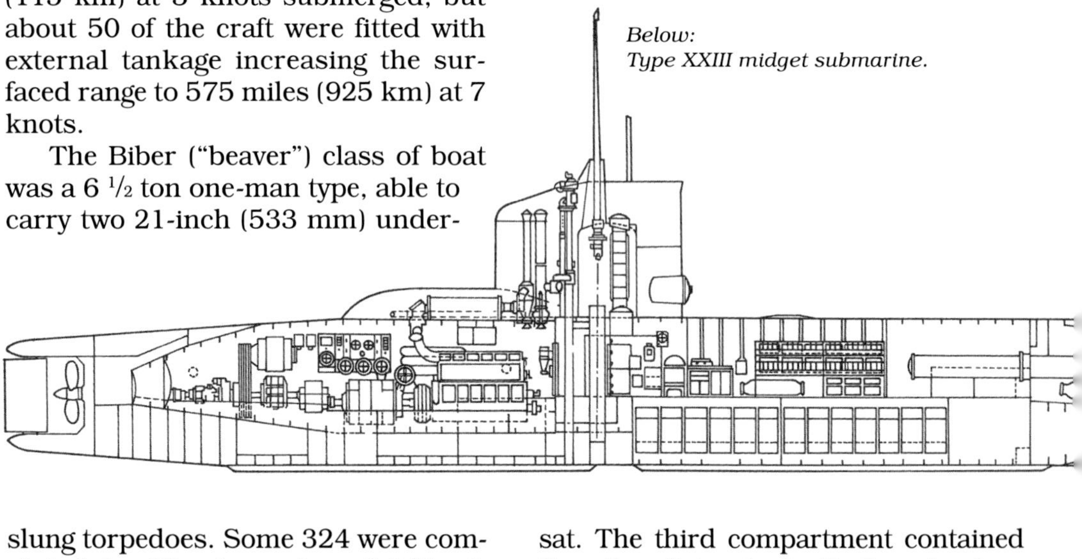

The Biber ("beaver") class of boat was a 6 ½ ton one-man type, able to carry two 21-inch (533 mm) underslung torpedoes. Some 324 were completed by Flenderwerke of Lübeck during 1944. The type was powered by one petrol engine delivering 32 hp (23.9 kW) for 6.5 knots surfaced and one electric motor delivering 13 hp (9.7 kW) for 5.25 knots submerged, and had a range of 150 miles (240 km) at 6 knots surfaced and 10 miles (16 km) 5 knots submerged. The boat could not launch its torpedoes while submerged as a result of depth-keeping problems.

The Biber was built in three sections bolted together. The bow section contained the main diving tank. Between the first and second bulkhead was the main compartment where the operator sat. The third compartment contained the after diving tank. Further developments of the Biber were planned as the two-man Biber II and Biber III, but these were not built.

The Molch ("salamander") class was an 11-ton one-man boat for coastal service with electric propulsion. Resem-

The Seehund Type XXVIIB midget submarine had a crew of two and two torpedoes.

bling a large torpedo, it had a range of only 47 miles (75 km) at 5 knots submerged, and was armed with two 21-inch (533 mm) underslung torpedoes. The first of 393 such boats was delivered in June 1944, and all the craft were built by A. G. Weser of Bremen, Germany.

The Molch craft were used in the Mediterranean against the Allied landing in the south of France in August 1944. Ten of the twelve craft were lost. Other operations followed, also without success, off Italy and in the Netherlands,

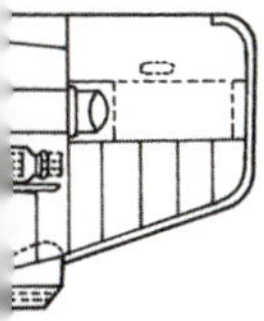

and between January and April 1945 Biber and Molch craft launched 102 sorties, losing 70 of their own number, sinking only seven small ships, and damaging two more. The Molch was later used only for training.

The Neger ("negro") and Marder ("pine marten") class craft, built to the extent of about 200 and 300 craft, respectively, in 1943 and 1945, were torpedo-carrying miniature submarines. The former operated awash, while the latter could run submerged, weighed 2.75 tons and carried one 21-inch (533 mm) torpedo. They could travel for 56 miles (90 km) at 4 knots surfaced. Their losses were very heavy and their victories very limited.

Seehund class

Type:	midget submarine
Tonnage:	15 tons
Dimensions:	length 39 ft. (11.9 m); beam 5 ft., 6 in. (1.7 m); draft 5 ft. (1.5 m)
Propulsion:	one diesel engine delivering 60 hp (44.7 kW) for 7.75 knots surfaced and one electric motor delivering 25 hp (18.6 kW) for 6 knots submerged
Armament:	two 21-inch (533 mm) torpedoes
Complement:	2

Gato class (1941)

In the 10 submarines of the Porpoise, Shark, and Perch classes launched in 1935-37, the two-shaft propulsion had been based on a diesel-electric layout with four diesel generators and four electric motors: this provided a speed of more than 19 knots surfaced with three of the diesel generators supplying current to the electric motors and the fourth used for recharging of the batteries, which allowed a submerged speed of 8 knots or more. The arrangement proved technically successful, and given that the preceding Cachalot class (two boats) had proved too small for Pacific operations at a length of 271 ft., 1 in. (82.9 m) with a displacement of 1,650 tons submerged, the new boats were increased in length to some 300 ft (91.4 m) with a displacements of just under 2,000 tons submerged.

There followed the 14 boats of the Salmon, Sargo, and Seadragon classes with small increases in displacement and length for higher surfaced speed and greater torpedo armament (four bow and four stern tubes rather than four bow and two stern tubes). The first two of these three classes reverted to a composite propulsion arrangement: of each pair of diesel engines, one powered a propeller shaft via gearing and the other powered a generator. The third class had geared diesel-electric drive with a single electric motor on each shaft. This last was more economical in volume and length, allowing a doubling of the battery capacity and use of lengthened torpedo tubes.

This process was taken one step further in the following and closely related Tabor and Gar classes with direct rather than geared drive and two more bow tubes.

Heavy deck armanent is clear in this photograph. The 1 ½ inch (40 mm) anti-aircraft gun is on the "bandstand" behind the bridge.
Photo: U.S. Navy.

The success of the Gar class led to the Gato class which, with the only slightly different Balao and Tench classes, constituted the main strength of the U.S. Navy's submarine arm in World War II and, as such, were the primary fleet submarines of the Pacific campaign.

First ordered in the Fiscal Year 1941 program and until the end of World War II, the

Gato and two companion classes were slightly improved Gar-class boats with an increase in length for improved stability and to allow the subdivision of the engine rooms into two compartments separated by a pressure-and water-tight bulkhead. The size of auxiliary ballast tanks was also increased to compensate for the considerable variation in weights resulting from the carriage and use of 24 torpedoes or 40 mines. The longer and more stable hull made possible the installation of diesel generators up to a rating of 2,000 hp (1491 kW) rather than 1,600 hp (1193 kW), but the more powerful engines planned for the boats ordered in the FY1942 and later programs were

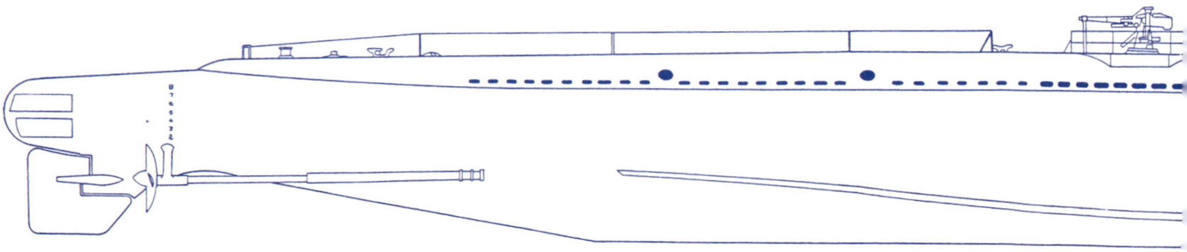

never installed, although more powerful generators were fitted. The propulsion arrangement was thus of the diesel-electric type with four diesel generators delivering current to two electric motors coupled to the two propeller shafts by reduction gearing or, in SS-343/352, 365/367, 377, 405/410 and all boats from SS0415 onward, direct drive.

The Gato class of submarines typically carried some 480 tons of diesel

Right:
The plotting table in the main control room of a Gato-class boat.

Left:
A fleet boat at speed.

Bottom left:
The Torpedo room of a Gato-class boat.

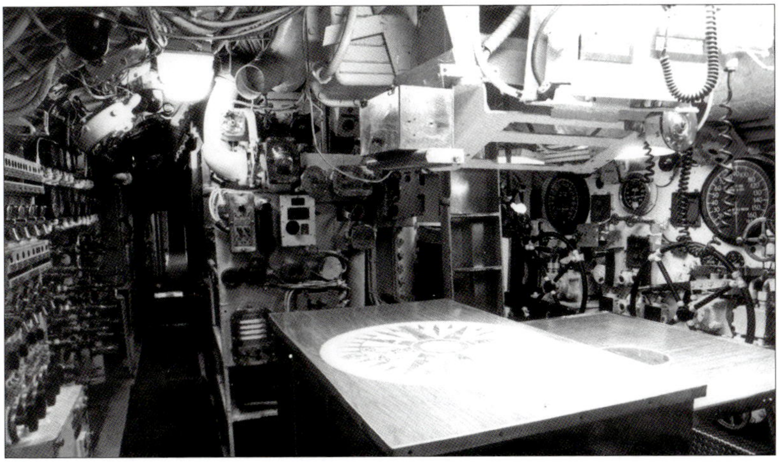

fuel, providing a range of 12,665 miles (20380 km) at 10 knots. The submerged range was 110 miles (177 km) at 2 knots. The underwater endurance was 48 hours with the air conditioning and all necessary auxiliary machinery functioning.

The Gato-class boats were designed to operate at 300 feet (91 m), and the weight saved in later boats allowed heavier hull construction, with the result that all of the boats from SS-285 onward were designed for operation at 400 feet (122 m). In 1945 it was claimed that from SS-475 onward the operational depth was 450 feet (137 m) and the collapse depth 750 feet (229 m).

The Gato class consisted of 77 boats launched by Electric Boat, Portsmouth and Mare Island Navy Yards, and Manitowoc Shipbuilding between August 1941 and December 1943 in the range between SS-212 and SS-284, and all named after creatures living in water, as were the Balao and Tench class boats.

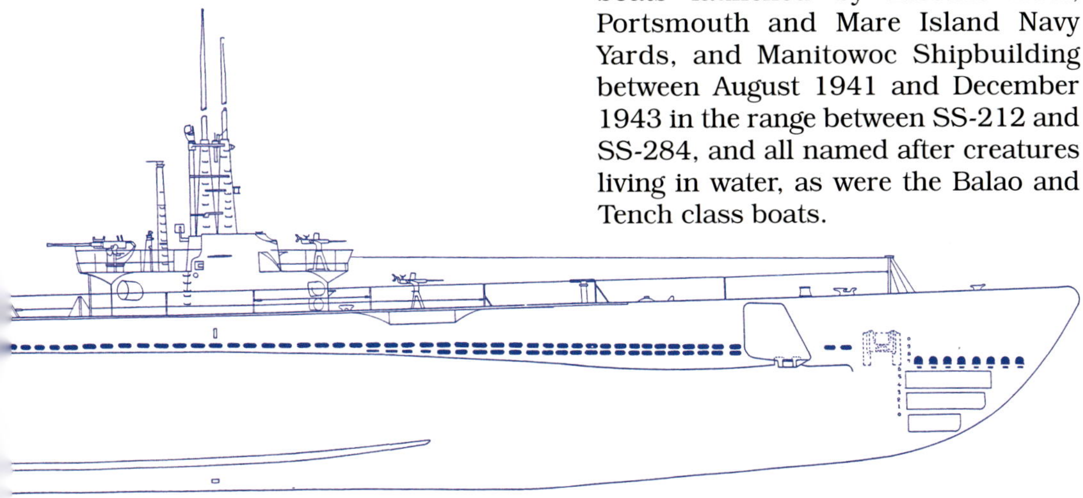

The following Balao class consisted of 122 boats, 10 being cancelled, launched by Cramp, Electric Boat, Portsmouth and Mare Island Navy Yards, and Manitowoc between October 1942 and September 1947 in the range between SS-285 and SS-416. Large numbers were later transferred to the Allied navies.

The final Tench-class boat was an evolutionary improvement over the Gato and Balao classes of boats, only

about 35 to 40 tons larger, but more strongly built and with a slightly improved internal layout. Further improvements were made beginning with SS-435, resulting in the unofficial designation of "Corsair" class. The first plan called for 146 Tench-class boats, but 115 were cancelled in 1944-45 when it became apparent that they would not be needed to defeat Japan. Tench-class boats were later transferred to Brazil (5), Canada (1), Greece (1), Italy (2), Peru (1), Taiwan (2), Turkey (2) and Venezuela (1). The Tench class of submarines thus consisted of 31 boats launched by Cramp, Electric Boat, and Portsmouth and Boston Navy Yards between July 1944 and January 1946 in the range between SS-417 and SS-525.

War modifications to the earlier boats included considerable reductions

in their bridges. This was undertaken in part to allow the boats to ship 20 mm and 1 ½ inch (40 mm) light and medium anti-aircraft guns on a so-called "cigarette deck" fore and aft of the main coning tower. As with the preceding classes of American long-range submarines, these boats were at first armed with a single 3-inch (76 mm) L/50 gun abaft the conning tower, but the design had been prepared with provision for larger-caliber deck guns, and later a 4-inch (102 mm) L/50 and finally 5-inch (127 mm) L/25 guns were installed. The later boats were completed with alternative gun mount positions fore and aft of the conning tower, and at a time late in World War II some boats mounted two 5-inch (127 mm) guns. In overall terms, therefore, SS-285 to SS-291 were equipped with one 4-inch (102 mm) L/50, one 1 ½ inch (40 mm) and two half-inch (12.7 mm) guns; SS-292 to SS-312 had one 5-inch (127 mm) L/25, one 1 ½ inch (40 mm) and two half-inch (12.7 mm) guns; and

SS-313 to SS-352, SS-365 to SS-378, SS-381 to SS-426, SS-435, SS-475 to SS-490 and SS-522 to SS-525 were fitted with one 5-inch (127 mm) L/25, one 1 ½ inch (40 mm) and one 20 mm guns.

Some 20 of the Gato-class boats, 12 of the Balao-class boats, and none of the Tench-class boats were lost in World War II. The Gato-class submarines gained many distinctions in World War II, in which they and they successors were instrumental in the defeat of Japan, but four of the most notable were the *Flasher,* which was the top-scoring U.S. boat of the war, with 100,231 tons officially credited to it; the *Harder,* which was skippered by Commander Samuel D. Dealey, the only submariner of the war (and probably the only commander ever) to sink five destroyers, four of them in the course of a single patrol; and the *Archerfish* which sank the 71,890-ton carrier *Shinano* on November 29, 1944. All the submarines of the classes preceding the Gato class were stricken after the end of World War II, but most of the very successful Gato, Balao, and Tench boats were retained, many being rebuilt as "Guppy" boats with improved streamlining and other features for greater underwater speed, or as "fleet snorkel" boats with a snorting mast providing the ability to run on the diesel engines at periscope depth.

Gato class

Type:	fleet submarine
Tonnage:	1,526 tons surfaced and 2.424 tons submerged
Dimensions:	length 311 ft., 9 in. (95 m); beam 27 ft., 3 in. (8.3 m); draft 15 ft., 3 in. (4.65 m)
Propulsion:	four General Motors or Fairbanks-Morse diesel generators delivering 5,400 hp (4026 kW) for 20.25 knots surfaced and General Electric, Elliot Motor or Allis-Chalmers electric motors delivering 2,740 hp (2043 kW) for 8.75 knots submerged
Armament:	one 3-inch (76 mm) gun and 10 21-inch (533 mm) tubes for 24 torpedoes or 40 mines
Complement:	80 to 85

Japanese submarines of World War II

Between 1905, when it received its first Holland-type submarines, and 1945, when it was comprehensively defeated at the end of World War II, Japan operated 49 classes of submarine excluding ex-German reparations at the end of World War I, and in World War II transferred or seized German and Italian submarines, four classes of midget submarines and five classes of suicide submarines. The classes used in World War II ranged from the tiny suicide craft intended solely for short-range defense to the largest conventionally powered submarines ever built. The last had huge range and, in some cases, were optimized for the carriage of attack aircraft (with which the Imperial Japanese navy hoped to decimate U.S. task forces in their atoll fleet anchorages) and also fixed strategic targets such as the Panama Canal, forcing U.S. shipping to use the far longer and more difficult route around Cape Horn.

In the 1930s the Imperial Japanese navy's thinking at the strategic and operational levels was based on offensive operations to create and hold the outer reaches of an expanded Japanese empire, and this required submarines large enough to roam deep into the Pacific, operate there for some time with an adequate number of weapons, and then return to base. Only after Japan had created this outer perimeter and was faced with the prospect of having to defend it against a steadily strengthening U.S. Navy, whose primary weapons

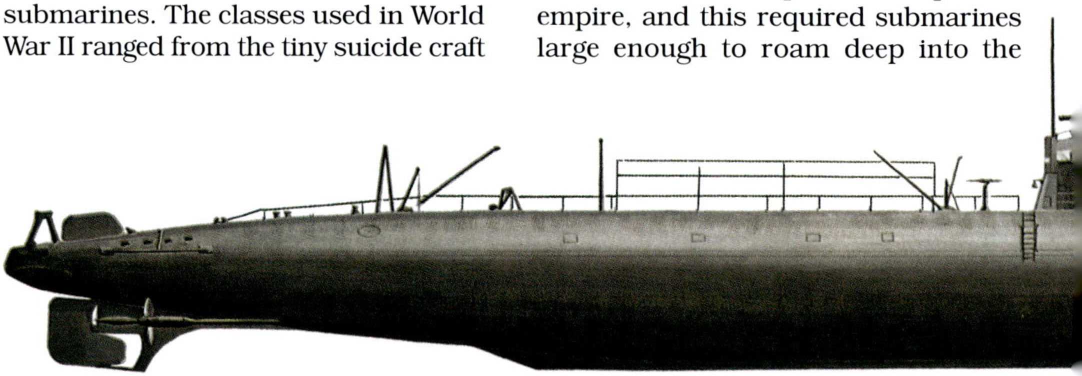

Line section drawing shows the I-58 that sank the USS Indianapolis.

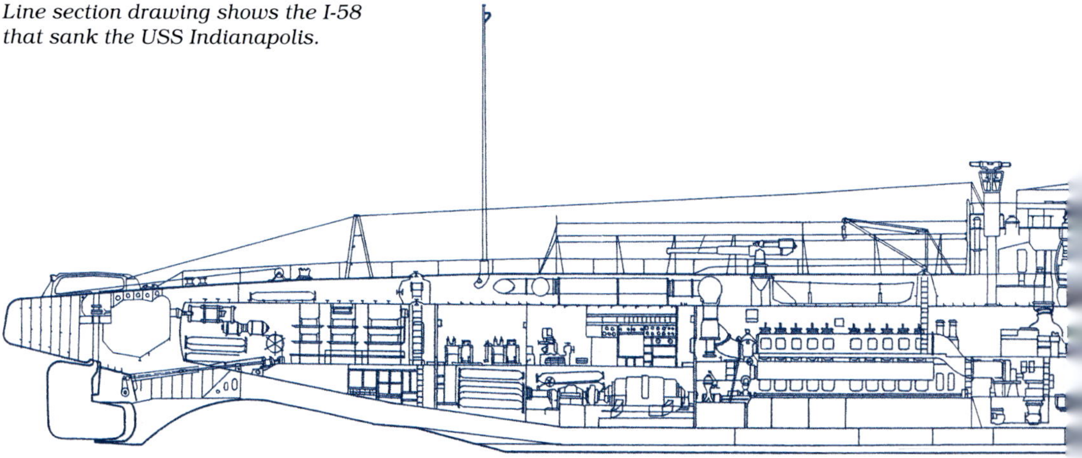

were the aircraft carrier and the fleet submarine, did the Imperial Japanese navy start to appreciate fully the need for smaller and more agile submarines with improved underwater speed and endurance. It had a modest number of such submarines as second-class boats, but these were generally old and deemed largely inadequate for modern service; they were therefore first to be supplemented and then succeeded by more advanced boats.

This type of modestly sized submarine is epitomized by the K6 group of second-class submarines, laid down in 1941-43 by a number of commercial yards and completed between March 1943 and November 1944 as the *RO-35* to *RO-50*, *RO-55* and *RO-56*. This was an enlarged and improved version of the K5 class (*RO-33* and *RO-34*), was the last Japanese medium submarine design, and had ranges of 5,750 miles (9255 km) at 16 knots surfaced and 52 miles (83 km) at 5 knots submerged. A 3-inch (76 mm) AA gun was added during construction. Only one of the class survived the war; all the rest succumbed to U.S. forces in the Pacific. Another 61 units of this class approved in the 1941 and 1942 Modified Programs, and nine proposed in the 1942 Program, were not even laid down.

The data for the K6 class included a displacement of 1,115 tons surfaced and 1,447 tons submerged, length of 264 ft., 1 in. (80.5 m), beam of 23 ft.,

2 in. (7.05 m) and draft of 13 ft., 4 in. (4.1 m), propulsion by two diesel engines delivering 4,200 hp (3132 kW) for 19.7 knots surfaced and two electric motors delivering 1,200 hp (895 kW) for 8 knots submerged, armament of one 3-inch (76 mm) gun, two 25 mm AA cannon and four 21-inch (533 mm) bow tubes for 10 torpedoes, and complement of 62.

Greater capability was offered by the I-200 or ST class boats, of which eight were laid down by the Kure Navy Yard in May 1944 but only three completed as the *I-201*, *I-202* and *I-203*. The I-200 class of submarine bore little resemblance to earlier the I-type boats, which had been optimized for a high surfaced speed for minimum transit times and a long range for maximum patrol endurance

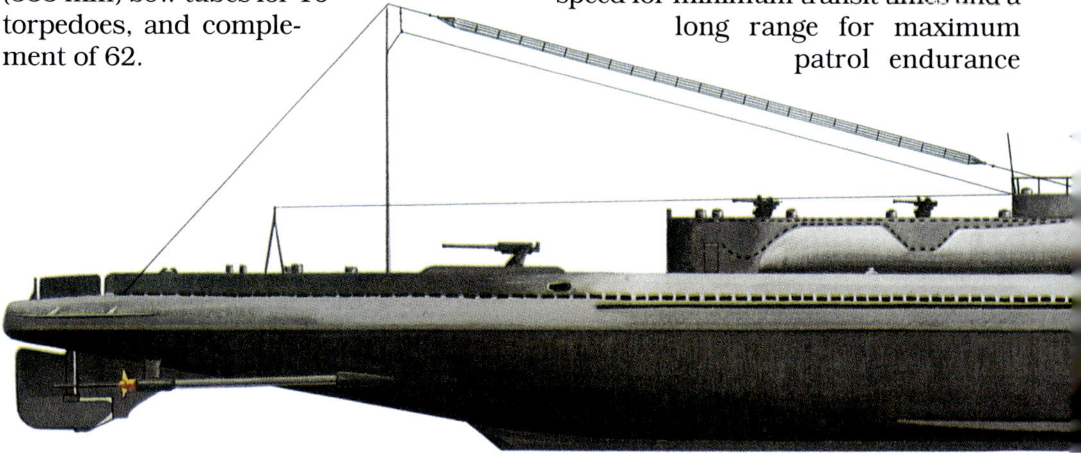

After total surrender in 1945, the I-400 is seen bow on. In the middle is the hanger where the Aichi M6A1 Seiran was stored. In the foreground are the rails along which the floatplane was launched. Note the offset conning tower.
Photo: U.S. Navy.

deep in the Pacific Ocean. The I-200 design emphasized maximum possible submerged performance and can be regarded as the first class of Japanese submarines designed for the true submarine rather than submersible role. The design was based on an all-welded hull assembled from prefabricated sections and of good streamlining, powerful electric motors and a high-capacity battery consisting of 4,192 cells. The maximum submerged speed of 19 knots was double that of contemporary U.S. Navy boats, and the I-200-class boats were also transported to the slip for final assembly. Some 23 units were ordered from the Kure Navy Yard under the 1943 construction program but, as noted, due to the deteriorating war situation, only eight were laid down, six launched, and just three completed before the end of the war. None of them saw operational use. Two of the submarines, the *I-201* and *I-203*, were seized and inspected by the U.S. Navy at the end of the hostilities. They were part of a group of four captured submarines, including the giant *I-400* and *I-401*, sailed to Hawaii

Aichi M6A1 Seiran submarine-launched floatplane.

equipped with a primitive snorting system allowing underwater diesel operation while recharging batteries.

The I-200-class boat had a test diving depth of 360 feet (110 m), and was fitted with four 21-inch (533 mm) bow tubes for 10 torpedoes; all-important anti-aircraft defense was entrusted to a pair of 25 mm cannon on mounts that could be retracted to maintain streamlining. The submarine was designed for mass production, with large sections prefabricated in factories and by U.S. Navy technical specialists for further inspection. On March 26, 1946, the U.S. Navy decided to scuttle all captured Japanese submarines: on April 5 the *I-202* was scuttled in Japanese waters, on May 21 the *I-203* was torpedoed and sunk by *Caiman* off the Hawaiian Islands, and on May 23 the *I-201* was torpedoed and sunk by the *Queenfish*.

The data for the I-200 submarine included a displacement of 1,291 tons surfaced and 1,450 tons submerged, length of 259 ft., 2 in. (79 m), beam of 19 ft. (5.8 m), draft of 17 ft., 11 in. (5.45 m), propulsion by two diesel engines delivering 2,750 hp (2050 kW) for 15.8 knots and two electric motors delivering 5,000 hp (3728 kW) for 19 knots, range of 6,680 miles (10750 km) at 16 knots surfaced, and complement of 31.

Typical of the latest type of large ocean-going fleet submarine in service at the time of Japan's December 1941 entry into World War II was the A1 class of three boats. The design was developed from that of the J3 class (two boats) with the hangar for the embarked reconnaissance floatplane opening forward of the conning tower. Three such boats were built, and equipped with communication facilities allowing them to operate as the command ships for groups of submarines. The *I-9* was sunk by the U.S. destroyer *Frazier* in the Aleutians on June 11, 1943, the *I-10* was sunk by the U.S. destroyer *David W. Taylor* and destroyer escort *Riddle* east of Saipan on July 4, 1944, and the *I-11* disappeared off Ellice Island (in Tuvalu, Polynesia) on January 11, 1944. The data for this class included a displacement of 2,919 tons surfaced and 4,149 tons submerged, length of 373 ft. (85.2 m), beam of 31 ft., 4 in. (9.565 m), draft of 17 ft., 7 in. (4.4 m), propulsion by two diesel engines delivering 12,400 hp (9245 kW) for 23.5 knots surfaced and two electric motors delivering 2,400 hp (1789 kW) for 8 knots submerged, range of 18,425 miles (29650 km) at 16 knots surfaced, armament of one 5 1/2 inch (140 mm) gun, one Yokosuka E14Y reconnaissance floatplane and six 21-inch (533 mm) bow tubes for 18 torpedoes, and complement of 114.

The single A2-class submarine *I-12*, sunk in January 1945, was similar to the A1 class boats except for its considerably less powerful engines for reduced surfaced and submerged speed, but considerably greater range.

The I-400 or Sto class of submarines consisted of the largest boats of World War II, and the largest conventionally powered submarines ever built. There were in essence submarine aircraft carriers each able to accommodate three Aichi M6A Seiran attack aircraft, which could thus be launched close to their targets far from Japan. The boats also carried torpedo armament for close-range combat and were designed to surface, launch their aircraft and then submerge once again before they were discovered.

The I-400 class was originally conceived for the task of reaching any point in the world and then returning to Japan,

Two giant aircraft-carrying submarines alongside a depot ship after surrender. Photo: U.S. Navy.

and more specifically to destroy the U.S.-controlled Panama Canal. A force of 18 such boats was planned in 1942, and work on the first was started in January 1943 at the Kure Navy Yard. Within a year, the plan had been trimmed to five boats, and finally only three boats were completed as the *I-400* at Kure, and the *I-401*, and *I-402* at the Sasebo Navy Yard.

Each boat had a figure-eight hull shape for additional strength to handle the on-deck hangar for the three aircraft, which were catapult-launched. Only limited use was made of the boats, which survived the war and were scuttled by the U.S. Navy in 1946.

I-400 class

Type:	long-range special-purpose submarine
Tonnage:	5,223 tons surfaced and 6,560 tons submerged
Dimensions:	length 400 ft., 3 in. (122 m); beam 39 ft., 4 in. (12 m); draft 23 ft., 0 in. (7 m)
Propulsion:	four diesel engines delivering 7,700 hp (5741 kW) for 18.75 knots surfaced, and electric motors delivering 2,400 hp (1789 kW) for 6.5 knots submerged
Armament:	one 5 ½-inch (150 mm) gun, three triple and one single 1-inch (25 mm) AA cannon, three Aichi M6A Seiran attack aircraft, and eight 21-inch (533 mm) tubes (all bow) for torpedoes
Complement:	144

Focke-Achgelis Fa 330 Bachstelze (1942)

One of the main problems associated with submarine warfare in World War II was the short optical horizon for lookouts on the low conning tower. It was difficult to acquire targets at more than short ranges and, more dangerously, there was little visual warning of the advent of high-speed attacking warships. Early in 1942, therefore, the German submarine arm suggested to the Focke-Achgelis helicopter company that it design a gyro-kite that could be towed aloft by a surfaced U-boat to extend the optical horizon of the pilot, who was in telephone contact with the boat.

Focke-Achgelis showed great ingenuity in the creation of this type, which was based on components that could be easily manhandled through a deck hatch for rapid assembly (and later disassembly) on the boat's deck. The fuselage contained two steel tubes, one horizontal and the other vertical: on the horizontal tube were installed the pilot's seat, the austere instrument panel, the landing skids, and the empennage consisting of a small tailplane and a vertical surface with hinged rudder; behind the pilot's seat, the vertical tube was the pylon for the windmilling rotor with three blades, each based on a tubular steel spar with wooden ribs and a covering of plywood and fabric, attached to the hub by flap and drag hinges and controlled by the pilot by means of a simple control column for tilt in the longitudinal and lateral planes. The gyro-kite was connected to the U-boat by 165 yards (150 m) of cable with attached telephone wire, and the operational procedure was for the rotor to be spun up by hand or pull rope before the machine was tilted backward so that the forward speed of the U-boat would then lift the gyro-kite into the air to a maximum height of 395 feet (120 m): this extended the U-boat's effective optical horizon from 5 miles (8 km) to 25 miles (40 km).

Escape from this machine was not without its dangers. Photo: John Batchelor.

Not the most enviable job in the German U-boat force in WWII. Photo: Paul Hertz Collection.

Landing was achieved by the simple expedient of winching the gyro-kite down onto the U-boat's deck, although for emergency use the pilot was provided with an overhead handle whose actuation jettisoned the rotor and extracted the parachute of the pilot, who released his seat belt only after the deployment of the parachute to allow the rest of the airframe to precede him into the water.

The first Fa 330 Bachstelze ("water wagtail") flew in 1942, and the type entered service in the middle of that year. The Fa 330 was built by Weser-Flugzeugbau, and slightly more than 200 machines were delivered. The later Fa 330s had a slightly larger rotor with a diameter of 27 ft., 11.75 in. (8.53 m).

Although the Fa 330 was practical in its designed role, the type was not popular with U-boat crews, as a crash dive with the Bachstelze aloft almost invariably meant the loss of the pilot.

Focke-Achgelis Fa 330A-1 Bachstelze

Type:	submarine-launched observation gyro-kite
Accommodation:	pilot on an open seat
Rotor:	diameter 24 ft. (7.315 m); disc area 452.38 ftÇ (42.03 m^2)
Fuselage:	length 14 ft., 6 in. (4.42 m)
Weights:	empty 180 lb. (82 kg); normal take-off 331 lb. (150 kg)
Performance:	operational airspeed between 17 and 25 mph (27 and 40 km/h)

Hedgehog anti-submarine projector (1943)

The most important method for the detection and subsequent attack on a submerged submarine at the start of World War II was the combination of sonar for the detection and initial assessment of the submarine's position, depth and course, and the depth charge fired in small patterns for the attack with its hydrostatic pistol firing the charge at the estimated depth of the submarine.

The major limitation of the combination of sonar and depth charge attack was the two types of "blind time." The first type resulted from the time it took the flat-ended cylindrical depth charge to sink to the depth at which it exploded. This time gap increased with the presumed depth of the contact, and could often result in the submarine evading the attacks. The second type was related to the attack method used by single destroyers, frigates, sloops, and corvettes. Once the ship had acquired its target on sonar, it headed toward the contact at speed. However, at a certain distance ahead of the oncoming warship, the target was too close to be held by sonar and, in combination with the slow descent of the depth charges dropped and/or fired as the ship passed over the presumed position of its target, this provided the submarine's captain with the chance to maneuver evasively in course and depth. For the attacker, this problem was compounded by the fact that the minimization of the dead time required a high-speed approach which further degraded the performance of the sonar and also warned the submarine.

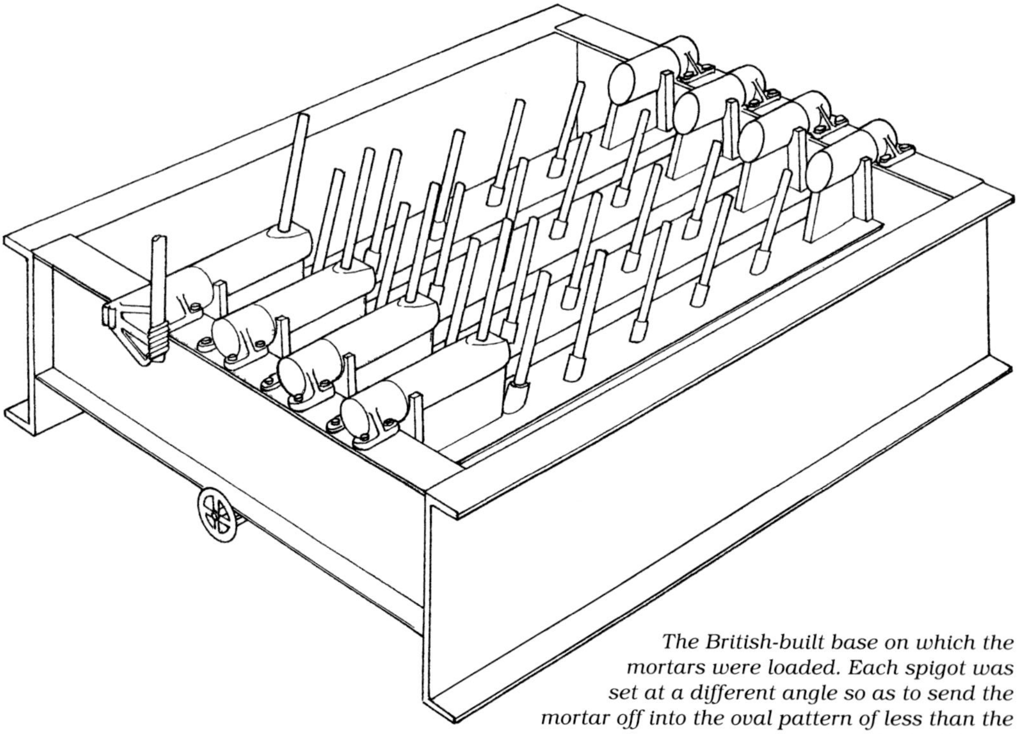

The British-built base on which the mortars were loaded. Each spigot was set at a different angle so as to send the mortar off into the oval pattern of less than the length of a U-boat.

The Hedgehog bombs were ripple fired, because if they all fired together they would have caused serious damage to the deck below.

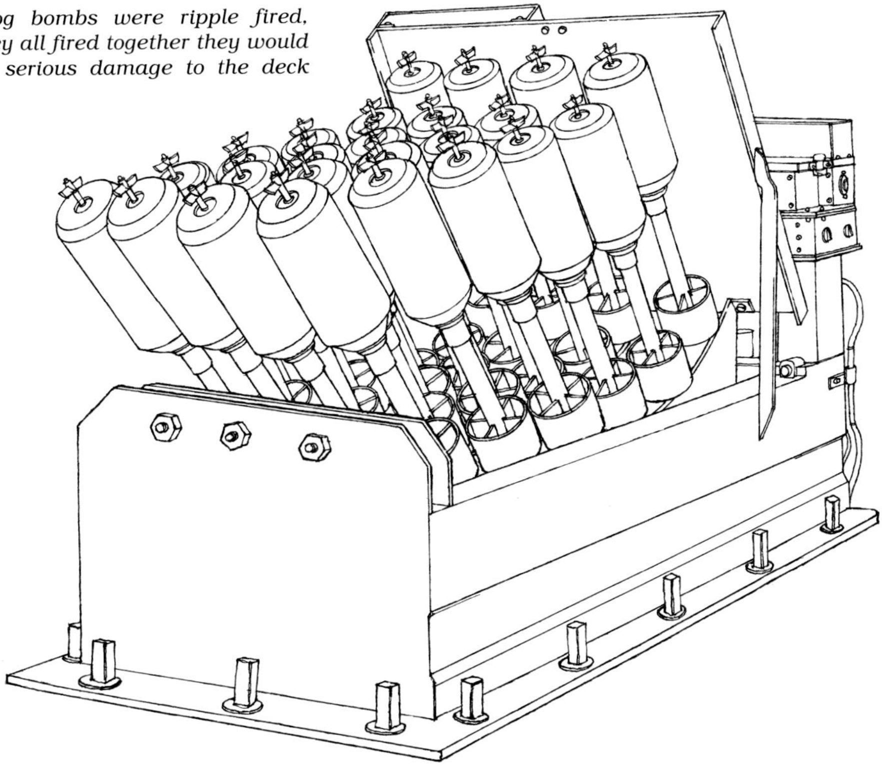

There were ways in which this problem could be mitigated if not overcome by the attacker: a teaming arrangement, for example, allowed one ship to hold the contact and pass information to another ship, which could then make a slow, and thus effectively silent, attack. For single ships, this was no solution, and what was needed was a weapon which could fire anti-submarine bombs ahead of the vessel with the target still in sonar contact, thereby removing the need to cross over the target and drop depth charges. The weapon created to meet this need was the Anti-Submarine Projector Mk 10, inevitably known for its appearance as the "Hedgehog." This was developed by the Royal Navy during World War II, and was deployed on warships operating as convoy escorts, such as destroyers and frigates, to supplement the depth charge. The weapon worked by firing a number of small spigot mortar bombs from spiked fittings in a frame with the fittings set at slightly different angles in elevation and azimuth to create an oval pattern of falling bombs. Rather than a hydrostatic or time fuse, such as were used on depth charges, the Hedgehog's bombs were impact-fused to explode on contact with the target's hull, and achieved a higher success rate than was ever achieved by depth charges.

The Hedgehog was developed by the Directorate of Miscellaneous Weapons Development and entered service in 1943. The Hedgehog was in its turn replaced from 1944 by the Squid mortar, firing 12-inch (305 mm) bombs from three elevating barrels, and this in turn was replaced by the improved three-barrelled Limbo, with automatic reloading and other improvements, during the

1950s. The U.S. produced a weapon similar to the Hedgehog, the Mousetrap, which fired rocket-propelled bombs whose launch did not impose the same recoil forces as the Hedgehog and could therefore be installed on smaller vessels.

The Hedgehog fired a salvo of 24 bombs in an arc aimed to land in an elliptical pattern measuring about 140 by 120 feet (40 by 35 m) at a fixed point about 200 yards (180 m) directly ahead of the attacking ship. The initial Mk 10 mounting was fixed, and was supplemented by the Mk 11 mounting which fired a circular pattern measuring 200 feet (60 m) in diameter out to a range of about 190 yards (175 m). The Mk 15 mounting fired the same pattern as the Mk 11 but was fitted on a gyro-stabilized platform able to compensate for the ship's rolling and pitching. The Mk 15 could also be fired from the ship's plotting room. The launcher comprised four "cradles," each with six launcher spigots. The firing sequence was staggered so that all the bombs would land at roughly the same time. Reloading took three minutes.

The primary advantages of the Hedgehog over the depth charge were that the target's depth did not need to be known, as the Hedgehog's bombs exploded only on contact, at the same time producing concrete evidence that the target had indeed been struck; as an ahead-firing weapon, the Hedgehog gave the submarine no warning of the attack, and therefore the opportunity to take evasive action, as there was no dead period as the warship ran the final part of its attack over the submarine's presumed location; and direct hits by one of two Hedgehog bombs was generally sufficient to sink a submarine. The weapon was also very economical, for an attack required far less weight of casing and explosive. Many depth charges were often required in order to inflict the cumulative damage sufficient to sink a submarine. Many U-boats survived hundreds of detonations over many hours: in April 1945, the U-427 survived 678 depth charges. The depth charge generally exploded at some distance from its target, and there was thus a water cushion between the detonation and the pressure hull; the detonation of a contact-fused charge, on the other hand, had the cushion on the other side, increasing the explosive shock.

The Hedgehog did not have the advantage of the cumulative damage effect of repeated explosions just outside the lethal distance that could make it harder for the target to dodge

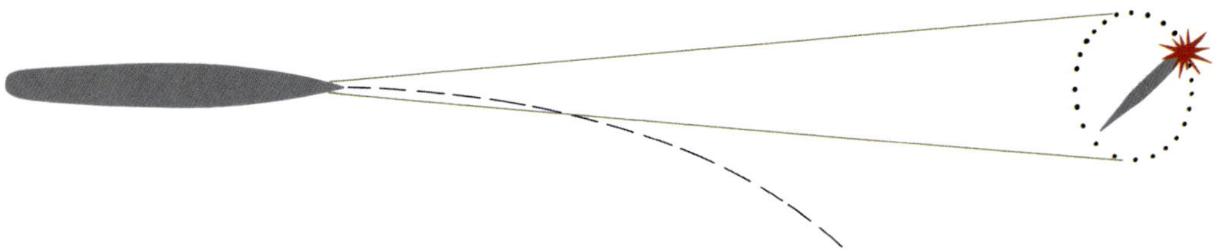

The spread of the mortars and how the Hedgehog can target the U-boat.

later attacks or force it to return to base for repairs when it did escape. The Hedgehog was much more successful than the depth charge, the best kill rate being about 25% to the depth charge's 7%.

Hedgehog Mk 10

Bomb caliber:	7 in. (178 mm)
Bomb weight:	65 lb. (29 kg) including 30 lb. (13.6 kg) of TNT or 35 lb. (15.9 kg) of Torpex
Bomb range:	220 to 285 yards (200 to 260 m)
Bomb sinking speed:	22 to 23 ½ ft. (6.7 to 7.2 m) per second
Mount weight:	28,780 lb. (13055 kg) with 24 spigots

Japanese midget submarines (1941)

Inferior to the British and U.S. navies in numerical and tonnage terms, the Japanese navy considered a number of special weapons. One of these was the midget submarine: this could be carried in useful numbers by parent vessels and released just outside the combat area to move in and attack the opponent's major warships, or outside a fleet anchorage to attack warships lying at anchor.

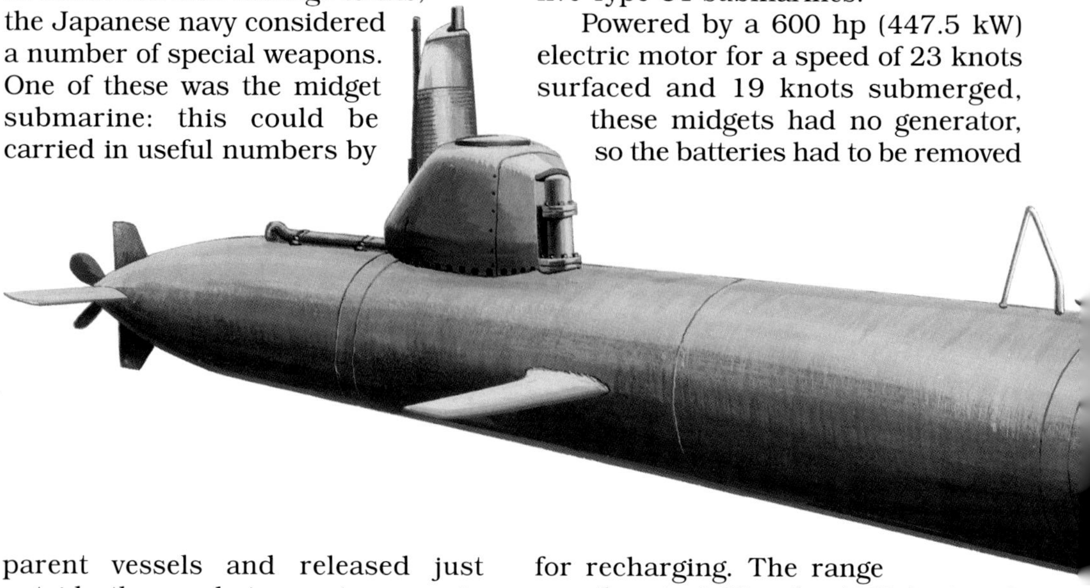

In 1932 two prototypes were built with cover names such as *Taisen Bagukai Hyoteki* ("anti-submarine bomb target"), *TB Mokei* ("model TB"), and *Tokushu Hyoteki* ("special target"). Based on torpedoes, these were electrically powered and had no conning towers. In1936 two more *Ko Hyoteki* ("target A") prototypes, based on the first two experimental craft were built, and these *Ha-1* and *Ha-2* boats had a superimposed pair of 18-inch (457 mm) torpedo tubes and small conning towers. Forty-one boats were ordered from a new facility at Ourazaki. The Type A class was based on the prototypes but optimized for deployment from seaplane tenders such as the *Chitose* and *Mizuho* then being refitted to handle them. The first trials were effected in 1941, and the boats were also to be carried and launched on attack missions by the five Type C1 submarines.

Powered by a 600 hp (447.5 kW) electric motor for a speed of 23 knots surfaced and 19 knots submerged, these midgets had no generator, so the batteries had to be removed for recharging. The range was thus just 93 miles (150 km) at 6 knots submerged. There were minor differences between the craft; for example, craft completed before Japan's entry into World War II had tubes open to the sea. War-built craft had enclosed torpedo tubes and other enhancements.

By early in 1942, the limitations of this early type had become evident, especially during involvement in the Japanese attack on Pearl Harbor, so the surviving craft were relegated to base defense. Another 16 boats were then ordered to an improved standard with inbuilt wire cutters, jumper wires and tubes with bow caps. There was still no onboard battery recharging capability, however, and the range was 93 miles (150 km) at just 2 knots submerged, falling at the full speed of 19 knots to 19.9 miles (32 km).

In October 1942 the *Ha-45* was laid down as an experimental development of the Type A with a 53.5 hp (40 kW) diesel generator to recharge

A photograph of the Kairyu midget submarine at the Washington D.C. Navy Yard. Photo: John Batchelor.

Kaiten midget sub. "Kamikaze" version of long-range 93 torpedo.

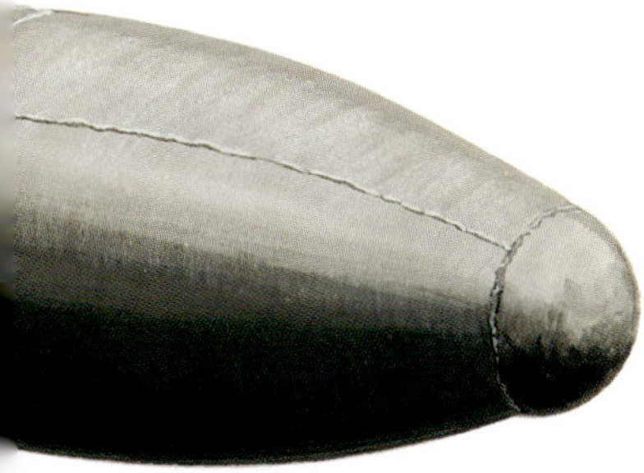

the batteries. This *Ko Hyoteki Otsu Gata* ("target A, type B") had displacement and length increased slightly over those of the Type A, but the diesel generator effected considerable improvements in range. The main failing was that battery recharging took 18 hours. The *Ha-45* was the only Type B craft, the *Ha-62* to *Ha-76* being of the *Ko Hyoteki Hei Gata* ("target A, type C") class and completed between 1942 and 1944 to a standard slightly improved over that of the Type B. More fuel gave them an extra 59 miles (95 km) of range at 6 knots surfaced and the recharging time for the batteries was reduced slightly. The Type C craft were designed to be launched from Type 1 landing ships, and immediately replaced the Type A craft. Some Type C craft were equipped with a long conning tower and two periscopes for training purposes.

Though the Type C was far superior to the Type A, it nonetheless possessed several poor features, such as the diesel engine. In 1943 the Japanese started on the design of a new midget submarine. This was finalized in December 1943, and in

Kairyu-type midget submarine.

Japanese midget submarines *continued*

The most important midget submarine, the Type C. It had a crew of three.
Photo: U.S. Navy.

June 1944 work began on the *Ha-77* as the prototype of the *Ko Hyoteki Tei Gata* ("target A, type D") generally known as the *Koryu* ("scaly dragon"). This was completed in January 1945 and was larger than the Type C with length increased by 4 ft., 3 in. (1.3 m) to accommodate a 150 hp (112 kW) diesel and two more crew. The higher-powered diesel gave the boat 2 knots more on the surface but a smaller bank of batteries and a lower-powered electric motor, delivering 500 hp (373 kW), meant a drop of 2 knots in submerged speed. A major advantage with the more powerful diesel was a battery recharging time of only eight hours. Range was also increased, and the diving depth became 330 feet (100 m).

The design was altered very slightly so that the units could be mass-produced in five sections for final assembly. Japan hoped to have 540 of the new craft in service by September 1945, and by then to have reached a steady production rate of 180 per month. Many delays, shortages of materials and heavy bombing attacks curtailed construction, however; by September 1945, only 115 had been completed.

Beginning in 1943, the Japanese also planned the two-man Kairyu

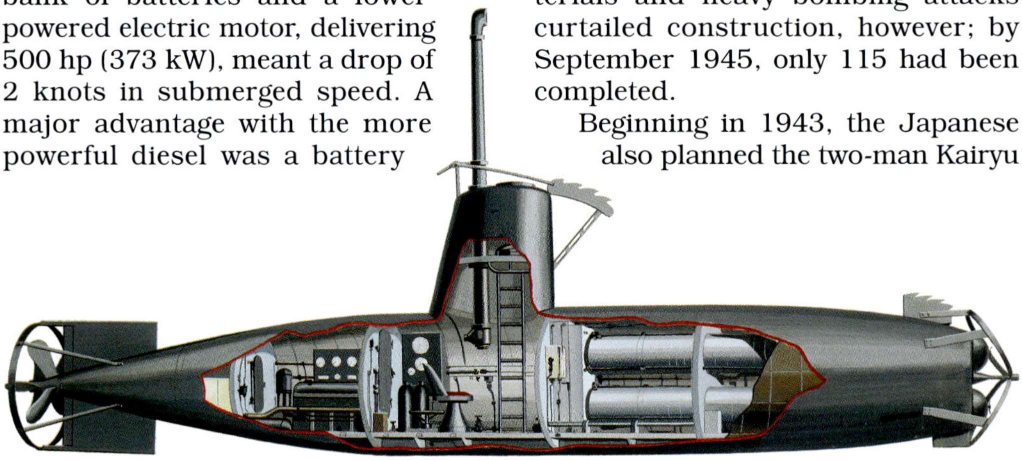

Diagram shows the Type A midget submarine with its net cutters on the bow and on the top of the conning tower. It carried two torpedoes.

Diagrams shows 3 views of the 'Type A' midget submarine.
Note the volume of batteries required to give it operational range,

("sea dragon") class of suicide submarine, of which two prototypes were built on the basis of the Type A with two underslung torpedoes. There were engine problems, though, and with the arrival of the smaller Kaiten ("turn toward heaven") classes, only 215 were completed, often with a large explosive charge instead of two torpedoes, and 40 were adapted as trainers. The first true suicide craft was designed in the spring of 1944 on the basis of the 24-inch (610 mm) Type 93 torpedo. Large numbers of this Kaiten 1 were produced, but many could not be completed for lack of engines. Three other Kaiten models were built, the first passing its acceptance trials in March and April 1945. These were propelled by a new engine running on hydrogen peroxide and developing between 1,500 and 1,800 hp (1118 and 1342 kW) to produce a speed in the order of 40 knots. Once more, there were serious production problems with the engine and its fuel. Many craft were left incomplete as a result of this and the situation became so bad that the Kaiten 4 was fitted with a conventional torpedo motor and carried a heavier warhead. The Kaiten 3 was used as a test model and did not enter production.

Type D Koryu class

Type:	midget submarine
Tonnage:	59.33 tons submerged
Dimensions:	length 86 ft. (26.2 m); beam 6 ft., 7 in. (2 m); draft 9 ft., 2 in. (2.8 m)
Propulsion:	one diesel engine delivering 150 hp (118 kW) for 8 knots surfaced and one electric motor delivering 500 hp (373 kW) for 16 knots submerged
Armament:	two 18-inch (457 mm) torpedoes
Complement:	5

Submarine deck guns of World War II

The torpedo of World War II was, in general, a highly effective anti-ship weapon, although each country that made large-scale use of submarines had first to overcome a number of teething problems, major and minor, with technical aspects of their weapon's propulsion and fusing systems. But for service as the primary weapon of a submarine, the torpedo suffered from several limitations. First, the torpedo was very expensive to manufacture. Second, it was large and weighty, difficult to handle on board a submarine whenever it was necessary to withdraw an unlaunched torpedo from a tube or load a fresh weapon into a tube from which a torpedo had been launched. Third, the size of the standard torpedo was so great that the number of such weapons that could be carried was very limited. And fourth, the torpedo was often "too much weapon" and therefore not cost effective when a small vessel was to be attacked.

The experience of World War I had proven that it was cost effective to fit submarines with a medium-caliber deck gun for the destruction of smaller vessels,

U.S. 5-inch (127 mm) deck gun.

A bewhiskered crew on their return from a long cruise, standing beside their 4-inch (100 mm) deck gun. Note the 4 small Japanese flags on each side of the conning tower, indicating 2 warships and 2 merchantmen sunk.
Photo: U.S. Navy.

especially of the mercantile type, and to provide at least a measure of self-protection capability if the submarine was caught on the surface or forced up to it. The world's navies therefore retained the concept during the 1920s and 1930s, and, in general, maintained their faith in the deck gun through World War II, often on the grounds that such a weapon also had other purposes such as the provision of a capability for the shelling of coastal targets of opportunity.

Two of the standard guns in British submarine service in the first part of World War II were the 4-inch (102 mm) QF Mk IV (or, later, Mk XII or Mk XXII) weapon for larger boats, and the 3-inch (76 mm) 20 cwt weapon for smaller boats. Some of the latter even carried a gun as light as the 12 pdr, 12 cwt weapon. There was also provision for light anti-aircraft armament, normally in the form of machine guns, although later in the war the 20 mm cannon become fairly common.

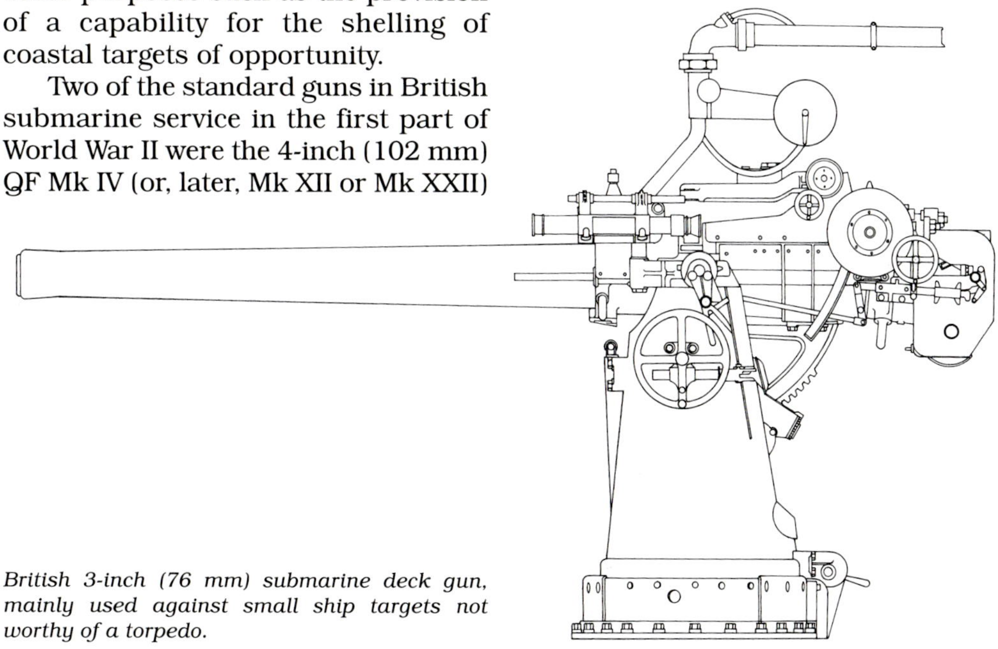

British 3-inch (76 mm) submarine deck gun, mainly used against small ship targets not worthy of a torpedo.

Submarine deck guns of World War II *continued*

While the AA guns were usually fitted on mounting on or abaft the conning tower, the single deck gun was generally mounted in an open mounting forward of the conning tower. Given their use in a vessel of this type, the guns had to feature special adaptations to make it impossible for seawater to seep into the barrel when the boat was submerged, and for the rapid fitment of items such as sights, detachable so that they could be kept safely inside the submarine when not needed. Another requirement of a deck gun was that the crew be able to man the weapon and bring it into action as rapidly as possible; this meant that the hatch for the gun crew and the weapon's ammunition had to be located as close to the gun as possible.

The U.S. pursued a generally similar pattern of gun disposition, although some of their later pre-World War II boats had two 6-inch (152 mm) L/53 guns in mountings fore and aft of the conning tower. The fleet boats of the Gato class and related classes generally started with a single 3-inch (76 mm) L./50 gun abaft the conning tower, but the boats were designed with provision for the mounting of heavier weapons, forward as well as abaft the conning tower, and later in the war 4-inch (102mm) L/50 and 5-inch (127 mm) L/25 weapons were introduced. The American boats entered the war with modest machine gun armament for AA use, but the threat of Japanese air attack in the Pacific, whose size meant that much time had to be

Top and right:
German deck gun. Designed in WWI, this 6-inch (15 cm) deck gun was still in use in WWII.
Photos: John Batchelor.

Twin 3/4-inch (20 mm) Oerlikon Cannon mount, fitted to many U.S. submarines.

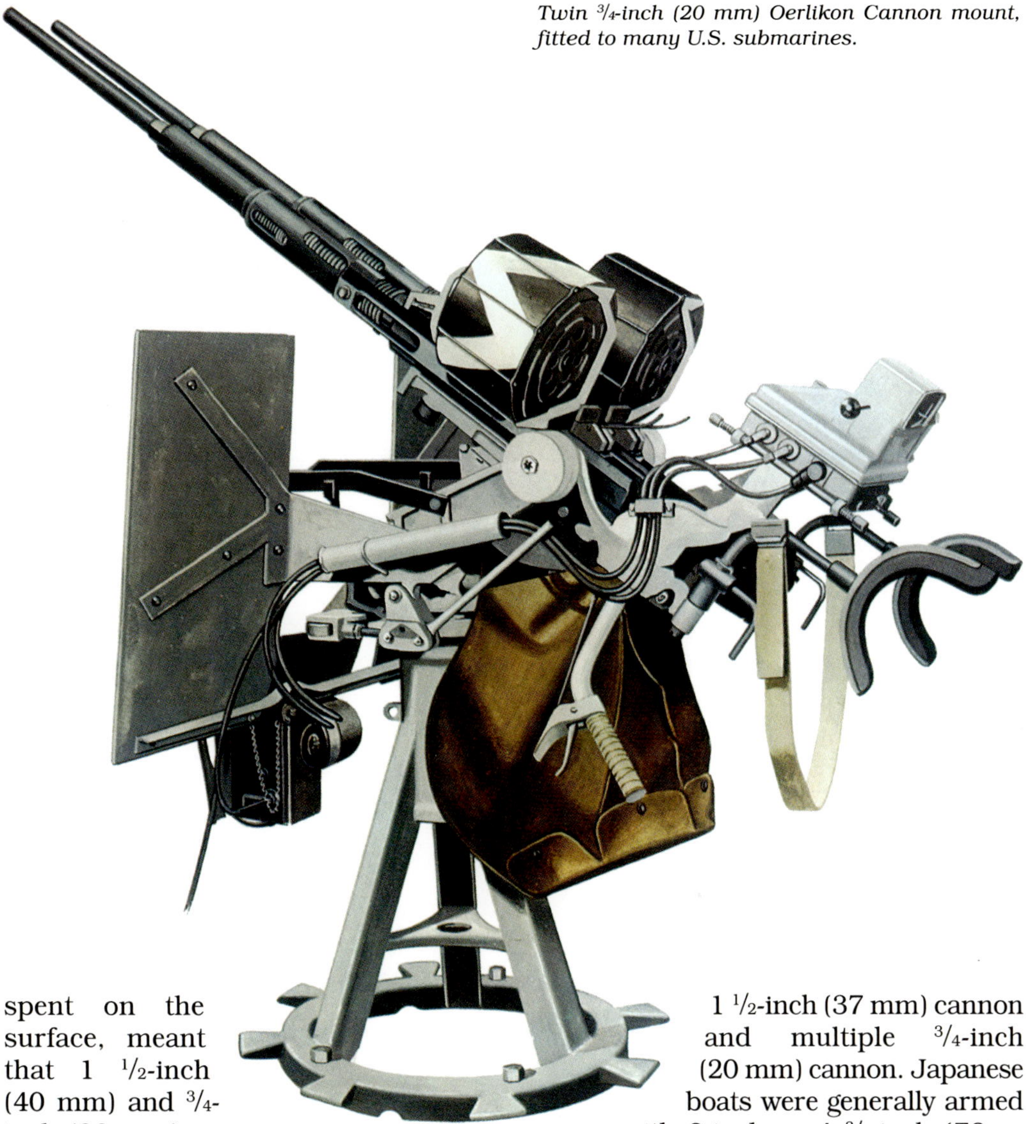

spent on the surface, meant that 1 1/2-inch (40 mm) and 3/4-inch (20 mm) weapons were later shipped.

The German U-boats generally carried one 3 1/2-inch or 4-inch (88 mm or 105 mm) deck gun and an AA armament which gradually came to include a 1 1/2-inch (37 mm) cannon and multiple 3/4-inch (20 mm) cannon. Japanese boats were generally armed with 3-inch or 4 3/4-inch (76 or 120 mm) deck guns, although larger boats carried one or two 5 1/2-inch (140 mm) guns, and the strength of the AA armament was steadily increased to include multiple 25 mm cannons.

Japanese 4 3/4-inch (120 mm) gun

Type:	anti-ship and anti-aircraft gun
Bore:	4 3/4 inches (120 mm) L/45
Weight of shell:	45 lb. (20.5 kg)
Range:	17,060 yards (15600 m) horizontally or 27,725 ft (8450 m) vertically
Rate of fire:	10 to 12 rounds per minute

Interior of submarines

No matter the type, year, or size, there never seems to be enough room on a submarine for the machinery or the crew!

A class (1944)

The A or Amphion-class submarine was of the conventional type with diesel-electric propulsion, and was ordered by the Admiralty in 1943 after realization that the Royal Navy's submarine arm lacked any class offering a useful capability for Pacific Ocean operations. The A class was designed to replace the S and T classes, which were too slow and too shallow-diving for Pacific service. The A class was essentially an enlarged T class optimized for speed and ease of construction and to make use of the materials and equipment of the T class. The A-class design featured a high and widely flared bow for good performance and seakeeping, and high-capacity air conditioning. Some 46 boats were ordered, but just 18 were launched and of these only 16 (10 by Vickers, three by Cammell Laird at Birkenhead, two by Scotts at Greenock, and one by Chatham Dockyard) were commissioned, the other two hulls being used for crush testing. The class was designed for speed of construction, as noted above, on the basis of an entirely welded hull assembled from prefabricated sections. At the time, this was a new concept in British shipbuilding although already widely employed in the German industry.

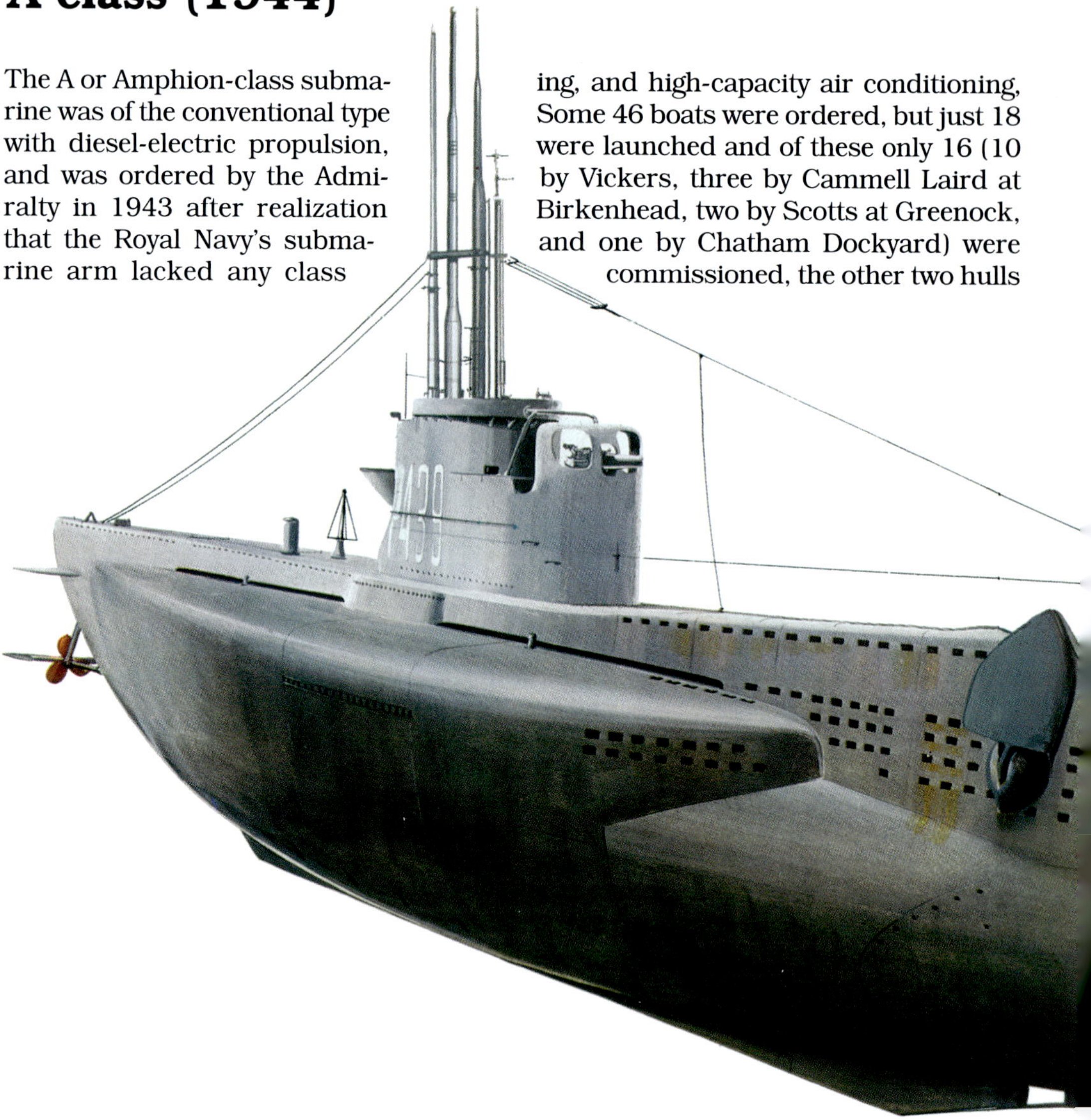

Each submarine needed about eight months between the laying of the keel and the launch, whereas the comparable time had been 15 months for the T-class boats, but only two A-class submarines were completed before the end of World War II. These were the *Amphion*, laid down as the *Anchorite* and launched on August 31, 1944, in the Vickers yard at Barrow-in-Furness, and the *Astute* on January 30, 1945, from the same yard. Neither of these boats saw action in World War II. The other Vickers-built boats were the *Auriga*, *Aurochs*, *Alcide*, *Alderney*, *Alliance* (now at the Royal Navy Submarine Museum, Gosport), *Ambush* and *Andrew*, the Cammell Laird-built *Affray* (the last British submarine lost at sea, on April 17, 1951), *Aeneas* and *Alaric*, the Scotts-built *Artemis* and *Artful*, and the Chatham-built *Acheron*. The two hulls launched by Plymouth Dockyard, but not completed, were the *Ace* and *Achates*.

The A class was one of only two wholly new submarine designs produced in the UK during World War II; the other was the X-class midget submarine. Early wartime experience had revealed the fact that submarines were now faced with the prospect of operating farther from the UK, especially in the Mediterranean and the Far East, and across larger patrol areas than had been foreseen. The resulting A class met this new situation with greater habitability, the ability to dive to 500 feet (150 m), and the surfaced range extended to 12,055 miles (19400 km) at 11 knots; the submerged range was 104 miles (167 km) at 3 knots or 18 miles (29 km) at 8 knots.

After World War II various modifications were made to the boats, which became known as "overseas patrol" submarines: these included a snorting mast based on the *Schnorchel* used by U-boats during the war, a radar which could be used from periscope depth, and a night periscope. The surviving boats were stricken beginning in 1969.

A class

Type:	patrol submarine
Tonnage:	1,385 tons surfaced and 1,620 tons submerged
Dimensions:	length 280 ft., 6 in. (85.5 m); beam 22 ft., 4 in. (6.8 m); draft 16 ft., 10 in. (5.1 m)
Propulsion:	two Admiralty of Vickers diesel engines delivering 4,300 hp (3206 kW) for 18.5 knots surfaced and two electric motors delivering 1,250 hp (932 kW) for 8 knots submerged
Armament:	one 4-inch (102 mm) gun, one 3/4-inch (20 mm) AA cannon, and 10 21-inch (533 mm) tubes for 16 torpedoes or 26 mines
Complement:	61

Underwater weapons of World War II

Until the arrival of ahead-throwing weapons such as the Hedgehog and Squid in service with the Royal Navy and US Navy from the middle part of the war, the standard anti-submarine weapon of World War II was the depth charge, as first developed in World War I.

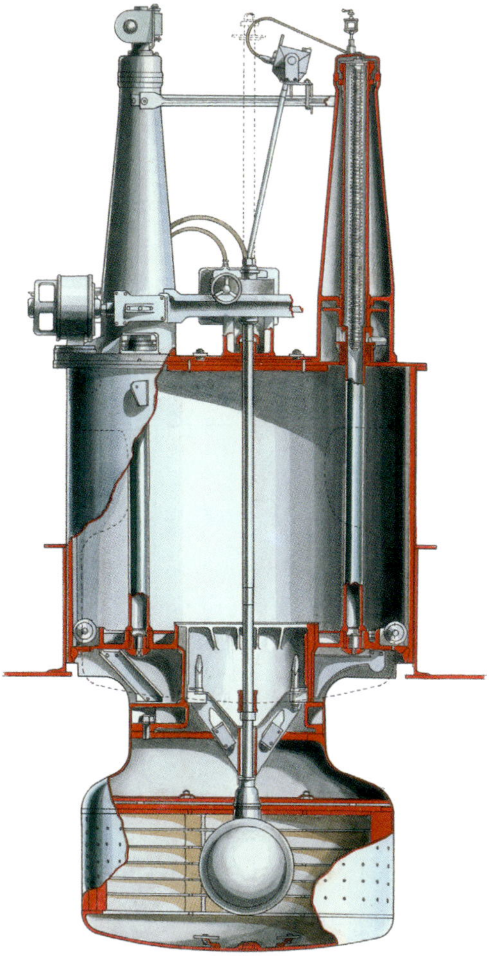

ASDIC/Sonar derived from the name given to the Anti-Submarine Detection Investigation Committee device used to detect submarines.

The depth charge was created specifically for the anti-submarine role, and destroyed its target by the shock of its explosion close to the target. For this purpose, the depth charge contained a large HE charge and a fuse that could be set to initiate the charge at a pre-set depth. The idea of a "dropping mine" emerged in 1910, and the depth charge was made a practical reality to satisfy the 1914 demand of Admiral of the Fleet Sir George Callaghan, commanding the Grand fleet. The concept was perfected by Herbert Taylor at the Torpedo and Mine School at Portsmouth, and the first genuinely effective depth charge was the Type D weapon developed in 1916 as a 300 lb. (136 kg) cylindrical casing filled with HE (normally TNT) and fitted with a hydrostatic pistol to trigger the detonation at the desired depth up to 300 feet (91 m).

So successful was the new weapon that it soon caught the attention of the U.S. Navy, which requested complete blueprints in March 1917. Commander Fullinwider of the Bureau of Naval Ordnance and a U.S. Navy engineer named Minkler incorporated a number of revisions to the British design and then secured a U.S. patent, possibly so that the U.S. would not have to pay royalties to Taylor.

The depth charge remained essentially unaltered, except in detail, right into 1943, when Torpex (50% more powerful than TNT) and a more streamlined casing were introduced, the latter to allow the depth charge to sink more rapidly. The standard 600 lb. (272 kg) depth charge of World War II would not typically ensure the rupture of an undamaged

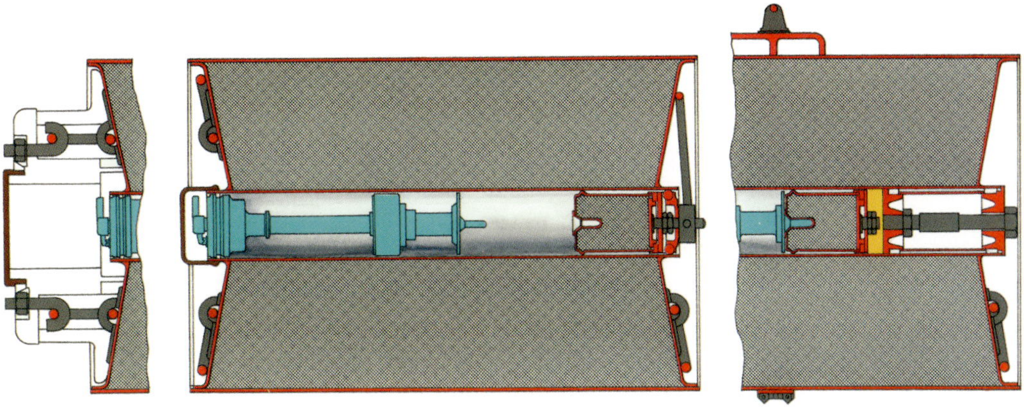

Above and right: British Type D Mk III Depth Charge. A hydrostatic device was preset so that the explosive charge detonated at a required depth.

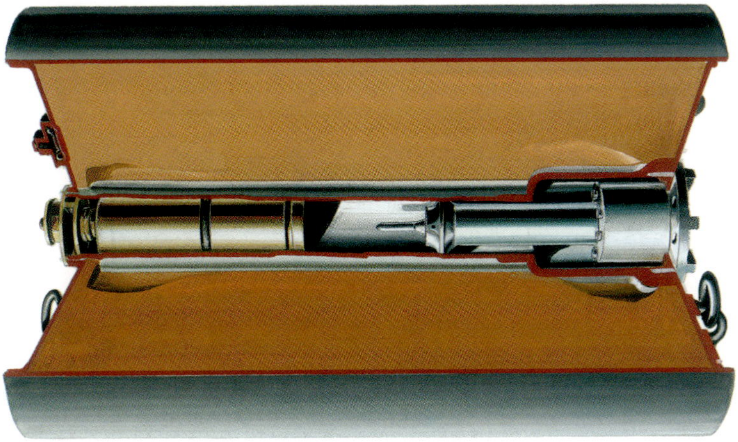

U-boat's hull unless it detonated within about 17 ½ feet (5.3 m). This was difficult to achieve, especially against a maneuvering target, and the evidence indicates that most of the U-boats which succumbed to depth charge attack were finally destroyed by cumulative damage suffered during a prolonged engagement rather than by a single explosion right beside the boat. The survivability of U-boats was in fact very high: the *U-427*, for example, survived an attack in which 678 depth charges were dropped.

The initial method of delivering depth charges was simply to roll them off racks at the stern of the attacking warship. The depth charges were at first placed at the top of ramps and allowed to roll over the stern. Late in World War I, though, there appeared an improved pattern of rack, holding a number of depth charges for remotely controlled release. This pattern of rack was used right through World War II.

In the last two years of World War I, some of the trawlers used for anti-submarine work were fitted on their forecastles with a thrower for one depth charge. More versatile projectors were then built to offer a wider pattern of depth charges when used in association with the stern racks. Appearing in 1918, the first of these

Underwater weapons of World War II *continued*

U.S. air-drop depth charge of WWII.

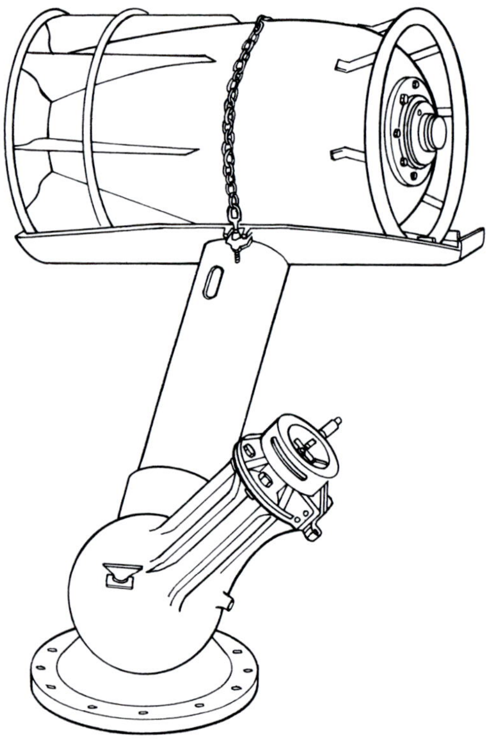

was the Y-gun, so called from its shape. Mounted on the ship's centerline with the two arms pointing outward, the gun carried one depth charge cradled on a shuttle in each arm. A charge ignited in the Y-gun's vertical section then propelled the depth charges about 50 yards (45 m) to each side of the ship.

Because of its nature, the Y-gun had necessarily to be mounted on the centerline, occupying an area which could otherwise be used for other purposes. The Y-gun was thus replaced starting in 1942 by the K-gun, which could be mounted along the edge of the deck. K-guns were often used with the stern racks to create a pattern of six to ten charges.

In all depth charge attacks, the attacking ship had to be moving at more than a certain speed to avoid damage from the explosion of its own depth charges.

The depth charge was also used by anti-submarine aircraft after early use had revealed that the standard 100 lb. (45 kg) anti-submarine bomb were ineffective, and in a low-level

Seeing a U-boat periscope would be a great temptation to a warship captain, who would want to ram it, only to find that it is false and attached to a mine.

The problem with depth charge attacks by surface ships was not the weapon but the manner of its delivery. An attacker normally detected a submerged submarine by sonar. The attacker then had to pass over the position of its target to drop its stern charges, which produced a hiatus in the sonar contact just before the depth charges were dropped, providing the target submarine with the opportunity to maneuver laterally or vertically out of its known position. It was this factor that led to the development of ahead-throwing weapons, which the attacker fired while still in contact with the target.

In the Pacific, Japanese depth charge attacks initially proved fairly unsuccessful against U.S. submarines. Unless caught in shallow water, a U.S. submarine could generally dive to a depth greater than the setting typically used by the Japanese for their depth charges. This fact was then betrayed by the indiscretion of a member of the U.S. Congress, and the Japanese revise their setting to an average of 250 feet (76 m). The U.S. Navy estimated that this cost it as many as 10 submarines and up to 800 men.

Allied Mk X 1-ton depth charge.

attack could skip off the water to hit the airplane which had dropped it. The Royal Navy's 450 lb. (204 kg) Depth Charge Mk VII was thus adapted for aerial use by the addition of a streamlined nose fairing and a tail-mounted set of stabilizing fins. Purpose-designed depth charges were later developed specifically for aerial use.

Type XVIIB class (1944)

The main problems with the submarines of the era before nuclear power were limited submerged endurance and a poor speed to range equation. Given the nature of the batteries of the day, the latter translated as a higher speed for a shortened distance or a slower speed for a lengthened distance, although in both cases speed and range were still low.

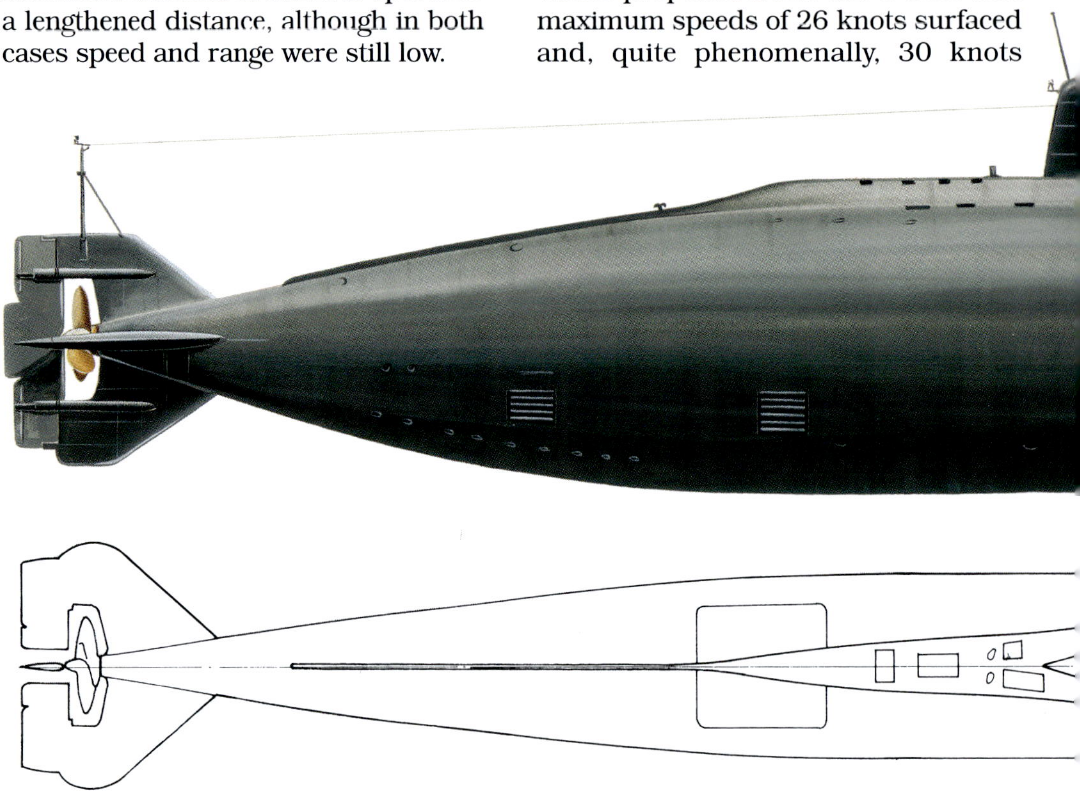

This situation affected the German U-boat arm as much as that of any other combatant in World War II. Professor Hellmuth Walter, an engineer who in 1933 was working on a new gas turbine at the Germaniawerft yard in Kiel, took an interest in the problem. Walter conceived the idea of closed-circuit propulsion based on the use of hydrogen peroxide in a stabilized form called Perhydrol. The combustion of Perhydrol and oil was complex, but offered the possibility of engines smaller and lighter than the diesel-electric arrangement of current U-boats, able to generate greater power, and able to free the boat from spending many hours on the surface every time the batteries needed recharging. In October 1934 Walter proposed a 300-ton U-boat with maximum speeds of 26 knots surfaced and, quite phenomenally, 30 knots submerged, as well as ranges of 2,880 miles (4635 km) at 15 knots surfaced and 575 miles (925 km) at the same speed submerged.

Walter's concept was rejected as too radical. Walter remained optimistic, and in 1937 shared his ideas with *Kapitän zur See* Karl Dönitz, commanding a U-boat training flotilla. Dönitz was very impressed and submitted Walter's ideas more formally, and in 1939 there emerged the contract for a small research boat, the *V-80*.

This was built in Kiel by Germaniawerft in great secrecy, and launched on April 14, 1940. With a displacement of 75 tons submerged, length of 72 ft., 2 in. (22 m) and crewed by four men, the *V-80* was unarmed and powered by a Walter turbine delivering 2,000 hp (1491 kW). In the following spring, the boat's trials, with Walter himself in command, revealed a speed of 28 knots, more than double that of any submarine in service anywhere.

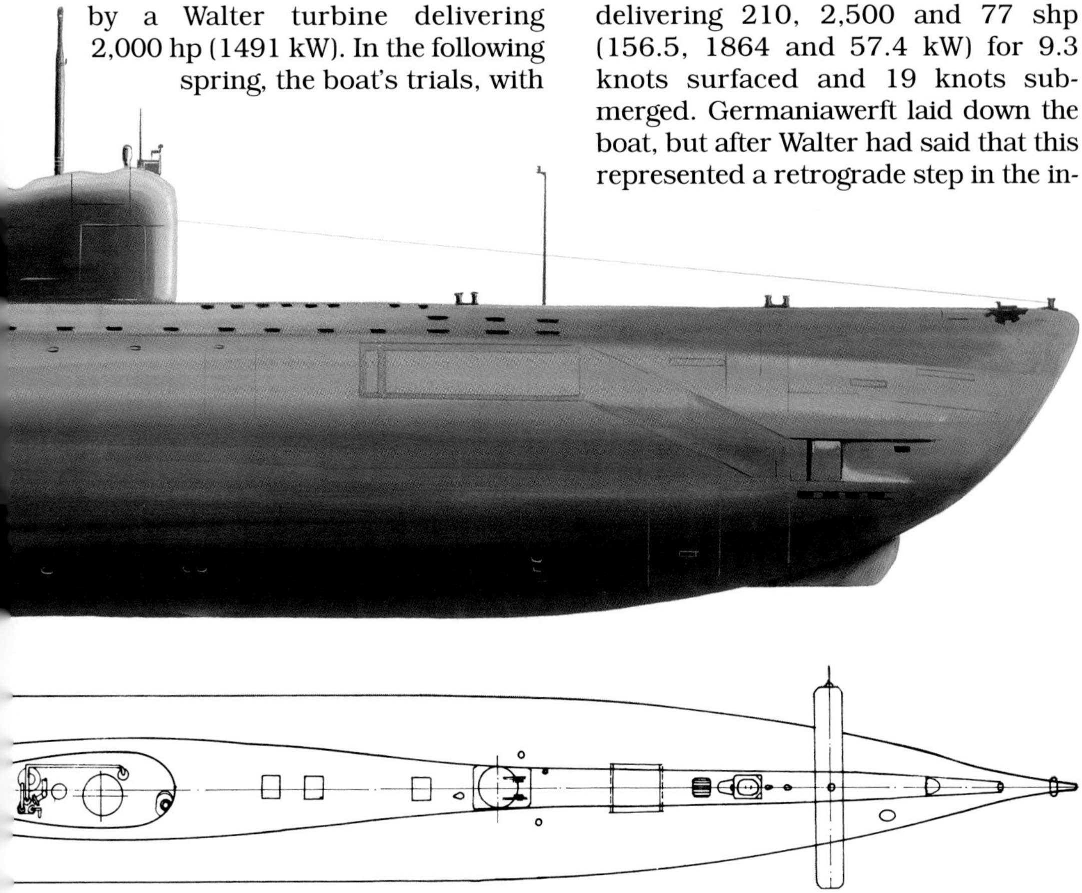

The German navy was so impressed by the test results from *V-80* that it recommended the construction of six coastal-type boats based on that design, but doubts emerged about the sense of proceeding straight to an operational type from a wholly experimental prototype. One Type XVII pre-production boat was then ordered with a displacement of 645 tons submerged, length of 170 ft., 11 in (52.1 m), two 21-inch (533 mm) bow tubes for six torpedoes, complement of 25, and single-shaft propulsion by two diesel engines, two Walter turbines and two electric motors delivering 210, 2,500 and 77 shp (156.5, 1864 and 57.4 kW) for 9.3 knots surfaced and 19 knots submerged. Germaniawerft laid down the boat, but after Walter had said that this represented a retrograde step in the introduction of diesel-electric back-up machinery, it was scrapped.

After a January 1942 meeting between Walter and Dönitz, head of the U-boat arm, contracts were awarded for four improved pre-production boats, with mixed propulsion, to be built by Germaniawerft to the Wk 202 class standard as the *U-792* and *U-793* and by Blohm & Voss of Hamburg to the Wa 201 class standard as the *U-794* and *U-795*. The keels were laid down in December 1942, and the first to enter the water, on September 28, 1943, was the *U-792*. Though armed, the boats were used only for trials and training.

The Walter boats did offer exceptional performance, but were very complex and therefore difficult and costly to build and maintain; additionally, they relied on uncertain supplies of Perhydrol, which was very dangerous.

The only three Walter-type boats to enter service before the end of World War II, and then without entering operational use, were three of five Type XVIIB coastal boats ordered from Blohm & Voss. These were the *U-1405*, *U-1406*, and *U-1407*. The small Walter boats thus did not have any real effect on the war, and were all scuttled in May 1945. The *U-1406* and *U-1407* were later salvaged, the former being allocated to the U.S. and the latter to the UK, which placed the boat in trials service with the name *Meteorite* in 1949.

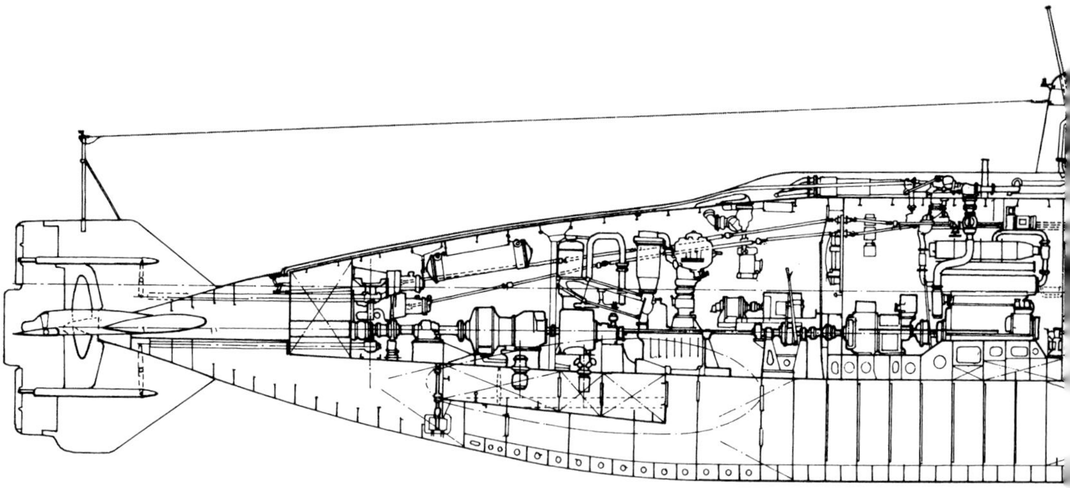

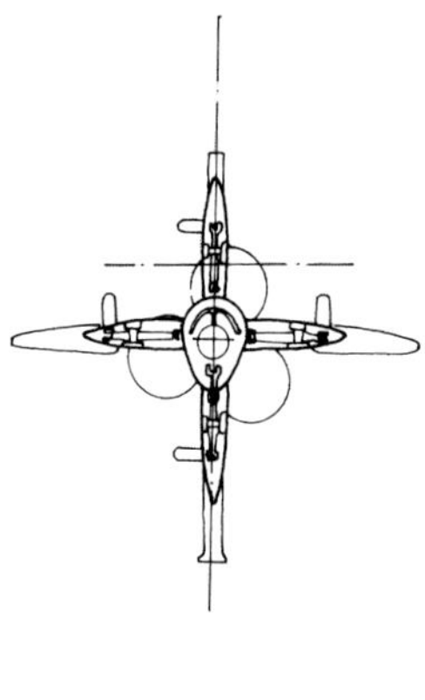

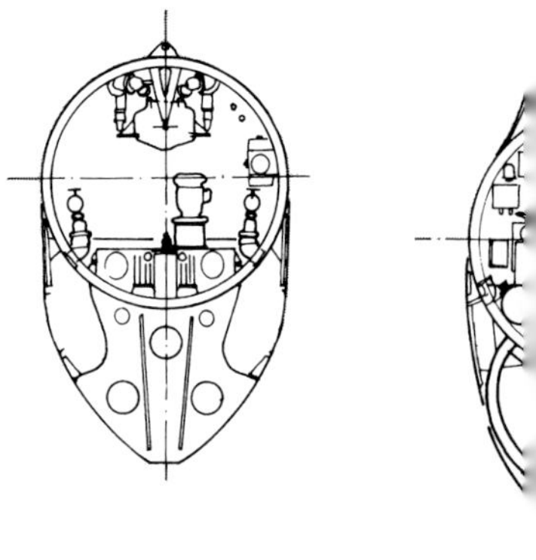

Type XVIIB class

Type:	coastal attack submarine
Tonnage:	307 tons surfaced and 340 tons submerged
Dimensions:	length 136 ft., 2 in. (41.5 m); beam 11 ft., 2 in. (3.3 m); draft 14 ft., 1 in. (4.3 m)
Propulsion:	one Deutz diesel engine delivering 210 hp (157 kW) for 8.5 knots surfaced, and one Walter turbine delivering 2,500 hp (1864 kW) for 21.5 knots submerged; there was also one electric motor delivering 77 hp (57.4 kW)
Armament:	two 21-inch (533 mm) tubes (both bow) for four torpedoes
Complement:	19

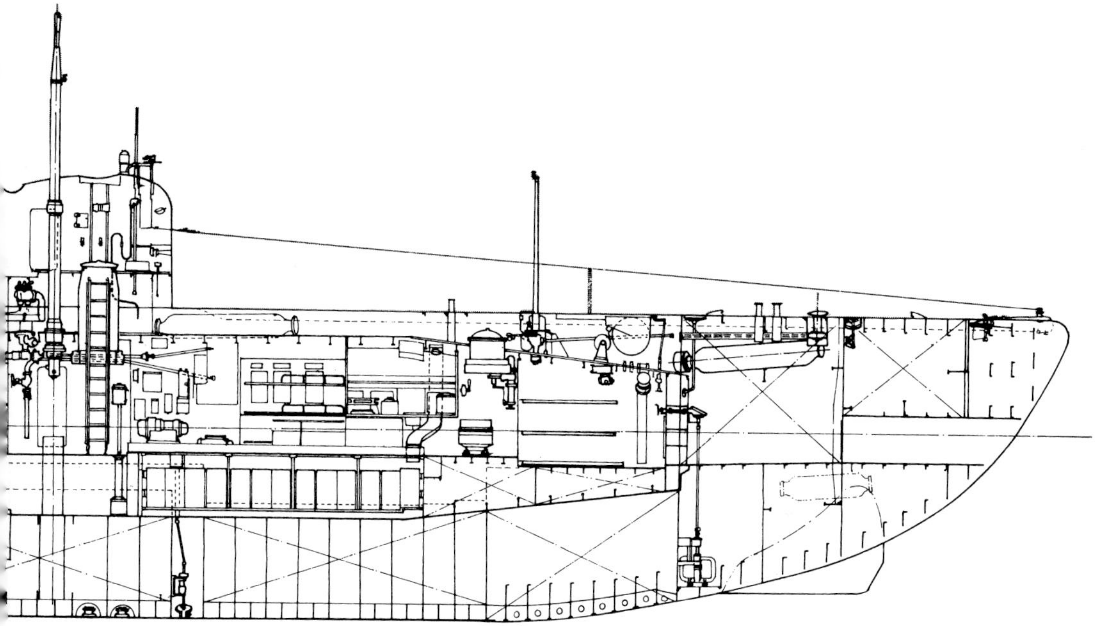

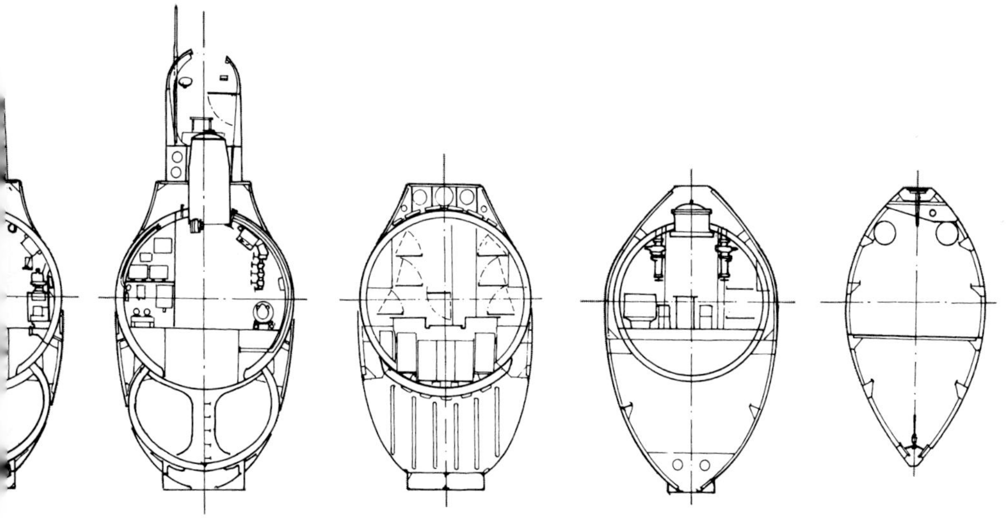

Type XXI class (1944)

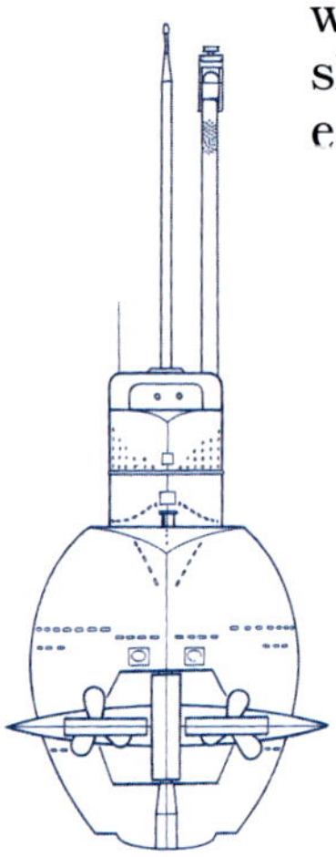

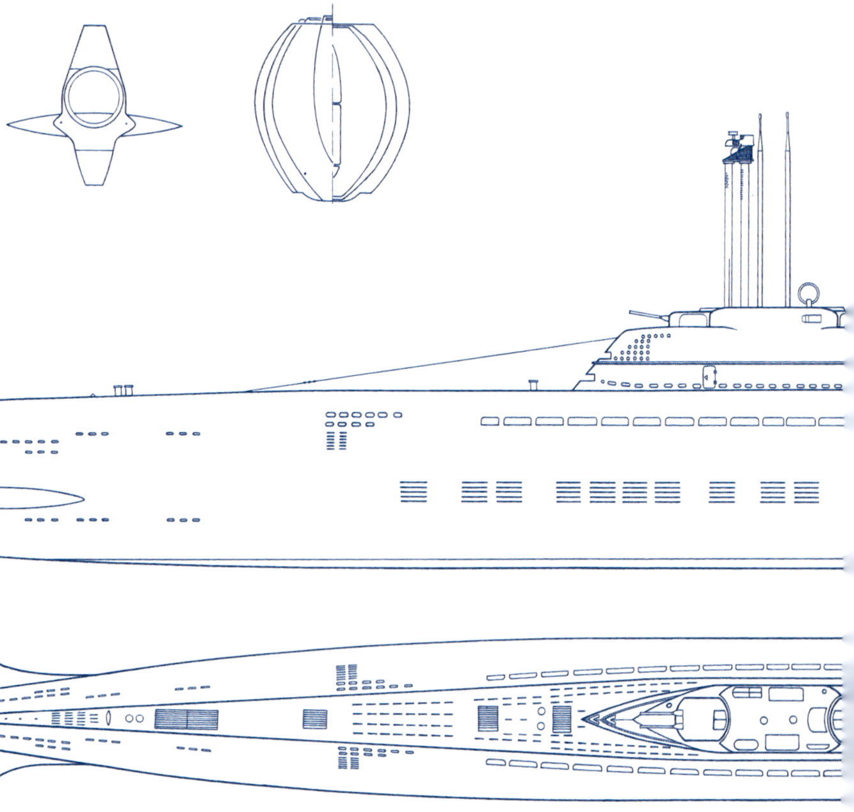

Also known as the "Elektroboote," the Type XXI class of U-boats were the first boats designed specifically to operate entirely submerged, rather than as submersibles (surface ships which could dive as a short-term expedient to escape detection or to launch an attack). The boats can be regarded only as revolutionary at the time they were designed, built, and first introduced. Had Germany been in the position to build the type at an earlier date and in larger numbers, the Type XXI class of U-boat could have made the Allied success in the Battle of the Atlantic very problematic.

By comparison with earlier U-boat classes, the most important change in the Type XXI class of boat was battery capacity enlarged to approximately three times the figure for the Type VIIC-class boats which where the mainstay of the U-boat arm throughout World War II. This increase of battery capacity gave the boats much enhanced underwater performance in speed and range, the latter significantly reducing the amount of time the boats had to spend on or just under the surface: in practical terms, this meant that the boats could travel submerged at about 5 knots for two or even three days before having to recharge their batteries, which took less than five hours using the *Schnorchel* (snorkel or snorting) mast as the boat cruised just below the surface. This reduced the chance of detection even by radar-equipped Allied warships and aircraft. The Type XXI-class U-boat was also much quieter than the Type VIIC-class boat,

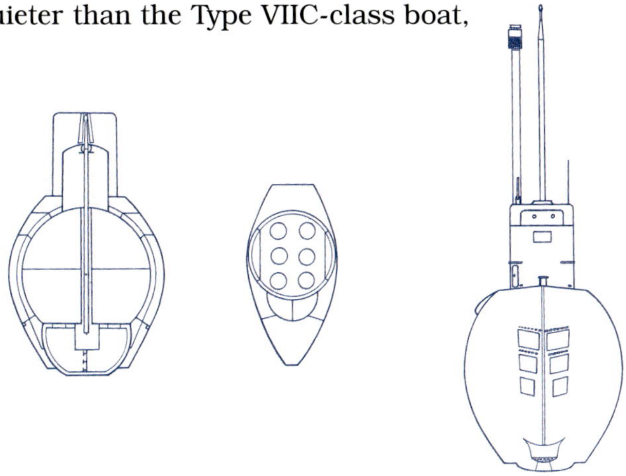

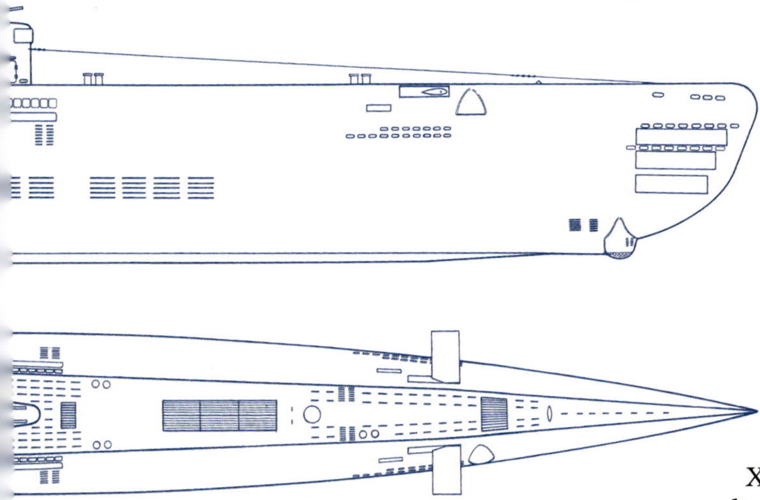

making it more difficult for the sonar of Allied warships to detect the type at longer ranges.

The boats' diesel-electric propulsion arrangement, driving two shafts, was based on two diesel engines and two electric motors; there were also two electric motors to provide 222 hp (165.5 kW) for a silent creeping speed of 5 knots. The range of the boats was 17,820 miles (28675 km) at 10 knots surfaced and 390 miles (630 km) 340 miles at 5 knots submerged.

Another key to the high underwater performance of the Type XXI-class boats was a hull of much better streamlining than those of earlier classes, a fact which reduced both drag and noise and made it possible for the Type XXI-class boats to travel faster under the water than on the water's surface. The combination of high underwater speed and reduced diving time made the Type XXI-class boats much more difficult to chase and destroy. The high underwater speed also produced a "sprint" capability to position itself most advantageously before launching a torpedo attack. Older boats had to surface in order to sprint into position, a fact which often betrayed them, especially after aircraft had become standard as part of the convoy escort force.

The design of the Type XXI-class submarine had a direct influence on the planning of the *Nautilus* (the world's first nuclear-powered submarine), and the *Albacore* (the first submarine with a teardrop hull).

Another positive feature of the Type XXI-class boats was their much improved habitability over the standards of earlier classes: there was a freezer for food, and minor crew conveniences such as a shower and washing facilities—at a time when the crews of older boats often had to spend weeks without bathing or shaving.

The advanced features of the Type XXI-class submarine included a hydraulically operated torpedo reload system which allowed all the torpedo tubes (six bow units) to be reloaded more quickly than a Type VIIC class of boat could reload a single tube by manpower. The Type XXI could fire 18 torpedoes in less than 20 minutes, and the boat's maximum warload was 23 torpedoes, or 17 torpedoes and 12 mines. The Type XXI class boat also incorporated a sonar system so advanced that it made it possible to create an accurate plot for torpedo launch without using the periscope, thereby increasing the boat's stealthiness. The anti-aircraft armament comprised four ¾-inch (20 mm) cannons in a pair of remotely controlled barbettes in a low-drag arrangement on the conning tower fore and aft of the periscope/snort array. There were also good electronics involving five activc and passive equipments with their antennae carried by retractable masts.

Between 1943 and 1945, 118 boats of the Type XXI class were built by Blohm & Voss of Hamburg, A. G. Weser of Bremen, and F. Schichau of

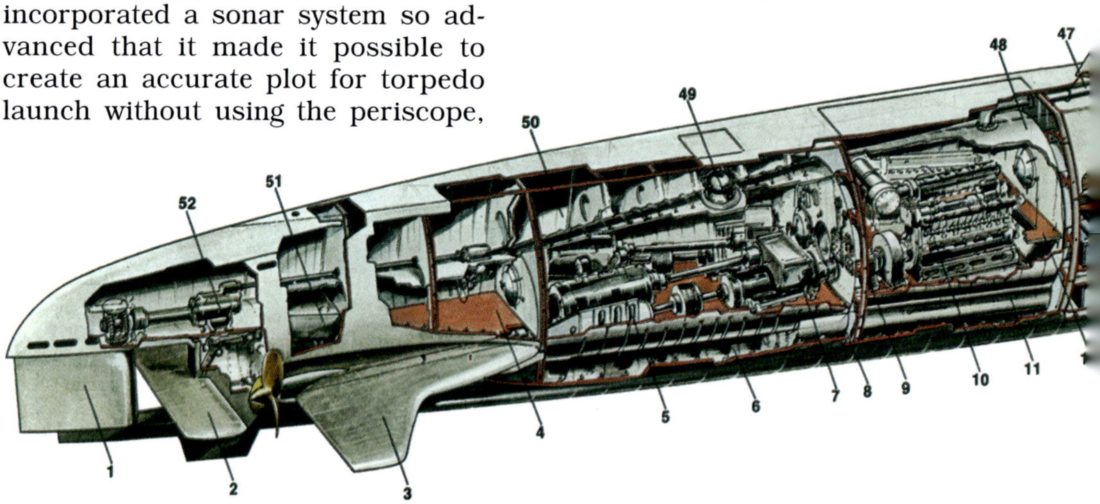

Key:
(1) *Rudder* (2) *Aft hydroplane* (3) *Stern plane* (4) *Aft emergency steering room*
(5) *Electric propulsion motors* (6) *Fuel saddle tanks* (7) *Electric motor gearing* (8) *Oil sump*
(9) *Diesel engine gearing* (10) *Main engine room* (11) *Ballast tank.*
(12) *Catwalk giving repair access to the upper parts of the engine* (13) *Accumulators*
(14) *Refrigerator* (15) *Galley* (16) *Potato store (starboard) and ammunition magazine (port)*
(17) *Periscope machinery* (18) *Main control room* (19) *Steering position*
(20) *Watertight bulkhead door* (21) *Radio room* (22) *Forward lower accumulator stores*
(23) *Junior officers' cabin* (24) *Ballast blowing vents* (25) *Torpedo crew quarters*
(26) *Upper forward accumulator room* (27) *Compressed air bottle* (28) *Torpedo storage room*
(29) *Six forward-firing torpedo tubes angled downward to avoid observation of torpedoes in the water* (30) *Torpedo tube doors mechanism* (31) *Forward pressure bulkhead*
(32) *Forward hydroplane* (33) *Water- and pressure-tight torpedo loading hatch*
(34) *Space between twin hulls used for ballast* (35) *Forward main pressure hull*
(36) *Two 37 mm cannon* (37) *Hatch into conning tower* (38) *Periscope trunking*
(39) *Hatch to bridge* (40) *Periscope pedestal* (41) *Search periscope (raised)* (42) *Schnorchel*
(43) *Antenna* (44) *Two 37 mm cannon* (45) *Escape hatch* (46) *Crew room*
(47) *Air trunking from Schnorchel to engine room* (48) *After pressure hull*
(49) *Engine room escape hatch* (50) *Fuel tank* (51) *After trim tank* (52) *Rudder steering gear*

Danzig. The boats were built more quickly than earlier types as the hull was assembled from eight pre-fabricated transported to the relevant yard after being made by various factories in a diversified production process. Only two of the boats, the *U-2511* and *U-3008*, had embarked on a operational patrol before the end of World War II in May 1945. This resulted in part from longer training process for the boats as the crews had to be trained in the operation of the many new and more advanced technological features.

Most of the boats were scrapped or scuttled after the war, but eight were taken by the Allies for evaluation and trials. The U.S. received *U-2513* and *U-3008*, which were commissioned into the U.S. Navy. The *U-3017* was commissioned into the Royal Navy as the *N41*, and the *U-2518* became the French *Roland Morillot*. The *U-3515*, *U-2529*, *U-3035* and *U-3041* became the Soviet navy's *B27*, *B28*, *B29* and *B30* respectively. A ninth Type XXI-class boat also saw service after the war: the *U-2540*, which had been scuttled at the end of the war, was raised in 1957 to become the West Germany's navy's research submarine *Wilhelm Bauer*, and this is the only remaining Type XXI boat; it became an exhibit of the German Maritime Museum in Bremerhaven.

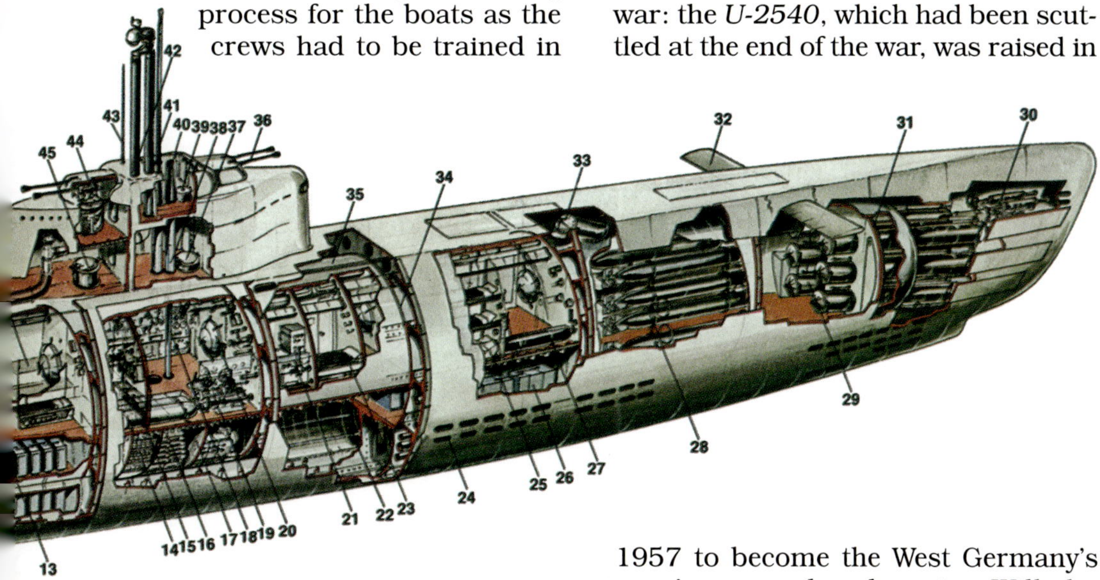

Type XXI class

Type:	attack submarine
Tonnage:	1,621 tons surfaced and 2,100 tons submerged
Dimensions:	length 251 ft., 7 3/4 in. (76.7 m); beam 26 ft., 3 in. (8 m); draft 20 ft., 8 in. (6.3 m)
Propulsion:	two MAN diesel engines delivering 4,000 hp (2982 kW) for 15.6 knots surfaced and two Siemens electric motors delivering 5,496 hp (4098 kW) for 17.2 knots submerged
Armament:	six 21-inch (533 mm) tubes with 23 torpedoes, and four 1-inch (20 mm) AA guns
Complement:	57

T Group 3 class (1943)

A further development of the second group of T-class boats (16 units of the War Emergency and 1940 Programs), the 22 boats of the Royal Navy's third group of T-class submarines were laid down between 1941 and 1944 for completion between 1943 to 1946 in the 1941 Program (17 boats) and 1942 Program (14 boats, of which nine were later cancelled). As in the preceding Group 2 boats, wartime austerity meant that the boats lacked many peacetime refinements such as jackstaffs (flagpoles) and guardrails, and had only one anchor. For the same reason, a major part of the internal pipework was of steel rather than copper.

The boats were constructed at a time when riveting was being replaced by welding, and as a result the *Taciturn*, *Talent* (ex-*Tasman*), *Tapir*, *Tarn*, *Teredo*, *Tiptoe*, *Trump*, *Tabard*, *Thermopylae*, *Totem*, *Truncheon* and *Turpin* were completed with pressure hulls of welded three-quarter-inch (19 mm) steel for an operating diving depth of 350 feet (107 m) though they were tested to a depth of 400 feet (122 m). With the possible exception of the *Tarn*, the boats carried 86 tons of additional fuel in external tanks, which in most cases were welded. Three of the boats were transferred to the Netherlands, the first *Talent* becoming the *Zwaardvisch* (resulting of the renaming of the *Tasman* as the *Talent* for British service), the *Tapir* becoming the *Zeehond* (in 1948) and the *Tarn* becoming the *Tijgerhaai*. The *Totem*, *Truncheon* and *Turpin* were transferred to Israel in 1964-68 to become the *Dakar*, *Dolphin* and *Leviathan*, respectively.

The armament was essentially similar to that of the Group 2 boats; all but the *Zwaardvisch* are listed with the alternative warload of 12 instead of 18 M2 mines, even though the torpedo total remained unaltered at 17. The reason for this is not certain, but it is probable that this was a result of the decision to use the boats against the Japanese in Far Eastern waters, which demanded additional equipment such as higher-capacity air conditioning and improved radar. This made it more difficult to trim the boats in the fresher (and therefore less dense) waters off the estuaries of the great rivers of the region, and thus favored locations for mine-laying, suggesting a reduction in load.

The boats of the 1941 Program were the *Telemachus*, *Talent*, *Tasman*, *Terrapin*, *Thorough*, *Thule*, *Tudor*, *Tireless*, *Token*, *Tradewind*, *Trenchant*, *Tiptoe*, *Trump*, *Taciturn*, *Tapir*, *Tarn*, *Talent*, and *Teredo*. The only boats of the 1942 Program to be completed were the *Tabard*, *Totem* (lost in accident on passage to Israel), *Truncheon*, *Turpin* and *Thermopylae*, while the nine which were cancelled in October 1945 after the surrender of Japan would have been the *Thor*, *Tiara*, *Theban*, *Talent*, *Threat* and four as-yet unnamed boats.

The *Terrapin* was severely damaged in a Japanese attack during May 1945 and considered not to be worth the cost of repair, but the other Royal Navy boats either survived or were not commissioned in time for service in World War II, and were decommissioned and broken up between the mid-1950s and mid-1970s.

T Group 3 class

Type:	patrol submarine
Tonnage:	1,290 tons surfaced, 1,560 tons submerged
Dimensions:	length 276 ft., 6 in. (84.3 m); beam 25 ft., 6 in. (7.8 m); draft 14 ft., 7 in. (4.45 m)
Propulsion:	two Admiralty or Vickers diesel engines delivering 5,000 hp (3728 kW) for 15.5 knots surfaced and two electric motors delivering 2,900 hp (2162 kW) for 9 knots submerged
Armament:	one 4-inch (102 mm) gun and 10 31-inch (533 mm) tubes for 16 torpedoes
Complement:	48

USS *Torsk* (1944)

Now docked at the Baltimore Maritime Museum, the USS *Torsk* was built as a Tench-class boat. It was laid down at Portsmouth Navy Yard in June 1944, launched in September 1944, and commissioned on December 16, 1944. Completed on the last day of 1944, the Torsk trained until February 11, 1945, when it sailed for Florida, where it operated from Port Everglades in anti-submarine research before passing though the Panama Canal to reach Hawaii on March 23.

The boat left Pearl Harbor on her first war patrol, where it served on lifeguard duty off Kii Suido, finding no "trade." On May 11, it departed to patrol off the north-eastern coast of Honshu. Arriving on May 13, it spent two days attempting to make contact with the other members of the "Lewellen's Looters" wolf pack. On May 16, it met the *Sand Lance* and *Cero*, but in a period of more than two weeks the three boats patrolled without locating anything other than mines. But on June 2, the *Torsk* found a small Japanese coastal minelayer and fired a salvo of six torpedoes, which the Japanese vessel evaded, but was then not counterattacked. The *Torsk* was again disappointed on June 4 when, while patrolling off Kobe Saki, it fired four torpedoes at a small freighter without scoring. On the following day, it set course for home, reaching Pearl Harbor on June 16.

After refitting and the receiving new equipment, the *Torsk* departed on her second war patrol on July 17, passing through the minefields of the Tsushima Strait on August 10. On the following day, it recovered seven Japanese

The USS Torsk at her berth in Baltimore's Inner Harbor, where she now serves as a museum and memorial. The sub was the last U.S. naval vessel to sink an enemy warship in World War II.
Photo: John Batchelor.

Part of the control room with wheel for forward diving planes on left and "Christmas tree" panel upper right.
Photo: John Batchelor.

merchant seamen from the *Koue Maru*, sunk four days earlier. On the afternoon of the same day, the boat reached her patrol area and, on the following morning off Dogo Island, made a submerged periscope attack which sank a small coastal freighter. On August 13, it sank another small cargo vessel before later making an unsuccessful effort to sink a cargo ship. In the morning of August 14, off Amarubi Saki, the *Torsk* sighted a medium cargo ship and took up the chase despite the fact that the merchantman was escorted by a Kaibokan-class escort vessel. The *Torsk* launched one of the new experimental Mk 28 torpedoes at the escorting ship, which was hit and sank. As the freighter entered port some 30 minutes later, the *Torsk* attempted unsuccessfully to sink her. Around noon, another Japanese escort arrived and the *Torsk* fired another Mk 28 torpedo at her and then dived deep. Five minutes later, the *Torsk* fired another torpedo, an Mk 27 acoustic-homing weapon. Both weapons hit the escort vessel within a minute of each other. Thus, the *Torsk* sank the last Japanese warship to be lost in World War II. On August 15, the boat was informed of the war's end, and reached Guam at the end of her second patrol on September 3.

For the next seven years, the *Torsk* was a training boat and in 1952 was upgraded to "fleet snorkel" submarine. The boat remained in service until March 1968, when it was decommissioned and modified as a training boat until December 1971.

USS Torsk

Type:	fleet submarine
Tonnage:	1,570 tons surfaced and 2,416 tons submerged
Dimensions:	length 311 ft., 8 in. (95 m); beam 27 ft., 3 in. (8.3 m); draft 15 ft., 5 in. (4.7 m)
Propulsion:	four 4 x 1350 hp (1 MW) 10cyl Fairbanks-Morse diesel engines delivering 5,400 hp (4026 kW) for 20.25 knots surfaced and two General Electric electric motors delivering 2,740 hp (2043 kW) for 8.75 knots submerged
Armament:	one 5-inch (127 mm) L/25 guns, one 1 ½-inch (40 mm) Bofors AA gun, one ¾-inch (20 mm) AA cannon, two half-inch (12.7 mm) machine guns, and 10 21-inch (533 mm) tubes for 28 torpedoes
Complement:	81

A class (1945)

The A class (otherwise known as Amphion or Acheron) of diesel-electric submarines was ordered for the Royal Navy in 1943 to reflect the fact that the British needed a different type of submarine for Pacific operations with greater range and speed as well as improved habitability and a deeper diving depth than the S-class and T-class boats it was designed to replace. In design, the A class was in essence an enlarged version of the T class with changes to suit the type to fast construction making use of materials and equipment on hand for the T-class boats. The A-class boat had a high, flared bow for excellent sea performance and had high-capacity air conditioning for Far East submarine operations.

Some 46 were ordered, but only 18 were launched (10 of them by Vickers-Armstrong) and just 16 commissioned, the other two hulls being used for crush testing. The class was based on a welded hull assembled from pre-fabricated sections, so each boat progressed from keel-laying to launch in about eight months by comparison with 15 months for the T-class boats. Only two of the new boats were completed before the end of the war as the *Amphion* and *Astute*, but neither saw action.

The A class was one of only two new British submarine designs produced during World War II, the other being the X-craft. After

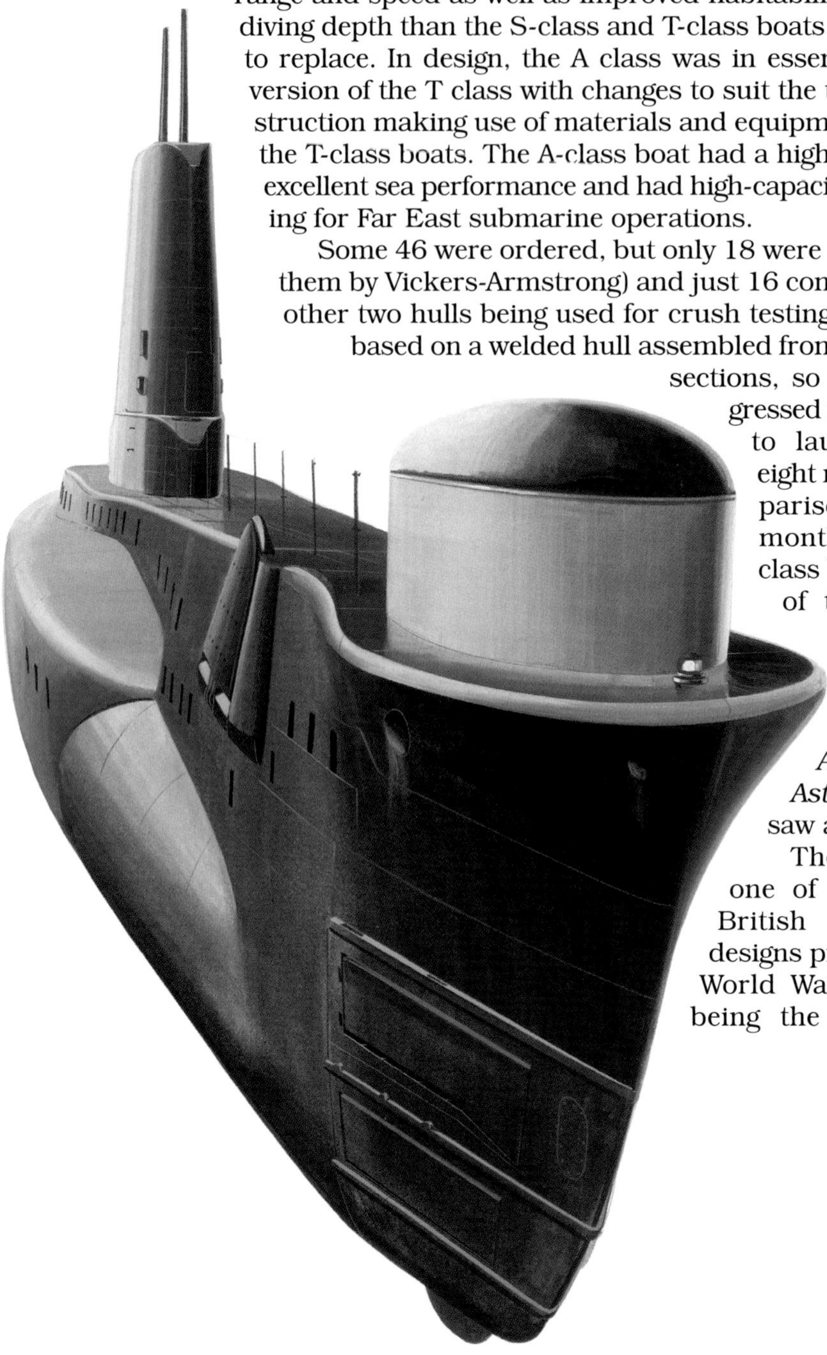

Stern of Alaric. Note the torpedo tube with cap open.
Photo: John Batchelor.

World War II, the boats were considerably modified with a snort mast based on the *Schnorkel* used by U-boats during the war, radar that could be used from periscope depth, and a night periscope. In the late 1940s, the primary target of the boats switched from surface vessels to submarines, thus reflecting the start of the Cold War with the USSR: the first role in this new tasking was defensive, by preventing the movement of Soviet boats out of Soviet northern waters, and the second was offensive, by mining Soviet ports. The A-class boats were revised for their new tasks in 1955-60, the forward and after parts of the hull being rebuilt, the deck and conning tower lengthened and streamlined, the deck guns removed to improve underwater speed and reduce noise, the two bow and two stern external torpedo tubes remove, and improved sonar fitted. The *Affray* was lost in 1951, but the other units served for almost three decades. There were supplemented and then replaced starting in 1958 by the Porpoise and Oberon classes of patrol boats, and the last operational A-class boat was the *Andrew*, decommissioned in 1974.

A class

Type:	patrol submarine
Tonnage:	1,385 tons surfaced and 1,620 tons submerged
Dimensions:	length 280 ft., 6 in. (85.5 m); beam 22 ft., 4 in. (6.8 m); draft 16 ft., 10 in. (5.1 m)
Propulsion:	two Admiralty of Vickers diesel engines delivering 4,300 hp (3206 kW) for 18.5 knots surfaced and two electric motors delivering 1,250 hp (932 kW) for 8 knots submerged
Armament:	one 4-inch (102 mm) gun, one 3/4-inch (20 mm) AA cannon, and 10 21-inch (533 mm) tubes for 16 torpedoes or 26 mines
Complement:	61

Whiskey class (1950)

The attack submarines of the Soviet navy generally known in the West by their NATO reporting designation as the "Whiskey" class, but in the USSR the Project 613, Project 644, and Project 665 classes were boats which the USSR designed and built during the first part of the Cold War during the 1950s and early 1960s. Created in the later 1940s to meet a requirement expressed in 1946, the design was apparently based in overall terms on that of the German Type XXI-class U-boat dating from the period late in World War II, but was downgraded in many respects to accord better with the USSR's less sophisticated submarine building and operating capabilities.

Between 1949 and 1958, a total of 236 submarines of this type were built by the Baltic, Gorkiy, Komsomolsk, and Nikolayev yards, 215 of them for service with all of the Soviet navy's main fleets and the other 21 delivered in prefabricated form to the Chinese navy for local assembly. The Whiskey-class boats were designed as the Project 613 type for the coastal patrol task in variants known in the West as the Whiskey I, Whiskey II, Whiskey III, Whiskey IV, and Whiskey V classes. The boats had two electric motors for silent running at low speed, and had a submerged speed of 7 knots while using the snorkel. The maximum range on the surface was 15,545 miles (25,015 km), the snorting range 6,920 miles (11,120 km), and the submerged range 385 miles (620 km) at 2 knots. The maximum underwater endurance with snorting was 166 hours, and each boat carried stores for a 30-day patrol.

During the 1950s and 1960s, some of these patrol boats were converted for the carriage and firing of two or four SS-N-3 Shaddock anti-ship cruise missiles. In the Whiskey Twin Cylinder class of boats, each boat carried a pair of containers for the missiles abaft the conning tower, while the Whiskey Long Bin class conversions, lengthened by 23 ft., 11.5 in. (7.3 m) to 273 ft., 3.5 in. (83.3 m), carried two twin sets of missile container/launchers. The prototype of this development was trialed in 1956 as the Whiskey Single Cylinder class boat with one container/launcher abaft the conning tower (or sail). In 1958-60, six more boats were converted to the initial Whiskey Twin Cylinder or Project 644-class operational stan-

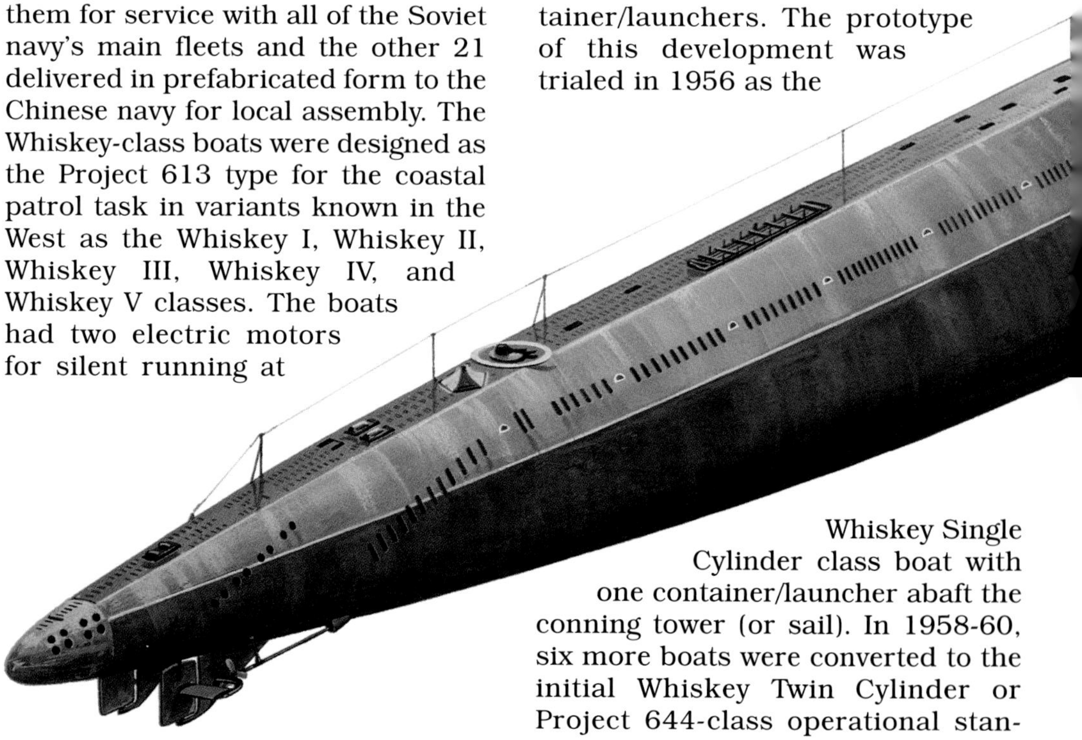

dard. Then in 1960-63, another six boats were converted to the Whiskey Long Bin or Project 655-class standard with a lengthened hull and conning tower for the accommodation of four container/launchers in the horizontal position. These missile boats could launch their weapons only on the surface, and it took up to 40 minutes to elevate the missile containers to the required launch angle and to prepare the missile guidance packages for launch. Each missile carried a 200-kiloton nuclear warhead.

The Whiskey Long Bin boats did not handle well below the surface, and the passage of water in the area of the missile container/launchers was very noisy. This was deemed a major operational failing at a time when Western sonars were improving rapidly in capability, and the boats were soon retired from service. Four were converted to the Whiskey Canvas Bag or Project 640 radar picket standard, and two more were adapted as special reconnaissance boats with the supposed tasks of fishery research and oceanographic research.

In Soviet service the Whiskey-class boats were replaced in the patrol task by the Romeo-class boats, and in the missile role by the Juliett-class boats.

Export of the Whiskey class in its basic patrol role were numerous, including two to Albania (where another two were seized in 1961 as that country broke with the USSR on adopting the Maoist concept of communism), two to Bulgaria, five as well as the 21 prefabricated boats to China where they were known as the Type 03-class boats, seven to Egypt, 12 operational boats to Indonesia as well another two non-operational vessels for cannibalization, four to north Korea, and four to Poland. Cuba and Syria also received elderly Whiskey-class boats for service in the battery-charging role. The missile and radar picket types were never exported.

Whiskey class

Type:	attack submarine
Tonnage:	about 1,080 tons surfaced and about 1,350 tons submerged
Dimensions:	length 249 ft., 4 in. (76 m); beam 20 ft., 8 in. to 21 ft., 4 in. (6.3 to 6.5 m); draft 16 ft., 1 in. (4.9 m)
Propulsion:	two Type 37D diesel engines delivering 4,000 hp (2982 kW) for 18.5 knots surfaced and two electric motors delivering 2,700 hp (2013 kW) for 13 knots submerged
Armament:	two 2 ¼-inch (57 mm) AA guns, two 1-inch (25 mm) AA guns and six 21-inch (533 mm) tubes for 12 torpedoes or 22 mines
Complement:	54

Zulu, Golf, and Juliett classes (1952–62)

The Zulu or Project 611-class submarine was the larger brother of the Whiskey class for the oceanic rather than coastal role, and 26 such boats were delivered beginning in 1952. Six were later converted as the world's first ballistic missile submarines, one of them carrying one F-11FM Scud missile and the other five each carrying two such missiles. The missiles were too long to be contained within the boat's hull, and so extended into the enlarged sail. One of the boats successfully launched a missile on September 16, 1955. The design was influenced by the German Type XXI-class U-boat of the World War II era, and the basic details of these diesel-electric submarines included displacements of 1,900 tons surfaced and 2,350 tons submerged, length of 295 ft., 3 in. (90 m), speeds of 18 knots surfaced and 16 knots submerged, and six bow and four stern 21-inch (533 mm) tubes for 22 torpedoes or 44 mines.

The success of the converted Zulu-class boats led to the design of the Project 629 or Golf-class diesel-electric missile submarines. Work on the design began in the mid-1950s, together with the D-2 missile system it was to carry, and the design was derived from that of the Foxtrot-class attack submarine. The type was originally designed to carry three R-11FM ballistic missiles with a range of around 93 miles (150 km). These were carried in three silos fitted in the rear of the large sail behind the bridge. They could only be fired on the surface, though the boat could be under way at the time. Only the first three boats were equipped with the R-11 missiles, the others having the longer-ranged R-13 (SS-N-4 Scud).

The first boats were commissioned in 1958 and the last in 1962, and were built at two yards (16 in Severodvinsk

Golf II class

Type:	ballistic missile submarine
Tonnage:	2,820 tons surfaced and 3,553 tons submerged
Dimensions:	length 324 ft., 6 in. (98.9 m); beam 26 ft., 11 in. (8.2 m); draft 27 ft., 11 in. (8.5 m)
Propulsion:	three diesel engines delivering 6,000 hp (4474 kW) for 17 knots surfaced and three electric motors delivering 5,200 hp (3877 kW) for 12 knots submerged
Armament:	three tubes for three R-21 (SS-N-5 "Serb" ballistic missiles, and 10 21-inch (533 mm) tubes for 16 torpedoes
Complement:	83

and seven in Komsomolsk). Some 14 were greatly modified in 1966-72 as Project 629A or Golf II-class boats, whose major changes were the upgrade of the missile system to carry the R-21 missiles, and improved propulsion and streamlining for higher speed. A few of the other boats were modified to different standards: one was adapted into a Project 629E class of mine-laying submarine, for example. All the boats had left Soviet service by 1990. In 1993, 10 were sold to North Korea for scrapping.

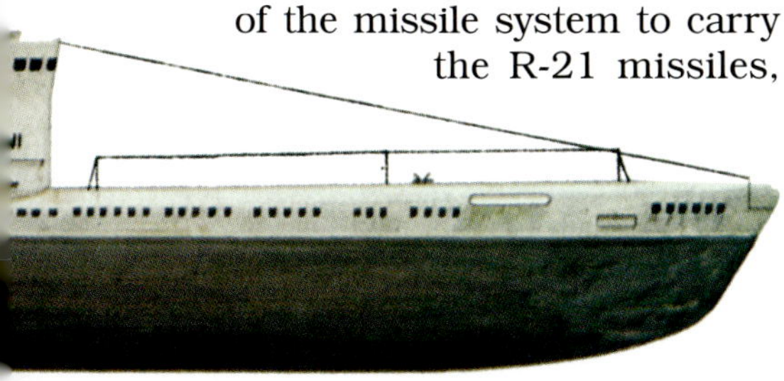

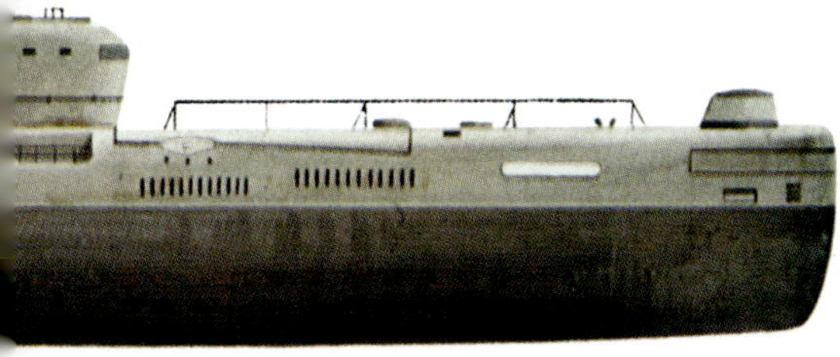

The Juliett or Project 651-class diesel-electric submarines were designed in the 1950s to provide the Soviet navy with a nuclear strike capability against the east coast of the U.S., a task for which they carried four SS-N-3 Shaddock cruise missiles, which could be launched while the submarine was surfaced and under way at less than 4 knots. The missiles were later replaced by SS-N-12 Sandbox anti-ship cruise missiles designed for use against U.S. aircraft carriers. Initial plans called for 35 boats, each with a full-load displacement of 4,137 tons, but only 16 were built. The boats were commissioned in 1962-68 and the last boat was decommissioned in 1994. The Project 675 or Echo II nuclear-powered class was a larger and nuclear-powered version of the Juliett class.

USS *Albacore* (1953)

The USS *Albacore* was a research submarine pioneering the U.S. form of the "teardrop" hull (sometimes known as the "albacore hull"), and was intended to pave the way toward the introduction of high-speed submarines with nuclear propulsion as currently under final development. The concept was derived directly from the design of the German Type XXI class of U-boat of World War II, and was intended to offset the technical lead the USSR had gained by the production of several designs using this type of hull form. The new boat was laid down in March 1952 at the Portsmouth Navy Yard, launched in August 1953, and commissioned in December of the same year.

The other key feature of the *Albacore*'s design was the diesel-electric propulsion arrangement with two comparatively low-powered diesel engines and one very powerful enteric motor driving a single shaft. The diesel engines were installed primarily to charge the boat's huge banks of batteries feeding current to the electric motor for very high speed under the water.

After completing her initial trials, the boat departed Portsmouth, New Hampshire, on April 8, 1954, for shakedown training before embarking on the first part of a career in which the boat was trialed to the limits of a particular configuration and then retuned to the builder for modifications, followed by another full-limit period of trials, etc, This provided a mass of experimental data, and paved the way for the evolution of improved hull configurations for later submarine classes.

The *Albacore* initially operated from New London, Connecticut, before traveling to Key West, Florida, for trials off Florida and Cuba. The boat returned to Portsmouth on July 3 for more than a

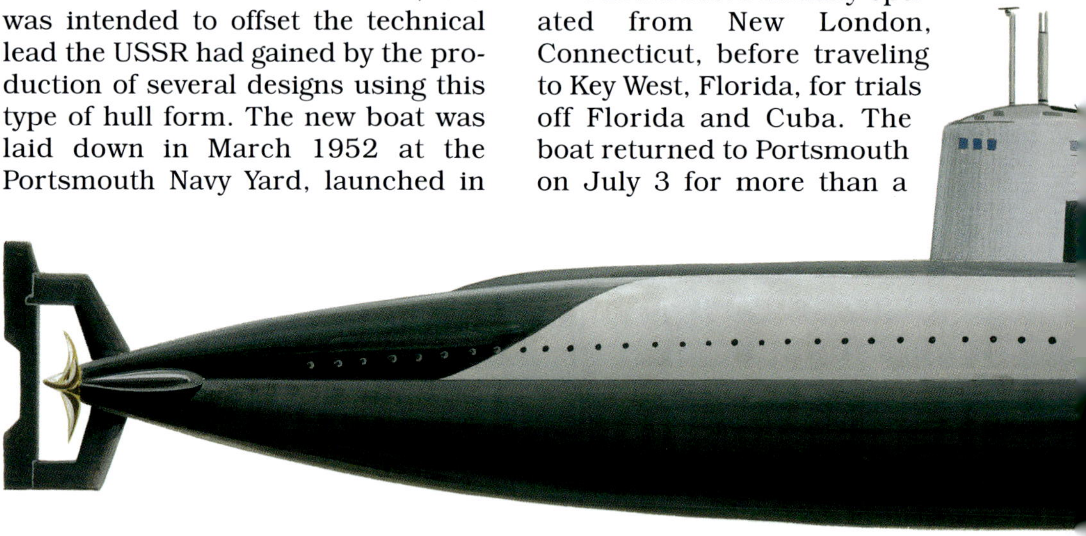

year of trials as well as repairs and modifications to rid her of technical problems.

In October 1955 the submarine again left Portsmouth for Key West, where it was involved in anti-submarine warfare evaluation and to provide target services for the development of anti-submarine tactics by surface warships. The boat returned in November 1955 to Portsmouth.

From December 1955 to March 1956, the *Albacore* was fitted with a new stern. Up until then, the propeller had been surrounded by the rudder and stern plane control surfaces, but now the propeller was abaft all these surfaces, raising the maximum speed from 27 to 33 knots. Operation with her new stern began in April 1956 and continued until a time late in the same year when, in November, it was again taken in hand for modification, this time for engine conversion, More trials followed in March and April 1957 from off San Juan, Puerto Rico, and Guantánamo Bay, Cuba, and then from Boston and Portsmouth until early 1958, when a new dockyard period began. Beginning in June 1958, the boat was used for noise-reduction trials, including an evaluation of Aquaplas sound-dampening elastic applied to the ship's superstructure and the inside of her tanks. In October 1958, the bow planes were removed for firth noise reduction.

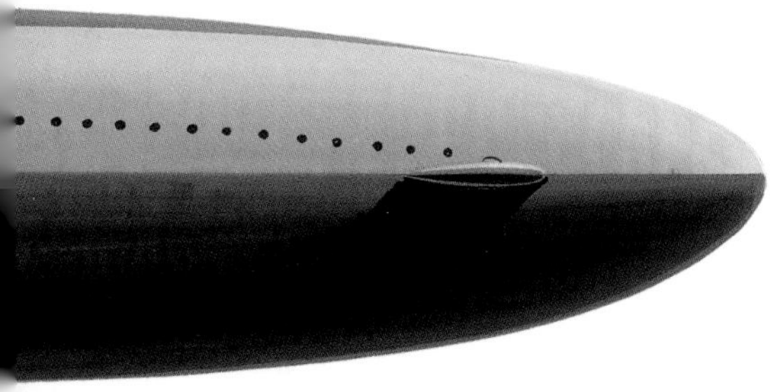

In 1959 a new propeller was installed and tested, and the boat spent the rest of 1959-60 in further trials before retuning to Portsmouth Navy Yard in November 1960 for a major overhaul and changes including X-type tail surfaces, an array of 10 dive brakes around her hull, a new bow with modified ballast tanks, new sonar systems, and a large auxiliary rudder in the after part of her sail. These changes were completed in August 1961, and the boat then operated off the U.S.'s eastern seaboard to establish the effect of her new layout and equipment on performance and capability. In 1962 the boat received new sonar, and from the last month of the year was cycled through her fourth conversion to include a contra-rotating propeller assembly, higher-capacity batteries, an upgraded electric motor, BQS and BQR sonars, an emergency recovery system, and a new main ballast tank blowing system. This work was completed in March 1965, and a further round of trials followed, followed by a number of experimental tasks interspersed by upgrades until September 1968.

Further development work occupied the period from April to August 1971, by which time the frequency of the diesel engine failures it was suffering prompted her decommissioning at Philadelphia, Pennsylvania, in December 1972. The boat was struck off in May 1980 and in 1985 became a memorial at the Port of Portsmouth Maritime Museum.

USS Albacore

Type:	experimental submarine
Tonnage:	1,500 tons surfaced and 1,850 tons submerged
Dimensions:	length 204 ft. (62.1 m); beam 27 ft. (8.2 m); draft 22 ft. (6.7 m)
Propulsion:	two General Motors diesel engines delivering 1,500 hp (1118 kW) for 25 knots surfaced and one Westinghouse electric motor delivering 15,000 hp (11184 kW) for 33 knots submerged
Armament:	none
Complement:	54

USS *Nautilus* (1954)

The USS *Nautilus* was the world's first operational nuclear-powered submarine, and the first vessel to complete a submerged transit of the Arctic Ocean under the North Pole.

In July 1951 the construction of a nuclear-powered submarine for the U.S. Navy was authorized, and the boat was designed and built under the supervision of Admiral Hyman G. Rickover. The boat was laid down at the Groton, Connecticut, yard of the Electric Boat Division of the General Dynamics Corporation in June 1952, launched in January 1954, and commissioned September of the same year.

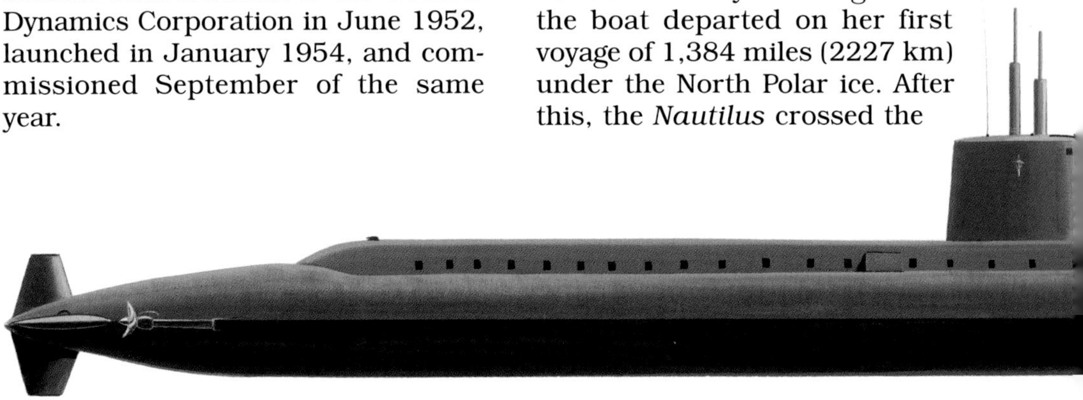

The key to the boat's revolutionary propulsion was the Westinghouse S2W pressurized water reactor that supplied steam to two geared turbines powering two shafts. After it had been commissioned, the *Nautilus* remained alongside for testing, and first got under way on nuclear power on January 17, 1955. In May the boat headed south on her shakedown cruise, and remained submerged for the whole 1,250-mile (2010 km) passage from New London to San Juan, a distance it covered in fewer than 90 hours.

In 1955-57 the *Nautilus* was operated to investigate the effects of increased submerged speeds and endurance, and the boat's capabilities in terms of submerged speed and endurance overnight rendered obsolete all the anti-submarine developments of World War II. Anti-submarine aircraft could not detect the submerged boat, which was invisible to radar, and her speed allowed the boat to evade anti-submarine warships with ease. In May 1957 the *Nautilus* traveled to the Pacific for use in the anti-submarine training role with the warships of the Pacific Fleet, and returned to New London in July. On August 19 the boat departed on her first voyage of 1,384 miles (2227 km) under the North Polar ice. After this, the *Nautilus* crossed the Atlantic for NATO exercises and to tour a number of British and French ports to be inspected by naval personnel of those countries. The boat arrived back at New London late in October, was refitted, and undertook coastal operations until spring 1958.

On April 25, 1958, the boat left once again for the West Coast, and after stops at San Diego, San Francisco, and Seattle, got under way on Operation Sunshine, her epoch-making transit under the ice of the North Pole. Her first attempt was stymied by deep pack ice in shallow water, but the *Nautilus* left Pearl Harbor. Hawaii, on July 23, submerged in the Barrow Sea Valley on August 1, and on August 3 became the first vessel to reach the geographic North Pole, from which the boat continued, and, after 96 hours and 1,830 miles (2945 km) under the ice, surfaced to the northeast of Greenland.

This voyage below the ice was important as a boost to the U.S., as the USSR had recently launched its Sputnik satellite into space but as yet had no nuclear submarine of its own.

The *Nautilus* now headed from Greenland to the Isle of Portland, England, and west across the Atlantic to reach the estuary of the Thames River at New London on October 29. For the remainder of the year, the boat operated from her home port of New London. After involvement in fleet exercises early in 1959, the *Nautilus*

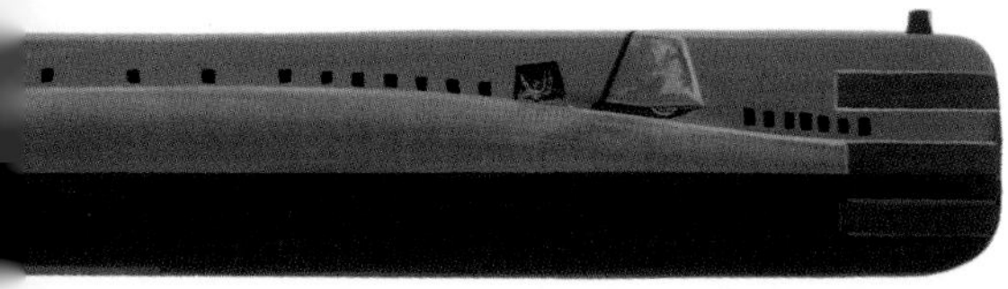

entered the Portsmouth Navy Yard at Kittery, Maine, for her first complete overhaul between May 1959 and August 1960. The *Nautilus* left New London, Connecticut, for her first operational deployment, in this instance with the U.S. 6th Fleet in the Mediterranean, before returning to her home port in December. The *Nautilus* operated in the Atlantic for an evaluation of improved anti-submarine tactics, was involved in NATO exercises and, during the autumn of 1962, in the U.S.'s naval quarantine of Cuba during the Cuban Missile Crisis, until it headed east again for a two-month tour of duty in the Mediterranean in August 1963. On its return, the boat joined in fleet exercises until entering Portsmouth Navy Yard for her second overhaul from January 1964.

Early in May 1966, the *Nautilus* returned to home port to resume operations with the Atlantic Fleet, and up to the middle of 1967 undertook special operations for ComSubLant (Commander, Submarine Forces, Atlantic fleet) and then in August 1967 returned to Portsmouth for another year of refit before being cycled through exercises off the mid-Atlantic and Eastern Seaboard, returning to New London in December 1968.

In the spring of 1979, the *Nautilus* left Groton, Connecticut, on her final voyage. It reached the Mare Island Navy Yard in California on May 26, 1979, and was decommissioned and stricken in March 1980. The boat is now a museum.

USS Nautilus

Type:	nuclear-powered fleet submarine
Tonnage:	3,533 tons surfaced and 4,092 tons submerged
Dimensions:	length 323 ft., 9 in. (98.7 m); beam 27 ft., 8 in. (8.4 m); draft 21 ft., 9 in. (6.6 m)
Propulsion:	one S2W nuclear reactor and two steam turbines delivering about 15,000 hp (11184 kW) for 23 knots submerged
Armament:	six 21-inch (533 mm) torpedo tubes (all bow)
Complement:	105

Oberon class (1959)

The Oberon class consisted of 13 diesel-electric submarines built for the Royal Navy. The type was based on the technically successful Porpoise-class submarine, but the Oberon class was considerably more successful in the export market, some 14 boats being bought by Australia (*Oxley*, *Otway*, *Onslow*, *Ovens*, *Orion* and *Otama*), Canada (*Ojibwa*, *Okanagan*, *Onondaga*, *Olympus* and *Osiris*), Brazil (*Humaitá*, *Tonelero* and *Riachuelo*), Egypt and Chile (*Hyatt* and *O'Brien*).

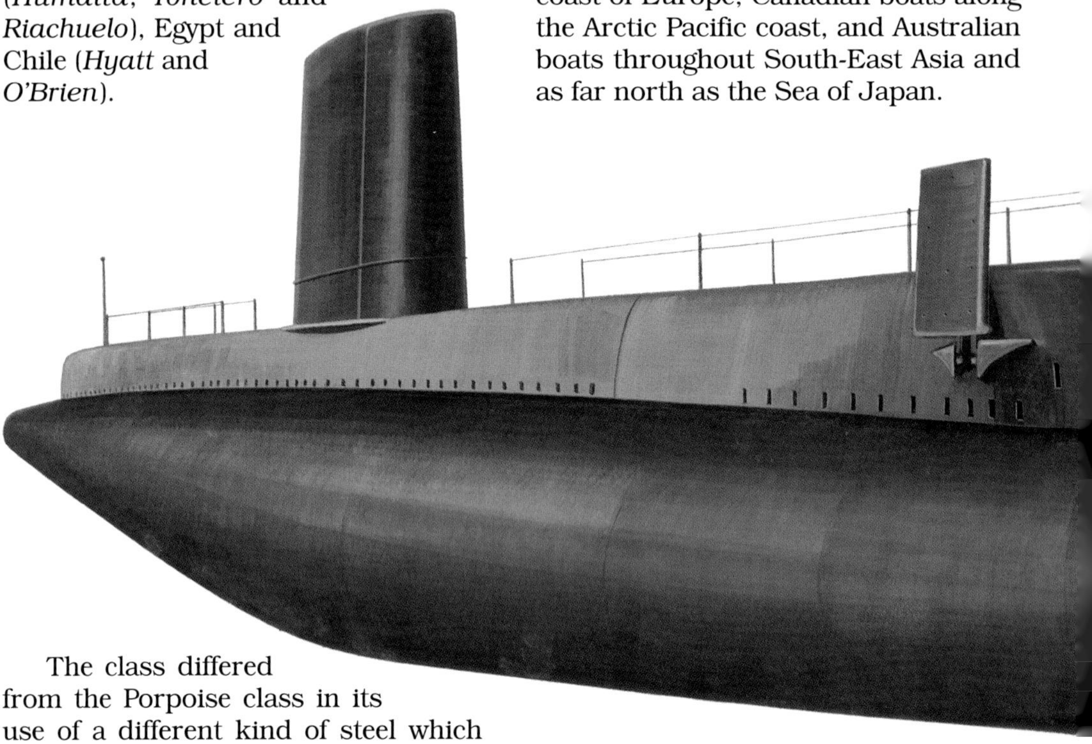

The class differed from the Porpoise class in its use of a different kind of steel which eased fabrication and offered a major increase in diving depth. Additionally, they made used of fiberglass in the casing, and other refinements helped the class become still quieter than the Porpoise class, while the steady introduction of new electronics and weapons including, in 1970, the Mk 24 Tigerfish torpedo or, in the case of the Australian and Canadian boats, the U.S. Mk 48 torpedo, and the Australian boats were later upgraded with the tube-launched version of the Harpoon anti-ship missile.

Like the Porpoise class, the Oberon class was notably quieter than its U.S. counterparts, and the boats therefore did excellent work in covert operations, performing surveillance and inserting special forces during the Cold War. These operations were undertaken primarily by British boats along the Arctic coast of Europe, Canadian boats along the Arctic Pacific coast, and Australian boats throughout South-East Asia and as far north as the Sea of Japan.

The Oberon class was arguably the finest diesel-electric type of its day, with an astonishing reputation for quietness that allowed it to exist into the twenty-first century until replaced by newer classes such as the Collins and Victoria classes in Australia and Canada, respectively.

The first of the class to be commissioned into the Royal Navy was the

The dramatic change in shape from the WWII-era conning towers to the modern "sail," as it is known today, can be seen in this photograph of an O-class boat.
Photo: Ministry of Defence.

Orpheus in 1960, followed by the *Oberon* in 1961. There followed the *Odin*, *Olympus*, *Osiris*, *Onslaught*, *Otter*, *Oracle*, *Ocelot*, *Otus*, *Opossum*, and *Opportune* before the *Onyx* was commissioned as the final boat in 1967. The *Onyx* took part in the Falklands War (1982) as the only conventional boat of Royal Navy's task force, and was used to land Special Boat Service personnel on clandestine missions. All of the Oberon-class boats have now been decommissioned, the last British boats in 1993, and the final Australian and Canadian boats in 2000.

As of 2007, 10 Oberon class boats survive, nine as complete units and two of them as museum vessels in the UK.

Oberon class

Type:	patrol submarine
Tonnage:	2,030 tons surfaced and 2,410 tons submerged
Dimensions:	length 295 ft. (90 m); beam 26 ft., 6 in. (8.1 m); draft 18 ft. (5.5 m)
Propulsion:	two 3,680 hp2744 kW) Admiralty Standard Range diesel generators and two English Electric electric motors delivering 12,000 hp (8947 kW) for 12 knots surfaced and 17 knots submerged
Armament:	eight 21-inch (533 mm) tubes (six bow and two stern) for 24 torpedoes
Complement:	62

USS *Growler* (1957)

The USS *Growler* was built as the second Grayback-class strategic submarine, thus sisters to the USS *Darter* diesel-electric attack submarine, but were taken in hand during construction for completion as strategic submarines with their hulls lengthened for the carriage of four Regulus surface-launched strategic cruise missiles: the *Grayback* was lengthened by 50 feet (15.2 m), and the *Growler* by 54 feet (16.5). The *Growler* was laid down at the Portsmouth Navy Yard of Portsmouth, New Hampshire, during February 1955, launched in April 1958, and commissioned in August 1958.

After completing training exercises off the Eastern Seaboard, the Growler sailed south for her shakedown cruise, reaching the Roosevelt Roads Naval Station, Puerto Rico, in February 1959. After a brief voyage back to Portsmouth, it returned to the Caribbean Sea in March to train in the care and operation of the SSN-N-8 Regulus I guided cruise missile. This was a turbojet-powered winged weapon of subsonic speed and able to carry a nuclear warhead over a distance of 575 miles (925 km) with guidance controlled by two ground stations or, later, one submarine.

The *Growler* returned to Portsmouth on April via Fort Lauderdale, Florida, and New London, Connecticut. The boat then traveled to the Pacific via Norfolk, Virginia, Key West, Florida, and the Panama Canal, reaching Pearl Harbor, Hawaii, in September as the flagship of the Pacific Fleet's Submarine Division 12. At Pearl Harbor, the *Growler* was involved in a wide assortment of battle and torpedo exercises as well as missile practice before beginning her first operational patrol as part of the U.S. nuclear deterrent force. On this patrol, between March 12 and May 17, 1960, the *Growler* departed Hawaii with a full store of four Regulus II much-improved Mach 2 missiles able to reach 1,380 miles (2,220 km) with a nuclear warhead. This missile did not become fully operational, the Polaris submarine-launched ballistic missile being preferred, but the *Growler* nonetheless patrolled under tight security and secrecy. A Regulus-armed patrol could last two months or more at a time, and it was necessary for the boat to remain submerged for days at a time, which was no means feat in a comparatively boat with diesel-electric propulsion and associated systems.

Between May 1960 and December 1963, the *Growler* completed nine such deterrent patrols, of which the fourth ended at Yokosuka, Japan, in April 1962 as the U.S. Navy displayed one of its newest weapons.

Returning to Mare Island, California, the *Growler* was decommissioned in May 1964 and placed in reserve.

The Regulus II cruise-type missile being launched in the Pacific from USS Grayback on September 16, 1957. Photo: U.S. Navy.

Thought was given to the boat's conversion as a special forces delivery/recovery platform, as the *Grayback* had been adapted with her hull lengthened by 11 ft., 8 in. (3.6 m), and the two missile hangars converted for "lock out" units for swimmers and swimmer delivery vehicles. It was decided that this would be too costly for the capability that would thus be offered, and the *Growler* was later moved to the Inactive Fleet section in the Puget Sound Navy Yard of Bremerton, Washington, was stricken on August 1, 1980, and was scheduled for disposal as a torpedo target. However, on August 8, 1988, Congress gave the hulk to Zachary Fisher, chairman of the Intrepid Sea, Air & Space Museum, New York, as a museum exhibit.

USS Growler

Type:	strategic missile submarine
Tonnage:	2,174 tons light and 3,387 tons submerged
Dimensions:	length 317 ft. (96.6 m); beam 27 ft., 2 in. (8.3 m); draft 17 ft. (5.2 m)
Propulsion:	three FM diesel engines delivering 4,600 hp (3429 kW) for 15 knots surfaced and two Elliott electric motors delivering 6,600 hp (4921 kW) for 12 knots submerged
Armament:	four Regulus I or two Regulus II surface-to-surface missiles, and six 21-inch (533 mm) torpedo tubes (four bow and two stern)
Complement:	87

Leninskiy Komsomol (1957)

The Project 627 class, known in the West as the November-class submarine was the USSR's first nuclear-powered attack submarine type. The boats of this class, totaling 14, were built primarily for performance rather than stealth, and were created for the specific task of entering U.S. ports and destroying them with nuclear torpedoes. The task was then revised to the destruction of the aircraft carriers constituting the primary element of the U.S. Navy's surface power-projection capability.

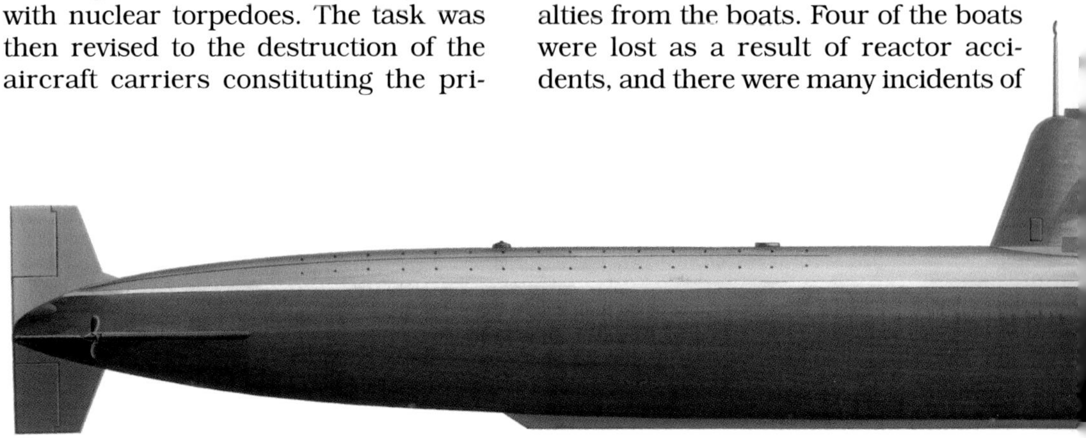

By even only slightly later standards, the November-class boats were very noisy as a result of their hull form, the use of an obsolescent reactor design, and the many free holes in the casing. Later changes included the addition of a pair of retractable hydroplanes just abaft the bow sonar, and two 16-inch (406 mm) stern tubes for two anti-escort torpedoes.

The first of the class was the *K-3*, later named as the *Leninskiy Komsomol*. This was laid down in May 1954, launched in August 1957, and delivered in March 1959. The boat was the first Soviet submarine to reach the North Pole in 1962, some four years after the USS *Nautilus* had first achieved this feat. Like the other 13 boats of the class, the *K-3* suffered reactor problems right through its career.

Like the Echo-class cruise missile and Hotel-class ballistic missile submarines, the November-class boats were a decided radiation hazard to their crews as a result of a combination of poor shielding and defects in the reactors. Because of this, special hospitals were set up to treat the radiation casualties from the boats. Four of the boats were lost as a result of reactor accidents, and there were many incidents of machinery breakdown and other problems while the boats were at sea on operational patrols.

The November-class boats served first with the Northern Fleet, but four of the class were transferred to the Far Eastern Front during the 1960s. On September 8, 1967, while it was in the Norwegian Sea, the *K-3* suffered a fire that broke out in the boat's hydraulic system, and crew members had to evacuate the relevant compartment. The flames spread to other parts of the boat, and the automatic extinguishing system was used. This was based on carbon dioxide gas, which killed the members of the crew in the two most forward compartments. When the door in the bulkhead separating the second and third compartments was opened, the gas spread, and more of the crew lost consciousness. The foremost compartments were then completely sealed off,

Soviet Tango Class boats on parade.
Photo: U.S. Navy.

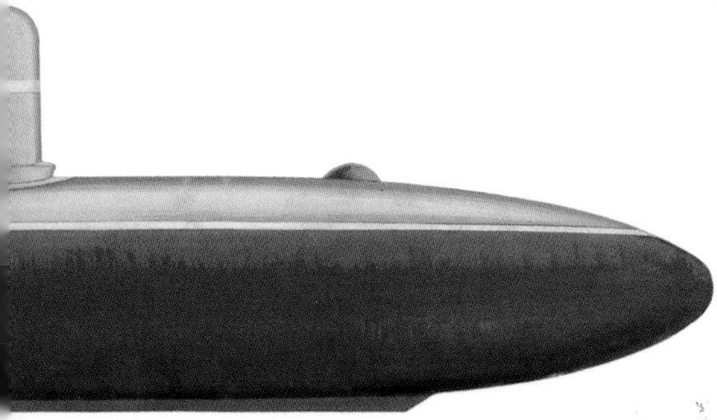

and the submarine surfaced. Four days later, the *K-3* returned to base with 39 dead on board.

The surviving vessels were decommissioned in 1988-92. All of the survivors, except the *K-3*, which was preserved as a museum, remain radioactive hulks in Russian ports.

A single vessel of this class, the *K-27*, was modified in Project 645 with two liquid metal-cooled VT-1 reactors. In August 2003 the *K-159* sank while being towed to the Polyarniy yard for scrapping, nine men being lost. There are currently plans to salvage the wreck for environmental reasons. It was reported in mid 2006 that the *K-60*, derelict for some years, had been delivered to a Polyarniy yard to be scrapped.

November class

Type:	nuclear-powered attack submarine
Tonnage:	3,065 tons surfaced and 4,570 tons submerged
Dimensions:	length 359 ft., 11 in. (109.7 m); beam 29 ft., 10 in. (9.1 m); draft 22 ft. (6.7 m)
Propulsion:	two pressurized water-cooled reactors powering geared two steam turbines delivering 30,000 hp (22368 kW) for 15 knots surfaced and 30 knots submerged
Armament:	eight 21-inch (533 mm) tubes for 14 conventional and six 15-kiloton nuclear anti-ship weapons torpedoes, and two 16-inch (406 mm) tubes for two torpedoes
Complement:	110

Yankee class (1966)

The Project 667A class of nuclear-powered ballistic missile boats, built in 1964-72, were known in the West as Yankee-class boats. Of the 34 submarines, 24 were built at Severodvinsk for the Northern Fleet, and the other 10 at Komsomolsk-na-Amur for the Far East Fleet. The Yankee-class boats were the first Soviet missile submarines with a missile battery comparable with those of their U.S. counterparts. The submarines were quieter than their Hotel-class predecessors, but still louder than NATO submarines, and had more streamlined lines for enhanced underwater performance.

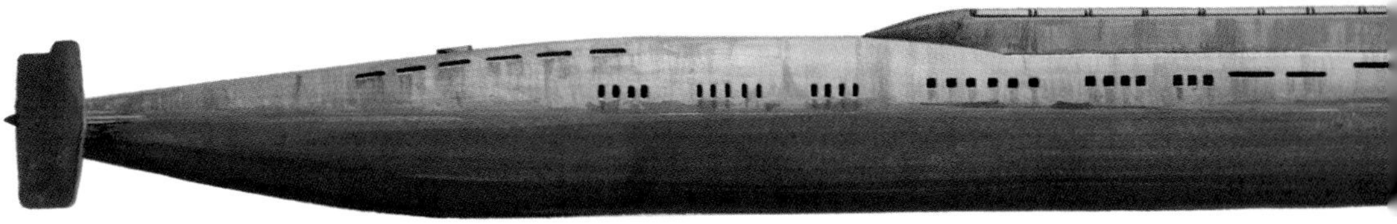

The boats carried 16 nuclear-armed ballistic missiles in vertical tubes abaft the sail, and during the 1970s up to three Yankee-class boats were stationed in a constantly maintained "patrol box" to the east of Bermuda and therefore within missile range of the eastern U.S. This forward deployment was seen as a balance against the presence of U.S. and NATO nuclear weapons in Western Europe.

One of the boats, *K-219*, was lost on October 6, 1986. The boat was off Bermuda when it suffered and explosion and fire, and was scuttled after attempts at towing had failed. Four crewmen died before rescue arrived. At least one other ship in the class was involved in a collision with a U.S. submarine. As a result of the SALT I and START I-II treaties, the boats were decommissioned and/or disarmed.

There were seven different variants within the Yankee class. The Yankee I class constituted the baseline configuration. The Yankee II or Project 667AM class comprised one Yankee I conversion, the *K-140*, to carry 12 SS-N-17 missiles, The Yankee Notch or Project 667AT class comprised six Yankee I conversions to the attack submarine role by the introduction of a notch-waisted central hull section in place of the missile compartment: the change increased the length to 464 ft., 3 in. (141.5 m) and changed the submerged displacement to 11,500 tons. The new central hull section had eight 21-inch (533 mm) tubes for up to 40 SS-N-21 anti-ship missiles or additional torpedoes. The bow tubes were retained, and some reports suggest the ability to launch 26 ½-inch (650 mm) torpedoes. The Yankee Sidecar, or Project 667AM class was a conversion of the *K-420* from 1980 in cruise missile standard with a submerged displacement of 13,650 tons and primary armament of 12 SS-NX-24 nuclear-armed cruise missiles in place of the original ballistic missiles. The SS-NX-24 was an experimental weapon, capable of supersonic flight and carrying twin nuclear warheads. It was meant as a tri-service strategic weapon, and thus would have filled a rather different role to the tactically oriented Oscar-class cruise missile

A Yankee class submarine on the surface. Photo: U.S. Navy.

boats of the same period. The missile was not adopted, in the end, as a standard type. The converted *K-420* was 501 ft., 11 ½ in. (153 m) long.

The Yankee SSN designation was applied to 16 conversions from Yankee I standard with all missile capability removed, leaving them with only their bow torpedo tubes, the central missile sections having been removed.

The Yankee Pod or Project 09774 was another conversion, in this instance as a trials boat for sonar equipment, with eponymous pod at the head of the rudder. It had other sensor systems, notably beside the sail. The Yankee Stretch or Project 09780-class boat was the *K-411* converted as the "mothership" for Paltus-class mini-submarines. The boat was 524 ft., 11 ¼ in. (160 m) long, and had no missile armament. Its task was probably oceanographic research, search and rescue, and intelligence gathering.

Yankee I class

Type:	nuclear-powered ballistic missile submarine
Tonnage:	7,637 tons surfaced and 11,320 tons submerged
Dimensions:	length 419 ft., 11 ½ in. (128 m); beam 38 ft., 4 ½ in. (11.7 m); draft 29 ft., 6 in. (9 m)
Propulsion:	two VM-4 pressurized water-cooled reactors powering four geared steam turbines delivering 50,000 hp (37280 kW) for 13 knots surfaced and 28 knots submerged
Armament:	16 launch tubes for 12 R-27 (SS-N-6 "Serb") SLBMs, and six 21-inch (533 mm) tubes for 18 torpedoes
Complement:	114

Daphné class (1959)

hull design, and the requirement which led to the class placed special importance on underwater agility, low noise, limited manning requirement and easy maintainability. This last requirement led to the adoption of a weapons layout with 12 tubes (eight bow, four stern) without reloads. Further reductions in complement were effected by the adoption of a maintenance system based on modular replacement. The last two boats, the *Psyché* and *Sirène* built by the Arsenal de Brest, incorporated a number of improvements, and had the PA4-135 diesel engines in place of the

Ordered by the French navy for the patrol task, the 11 small boats of the Daphné class were based on a design developed from that of the small hunter-killer boats of the Aréthuse class. The Daphné class was thus designed as a second-class partner to the Narval class of ocean-going submarines dating from the period following World War II's end. The Daphné class was based on a double-

PA1 engines of the other nine boats, which were *Daphné*, *Diane*, and *Minerve* built by the Aciers et Chantiers Dubigeon, and the *Doris*, *Eurydice*, *Flore*, *Galatée*, *Junon* and *Venus* built by the Arsenal de Cherbourg. The boats were laid down in 1958-1965, completed in 1959-1969, and completed in 1964-1970. Of these, the *Eurydice* and *Minerve* were lost in accidents in the western end of the Mediterranean during 1970 and 1968, respectively, probably as a result of a fault in the design of the snorkel, and the others were decommissioned between the late 1980s and mid-1990s.

Beginning in 1971, all the boats except the *Daphné* were extensively modernized with more advanced search-and-attack sonar in a large dome above the bow, and a more capable torpedo fire-control system. Seven of the nine boats left after the loss of the *Eurydice* and *Minerve* were on the strength of the Mediterranean Squadron, the two others being the *Psych* and *Sirène*, which were based at Lorient.

The type was also successful on the export market. Ten were built in France for Portugal in the late 1960s (*Albacora*, *Baraccuda*, *Cachalote* and *Delfim* decommissioned in the first five years of the twenty-first century), Pakistan in 1970 (*Hangor*, *Shushuk* and *Mangro*, later joined by the Ghazi ex-Cachalote decommissioned in the first decade of the 21st century) and South Africa in the early 1970s (*Maria van Riebeeck*, later renamed *Spear*; *Emily Hobhouse*, later *Umkhonto;* and *Joanna van de Merwe*, later *Assegai*, decommissioned by 2003). Another four boats were built under license at Cartagena by Bazan for service with the Spanish navy as the *Delfín*, *Tonina*, *Marsopa*, and *Narval*, and these boats were decommissioned between 2003 and 2006. The Daphné-class boat might well have gained other export orders but for the loss of the two French boats.

Daphné class

Type:	patrol submarine
Tonnage:	860 tons surfaced and 1,038 tons submerged
Dimensions:	length 189 ft., 8 in. (57.8 m); beam 22 ft., 4 in. (6.8 m); draft 15 ft., 1 in. (4.6 m)
Propulsion:	two SEMT-Pielstick diesel engines delivering 1,300 hp (969 kW) for 13.5 knots surfaced and one electric motor delivering 1,600 hp (1193 kW) for 16 knots submerged
Armament:	12 22-inch (550 mm) tubes (eight bow and four stern) for 12 torpedoes or missiles
Complement:	45

Dolfijn class (1959)

The four patrol boats of the Dolfijn class were the *Dolfijn* and *Zeehond* built by the Rotterdam Dry Dock Company between December 1954 (laid down) and March 1961 (completed), and the *Potvis* and *Tonijn* built by the Wilton-Fijenoord yard of Schiedam, Netherlands, between September 1962 (laid down) and February 1966 (completed).

These were also the first submarines designed and built after the end of World War II for the Royal Netherlands navy, and were interesting at the technical level for their novel triple-hulled design with three long pressure hulls of cylindrical section disposed in a triangular shape and enclosed within an outer casing to provide the designed hydrodynamic shaping. The upper cylinder accommodated the crew, the control spaces and the armament (four bow and four stern torpedo tubes), while the side-by-side pair of lower cylinders, both shorter than the upper cylinder, each carried one of the wholly independent halves of the two-shaft propulsion arrangement, each half comprising one 12-cylinder diesel engine, one electric motor, and one 168-cell battery. The boats had a diving depth of 985 feet (300 m), and their sails incorporated a retractable snorkel mast as well as a folding communications antenna and two periscopes.

The order for the second pair of boats was placed but then deliberately delayed by a short time while the possibility of an alternative propulsion arrangement, based on nuclear power, was considered, evaluated, and then finally rejected as being inappropriate for the Netherlands, as well as more expensive to procure and to operate.

The order for the second pair of boats thus was reinstated in 1962, and the resulting *Potvis* and *Tonijn* were completed with a number of improved features retrofitted on the earlier boats. As initially completed, the early boats had a length of 257 feet (78.3 m) and retained their original MAN 12-V6V 22/30 diesel engines until their demise, the *Dolfijn* being broken up in 1985 and the Zeehond being reclassified as a test hulk in 1990. The *Potvis* and *Tonijn* had their original diesel engines replaced in 1978/70 by SEMT-Pielstick units.

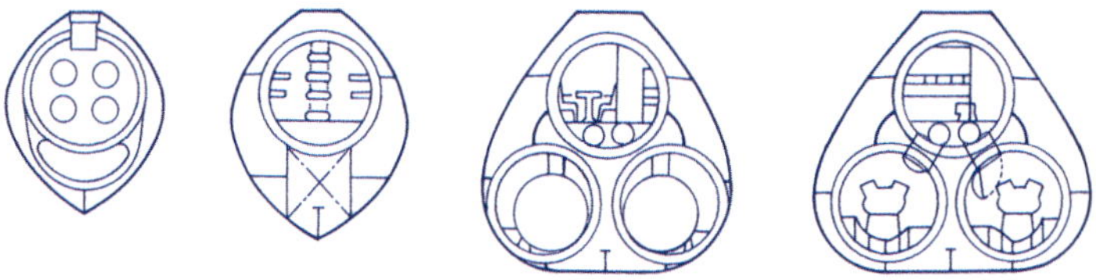

In the early 1970s, the *Zeehond* had a new sonar fitted in a dome atop the forward casing, but this equipment was later removed once again. The boat was to have been decommissioned in 1987, but a fire then delayed the completion of the *Walrus*, lead boat of a four-strong class of advanced diesel-electric submarines, led to the decision to extend her service life until 1990. Since then, the boat has been used by RDM as a trials platform in the development of an air-independent propulsion system of the type that provides enhanced underwater endurance and propulsion without recourse to nuclear power. This type of propulsion has now started to become a practical proposition, turning the conventionally (i.e. non-nuclear) powered submarine from an advanced submersible into what can be regarded as true submarine of a limited but still very useful type.

Dolfijn class

Type:	patrol submarine
Tonnage:	1,494 tons surfaced and 1,826 tons submerged
Dimensions:	length 261 ft. (79.5 m); beam 26 ft. (8.2 m); draft 16 ft. (5 m)
Propulsion:	two MAN 12-V6V 22/30 diesel engines delivering 2800 hp (1864 kW) for 14.5 knots surfaced and two electric motors delivering 4,000 hp (2982 kW) for 17 knots submerged
Armament:	eight 21-inch (533 mm) tubes (four bow and four stern)
Complement:	64

George Washington class (1969)

When it became clear in the mid-1950s that the technology was maturing for submarine-launched ballistic missiles offering greater range and accuracy with a nuclear warhead than the current interim-generation cruise missiles, which were also armed with nuclear warheads but had to be launched on the surface as they were winged weapons. The SLBM could be carried in vertical tubes incorporated in the hulls of large nuclear-powered submarines for launch under the water, thereby reducing the vulnerability of the submarine and increasing its operational range and patrol endurance.

The U.S. Navy accordingly ordered a class of nuclear-powered boats armed with long-range strategic missiles on December 31, 1957, and contracted with the Electric Boat Division of the General Dynamics Corporation for the task of converting two existing attack submarine hulls to ballistic missile-carrying standard as rapidly as possible to lay the foundations of the services new type of nuclear deterrent force.

To aid it in accomplishing the task, Electric Boat persuaded the U.S. Navy in January 1958 to slip the launch dates of two Skipjack-class nuclear-powered attack submarines, the *Scorpion* which had just been laid down and the *Sculpin*, which had not yet been laid down. On February 12, 1958, President Dwight D. Eisenhower signed funding for three more ballistic missile submarines of the same class, and on July 29, 1958, for two more. The class thus came to comprise, in all, the *George Washington* and *Patrick Henry* from Electric Boat, the *Theodore Roosevelt* from the Mare Island Navy Yard, the *Robert E. Lee* from Newport News, and the *Abraham Lincoln* from the Portsmouth Navy Yard.

The George-Washington- class boats were in essence Skipjack-class attack boats cut in half and lengthened by 130 feet (39.6 m) for the insertion of a 16-tube missile compartment between the boast's control and navigation areas and its reactor compartment. In the case of the lead unit, the *George Washington*, the keel already laid by Electric Boat at Groton, Connecticut, for the *Scorpion*, was cut apart and extended to become the keel for the *George Washington*. Then, Electric Boat and the Mare Island Navy Yard began construction of one other boat each from extended plans.

The *George Washington* was launched in June 1959, completed in

A photograph of USS Abraham Lincoln on the surface. *Official U.S. Navy photograph.*

December 1959, and began the first strategic deterrent patrol in November 1960, followed by the SS *Patrick Henry* in January 1961. The *George Washington* returned from its patrol in January 1961 at New London, Connecticut, the *Patrick Henry* returning in March 1961 to the new base at Holy Loch, Scotland, beginning the use of Holy Loch as a refit and upkeep anchorage.

The George Washington class of boats carried the Polaris A-1 missile on their patrols until June 1964, when the *George Washington* switched to the improved Polaris A-3 missile. The last of the class, the *Abraham Lincoln*, switched to the Polaris A-3 missile in October 1965.

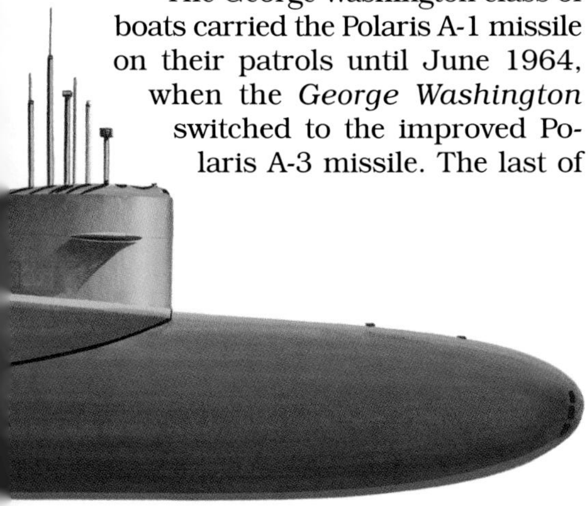

Early in the 1980s, to make room within the limitations imposed by SALT II for the Ohio-class ballistic missile submarines, the *George Washington*, *Patrick Henry*, and *Robert E. Lee* had their missiles removed and were reclassified as SSNs (nuclear-powered attack submarines), a role in which they served for several years before being decommissioned by January 1985. The *Theodore Roosevelt* and *Abraham Lincoln* were both decommissioned in February 1981.

George Washington class

Type:	nuclear-powered ballistic missile submarine
Tonnage:	5,959 tons surfaced and 6,709 tons submerged
Dimensions:	length 381 ft., 8 in. (116.4 m); beam 33 ft. (10.1 m); draft 26 ft., 8 in. (8.1 m)
Propulsion:	one Westinghouse S5W pressurized water-cooled reactor powering geared steam turbines delivering about 15,000 hp (11184 kW) for 18 knots surfaced and over 25 knots submerged
Armament:	16 tubes for 16 Polaris submarine-launched ballistic missiles, and six 21-inch (533mm) tubes (all bow) for torpedoes
Complement:	112

Skipjack class (1958)

The Skipjack class of six nuclear-powered attack submarines was ordered for service with the U.S. Navy as successor to the four boats of the Skate class, which had been built as the service's first "production"-standard SSNs to a design derived from that of the pioneering but essentially experimental *Nautilus*.

The Skipjack class was therefore only the second class of SSN to be built for the U.S. Navy, and at the same time it was the first nuclear-powered class to be based on the teardrop-type hull form validated in another experimental type, the conventionally powered *Albacore*. Another feature inherited from the *Albacore* was the configuration of the stern control surfaces and propeller: the former was of the symmetrical cross type with horizontal surfaces to port and starboard and vertical surfaces above and below the finely tapered cylindrical terms, which terminated in the propeller abaft the control surfaces. The nature of the stern made it impossible for torpedo tubes to be fitted in this part of the hull, so the entire torpedo armament was grouped in the bow.

Based on a design structurally new from the keel up, the six Skipjack submarines also introduced a new location for the forward diving planes, which were relocated from the bow section to the sail. This change greatly reduced the flow noise round the bow-mounted sonar, thereby yielding significantly improved sonar performance and also enhancing the survivability of the boats, and at the

same time providing greater underwater maneuverability. The ability to dive to 900 feet (275 m) and to reach 29 knots submerged resulted from the use of HY-80 steel in the structure and the new S5W reactor as the heart of the propulsion system. All the engine room fittings except the reactor and steam turbines were duplicated to reduce the chances of a catastrophic propulsion system breakdown.

The class was built between May 1956, when the *Skipjack* was laid down by the Electric Boat Division of the General Dynamics Corporation, and October 1961, when the *Snook* was completed by Ingalls Shipbuilding. The other four boats were the *Scamp* from the Mare Island Navy Yard, the *Scorpion* from Electric Boat,

Skipjack in 1959. Official U.S. Navy photograph.

the *Sculpin* from Ingalls, and the *Shark* from Newport New Shipbuilding. The boats served at various times with the Atlantic and Pacific Fleets; the *Scorpion* was lost with all 99 hands off the Azores Islands in May 1964 while on passage from the Mediterranean to Norfolk, Virginia.

The Skipjack boats were the fastest submarines in service with the U.S. Navy until the advent of the altogether more modern Los Angeles class of boats in the second half of the 1970s, and in the final stages of their lives, the five surviving submarines of the class, now old and technically obsolete in many of their features, though still fast, were relegated for use mainly for crew training and as high-speed targets for anti-submarine warfare development and training. The boats were decommissioned between May 1986 and August 1990.

Skipjack class

Type:	nuclear-powered attack submarine
Tonnage:	3,075 tons surfaced and 3,500 tons submerged
Dimensions:	length 251 ft., 8 in. (76.8 m); beam 31 ft., 8 in. (9.7 m); draft 25 ft., 3 in. (7.7 m)
Propulsion:	one Westinghouse S5W pressurized water-cooled reactor powering geared steam turbines delivering 15,000 hp (11914 kW) for 15 knots surfaced and 29 knots submerged
Armament:	six 21-inch (533 mm) tubes (all bow) for 24 torpedoes
Complement:	between 85 and 114

Typhoon class (1980)

The Russians have long possessed a particular interest in the largest possible examples of weapons, as evident in World War I with the Sikorsky Ilya Muromets, the world's first four-engined bomber, and in World War II with a number of very heavy and well protected tank types armed with guns of up to 6-inch (152 mm) caliber. The same tendency was also been evident in a number of the vessels built for the Soviet navy, but nowhere has it been more strongly revealed than in the Typhoon class of nuclear-powered ballistic missile submarines.

Known in the USSR and now Russia as the Project 941 Akula class, the Typhoon-class submarine entered service in the early 1980s and, with a maximum submerged displacement in the order of 48,000 tons, is by far the most massive type of submarine ever built. "Typhoon" is the NATO reporting name for the class, and was derived from the fact that the Russian word was used by Leonid Brezhnev, the General Secretary of the Communist Party of the Soviet Union, and thus the political leader of the USSR, in a 1974 speech while describing a new type of nuclear-powered ballistic missile submarine. The new Project 941 submarine was developed with the Russian name "Akula," ("shark"), and this has sometimes led to confusion with another class of submarine, as the Akula designation is used by NATO for the Project 971 class of nuclear-powered attack submarines.

Despite their huge size, the Typhoon-class submarines are among the quietest vessels in current operation, considerably less noisy than their Soviet SSBN predecessors; they are also more maneuverable than the

earlier boats. This double advantage results in part from the submarines' great size, which allows them to minimize the noise caused by water flowing past the hull.

As well as their primary ballistic missile armament, carried in two longitudinal rows of 10 hatch-covered launchers forward of the sail, the Typhoon-class submarines each have six torpedo tubes; two of these are 21-inch (533 mm) units designed to fire the RPK-2 (SS-N-15) cruise missile or Type 53 torpedo, and the other four are 26-inch (650 mm) units designed to fire the RPK-7 (SS-N-16) anti-ship missile, Type 65 heavy-weight anti-ship torpedo, or any of several types of sea mine.

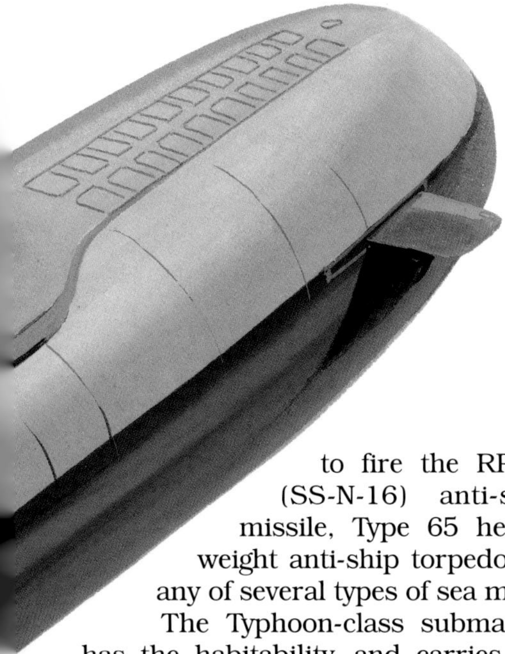

The Typhoon-class submarine has the habitability, and carries the personnel and consumables, to remain submerged and operationally effective for a period of up to 180 days under normal conditions, and somewhat more should this be made necessary by conditions such as the outbreak of a nuclear war. Most Western SSBNs are optimized for a patrol of 90 days.

The Typhoon-class submarine incorporates multiple pressure hulls in an arrangement that simplified the problems of creating the desired internal design, but also made the submarine very much wider than a normal submarine. In the main part of the submarine, two Delta-class titanium pressure hulls are arranged side-by-side in parallel with each upper, and above and between them is a third but somewhat smaller pressure hull, and this protrudes just below the sail, which is notably long and surmounted by periscopes, radar and radio antennae, and other items. This arrangement of multiple hulls, almost wholly wrapped in an outer hull offering the optimum hydro-dynamic shaping consonant with the submarine's nature and other features, also greatly improves the survivability of the Typhoon-class submarine: thus the breach of one pressure hull leaves the personnel in the others safe, and this also reduces the chances for any catastrophic flooding. The propulsion arrangement consists of two entirely separate pressurized water-cooled reactors powering two sets of geared steam turbines which each drive one shaft and its seven-blade shrouded propeller.

The great internal volume also makes it possible for the Typhoon-class submarine to be optimized in terms of crew habitability with features such as sports facilities, a sauna, a swimming pool and a smoking room.

Six Typhoon-class submarines were built, all of them at Severodvinsk, and were laid down between March 1977 and January 1987, launched between September 1980 and July 1988, and completed between December 1981 and September 1989 as the *TK-208*, (*Dmitriy Donskoy*), *TK-202*, *TK-12*, *TK-13*, *TK-17* (*Arkhangyel'sk*) and *TK-20* (*Severstal*), respectively; a seventh unit was ordered, as the *TK-210* was cancelled. As completed, each of the boats carried the primary armament of 20 R-39 (SS-N-20) SLBMs, each carrying a maximum of 10 MIRVed nuclear warheads. The submarines were at first designated only by their hull numbers, but names were later assigned to the four units retained by the Russian navy after the collapse of the USSR at the end of the Cold War. These submarines were each sponsored by a city or company. Only the first of these submarines to be constructed, now known as the *Dmitriy Donskoy*, is still in service with the Russian navy, which operates it as a test platform for the 45-ton Bulava (SS-NX-30) submarine-launched ballistic missile currently under development as a variant of the new Topol-M inter-continental ballistic missile). All the R-39 missiles have been retired, and the Typhoon-class submarines are scheduled for replacement by the units of the Borei class beginning in 2008.

With a primary armament of 16 Bulava missiles, displacement of 24,000 tons submerged, length of 557 ft., 9 in. (170 m) and submerged speed of 25 knots with one pump-jet driven by one geared steam turbine powered by one pressurized water-cooled reactor, the Borei-class submarine is planned as the successor to the Delta III and Typhoon classes. Design of this Project 935 class began in 1996 in parallel with a new missile designated as the SS-NX-28 in the West. The missile was cancelled and replaced by the heavier Bulava missile, a change forcing a reduction in the primary armament from 20 to 16 missiles, and the revised Project 935 became the Project 955. The three submarines currently planned are being built in Sevmash, Russia, under the supervision of the Rubin Design Bureau.

The enormous beam of over 75 feet (22 m) can best be seen in this NATO photo of a surfaced Typhoon boat.

With the eight crew on the bridge, the Typhoon shows the sheer scale of its 18,500 tons.
Photo: U.S. Navy.

Some consider the Borei to be state of the art, incorporating characteristics superior to any submarine currently in service in terms of quietness and minimal sonar signature. Advances include a compact and hydrodynamically efficient hull for reduced noise, and the first use of pump-jet propulsion on a Russian nuclear submarine.

After considerable delays, first-of-class *Yuri Dolgorukiy* was launched in April 2007. The next two submarines are the *Aleksandr Nevskiy* and *Vladimir Monomakh*.

Typhoon class

Type:	nuclear-powered ballistic missile submarine
Tonnage:	23,200 to 24,500 tons surfaced and 33,800 to 48,000 tons submerged
Dimensions:	length 574 ft., 2 in. (175 m); beam 75 ft., 6 in. (23 m); draft 39 ft., 4 in. (12 m)
Propulsion:	two OK-650 pressurized water-cooled reactors powering two VV-type geared steam turbines delivering 99,250 hp (74000 kW) for 12 knots surfaced and 27 knots submerged
Armament:	tubes for 20 RSM-52 submarine-launched ballistic missiles, one Igla launcher for surface-to-air missiles, four 25 ?-inch (650 mm) tubes for heavy-weight anti-ship torpedoes and RKP-7 Vodopad anti-ships missiles, and two 21-inch (533 mm) tubes for standard-weight anti-ship torpedoes and RPK-2 Viyoga cruise missiles
Complement:	163

Juliett class (1960)

Known in the West from its NATO reporting name as the Juliett class, the Project 651 class of diesel-electric submarines was designed in the 1950s to provide the Soviet navy with a nuclear strike capability against targets on the eastern seaboard of the U.S., and later against U.S. Navy carrier task forces.

The core of the armament scheme for these 16 boats was four nuclear-armed cruise missiles, which had to be launched with the boat on the surface and moving at a speed of less than 4 knots. Once the boat had surfaced, each of the four missile container/launchers, disposed as two on each beam, had to be elevated to about 20°. It was five minutes before the first missile could be launched, and the other three could then follow at 10-second intervals. Although designed to carry six examples of the P-500 (SS-N-12 Sandbox) cruise missile, this weapon was delayed in development so the missile type first carried by the Juliett-class boats was the larger P-5, known in the West as the SS-N-3 Shaddock. This had basic flight control by an autopilot, with command guidance for mid-course update and either a radar or infrared seeker unit for terminal guidance. The 350-kiloton warhead could be delivered over a range of 250 miles (400 km). With the advent of nuclear-powered boats carrying submarine-launched ballistic missiles, the P-5 was rendered obsolescent, and one of the boats was revised to the Project 651M standard with the P-500 anti-ship missile. Optimized for attacks on carrier battle groups, the P-500 also carried a 350-kilon warhead but at higher speed and over a range of 300 miles (480 km) with autopilot basic control, mid-course command guidance and active radar homing. A special target guidance radar was built into the forward edge of the sail structure, which opened by rotating, and the boat was eventually fitted with the Kasatka "Punch Bowl" satellite down-link for targeting information.

The boats of the Juliett class had a steel double hull, covered by two-inch-thick (50 mm) black tiles made of sound-absorbing hard rubber, and possessed a notably low magnetic signature. The boats were characterized by very high reserve buoyancy, and were divided into eight watertight compartments, from bow to stern the forward torpedo room with six 21-inch (533 mm) tubes; the quarters for the officers and chiefs, and the forward batteries; the missile control room and batteries; the control room; the crew quarters and batteries; the forward engine room containing the diesel engines and generators; the after engine room with the electric motors; and the aft torpedo room with four 16-inch (406 mm) tubes.

The initial plan called for 35 boats, but only 16 were built, all of them by the Krasnoye Sormovo shipyard in Gorkiy from 1960. The Juliett-class submarines were commissioned between 1962 and 1968, and served through the 1980s. The boats were generally deployed as part of the Baltic Fleet, with patrols taking them out into the open sea in preparation for possible operations against the eastern U.S., but later the submarines were seen in the Mediterranean Sea and Indian Ocean, both of them areas used by US aircraft carriers. The last of the submarines was decommissioned in 1994.

The Project 675 or Echo II submarines were in effect nuclear-powered counterparts of the Juliett-class submarines, but were larger and carried eight missile launchers.

Juliett class

Type:	ballistic missile submarine
Tonnage:	3,174 tons surfaced and 4,137 tons submerged
Dimensions:	length 281 ft., 9 in. (90 m); beam 31 ft., 10 in. (10 m); draft 23 ft. (7 m)
Propulsion:	two D-43 diesel engines delivering 8,000 hp (5965 kW) for 16.8 knots surfaced, one 2D-42 diesel engines delivering 1,750 hp (1305 kW), two PG-141 electric motors delivering 6,000 hp (4474 kW) for 18 knots submerged, and two PG-140 electric motors delivering 1,000 hp (746 kW) for creeping speed
Armament:	four SS-N-3 Shaddock nuclear-armed cruise missiles, six 21-inch (533 mm) tubes for 18 torpedoes, and four 16-inch (406 mm) tubes for four torpedoes
Complement:	82

Ohio class (1979)

The U.S. Navy currently operates 18 Ohio-class nuclear-powered submarines, most of them constituting the heart of the service's nuclear-armed deterrent force. All built by Electric Boat in 1976-1997, the submarines fall into two subclasses with differing armament. There are 14 SSBNs, each carrying 24 Trident II ballistic missiles, and known as Trident submarines, which are the sea-based leg of the nuclear triad of the U.S. strategic nuclear arsenal. The other four are SSGNs, each armed with 154 Tomahawk cruise missiles carrying conventional warheads.

Between them, the SSBNs carry about half the total U.S. strategic warhead inventory. Though the missiles have no pre-set targets when the submarine goes on patrol, the submarine can, when required, undertake rapid targeting using its onboard system and data provided by secure communication links.

The Ohio-class submarine is the largest submarine type yet built for the U.S. Navy, and is excelled in size and displacement only by Russia's Typhoon-class SSBNs. The Ohio-class submarine was designed specifically for extended patrols, and thus possesses great habitability. Each submarine has alternating "Blue" and "Gold" crews, which replace each other at 100-day intervals when the submarine puts in for consumables such as food. To decrease the time spent in port for crew change and resupply, there are three large hatches to ease the movement of supply pallets, equipment modules and machinery components.

The design allows the submarine to operate for more than 15 years between overhauls, and the design is said to offer the same degree of radiated noise at the 20-knots cruising speed as previous submarines at just 6 knots.

The first eight Ohio-class submarines were initially outfitted with 24 Trident I C-4 SLBMs, but from the ninth, the *Tennessee*, the standard switched to the much-improved Trident II D-5 missile with MIRVed warheads and greater accuracy. Starting with the *Alaska* in 2000, the remaining Trident I submarines have been converted to the Trident II.

The first eight submarines were home-ported in Bangor, Washington, to replace the Polaris A-3 SSBNs then being taken out of service. The other 10 were initially home-ported in Kings Bay, Georgia, replacing the Atlantic-based submarines carrying the Poseidon or, as a retrofit, the Trident I SLBM. During the conversion of the first four submarines as SSGNs, the *Pennsylvania*, *Kentucky*, *Nebraska*, *Maine*, and *Louisiana* were moved from Kings Bay to Bangor, Maine, with further changes occurring as required.

As the Cold War ended, the U.S. Navy anticipated that the *Ohio* would retire in 2002, followed by the *Michigan, Florida* and *Georgia*. The plan was then changed, and these first four boats were taken in hand for conversion to SSGN standard as with conventionally armed cruise missiles. In a program started in 2002 for completion in 2010, 22 of the 24 88-inch (2.2 m) diameter Trident missile tubes are each being adapted to carry one vertical launch system, one of whose layouts may be a cluster of seven Tomahawk cruise missiles for a total of 154 missiles. Other possibilities include new generations of supersonic cruise missiles, unmanned air vehicles, decoy missiles, sensors for anti-submarine warfare or missions such as intelligence, surveillance and reconnaissance, and other items. The tubes can also carry canisters extending the deployment time of Special Forces detachments.

The other two Trident tubes are converted to swimmer lock-out chambers. For special operations, the Advanced SEAL Delivery System and the Dry Dock Shelter can be mounted on a lock-out chamber, and the boat can carry up to 66 special operations personnel. The incorporation of enhanced communications also allows the SSGN conversions, which re-entered service in 2006–07, to serve as forward-deployed covert command centers for small-scale operations.

Ohio class

Type:	nuclear-powered submarine-launched ballistic missile submarine
Tonnage:	16,600 tons surfaced and 18,750 tons submerged
Dimensions:	length 560 ft., (170.7 m); beam 42 ft. (12.8 m); draft 35 ft., 6 in. (10.8 m)
Propulsion:	one General Electric S8G pressurized water-cooled reactor powering geared steam turbines delivering 35,000 hp (26096 kW) for 12 knots surfaced and 24 knots submerged and one 325 hp auxiliary motor, 44.8 MW output 1 shaft
Armament:	(Pacific-Fleet submarines) 24 Trident C-4 submarine-launched ballistic missiles with up to eight MIRVed 100-kiloton nuclear warheads or (Atlantic-Fleet submarines) 24 Trident D-5 SLBMs with up to 12 MIRVed 300/475-kiloton nuclear warheads, and four 21-inch (533 mm) tubes (all bow) for torpedoes
Complement:	155

Delta class (1972)

Four subclasses of the Delta-class nuclear-powered ballistic missile submarine have served with the Soviet and now the Russian navies, each with different capabilities and systems. The first subclass was the Project 667B or, to the West, Delta I class, of which 18 were built at Severodvinsk and Komsomolsk with a submerged displacement of 10,000 tons, length of 456 feet (139 m) and primary armament of 12 R-29 (SS-N-8 Sawfly) SLBMs. The range of this missile meant that the submarines did not have to enter the Atlantic or Pacific to threaten the U.S., and therefore patrolled in areas such as the Arctic Ocean, and the Norwegian and Barents Seas. The first entered service with the Northern Fleet in 1972, by 1991 the number of operational submarines had fallen to nine, and these were stripped of their missiles by 1997.

The four Project 667BD or Delta II class submarines were improved Delta I boats built by Severodvinsk with a submerged displacement of 10,500 tons, length of 508 ft., 6 in. (155 m) and primary armament of 16 R-29D SLBMs. As well as its four more missile tubes, the submarines had additional quietening features. All four had been decommissioned by 1996.

The 14 Project 667BDR or Delta III-class submarines were built by Severodvinsk with a submerged displacement of 18,200 tons, length of 544 ft., 7 in. (166 m), same missile armament as the Delta II class, and upgraded propulsion. Like the previous subclasses, it is a double-hulled

type with a thin outer hull of low-magnetic steel wrapped around a thicker inner pressure hull, and work on the type stated in 1972. The Delta III class is the first of the breed able to launch any number of missiles in a single salvo, and also the first submarine able to carry MIRVed warheads. The submarine carries 16 R-29R missiles each carrying three to seven MIRVs with a range of between 4,040 and 4,970 miles (6500 and 8000 km) depending on the number of re-entry vehicles. The Delta III class also carries a new fire-control system for the use of torpedoes in deep water. The submarines were commissioned in 1976-1981, and were allocated as 10 and four to the Pacific and Northern Fleets, respectively. Seven submarines are still in active service, the others being placed in reserve during the mid-1990s.

The Project 667BDRM or Delta IV class was designed for Northern Fleet service, and seven units were built by Severodvinsk in 1984-1992. The design of the Delta IV resembles that of the Delta III class but with greater displacement and length as well as a more modern missile type as its primary armament. The submarine has an operational diving depth of 1,050 feet (320 m) and a maximum depth of 1,315 feet (400 m), and the propulsion system drives two shafts each carrying a shrouded five-blade rather than seven-blade fixed-pitch propeller. Supplies are carried for a patrol length of 80 days, and like its predecessor the outer surface is coasted with a special coating to reduce the submarine's acoustic signature. During the development process, several measures were incorporated to reduce noise levels. The gears and associated equipment are located on a base unit isolated from the pressure hull, and the power compartments are also isolated. The efficiency of the hydro-acoustic coatings of the light outer hull and inner pressure hulls have been increased. Newly designed five-bladed propellers with improved hydro-acoustic characteristics are employed. The Delta IV-class submarines, all of which are still in service, each carry 16 R-29RM (SS-N-23 Skiff) missiles each carrying four to 10 100-kiloton MIRVs. The missile can be launched at depths down to 180 feet (55 m) as the submarine cruises at up to 7 knots, and all 16 missiles can be fired in a single salvo. The submarine is also capable of launching the SS-N-15 Starfish anti-ship missile with a 200-kiloton nuclear warhead, or the Mk 40 anti-ship torpedo.

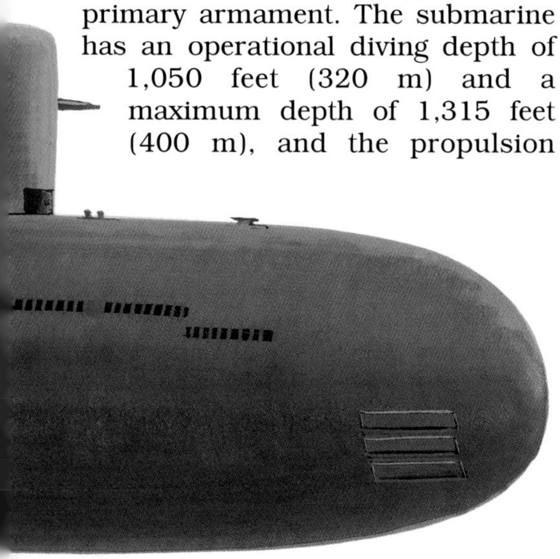

Delta IV class

Type:	nuclear-powered ballistic missile submarine
Tonnage:	13,500 tons surfaced and 18,200 tons submerged
Dimensions:	length 544 ft., 7 in. (166 m); beam: 39 ft., 6 in. (12.3 m); draft 29 ft. (8.8 m)
Propulsion:	two VM-4 pressurized water-cooled reactors powering two geared GT3A-365 steam turbines delivering 59,950 hp (44700 kW) for 14 knots surfaced and 24 knots submerged
Armament:	16 tubes for 16 SS-n-23 submarine-launched ballistic missiles, and four 21-inch (533 mm) tubes (all bow) for 18 torpedoes or anti-ship missiles
Complement:	135

Nuclear propulsion

Though submarines had the capability, almost from the time they emerged as practical vessels of war, to close on a target without detection and attack with a torpedo, this tactical advantage was for years offset by a number of disadvantages. First and foremost of these was the submarine's limited submerged speed, range, and endurance, which meant that the boat had to spend much of the time on the surface for higher-speed cruising, battery recharging, and replenishment of the air supply. These limitations were effectively overcome by the adoption of nuclear power in the 1950s, when submarines became faster underwater than on the surface, batteries became redundant, and constant electricity generation opened the way for better air recycling and/or the hydrolysis of sea water into oxygen and hydrogen, and desalination of sea water for use as drinking water.

Many have suggested, therefore, that the submarines of the period before the advent of nuclear power should be classified as submersibles

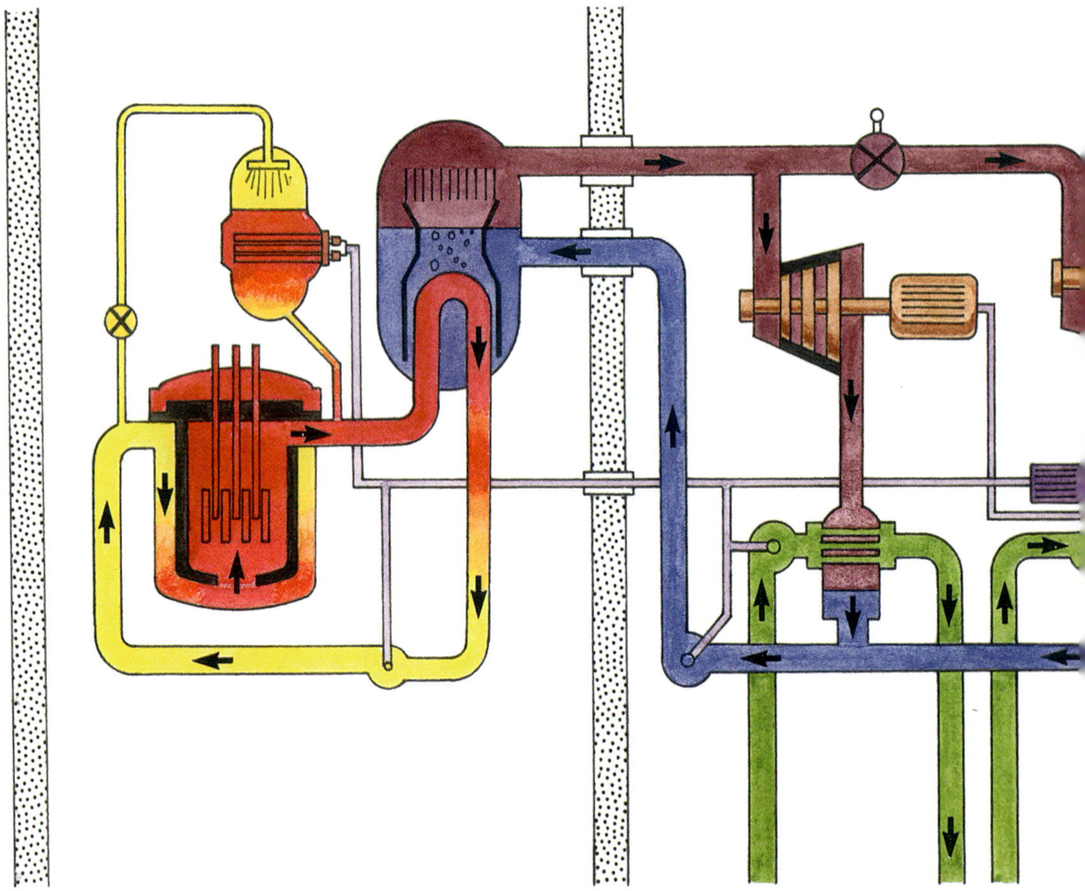

rather than true submarines as they were able to submerge and remain submerged for only a limited time.

Most nuclear submarines use the pressurized water-cooled type of reactor, in which water acts as both coolant and moderator. In such a system, water travels around a primary circuit, passing several times through the reactor and thence to a heat exchanger. The primary-circuit water is kept at a high pressure to prevent it from boiling and turning to steam, a condition provided by a pressurizer. In the heat exchanger, the heat energy is transferred from the pressurized water in the primary circuit to the unpressurized water in the secondary circuit, which then becomes steam and drives the turbine. Having driven the turbine, it passes to a series of condensers, becoming water once again and returning in liquid form to the steam generator to continue the cycle. The pressurized water-cooled reactor system's condensers use sea water as a heat sink and require a constant throughput, which is provided either by the submarine's forward motion or, at low speed, by pumps.

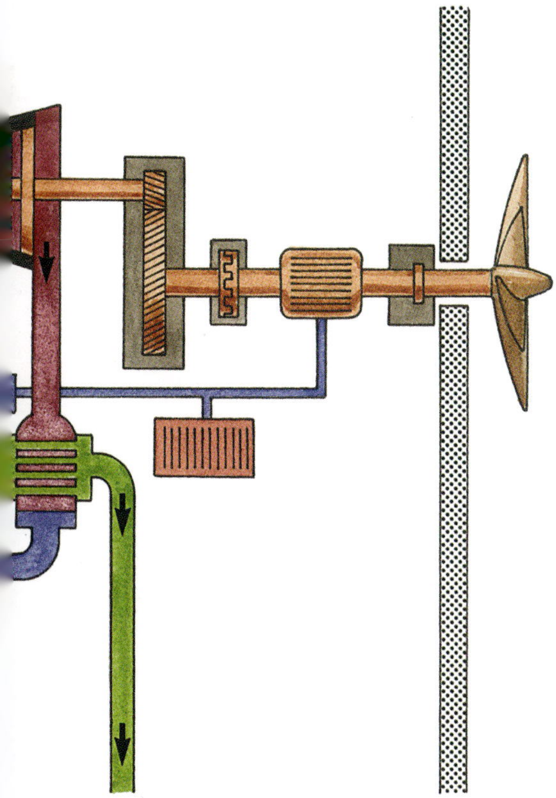

The operation of a reactor system of this nature needs significant auxiliary power, mainly to operate the circulation pumps in the primary circuit and the electrical heater elements in the pressurizer. The system can be designed to use natural circulation resulting from the thermal gradients from the nuclear reaction, but at higher power levels pumps have still to be used. To minimize noise and vibration, some systems use several pumps that can be selectively activated according to the power level. All these pumps create low-level noise, however, which can be detected by suitable sensors.

Other coolants have been evaluated. The *Seawolf*, launched in 1955, was fitted with an S2G reactor cooled by liquid sodium, which produced very efficient heat transfer but was troublesome in service: if the sodium was allowed to cool it became solid, ruining the primary circuit's pipes, and the system also had a propensity toward high-pressure steam leaks. After two years, the S2G was changed for an S2Wa pressurized water-cooled reactor.

Polaris & Poseidon SLBMs

The Lockheed UGM-27 Polaris was a submarine-launched, two-stage solid-propellant ballistic missile developed for the U.S. Navy's first-generation nuclear-powered ballistic missile submarines. The first Polaris flew from Cape Canaveral, Florida, in January 1960. The Polaris grew out of a plan to create a submarine-based missile force based on a liquid-propellant Jupiter missile (not the land-based Jupiter IRBM), which was to have been carried horizontally and launched from a surfaced submarine. At the suggestion of Edward Teller, a "father" of the thermonuclear device, the U.S. Navy switched to the smaller Polaris with solid propellants.

The U.S. Navy had originally preferred the cruise missile in the strategic role, but a major disadvantage of early cruise-missile launch systems was the need to surface, and remain surfaced for some time, for the launch. This left the submarines very vulnerable. It quickly became clear that solid-propellant ballistic missiles had advantages over cruise missiles in range and accuracy, and could also be launched from a submerged submarine.

The Polaris program was begun in 1956, and the *George Washington*, the first U.S. missile submarine, made the first submerged launch of a Polaris A-1 missile on July 20, 1960. The Polaris

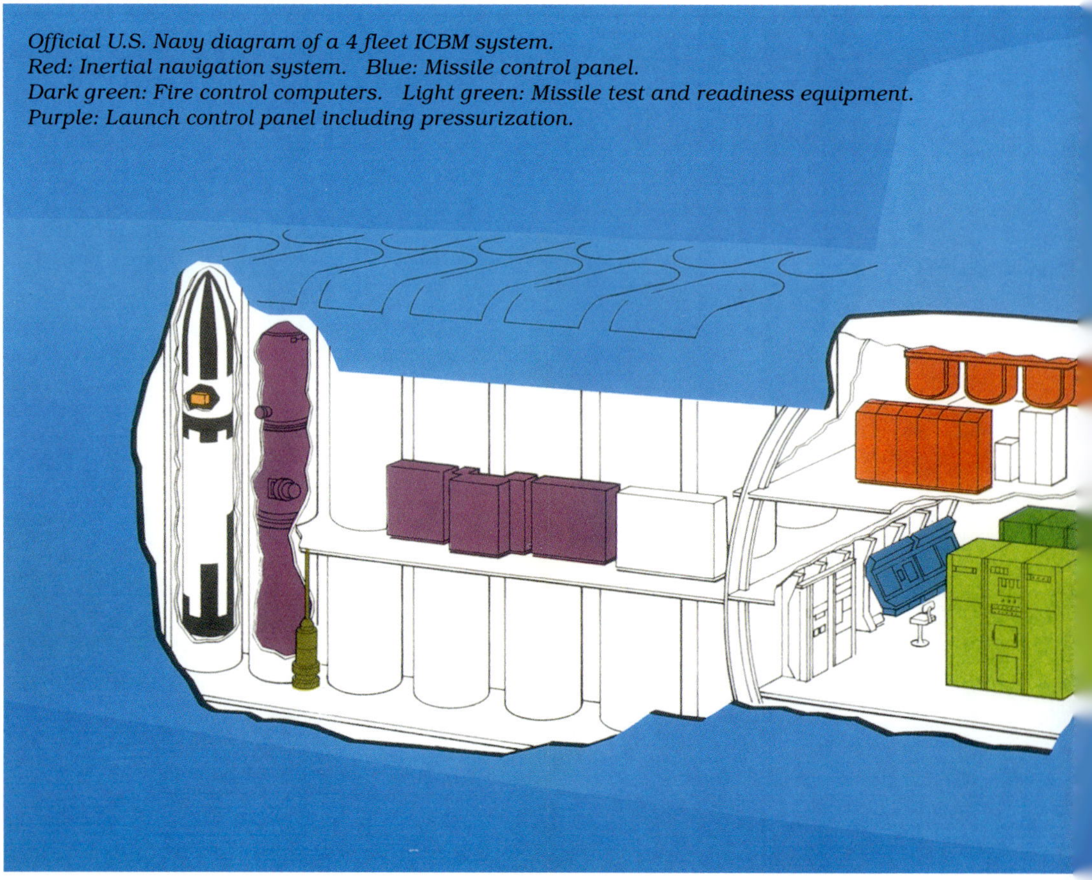

Official U.S. Navy diagram of a 4 fleet ICBM system.
Red: Inertial navigation system. Blue: Missile control panel.
Dark green: Fire control computers. Light green: Missile test and readiness equipment.
Purple: Launch control panel including pressurization.

A-2 was essentially an upgraded Polaris A-1 for service late in 1961, and was carried by 13 submarines up to June 1974. There had been many problems with and modifications of the 60-kiloton W47 warhead, so the U.S. Navy sought a replacement with either a larger yield or equivalent destructive power. The result was the 200-kiloton W58 warhead used as a cluster of three on the definitive Polaris A-3. This had a range of 3,150 miles (5070 km) and a new weapons bay housing three Mk 2 re-entry vehicles. Originally known as a "cluster warhead," this was later known as a "multiple re-entry vehicle" (MRV). The three warheads were spread about a common target and not independently targeted.

The Polaris A-1 had a range of 1,150 miles (1850 km) with its single Mk 1 RV, and the missile had a length of 28 ft., 6 in. (8.7 m), diameter of 54 in. (1.4 m) and launch weight of 28,800 lb. (13065 kg). Work on the W47 nuclear warhead began in 1957. The U.S. Navy accepted delivery of the first 16 warheads in July 1960, and on May 2, 1962, tested a missile with a live warhead in the Pacific.

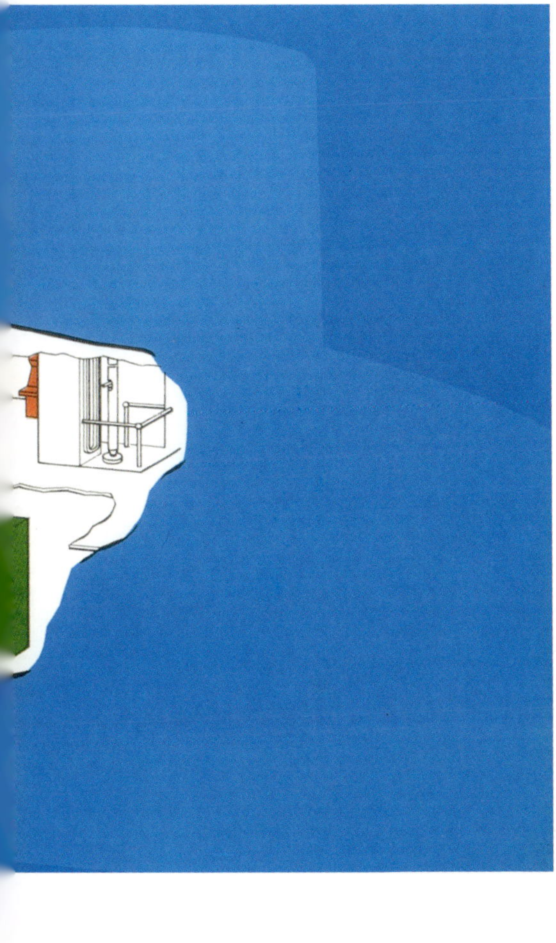

The two stages were each steered by thrust vectoring. Inertial navigation guided the missile to a CEP of about 985 yards (900 m), insufficient for use of the missile against hardened targets. The missile was therefore generally tasked with attacks on dispersed military surface targets (airfields or radar sites), so clearing the way for heavy bombers.

The later Polaris A-2, Polaris A-3 and Polaris B-3 versions were larger, heavier and had greater range. The range increase was most important: The Polaris A-2's range was 1,725 miles (2775 km), the Polaris A-3 2,875 miles (4625 km) and the Polaris B-3 2,300 miles (3700 km). The Polaris A-3 carried an MRVed payload, which spread the warheads about a common target, while the planned Polaris B-3 was to have penetration aids to counter Soviet anti-ballistic missile defenses. The Polaris B-3 was then evolved into the UGM-73 Poseidon C-3, in which the decoy concept was terminated in favor of using the missile's greater throw-weight for between 10 and 14) of hardened RVs with a high re-entry speed to overwhelm the Soviet defenses by sheer weight of numbers. The abandoned Antelope decoy system for the Polaris B-3 was known to the UK, by which it was adopted and evolved into Super Antelope, later redesignated as Chevaline.

The Poseidon succeeded the Polaris from 1972 and ushered in major warhead and accuracy advances. The Poseidon was in turn followed by the

UGM-96 Trident I and UGM-133 Trident II in 1979 and 1990. A development study for an extended-range version of the Polaris, through an enlargement of the basic missile to the maximum size compatible with the length and diameter of existing launch tubes, was started in 1963. Tests had already shown that the smaller-diameter Polaris missile could be operated without any problem in launch tubes with their fiberglass liners and locating rings removed. The initial Polaris B-3 designation later changed to Poseidon C-3. The Poseidon C-3 was the only version of the missile produced; about 620 such weapons were built and delivered to the U.S. Navy in 1970-1978.

Although slightly longer and considerably heavier and greater in diameter than the Polaris A-3, the Poseidon had the same range, but with greater payload weight. It also had improved accuracy and up to 14 W68 thermonuclear warheads in Mk 3 RVs of the multiple independently targeted RV (MIRV) type. The low-yield warheads were apparently selected to make the weapon unsuitable as a first-strike weapon against Soviet hardened targets. Given the role of the Poseidon C-3, it was felt that a newer and considerably more accurate combined celestial-inertial guidance system was not appropriate as a highly accurate and effectively invulnerable weapon system might be seen as a possible first-strike weapon.

As with the Polaris, it was thought dangerous to start the first-stage rocket motor inside the submarine, so a system was created to eject the missile from its launch tube by the expansion of high-pressure steam produced by a solid-fuelled boiler. The first test launch of the Poseidon C-3 took place on August 16, 1968, and the first test launch from a submarine was made from the *James Madison* on August 3, 1970. The Poseidon C-3 officially entered service on March 31, 1971, and eventually equipped all 31 Lafayette-class SSBNs. These submarines were initially operated with the Polaris missile, but it was replaced without undue difficulty by the Poseidon missile during the course of scheduled refits. Some 12 of these boats were later converted to carry the Trident I missile, and the entire class was deactivated in 1985-1994.

Photograph shows Polaris test round being launched.
Photo: U.S. Navy.

UGM-73 Poseidon

Type:	strategic submarine-launched ballistic missile
Launch weight:	64,400 lb. (29212 kg)
Dimensions:	length 34 ft., 1 1/4 in. (10.4 m); diameter 74 in. (1.9 m)
Propulsion:	two-stage solid-propellant rockets each with a single thrust-vectoring nozzle
Range:	2,875 miles (4625 km) with MIRV, or 3,685 miles (5930 km) with single RV
Warheads:	10 or 14 50-kiloton W68 warheads in Mk 3 MIRVed RVs
Guidance:	inertial for a CEP of 600 yards (550 m)

Resolution class (1966)

In the period from the early 1950s to the early 1960s, the UK's nuclear-deterrent capability rested with the Royal Air Force's V-bombers. During this time, though, developments in radar and surface-to-air missiles made it clear that the manned bomber was too vulnerable for assured delivery of nuclear weapons onto their targets. Therefore, in January 1963, the defense committee of the British cabinet decided that the nuclear-deterrent capability should be switched from the manned bomber to the ballistic missile, in this instance carried and launched by nuclear-powered submarines whose underwater endurance and mobility would ensure an effective inviolability which no fixed land base could offer. In February 1963 the government announced that it was to order four Resolution-class nuclear-powered submarines each armed with 16 Lockheed UGM-27 Polaris missiles. These submarines would take over the nuclear deterrent role from the V-bombers from 1968.

The first two pairs of boats were ordered in May 1963 from Vickers Shipbuilding Ltd. of Barrow-in-Furness (the *Resolution* and *Repulse*) and Cammell Laird & Co. Ltd. of Birkenhead (the *Renown* and *Revenge*). The option of buying a fifth unit, the *Ramillies*, was cancelled in February 1965. The four new submarines were allocated traditional battleship names, indicating that the Royal Navy felt that the new submarines were the capital ships of their time.

The construction of the submarines was unusual in that the bow and stern sections were constructed separately before being attached to the front and rear of the U.S.-designed missile compartment. In overall terms, the design was a modification of that used for the Valiant class of nuclear-powered attack submarines, but greatly lengthened to incorporate the missile compartment between the fin and the nuclear reactor compartment. This missile compartment accommodated the 16 container/launch tubes, each with its own hatch, in two longitudinal rows of eight tubes for a total of 16 Polaris A-3 missiles. A Rolls-Royce pressurized water-cooled reactor supplying steam to English Electric turbines gave the boats a speed of 25 knots submerged, and the boats had a maximum diving depth of 900 feet (275 m). In the event of a problem with the nuclear propulsion plant, the boats could revert to a conventional but strictly limited propulsion arrangement of one Paxman diesel generator unit delivering 4,000 hp (2982 kW), The submarines were designed to stay out of trouble, but a defensive ca-

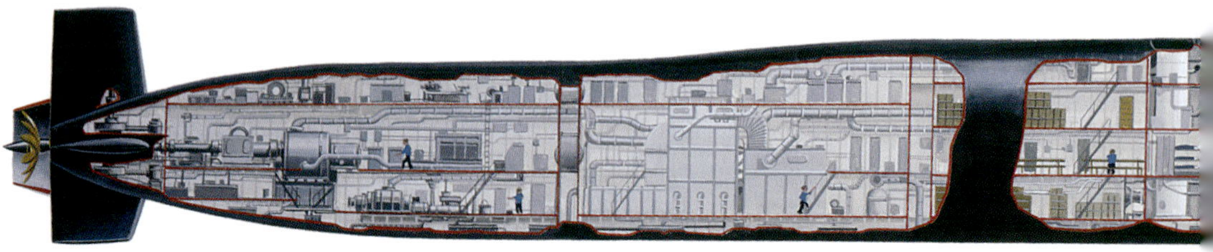

pability was provided by six 21-inch (533 mm) bow tubes to launch Tigerfish wire-guided homing torpedoes. A high level of habitability was built into the beats to ensure maximum efficiency was retained in long underwater patrols, and each submarine had two alternating crews each of 143 men. This ensured that the submarines could return to sea with the minimum delay needed to load stores and change crews.

The first of the submarines to be completed was the *Resolution*, which had been laid down in February 1964 and launched in September 1966. After being commissioned in 1967, the submarine underwent a long period of sea trials culminating in the test firing of a Polaris missile on February 15, 1968. The *Resolution* began its first operational patrol on June 15, 1968, and so inaugurated an eventual 28 years of Polaris patrols. The other three submarines were completed in September 1968, November 1968, and December 1969, and the four-strong class formed part of the Royal Navy's 10th Submarine Squadron, all based at Faslane, in Scotland.

All four submarines were revised in the 1980s for the Polaris A3TK missile fitted with the British-developed Chevaline MRV warhead. As the newer Vanguard-class submarines entered service in the mid-1990s, the Resolution class was retired and the submarines were laid up at Rosyth Dockyard with their reactors removed.

Resolution class

Type:	nuclear-powered ballistic missile submarine
Tonnage:	7,500 tons surfaced and 8,400 tons submerged
Dimensions:	length 425 ft., 0 in. (129.5 m); beam 33 ft., 0 in. (10.1 m); draft 30 ft., 1 in. (9.2 m)
Propulsion:	one Rolls-Royce PWR-1 pressurized water-cooled reactor supplying steam to two sets of English-Electric geared steam turbines delivering 27,500 hp (20504 kW) for 20 knots surfaced and 25 knots submerged
Armament:	16 vertical tubes for 16 Polaris submarine-launched ballistic missiles, and six 21-inch (533 mm) tubes (all bow) for torpedoes
Complement:	143

Akula class (1984)

Known to the Russians as the Project 971 or Shchuka-B ("pike B") class, this nuclear-powered attack submarine type is best known in the West by the NATO reporting designation "Akula" class. The lead submarine is the *Bars*, launched in 1984 and commissioned in 1986.

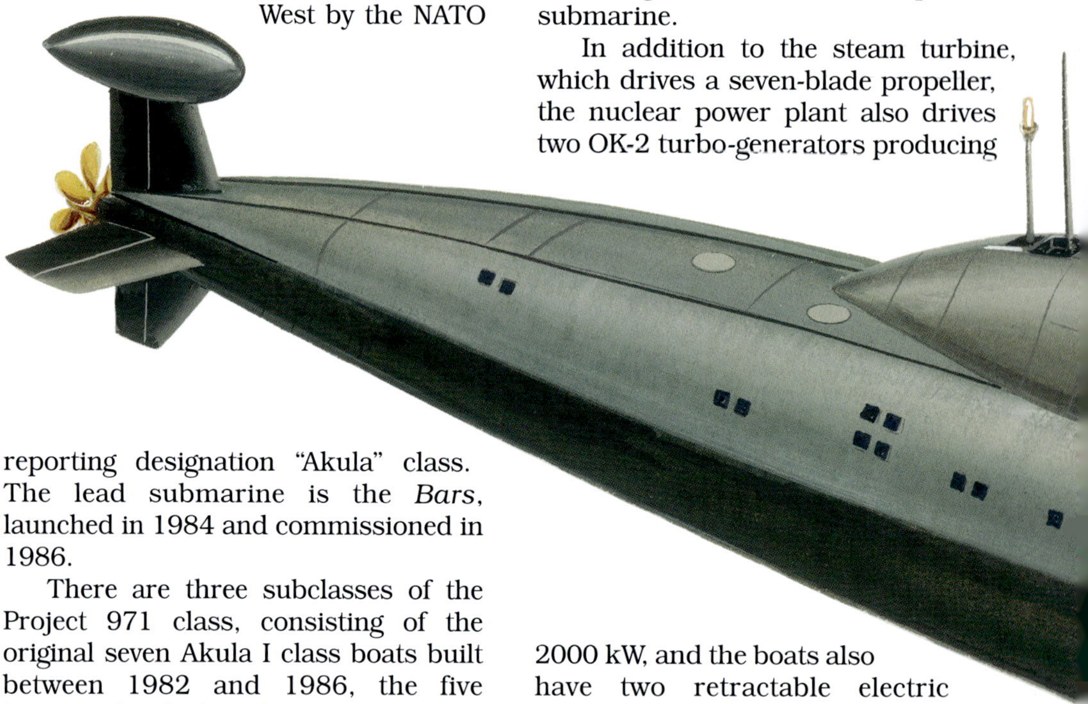

There are three subclasses of the Project 971 class, consisting of the original seven Akula I class boats built between 1982 and 1986, the five Improved Akula class boats built between 1986 and 1991, and the four Akula II-class boats built from 1991. It should be noted, though, that this is disputed, as not all authorities agree on the distinction between the Improved Akula and Akula II classes.

The Akula-class submarine is based on a special double-hull system which greatly increases the boat's strength reserve and thus allows the boat to dive to a greater depth than any other nuclear-powered attack submarine of the period: a test depth of 1,475 feet (450 m), a never-exceeded depth of 1,805 feet (550 m) and a calculated crush depth of 2,165 feet (600 m) have been reported. The Akula-class boat is also the quietest nuclear-powered attack submarine of Soviet design, and it is claimed that the noise radiated by the Akula II class boat is similar to that of the first examples of the U.S. Navy's Los Angeles class nuclear-powered submarine.

In addition to the steam turbine, which drives a seven-blade propeller, the nuclear power plant also drives two OK-2 turbo-generators producing 2000 kW, and the boats also have two retractable electric propulsors for low-speed maneuvering at 3 knots. The very noticeable and distinctive "bulb" at the head of the rudder of the Akula-class submarine accommodates the boat's Pelamida-towed sonar array in its retracted form. Other sonars are the MGK-503-M Skat active/passive suite, flank-array sonar, and the MG-70 mine detection sonar.

All of the Akula-class submarines are fitted with four 21-inch (533 mm) tubes which can launch the Type 53 heavy-weight anti-ship torpedo or the RPK-2 Viyuga (SS-N-15 Starfish) anti-submarine missile, and four 26-inch (650 mm) tubes which can launch the Type 65 torpedo, optimized for use against targets such as aircraft carriers, or the SS-N-16 Stallion missile in either its RPK-6 Vodopad anti-ship or RPK-7

Vorobei anti-submarine forms. All three of the missiles have a nuclear warhead option. The torpedo tubes are arranged in two rows of four tubes each. The Improved Akula and Akula II submarines have an additional six 21-inch (533 mm) tubes mounted externally, but it is uncertain if these are fully functional external launch tubes or more limited launchers for mines and decoys. These external tubes are mounted outside the pressure hull in one row, above the "standard" tubes, and can only be reloaded in port or with the assistance of a submarine tender. The 26-inch (650 mm) tubes can also be fitted with liners to allow the launch of 21-inch (533 mm) weapons. The "standard" tubes can also be used to deploy mines.

Of the seven original Akula I submarines, only three are known still to be in service. The K-284 *Akula* was decommissioned in 1995, the K-322 *Kashalot*, K-480 *Bars* and K-317 *Pantera* are thought to be in reserve. The five Improved Akula I boats, *Drakon*, *Volk*, *Tigr*, *Narval*, and one other, are thought still to be in service. The sole Akula II boat known to be in service is the *Vepr*, but construction continues at a slow rate. The Indian navy has ordered three Akula II submarines on a lease-buy arrangement, and should receive the first of the boats, named *Chakra*, in June 2008.

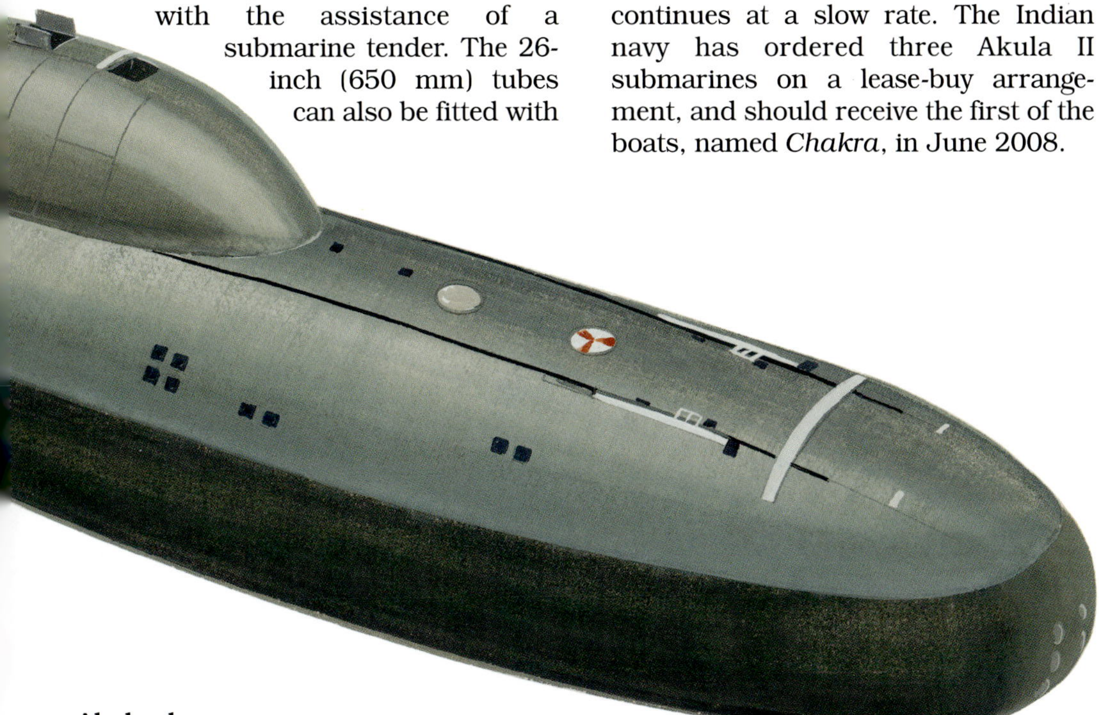

Akula class

Type:	nuclear-powered attack submarine
Tonnage:	5,700 to 7,500 tons surfaced and 7,900 to 9,100 tons submerged
Dimensions:	length between 354 ft., 4 in. (108 m) and 366 ft., 6 in. (111.7 m); beam 44 ft., 3 in. (13.5 m); draft 31 ft., 6 in. (9.6 m)
Propulsion:	one OK-650B pressurized water-cooled reactor delivering steam to one OK-7 geared steam turbine delivering 43,000 hp (32060 kW) for 20 knots surfaced and 35 knots submerged
Armament:	four 21-inch (533 mm) tubes and four 26-inch (650 mm) tubes for 40 torpedoes, missiles, and mines, and one launcher for SA-18 Igla-M surface-to-air missiles
Complement:	51

Xia class (1981)

The single example of the Type 092 Daqinu or Type 092-II submarine is generally known in the West by the U.S. Department of Defense reporting designation "Xia"-class submarine. This was the first nuclear-powered ballistic missile submarine class built for and operated by the Chinese People's Liberation Army Navy, and also the first type of SSBN to be designed and built in Asia. The design was derived from that of the Type 091 or Han-class nuclear-powered attack submarine, of which five were delivered from mid-1974, with the hull lengthened by some 72 ft., 2 in. (22 m) to allow the insertion of 12 vertical missile tubes.

The first of this new breed of submarine was the *Changzheng 6*, which was laid down in 1978 at the Huludao Shipyard, 120 miles (195 km) northeast of Beijing, in the same yard which had built the Han-class submarines. The *Changzheng 6* was launched in 1981, and then required some six years, up to 1987, for its fitting out to be completed and initial trials to be undertaken.

The primary armament was initially the JL-1 SLBM, a type known to the West by the U.S. reporting designation "CSS-N-3" and carrying a nuclear warhead of some 200-300 kilotons over a distance of more than 1,100 miles (1770 km), but the submarine was then cycled through number of considerable number of upgrades to achieve a process of steady, incremental improvements. These upgrades included the installation of a much-improved main sonar, the Type H/SQ2-262B equipment, in place of the original Type 604 sonar.

The *Changzheng 6* has also undergone numerous refits, and in 2007 was characterized by a new black paint finish, possibly the introduction of some comparatively simple quieting technologies, French-designed sonar, and the improved longer-range JL-1A SLBM. It is reported that the *Changzheng 6* has not cruised to any point outside Chinese regional waters, suggesting major problems, and this seems to be indicated by the fact that two such boats were built and one of these was lost in an accident.

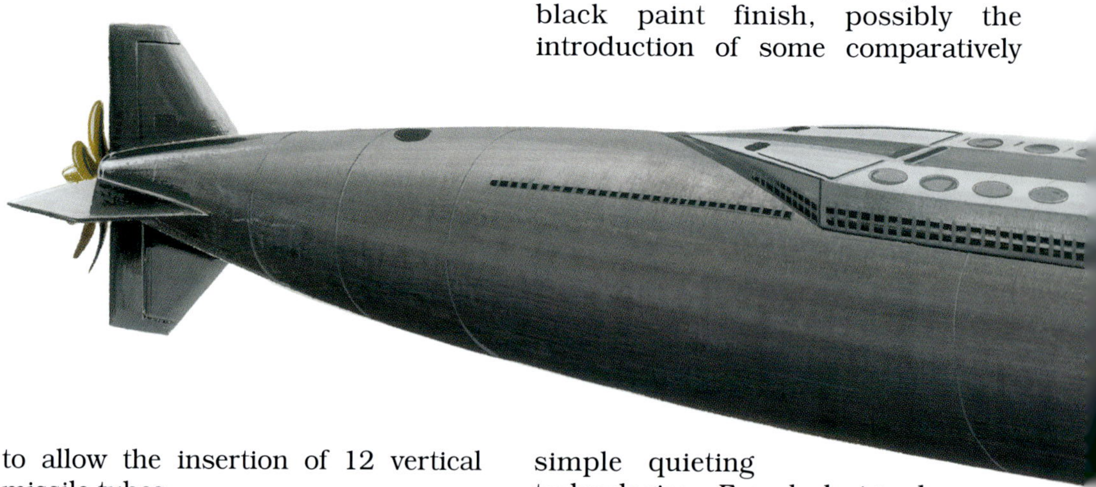

The Xia class is now technically obsolete, and the single surviving example is thought not to be operational. A new SSBN type has been created to succeed the Xia class, the Type 094 class which has the Western reporting designation, "Jin" class. The first of the new vessels, with a displacement in the order of 9,000 tons submerged, was laid down at the Huludao Shipyard in 1999, and was launched in July 2004. Late in 2006, a commercial satellite photographed what is believed to be the new Jin-class submarine alongside at Xiaopingdao Submarine Base. In comparison with the Xia class, the Jin class is 36 ft., 1 in. (11 m) longer to house the tubes for the 12 JL-2 missiles and part of the part of the reactor.

The JL-2 (CSS-N-4) has a range of about 4,970 miles (8000 km), and is thus capable of targeting much of the Western Hemisphere, some of it from areas close to the Chinese coast. The Jin-class submarine is thought to use Russian technology, and the U.S. Office of Naval Intelligence indicates that another five Jin-class submarines may be built. This is only an estimate, however, and has not been accepted by all U.S. intelligence agencies. The Jin class, however, marks a major improvement over the Xia class, and the U.S. government has expressed its concern about the new type, on the grounds that the Chinese government has not been transparent about the program and is therefore destabilizing the current balance of power in the Pacific region.

Further commercial satellite imagery reveals potentially two more Jin-class submarines in drydock, though one of these may be the Jin-class submarine identified at an earlier time. In October 2007 the first photograph of the Jin-class submarine was published on the Internet, revealing that the primary missile armament is 12 JL-2 missiles rather than the 16 previously estimated.

Xia class

Type:	nuclear-powered ballistic missile submarine
Tonnage:	6,500 tons surfaced and 7,000 tons submerged
Dimensions:	length 393 ft., 8 in. (120 m); beam 32 ft., 10 in. (10 m); draft 26 ft., 3 in. (8 m)
Propulsion:	one pressurized water-cooled reactor powering two geared steam turbines for about 22 knots submerged
Armament:	12 tubes for 12 JL-1 or later JL-2 submarine-launched ballistic missiles, and six 21-inch (533 mm) tubes (all bow) for torpedoes
Complement:	100

Seawolf class (1995)

The Seawolf class of nuclear-powered attack submarines was conceived as a successor to the Los Angeles class of submarines with greater speed and better armament. The alternative designation, SSN-21 class, and out-of-sequence designation (SSN-21, SSN-22 and SSN-23) reflect the fact that the type was planned as the U.S. Navy's "Nuclear-Powered Attack Submarine for the Twenty-First Century." The first of the class, the *Seawolf*, was ordered from the Electric Boat Division of General Dynamics, Connecticut, in January 1989, launched in June 1995, and commissioned in July 1997. The *Connecticut* was laid down in September 1992, launched in September 1997, and commissioned in December 1998. The *Jimmy Carter*, third and last unit of the class, was laid down in December 1998, christened in June 2004 after the program had been delayed so that extensive changes could be incorporated, and commissioned in February 2005. These changes included a submerged displacement of 12,139 tons and a hundred-foot (30.5 m) increase in length to allow the insertion of a section known as the Multi-Mission Platform allowing the launch and recovery of remotely operated vehicles and U.S. Navy SEAL Special Forces. The plug features a fairing over a wasp-waist passageway, allowing members of the crew to pass between the fore and aft sections of the hull while providing sufficient volume for the storage of ROVs and any special equipment needed to allow their launch from and recovery by the submarine. The MMP may also be used as an underwater splicing chamber for tapping of undersea fiberoptic cables. The *Jimmy Carter*'s other changes include modifications to the ballast control and mission management spaces, and the

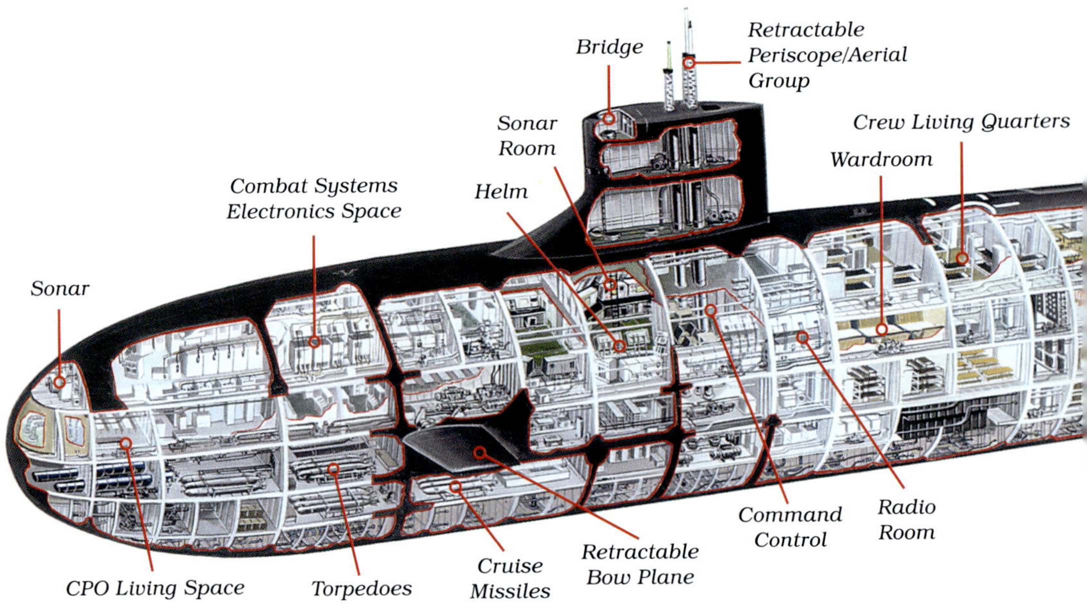

addition of a new high-capacity communications mast.

The Seawolf class was a product of the Cold War, conceived to maintain the U.S. Navy's acoustic advantage over Soviet submarines: it is claimed that a Seawolf-class submarine cruising at 25 knots submerged is quieter than a Los-Angeles-class submarine quiescent alongside a pier. With the end of the Cold War and a change of emphasis from oceanic to littoral operations, the Seawolf class submarines' cost was deemed too high, so the program was trimmed to just the three submarines, to expedite the design and construction of the Virginia class of smaller and

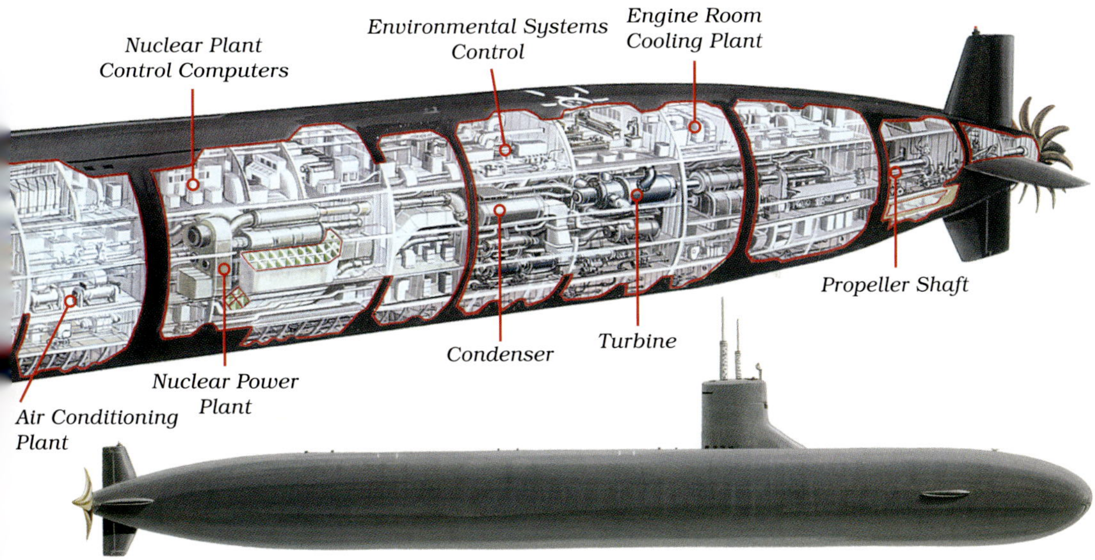

cheaper nuclear-powered attack submarines.

The modular design of the Seawolf class pioneered major improvements and innovations for enhanced maneuverability, volume for later upgrades and weapons developments, and better sonar. The submarines are coated with a full acoustic cladding, had a maximum "silent" submerged speed of 20 knots, possess a maximum diving depth of 2,000 feet (610 m), and have the capability for operations under the Arctic ice. The submarines have retractable bow hydroplanes.

The core of the Seawolf-class submarine's operational capability is its combat data system, initially the Lockheed Martin BSY-2 system with a network of some 70 or so Motorola

Left:
The seawolf is steered from the right when submerged.
Photo: Electric Boat Company.

Right:
On the surface the helm shifts to the left.
Photo: Electric Boat Company.

68030 processors, now being replaced by the Raytheon BYG-1 system. Weapons control is managed by the Raytheon Mk 2 fire-control system. Like the improved Los Angeles submarines, the Seawolf-class submarine lacks any external weapons.

The Seawolf-class submarine has eight 26-inch (660 mm) tubes to launch missiles and torpedoes, of which it carries 50. The submarine is armed with both the land-attack and anti-ship version of the Raytheon Tomahawk missile, whose land attack variant has a range of 1,550 miles (2495 km) and TAINS (Terrain-Comparison Aided Inertial Navigation System) to guide the missile toward its target at high subsonic speed at between 65 and 330 feet (20 and 100 m). The Tomahawk can be fitted with a nuclear warhead normally not carried. Missile improvements include an upgraded propulsion system and the Navstar Global Positioning System guidance capability. The anti-ship Tomahawk missile had a range of 280 miles (450 km) and is fitted with an inertial guidance package as well as active radar and anti-radiation homing terminal guidance.

The first submerged launch of the new Raytheon Tactical Tomahawk Block IV missile took place in November 2002, this development including a two-way satellite link that makes possible the reprogramming of the missile in flight and transmission from the missile of battle damage indication imagery. The missile entered service with the U.S. Navy surface warships in September 2004.

The Seawolf class of submarines also carries the Boeing Harpoon anti-ship missile, in its so-called Sub-Harpoon variant for encapsulated launch from under the surface. This missile has active radar homing to deliver a 500 lb. (227 kg) warhead at high subsonic speed over a range of 80 miles (130 km).

The Gould Mk 48 ADCAP (Advanced Capability) torpedo is designed to tackle both high-performance surface ships and high-speed submarines with deep-diving capability. The torpedo carries a 589 lb. (267 kg) warhead, is capable of

operating with or without wire guidance, and employs either or both active and passive homing. The torpedo's range is 31 miles (50 km) in active mode and 24 miles (38 km) in passive mode.

Countermeasures are vitally important to the modern submarine's survival, and in the Seawolf-class submarine these include the Northrop Grumman WLY-1 torpedo decoy system and the GTE WLQ-4(V)1 electronic countermeasures system.

The submarine's sonar suite is the BQQ-5D with bow-mounted active-passive arrays and wide-aperture passive flank arrays. Also fitted are the TB-16 surveillance and TB-29 tactical towed arrays, which will be replaced by the TB-29A thin-line towed-array being developed by Lockheed Martin, and the BQS-24 active sonar system for a close-range detection capability. The Seawolf-class submarines are being upgraded with the Lockheed Martin BQQ-10(V)4 sonar processing system under the Acoustic-Rapid Commercial-of-the-shelf Insertion (A-RCI) program. BPS-16 radar is fitted for navigation.

The Seawolf-class submarine has, as its primary power source, the Westinghouse S6W pressurized water-cooled reactor system whose steam is used to drive two sets of geared steam turbines powering the pump-jet propulsor. Each submarine also has a secondary motor for submerged propulsion.

Seawolf class

Type:	nuclear-powered attack submarine
Tonnage:	8,600 tons surfaced and 9.142 tons submerged
Dimensions:	length 353 ft., 0 in. (107.6 m); beam 40 ft., 0 in. (12.2 m); draught 35 ft., 0 in. (10.7 m)
Propulsion:	one Westinghouse S6W pressurized water-cooled reactor supplying steam to two geared steam turbines delivering 52,000 hp (38771 kW) for 18 knots surfaced and 35 knots submerged
Armament:	eight 26 in. (660 mm) tubes (all bow) for 50 weapons including torpedoes, Tomahawk land attack and anti-ship cruise missiles and Harpoon anti-ship missiles, or 100 mines
Complement:	134

Oscar class (1980)

The nuclear-powered cruise missile submarines known to their Soviet originators as the Project 949 Granit and Project 949A Antei classes are better known in the West by their NATO reporting designations, the Oscar I and Oscar II classes, respectively. In 2007 the Oscar-class submarine was the largest attack submarine type in current service, for it is slightly larger than the converted Ohio-class submarine of the U.S. Navy, displacing less when surfaced but more when submerged, and in dimensional terms it is of slightly less length but greater beam. The primary task of the Oscar-class submarines from the start of their careers was the destruction of the U.S. Navy's main battle groups centered on aircraft carriers.

In 1970 the Soviet shipyard at Severodvinsk launched a single Project 661 Anchar-class nuclear-powered attack submarine, which received the Western designation, "Papa" class, and was the subject of considerable uncertainty as to its role. It was considerably larger than the Charlie-class cruise missile submarines and carried two more launchers for an unidentified type of missile: the one Papa-class submarine had been a prototype to test and prove a new nuclear propulsion arrangement and a new type of missile, a submarine-launched version of the P-50 Malakhit (SS-N-9 Siren) anti-ship missile. The Papa-class submarine was thus a very fast attack submarine, reaching 44.7 knots on trials, and equipped with 10 anti-ship cruise missiles in individual tubes forward of the sail, between the inner and outer hulls.

The Oscar-class design introduced other improvements, especially in the armament. The primary element of this was two 12-tube banks of tubes for the SS-N-19 long-range anti-ship missile, which could be launched while the submarine was submerged. These tubes were located on each side of the sail and set at a 40° elevation between the inner pressure hull and the outer hydrodynamic hull. One less fortunate aspect of this arrangement was that the pressure hull is probably only 27 ft., 11 in. (8.5 m) in diameter, adversely affecting habitability.

The missile was designed for launch on the basis of radar data provided via the "Punch Bowl" antenna

from a satellite, or via a towed VLF buoy normally housed abaft the sail.

Severodvinsk built two Oscar I submarines for the Northern Fleet. These were the *K-525* (later *Arkhangyel'sk*), which was laid down in 1978, commissioned in 1980, decommissioned in 1997, and scrapped at Sevmash during 2001; and the *K-206* (*Murmansk*, ex-*Minsky Komsomolets*) commissioned in 1981, decommissioned in 1997, and scrapped at Zvezdochka in 2004.

The same yard also built 11 Oscar II class submarines as five and six units for the Northern and Pacific Fleets respectively. The Northern Fleet submarines comprised the *K-148* (*Krasnodar*) commissioned in 1986, the *K-119* (*Voronezh*) commissioned in 1988, the *K-410* (*Smolensk*) commissioned 1990, the *K-266* (*Orel*, ex-*Severodvinsk*) commissioned 1992, and the *K-141* (*Kursk*) laid down in 1992, launched in 1994, commissioned in December 1994, and lost on August 12, 2000.

The Pacific Fleet submarines were the *K-132* (*Irkutsk*) commissioned in 1987 and in inactive reserve from 1997, the *K-173* (*Krasnoyarsk*) commissioned 1989 and in inactive reserve from 1998, the *K-442* (*Chelyabinsk*) commissioned in 1990, the *K-150* (*Tomsk*) commissioned in 1991, the *K-186* (*Omsk*) launched in May 1993 and commissioned in October 1993, and the *K-456* (*Viluchinsk*, ex-*Kasatka*) commissioned into the Northern Fleet in 1991 but transferred to the Pacific Fleet September 1993.

One more Oscar II class submarine, the *K-530* (*Belgorod*), was laid down in July 1992, and is still under construction at Severodvinsk; work on this submarine has been frozen for several periods as a result of the lack of adequate funding. In July 2006 the Russian minister of defense announced that the "Ministry of Defense does not need *Belgorod*, therefore it does not intend to finance its construction." It is not clear whether the submarine will be completed and, if so, for whom.

It was once planned to develop a new fourth-generation follow-on to the Oscar class, but this plan was scrapped.

Oscar class

Type:	nuclear-powered strategic cruise missile submarine
Tonnage:	13.900 tons surfaced and 18,300 tons submerged
Dimensions:	length 505 ft., 3 in. (154 m); beam 59 ft., 9 in. (18.2 m); draft 29 ft., 9 in. (9 m)
Propulsion:	two pressurized water-cooled reactor powering two geared steam turbines delivering 98,000 hp (73070 kW) for 15 knots surfaced and 29 knots submerged
Armament:	two 25.6 in. (650 mm) and four 21 in. (533 mm) tubes (all bow) for 28 weapons including the Tsakra (SS-N-15 Starfish) anti-submarine missile with a 15-kiloton warhead, Vodopad/Veder (SS-N-16 Stallion) anti-ship missile with 200-kiloton warhead, or Type 40 anti-submarine torpedo, or 32 ground mines.
Complement:	107

Soviet concrete concept submarine (1998)

In the late 1990s, there were suggestions that the Russian navy was considering the development of small submarines fabricated largely of concrete. The idea of such submarines was first mooted by a German engineer, Heinz Lipschutz, in 1957. At the time, he was working for a British airline as a pilot, and tried without success to interest the Royal Navy. The advantage of such a boat was thought to lie in the ease and cheapness with which it could be built, thereby offering a poorer nation the opportunity to rival an affluent nation in the defense of its national maritime interests.

The Russians looked seriously at the notion of a six-crew concrete boat, which would have differed from other submarines of the period in several important ways. While conventional boats with nuclear or diesel-electric propulsion float until they take on ballast water, the concrete submarine was designed to be heavier than the water it displaced and lift off the bottom using four electric turbine pumps to draw in external water and accelerate it to emerge as thrust from vectoring nozzles: there would have

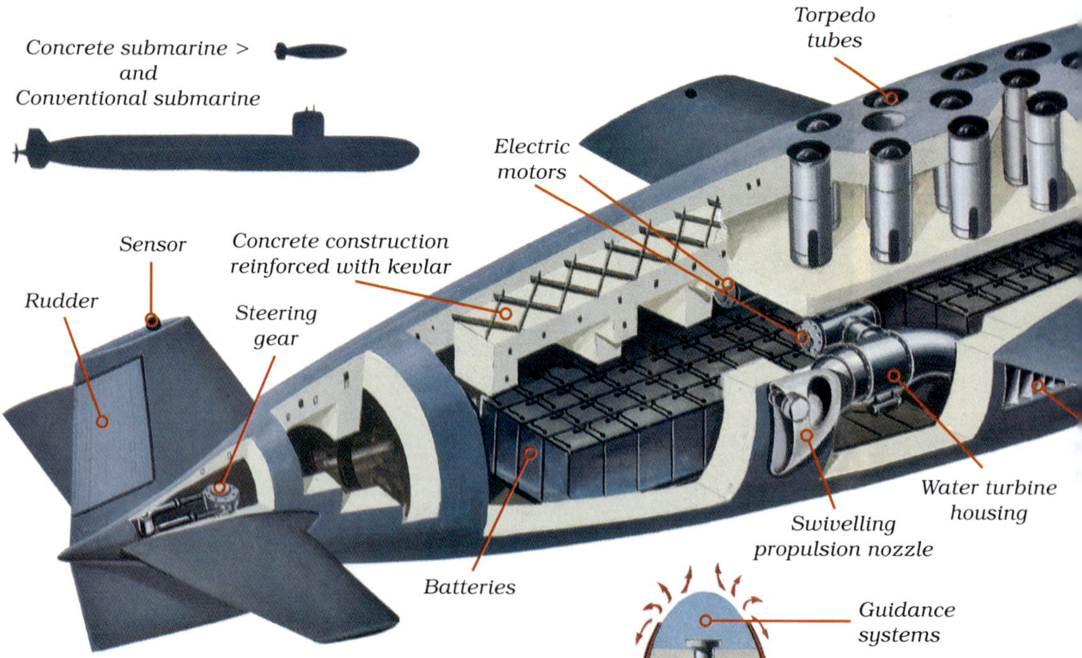

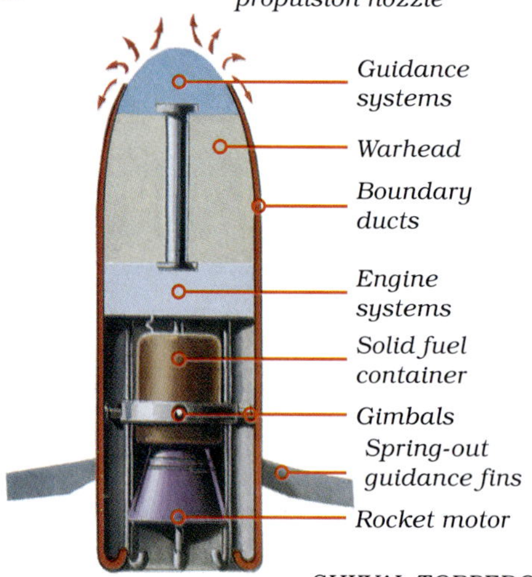

SHKVAL TORPEDO

been two nozzles on each beam fore and aft of the central "wing," itself providing lift when the boat was moving forward. As the concrete boat would have been designed for negative buoyancy, there would have been no limit other than available volume, to the size and weight of the batteries installed.

The concrete boat would also have fought in a different manner. Conventional submarines roam the sea on patrols, but on a typical patrol a concrete submarine would have sunk offshore and waited for an opponent's vessels to pass overhead, and then fire one of its vertical-launch Shkval torpedoes. Guided by pop-out fins and propelled by a solid-propellant rocket, this would have incorporated ducts to carry a small part of the rockets gases though the weapon's sides to emerge at the nose before streaming back and allow the torpedo to move through gas rather than water. A speed of some 230 mph (370 km/h) was suggested, which is four times greater than that of any conventional torpedo with propeller or pump-jet propulsion.

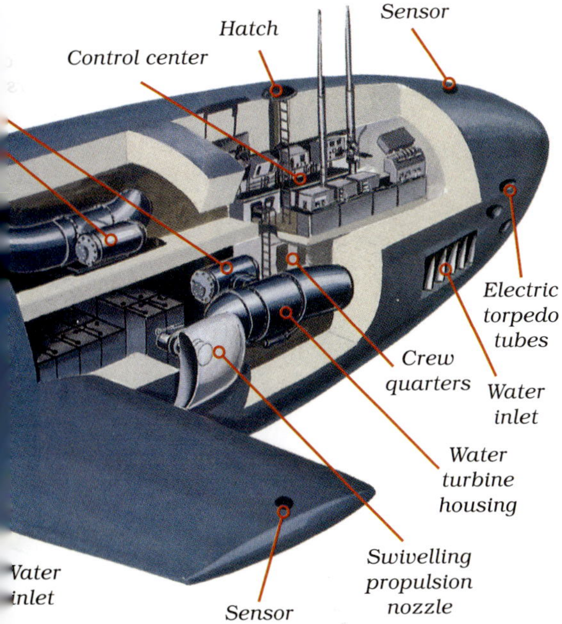

Because concrete is strong in compression, and in the concrete boat would have been of the reinforced type with a mesh of Kevlar or a similar material rather than a mesh of steel rods, the concrete boat would have been able to operate well below the crush depth of a steel- or even titanium-hulled boat. Moreover, sonar would have been hard pressed to differentiate the concrete boat from a sandy or rocky seabed. Concrete boats could also have been left on the bottom to be manned by their crews only in times of crisis or war. Groups of concrete submarines could have kept in contact on the bottom by means of practically undetectable tight-beam sonar, also allowing the boats' passive sonars to work as a giant listening network.

Concrete submarine

Type:	coastal and oceanic defense submarine
Tonnage:	variable
Dimensions:	variable
Propulsion:	four electrically powered water turbines for more than 60 knots
Armament:	variable number of vertical-launch torpedoes
Complement:	6

U.S. aircraft-carrier submarine

There have been many suggestions over the years about ways in which the submarine could be used for purposes other than the naval attack and missile roles. The Germans pioneered the transport submarine in World War I and supply submarine in World War II, and these basic concepts have been updated with proposals for nuclear-powered transport submarines. Taken one step further forward and slightly off to one side is the concept of the aircraft between 200 and 400 feet (61 and 122 m) on the presupposition that the submarine could manage a surfaced speed of more than 20 knots, which seems feasible with nuclear propulsion. To avoid obstructing the flight deck, the sail would have been omitted or made retractable, and there would also have been two catapults.

The maintenance of hull integrity against water ingress, especially at depth, would have been a major factor,

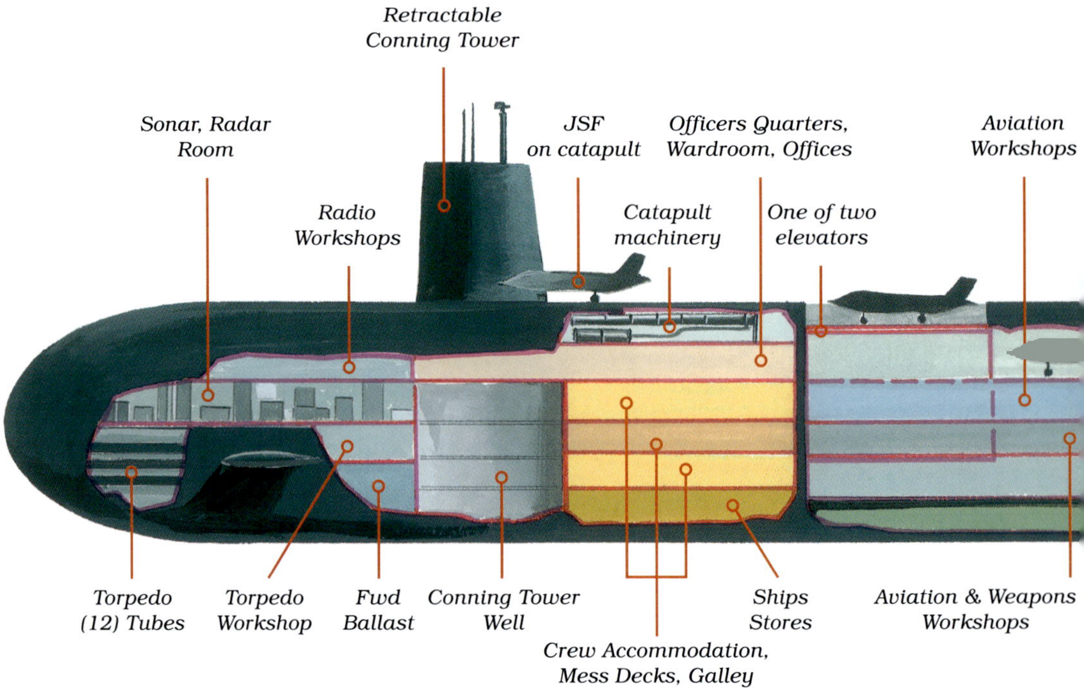

carrier submarine, which would have to surface only to launch and recover its aircraft. These would be of the STOL (short take-off and landing) type to minimize the length of the flight deck which would be required, and thus the length of the submarine, One concept envisaged a flight deck length of complicated by the fact that there would have had to be at least one and almost certainly two aircraft elevators so that aircraft could be moved between the flight ands hangar decks. Each elevator would thus have been only slightly larger than the "footprint" of the folded airplane, sealed by hatches measuring about 12 by 25 feet (3.7 by 7.6 m).

The need to incorporate a hangar deck and flight deck would have dictated the hull design, especially in terms of its shape. While a good shape for a pressure hull is cylindrical with hemispherical ends, the need to carry and operate aircraft would suggest a much flattened cylinder modified by a substantial rounding-off of the bottom corners and slightly rounding the top corners, and terminating fore and aft in streamlined sections. The shaped stern section of the aircraft carrier submarine would have been unsuited for any rearward extension of the hangar deck, but could have been used to carry intermediate-range ballistic missiles. The hull would have had four or five decks, the hangar deck having twice the height of the other decks.

Such a vessel could also have been used for cargo carrying in the military supply or mercantile roles.

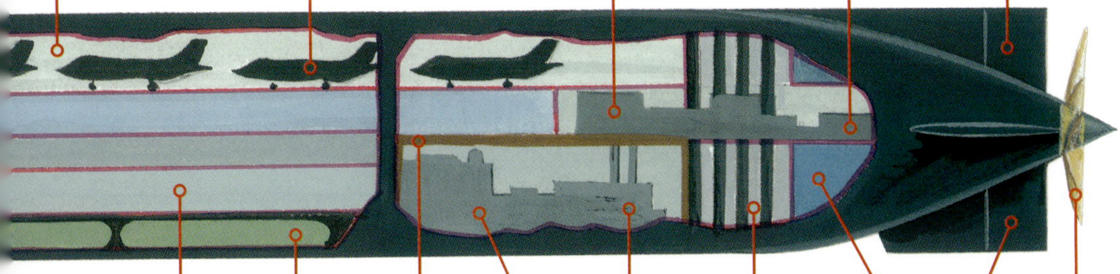

Aircraft-carrier submarine (concept)

Type:	aircraft-carrier submarine
Tonnage:	12,000 tons submerged
Dimensions:	length 500 ft. (152.4 m); beam 80 ft. (24.4 m); draft 40 ft. (12.2 m)
Propulsion:	probably two pressurized water-cooled reactors powering two steam turbines for 30 knots surfaced and 35 knots submerged
Armament:	up to 30 STOL warplanes and tubes for 27 intermediate-range ballistic missiles
Complement:	not available

Sonar (Asdic) in World War II

Known at the time to the British as "Asdic," sonar uses under-water sound propagation to provide for navigation, communication, or detection of other vessels. There are two kinds of sonar: active (in which a sound pulse is transmitted by equipment which then listens for a returning echo) and passive (in which the equipment merely listens for noise radiated by a target).

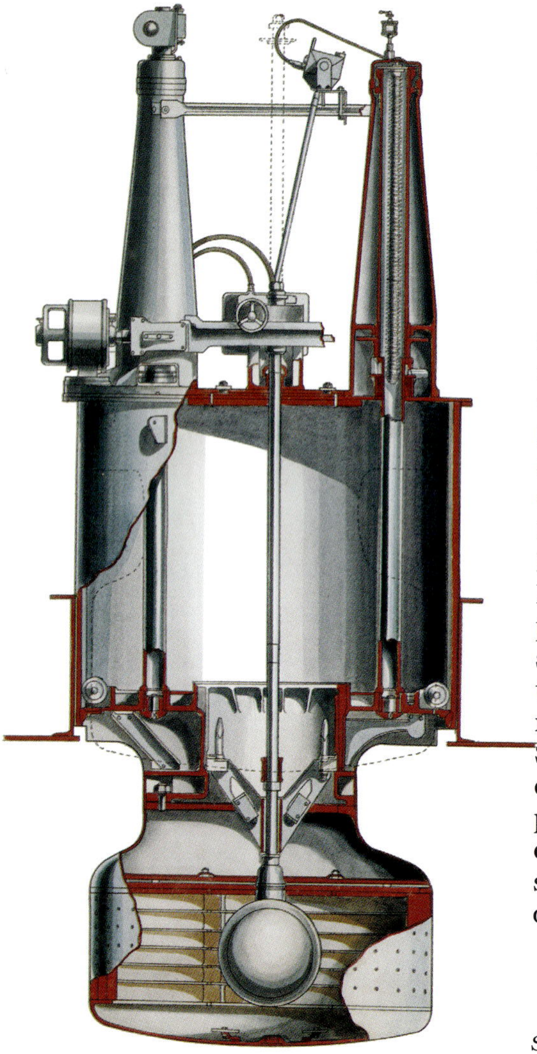

Sonar dome below ship's bottom plates.

The use of sound to "echo locate" underwater was spurred by the 1912 sinking of the liner *Titanic* after it had struck the submerged part of an iceberg. The world's first patent for an underwater echo-ranging device was received by the British patent office just one month after the sinking of the *Titanic*, and a German patent for an echo sounder followed in 1913. While working for the Submarine Signal Company in Boston, Reginald Fessenden, a Canadian, developed the concept in 1912, later testing a pioneer system in Boston harbor, and finally in 1914 from the U.S. Revenue Service (now the U.S. Coast Guard) cutter *Miami* on the Grand Banks off Newfoundland. This latter proved the concepts of depth sounding, communication using Morse code, and echo ranging.

The need in World War I to detect submerged submarines led to further research. The British used early underwater hydrophones, and a French team worked on the use of quartz in an active sound device during 1915. Under the auspices of the British Board of Invention and Research, the Canadian physicist Robert Boyle embarked in 1916 on the practical development of an active sound detection equipment. A prototype was ready for evaluation in mid-1917. Performed for the Anti-Submarine Division, the work was continued in great secrecy, and used piezoelectric quartz crystals in the first effective underwater system for active sound detection. To avoid any mention of sound or quartz, the work was

Crew members watch for results from dropping a pattern of depth charges.
Photo: Ministry of Defence.

described as being connected with "supersonics," later changed to "ASDics." From this came the British acronym ASDIC, or Asdic. By 1918, both the British and Americans had manufactured active systems, the former being well ahead of the latter. Asdic was first trialed in 1920, entered production in 1922, and was introduced in 1923. The U.S. Navy introduced its QB sonar during in 1931.

By the outbreak of World War II, the Royal Navy had five different equipments in surface vessels and others in submarines, all used within the context of a complete anti-submarine warfare system including depth charges as the primary weapons. This last limited the utility of sonar, for the vessel had to pass over the target (the "contact") before the depth charges could be fired, resulting in loss of sonar contact just before the attacker passed over its supposed position. This meant that the attacking vessel was effectively deaf at this time, and fired the depth charges on the basis of earlier estimates of the target submarine's position, course, speed, and depth. The submarine's commander thus had the change to evade an attack.

The attacker's capability was improved by the use of several ships co-operating (at least one keeping "contact" and sending information to the attacking vessel by voice radio) and the adoption of "ahead-throwing weapons" such as the Hedgehog and the later Squid launching impact-fused weapons, smaller than depth-fused depth charges, in a pattern ahead of the vessel, which could therefore still maintain "contact" with the target.

At the beginning of World War II, British technology was transferred without charge to the U.S., whose efforts complemented the British work. Among the many new types of equipment thus developed were sonobuoys first developed by the British in 1944, dipping/dunking sonar, and mine-detection sonar. Work on sonar had also been carried out in the Axis counties, notably Germany, and included countermeasures. At the end of the war, this German work was assimilated by the UK and U.S.

Index

Classes A - Z

A
A class 88, 92, 102
A class (1944) 280-281
A class (1945) 298-299
A2 class 262
Acciaio class 190-191
Acheron class 298-299
Adua class 190
Agosta 90B class 18
Akula class 87, 112-113
Akula class (1984) 342-343
Amphion class 298
Amphitrite class 129
Archimede class 226
Aréthuse class 316
Argonauta class 190
Argonaut class (1927) 176-179

B
B class 87, 92, 102-103
B class (1915) 186-187
B class (1940) 200-201
Balao class 252
Bars class 87
Bernardis 600-ton type 190
Biber class 250
Borei class 326
Brin class 226
Brumaire class 97, 128-129

C
C class 88, 92, 118
Collins class 308

D
D class 88-89, 92, 124, 140, 162
D, K, and M classes (1917) 162-163
Daphné class 316-317
Delfin class 97
Delta class 332-333
Dolfijn class 318-319

E
E class 90, 92, 124-127, 158, 194
Echo class 312, 329

F
F class 140-141
F class (Italy) 98-99
Farfadet class 77
Ferre class 94-95
Foca class 226

G
Gar class 252
Gato class 252-257
George Washington class 320-321
Golf class 302
Gotland class 18

H
Han class 344
Hotel class 312

I
I-200 class 260
I-400 class 262
Improved H class 148

J
J class 138-139
J3 class 262
Juliett class 302, 328-329

K
K class (1938) 202-203
K class 12, 132, 152, 162
K6 class 259
Kaiman class 86, 112
Kairyu class 272
Kaiten class 273
Kalev class 194-195
Karp class 84, 86
Kasatka class 87

L
L class 146-147, 158-159, 194, 204
Los Angeles class 346

M
M class 132, 134-137, 162
Major General Bubnov class 87
Marder class 251

Minoga class 87
Molch class 250
Morse class 77
Morzh class 87

N
Naïade class 76-77
Narwal class 176-179
Nautilus class 176-179
Neger class 251
November class 312

O
O class 174-175
O-19 class 188, 234-235
Oberon class 308-309
Odin class 204-205
Ohio class 321, 330-331
Orzeł class 188-189
Oscar class 350-351

P
Papa class 350
Perch class 252
Perla class 190
Pluviôse class 128
Porpoise class 252, 308
Project 627 class 312
Project 651 class 328
Project 667 class 314
Project 667 class 332
Project 675 class 329
Project 941 Akula class 324
Project 949 class 350
Project 971 class 342

R
R class 148-149
Redoutable class 192, 198-199
Requin class 198
Resolution class 340-341

S
S War class 240
S class 146, 182, 212
S class (1918-21) 182-183
S class (1931) 212-215
S class (1941) 240-241
Salmon class 252
Saphir class 192
Sargo class 252
Seadragon class 252
Seawolf class 346-349
Shark class 252
ShCh class 196-197
Shchuka-B class 342
Sirena class 190
Sirène class 77
Sjölejonet class 184-185
Skipjack class 92-93
Skipjack class (1958) 320-322
SSN-21 class 346
ST class 260
STo class 262

T
T Group 3 class 294
T class 206
Tabor class 252
Tench class 252, 296
Triton class 206-209
Type 091 class 344
Type 092 Daqingyu class 344
Type 092-II class 344
Type 204 class 18
Type 209 class 18
Type 212A class 18
Type 214 class 18
Type A class 270
Type B class 271
Type C class 271
Type C1 class 270
Type II class 216-217
Type VII class 218-221
Type IX class 222-225
Type XIV class 228-229
Type XVIIB class 286-289
Type XXI class 16, 290-293
Type XXVIIA Hecht class 248
Type XXVIIB Seehund class 249
Typhoon class 324-327, 330

U
U class 210-211
U-5 class 85
U-9 class 108-111
U-31 class 120-123
U-139 class 160-161
U-151 class 142-145
UB I class 100-101, 104, 130
UB II class 104-105
UB III class 104-107

UB type 12
UC I class 130-133
UC II class 130-133
UC III class 130-133

V
V class 242
Vampire class 242-243
Victoria class 308
Virginia class 11, 347

W
Whiskey class 300-301

X
X 1 class 172-173
X class 236-239
Xia class 344-345

Y
Yankee class 314-315

Z
Zulu class 302-303

General Index

A
Abdul Hamid 58, 60
Abdul Medjid 58-59, 62
Air Independent Propulsion 17
Akula 112-113
Albacore 304, 322
Alligator 38
Alligator 73
Almirante Lynch 47
Alstitt boat 38-39
American Diver 42
Aquidaban 47
Argonaut Junior 66
Argonaut 66-67, 78, 176
Arnauld de la Perière, Kapitänleutnant Lothar 122
Aube, Admiral 62

B
Bauer, Wilhelm 36, 56, 84
Blanco Encalada 23, 47
Blume, Federico 95
Bonaparte, Napoleon 34
Borelli, Giovanni 29
Bourne, William 7, 26
Brandtaucher 36-37, 84
Brennan, Louis 23
Breslin, John J. 52
Bubnov, I. G. 86, 113
Bushnell, Cornelius S. 44
Bushnell, David 7, 30, 56
Bushnell, Ezra 32

C
Chariot human torpedo 244-247
Clermont 34

D
D'Alton, Captain P. W. 58
d'Equevilley-Montjustin, Raymondo Lorenzo 84, 108
Davey, Marie 10
David 40-41
de Lôme, Henri Dupuy 63, 64
de Son, M. 28-29
de Villeroi, Brutus 38
deck guns of World War I 164-167
deck guns of World War II 274-277
Doughty, Thomas H. 10

E
Eagle 32
Edwards, Mark 27
El Ictineo 56

F
Fenian Ram 52-53
Fisher, Admiral Sir John 'Jackie' 118
Focke-Achgelis Fa 330 Bachstelze 264-265
Forel 80-81
Franklin, Benjamin 32
Fulton, Robert 7, 34, 63

G
G/6 torpedo 150-151
Garcia, Cosma 56
Garrett, Reverend George 48, 56, 58, 60
German midget submarines 248-251
Glassell, Lieutenant William T. 40
Goubet I 54
Goubet II 54-55, 98
Goubet, Claude 54, 56, 68, 98
Growler 310-311

Gustave Zédé 63, 64-65
Gustave Zédé 10, 64, 66, 68, 76
Gustavo Sampaio 47
Gymnote 10, 62-63, 68, 76

H
H. L. Hunley 21, 42-43
Hajen 82-83
Halsey, Silas 36
Hedgehog projector 266-269
Holland No. 1 52, 70-71
Holland VI 70-75
Holland 72
Holland, John P. 45, 52, 62, 69, 70, 82, 92
Housatonic 42
Howe, Vice Admiral Richard 33
Huascar 22
Hunley, Captain Horace Lawson 42

I
Intelligent Whale 44-45, 73

J
Japanese midget submarines 270-273
Japanese submarines of World War II 258-263

K
Kobben 85
Kophamel, Kapitänleutnant Waldemar 122
Krab 114-117
Krebs, Captain Arthur 10

L
Lake, Simon 10, 66, 69, 78, 82, 112, 114
Laubeuf submarines 96-97
Laubeuf, Maxime 69, 76, 84, 96, 128
Laurenti-Fiat type 98
Lee, Sergeant Ezra 32
Leninskiy Komsomol 312-313
Luppis, Giovanni Biagio 21, 46
Lyons, Thomas W. 42

M
McClintock, Captain James R. 42
Memphis 41
Meriam, Scovel S. 44
Minoga 86-87, 113
missiles 17
Monturiol, Narsisco 56
Morse 76

N
Naletov, M. N. 114
Narval 38, 68-69, 76, 96
Nautilus 15, 21, 34-35, 176
Nautilus (1954) 306-307
New Ironsides 40
Nordenfelt I 58
Nordenfelt II 58
Nordenfelt III 58-59
Nordenfelt IV 60-61
Nordenfelt submarines 60-61
Nordenfelt, Thorsten 58-60
North River Steam Boat 34
nuclear propulsion 334-335

O
Obry, Ludwig 23, 46

P
Palmcrantz, Helge 60
Papin, Denis 29
Park, Thomas B. 42
Payne, Lieutenant John A. 42
Peral y Caballero, Lieutenant Isaac 56
Peral 56-57
Périer, J. C. 34
periscope 10
Pioneer 42
Pitt, William 35
Planet, Gaston 54
Plongeur Marin 36
Plunger 38
Polaris SLBM 336-339
Poseidon SLBM 336-339
Protector 78-79

R
Resurgam 48-51
Richson, Carl 82
Romazotti. M. 64, 76
Roosevelt, Secretary of the Navy Theodore 72

S
Schnorchel 15
Shilder, Karl 36
Shkval torpedo 352

Siluro and Lenta Corsa torpedo 230-233
Skate 21
Sonar (Asdic) in World War II 356-357
Soviet concrete submarine 352-353
Stoney, T. 40
Submarine Propeller 73
submarine-launched aircraft 168-171
Surcouf 180-181
Swordfish 152-157

T
Ting Yuen 47
torpedo 21, 46
Torsk 296-297
Turtle 30-33

U
U-1 18, 84-85
U-2 84
U-3 & *U-4* 85
U-31 18
U-1407 18
underwater weapons of World War II 282-285
U.S. aircraft-carrier submarine 354-355

V
van Drebbel, Cornelius 7, 27
von Heimburg, Kapitänleutnant Heino 122
von Tirpitz, Admiral Alfred 84

W
Walter turbine 18
Wanklyn, Lt/Cdr Malcolm 211
Washington, George 32
Weddigen, Kapitänleutnant Otto 111
Whitehead, Robert 22, 46-47